American Swords & Sword Makers

Volume II

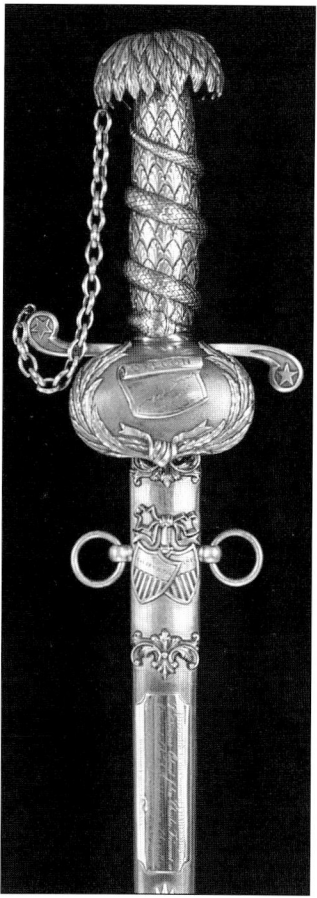
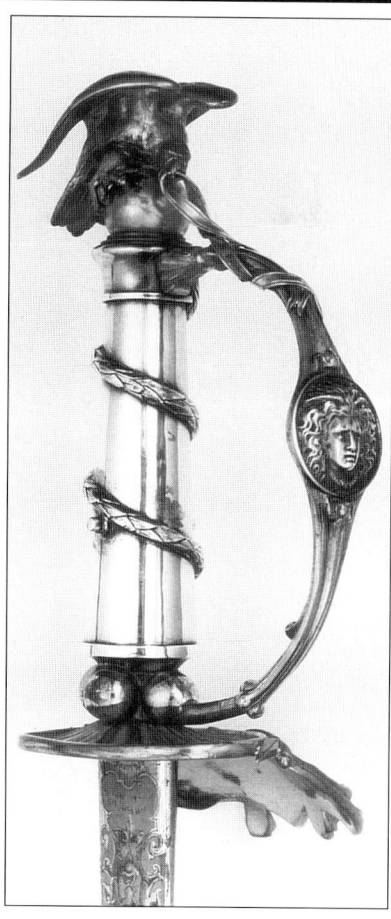

Richard H. Bezdek

Paladin Press • Boulder, Colorado

To Ann Elizabeth.
Thank you for all your help with this book.
Love, Papa

Other books by Richard H. Bezdek:
> *American Swords and Sword Makers*
> *Swords and Sword Makers of the War of 1812*

American Swords and Sword Makers, Volume II
by Richard H. Bezdek

Copyright © 1999 by Richard H. Bezdek

ISBN 1-58160-016-X
Printed in the United States of America

Published by Paladin Press, a division of
Paladin Enterprises, Inc., P.O. Box 1307,
Boulder, Colorado 80306, USA.
(303) 443-7250

Direct inquiries and/or orders to the above address.

PALADIN, PALADIN PRESS, and the "horse head" design
are trademarks belonging to Paladin Enterprises and
registered in United States Patent and Trademark Office.

All rights reserved. Except for use in a review, no
portion of this book may be reproduced in any form
without the express written permission of the publisher.

Neither the author nor the publisher assumes
any responsibility for the use or misuse of
information contained in this book.

Photos on front cover, left to right:
  Sword presented to Brig. Gen. Godfrey Weitzel, October 1863. (Photo courtesy of Donald R. Tharpe, Tharpe Collection of American Military History, © Donald R. Tharpe)

  Sword presented to Lt. Col. John Charles Fremont by the citizens of Charleston, SC. (Arizona Historical Society collection)

  Sword presented to Gen. John C. Robinson, July 4, 1865. (Photo courtesy of Donald R. Tharpe, Tharpe Collection of American Military History, © Donald R. Tharpe)

Illustration on back cover:
  Civil War naval presentation sword illustration from the Tiffany & Co. sword design book of silversmith Edward C. Moore. (© Tiffany & Co., from the archives)

Illustration on endsheets:
Presentation sword illustration from the Tiffany & Co. sword design book of silversmith Edward C. Moore. (© Tiffany & Co., from the archives)

Contents

INTRODUCTION · 1

CHAPTER 1 · 3
Fabricators of the M1832 Artillery Sword, M1833 Cavalry Sword, M1840 Cavalry Sword, M1840 Light Artillery Sword, M1840 Noncommissioned Officer Sword, and M1840 Musician's Sword

CHAPTER 2 · 5
Fabricators of M1860, M1906, and M1913 Cavalry Swords

CHAPTER 3 · 7
U.S. Armories and Arsenals Fabricating Swords and Edged Weapons

CHAPTER 4 · 9
State Armories and Arsenals Fabricating Swords and Edged Weapons

CHAPTER 5 · 11
Federal Period (1795-1815) U.S. Government Cavalry Saber Contracts

CHAPTER 6 · 13
Civil War (1861-1865) U.S. Government Cavalry Saber Contracts

CHAPTER 7 · 15
U.S. Sword Makers

CHAPTER 8 · 93
European Sword Makers and Dealers Who Exported Swords to Union Dealers during the Civil War

CHAPTER 9 • 95
U.S. Sword Dealers

CHAPTER 10 • 159
U.S. Silversmiths Who Mounted Swords

CHAPTER 11 • 185
Confederate Sword Makers

CHAPTER 12 • 203
European Sword Makers and Dealers Who Exported Swords to
Confederate Dealers during the Civil War

CHAPTER 13 • 205
Confederate Sword Dealers

CHAPTER 14 • 209
Bibliography and List of Reference Material on Edged Weapons Makers and Dealers

APPENDIX A • 215
U.S. Cavalry Sword Makers

APPENDIX B • 219
U.S. Naval Cutlass Makers

APPENDIX C • 221
U.S. Bowie Knife Makers

APPENDIX D • 225
U.S. Tomahawk & Belt Axe Makers

APPENDIX E • 229
U.S. Pike Makers

APPENDIX F • 231
Tiffany & Co.

U.S. SWORD PHOTOS • 261

CONFEDERATE SWORD PHOTOS • 303

SWORD ILLUSTRATIONS FROM OLD MILITARY DEALER CATALOGS • 317

**SWORD ILLUSTRATIONS FROM THE VERY RARE F.W. WIDMANN AND
WILLIAM H. HORSTMANN & SONS SWORD CATALOGS • 363**

**MOUNTED CAVALRY SABER EXERCISE ILLUSTRATIONS FROM
AN 1843 PHILADELPHIA SWORD MANUAL • 367**

Contributors

No book of this kind can be completed without the help of many people, especially in the area of sword photos and illustrations. I must give my special thanks to the following people and organizations for their contributions to this book.

Jay P. Altmayer, author of *American Presentation Swords*.

Don Ball, expert on American swords and military antiques dealer.

Bruce S. Bazelon, curator of the Pennsylvania Historical and Museum Commission and author of *Directory of American Military Goods Dealers & Makers—1785-1915* and several other books.

Jim Brown, expert on American swords and sword restorer.

Norm Flayderman of N. Flayderman & Co., Inc., America's oldest and most respected purveyor of military and nautical antiques.

Leonard J. Garigliano, expert on American swords, president of the Association of American Sword Collectors, and author of *Abstract Review and Notes Regarding Principal Sword Contractors during the American Civil War* and other books.

Kevin Hoffman, expert on American swords.

Harry Hunter, Museum Specialist, The Smithsonian Institution, Armed Forces History Division, Museum of American History.

C. Philip Johnson, collector of American swords.

George W. Juno, **Russ Pritchard Jr.**, and **Russ Pritchard III**, of The American Ordnance Preservation Association Ltd. (AOPA) and dealers in military antiques.

Dave Kleiner, information on silversmiths who mounted swords.

George C. Nuemann, author of *Swords and Blades of the American Revolution* and several other books.

Seward R. Osborne, historian and author.

Bob Owens, expert on Confederate swords.

C. Allen Russell, information on Confederate sword makers and dealers.

Annamarie V. Sandecki, Chief Archivist, Tiffany & Co., New York, NY.

David V. Stroud, author of *Inscribed Union Swords*.

Don Tharpe, expert on American swords.

Marybelle Bolger Tutt, genealogist, information on Longview, Texas, and G.A. Kelly.

Introduction

Since my first book, *American Swords and Sword Makers,* was published in 1994, I have obtained a large amount of new information on sword makers, sword dealers, and silversmiths who mounted swords. Volume II contains all of this new data. Collectors of bowie knives, dirks, and tomahawks will also find many new listings concerning these important areas.

Volume II is designed to make it easy for the reader and researcher to find the new information. All listings are labeled in the left margin as "New" (N), "Addition" (A), or "Correction" (C). New information was uncovered after the publication of Volume I. Additional information supplements data already listed in Volume I. Corrected information replaces inaccurate information in the first volume.

Volume II contains a lot of exciting new features. The photo section contains all new photos, most of which have never been shown in any book. In Volume I, I listed many old military dealer catalogs in the bibliography; in this new book, I actually show pages that advertise swords from some of these catalogs. Finally, I have included a fantastic new appendix (F) covering Tiffany & Company of New York featuring many photos and illustrations of highly prized presentation swords, including those presented to Ulysses S. Grant, William Tecumseh Sherman, and Admiral David G. Farragut.

Volume II has the same chapter names as Volume I; only the number of chapters has been reduced. The reason for this is that there is no new information pertaining to several of the chapters in Volume I so they are not relisted. The old chapter numbers are shown below so you can cross-reference the information.

CHAPTER 1 (CHAPTER 8 IN VOLUME I)
Fabricators of the M1832 Artillery Sword, M1833 Cavalry Sword, M1840 Cavalry Sword, M1840 Light Artillery Sword, M1840 Noncommissioned Officer Sword, and M1840 Musician's Sword

CHAPTER 2 (CHAPTER 9 IN VOLUME I)
Fabricators of M1860, M1906, and M1913 Cavalry Swords

CHAPTER 3 (CHAPTER 11 IN VOLUME I)
U.S. Armories and Arsenals Fabricating Swords and Edged Weapons

CHAPTER 4 (CHAPTER 12 IN VOLUME I)
State Armories and Arsenals Fabricating Swords and Edged Weapons

CHAPTER 5 (CHAPTER 13 IN VOLUME I)
Federal Period (1795-1815) U.S. Government Cavalry Saber Contracts

CHAPTER 6 (CHAPTER 15 IN VOLUME I)
Civil War (1861-1865) U.S. Government Cavalry Saber Contracts

CHAPTER 7 (CHAPTER 17 IN VOLUME I)
U.S. Sword Makers

CHAPTER 8 (CHAPTER 20 IN VOLUME I)
European Sword Makers and Dealers Who Exported Swords to Union Dealers during the Civil War

CHAPTER 9 (CHAPTER 22 IN VOLUME I)
U.S. Sword Dealers

CHAPTER 10 (CHAPTER 24 IN VOLUME I)
U.S. Silversmiths Who Mounted Swords

CHAPTER 11 (CHAPTER 31 IN VOLUME I)
Confederate Sword Makers

CHAPTER 12 (CHAPTER 32 IN VOLUME I)
European Sword Makers and Dealers Who Exported Swords to Confederate Dealers during the Civil War

CHAPTER 13 (CHAPTER 33 IN VOLUME I)
Confederate Sword Dealers

CHAPTER 14 (CHAPTER 34 IN VOLUME I)
Bibliography and List of Reference Material on Edged Weapons Makers and Dealers

CHAPTER 1

Fabricators of the M1832 Artillery Sword, M1833 Cavalry Sword, M1840 Cavalry Sword, M1840 Light Artillery Sword, M1840 Noncommissioned Officer Sword, and M1840 Musician's Sword

U.S. Ordnance Department Sample Sword Purchases in Europe (1838-1839)
(C)   Swords purchased in London in 1839 were from W. (William) L. (Lucus) & H. (Henry) Sargant, 74 Edmond St., Birmingham, England (not Robert Mole & Sons).

U.S. Fabricators of the M1840 Cavalry Saber (with government contracts)
(A)   Ames Manufacturing Co.
       William Glaze & Co.
       Horstmann Brothers
       P.S. Justice

U.S. Fabricators of the M1840 Cavalry Saber (no government contracts)
(A, C) S. (Samuel) Collins & Co. (Variation)
       Sheble & Fisher (Variation)
       Charles Hammond (Variation)
       Henry Sauerbier (Variation)

CHAPTER 2

Fabricators of the M1860, M1906, and M1913 Cavalry Swords

U.S. Fabricators of M1860 Cavalry Sabers (with government contracts)
(A, C) Ames Mfg. Co.
     Mansfield & Lamb
     C. Roby & Co.
     Emerson & Silver
     D.J. Millard
     Providence Tool Co.

Other Civil War Cavalry Saber Fabricators, probably M1860 (no government contracts)
(A, C) Gilbert Dubois
     Henry Disston & Sons
     William T. Clement
     Hamilton Ruddick

CHAPTER 3

U.S. Armories and Arsenals Fabricating Swords and Edged Weapons

(A) **U.S. Philadelphia Armory and Magazine**
- Established by the Second Continental Congress in Philadelphia (1775).
- Originally a private armory on Water Street on the west side of Philadelphia next to the Schuylkill River.
- Also called the Water Street Armory and the Continental Armory.
- On July 19, 1777, the following advertisement appeared in the *Pennsylvania Evening Post* (Philadelphia):
  Butler, Thomas (Armourer)—Water Street Armoury
  Wanted: two or three Gunlock Filers and a good stocker or two, who by applying as above,
  shall be properly encouraged by Thomas Butler, Chief Armourer of the United States.
- On August 18, 1777, the following advertisement appeared in the *Pennsylvania Evening Post*:
  Butler, Thomas (Armourer)—Continental Armoury
  Wanted: a quantity of Walnut Plank. Any person who has plank for sale, by applying to Thomas Butler,
  said armoury, shall have ready money and a good price for the same.
- The U.S. Philadelphia Armoury and Magazine was closed and became the Pennsylvania State Arsenal (1821).

(A) **U.S. Philadelphia Arsenal**
- Established in 1799.
- Located on Gray's Ferry Road and Arsenal Street on the outskirts of Philadelphia next to the Schuylkill River. (It was also known as the Schuylkill Arsenal.)
- The office of U.S. Purveyor of Public Supplies was located at the U.S. Philadelphia Arsenal until 1812. After 1812 it was called the Office of the Commissary General of Purchases. It is now called the U.S. Department of the Quartermaster Department of the U.S. Army.
- Arsenal quartermaster: William Linnard (1812-1815).
- During the Civil War the arsenal had four branch warehouses in the city of Philadelphia.

(A, C) **U.S. New London, Virginia, Arsenal (Bedford County)**
- Reports of two horseman swords (reverse-P, half-wagon-wheel hilt and plain reverse-P hilt) being made at the New London Arsenal were incorrect. They have now been attributed to Dunbar and Leonard of Canton, MA.

- During the U.S. Revolutionary War, a state of Virginia purchasing agent in France, Jacques Le Maire, sent back to Virginia swords and blades he purchased at the Klingenthal manufactory (1779). He purchased cavalry sword blades marked "Dragoon of Virginia" and two short swords (hangers) marked "Grenadier of Virginia" and "Artillery of Virginia." Some were issued immediately, and the rest were stored temporarily at the U.S. New London arsenal in Virginia.
- When the British were raiding near the New London Arsenal, 557 of the "Grenadier of Virginia" and "Artillery of Virginia" swords were transferred to the Point of Fork, Virginia, State Arsenal, which had just opened (July 1782).
- The balance of the short swords and the "Dragoon of Virginia" blades were transferred to the Point of Fork arsenal in 1783. I believe the "Dragoon of Virginia" blades were mounted at the arsenal.

(N) U.S. Frankford Arsenal, Bridesburg, Pennsylvania
- Located on the Frankford Road (near Philadelphia) next to the Delaware River.
- Commandant: Maj. T. (Theodore) S. Laidley.
- Ordnance officer: 1st Lt. T.J. Treadwell.
- A large Civil War depot taking delivery and inspecting military accouterments, firearms, and swords from domestic and foreign makers and dealers.

(N) U.S. New York Arsenal, Governor's Island, New York
- Commandant: Maj. R. (Robert) H. (Henry) K. (Kirkwood) Whiteley.
- A large Civil War depot taking delivery and inspecting military accouterments, firearms, and swords from domestic and foreign makers and dealers.

(N) U.S. Washington Arsenal, Washington, D.C.
- Commandant: Lt. Col. George D. Ramsey.
- A large Civil War depot taking delivery and inspecting military accouterments, firearms, and swords from domestic and foreign makers and dealers.

CHAPTER 4

State Armories and Arsenals Fabricating Swords and Edged Weapons

(A) **State of Virginia Manufactory of Arms**
- In operation from 1801-1900 in Richmond, Virginia.
- Called the Virginia Manufactory.
- In 1801, when the Virginia Point of Fork Arsenal closed, the equipment and machinery and 900 short swords marked "Grenadier of Virginia" and "Artillery of Virginia" (purchased by the state of Virginia at the Klingenthal manufactory in France in 1778 and arriving in Virginia in 1779) were transferred to a temporary storage area in the attic of the capital building in Richmond. In 1806 there were 600 on hand.
- In 1806, 187 "Grenadier of Virginia" short swords were transferred from the capital storage area to the Virginia Manufactory. They were cleaned up and the blade markings were removed. New belts and scabbards were made. Eighty were marked "7 VA. REGT." and 107 were marked "4 VA. REGT." They were all issued to three artillery companies in Norfolk County, Virginia. Eventually, the remaining 413 short swords were moved to the Virginia Manufactory.
- By 1808 all of the short swords had been issued to sergeants in the Virginia militia.
- During the Revolutionary War, infantry and foot artillery soldiers still carried short swords (hangers). After the war, only sergeants of infantry and artillery carried swords (non-comm. swords). The Virginia Manufactory began making its own cavalry and non-comm. swords in 1804.
(See State of Virginia)
(See Point of Fork, Virginia, Arsenal)

(A) **Point of Fork, Virginia, State Arsenal, Fluvanna County**
- Opened in early 1781.
- In July 1781, when the British were raiding near the U.S. New London arsenal, the commanding officer transferred 557 short swords marked "Grenadier of Virginia" and "Artillery of Virginia" (purchased in France by the state of Virginia in 1779 and stored at New London) from New London to the Point of Fork Virginia Arsenal.
- In 1783, all the state of Virginia military supplies (including the "Grenadier of Virginia" and "Artillery of Virginia" swords and "Dragoon of Virginia" saber blades) were transferred to the Point of Fork Virginia Arsenal. I believe the "Dragoon of Virginia" blades were then mounted and distributed.

- In April 1791, the arms report showed 25 horseman ("Dragoon of Virginia") swords and 1,214 sergeant swords ("Artillery of Virginia" and "Grenadier of Virginia") on hand at the Point of Fork Arsenal. During the Revolutionary War, infantry and foot artillery soldiers carried short swords (hangers). After the Revolutionary War, only sergeants carried swords (non-comm. swords).
- When the Point of Fork Arsenal was closed in 1801, 900 "Grenadier of Virginia" and "Artillery of Virginia" swords were transferred to a temporary storage area in the attic of the capitol building in Richmond, Virginia. Eventually they were transferred to the Virginia Manufactory of Arms in Richmond.

(See State of Virginia)

(See Virginia Manufactory)

CHAPTER 5

Federal Period (1795–1815) U.S. Government Cavalry Saber Contracts

	Contract Amount	Date of Contract	Sword Maker
(A)	500 (only 22 accepted)	1810	James Winner Philadelphia, PA
	478 (finished the Winner contract)	1811	J. Abraham Nippes Philadelphia, PA

CHAPTER 6

Civil War (1861–1865) U.S. Government Cavalry Saber Contracts

	Company	Number	Model
(C)	P.S. Justice	13,685	M1840 (Variation)

CHAPTER 7

U.S. Sword Makers

(N) **SAMUEL ABBOT**　　　　　　　**FORT MICHILIMACKINAC**　　1839-1845
　　　　　　　　　　　　　　　　　　STRAITS OF MACKINAC
* Fort Michilimackinac was originally a French fort and trading post, becoming a British fort at the end of the French and Indian War (1763).
* The fort was ceded to the U.S. at the end of the Revolutionary War (1783).
* Abbot made tomahawks for the local Huron Indians.

(Blacksmith)

(A) **EZEKIAL ADAMS**　　　　　　　**WEBSTER, NH**　　　　　　1860-1868
* Made bowie knives and belt axes (tomahawks).

(Cutler)

(N) **R. (ROBERT) ADAMS**　　　　　**BALTIMORE, MD**　　　　　1790-1810
* Made riflemen's belt axes (tomahawks).

(Cutler, Silversmith)

(A) **JOSEPH ALBOT**　　　　　　　　**NEW YORK, NY**　　　　　　1755-1765
　　　　　　　　　　　　　　　　　　(under British dominion)
* Made tomahawks and scalping knives for the British Indian Service.

(Blacksmith)

(A) **SAMUEL ALEXANDER**　　　　　**PHILADELPHIA, PA**　　　　1804-1830
* Shop located at 119 Walnut Street.
* Made presentation swords for the state of Virginia.

(Silversmith)

(A) **JACOB ALLEN**　　　　　　　　**NEW YORK, NY**　　　　　　1773-1783
* Probably made cavalry sabers.

(N) J.B. ALLERE   **CHICAGO, IL**   **1810-1840**
- Made tomahawks for the U.S. Office of Indian Trade.

(Blacksmith)

(A) AMEDEE ALVISET   **NEW YORK, NY**   **1840-1856**
- Located at 556 Pearl Street.

(N) AMERICAN CUTLERY CO.   **NEW YORK, NY**   **1900-1925**
- Had a branch in Chicago, IL.
- Made M1917 and M1917C bolo knives and M1917 and M1918 trench knives.

(N) AMERICAN FLASK & CAP CO.   **NEW YORK, NY**   **1857-1900**
- Located at 52 Beekman Street.

Made powder flasks, percussion caps, shot belts and pouches, pistol holsters, and bowie knives.

(N) AMERICAN KNIFE CO.   **REYNOLDS BRIDGE, CT**   **1849-1865**
- General knife maker, including bowie knives.
- Sales agent: Miles Morse.
- President: George B. Pierpont.
- Purchased by the Northfield Knife Co. of Northfield, CT (1865).

(A) N.P. AMES   **CHICOPEE FALLS, MA**   **1829-1834**
- While Ames was in Chicopee Falls with his shop at Edmond Dwight's textile mill (Chicopee Mfg. Co.), he had eight employees (1829).

AMES MFG. CO.   **CABOTVILLE, MA**   **1834-1848**
- The Ames Manufacturing Co. was formed by Nathan P. Ames Jr. and James Tyler Ames (1834). Soon after they moved to an area that became known as the Cabotville Works and then the town of Cabotville. However, the swords produced between 1834-1848 at Cabotville were marked "N.P. Ames Springfield Mass." (Cabotville was near Springfield) or "N.P. Ames Cabotville Mass."
- When Cabotville was incorporated into the town of Chicopee (1848), the swords were marked "Ames Mfg. Co. Chicopee Mass."
- Ames won a silver medal for the best edged tools at the American Institute Exposition in New York (1835).
- Had 68 employees (1836).
- Nathan P. Ames Jr. took a trip to England, where he studied English sword making techniques. He also learned about and brought back to the U.S. the process of silver plating with electricity known as electroplating (1837).
- A Nathan P. Ames business card from c. 1837 reads as follows:

N.P. Ames
Cabotville Works
Springfield
Mass

Manufacturer of swords, cutlery and edged tools. Swords manufactured for the general, staff and regimental officers of the Army of the United States of every pattern. Also Dragoon sabres, and Artillery swords for the United States service of the latest patterns. Swords of any pattern made to order.

- Ames won the "Best Sword Display" award at the Massachusetts Charitable Mechanics Association Exposition at Boston's Quincy Market (1837).
- The Ames Company began making quality hunting knives, some with rosewood grips and brass scabbards.
- They also made lion-head pommel bowie knives as well as other styles (beginning c. 1840).

| AMES MFG. CO. | CHICOPEE, MA | 1848-1881 |

- Before the Civil War started, Ames had contracts with Alabama (approximately 500) and Georgia (approximately 1,000) for M1840 cavalry sabers (late 1860 and early 1861).
- The 10,000 sabers Ames imported from Solingen, Germany (through the New York importer G.A. & E. Scheidt), and sold to the U.S. government were M1840 cavalry sabers (1862). They had both the Ames and German maker's name (probably S&K) stamped on them. There were no U.S. government marks.
- The sabers were delivered to the U.S. New York Arsenal at Governor's Island and inspected by Maj. R. (Robert) H. (Henry) K. (Kirkwood) Whiteley (initials "R.H.K.W." stamped on the swords).
- After the Civil War, Ames continued to sell M1860 cavalry sabers in the United States to city and state militia cavalry units and other customers. They were stamped "Ames Mfg. Co." sideways on the blade near the hilt and had no government marks or inspector stamps.
- An Ames Business Card (c. 1870) reads as follows:
  Ames Manufacturing Co. Chicopee
  Manufacturers of cotton machinery of every description with shafting and
  apparatus for cotton mills complete.
  Lathes, turning and milling engines.
  Planing machines and machinery tools in general.
  Brass and iron castings of every variety.
  Swords of all descriptions used by the United States Army,
  rich presentation swords and every variety of fancy swords and belts.
  Bronze cannon of any size or kind made to order.
- The Chicopee, MA, city directory (1875) showed the following:
  Ames Manufacturing Company
  Chicopee, Mass
  Manufacturers of:
    Sewing machines
    Gun stocking machinery
    Gun making machines
    Bronze cannon
    Regulation and society swords
    Mill Shafting
    Pulleys and gearing
    Boydens turbine wheel
    Mill power pumps
    Mining power pumps
    Reservoir power pumps
    Iron and brass castings
    Bronze statuary
    Silver and plated ware
    Machinists tools
- Advertised in the *Manufacturer and Industrial Gazette* (May 1880) as follows:
  Ames Manufacturing Company
  Chicopee Massachusetts
  A.C. Woodworth—President
  Luther White—Treasurer
  Manufacturers of:
    "Boyden" turbine water wheel
    Gears, pulleys, shafting, hangers
    General mill supplies
    Iron and brass castings

(we have one of the largest pattern lists in New England)
Machinists and special tools
Lathes
Planers
Upright drills
Vertical gang drills
Drill and slotting machines
2 spindle edge milling machines
Common milling machines
Hand milling machines
Horizontal boring machines
Compound planers or shapers
Jigging or die sinking machines
Special tools and machinery made to order
"Martin's" improved brick machines kept constantly on hand

<u>Sword Department</u>

The Ames Manufacturing Co. are the largest manufacturers of swords in the United States, and the only ones that make swords complete from raw materials. They have, during the past two years, furnished Foreign Governments more than 250,000 sabers and bayonets. One department of their works is devoted exclusively to this branch of their business and includes the manufacture of:
Regulation swords
Presentation swords
Society swords
Regalia materials and trimmings in every variety
Bronze statuary and monumental works a specialty

THE AMES SWORD CO.　　　　　　　　　**CHICOPEE, MA**　　　　　　　　1881-1925

- The Ames Sword Co. catalog issued on September 25, 1883, lists the following:
  Designers and manufacturers of:
  Presentation swords
  Masonic swords
  Military regulation swords
  Independent Order of Odd Fellows swords
  Knights of Pythias swords
  Military association swords
  Miscellaneous society swords
  Theatrical and combat swords
  Foils
  Daggers
  Bayonets
  Sword belts and mountings
  Link and barrel chains
  Baldric stars, fasteners and hangers
  Commandry, chapter and regalia jewels
  Flag rod tops
  Society badges
  Stone hammers
  Bronze and brass castings
  Gold, silver and nickel plating
  Engraving, modeling and die sinking
  Repairing and replating

- In 1891 the Ames Sword Company of Chicago, IL, issued catalog #51 supplies for Masonic lodges. It listed over 140 different items, including swords, sword belts, badges and pins, jewelry, costumes and outfits, furniture, turbans and headdresses, and tools. It also advertised uniforms and equipment for the Knights Templer; regalia and paraphernalia for the Independent Order of Odd Fellows (IOOF), including swords, costumes, and uniforms; paraphernalia and supplies for the Knights of Pythias; regalia, paraphernalia, uniforms and equipment "for all the societies"; military and band equipment; Grand Army of the Republic (GAR) and Sons of Veterans supplies; uniforms for schools, letter carriers, colleges, police, firemen, and streetcar employees; and badges, flags, and banners (printed, painted, and embroidered).
- The Ames Sword Co. advertised, in their Chicago location, the manufacture of military trappings (1893).
- Military sales department manager: Edward Bickerstaff.
- The company's main offices were in Boston, MA.
- An Ames Sword Co. letterhead (1903) shows the following:

    Ames Sword Company, Chicopee, Mass
    John D. Bryant—President (Boston, Mass offices)
    Gamaliel Bradford—Treasurer (Boston, Mass offices)
    Charles A. Buckley—Superintendent (Chicopee, Mass manufactory)
    Manufacturers of:
    Military, society and presentation swords
    Perfection padlocks and key holders
    Belts (Sword)
    Mountings (Society)
    Regalia (Society)
    Jewels (Society)
    Designing
    Modeling
    Engraving

(N) **JEAN BAPTISTE AMVOT**	FORT MICHILIMACKINAC STRAITS OF MACKINAC (under French dominion)	1742-1750

- Made pipe tomahawks for local Huron Indians.

(Blacksmith)

(A) **PETER ANGSTADT (ANSTADT)**	BERKS CO., OHIO	1800-1810
PETER ANGSTADT	MONTGOMERY CO., OHIO	1810-1850

- Made Kentucky flintlock rifles and exquisite pipe tomahawks with silver-inlayed bowls, blades, and halfs, some engraved "American Horse."

(Gunsmith, silversmith, tomahawk maker)

(A) **FRANCIS AREIS**	PHILADELPHIA, PA	1795-1836

- Shop located at 60 South Street (near 2nd Street).
- Advertised in the *American Advertising Directory* (1831) that he manufactured and repaired firearms, pistols, swords, gunlocks, etc.

(A) **GEORGE ARMITAGE**	PHILADELPHIA, PA	1796-1836

- Located at 438 Sassafras Street.
- Made naval officer sabers with eagle-head pommels.

(A) **E.A. ARMSTRONG**	DETROIT, MI	1870-1894

- Located at 176 Jefferson Avenue.

(A) **T.H. ARMSTRONG**   DETROIT, MI   1854-1870
- Located at 176 Jefferson Avenue.

(A) **WILTON ATKINSON**   LANCASTER, PA   1745-1783
- Located on Queen Street.

(A) **L.W. BABBITT**   CLEVELAND, OH   1832-1840
- Located at 14 Bank Street.
- Made bowie and hunting knives and percussion rifles.

(A) **WILLIAM BACON**   NEW YORK, NY   1825-1845
- Located at 213 Water Street.
- Made bowie knives.

(A) **JOHN BAILEY (BAYLEY)**   PHILADELPHIA, PA   1757-1799
- Shop located at 4 South Front Street (at Chesnut Street).
- Made silver-hilted small swords.

    JOHN BAILEY (BAYLEY)   NEW CASTLE, DE   1799-1806

(Goldsmith, silversmith, whitesmith, sword hiltor)

(A) **JOHN BAILEY**   FISKKILL, NY   1778-1784
- Set up a forge, cutlery, and blacksmith shop on a tributary of the Hudson River now called Forge Brook.

    JOHN BAILEY   NEW YORK, NY   1784-1794
- Shop located at 22 Little Dock Street (at the sign of the crossed swords).
- Made iron, hussar hilt cavalry sabers.

    JOHN BAILEY & G. HEDDERLY   NEW YORK, NY   1794-1798
- Located at 60 Water Street.

(Bell founders)

(A) **J. (JACOB) S. BAKER**   PHILADELPHIA, PA   1796-1860
- Factory located at 516 North Front Street.

(A) **MELCHIOR BAKER &**   NICHOLSON TWSP.   1781-1801
    ALBERT GALLATIN   FAYETTE CO., PA
- Made cavalry broadswords.

(N) **SAMUEL BALL**   FELLS POINT, MD   1790-1820
- Located on Duke Street.
- Advertised in the Baltimore city directory as a cutler (1796).

(N) **ETTIENNE BALLARD**   DETROIT, MI   1775-1783
    (under British dominion)
- Made tomahawks for the British Indian Service.

(Blacksmith)

(A) **PIERRE BARRELL**   PARIS, FRANCE   B1799-1820
- Changed his name to Peter Bammell when he immigrated to Philadelphia, PA, (1820).

    PETER BAMMELL   PHILADELPHIA, PA   1820-1836
- Made silver-mounted officer hangers (short swords) with stag horn grips.

(N) **FRANCES BAXLER** BALTIMORE, MD 1800-1830
- Made tomahawks for the U.S. Office of Indian Trade (1820).

(Blacksmith)

(N) **BAY STATE HARDWARE CO.** NORTHAMPTON, MA 1863-1871
- Purchased by H.R. Hinckley (1871) and changed the name to Northampton Cutlery Co.

NORTHAMPTON CUTLERY CO. NORTHAMPTON, MA 1871-1997
- President in early years: H.R. Hinckley.
- Made table cutlery, surgical instruments, carver's knives, butcher's knives, hunting knives, and bowie knives.
- Made bayonets during World War II.
- New York offices located at 122 Chambers Street.

(A) **WILLIAM BEATTY** PHILADELPHIA, PA 1810-1813
- Operated a hammer mill on Ridley Creek making edged tools and cutlery.

(N) **CHRISTIAN BECK SR. I** PHILADELPHIA, PA Bc1733, 1767-1780
    CHRISTIAN BECK SR. I LANCASTER, PA 1780-1786
- Made Kentucky flintlock rifles.

(N) **CHRISTIAN BECK JR. II** PHILADELPHIA, PA 1770-1786
- Son of Christian Beck Sr. I.

    CHRISTIAN BECK JR. II LEBANON CO., PA 1786-1812
- Made Kentucky flintlock rifles.

(N) **CHRISTIAN BECK III** LEBANON CO., PA B1787-1807
    CHRISTIAN BECK III DAUPHIN CO., PA 1807-1813
    CHRISTIAN BECK III FRANKLIN CO., PA 1813-1827
    CHRISTIAN BECK III MARTINSBURG, VA 1827-1830
- Son of Christian Beck Jr. II and nephew of John Philip Beck.
- Made Kentucky flintlock rifles.
- Made pipe tomahawks.

(C) **JOHN PHILIP BECK** LEBANON CO., PA B1751, 1770-D1821
- Son of Christian Beck Sr. I.
- Brother of Christian Beck Jr. II.

(Gunsmith)

(A) **S. (SAMUEL) BECK** PHILADELPHIA, PA 1775-1783

(Gunsmith)

(A) **THOMAS BECK** PHILADELPHIA, PA 1760-1780
- Located on Chesnut Street (between 2nd and 3rd Streets).

(N) **JOHN & AMOS BELKNAP** ST. JOHNSBURY, VT 1879-1887
- General knife makers, including bowie knives.

(N) **SAMUEL BELL** KNOXVILLE, TN 1830-1845
    SAMUEL BELL SAN ANTONIO, TX 1845-1850
    J. (JOSEPH) & S. (SAMUEL) BELL SAN ANTONIO, TX 1850-1860
- Made silver-hilted swords and silver-mounted bowie knives.

(Silversmith, cutler, sword hiltor, bowie knife maker)

(N) GEORGE BENEKE　　　　　　　　　　　　　PHILADELPHIA, PA　　　　　　　1810-1820
- Located on 13th Street (near Filbert Street).
- Advertised in the Philadelphia city directory as a cutler (1811-1815).

(N) GEORGE C. BENNER　　　　　　　　　　　PHILADELPHIA, PA　　　　　　　1810-1820
- Located at 104 North Front Street.
- Advertised in the Philadelphia city directory as a cutler (1811-1815)

(A) ISAAC BERLIN　　　　　　　　　　　　　　NORTHAMPTON COUNTY　　　B1755-1781
　　　　　　　　　　　　　　　　　　　　　　　　EASTON, PA
- Apprenticed as a gun maker with his father Abraham Berlin (1768-1773).
- Worked in his father's gun shop (c. 1773-1776).
- Served along with his father in Capt. Henry Alshouse's 5th (Easton) Company, Northampton County Militia (1776-1781). Began as a private, promoted to sergeant, and finally became company adjutant.
- Made swords for his fellow officers.
- Captured by the British at the Battle of Long Island and put on a prison ship (1776). He was one of the few who survived and was part of a prisoner exchange (1777). Returned to Easton in poor health.
- Tax lists show him as a blacksmith (1779), a swordsmith (1780), and again a blacksmith (1781).
- Officially discharged from the Northhampton County Militia (November 1781).
- Moved with his family to Tract #1501 in Randolph Township, PA (1781). The land was given to him for his services in the Revolutionary War.

ISAAC BERLIN　　　　　　　　　　　　　　　　RANDOLPH TWSP., PA　　　　　1781-1784
- The land proved to be marshy and could not be farmed.
- Returned to Easton, PA (1784).

ISAAC BERLIN　　　　　　　　　　　　　　　　NORTHAMPTON CO.　　　　　　1784-1786
　　　　　　　　　　　　　　　　　　　　　　　　EASTON, PA
- Listed in the tax lists as a gunsmith.
- Moved to Berwick Township, Abbottstown, in Adams County, PA (1786).

ISAAC BERLIN　　　　　　　　　　　　　　　　BERWICK TWSP.,　　　　　　　　1786-1806
　　　　　　　　　　　　　　　　　　　　　　　　ABBOTTSTOWN, PA
- Bought 10 acres in Northampton County, Lehigh Township, from his father Abraham Berlin (1806).

ISAAC BERLIN　　　　　　　　　　　　　　　　NORTHAMPTON CO.　　　　　　1806-1820
　　　　　　　　　　　　　　　　　　　　　　　　LEHIGH TWSP., PA
- Bought a farm from George Reiffer on French Creek, two miles below Saegertown, in Mead Township, Crawford County, PA (1820).

ISAAC BERLIN　　　　　　　　　　　　　　　　CRAWFORD CO.　　　　　　　　1820-1829
　　　　　　　　　　　　　　　　　　　　　　　　MEAD TWSP., PA
- Moved to Woodcock Township (1829).

ISAAC BERLIN　　　　　　　　　　　　　　　　CRAWFORD CO.　　　　　　　　1829-D1831
　　　　　　　　　　　　　　　　　　　　　　　　WOODCOCK TWSP., PA
- Isaac Berlin died (June 16, 1831).

(Flintlock rifle and gun maker, sword maker, farmer)

(N) CHARLES E. (ETHAN) BILLINGS　　　　WETHERFIELD, VT　　　　　　　B1835-1865
- Tool maker for Colt Firearm Co. (1856–1862).
- Tool maker for E. Remington Arms Co. of Ilien, NY (1862-1865).

CHARLES E. BILLINGS　　　　　　　　　　　HARTFORD, CT　　　　　　　　　1865-1868
- Patented a pistol/bowie knife combination (1868).

ROPER REPEATING RIFLE CO.　　　　　　　AMHERST, MA　　　　　　　　　1868-1869
- Established by Sylvester M. Roper (1866), with Christopher M. Spencer as agent.

- Made repeating rifles and shotguns.
- President: Charles E. Billings (1868).
- Reorganized as Billings & Spencer (1869).

BILLINGS (CHARLES E.) & SPENCER   HARTFORD, CT   1869-1873
(CHRISTOPHER M.)
- Located at 142 Russ Street (corner of Lawrence Street).
- Made Ballard, Marlin, and Roper firearms and parts.
- Made Prussian needleguns.

(A) **JAMES BIRD**   WILLIAMSBURG, VA   1720-1770
- Located at Woodsides Wharf (between Goldberry and Hackett Streets).

(N) **JAMES BLACK**   PHILADELPHIA, PA   B1800-1822
- Apprentice to silversmith Stephen Henderson (c. 1814-1818) at 91 North 9th Street.
- Journeyman to Henderson (Stephen) & Field (Samuel) & Co., silversmiths (c. 1818-1820) at 89 South 2nd Street.

JAMES BLACK   PHILADELPHIA, PA   c1820-1822
- Located at 123 Chestnut Street.
- Moved west (1822-1824).

JAMES BLACK   HEMPSTEAD CO.   1824-D1872
                                WASHINGTON, AR
- Worked for blacksmith William Shaw.
- Married Shaw's daughter Anne (1828).
- Opened his own cutlery shop (1828).
- Became a well-known knife maker.
- Supposedly made two hunting knives for James Bowie, one to Bowie's design and one of his own design (c. 1830). There is no proof of this story.
- Perfected a 12-step steel tempering process, which made for excellent blades.

(Silversmith)

(N) **JOHN BLACK**   PHILADELPHIA, PA   1780-1820
- Located at 120 South Front Street.
- Advertised in Philadelphia city directory as a cutler (1811-1815).
- Possibly James Black's father.

(N) **CHARLES BLAIR**   EAST AMHERST, MA   1816-1836
MORRILL (HENRY A.), MOSMAN   EAST AMHERST, MA   1836-1838
(SILAS A. JR.), & BLAIR (CHARLES)
- Made pistols, George Elgin's cutlass pistols, and bowie knife pistols.

MORRILL (HENRY A.) & BLAIR   EAST AMHERST, MA   1838-1839
(CHARLES)
- Pistol makers.

CHARLES BLAIR   COLLINSVILLE, CT   1839-1885
- Became factory superintendent for cutler and edged weapon maker S. (Samuel) Collins & Co. (1839-1885).
- In 1857 John Brown, infamous abolitionist and tannery operator, of Osawatomie, Kansas, ordered 1,000 pikes at $1 each from Charles Blair on a separate contract (not from Collins & Co.). Brown, who was born in Torrington, CT, in 1800, was aware of cutler Blair.
- Blair made 12 sample pikes (1857) and 954 pikes (1858) for Brown.
- The pikes had 9-inch double-edged blades that were 2 inches wide, cross guards, and 6-foot ash poles.
- Blair made the cross guards and the poles. A Charles Hart of Collinsville (probably another Collins

employee) made the blades. A company in New Haven, CT, made the ferrules.
- They were to be shipped to Isaac Smith of Chambersburg, PA.

(A) **C. (CHARLES) J. BLITTERSDORF** **PHILADELPHIA, PA** 1780-1865
- Located at 143 North 4th Street.
- Made bowie knives during the Civil War.

(A) **H. (HERMAN) BOKER & CO.** **NEW YORK, NY** 1837-1971
- Dealer and importer in guns, pistols, hardware, and swords.
- Imported hardware and cavalry sabers from his brother Henry (Heinrich) Boker (Solingen, Prussia). The cavalry swords were marked "H. Boker" or "Henry Boker."
- Located at 50 Cliff Street (1837-1861), 101 and 103 Duane Street (1862-1971).
- Had offices in Liege, Belgium; Birmingham, England; Solingen, Prussia; Remscheid, Prussia; and Bonn, Westphalia (1861).
- Partners: H. (Herman) Boker Jr., Herman Funke (1861).
- Sales agent: John Schleicher (1861).
- H. Boker & Co. bought the Lamson & Goodnow Co. of Shelburne Falls, MA (1872). The company was sold in 1971.
- Partners: F. (Friedrich) A. Boker, Herman Funke, F. Schumacker (1872).
- Their invoices (c. 1875) read:

    Herman Boker & Co.
    American Cutlery Dept.
    Lamson & Goodnow Mfg. Co.
    Cutlery
    Guns
    Hardware

- Made bowie knives.
- Company executives: John Boker Sr., John Boker Jr. (early 1900).

(See Lamson & Goodnow Co.)

(N) **JOHN BOOK** **LANCASTER CO., PA** 1785-1790
- Advertised as a gunsmith, whitesmith, iron worker, and sickle maker.
- Also made belt axes (tomahawks) for the local Indians.

(A) **SQUIRE BOONE** **ROMAN CO., NC** 1744-1790
    SQUIRE BOONE **HARVARDSBURY, KY** 1790-1815
- Brother of Daniel Boone.
- Made pipe tomahawks and rifles.

(Gun maker, cutler)

(N) **WILLIAM BOOTH** **NAZARETH, PA** 1781-1797
- Musket maker for William Henry Jr. at Henry's gun factory in Nazareth, PA.

    BOOTH (WILLIAM) & CO. **PHILADELPHIA, PA** 1797-1817
- Partner and son: Richard Booth.
- Gun shop located at 85 South 2nd Street (1797-1799), 88 South 2nd Street (1799-1817).
- Made and sold military and dueling flintlocks pistols.
- Bought 12 boarding pikes at $1 each and 12 naval cutlasses at $2.50 each from John Joseph Henry, Philadelphia, PA (March 11, 1816).
- Sold out his business to Richard Constable (1817).

(Gunsmith, goldsmith, silversmith, military goods dealer)

(N) **JOHN BORDEAU** FT. LARAMIE, DAKOTA TERR. 1730-1750
- Made and traded tomahawks to local Indians for beaver skins.

(Blacksmith)

(N) **HENDRICK BOSCH** NEW YORK, NY 1650-D1701
- Located on Pearl Street (near Broad Street).
- Advertised as a sword cutler.
- Probably made cavalry swords.

(N) **ANTHONY BOUCHET (BOUCHETTE)** BALTIMORE, MD 1810-1820
- Shop located on Water Street.
- Advertised in the Baltimore city directory as a cutler.

(N) **R. (RYER) BOWEN SR.** FORT PITT Bc1736, 1756-1800
(LATER PITTSBURGH, PA)
- During the French and Indian War (1756-1763), had a contract with the British Indian Service for 51 brass tomahawks, which were provided to Indians friendly to the British.
- Related to William Bowen.

(Blacksmith, cutler, tomahawk maker)
(See William Bowen)

(N) **R. (RYER) BOWEN JR.** PITTSBURGH, PA 1780-1819
- Son of Ryer Bowen Sr.
  R. (RYER) BOWEN JR. WHITING, PA 1819-1828
- Succeeded edged weapons maker William Stackpole.
  R. (RYER) BOWEN JR. PITTSBURGH, PA 1828-1830
- Located on the corner of Pennsylvania Street and Cecils Alley.

(Blacksmith; cutler; knife, axe, and tomahawk maker)
(See William Stackpole)

(N) **WILLIAM BOWEN** FORT PITT 1736-1770
(LATER PITTSBURGH, PA)
- Related to Ryer Bowen Sr.
- Had a contract with the British Indian Service for tomahawks, which were provided to Indians friendly to the British (1770).

(Blacksmith; knife, axe, and tomahawk maker)
(See Ryer Bowen Sr.)

(N) **ISAAC BRABANT** PURYSBURGH, SC 1750-1760
(under British dominion)
- Made tomahawks for local Indians.

(Blacksmith)

(A) **DAVID BRADY SR.** MT. JOY, PA 1829-1870
- Located at 60 Main Street (with son David Jr.).
- Made edged tools.

(A) **DAVID BRADY JR.** MT. JOY, PA 1848-1882
- Located at 60 Main Street (1848-1870), 125 E. Walnut Street (1870-1882).
- Made knives and edged tools.

(Cutler)

(A) **JAMES BREARLEY**   PHILADELPHIA, PA   1780-1825
- Located at 78 North 3rd Street (1780-1813), 113 1/2 North 3rd Street (1813-1825).

(N) **BRIDGEPORT GUN IMPLEMENT CO.**   BRIDGEPORT, CT   1900-1910
- Marked their products "B.G.I.C.O."
- Made brass-mounted bowie knives with short 8 1/2-inch blades and hard rubber grips riveted on the tang.

(N) **BRIDGEPORT KNIFE CO.**   BRIDGEPORT, CT   1878-1900
- Located at the corner of Washington and Hallett Streets.
- Knife maker, including bowie knives.
- Exported to South America.

(N) **JAMES (JIM) BRIDGER**   RICHMOND, VA   1804-1816
    JIM BRIDGER   ST. CLAIRE CO., IL   1816-1822
- Apprenticed to gunsmith Philip Creamer at St. Claire Co., IL, across the river from St. Louis, MO.

    JIM BRIDGER   NORTHWEST U.S.   1822-1843
- Traveled as a fur trapper for several fur companies.

    JIM BRIDGER   FORT BRIDGER, WY   1843-1853
- Established a gun shop and blacksmiths forge among the Shoshone Indians.
- Made and traded guns.
- Made knives and tomahawks.
- Fort Bridger was a trading post, hostelry, and supply point for pioneers on the Oregon Trail traveling to Oregon.

    JIM BRIDGER   WESTERN U.S.   1853-1868
- Retired in 1868.

    JIM BRIDGER   KANSAS CITY, MO   1868-D1881

(C) **CHAUNCEY BROCKWAY**   SOUTH CHARLESTON, NH   1840-1844

(N) **R. BRODERICK**   PIQUA, OH   1815-1825
- Made tomahawks for the U.S. Office of Indian Trade (1820).

(Blacksmith)

(A) **FRANCIS BROOKS**   PHILADELPHIA, PA   1770-1795
- Had two shops: one for his business as a pistol maker and gunsmith at 87 Bankside South and the other for his business as a cutler and hardware and jewelry importer at 86 Water Street.

(A) **NICHOLAS BROOKS**   PHILADELPHIA, PA   1775-1815
- Located on 2nd Street (between Market and Chesnut Streets).

(N) **ALBERT BROWN**   NEW CASTLE, PA   1861-1865
    BROWN (ALBERT) & SON   NEW CASTLE, PA   1865-1870
- Gun and bowie knife maker.
- Shop located on Grey Street.

(A) **JAMES BROWN**   PITTSBURGH, PA   1812-1814
- Located on Marbury Street (between Liberty and Pennsylvania Streets).

(Cutler)

    BROWN (JAMES), BARKER (ABNER) & BUTLER (JAMES R.)   PITTSBURGH, PA   1814-1816

(Blacksmith, cutler, and knife maker)

(A) **J.M. BROWN**   **GREEN BAY, WI**   **1815-1830**
- Made tomahawks for the U.S. Office of Indian Trade (1820).

(Blacksmith)

(N) **WILLIAM BROWN**   **NEWARK, NJ**   **Bc1824-1844**
    WILLIAM BROWN   **NEWARK, NJ**   **1844-1851**
- Locations:
    - 14 Clay Street (1844-1845)
    - 85 Quarry Street (1845-1848)
    - 8 Webster Street (1848-1851)

    CRAWFORD (AARON), BROWN   **NEWARK, NJ**   **1851-1852**
    (WILLIAM) & SAUERBIER (HENRY)
- Located at 7 Mechanic Lane.

(Cutler)
(See Aaron Crawford & Henry Sauerbier)

(A) **CHARLES OLIVER BRUFF**   **CHARLESTOWN, MD**   **B1731-1760**
        TALBOT COUNTY
    CHARLES OLIVER BRUFF   **ELIZABETHTOWN, NJ**   **1760-1765**
    CHARLES OLIVER BRUFF   **NEW YORK, NY**   **1765-1776**
- Advertised in the *New York Gazette* (June 19, 1775):
    > On Maiden Lane, near the Fly Market
    > *Those gentlemen who are forming themselves into companies, in defense of their liberties, and others that are not provided with swords, may be suited therewith by applying to Charles Oliver Bruff. Small swords, silver mounted.*
    > *Cut and thrust swords.*
    > *Cutteau de chase (hunting swords) mounted with beautiful green (ivory) grips.*
    > *Broadswords with the heads of Lord Chattham and John Wilkes esquire; with shells (guard).*
    > *Pierced and ornamented with Mottoes:* "For Pitt's Head"
    >   "Magna Carta and Freedom"
    >   "For Wilke's Head"
    >   "Wilkes and Liberty"
    > *Or in whatever form a gentleman may fancy, being a collection of most elegant swords made in America, all manufactured by the said Bruff.*
- Advertised in the *New York Gazette* (July 8, 1726):
    Wanted: Silversmiths, a cutler, chapeforgers, filers and whitesmiths.

(N) **JACOB BUCHANON**   **BALTIMORE, MD**   **1790-1810**
- Located at 9 Queen Street (1790-1796), 24 Queen Street (1796-1810).
- Had a brass and iron forge.
- Advertised brass-, iron-, and silver-mounted knives.

(N) **JOHN, CHARLES & RICHARD BUCK**   **SHEFFIELD, ENGLAND**   **c1825-1849**
- John and Charles immigrated to Rochester, NY (1849).
- Richard immigrated to Rochester, NY (1853).
- Moved to Worchester, MA (1853).

    BUCK BROS.   **WORCESTER, MA**   **1853-1864**
- Partners: John, Charles, and Richard Buck.
- Made fine edged tools and bowie knives.
- Charles left the company (1864).
- John and Richard moved to Millbury, MA.

BUCK BROS.	MILLBURY, MA	1864-1893

- Partners: John and Richard Buck.
- Richard Buck died (1893).

(A) **ELISHA BUELL (BUEL)**	HEBRON, CT	1775-1797

- Made 40 muskets for the U.S. privateer *Oliver Cromwell* (1776).
- Made brass-mounted artillery officer swords with spiral green ivory grips and eagle-head pommels during the Revolutionary War.
- Moved to Marlborough, CT (1797).

ELISHA BUELL	MARLBOROUGH, CT	1797-1833

- Established a gun factory on the Turnpike Road (1810).
- Had U.S. contracts for M1795 and M1808 muskets.

(Gunsmith, sword maker)

(N) **BURKINSHAW KNIFE CO.**	PEPPERELL, MA	1853-1923

- President: Aaron Burkinshaw.
- General knife maker, including bowie knives.

(A) **WILLIAM BURNETT (BURNETTE)**	GREEN BAY, WI	1815-1830

- Made tomahawks for the U.S. Office of Indian Trade in 1820.

(Blacksmith)

(N) **THOMAS BURNEY**	OHIO FRONTIER	1740-1750

- Had a blacksmith shop on the Muskingum River.
- Made and repaired tomahawks, knives, and guns for local Indians.

THOMAS BURNEY	PICKAWILLANY, OHIO FRONTIER	1750-1752

- Moved to Pickawillany at the request of the Ohio Land Co., which had established a trading post there. The Miami Indians at Pickawillany had asked the Ohio Land Co. to post a smith there to make and repair their tomahawks and guns.

THOMAS BURNEY	WESTMORELAND CO., PA	1752-D1755

- Set up a blacksmith shop (forge), probably on Turkle Creek, and was an agent for the British Indian Service dealing with local Indians. Here again he made and repaired tomahawks, knives, and guns for local Indians.
- Became a member of the Pennsylvania militia.
- Joined British Gen. Edward Braddock's expedition with two regiments of British foot soldiers against the French Fort Duquesne (later British Fort Pitt, later Pittsburgh). After they crossed the Monongahela River, they met the French and their Indian allies. Burney and General Braddock both were killed (July 9, 1755).

(N) **JOHN B. BURROWS**	PHILADELPHIA, PA	1800-1820

- Located on the corner of 6th Avenue and Fitzwalter Street.
- Advertised in the Philadelphia city directory as a cutler.

(N) **JAMES BURT**	BOSTON, MA	1770-1790

- Made guns and swords during the Revolutionary War.

(Gun maker, cutler, sword maker)

(A) **RICHARD & WILLIAM BUTLER**	LANCASTER CO., PA	1745-1759
RICHARD & WILLIAM BUTLER	CARLISLE, PA	1759-1765
RICHARD & WILLIAM BUTLER	FORT PITT (LATER PITTSBURGH, PA) (under British dominion)	1765-1770

- Sons of Thomas Butler Sr.
- Formed a partnership and opened a gunsmith shop.
- Made small and large pipe tomahawks.

(A) **THOMAS BUTLER SR.**   LANCASTER CO., PA   B1720, 1759-D1791
     THOMAS BUTLER SR.   CARLISLE, PA
     (under British dominion)

(Gunsmith, cutler, tomahawk maker)

(N) **JOHN CAMPBELL**   FORT MICHILIMACKINAC   1822-1830
     STRAITS OF MACKINAC
     U.S. NORTHWEST TERRITORY

- Fort Michilimackinac was originally a French fort and trading post. It became a British fort at the end of the French and Indian War (1763) and was ceded to the U.S. at the end of Revolutionary War (1783).
- Campbell made tomahawks for the U.S. Office of Indian Trade (1822).

(Blacksmith)

(A) **WILLIAM CAMPBELL**   FREDERICK CO., VA   1766-1780
     WILLIAM CAMPBELL   ANNAPOLIS, MD   1780-1781
     (under British dominion)
     WILLIAM CAMPBELL   HAMPSHIRE CO., VA   1781-D1799

- Made knives and tomahawks for local Indians.

(N) **CANTON CUTLERY CO.**   CANTON, OH   1880-1930
- General knife makers, including bowie knives.

(A) **P.S. CANU**   WILMINGTON, NC   1806-1807
(Gunsmith)

(A) **ROBERT CARR**   PHILADELPHIA, PA   1779-1815
- Locations:
  - Meade Alley (1779-1799)
  - 334 South 2nd Street (1799-1810)
  - 9 German Street (1810-1815)

(A) **DANIEL CARRELL**   PHILADELPHIA, PA   1764-1784
     JOHN & DANIEL CARRELL   PHILADELPHIA, PA   1784-1785
- Located on Market Street (1784), Front Street (1785).
     DANIEL CARRELL   CHARLESTON, SC   1785-1801
     DANIEL CARRELL   PHILADELPHIA, PA   1801-1806

(A) **JOHN CARRELL**   PHILADELPHIA, PA   1760-1784
     JOHN & DANIEL CARRELL   PHILADELPHIA, PA   1784-1785
- Located on Market Street (1784), Front Street (1785).
- Advertised as goldsmith, jeweler, watch and clock maker (1784).
     JOHN CARRELL   PHILADELPHIA, PA   1785-1796
- Located at 32 Market Street (at Lucretia Street).
- Advertised in the *Pennsylvania Packet* silver-mounted swords, watches, clocks, gold and silver work, and jewelry (1787).

(A) **JOHN CARTWRIGHT**   PITTSBURGH, PA   1830-1858

- Located at 140 Wood Street (1830-1840), 83 Wood Street (1840-1858).
- Advertised in the *Pittsburgh Daily Morning Post* (May 13, 1847) as follows:
    Importer and manufacturer of cutlery. Lately received a large assortment of pen and pocket cutlery, knives, tableware, guns, rifles, pistols, powder flasks, shot belts, percussion caps, bowie and hunting knives and dirks.

CARTWRIGHT (JOHN) & YOUNG (WILLIAM W.)	PITTSBURGH, PA	1858-1861

- Located at 83 Wood Street.
- Advertised as successors to John Cartwright.

W. (WILLIAM W.) YOUNG	PITTSBURGH, PA	1861-1865

- Advertised in the *Waynesburg Messenger* (September 11, 1861) as successor to Cartwright & Young.
- Manufacturer of and dealer in tools, cutlery, surgical and dental instruments, guns, and pistols.

(A) **CARVER (WILLIAM) & HALL (THOMAS)** — ALEXANDRIA, VA — 1795-1797
- Located on Saint Asaph Street.

(N) **CASE BROTHERS** — LITTLE VALLEY, NY — 1880-1890
- Knife makers, including bowie knives.

(N) **R. (RANDELL) H. CASHWELL (CASHELL, CASKELL)** — PHILADELPHIA, PA — 1790-1810
R.H. CASHWELL — BALTIMORE, MD — 1810-1811
R.H. CASHWELL — FREDERICK, MD — 1811-1818
- Located on Market Street, fourth house below the turnpike.
- Advertised "*guns and pistols bronzed, blued and blackened in such a manner that they cannot rust.*" Also advertised firearms cleaned and repaired; swords cleaned and polished; new swords mounted, gilt, or plated; and blades blued (1814).

(Silversmith, gunsmith, whitesmith, sword hiltor)

(N) **JOHN F. (FRANKLIN) CASSELL** — BALTIMORE, MD — 1838-1848
- Made tomahawks and repaired guns for local Indians.

JOHN F. (FRANKLIN) CASSELL — CLAYTON, IL — 1848-1886

(Gunsmith, blacksmith)

(N) **CATTARAUGUS CUTLERY CO.** — LITTLE VALLEY, NY — 1880-1960
- General knife makers, including bowie knives.

(N) **CENTRAL CITY KNIFE CO.** — PHOENIX, NY — 1880-1920
- General knife makers, including bowie knives.

(N) **JAMES CHAMBERS** — LANCASTER CO., PA (under British dominion) — B1738, 1750-D1763
- Made knives and tomahawks and repaired guns for local Indians.

(Gunsmith, blacksmith)

(A) **GOLDSMITH CHANDLEE SR.** — WINCHESTER, VA — 1775-D1821
- Located at corner of Cameron and Piccadilly Streets.

(Silversmith, sword hiltor, clock maker, mathematical instrument maker)

(N) **LEFEVRE CHAPARO**		DETROIT, MI (under British dominion)	1775-1783

- Made tomahawks for the British Indian Service (1778).

(Blacksmith)

(A) **ROBERT CHAT** — PHILADELPHIA, PA — 1780-1800
- Located at 33 Mead Alley.

(A, C) **JACOB D. CHEVALIER** — NEW YORK, NY — 1823-1835
- Moved from Dealer listing in Volume I.
- Located at 151 Reade Street.

(Cutler, dental instrument maker)

JOHN D. CHEVALIER — NEW YORK, NY — 1835-1861
- Located at 151 Reade Street (1835-1845).
- Located at 360 Broadway (1845-1860).
- Showroom located at 639 Broadway, factory at 14-16 Amity Place (1860-1861).
- Made high-quality bowie knives.
- Some marked "Chevaliers California Knife," others marked "Chevaliers Union Knife."

JOHN D. CHEVALIER & SONS — NEW YORK, NY — 1861-1871
- Showroom located at 639 Broadway.
- Factory located at 14-16 Amity Place.

(Cutler, knife maker, surgical instrument maker, fancy hardware maker)

(N) **JAMES CHRISTIE** — PHILADELPHIA, PA — 1775-1783
- Pennsylvania Committee of Safety musket and bayonet maker.

(C) **JOSIAH CLAPHAM** — POINT OF FORK, VA
FLUVANNA CO. — 1739-1783

(A) **BENJAMIN CLARK** — PHILADELPHIA, PA — 1790-1811
- Located at 36 Market Street.

(C) **JOHN CLARK** — SHIPPENSBURG, PA — 1811-1818

(A) **DANIEL CLARKE** — PHILADELPHIA, PA — 1820-1856
- Made bowie knives.

(A) **WILLIAM T. CLEMENT** — GREENFIELD, MA — 1816-1843
WILLIAM T. CLEMENT — SHELBURNE FALLS, MA — 1843-1857
- Factory superintendent at Lamson & Goodnow Mfg. Co. (cutler) (1843-1857).
- Purchased the Bay State Tool Co. with his partner C.H. Hawkes (1857).

WILLIAM T. CLEMENT & C.H. HAWKES — NORTHAMPTON, MA — 1857-1866
- Tool company making hoes, rakes, and hay forks.
- Made bayonets and gun barrels during the Civil War.

**SAMUEL NORRIS &
WILLIAM T. CLEMENT** — SPRINGFIELD, MA — 1862-1866
- A separate company making muskets.
- Had Massachusetts contracts for 3,000 Springfield muskets at $18.50 each (1862-1864).
- Also made percussion pistols.

**CLEMENT (WILLIAM T.),
HAWKES (C.H.) MFG. CO.** — NORTHAMPTON, MA — 1866-1882

- Made table cutlery.
- Built a new factory.
- Exhibited table knives at the New York Fair (1867).
- Made bowie knives.

THE CLEMENT CUTLERY CO.   NORTHAMPTON, MA   1882-1956
- Made knife blanks for other cutlery companies.

THE CLEMENT CO.   NORTHAMPTON, MA   1956-1998
- Make Delvin knives and other cutlery.

(N) **JAMES CLIFFE**   OPELOUSAS DISTRICT, LA   c1800-1840
- A blacksmith at the sugar plantation of Rezin Bowie (father of Rezin Pleasant Bowie and James Bowie).
- Rezin Bowie had Cliffe make him a hunting knife out of a file (c. 1818). It had a single-edged 9 1/4 x 1 1/2" blade. The blade had an almost straight back and a curved edge coming to a saber type point. Bowie had Cliffe incorporate a cross guard between the blade and handle to prevent the hand from slipping down on the blade when killing an animal (Bowie had his hand injured in such a manner). It did not have the concave "clipped" point that eventually became known as the bowie knife. (The first bowie knife was made by Henry Sheirley of Philadelphia, PA.)
- When Rezin's brother James was involved in a feud with a Maj. Morris Wright and his friends, Rezin gave James a hunting knife for additional self-protection (1827). It was in the same style that Rezin had had made by James Cliffe. This was the knife James Bowie used in the famous Sand Bar duel, where he fought four adversaries and killed one. He almost died from wounds received in the fight.

(See Henry Sheirley)

(N) **WILLIAM CLINTON**   PHILADELPHIA, PA   1750-1770
                                     (under British dominion)
- During the French and Indian War (1756-1763), sold pitching axes (throwing axes/tomahawks) to Pennsylvania Lt. Governor Thomas Penn for use by Indians friendly to the British.

(Blacksmith)

(A) **JAMES COATS (COATES)**   PHILADELPHIA, PA   1790-1815
- Gunsmith shop located at 47 Tammany Street.
- Worked for gun and sword maker John Joseph Henry Sr. (1814-1815).

(Gunsmith, sword maker)

(A) **MOSES COATS (COATES)**   EAST CALN, CHESTER CO., PA   1785-1796
- Made scalping knives and tomahawks for the local Indians.

(Cutler, blacksmith)

(A) **SANFORD B. COCKE**   RICHMOND, VA   B1822-1850
- Located at 162 Main Street.

(A) **JOHN COLER**   BALTIMORE, MD   1775-1797
- Blacksmith shop located at 36 Light Street.

JOHN COLER   PHILADELPHIA, PA   1797-1805

(Blacksmith, pike maker)

(A) **DANIEL C. COLLINS**   HARTFORD, CT   B1802-1826
- Worked at a local hardware store (David Watkinson & Co.) with his brother Samuel (c. 1820-1826).

SAMUEL W. (WATKINSON) COLLINS   HARTFORD, CT   B1805-1826
- Worked at a local hardware store (David Watkinson & Co.) with his brother Daniel (c. 1820-1826). Watkinson was a relative.

- The Collins brothers decided to mass produce presharpened (cast) axe heads. (Previously, axe heads were hand-hammered and unsharpened.)
- Bought the old Humphrey Grist Mill in South Canton, CT, on the Farmington River, 15 miles west of Hartford, and converted it into an axe head factory (1826).

COLLINS & CO.   **SOUTH CANTON, CT**   1826-1828
(SAMUEL W. & DANIEL C.)

- Partners and cousins: William Wells, John F. Wells.
- South Canton became Collinsville (1828).

COLLINS & CO.   **COLLINSVILLE, CT**   1828-1834

- Main office located on the corner of Front and Main Streets.
- President: Samuel W. Collins.
- Forging shop foreman: B.T. Wingate.
- Machinist: Elisha K. Root.
- Opened a depot and sales office in Hartford, CT (1828).
- Installed the first trip hammer (1828).
- Built duplex houses for their employees (1831-1832).
- The company grew and began making picks, shovels, farm tools, and plows.
- As the years passed, machetes, dirks, bayonets, Indian belt knives, and bowie knives were added.

COLLINS MFG. CO.   **COLLINSVILLE, CT**   1834-1843

- Office located on the corner of Front and Main Streets.
- The company was reorganized; Samuel W. Collins forced to step down from president to superintendent of operations.
- Began making iron and cast steel (1842).
- All products were marked "Collins & Co. Hartford, CT."
- Factory superintendent: Charles Blair (1839-1885).

THE COLLINS CO.   **COLLINSVILLE, CT**   1843-1966

- Office located on the corner of Front and Main Streets.
- The company was again reorganized with Samuel W. Collins as president.
- All products were still marked "Collins & Co. Hartford, CT."
- Began to ship products abroad, especially South America (1840).
- Opened a new depot and sales office in New York (1846).
- Located at 1912 3rd Avenue (1846-1862), 212 Water Street (1862-1966).
- Began making bowie knives (1847).
- Hartford sales office and depot closed (1848).
- Began to use cast steel purchased from Thomas Firth & Sons, Sheffield England (1849).
- Exhibited axes and edged tools at the Great International Exposition, London, England (1851).
- Charles Blair, Collinsville factory superintendent, had a separate contract (not Collins contract) with the infamous abolitionist John Brown for 1,000 pikes (1857).
- Had 350 employees (1860).
- Made over 300 different patterns of machetes (1860).
- Built new shops with steam engine, steam boilers, trip hammers, and rollers (1863-1864).
- During the Civil War, had U.S. contracts for 1,000 M1840 musician's swords ($4 and $4.25 each) and 650 non-comm. swords ($4.50, $4.75, and $5 each).
- Also made M1850 foot officer swords, M1850 staff and field officer swords, M1852 naval officer swords, and M1840 (variation) cavalry sabers.
- Imported M1860 cavalry officer sabers.
- Sold M1850 foot officer swords and many blades (plain and engraved) to Tiffany & Co., Schuyler, Hartley & Graham, and James P. Fitch, all of New York.
- Made gun parts (including butt plates, trigger guards, and barrel bands) for Eli Whitney & Co. of New Haven, CT (1862).

- Had Civil War contracts for crowbars, picks, axes, and sledgehammers.
- Made bowie knives during the Civil War. One has been seen with a lion-head pommel and etched blade ("The Union Now & Forever"). It also has the name "S.M. Tatro" on it. He was Collins' inspector of grinding.
- Built a two-story plow warehouse next to the main office building in Collinsville (1865).
- Tore down the main offices and built new three-story offices on the same site (1867).
- Had 638 workmen (1868).
- Began publishing catalogs (1870).
- Began to use traveling sales representatives (1870).
- Samuel W. Collins died (1871).
- Exhibited at the Philadelphia Exposition, including swords and bayonets (1876).
- Exhibited at the Paris International Exposition (1878).
- During World War II, Collins & Co. made 1,050,000 machetes for the U.S. government for use by the U.S. Army, Navy, and Marine Corps.
- Also had contracts for axes, picks, shovels, and sledgehammers.
- Sold four million machetes to Latin America and made 12,000 tools per day (1946).
- Opened a factory in Mexico City, Mexico (1954).
- Opened a factory in Sao Paolo, Brazil (1956).
- Opened a factory in Palmira, Columbia (1961).
- Opened a factory in Amatitlan, Guatemala (1965).
- Collins & Co. was purchased by the Mann Edged Tool Co. (1966).

(See Charles Blair)

Collins Products

(The numbers next to the items are Collins model numbers from their catalog.)

U.S. Military Swords
M1840 musician's swords
M1840 non-comm. swords
M1850 foot officer swords
M1850 staff and field officer swords
M1852 naval officer swords
M1840 (variation) cavalry sabers
M1860 officer cavalry sabers (were imported)

Foreign Military Short Swords
#66 Mexican Army sword
#86 Spanish Regulation sword
#87 Cuban Rebel officer sword
#87 Cuban other ranks sword
#87 Mexican Army sword

Nonmilitary Short Swords
#135 reverse-P hilt sword
#169 and #192 "D" guard hilt sword
#375 cross guard hilt, lion-head pommel sword

Bowie Knives (c. 1847-1968)
#18 bronze cast hilt bowie knife
#18 Elefante model bowie knife

#18 Galo model bowie knife
#18 corrugated leather grip bowie knife
    Lion-head pommel bowie knife (Civil War)
#17 cast bronze hilt bowie knife
#17 corrugated leather grip bowie knife

U.S. Military Knives
M1904-1905 Hospital Corps knife
M1887 Hospital Corps knife
Pre WWII Hospital Corps knife
WWII Hospital Corps knife
M1904 Philippine scout cavalry knife
M1906 Signal Corps (brush cutting) knife
1934 Air Corps survival bowie knife
1942 Air Corps survival bowie knife
1942 Marine Corps "Gung Ho" raider bowie knife
1942 Air Corps survival bowie knife (horn grip)
Post WWII Air Corps survival bowie knife (plastic grip)
Canadian WWII bush knife

U.S. Military Machetes
#191 Marine Corps machete
M1943 Engineer machete bolo knife
M1909 machete bolo knife
Army Air Force Corps survival machete
#127-#128-#151-#623 Army experimental machetes
M1939 Army Quartermaster Corps machete
#23-#35-#85-#128 Marine Corps experimental machetes
M1942-1943-1944 Navy K1 machetes
M1943-1944-1945 Navy K2 machetes
#1253 paratrooper machetes type 1, 2 and 3
M1942 Army machetes

Bayonets
- During the Civil War, Collins made more than 200,000 bayonets.
- Made saber bayonets for the Plymouth-Whitneyville M1861 navy rifle; Spencer navy rifle; Colt M1855 revolving rifle and carbine; Sharps M1860 rifle; and Sharps & Hankins M1863 rifle.
- Made angular socket bayonets for the Springfield M1855 rifle-musket; Sharps M1863 rifle; Colt special M1861 rifle; and Colt M1855 revolving rifle and carbine.

Collins Hunting Knives
- Numbers in their catalog were #39, #165, #363, #376, #396, #397, #398, #443, #444, #450, #457, #490.

Other Collins Weapons
8mm pistol (copy of Colt Police Special) (c. 1919)
Pike and lance heads
Daggers

Collins Tools (over 1,200 items)
Axes

Hatchets
Hook knives
Machetes (over 300 styles)
Machete knives
Hand hammers
Sledgehammers
Cane knives
Cloth knives
Picks
Chisels
Shovels
Crowbars
Hoes
Adzes
Pole knives
Wedges

(N) JOHN CONCKLIN	BALTIMORE, MD	1790-1800

- Made tomahawks for local Indians.

(Blacksmith)

(A) JOHN CONEY	BOSTON, MA	B1655, 1675-D1722

- Appollos Rivoire (Paul Revere I, father of the famous Paul Revere II) apprenticed as a goldsmith and silversmith with Coney (1715-1722).

(See Paul Revere I in Silversmith listings)

(N) RICHARD CONSTABLE	PHILADELPHIA, PA	1817-1851

- Bought out Booth & Co. (1817).
- Located at 88 South 2nd Street (1817-1833), 83 South 2nd Street (1833-1851).
- Imported guns from England.
- Made flintlock dueling pistols and muskets.

(N) JOHN CORBY	CHARLESTON, SC	B1792-1812
GRAY (WILLIAM) & CORBY (JOHN)	CHARLESTON, SC	1812-1820

- Bought out William Gunn (1812).
- Located at 5 Queen Street.

JOHN CORBY	CHARLESTON, SC	1820-1823

- Located on the corner of Pritchard Street and Knox's wharf.
- Sold ships chandlery.

(Gunsmith, blacksmith, cutler)
(See William Gunn)

(N) W. (WILLIAM) M. COTTON	LEOMINSTER, MA	1820-1850

- Rifle, gun, and bowie knife maker.

(A) C. (CHARLES) COWAN	PITTSBURGH, PA	1800-1819

- Located on the corner of Pennsylvania Street and Cecils Alley.
- Made steel axes and tomahawks.
- Had a slitting mill and hammer mill.

(Cutler)

(N) **AARON CRAWFORD**   NEWARK, NJ   B1818-1838
    A. (AARON) CRAWFORD   NEWARK, NJ   1838-1844
- Operated a tool factory.
- Factory located on Washington Street (1838-1839).
- Factory located on Nesbitt Court (1839-1844).

    AARON CRAWFORD   NEWARK, NJ   1844-1846
- Changed production to saddlery hardware.
- Factory located at 342 Broad Street (1844-1845), 346 Broad Street (1845-1846).

    AARON CRAWFORD   NEWARK, NJ   1846-1851
- City directories show Crawford in saddlery hardware and cutlery.
- Located at 7 Mechanic Lane.

    CRAWFORD (AARON), BROWN (WILLIAM) & SAUERBIER (HENRY)   NEWARK, NJ   1851-1853
- Listed as cutlers in Newark city directories.
- Located at 7 Mechanic Lane.

    AARON CRAWFORD   NEWARK, NJ   1853-1866
- Listed as a cutler in Newark city directories.
- Located at 212 Market Street (1853-1861), 10 Mechanic Lane (1861-1866).

(See William Brown & Henry Sauerbier)

(N) **JOHN G. CRAWFORD**   NEWARK, NJ   1851-1852
- Located at 98 Washington Street.

(Cutler)

(N) **PETER CREMAR**   FORT PITT (LATER PITTSBURGH, PA)   1758-1770
- During the French and Indian War (1756-1763), had a contract with the British Indian Service to provide tomahawks to Indians friendly to the British.

(Blacksmith; knife, axe, tomahawk maker)

(N) **PETER CRONIN (COCIN-CONIN)**   FORT PITT (LATER PITTSBURGH, PA)   1758-1770
- During the French and Indian War (1756-1763), had a contract with the British Indian Service to provide tomahawks to Indians friendly to the British.

(Blacksmith; knife, axe, tomahawk maker)

(N) **WILLIAM H. CUMMINGS**   PHILADELPHIA, PA   1820-1855
- Gun shop located at 45 Green Street.
- Made flintlock muskets and inlayed-pewter pipe tomahawks.

(Gunsmith, blacksmith)

(N) **ROBERT CUNIE**   WEST AUGUSTA, VA   1775-1783
- Made riflemen's belt axes (tomahawks) (1777).

(Blacksmith)

(A) **JOHN CUTLER**   BOSTON, MA   1740-1790
- Located at 39 Marlborough Street.
- Also a brassfounder.

(A) **BAPTISTE DARTNELL**   PHILADELPHIA, PA   1799-1800
- Located at 39 Plumb Street.

(A) **THOMAS DAVIS**　　　　　　　　　　　　　　PHILADELPHIA, PA　　　　　　　1750-1760
- Located on Market Street.

(A) **WILLIAM DAWSON**　　　　　　　　　　　　PHILADELPHIA, PA　　　　　　　1749-1783
- Located on 3rd Street (between Market and Arch Streets).

(A) **DEMOULIN BROS.**　　　　　　　　　　　　　GREENVILLE, IL　　　　　　　　1905-1997
- Located at 1105 South 4th Street.

(A) **HENRY DERINGER JR.**　　　　　　　　　　　PHILADELPHIA, PA　　　　　　　1808-D1868
- Home located at 33 Coates Street (1808-1812), 612 North Front Street (1812-1868).
- Gun shop located at 307 North Front Street (1808-1811), 29 Green Street (1811-1812).
- Pistol, rifle, sword factory, and military store located at 374 North Front Street (1812-1819).
- Pistol, rifle, and sword factory located at 370 North Front Street (1819-1868).
- Second rifle factory located at 607 Tamarind Street (between Green and Coates Streets) behind his home at 612 North Front Street (1847-1868).
- Son-in-law Jonathon Clarke was superintendent in his main factory at 370 North Front Street (c. 1854-1868).
- In 1812 Deringer advertised as follows:

    Rifle Manufactory
    Henry Deringer informs his customers and the public in general, that he has on hand and intends to keep at his military store, 374 No. Front Street, an assortment of:
    Rifles
    Muskets
    Fowling pieces
    Pistols
    Swords
    Cutlasses
    Boarding pikes
    and Boarding axes of every description

- Deringer also sold tomahawks to the U.S. Office of Indian Trade.
- Purchased pistol making machinery from N.P. Ames of Chicopee, MA, to make M1843 boxlock pistols for the U.S. Navy (1845).
- Made 5,250 pair of his famous Deringer pocket pistols (1849-1868).
- When Henry died, his rifle factory at 607 Tamarind Street was willed to his son Bronaugh (1868).
- His son-in-law Jonathon Clarke, who was his factory superintendent at his main factory (370 North Front) continued that business (c. 1854-1868).

　　BRONAUGH W. DERINGER & CO.　　　　　PHILADELPHIA, PA　　　　　　　1868-1881
- Factory located at 607 Tamarind Street.
- Son and successor to Henry Deringer Jr.

(Gunsmith)
　　THE DERINGER RIFLE & PISTOL WORKS　PHILADELPHIA, PA　　　　　　　1868-1870
- Factory located at 370 North Front Street.
- President: Jonathon Clarke.
- When Clarke died his son took over (c. 1870).

　　THE DERINGER RIFLE & PISTOL WORKS　PHILADELPHIA, PA　　　　　　　1870-1881
- Factory located at 370 North Front Street (1870-1880), 611 Tamarind Street (1880-1881).
- President: I. Jones Clarke (son of Jonathon).
- Sold cartridge revolvers and single shot pistols.

(N) **JACOB DERINGER** PHILADELPHIA, PA 1861-1865
  19th WARD
- Probably son of Philip Deringer.

(Gunsmith)

(N) **JOHN HENRY DERINGER** EASTON, PA B1788-1833
- Sometimes used German spelling "Johan Heinrich Deringer."
- Apprenticed to and worked for his father Henry Deringer Sr. in Easton, PA (c. 1803-1833).
- When his father died, he moved to Philadelphia, PA (1833).

JOHN H. (HENRY) DERINGER PHILADELPHIA, PA 1833-1840
- Gun shop located on North Front Street (near Coates Street), next to his brother Henry Deringer Jr.'s gun factory at 370 North Front Street.

(N) **PHILIP DERINGER** EASTON, PA Bc1794-1861
- Son of Henry Deringer Sr. (brother of Henry Jr.).
- Apprenticed to and worked with his father in Easton, PA (c. 1809-1833).
- When his father died (1833), he probably moved to Philadelphia, PA, to work with his famous brother Henry Deringer Jr. at his gun shops (c. 1833-1861).
- Opened his own gun shop in Reading, PA (1861).

PHILIP DERINGER READING, PA 1861-1885
- Gun shop located on North Fourth Street (above Washington Street).

(N) **T. (THOMAS) T. DERINGER** PHILADELPHIA, PA 1840-1847
- Probably son of John Henry Deringer.
- Located at 8 Coates Street.

(Gunsmith)

(A) **GEORGE DEWSNAP** PITTSBURGH, PA 1821-1824
- Located on Liberty Street.

(A) **DINGEE (ROBERT) & UNDERHILL** NEW YORK, NY 1803-1805
  (SAMUEL)
- Located at 169 Broadway.

ROBERT DINGEE SR. NEW YORK, NY 1806-1843
- Locations:
  169 Broadway (1806-1814)
  65 Dey Street (1814-1816)
  3 Cumber Street (1816-1839)
  23 Spruce Street (1839-1843)

(N) **JOHN DODD** PON PON 1750-1755
  (British Providence of South Carolina)
- Made and repaired guns, knives, and tomahawks for local Indians.

JOHN DODD CHARLESTOWN 1755-D1771
  (British Providence of South Carolina)
- Gun shop on Meeting Street near the market at the sign of the gun and pistols (1755-1762).
- Gun shop on the corner of Meeting and White Streets at the sign of the gun and pistols (a little higher up on Meeting Street) (1762-1771).
- Advertised in the *South Carolina Gazette* "*making and mending of guns in the neatest and best manner at reasonable prices*" and "*the best new spare barrels and the best stocks of curled walnut*" (1755 and 1762).

(Gunsmith, blacksmith, knife and tomahawk maker)

(A) **SAMUEL DORSEY**   ELKRIDGE, MD   1775-1783
- Committee of Safety contract for 10 four-pound cannon with swivels (1777).

(N) **A. (AUGUSTINE) J. DRAKE**   BOSTON, MA   1861-1869
- Located at 70 Albany Street.
- Massachusetts contract for 900 Whitney rifle bayonets, 200 Enfield rifle bayonets, and 30 Springfield rifle bayonets (1862).

(Machinist, gunsmith, gun repair, bayonet maker)

(N) **GILBERT DUBOIS**   NEW YORK, NY   B1819-c1840
    GILBERT DUBOIS   NAPANOCK, NY   c1840-1867
- Became owner of the Napanock Axe factory.
- Had 100 employees and made approximately 600 axes daily (1860).
- Dubois also made some Civil War cavalry sabers.
- Two Civil War M1860 cavalry sabers are known, marked "G. Dubois Napanock, NY."
- The sabers have hard rubber grips with fish scales cut into them.

(Edged tool maker)

(N) **LOUIS DUPLESIS**   OVIANTENON, IN   1775-1783
    (under British dominion)
- Made tomahawks for the British Indian Service (1778).

(N) **J. DURANT**   PHILADELPHIA, PA   1775-1783
- Made riflemen's belt axes (tomahawks) for the Pennsylvania Committee of Safety (1778).

(Blacksmith)

(N) **FRANCOIS DYELLE**   OHIO TERRITORY   1775-1783
    (under British dominion)
- Made tomahawks for the British Indian Service to be provided to Indians friendly to the English (1778).

(Blacksmith)

(A) **CHARLES EBERLE**   PHILADELPHIA, PA   1790-1808
- Arms inspector at the U.S. Philadelphia Armory (1807-1808).

    CHARLES EBERLE   PHILADELPHIA, PA   1808-1815
- Shop located at 11 North 6th Street.
- Made surgical instruments.
- May have made cavalry sabers.

(Gun maker, general cutler)

(A) **GEORGE & HENRY EBERLE**   PHILADELPHIA, PA   1799-1800
- Located on 4th Street (between Market and Arch Streets).

(A) **HENRY EBERLE**   PHILADELPHIA, PA   1800-D1822
- Located on Vine Street (above 7th Street) (1800-1810), 72 North 8th Street (1810-1822).

(Cutler, knife and bayonet maker)

(A) **JOHN EBERLE**   ELIZABETHTOWN, PA   1760-1780
- Made bayonets.

(C) **S. (SAMUEL) E. (EARLE) EBY & CO.**   PHILADELPHIA, PA   1925-1946

(A) **EMERSON (JAMES E.) & SILVER**   TRENTON, NJ   1860-1865
(JOSEPH S.)
- New York offices located at 447 Broome Street (second door west of Broadway).
- Displayed presentation swords at the New York Fair (1864).
- Made bowie knives.
- Had a New Jersey state contract for M1840 light artillery sabers with slightly curved M1860 cavalry saber blades.
- Testified to the Commission of Ordnance that in the last six months, he had provided 5,000 M1840 cavalry saber blades to Horstmann Brothers & Co., Philadelphia, PA. They were marked with a "keystone mark" because they were made at their Keystone Tool Works (April 7, 1862).
- Made many custom-order officer swords.
- Sold blades to George W. Simons & Co., Philadelphia, PA.
- Advertised in the *Army-Navy Journal* (November 28, 1863):
Manufacturers of rich presentation, masonic and regulation swords, fine spurs, belts, jewels, flags, banners, etc. Our facilities are unsurpassed. We make every part within our establishment, and are constantly getting up new and superior designs.
- Advertised in the *Army-Navy Journal* (August 27, 1864):
> *Manufacturers of all kinds of presentation and regulation swords, masonic and military goods and edged tools.*
> *New York Agents: Messrs, Schuyler, Hartley & Graham*
> *Shop—19 Maiden Lane.*
> *Factory—Trenton, NJ.*
> *Particular attention paid to presentation swords of new patterns, unsurpassed in richness and design. Blades or scabbards ornamented with camp or battle scenes, or correct likeness from photographs, put up in rosewood, mahogany, ebony or other fancy wood. Cases lined with velvet with room on top for belts, gloves, etc. All kinds of regulation swords on hand and made to order. We manufacture every part of our goods within our own establishment and we warrant our swords to stand government proof. We have made over 50,000 swords for the U.S. government.*
- Made a silver-hilted M1850 staff and field nonregulation sword for Gen. Samuel Wylie Crawford.

(N) **NATHANIEL EMMES SR.**   BOSTON, MA   1780-D1825
- Locations:
    Hancock's wharf (1789-1796)
    5th Street (1796-1798)
    Market Square (1798-1815)
    5th Street (1815-1824)
    Washington Street (1824-1825)

(Gunsmith, cutler)

(N) **NATHANIEL EMMES JR.**   BOSTON, MA   1816-1840
- Son of Nathaniel Sr.
- Located at 25 Fish Street (1816-1825), Washington Street (1825-1840).

(Gunsmith, cutler)

(N) **EMPIRE KNIFE CO.**   WINSTED, CT   1852-1856
- Owners: Mr. Thompson, Mr. Gascoigne.
- Made pocket knives.
- James Alvord and Elliott Beardsley purchased the Empire Knife Company (1856).

EMPIRE KNIFE CO.   WINSTED, CT   1856-1876
- Owners: James Alvord, Elliott Beardsley
- Elliot Beardsley died (1876).

EMPIRE KNIFE CO.   WEST WINSTED, CT   1876-1890

- Owner: James Alvord.
- Made shears, scissors, kitchen knives, razors, pocket knives, and bowie knives.

EMPIRE KNIFE CO.	WEST WINSTED, CT	1890-1930
(N) **JOHN ENDSOR**	BALTIMORE, MD	1790-1800

- Made tomahawks for the local Indians.

(Blacksmith)

(A) **JOHN ENGLES**	SOLINGEN, PRUSSIA	1735-1765

- Immigrated to Maryland.

JOHN ENGLES	MONOCACY, FREDERICK CO., MD	1765-1796
JOHN ENGLES	ALLEGHENY CO., MD	1796-1799
(A) **PETER ENGLES SR.**	SOLINGEN, PRUSSIA	1755-1765

- Immigrated to Maryland.

PETER ENGLES SR.	MONOCACY, FREDERICK CO., MD	1765-1796
PETER ENGLES SR.	GREENSBORO, PA SOMERSET CO.	1796-D1833
(N) **J. (JOHN) ENGLISH**	PHILADELPHIA, PA	c1800-1820

- Had a factory called Sheffield Works #2.
- Made quality knives and edged tools.

ENGLISH (JOHN) & HUBER (HENRY JR.)	PHILADELPHIA, PA	1820-1866

- Made quality bowie knives (some silver-mounted) and edged tools.

HENRY HUBER JR.	CHAMBERSBURG, PA	1866-1870

- Bought the John Shugart & Co. (1866).
- A cutlery and knife-making company.

HUBER (HENRY JR.) & CO.	CHAMBERSBURG, PA	1870-1876
HUBER (HENRY SR.) TOOL WORKS	CHAMBERSBURG, PA	1876-1880

(Silversmith, knife maker, axe and edged tool maker)

(N) **JOSEPH ENGLISH**	PHILADELPHIA, PA	1830-1840

- Made pipe tomahawks for the local Indians.

(Blacksmith)

(A) **DAVID P. ESTEP JR.**	PITTSBURGH, PA	1809-1838

- Son of Ephraim Estep.
- Became partner in E. Estep & Co. (1838).

(A) **EPHRAIM ESTEP**	PETERS TWSP. ALLEGHENY CO., PA	B1788-1809
E. ESTEP	LAWRENCEVILLE, PA	1809-1838
E. ESTEP & CO.	LAWRENCEVILLE, PA	1838-1842
ESTEP & MORGAN	PITTSBURGH, PA	1842-1844

- Factory located in Lawrenceville, PA.

E. (EPHRAIM) ESTEP & SONS	PITTSBURGH, PA	1844-1856

- Factory located in Lawrenceville, PA.

- Pittsburgh offices located on 5th Street.
- Pittsburgh sales agent: George Cochran, 26 Wood Street (Estep warehouse).
- Advertised edged tools, coopers, and carpenters tools and extra large knives (bowie knives?) "constantly on hand or made at short notice" (1844).

(A) **DANIEL EVANS**   PHILADELPHIA, PA   1753-1783
- Located on 5th Street (near Market Street).
- Had a Pennsylvania Committee of Safety contract for riflemen's belt axes (tomahawks) (1776).

(Blacksmith)

(A) **DANIEL EVANS**   BALTIMORE, MD   1776-1796
- Located on Gay Street.

(A) **GEORGE EVANS SR.**   LONDON, ENGLAND   1776-1796
    GEORGE EVANS SR.   PHILADELPHIA, PA   1796-D1798
- Located at 33 North Front Street.

    GEORGE EVANS & CO.   PHILADELPHIA, PA   1798-1905
- Located at 132 North 5th Street.

(N) **RICHARD FAXON**   BOSTON, MA   1810-1816
- Located at 11 Orange Street.

    CHARLES FAXON   BOSTON, MA   1816-1820
- Son of Richard Faxon.
- Located at 121 Broad Street.

(Blacksmith, edged tool and knife maker)

(N) **JOSEPH FEINOUR**   LANCASTER CO., PA   1775-1783
- Made tomahawks for the local Indians during the Revolutionary War.

(Blacksmith)

(N) **AUGUSTINE FELTCAN**   FORT MICHILIMACKINAC   1775-1783
    STRAITS OF MACKINAC
    (under British dominion)
- Fort Michilimackinac was originally a French fort and Indian post. It became a British fort at the end of the French and Indian War (1763) and was ceded to the U.S. at the end of the Revolutionary War (1783).
- Made tomahawks for the British Indian Service to be provided to Indians friendly to the British (1779).

(Blacksmith)

(A) **JOSEPH FENTON**   FRANKLIN, OH   1840-1842
    JOSEPH FENTON   COLUMBUS, OH   1842-1865
- Located at west side of High Street (1842-1852).
- Located on east side of High Street (near Town Street) (1852-1865).
- Made hunting and bowie knives.

(Cutler, knife maker)

(A) **PHILIP FINK**   BETHEL TWSP., PA   1850-1880

(N) **JESSE FISHPAW**   BALTIMORE, MD   1800-1815
- Made tomahawks for the U.S. Office of Indian Trade (1810).

(Blacksmith)

(A) **JOHN FITCH** TRENTON, NJ 1769-1776
- Located on King Street.

(A) **HENRY FLOWER** PHILADELPHIA, PA 1733-1766
- Located on 2nd Street (at the sign of the dial).

(A) **ABRAHAM GERRITZE FORBES** NEW YORK, NY 1765-1795
- Made silver-hilted small swords.

(Silversmith, sword hiltor)

(A) **GILBERT FORBES** NEW YORK 1750-1775
(under British dominion)
- Made belt axes (tomahawks), bayonets, muskets, rifles, and pistols.

(Gunsmith, cutler, blacksmith)

(A) **WILLIAM GARRETT FORBES** NEW YORK B1751-1773
FORBES (WILLIAM GARRETT) & NEW YORK, NY 1773-1799
LOCKWOOD (JAMES)
W. (WILLIAM) G. (GARRETT) FORBES NEW YORK, NY 1799-1838
- Made silver-hilted, hussar-hilted cavalry officer sabers.

(Silversmith, sword hiltor)

(A) **WILLIAM FOSBROOK** NEW YORK, NY 1768-1792
- Located at 58 Queens Street near Pecks slip.
- Advertised in the *New York Daily Gazette* (March 19, 1789):
  Light horse swords of Potter's make to be sold cheap by the quantity
- Advertised in the *New York Weekly Museum* (April 13, 1792):
  400 light horse and hanger blades for sale.

(See James Potter)

(N) **FOSTER & MURRAY** PITTSBURGH, PA 1800-1814
- Made axes, belt axes (tomahawks), and knives.

(Blacksmith, cutler)

(N) **JOSIAH FOWLE** BOSTON, MA 1810-1815
- Located at 17 Newbury Street.
- Advertised as a cutler in Boston the city directory.

(N) **JAMES D. FRARY** MERIDAN, CT B1833-1848
JAMES D. FRARY NEW YORK, NY 1848-1852
- Served apprenticeship and was a clerk in a hardware company.
JAMES D. FRARY MERIDAN, CT 1852-1854
- With his father, organized the Meridan Britannia Co.
- Sold his interest in the company and purchased the Meridan Hardware Co. (1854).
MERIDAN HARDWARE CO. MERIDAN, CT 1854-1857
- Also known as Frary, Benham & Co.
- Made powder flasks, game bags, and sporting goods.
FRARY (JAMES D.) & CO. MERIDAN, CT 1857-1862
- Hardware maker (e.g., scales, faucets, tools).
- George M. Landers purchased Frary & Co. (1862).

GEORGE M. LANDERS & CO. NEW BRITAIN, CT 1862-1865
- President: George M. Landers.
- Treasurer: James D. Frary.
- Secretary: William H. Smith.

LANDERS (GEORGE M.), FRARY NEW BRITAIN, CT 1865-1965
(JAMES D.) & CLARK (JOHN W.)
- President: George M. Landers.
- Secretary-treasurer: James D. Frary.
- Partner: John W. Clark.
- Frary became treasurer (1868).
- Frary became president (1870).
- Frary left to form his own company (1876).
- Made bowie knives

FRARY (JAMES D.) CUTLERY CO. BRIDGEPORT, CT 1876-1879
- Made table cutlery.
- Probably made bowie knives.

FRARY (JAMES D.) & SON BRIDGEPORT, CT 1879-D1895
- Made table cutlery, pocket knives (mass produced), and razors.
- Probably made bowie knives.
- James D. Frary died (1895).

(N) **JOHN FRASER (FRAZIER)** SCOTLAND B1721-1735
- Immigrated to Paxton Township, Lancaster County, PA (1735).

JOHN FRASER PAXTON TWSP. 1735-1746
  LANCASTER CO., PA
- Worked on a farm and also apprenticed as a gunsmith.

JOHN FRASER VENANGO, CHESTER CO., PA 1746-1753
- Set up a gun and blacksmith shop in Venango, a settlement near an Indian village on the Ohio River.
- Traded with the Indians for furs.
- Venango was captured by the French during the French and Indian War (1753).
- Fraser moved to Turtle Creek.

JOHN FRASER TURTLE CREEK, PA 1753-1754
  WESTMORELAND CO.
- Turtle Creek was near the French Fort Duquesne.
- Set up a gun and blacksmith shop.
- Made guns, knives, tomahawks, and tools, which he traded with Indians, friendly to the British for furs.
- Also repaired guns for the Indians.
- Made a lieutenant in the Pennsylvania militia by Col. George Washington.
- Washington stationed Fraser at the Ohio Company warehouse at the fork of the Allegheny and Monongahela Rivers, which becomes the Ohio River (near Fort Duquesne).
- French captured Turtle Creek (1754).
- Fraser moved to Winchester, VA.

JOHN FRASER WINCHESTER, VA 1754-1755
- Set up a gun and blacksmith shop.
- Col. George Washington contracted with Fraser to make guns for the Virginia militia.
- Married Jane McClain, moved to Evitts Creek, MD, and formed a partnership with George Croghan (1755).

FRASER (JOHN) & CROGHAN EVITTS CREEK, MD 1755-1768
(GEORGE)
- Situated on Evitts Creek, a tributary of the Potomac River.
- Evitts Creek was near Fort Cumberland.

- Set up a gun and blacksmith shop.
- When British Gen. Edward Braddock mounted a military expedition against French Fort Duquesne, Fraser (knowing the country) and Croghan acted as guides (1755).
- Another famous gun maker from Pennsylvania, William Henry Sr., was armorer to the expedition.
- Braddock was killed and the expedition was unsuccessful in capturing the fort.
- British General Forbes mounted a second military expedition against Fort Duquesne (1758).
- William Henry Sr. was armorer again.
- Fraser stayed home.
- The British captured the fort and renamed it Fort Pitt after British Prime Minister Pitt. It later became Pittsburgh, PA.

JOHN FRASER   **COLERIN TWSP. CUMBERLAND CO., PA**   1768-D1773

- Purchased 300 acres of land and built a tavern and a gun and blacksmiths shop.

(N) **C. (CHARLES) C. FULLER**   **WORCESTER, MA**   1885-1902
FULLER (CHARLES C.) REGALIA & COSTUME CO.   **WORCESTER, MA**   1902-1920

- Located at 5 Pleasant Street (at the corner of Main Street).
- Made and sold uniforms, flags, regalia, and swords.

(A) **JACOB FUNK**   **MUSKINGUM CO., OH**   1790-1816

- Probably made cavalry sabers.

(N) **J. GALLARNO**   **GREEN BAY, WI**   1785-1800

- Made knives and tomahawks for local Indians.

(Cutler, blacksmith)

(A) **EMERSON GAYLORD**   **SOUTH HADLEY, MA**   B1819-1833
EMERSON GAYLORD   **AMHERST, MA**   1833-1841

- Apprenticed to, and worked for, a harness maker.

EMERSON GAYLORD   **CHICOPEE, MA**   1841-1863

- Gaylord began working as a leather dresser for the Ames Manufacturing Company in its leather products shop (1841).
- Took over the leather products shop and subcontracted with Ames for all the products (1843).
- Hired his own men and supervised all works. Made assorted leather products, including harness and sword scabbards.
- Purchased the leather products business from Ames and rented their leather shop building (1856).
- Had a U.S. contract for M1855 rifled musket bayonet scabbards.
- Had a U.S. contract for mail bags (1859).
- Prior to the outbreak of the Civil War, made leather military accouterments for the states of Maryland, Virginia, Georgia, Alabama, and Mississippi (1861).
- When the Civil War began, he immediately received orders for military accouterments from Col. William A. Thornton (U.S. Arsenal, Governors Island, NY) and from the governor of Massachusetts.
- Received U.S. government orders for such items as artillery harness and cavalry saddles (1861).
- During the Civil War he sold the U.S. government over 200,000 leather products valued at over $2,000,000.
- Gaylord's Civil War production included carbine and pistol cartridge boxes, saber belts and plates, NCO belts and plates, pistol holsters, cavalry accouterment sets, carbine slings and swivels, sword knots, Blakeslee & Mann cartridge boxes, Hoffman bayonets (5,000), cavalry cartridge boxes, and bayonet scabbards.
- Formed the Gaylord Mfg. Co. and purchased the Ames leather shop building (1863).

GAYLORD MANUFACTURING CO. CHICOPEE, MA 1863-1881
- Director and president: Emerson Gaylord.
- Director and treasurer: Jerome Wells.
- Directors: T.W. Carter, James T. Ames (president of Ames Mfg. Co.), E.N. Snow.
- Made a complete line of harness and leather products, including leather fire hoses and leather machine belting.
- Serano Gaylord, who was working for Eagle Lock Co. in Terryville, CT, joined the company (c. 1865). Emerson Gaylord was a stockholder in the Eagle Lock Co.
- Serano Gaylord introduced the manufacture of cabinet locks, trunk locks, and trunk trimmings to Gaylord Mfg. Co.
- Gaylord Mfg. Co. began making steel pens and mailboxes (1865).
- Purchased the Chicopee Malleable Iron Co. (1865).
- Eventually made over 350 styles of cabinet locks.
- Emerson Gaylord became a major stockholder in the Ames Mfg. Co. (1867).
- Gaylord was president of the Ames Mfg. Co. (1872-1874).
- Began to manufacture military and society swords (1876).
- Initially bought surplus sword blades from Ames Mfg. Co.
- Gaylord Mfg. Co. advertisement in the Chicopee, MA, business directory (1879) reads:

    Manufacturers of cabinet locks in every variety
    Regulation Army and Navy swords and belts
    Knights Templar swords and belts
    Grand Army swords and belts
    Odd Fellow swords and belts
    and other society swords and belts
    Cartridge boxes
    Scabbards
    Military accoutrements
    Designing, modeling, diesinking, engraving, etc.
    Brass castings made to order

- Sold lock division, including machinery, factory, and real estate, to the Eagle Lock Co., Terryville, CT, for $107,000 (1881).
- Sold sword factory and machinery to the Ames Mfg. Co. They then formed the Ames Sword Company (1881).
- Gaylord retired and his son, Arthur Gaylord, formed a small company (1881).

GAYLORD (ARTHUR) & CHAPIN (FREDERICK) CHICOPEE, MA 1881-1886
- Continued to operate the Gaylord brass foundry and made some society swords.

(A) **DAVID & WILLIAM GEDDY** WILLIAMSBURG, VA 1738-1751
- Advertised in the *Virginia Gazette* (1751) as "*gunsmiths, cutlers, and founders*" offering for sale in their shop:

    Gunwork:
        Gun and pistol stocks varnished, locks, mountings and barrel, blued, bored and rifled
    Founderswork:
        Harness buckles
        Coach knobs
        Hinges
        Squares
        Fire dogs
        House bells
        Dials
        Nails

Cutlers work:
 Razors, lancets, shears and surgeon's instruments, ground, cleaned and
 glazed, sword blades polished, blued and gilted
 Scabbards for swords
 Needles and sights for compasses
 Rupture bands

(N) WILLIAM GILCHRIST   PHILADELPHIA, PA   1860-1865
- Located at 529 Commerce.
- Advertised as a brass founder and fine cutlery maker.

(N) JACOB GLASSER   BALTIMORE, MD   1800-1815
- Made tomahawks for the U.S. Office of Indian Trade (1810).

(Blacksmith)

(A) JACOB GMINDER   BALTIMORE, MD   1848-D1899
- Locations:
    10 1/2 South Calvert Street (1848-1864)
    10 South Calvert Street and 117 W. Baltimore Street (1864-1867)
    10 South Calvert Street (1867-1885)
    14 South Calvert Street (1885-1899)
- Advertised as silver plater, maker of coffin trimmings and military ornaments.
- During the Civil War advertised as a silver plater, manufacturer and dealer in military equipment, embroidered and metal hat and cap ornaments, corp. badges, shoulder straps, buttons, and "fine swords of elegant design for presentation."

(A) CHRISTIAN GOBRECHT   PHILADELPHIA, PA   1815-1845
- Located on Baltimore Street.

(N) JOHN GODFRIED   FREDERICK CO., MD   1791-1816
- Made tomahawks for the local Indians.

(Blacksmith)

(A) JOHN GOODMAN SR.   PHILADELPHIA, PA   1758-1805
- Located at 261 North Front Street.

(A) JOHN GOODMAN JR.   PHILADELPHIA, PA   1780-1850
- Located at 194 North Front Street.

(A) GORE (CHARLES) & CO.   DENVER, CO   1862-1882
- Gun shop locations:
    corner of 16th and Larimer Streets (1862-1867)
    12 Edward Street (1867-1871)
    12 Blake Street (1871-1882)

(N) RICHARD GOSLING
(See Richard Ghiselin, Volume I)

(A) W. (WILLIAM) R. GOULDING   NEW YORK, NY   1850-1855

- Locations:
    - 21 Fulton Street (1850-1852)
    - 85 Fulton Street and 33 Gold Street (1852-1853)
    - 85 Fulton Street (1853-1855)
- Made bowie knives.

GOULDING (WILLIAM R.) & FORD (JAMES) NEW YORK, NY   1855-1866
- Two locations at 85 Fulton Street and 139 Elm Street.
- Made iron-spiked tomahawks.

(A) **WILLIAM GRAY**   CHARLESTON, SC   B1722-1812
    GRAY (WILLIAM) & CORBY (JOHN)   CHARLESTON, SC   1812-1820
- Bought out William Gunn.
- Shop located at 5 Queen Street.

    WILLIAM GRAY   CHARLESTON, SC   1820-D1822
- Located on the corner of Laurens and Washington Streets.

(See John Corby)
(Gunsmith, blacksmith, cutler)

(A) **WILLIAM GREAVES & SON**   PHILADELPHIA, PA   1845-1865
- Located at 25 North 6th Street.
- Made bowie knives.
- Possible branch of a Sheffield, England, company.

(N) **JOHN A. GRIFFITHS**   LONDON, ENGLAND   c1810-1830
- Immigrated to Cincinnati, OH (1830).

    JOHN A. GRIFFITHS   CINCINNATI, OH   1830-1852
- Gun shop located at 279 Main Street (between 6th and 7th Streets).

    GRIFFITHS (JOHN A.) & SIEBERT (HENRY L.)   CINCINNATI, OH   1852-1854
- Gun shop located at 279 Main Street between (6th and 7th Streets).

    JOHN A. GRIFFITHS   CINCINNATI, OH   1854-1866
- Gun shop located at 279 Main Street (between 6th and 7th Street) (1854-1861), 165 Main Street (1861-1866).
- Made shotguns, rifles, and bowie knives.

(A) **GEORGE GRUBB**   PHILADELPHIA, PA   1780-1815
- Located at 316 South 2nd Street (1780-1806), 225 Swanson (1806-1815).

(Cutler, gunsmith)

(A) **HENRY BROWN GUEST**   PHILADELPHIA, PA   1777-1780
- Located at 2nd Street (near Chesnut Street).

(A) **WILLIAM GUNN**   CHARLESTON, SC   B1778-1792
    WILLIAM GUNN   CHARLESTON, SC   1792-1801
- Shop located at 6 Queen Street.

    GUNN (WILLIAM) & BEAUCHRE (FRANCIS D.)   CHARLESTON, SC   1801-1812
- Shop located at 5 Queen Street.

    WILLIAM GUNN   CHARLESTON, SC   1812-D1813
- Shop located at 5 Queen Street.

- William Gray (Gunn's son-in-law) and John Corby bought out William Gunn (1812).

(Gunsmith, blacksmith, cutler)

(N) **JOHN HAGEN JR.** MOUNT NEBO, MARTIC TWSP., PA 1850-1885
- Made $400 worth of edged weapons, possibly including bowie knives and bayonets (1870).

(N) **CHARLES HALBACK** SOLINGEN, PRUSSIA B1810-1835
- Immigrated to Baltimore, MD (1835).

  CHARLES HALBACK BALTIMORE, MD 1835-1856
- Located at 12 Mercer Street.
- Made surgical instruments and knives, including bowie knives.

(Cutler, knife, gun, and hardware dealer and importer)

(A) **HALBACK & SONS** BALTIMORE, MD 1780-1820
- Made pistols with bronze cannon type barrels.

(Gunsmith)

(N) **WILLIAM A. HALL** CHICAGO, IL 1820-1840
- Made pipe tomahawks for the U.S. Office of Indian trade (1820).

(Blacksmith)

(A) **C. (CHARLES) HAMMOND & SON** PHILADELPHIA, PA 1862-1864
- Located at 501 Commerce Street.
- Bought M1840 type cavalry saber blades from Sheble & Fisher, Philadelphia, PA.

  GEORGE HAMMOND & SONS PHILADELPHIA, PA 1864-1901
- Located at 18 North 5th Street.

(N) **HENRY HARRINGTON** SOUTHBRIDGE, MA Bc1800-1850
- Had a gun and cutlery shop.
- Made butcher knives, surgical instruments, and razors.
- Patented a three-barrel, breech-loading percussion pistol and rifle (1837).
- Edged tools and shoe knives made later.

  HARRINGTON CUTLERY CO. SOUTHBRIDGE, MA 1850-1933
- Made bowie knives during the Civil War.
- President: John Harrington (1850-1884).
- President: Dexter Harrington (1884-1933).
- Located at 37 South Marcy Street.
- Made over 1,000 cutlery products.
- Merged with the John Russell Cutlery Co. (1933) and became Russell, Harrington Cutlery Co.

(A) **GEORGE HARRIS** PITTSBURGH, PA 1795-1850
- Located at the southwest corner of Liberty and Smithfield Streets.
- Made militia officer swords with silver reverse-P hilts and eagle-head pommels.
- Bought blades from William Rose & Sons, Blockley Township, PA.
- Some swords are marked "G. Harris, Sterling, Pittsburgh."

  HARRIS (GEORGE) & CO. NEW YORK, NY 1850-1854
- Located at the southwest corner of Liberty and Smithfield Streets.
- Bought blades from Joseph Rose Jr., New York, NY (1850-1854).

(Silversmith, sword hiltor).

(A) **ISAAC HARROW** TRENTON, NJ 1710-1740
(under British dominion)
- Made knives, axes, and belt axes (tomahawks).
(Cutler, blacksmith)

(N) **FREDERICK HARTENSTEIN** BROOKLYN, NY 1860-1866
- Locations:
    131 1/2 Atlantic Avenue (1860-1861)
    151 Court Street (1861-1864)
    290 Atlantic Avenue (1864-1866)
  HARTENSTEIN (FREDERICK) & CO. BROOKLYN, NY 1866-1868
- Located at 290 Atlantic Avenue.
(Cutler, knife and dirk maker)

(N) **J. HAYES** FORT PITT 1760-1770
(LATER PITTSBURGH, PA)
(under British dominion)
- Made pipe tomahawks with thread-on removable bowls.
(Blacksmith)

(N) **M.J. HAYES & SON** SAN FRANCISCO, CA 1887-1901
- General knife maker, including bowie knives.

(A) **CALEB HEFFEY** ALEXANDRIA, VA 1807-1808
- Located on Royal Street.

(A) **GEORGE HEIGHBERGER** PHILADELPHIA, PA 1760-1790
- Sold Samuel Hodgdon, U.S. Commissary General of Military Supplies, 50 sword blades at $0.70 each and five sword blades at $0.80 each (October 30, 1781).

(N) **ROCHUS HEINISCH (SR.)** LEUTMERITZ, BOHEMIA Bc1795-c1815
- Immigrated to New York, NY (c. 1815).
  ROCHUS HEINISCH (SR.) NEW YORK, NY c1815-1820
- Worked as a cutler and surgical instrument maker.
- Moved to Elizabeth, NY (c. 1820).
  ROCHUS HEINISCH (SR.) ELIZABETH, NJ c1820-1825
- Worked as a cutler.
- Moved to Newark, NJ (1825).
  ROCHUS HEINISCH (SR.) NEWARK, NJ 1825-1865
- Built a cutlery factory on Quarry Street.
- Son Rochus Heinisch Jr. apprenticed and worked with him before and after serving as a lieutenant in Company A, 26 Regiment, of the New Jersey volunteer infantry.
- During the Civil War made bowie knives with 7 1/2" blades and brass-mounted black leather scabbards.
- Exhibited cutlery at the Hyde Park, NY, Crystal Palace Exhibition (1851).
  ROCHUS HEINISCH (SR.) NEWARK, NJ 1865-1871
- Cutlery factory located at 114 Market Street.
- Sons Albert and Henry apprenticed and worked with him.
- Advertisement in 1869 reads:
    Manufacturer of celebrated cutlery
    Warranted the best in the world

Specializing in scissors of all kinds
Tailors shears
Surgical instruments
Pocket knives
Razors

ROCHUS HEINISCH & SONS   NEWARK, NJ   1871-c1900
- Partners and sons: Albert, Henry, and Rochus Jr.
- Rochus Heinisch Sr. died (1874).
- The company was purchased by Wiss Cutlery (c. 1900).

(N) **OTTO HELMOLD**   PITTSBURGH, PA   1859-1872
- Located at 96 Smithfield Street.

(Cutler, bowie knife maker)

(A) **HENDERSON-AMES**   KALAMAZOO, MI   1893-1923
- Located on the corner of East Main and Edward Streets.

(A) **JAMES HENDRICKS**   PHILADELPHIA, PA   1746-1800
- Located on the corner of Church Alley and Market Street.

(A) **JOHN HENDRICKS**   ALBANY, NY   1735-1740
    JOHN HENDRICKS   PHILADELPHIA, PA   1740-1798
- Located at 53 Green Street.
- Made scalping knives and tomahawks for local Indians.
- Employee: William Ward (1767-1769).

(A) **ANTON HENINGER**   NEW HAVEN, CT   1861-1865
- Made bowie knives.

(Cutler, knife maker)

(A) **ANDREW G. HICKS**   MICHIGAN   B1807-1830
    A. (ANDREW) G. HICKS   CLEVELAND, OH   1830-D1866
- Listed in the Cleveland city directory as a manufacturer of planes, tools, and cutlery (1857-1866).
- Located at 45 Root Street and several other Root Street addresses.
- Made rifleman knives for the U.S. Allegheny Arsenal (purchased supplies for states west of the Allegheny mountains).
- Made belt and bowie knives.
- Made edged tools.

(Knife and tool maker, cutler)

(A) **GEORGE HINTON**   PHILADELPHIA, PA   1767-1790
- Located on Spruce Street.
- Made scalping knives.

(N) **F. HOFF**   LANCASTER CO., PA   1800-1815
- Made pipe tomahawks for the local Indians.

(Blacksmith)

(A) **CONRAD HOFFMAN**   PITTSBURGH, PA   1810-1812
- Located on Market Street.

(N) **ALEXANDER H. HOLLEY**   LAKEVILLE, CT   1836-1850
- Inherited a blast furnace that was used by Ethan Allen to cast cannon during the Revolutionary War.
- Tore down the furnace and bought pocket knife-making equipment from a failed company in Waterbury, CT (1843).
- Built a new knife factory (1844).

    HOLLEY & CO.   LAKEVILLE, CT   1850-1854
- Partners: Alexander H. Holley, Nathan W. Merwin, George B. Burrell.

    HOLLEY MFG. CO.   LAKEVILLE, CT   1854-1936
- Made pocket knives, hunting knives (including bowie styles), kitchen knives, pruning knives, and scissors.
- Used cast steel.
- Used Bloget, Clark & Brown as Boston agents and Quince & Delapierre as New York agents.

(C) **SAMUEL HOLMES**   PHILADELPHIA, PA   1775-1783
- Pennsylvania Committee of Safety contract for 50 naval cutlasses (1776).

(A) **THE HOPE FURNACE**   SCITUATE, RI   1765-1812
- Made cavalry sabers during the Revolutionary War (none for the War of 1812).

(A) **EZEKIAL HOPKINS**   SCITUATE, RI   1740-1765
- Made cavalry swords at the Hope Furnace.

(N) **CORNELIUS HOWARD**   ANNAPOLIS, MD   1750-1800
- A shipment of 251 tomahawks, made by Howard, was forwarded to a military post commander Col. R. Meigs as Indian trade goods (August 10, 1794).

(Blacksmith)

(A) **D. (DAVID) B. HOWELL**   NEW YORK, NY   1865-1874
- Offices located at 434 Broadway.
- Factory located at 6 Howard Street.

(A) **HENRY HUBER**
(See John English)

(A) **RUDOLPH HUG**   CINCINNATI, OH   1853-1882
- Located at 540 Central Street (1853-1862), 538 Central Street (1862-1882).
- Also made bowie knives.

(N) **ALFRED HUNTER**   NEW YORK, NY   1830-1834
- Shop located at 10 Amity Street (1830-1832), 12 Amity Street (1832-1834).

    ALFRED HUNTER   NEWARK, NJ   1834-1865
- Shop located at 145 Quarry Street (1834-1850), 25 Sheffield Street near State Street (1850-1865).
- Advertised as a *"manufacturer of strong and serviceable ivory and buffalo horn handled cutlery warranted of the best materials and manufacture, combining elegance with durability (including bowie knives)."*
- Also used rosewood and German silver-trimmed handles on his bowie knives.

(A) **JAMES & ADAM HUNTER**   SCOTLAND   c1710-1737
- Immigrated to Stafford County, VA (1737).

    JAMES & ADAM HUNTER   STAFFORD CO., VA   1737-1775
- Began as merchant.
- Bought a large farm.

- Farm superintendent: John Strode.
- Bought an iron forge near Falmouth, VA, and established Hunters Iron Works. It was located on the Rappahannock River across from the Virginia state gun factory at Fredericksburg, VA.
- Made farm tools, edged tools, nails, fullers, shears, shipbuilding supplies, anchors, camp kettles, and entrenching tools.
- Supplied pig iron to and did iron work for the U.S. Army and Navy.
- In 1770, Hunters Iron Works was the largest in the colonies.
- Dug a 3/4-mile-long canal from the Rappahannock River to his iron works to provide water power.
- Changed the name of company to the Rappahannock Forge (1775).

(See John Strode)

RAPPAHANNOCK FORGE   STAFFORD CO., VA   1775-1782

- Owner: James Hunter.
- Superintendent: Uri Banks.
- Clerk: Henry Banks (son of Uri).
- Foreman: John Strode.
- Arms foreman: Joseph Perkins (1775-1777).
- Uri Banks recruited skilled workmen in Philadelphia (1776).
- John Strode advertised for skilled craftsman, including small arms makers, file makers, blacksmiths, anchorsmiths, nailers, and coopers (1776).
- Offered new workers a half lot at a small rent and assistance in building a house (material cost deducted from future wages).
- Also advertised for Negro tradesmen.
- Received a Virginia contract for 200 stands of muskets (1776).
- Received a Virginia contract for all the muskets (with bayonets and ramrods) that the company could make in one year (1776).
- Because the Rappahannock River was obstructed by the British, Hunter convinced the Virginia general assembly to pass a bill allowing him to mine iron ore and forge pig iron at the Accokeck mine and furnace (formerly British owned) (1777).
- Also bought iron ore and pig iron from forges in Maryland.
- Started a major building project ultimately costing 40,000 British pounds (a staggering amount in that time) (1777). The project involved the building of a slitting and plating mill, wire mill, steel furnace, iron furnace, grist mill, saw mill, cooper's shop, saddler's shop, brass foundry and shop, wheel wright shop, and shoemaker's shop.
- Made horseman sabers for the 1st Regiment of Continental Dragoons under Col. Theodoric Bland (formerly the Virginia Light Horse) and the 3rd Regiment of Continental Dragoons under Col. George Baylor (1777-1778).
- Asked to repair muskets damaged at Richmond, VA, by an attack by British raider Benedict Arnold. Hunter declined because of a lack of skilled armorers (1780).
- Arms production was temporarily stopped because of a lack of skilled armorers (1780). Many workers had joined the army.
- Some British arms, including swords, were captured during the Battle of Guilford Courthouse (March 15, 1781).
- The Battle of Guilford Courthouse took place in northern North Carolina. British forces, under Gen. Lord Charles Cornwallis, fought against American Gen. Nathaniel Greene.
- Lt. Col. William Washington (third cousin of Gen. George Washington), in command of the 3rd Regiment of Continental Dragoons, ordered Maj. Richard Call to send a horseman saber, captured from British Col. Banastre Tarlton's light horse regiment at Guilford courthouse, to Virginia Governor Thomas Jefferson (March 28, 1781). Jefferson was to forward the saber to James Hunter at the Rappahannock Forge to use as a pattern for U.S. dragoon sabers. It had a hussar-type knucklebow, flat pommel cap, and split-and-divided guard.
- Hunter informed Jefferson that he would have to stop saber production again unless his sword cutlers and artificers were furloughed from the army (May 1781).

- Hunter told Jefferson that he was removing and relocating his tools, machinery, and equipment because British Col. Banastre Tarlton's light horse regiment (with 500 troopers) was raiding at Hanover Court near Bowling Green, not too far from Fredericksburg, on his way to destroy Hunter's iron works. The move was supervised by retired American General Weedon (June 1781).
- The tools, machinery, and equipment were returned after Tarlton left the area.
- Hunter then enlarged his main production facility, making it 350 feet long and four stories high.
- The first floor had the machinery (trip hammers and forges), which was driven by a waterwheel on the Rappahannock River.
- The second floor was the main assembly area. It was a completely open room with no partitions. The clerk sat in the center of the room on an elevated area. He logged in each workman's time worked, work done, and products finished.
- The third floor housed the storerooms for partly finished products and workmen's lodging.
- The fourth floor was a storage area for finished products.
- Hunter recalled all his armorers and workmen, who had left when he relocated in June 1781.
- Hunter informed the Virginia Committee of Safety and Governor Thomas Jefferson that he had on hand 1,000 horseman sabers made to the pattern saber sent to him by Lt. Col. William Washington (November 1781).
- Rappahannock Forge was closed (1782).
- James Hunter died (1785).

Products Made at the Rappahannock Forge

Domestic metal products
Farm tools
Spades
Shovels
Entrenching tools
Camp kettles
Ladles
Anchors
Files
Nails
Shears

Military metal products
Muskets
Bayonets
Carbines
Pistols
Horseman sabers
Wall guns
Spurs

Military and domestic leather products
Bridles
Riding boots
Harnesses

(N) **ISAAC P. HYDE** STAFFORD SPRINGS, CT B1853-1872
- Opened a knife factory in Southbridge, MA (1872).

ISAAC P. HYDE SOUTHBRIDGE, MA 1872-1875
- Theodore Harrington was the knife factory superintendent (possibly related to Henry Harrington).

HYDE (ISAAC P.) & JACOBS (FRANKLIN) SOUTHBRIDGE, MA 1875-1881
- Knife makers, including bowie knives.
- Also made and sold knife blades.

I. (ISAAC) P. HYDE MANUFACTURING SOUTHBRIDGE, MA 1881-1897
- President: Isaac P. Hyde.
- Treasurer: F.L. Chapin.
- Clerk: Franklin Jacobs.

- Made knives, shoe tools, and mechanical products.
- Isaac P. Hyde died (1897).

(See Henry Harrington)

(N) JACOB IRVIN NATCHITOCHES, LA 1820-1830
- Made tomahawks for the U.S. Office of Indian Trade (1822).

(Blacksmith)

(A) SAMUEL JACKSON BALTIMORE, MD 1831-1895
- Locations:
    corner of German and Liberty streets (1831-1833)
    11 N. Liberty Street (1833-1840)
    172 Fremont Street (1840-1847)
    194 Baltimore Street (1847-1895)
- Made silver-mounted bowie knives.

(N) A. JACOT & CO. NORFOLK, VA 1819-1835
- Located on Main Street.
- Made guns and gun locks.
- Made surgeons and dentists instruments and knives.

(General cutler, gunsmith)

(N) F. (FRANCIS) JAHN & BROS. PHILADELPHIA, PA 1849-1854
- Located at 4 Decatur Street.

FRANCIS JAHN PHILADELPHIA, PA 1854-1895
- Locations:
    165 Race Street (1854-1858)
    435 Race Street (1858-1863)
    506 Race Street (1863-1895)
- Brass founder, ornaments, plater.
- Made M1850 foot officer swords during the Civil War.

(N) RICHARD JELLERE BALTIMORE, MD 1800-1820
- Made tomahawks for the U.S. Office of Indian Trade (1810).

(Blacksmith)

(A) JOHN JENKINS PHILADELPHIA, PA B1735, 1750-D1796
- Located on Chesnut Street.

(N) JOSEPH JENKS SR. HOUNSLOW HEATH, ENGLAND 1642
- Sword and blade making center.
- Immigrated to Boston, MA, then to Lynn, MA (1642)

JOSEPH JENKS SR. LYNN, MA 1642-1660
- Made horseman swords, knives, and edged tools.

(A) JOSEPH JENKS JR. PAWTUCKET FALLS, RI 1650-1680
- Son of Joseph Jenks Sr.
- Made knives, axes, belt axes (tomahawks), edged tools, hammers, anchors, and assorted iron products.

(Cutler, blacksmith)

(A) **REYNALDO JOHNSON**   PHILADELPHIA, PA   1800-1808
     REYNALDO JOHNSON   AQUASCO, MD   1808-1815
- Had U.S. contract with the U.S. Office of Indian Trade for 22 tomahawks and 178 hatchets (1808).

(N) **SAMUEL JOHNSON**   CHICAGO, IL   1810-1830
- Had a contract for tomahawks with the U.S. Office of Indian Trade (1822).

(Blacksmith)

(N) **JOSEPH JOURDAIN**   THREE RIVERS, CANADA   1780-1796
     JOSEPH JOURDAIN   GREEN BAY, WI   1796-1834
     JOSEPH JOURDAIN   WINNEBAGO RAPIDS, WI   1834-D1866
- Made tomahawks for local Indians.

(Blacksmith)

(A) **P. (PHILIP) S. JUSTICE**   PHILADELPHIA, PA   1859-1888
- Imported 464 British M1821 cavalry sabers and sold them to the U.S. government (1861).
- Had U.S. contracts for 13,685 M1840 variation cavalry sabers.
- Approximately 9,685 were imported from Schnitzler & Kirschbaum, Solingen Prussia; approximately 4,000 made by Justice.
- Imported approximately 9,585 M1840 cavalry sabers from Schnitzler & Kirschbaum between November 1861 and March 1862.
- They were marked (in large letters) in two straight lines:
  P.S. Justice
  Phila
- Made approximately 4,000 M1840 variation cavalry sabers with M1840 style blades and M1860 type grips.
- They were marked (in small letters) in two curved lines:
  P.S. Justice
  Philad
- Bought M1840 type cavalry saber blades from Sheble & Fisher, Philadelphia, PA.
- Used Schnitzler & Kirschbaum scabbards on all cavalry sabers.
- None of the P.S. Justice sabers have U.S. government stamps or inspectors marks.
- Some Justice cavalry sabers were used by the state of Pennsylvania and are marked "C.P." (Commonwealth of Pennsylvania).

(A) **PETER KEENER & SON**   BALTIMORE, MD   1795-1806
- Located on North Green Street (old town).

(C) **DANIEL KENT**   WEST BRADFORD TWSP., PA   1690-1706

(A) **ADAM KETLER**   NORRISTOWN, PA   1815-1820
- Shop located on the corner of Germantown pike and Front Street.

(A) **ADAM KINSLEY**   CANTON, MA   1767-1789
     LEONARD (JONATHAN) & KINSLEY   CANTON, MA   1789-1799
     (ADAM)
- Operated a rolling and slitting mill on the Naponset River (iron products).
- Paul Revere Jr. bought their mill and converted it into a copper rolling mill (1799).

(A) **A. KIRCHNER**   PHILADELPHIA, PA   1830-1850
- Located at 66 Vine Street.

JOHN K. KIRCHNER	PHILADELPHIA, PA	1850-1865

- Located at 66 Vine Street.

(A) **JOHN GODFRIED KNECHT**	SOLINGEN, PRUSSIA	c1770-1790

- Immigrated to Richmond, VA (1790).

JOHN GODFRIED KNECHT	RICHMOND, VA	1790-1795

- Shop on Lexington Street.
- Boarded in the house of silversmith John Wilson.
- Wilson died and Knecht moved to Baltimore (1795).

JOHN GODFRIED KNECHT	BALTIMORE, MD	1795-1820

- Locations:
    2nd Street (1795-1809)
    10 Water Street (1809-1816)
    35 Harrison Street (1816-1870)

(Blacksmith, gunsmith, cutler, sword and sword blade maker)

J. (JOHN) KNECHT	ST. LOUIS, MO	c1820-1840

- Probably a relative of John Godfried Knecht.
- Made hunting swords and probably cavalry swords.
- Also made tomahawks for local Indians.

(A) **RUDOLPH KOCH**	FORT MICHILIMACKINAC STRAITS OF MACKINAC (under British dominion)	1765-1775

- Fort Michilimackinac was originally a French fort and trading post. It became a British fort at the end of the French and Indian War (1763) and was ceded to the U.S. at the end of the Revolutionary War (1783).
- Made and repaired axes and hatchets, including pipe tomahawks, for the British Indian Service (1768-1769).

(N) **AGUSTIN LAFAY (LEFOI)**	DETROIT, MI	1770-1780

- Made tomahawks for the British Indian Service (1778).

PIERRE LAMOTHE
(See Silversmith listings)

(A, C) **SILAS LAMSON SR.**	SHELBURNE FALLS, MA	1837-1840

- Made scythe snaths (handles for long-grass cutting scythes).

NATHANIEL LAMSON & SILAS LAMSON JR.	SHELBURNE FALLS, MA	1840-1843

- Sons of Silas Lamson Sr.
- Built a factory on Deerfield Street (on the Deerfield River).
- Made scythe snaths.
- Silas Jr. died and his brother Ebenezer G. Lamson became a partner in the company (1843).
- Cyrus Alden became a partner (1843).

LAMSON (NATHANIEL & EBENEZER G.) & ALDEN (CYRUS)	SHELBURNE FALLS, MA	1843-1851

- Located on Deerfield Street.
- Factory superintendent: William T. Clement (1843-1857).
- Began making shoe and butcher knives (1846).
- Began making table cutlery (1848).
- Ebenezer D. Goodnow and Abel P. Goodnow joined the company (1850).

LAMSON (NATHANIEL & EBENEZER G.)   SHELBURNE FALLS, MA   1851-1997
GOODNOW (EBENEZER D. & ABEL P.) MANUFACTURING CO.
- Built a new three-story cutlery factory (208′ x 48′) across the Deerfield River on Buckland Street (1851).
- Had 200 employees.
- Factory superintendent: Joseph W. Gardner (1857-1876).
- Had U.S. contracts for knives and bayonets during the Civil War.
- Made a 62-piece set of table cutlery for President Ulysses S. Grant (1869). Presented on Nov. 17, 1869.
- Factory destroyed by fire but rebuilt (1862). They had 300 workmen in the new factory.
- Lamson & Goodnow became the largest cutlery maker in the U.S., with 500 workers (1865).
- H. (Herman) Boker & Co., NY, purchased Lamson & Goodnow but did not change the name (1872).
- By 1900 was making 50 styles of knives, including bowie and hunting knives, as well as edged tools.
- New York offices located at 45 Murray Street.
- President: Clifton Field (1920-1946).
- President: John Woodsome (1946-1971).
- Rogers, Lunt & Bowlen (silversmiths) of Greenfield, MA, purchased Lamson & Goodnow from Herman Boker & Co. but did not change the name (1971).
- Companies executives in 1971:
    President: Lucius Nims.
    Chief engineer and vice president: Donald Elliot.
    Clerk: Deane Jones (later vice president).
    Board chairman: John Woodsome.
    Directors: Denham Lunt Sr., Denham Lunt Jr.

(A) **LAMSON (TRUMAN) & HUBBARD   BOSTON, MA   1865-1915**
    (COLEMAN S.)
- Located at 90-94 Bedford Street.

(A) **GEORGE M. (MARCELLUS) LANDERS   LENOX, MA   B1813-1820**
- Moved to New Britain, CT, with his father, schoolteacher Marcellus Landers (1820).
    GEORGE M. LANDERS   NEW BRITAIN, CT   1820-1825
- Marcellus Landers died, and George moved back to Lenox to live with his grandfather Thomas Landers (1825).
    GEORGE M. LANDERS   LENOX, MA   1825-1829
- At age 16, Landers, like most young men of the time, apprenticed at a trade (carpenter).
- Moved back to New Britain, CT (1829).
    GEORGE M. LANDERS   NEW BRITAIN, CT   1829-1842
- Became a carpenter's apprentice/cabinetmaker (1829-1834).
- Became a journeyman to Josiah Dewey (1834-1842).
- Dewey had a brass and iron foundry on Main Street (started in 1822).
- Dewey made cast hooks, cupboard latches, furniture casters, and other household items.
- Dewey took Landers in as a partner (1842).
    DEWEY (JOSIAH) & LANDERS   NEW BRITAIN, CT   1842-1847
    (GEORGE M.)
- Made same basic items as before.
- Landers' son, Charles S. Landers, was born (1846; died 1900).
- Josiah Dewey died and Landers opened his own company (1847).
    GEORGE M. LANDERS   NEW BRITAIN, CT   1847-1853
- Built his own foundry and factory.
- Enlarged the production.
- Went into partnership with Levi O. Smith (1853).

| **LANDERS (GEORGE M.) & SMITH (LEVI O.) MFG. CO.** | **NEW BRITAIN, CT** | **1853-1862** |

- President: George M. Landers.
- Secretary and treasurer: Levi O. Smith.
- Auditor: Samuel W. Hart.
- Stockholder: Francis Fenton.
- Levi O. Smith retired (1862).
- Landers bought the Frary (James D.) Co. of Meridan, CT, including tools and patterns (1862). Frary made scales, faucets, tools, etc.

| **GEORGE M. LANDERS & CO.** | **NEW BRITAIN, CT** | **1862-1865** |

- President: George M. Landers.
- Treasurer: James D. Frary.
- Secretary: William H. Smith (resigned in 1865).
- Factory superintendent: R.L. Webb.
- Factory enlarged to 700 feet long on two acres of land (1862-1864).
- Built a 250' x 40' foundry in New Britain, CT.
- Built a factory in Bristol, CT.
- Factory superintendent: D.E. Peck.
- Built a warehouse and sales office in New York at 31 Beckman Street.
- Warehouse superintendent: John W. Clark.
- Built a four-story grinding and finishing shop (45' x 43'), a forging shop (38' x 135'), and an engine and boiler building (37' x 120') in New Britain, CT.
- Now made faucets, Trumbull patent scales, mollasses and water gates, small bells, harness snaps, screws, tools, and household hooks.
- Had 300 employees.
- John W. Clark (New York warehouse and salesroom superintendent) was made a partner (1865).
- Landers, Frary & Clark incorporated (1865).

| **LANDERS (GEORGE M.), FRARY (JAMES D.) & CLARK (JOHN W.)** | **NEW BRITAIN, CT** | **1865-1965** |

- President: George M. Landers.
- Secretary and treasurer: James D. Frary.
- Partners: John W. Clark, S.W. Hall, C.B. Irwin, H.E. Russell, Joseph A. Pickett.
- Went into the cutlery business (1866).
- Built a four-story cutlery factory on Center Street called Aetna Cutlery Works.
- Landers, Frary & Clark bought the Meridan Cutlery Co. (formerly Pratt & Ropes) of Meridan, CT, makers of knives, tableware, and bowie knives (1866).
- Also bought the Bates Cutlery Mfg. Co. of Putnam, CT.
- Charles S. Landers became secretary and James D. Frary became treasurer (1868).
- George M. Landers retired as president and became vice president and director (1870).
- James D. Frary became president
- Made Perry's meat choppers, coffee mills, apple parers, screwdrivers, socket wrenches, hammers, tobacco cutters, etc. They made cutlery items such as hatchets, scissors, table cutlery of many types, carving knives, and military combination knife and fork utensils (1870).
- James D. Frary left the company to form Frary Cutlery Co., Bridgeport, CT (1876).
- Joseph A. Pickett became president and director.
- Charles S. Landers became president (c. 1895).
- Company adopted its trademark L.F. & C. (1897).
- Charles S. Landers died (1900). Charles F. Smith became new president.
- Landers, Frary & Clark bought several appliance companies and began to make electric percolators, electric toasters, electric ranges, vacuum cleaners, clothes washers, and refrigerators (1908-1933).

- Had New York salesroom at 302 and 304 Broadway, Chicago salesroom at 137 Wabash Avenue, and San Francisco salesroom at 134 Sutter Street (1905).
- Received a U.S. government contract for 15,000 M1913 cavalry swords (1913).
- Built a three-story cutlery factory, where the M1913 cavalry swords were made (1913).
- A company biographer indicates that 93,487 M1913 cavalry sabers were made by Landers, Frary & Clark.

World War I (1914-1918) Production
Gas mask parts: 8,448,800
Mess kits: 3,892,754
Mess kit knives: 7,825,212
Canteens: 3,192,500
Canteen cups: 3,500,000
Bayonets: 500,000
M1917 trench knives: 211,000
M1918 trench knives: 119,261
M1918 trench knives (Mark I): 119,424
Paratroopers knives: 5000
Saddlers knives: 2500
Amputating knives: 158,250
Bolo knife scabbards: 204,217
Surgeons lancets: ?
Surgeons operating knives: ?

- Charles F. Smith died (1938). New president: Arthur Kimball.
- Arthur Kimball died (1940). New president: Richard L. White. Other executives included Bret C. Neece (vice president), Francis L. Dabney (treasurer), Henry T. Burr (secretary), and Arthur E. Allen (chairman of board).

World War II (1941-1945) Production
Grenades (M17): 250,000 a month in 1944
Shell fuses (M54)
Parachute hardware
Bomb shackles
Incendiary bombs
Stuffing tubes for ships gun parts
Machine gun mounts (two-gun type)
Machine gun mounts (four-gun type)
Canteens
Canteen cups
Mess kits
First aid kits
Small motors for military use
Army fighting knives
Paratroopers knives
Commando knives for Great Britain
Navy steel cable

- Cutlery division was closed (1950).
- Bought several companies making small appliances (1951-1959).
- Executives in 1952: Richard L. White (chairman of the board), Bret C. Neece (president).
- Sold the major appliance division to Art Kraft Corp., Lima, OH (1957).

- Executives in 1958: Frederick W. Silverman (chairman of the board), Bret C. Neece (president).
- Executives in 1969: Harry T. Silverman (president), Bret C. Neece (chairman of the board).
- Landers, Frary & Clark was bought by the General Electric housewares division (1965).

(See Frary Cutlery Co.)

(N) **J. (JACQUES) P. LASSURE (LASSERRE)**   PARIS, FRANCE   Bc1800, 1820-1841
- Apprenticed as a cutler in Paris, France.
- Immigrated to New Orleans, LA (1841).

J. (JACQUES) P. LASSURE   NEW ORLEANS, LA   1841-1844
- Had a cutlery shop.
- Moved to Baltimore (1844).

J. (JACQUES) P. LASSURE   BALTIMORE, MD   1844-1850
- Wrote a letter to the U.S. Indian Department stating that he learned the trade of cutler in Paris and that he made all types of delicate mathematical and navigational instruments and cutlery (from swords to shears, including bowie knives) at his cutlery shop at 35 Water Street (c. 1844).
- Stated that he had on hand a variety of Indian tomahawks and rifleman belt axes (pipe and spear variations) at reasonable prices.

(Gunsmith, cutler, instrument maker, sword maker)

(A) **RICHARD LATHAM**   CHARLESTON, SC   1769-D1784
- Located on King Street.

H.G. LEISENRING
(See Dealer listing)

(A) **CHARLES LEONARD**   CANTON, MA   1808-1826
- Had a U.S. contract for 5,000 M1808 muskets.
- Partner and son: Rudolph Leonard.

(A) **J. (JONATHAN) W. LEONARD**   NEW YORK, NY   1845-1857
- Located at 384 Broadway.

(C) **RUDOLPH LEONARD**   CANTON, MA   1808-1826
- Not Robert.

(N) **JOHN LEWIS**   DETROIT, MI   1820-1840
- Made pipe tomahawks for the U.S. Office of Indian Trade.

(Blacksmith)

(A) **MITCHELL C. LILLEY**   AUGUSTA CO., VA   B1819-1829
    MITCHELL C. LILLEY   BROWN CO., OH   1829-1831
    MITCHELL C. LILLEY   COLUMBUS, OH   1831-1865
- Became a bookbinder (Masonic manuals) (c. 1839).

THE M.C. LILLEY & CO.   COLUMBUS, OH   1865-1931
- Regalia and sword makers.
- Locations:
    26 North High Street (1865-1869)

253 South High Street (1869-1873)
215 and 217 South High Street (1873-1888)
27 to 39 W. Gay Street (1888-1894)
261 Long Street (1894-1931)
- Advertised as a maker of military and band uniforms and swords and importer of laces, fringes, cords, silks, and velvets (1888).
- Also sold banners, flags, and lodge supplies and uniforms for all societies.

M.C. LILLEY (BRANCH) PITTSBURGH, PA 1900-1915
- Located at 204 North Avenue.

M.C. LILLEY (BRANCH) NEW YORK, NY 1893-1916
- Locations:
University Place (1893-1894)
818 Broadway (1894-1895)
842 Broadway (1895-1899)
13 W. 30th Street (1899-1909)
1123 Broadway (1909-1916)

(C) **COL. OLIVER LIPPINCOTT** CHICAGO, IL 1860-1880
- Locations:
190-192 Washington Street (1860-1872)
195-197 Lake Street (1872-1875)
81 Randolph Street (1875-1880)

(A) **NICODEMUS LLOYD** PHILADELPHIA, PA 1790-1820
- Had a contract with the U.S. Office of Indian Trade for 12 pipe tomahawks and 61 axes (1805).
- Had another contract for 1,050 tomahawks and 50 pipe tomahawks (1806).

(A) **JOSEPH LOWNES** PHILADELPHIA, PA B1758, 1792-1816
- Located at 133 South Front Street (1792-1811), 124 South Front Street (1811-1816).

(A) **F. (FRANCOIS) LUSIGNANT** FORT WAYNE, IN 1810-1830
- Made tomahawks for the U.S. Office of Indian Trade (1820).
(Blacksmith)

(N) **A. MADISON** NEW YORK, NY 1820-1830
- Made pipe tomahawks for local Indians.
(Blacksmith)

(N) **JOHN MALONY** BALTIMORE, MD 1785-1800
- Made tomahawks for local Indians.
(Blacksmith)

(N) **JOSEPH MANNING** NEW YORK, NY 1820-1845
- Made belt knives, including bowie knives.

(A, C) <u>**THE HISTORY OF MANSFIELD & LAMB**</u>

NEWTON DARLING SLATERVILLE, RI Bc1804-1830
- Learned scythe making from Col. Comstock Passmore of Branch Village, RI (c. 1820-1824).

- Established his own scythe factory on the Branch River, one mile below the village of Slaterville, RI (1824).
- A water wheel ran the factory grinders and equipment.
- Henry S. Manfield, a bank cashier from Branch Village, RI, joined (c. 1830).

DARLING (NEWTON) & MANSFIELD (HENRY S.)   SLATERSVILLE, RI   c.1830-1839

- Operated a scythe factory (mill).
- Ansel Holman joined the company (1839).

DARLING (NEWTON), MANSFIELD (HENRY S.) & HOLMAN (ANSEL)   SLATERSVILLE, RI   1839-1841

- Operated the scythe factory (mill).
- Darling sold his interest in the company to Mansfield & Holman (1841).

MANSFIELD (HENRY S.) & HOLMAN (ANSEL)   SLATERSVILLE, RI   1841-1846

- Operated the scythe factory (mill).
- Estus Lamb (former textile factory owner) joined the company as a major stockholder (1846).

MANSFIELD (HENRY S.) & LAMB (ESTUS)   SLATERVILLE, RI   1846-1860

- Partner: Ansel Holman.
- The scythe factory was refitted and enlarged to a 2 1/2-story building.
- Henry Mansfield owned a farm run by his sons Joseph and John Mansfield.
- Made 72,000 scythes and had 50 workers (1850).
- The factory complex had seven buildings, all located near Main and Maple Streets (1855).
- By c. 1859, a group of workers cottages had been built on Main Street.
- The factory complex and workers cottages became known as the village of Forestdale.

MANSFIELD (HENRY S.) & LAMB (ESTUS)   FORESTDALE, RI (NEAR SMITHFIELD)   1860-1872

- Partner: Ansel Holman.
- Built a large cotton factory (mill) on the Branch River above the scythe factory (1860). Lamb had a textile mill background. It was 3 1/2 stories and 166' x 68', with a 65' x 45' corner building forming an "L" shape.
- Began making cloth (1861).
- The scythe factory and office now located at 21 Main Street, Smithfield, RI.
- By 1861 a group of 2 1/2-story worker tenement houses had been built along Main Street.
- The scythe and cotton mill complex had 200 workers (1862).
- Obtained first U.S. government cavalry saber contract (August 28, 1861).

U.S. Civil War Cavalry Saber Contracts

August 28, 1861	10,000 M1860 cavalry sabers at $8.50 each
July 6, 1863	8,000 M1860 cavalry sabers at $5.75 each
March 15, 1864	4,300 M1860 cavalry sabers at $6 each
April 11, 1864	1,750 M1860 cavalry sabers at $4.50 each
June 2, 1864	7,950 M1860 cavalry sabers at $6.50 each
January 2, 1865	5,000 M1860 cavalry sabers at $6.75 each
February 11, 1862	80 M1840 imported German-made cavalry sabers at $7.50 each
June 19, 1862	378 M1860 imported German-made cavalry sabers at $6 each

(German sabers imported from W.R. Kirschbaum, Solingen, Prussia.)

- Cotton textile factory incorporated as the Forestdale Manufacturing Co. (1862).
- Owners: Henry S. Mansfield, Estus Lamb.

- Partner and factory superintendent: George W. Holt.
- Clerk: S.O. Tabor.
- Made 8,000 scythes and had 50 workers (1870).
- Cotton factory had 300 looms and 235 workers (1870).
- Had 61 worker tenement houses, a boarding house, and a company store on Main Street (1870).
- The J.&W. Stater textile company purchased the Forestdale Manufacturing Co. and the equipment and the real estate of Mansfield & Lamb (the scythe factory was closed) (1872).

(A) **GEORGE MANZ**   PITTSBURGH, PA   1818-1868
- Located on Killemoon's Court.

      GEORGE MANZ   WHEELING, WV   1868-1875
- Located at 168 Main Street.

(Gunsmith, whitesmith)

(N) **MARKS & REES**   CINCINNATI, OH   1815-1840
- Made silver-hilted bowie knives.

(Silversmith, cutler)

(A) **COLONY OF MARYLAND**
- Fifty broadswords with belts were ordered from England for his majesty's troops in the colony of Maryland (1758).

(N) **STATE OF MARYLAND**
- Obtained 600 cavalry sabers from U.S. federal arsenals (probably residue from the 1798 N. Starr and 1799 Buel & Greenleaf U.S. cavalry saber contracts) (1812).

(N) **ANTHONY MATELIN**   BALTIMORE, MD   1775-1800
- Located at 26 Light Street.
- Advertised as a cutler in Baltimore city directory.

(N) **J.H. McCLURE**   RICHMOND, VA   1810-1827
      J.H. McCLURE   RALEIGH, NC   1827-1837
- Advertised as pistol, gun, and knife blade maker, cutler, and repairer of all kinds of cutlery (1827).
- Located on Fayetteville Street.

(Cutler)

(N) **HUGH McCONNELL**   PHILADELPHIA, PA   1815-1850
      HUGH McCONNELL   SAN FRANCISCO, CA   1850-1863
- Locations:
    - 116 Pacific Avenue 1850-1854)
    - 233 Jackson Street (1854-1858)
    - 191 Jackson Street (1858-1861)
    - 605 Jackson Street (1861-1883)
- Made hunting and bowie knives (some silver and gold mounted) and surgical instruments.
- Will & Finck succeeded McConnell (1863).

(Silversmith, cutler)
(See Will & Finck)

(A) **GEORGE McGUNNEGLE**   PITTSBURGH, PA   1787-D1820
- Shop locations:

Market Street (1787-1796)
2nd Street (1796-1805)
corner of Liberty and Pennsylvania Streets (1805-1820)
- Advertised in the Pittsburgh Gazette that he carried on a whitesmith business in all its various branches, making locks, keys, hinges, pipe and squaw tomahawks, and scalping knives. Also ground swords, razors, and scissors and cleaned and polished guns and pistols (1789).

(Cutler, iron worker)

(A) **WILLIAM McKNIGHT**   PITTSBURGH, PA   1815-1820
- Made cavalry sabers.
- Shop located on 4th Street (between Wood and Smithfield Streets).

(Metal worker, tinsmith, coppersmith, sword maker)

(A) **WILLIAM McLAWS**   PHILADELPHIA, PA   1790-1803
- Two locations at 22 Chesnut Street and 22 Carter Alley.

(A) **JAMES McNAUGHT**   RICHMOND, VA   1817-D1825
- Located on East Street (between 19th and 20th Streets) (1817-1820), Main Street (1820-1825).

(A) **JOHN W. MEER**   PHILADELPHIA, PA   1790-D1834
- Located at 22 North Street (1790-1804), 4 South 7th Street (1804-1834).

(N) **NATHANIEL MELCHER (MELCHOIR)**   SOLINGEN, PRUSSIA   B1808-1814
- Immigrated from Solingen to Zlatoust, Russia (1814-1830).
- Immigrated from Zlatoust to Baltimore, MD (1830).

    N. (NATHANIEL) MELCHER   BALTIMORE, MD   1830-1872
- Shop located on Mercer Street at Grand Street.
- Advertised sporting, target, and Kentucky flintlock rifles, musket locks, and cutlery.

    NATHANIEL MELCHER   WILMINGTON, DE   1872-D1879

(Gunsmith, locksmith, cutler)

(N) **GEORGE MELDRUM**   FORT MICHILIMACKINAC STRAITS OF MACKINAC (under British dominion)   1775-1783
- Fort Michilimackinac was originally a French fort and trading post. It became a British fort at the end of the French and Indian War (1763) and ceded to the U.S. at the end of the Revolutionary War (1783).
- Made tomahawks for the British Indian Service.

(A) **HENRY MELLINGER**   LANCASTER CO., PA   1850-1883
- Located at the corner of Water and Market Streets.

(N) **JOHN PETER MENTA**   BALTIMORE, MD   1776-1810
- Located at 2 Harrison Street.
- Advertised in the city directory as a cutler.
- Made tomahawks for local Indians.

(Blacksmith)

(A) **BENJAMIN MEREDITH**   BALTIMORE, MD   1803-1817
- Locations:
    30 Light Street (1803-1809)

      6 Water Street (1809-1814)
      33 South Liberty Street (1814-1815)
      corner of Light and Banks Streets (1815-1817)
      Pace Street (1817)
(Cutler, whitesmith, instrument maker, gunsmith)

MERIDAN CUTLERY CO.
(See David Ropes)

(N) SOLOMAN MIGNERON   PHILADELPHIA, PA   1820-1840
- Made pipe tomahawks.

(A) D.J. MILLARD   CLAYVILLE, NY   1849-D1875
- Had a U.S. government contract for 10,000 M1860 cavalry sabers at $7 each (he delivered 10,031) (1861).
- The first 600 sabers and 1,100 scabbards delivered were purchased from other sword makers because his sword factory was not ready.

(N) NATHANIEL MILLER   WOODSTOCK CO., CT   1750-1770
- Made tomahawks for local Indians.

(Blacksmith)

(N) WILLIAM & GEORGE MILLER   YALESVILLE, CT   1868-1880
- Cutlery shop.

WILLIAM & GEORGE MILLER   WALLINGFORD, CT   1880-1885
- Cutlery shop.

MILLER BROS. (WILLIAM & GEORGE)   MERIDAN, CT   1885-1925
- Made pocket knives, farriers knives, and bowie knives.

(A) SAMUEL MILLER   BOSTON, MA   1725-1745
- Made silver-hilted small swords.
- Advertised as a maker of brass- and iron-hilted cavalry swords.

(A) WILLIAM H. MILNER   NEW YORK, NY   1850-1860
- Located at 384 Broadway.

(A) NATHANIEL MITCHELL   UNIONTOWN, PA   1814-1850
- Located on Pittsburgh Street.

(A) JOHN LEWIS MOISSON   CHARLESTON, SC   1807-D1830
- Locations:
      133 Queen Street (1807-1811)
      79 Meeting Street (1811-1812)
      79 E. Bay Street (1812-1815)
      corner of State Street and Chalmers Alley (1815-1830)

(A) FREDERICK MOLLER   NEW YORK, NY   1840-1850
- Located at 200 Division Street.

(N) BENJAMIN MOORE   SUTTON, MA   1800-1815
- Made tomahawks for the local Indians.

(Blacksmith)

(N) **JOSEPH MORDECAI**   CHARLESTON, SC   1809-1822
- Locations:
    4 Liberty Street (1809-1816)
    42 Beaufain Street (1816-1818)
    Meeting Street (1818-1819)
    Charleston fire destroyed shop but rebuilt (1819)
    25 Beaufain Street (1819-1822)

(Gun, bayonet, knife maker)

(A) **THEOPHILUS MUNSON**   NEW HAVEN, CT   B1675, 1697-D1747
- Bought a gun shop on the southeast corner of Elm and High Streets (1697).
- Made doglock muskets.
- Armorer for colony of Connecticut.
- Repaired guns, mounted cannon on new type carriages, made pikes.

(A) **JAMES MURRAY**   YORK, PA   1780-1805
- Located on Water Street.

(N) **GEORGE MUSCROFT**   LONDON, ENGLAND   c1810-1834
- Immigrated to Baltimore, MD (1834).

    GEORGE MUSCROFT   BALTIMORE, MD   1834-1850

(Cutler, knife maker)

(A) **SHELDON NASH**   CINCINNATI, OH   1853-1865
- Located on 8th Street (east of Broadway).
- Made bowie knives (some silver mounted).

(Silversmith, cutler, knife maker)

(N) **D. (DANIEL) B. NEAL**   MT. GILEAD, OH   1817-1858
- Made hunting knives.

(Gunsmith, cutler)

(N) **NEW YORK KNIFE CO.**   WALDEN, NY   1853-1870
- Established by a group of knife makers who immigrated from Sheffield, England.
- Made bowie knives.
- Changed name to Walden Knife Co. (1870).

    WALDEN KNIFE CO.   WALDEN, NY   1870-1923
- Their knife factory was located in Montgomery, Orange County, NY.
- Made bowie, hunting, and table knives.

(N) **A.D. NEWTON**   LA POINTE, WI   1825-1850
    A.D. NEWTON   DEPERE, WI   1850-1857
- Made tomahawks, knives, and half axes and repaired guns for the local Indians (a service requested by the Indians) while working for the American Fur Company.

(Gunsmith, blacksmith)

(C) **DANIEL NIPPES**   PHILADELPHIA, PA   1810-1811
- Did not have a U.S. contract for 1,000 cavalry sabers.

(N) **NORTHFIELD KNIFE CO.**   NORTHFIELD, CT   1858-1919

- President: John S. Barnes (1858-1862).
- President: Samuel Mason (1862-1865).
- President: Franklin H. Catlin (1865-1919).
- Factory superintendent: Charles Platts (1872-1919).
- Purchased the American Knife Company (1865).
- Exhibited at the Philadelphia Centennial Exposition (1876).
- Exhibited at the Paris Worlds Fair (1878).
- Purchased the Excelsior Knife Company (1884).
- Exhibited at the Chicago Columbian Exposition (1892).
- Made pocket and bowie knives.
- Clark Bros. Cutlery Co. purchased the company (1919).

(See American Knife Co.)

NORTHAMPTON CUTLERY CO.
(See Bay State Hardware)

(N) **ANDREW OLIVER** BOSTON, MA B1724, 1740-D1776
- Made silver-mounted hunting knives.

(Silversmith, knife maker)

(A) **WILLIAM OPY** FORT PITT 1755-1763
  (LATER PITTSBURGH, PA)
- During the French and Indian War, contracted with the British government to make and repair tomahawks for Indians friendly to the British.
- Delivered 32 dozen large and small tomahawks (1768).

(N) **SGT. JOHN ORDWAY** FORT MANDAN, ND 1804-1806
- Armorer with the Lewis and Clark expedition (1804-1806).
- Lewis had Ordway make Missouri war hatchets (tomahawks) and scalping knives while at Fort Mandan for trade with local Indians.

(Armorer, blacksmith, gunsmith)

(N) **LEBER & SYLVESTRE PAPIN** ST. LOUIS, MO 1825-1835
- Made pipe tomahawks for local Indians.

(Blacksmith)

(N) **WILLIAM PARKE** HUDSON BAY, CANADA 1770-1790
- Sold pipe tomahawks to the Hudson Bay Fur Co., which they traded to local Indians for furs.

(A) **JOSEPH, THOMAS & WILLIAM** WILLIAMS FORD 1750-1770
  PARKINSON (LATER WILLIAMSPORT, MD)
   (under British dominion)
- Had a gunsmith shop in the Conoccocheague settlement on the Potomac River near the Williams Ford.
- Moved to Yohogania Co., VA, which is now Washington Co., PA (1770).

  JOSEPH, THOMAS & WILLIAM YOHOGANIA CO., VA 1770-c1783
  PARKINSON (under British dominion)
- Had a gunsmith shop on the Monongahela River.
- During the Revolutionary War, the Virginia Committee of Safety contracted with them for rifles, tomahawks, scalping knives, and cutlery for the use of the Yohogania County militia (January 29, 1777).

  WILLIAM PARKINSON YOHOGANIA CO., VA c1783-1790

THOMAS PARKINSON	TYGART VALLEY, VA	c1783-D1808

- Traded with local Indians.

JOSEPH PARKINSON	YOHOGANIA CO., VA	c1783-1801
JOSEPH PARKINSON	DUNBAR TWSP. FAYETTE CO., PA	1801-1804
JOSEPH PARKINSON	SOMERSET TWSP. WASHINGTON CO., PA	1804-1806
JOSEPH PARKINSON	BROOKE CO., VA	1806-D1807

(N) **CHRISTOPHER PARRY** — PHILADELPHIA, PA — 1735-1760
- Apprentice: William Wright (1746-1751).

(Cutler, knife maker)

(A) **STEPHEN PASCHALL** — PHILADELPHIA, PA — 1750-1783
- Made sword blades, scythes, and sickles during the French and Indian War (1756-1763).

(A) **THOMAS PEARSON** — LONDON, ENGLAND — c1657-1677
- Blacksmith and knife maker.
- Immigrated to Philadelphia, PA (1677).

THOMAS PEARSON — PHILADELPHIA, PA — 1677-1690
- Set up shop in a cave on the west bank of the Delaware River below Philadelphia.
- Sold knives and belt axes (tomahawks) to the local trade Indians.

(Blacksmith, cutler)

(A) **DANIEL PEASE** — BLUE HILL, NY — 1860-1869
- Made bowie knives and belt axes (tomahawks).

(A) **DANIEL PECK** — PETERSBURG, VA — 1797-1808
- Located on Pocohontas Street.

(A) **WILLIAM PERKINS** — PHILADELPHIA, PA — 1775-1790
- Located on Water Street at South Street.
- Made standard axes, belt axes (tomahawks), and edged and regular tools.

(A) **PETTIBONE BROS. MFG. CO.** — CINCINNATI, OH — 1900-1976
- Located at 626-628-630-632 Main Street.
- Officers in 1911 were:
    President: L.H. Brooks.
    Vice-President: H.H. Hoffman.
    Secretary and General Manager: George A. Brooks.
    Directors: L.C. Goodwin, E.C. Jones, D.W. O'Neil.
- Had a branch in San Francisco, CA.
- Their sales receipt advertised military goods, uniforms, regalia and lodge supplies for all secret societies, banners and badges; also gold and silver trimming importer and sword maker.

(A) **DANIEL PETTIBONE** — BOSTON, MA — 1811-1815
- Had a U.S. contract for rifleman belt axes (tomahawks) (1812).

(A, C) **JAMES PETTIBONE** — CINCINNATI, OH — B1848-1872
- Employee of John Boner (1866-1871).
- Bought out Boner (1872).

JAMES PETTIBONE	**CINCINNATI, OH**	**1872-1878**

- Partner: William Pettibone (clerk).
- Located at 92 North 4th Street.

PETTIBONE (JAMES & WILLIAM) MFG. CO.	**CINCINNATI, OH**	**1878-1895**

- Located at 99 North 5th Street (1828-1885), 165 and 169 Elm Street (1885-1895).

PETTIBONE BROS.	**CINCINNATI, OH**	**1895-1976**

- Located at 274 Main Street (1895-1897), 626-632 Main Street (1897-1976).
- Made 10,000 swords annually (mostly fraternal).
- Charles B. Pettibone (born 1872) succeeded James (retired) (1900).
- Had branch in San Francisco at 3969 Washington Street (1906).
- Pettibone Bros. bought out by Schwartz Tailoring Co. but kept the Pettibone name (1955).

(N) JULIUS PETTIS	**TROY, NY**	**1865-1880**

- Located at 374 River Street.
- Made M1872 cavalry officer swords.

(Cutler, sword maker)

(N) J. (JOSEPH) PETTY	**LA CROSSE, WI**	**1835-1857**

- Rifle and halberd tomahawk maker.

(Gunsmith, blacksmith)

(A) JOHN PIM	**BOSTON, MA**	**1705-1730**

- Made silver-hilted small swords.
- Made brass- and iron-hilted cavalry swords.

(A) WILLIAM PINCHIN SR.	**PHILADELPHIA, PA**	**1784-1826**

- Located at 326 Sassafras Street.

WILLIAM PINCHIN JR.	**PHILADELPHIA, PA**	**1826-D1862**

- Locations:
    336 Sassafras Street (1826-1845)
    16 Jacoby Street (1845-1855)
    120 Jacoby Street (1855-1862)

(A) WILLIAM PINTARD	**PHILADELPHIA, PA**	**1780-1800**

- Located on the corner of North 3rd and Green Streets.

(A) FAYETTE R. PLUMB	**PHILADELPHIA, PA**	**1855-1875**
YERKES (JOHN) & PLUMB (FAYETTE)	**PHILADELPHIA, PA**	**1875-1888**

- Located on the corner of Trenton and Tucker Streets.

FAYETTE PLUMB	**PHILADELPHIA, PA**	**1888-1940**

- Locations:
    corner of Trenton and Tucker Streets (1888-1889)
    corner of Trenton and James Streets (1889-1890)
    4837 James Street (1890-1940)
- Had U.S. contracts for more than 58,000 M1909 bolo knives.
- Also had U.S. contracts for M1917 bolo knives as well as fighting knives.
- Ladew & Co. made the leather scabbards for Plumb's bolo knives.

(Cutler, edged tool maker, knife maker)

(N) **DANIEL POSE**   BALTIMORE, MD   1790-1800
- Made tomahawks for local Indians.

(Blacksmith)

(C) **JAMES POTTER**   NEW YORK, NY   1755-1786
- Advertised for a forger and two to three filers to make swords (June 13, 1778).

(A) **LEWIS PRAHL**   **BLOCKLEY TWSP. PHILADELPHIA CO., PA**   c1750-1784
- Made sabers with solid brass hilts, lion-head pommels, and eagle-head pommels with split and divided guards.
- The 1777 and 1781 Pennsylvania Committee of Safety cavalry saber contracts obtained by Prahl were for iron, hussar-hilt sabers with leather-covered grips and leather scabbards.

     LEWIS PRAHL   PHILADELPHIA, PA   1784-D1809
- Shop located at 131 Wood Street.

(A) **MICHAEL PRICE**   SAN FRANCISCO, CA   1840-D1888
- Locations:
  - 59 Montgomery Street (1858-1861)
  - 221 Montgomery Street (1861-1862)
  - 238 Montgomery Street (1862-1863)
  - 110 Montgomery Street (1863-1868)
- Showroom located at 415 Kearney; factory located at 23 Stevenson (1868-1888).
- Made bowie knives, push daggers, and carved ivory grip hunting knives, some with silver mountings.

(A) **WILLIAM PRICE**   NEW YORK, NY   1838-1858
- Located at 424 Broadway.
- Partner: Virgil Price, but a different address.

     WILLIAM PRICE & CO.   NEW YORK, NY   1858-1868
- Partner: Virgil Price.
- Located at 144 Green Street.
- Made presentation, fraternal, and Masonic swords.
- Also made M1860 staff and field officer swords.

     VIRGIL PRICE   NEW YORK, NY   1868-1871
- Located at 144 Green Street (1868-1870), 436 Broome Street (1870-1871).

(C) **WILLIAM PRINTUP**   NEW YORK, NY   1750-1770
- During the French and Indian War (1756-1763), had a contract with the British Indian Service for tomahawks to be provided to Indians friendly to the British.

(A) <u>THE HISTORY OF THE PROVIDENCE TOOL CO.</u>

JEREMIAH & JOSEPH ARNOLD   PAWTUCKET, RI   1834-c1840
- Hardware factory making iron nuts, washers, and machinery.
- Joseph retired (c. 1840).

WILLIAM FIELD & CO.   PAWTUCKET, RI   c1840-1846
- Partner: Jeremiah Arnold.
- Company moved to Providence, RI (1846).

PROVIDENCE TOOL CO.   PROVIDENCE, RI   1846-1885
- Partners: Jeremiah Arnold, William Field.

- Treasurer John B. Anthony negotiated all Civil War musket and saber contracts with the U.S. government.
- Purchased the Providence Forge and Nut Co. (1856).
- Made a complete line of hardware and ships chandlery.
- President: Richard Borden (1860).
- Had a musket and sword armory during the Civil War located at 148 West River Street.
- Had 200 men making muskets and 70 men making cavalry sabers in the armory.
- Sold the U.S. government 10,434 M1860 cavalry sabers.

(N) **PIERRE PROVINSABLE (PROVINSALLE)**　　SAGINAW, MI　　　　　　　　　　1810-1830
- Made pipe tomahawks for the U.S. Office of Indian Trade.

(N) **JOHN D. REED**　　　　　　　　　　　BALTIMORE, MD　　　　　　　　　　1800-1815
- Made tomahawks for the U.S. Office of Indian Trade (1810).

(Blacksmith)

(A) **JOHN FREDERICK REICHE**　　　　　GERMANY　　　　　　　　　　　　　　c1774-1794
　　　　　　　　　　　　　　　　　　　　　　(PROBABLY SOLINGEN, PRUSSIA)
- Immigrated to Philadelphia, PA (1794).

　　JOHN FREDERICK REICHE　　　　　PHILADELPHIA, PA　　　　　　　　　1794-1810
- Located at 84 4th Street.

(A) **LEONARD & JAMES REICHE**　　　　PHILADELPHIA, PA　　　　　　　　　1809-1815
　　(RICKEY)
- Made iron cavalry sabers with reverse-P hilts, flat 34″ clipped-point blades, and grooved walnut grips during the War of 1812.

(N) **CHARLES C. REINHARDT**　　　　　　BALTIMORE, MD　　　　　　　　　　1837-1850
- Locations:
    - 24 Lombard Street (1837-1841)
    - 8 Light Street (1841-1845)
    - 9 Light Street (1845-1850)

　　CHARLES C. REINHARDT & CO.　　　PHILADELPHIA, PA　　　　　　　　　1850-1865
- Locations:
    - 9 Light Street (1850-1855)
    - 11 Light Street (1855-1857)
    - 7 N. Gay Street (1857-1865)
- Charles C. Reinhardt retired (1865).

　　REINHARDT & BROTHER　　　　　　　PHILADELPHIA, PA　　　　　　　　　1865-1873
- Partners: William H. Reinhardt, J. (James) Reinhardt.
- Located at 7 North Gay Street (1865-1868), 2 Anthony Street (1868-1873).
- Made fine quality bowie knives.

(Cutlers, knife makers, surgical and dental instrument makers)

(N) **E. (ELIPHALET) REMINGTON & SONS**　ILION, NY　　　　　　　　　　　　1850-1900
- U.S. contract for 2,268 sword bayonets (1861).
- Bought a 50 percent interest in a sword blade rolling machine patented by John G. Richardson of Philadelphia, PA (1873). Probably used it to make bayonet blades.

(See John G. Richardson)

(C) **WILLIAM RICH**   SACO, ME   1741-1743
- Armorer to the Maine district of the Massachusetts Bay Colony.

(A) **FRANCIS RICHARDSON JR.**   PHILADELPHIA, PA   1717-D1782
- Made silver-hilted small swords.

(A) **JOSEPH RICHARDSON SR.**   PHILADELPHIA, PA   1725-D1770
- Located on Front Street.

(N) **F. RICHTER**   BOSTON, MA   1840-1850
- Knife maker, including bowie knives.

(N) **WILLIAM RIGHTMAN**   CHARLESTON, SC   1775-1783
- Made rifleman belt axes (tomahawks).

(Blacksmith)

(A) **BENJAMIN RITTENHOUSE**   PHILADELPHIA, PA   1777-1819
- Located on Pine Street (above 12th Street).

(A) **DAVID RITTENHOUSE**   PHILADELPHIA, PA   1770-D1796
- Located on the corner of 7th and Arch Streets.

(N) **JAMES ROBERTS**   VINCENT TWSP. CHESTER CO., PA   1745-1795
- Advertised as a cutler.

(N) **JAMES ROBERTS**   FELLS POINT, MD   1775-1800
- Located at 3 Thames Street.
- Advertised as an armorer in the Baltimore city directory.

(A) **C. (CHRISTOPHER) ROBY & CO.**   W. CHELMSFORD, MA   1853-1867
- During the Civil War, used Hooker & Co. (brass founder) to make brass sword hilts and mountings.
- Joseph Raynes & Co. were the sole agents for Roby swords in Lowell, MA.
- Blodget, Brown & Co. located at 83 Beckman Street, New York, NY, were the sole agents for Roby swords in New York.
- Made bowie knives.
- Made M1850 staff and field officer and M1852 naval officer presentation swords.
- Advertised in the *Chicago Tribune* as a manufacturer of U.S. regulation swords for line officers, staff officers, medical officers, paymaster officers, and general officers (December 3, 1867).
- Advertised in the *Army-Navy Journal* (May 7, 1884):

      Swords, belts, sashes, etc.
      C. Roby & Co.

Manufacturers of line, non-commissioned, field, navy, medical, paymaster, chaplains, and general officers United States regulation swords, also belts and sashes. Also U.S. regulation cavalry and artillery sabers, etc.

(A) **THOMAS RODE (ROD)**   PITTSBURGH, PA   1800-1815
- Located at Pennsylvania Street between Pitt and St. Clair Streets.

(N) **E. (ELISHA) ROGERS**   UTICA, NY   1815-1835
- Gun shop located at corner of General and Liberty Streets.

- Made quality rifles and spiked tomahawks.

(Gunsmith, blacksmith)

(N) J.B. ROGERS   YORK, ME   1861-1865
- Made bowie knives (called "mountain toothpicks").

(N) DAVID ROPES   SACCARAPA, ME   1832-1845
- Made belt and bowie knives.
- Bought ivory handles for his knives from ivory button maker Julius Pratt of Meridan, CT. They eventually formed a partnership.

    PRATT (JULIUS) & ROPES (DAVID)   MERIDAN, CT   1845-1855
    MERIDAN CUTLERY CO.   MERIDAN, CT   1855-1866
- President: Julius Pratt.
- Partner: David Ropes.
- Secretary and treasurer: J.B. Beadle.
- Employee: Homer A. Curtiss (knife maker).
- Landers, Frary & Clark bought out Meridan Cutlery Co. (1866).

(General knife makers, including bowie knives, and tableware makers)

(A) THE ROSE FAMILY–CUTLERS OF PHILADELPHIA

Name	Born	Died
William Rose	1754	1810
Joseph Rose Sr. (son of William Rose)	1778	1819
Benjamin F. Rose (son of William Rose)	c. 1784	c. 1840
William Rose Sr. (son of William Rose)	1783	1854

- William Rose married Susannah Frailey (1807).

Sons of William Rose Sr. by Susannah Frailey:

William Rose Jr.	1810	1883
Peter Rose	c. 1815	c. 1850

- William Rose married Catherine Frailey (1820).

Sons of William Rose Sr. by Catherine Frailey:

Joseph Rose Jr.	1823	1881
Rudolph F. Rose	1826	c. 1895
John W. Rose	1828	c. 1895

JOSEPH ROSE SR.
- Made iron hussar hilt cavalry sabers for state militias.
- His sabers had three blade types:
  1) Triple fuller imported blade with a "bird cage" leather scabbard, like the William Rose U.S. 1807 contract saber.
  2) Woolley & Co., Birmingham, England, M1796 English saber type blade.
  3) Woolley & Co., Birmingham, England, c. 1780 and M1788 type blade with a wide fuller from hilt guard to the tip of the blade.

The Career of Joseph Rose Jr. (1823-1881)

JOSEPH ROSE JR.   BLOCKLEY TWSP., PA   B1823-1840
- Son of William Rose Sr. by his second wife, Catherine Frailey.

| **WILLIAM ROSE (SR. & JR.)** | **WEST PHILADELPHIA, PA** | **1840-1849** |

- Originally West Philadelphia was the part of Philadelphia west of 33rd Street. It became a separate town (c. 1840).
- Joseph Rose Jr. apprenticed with his father William Rose Sr. and stepbrother William Rose Jr.

| **WILLIAM ROSE (SR.) & SON (WILLIAM JR.)** | **WEST PHILADELPHIA, PA** | **1849-1850** |

- Joseph Rose Jr. worked in the shop of his father William Rose Sr. and stepbrother William Rose Jr.

| **WILLIAM ROSE SR. & SONS** | **NEW YORK, NY** | **1850-1854** |

- Joseph Rose Jr. worked at his father's cutlery shop in New York, NY, as the manager.
- In addition to surgical instruments, they made swords, blades, and bowie knives.
- Joseph Rose Jr. made a naval presentation sword with his name on it during this period.
- Joseph Rose Jr. sold sword blades to Harris (George) & Co., NY.
- A silver-mounted bowie knife marked "Rose, NY" is known.
- When his father William Rose Sr. died (1854), Joseph Rose Jr. went back to West Philadelphia to work with his stepbrother William Rose Jr. and brothers Rudolph F. Rose and John W. Rose.

| **WILLIAM ROSE (JR.) & BROS.** | **WEST PHILADELPHIA, PA** | **1854-1881** |

- Partners:
    William Rose Jr. (first marriage).
    Joseph Rose Jr. (second marriage).
    Rudolph F. Rose (second marriage).
    John W. Rose (second marriage).
- Listed as cutlers in city directory (1854-1861).
- Listed as trowel makers and makers of other edged tools such as round knives (1861-1890).
- Joseph Rose Jr. died (1881)

The Rose Family–Cutlers of Philadelphia: Their New York Cutlery Shops and Offices

| **WILLIAM ROSE & SONS** | **NEW YORK, NY** | **1815-1890** |

- The name of the New York office seems to have remained the same, even though the name of the Rose shops in Blockley Township and West Philadelphia changed several times between 1815 and 1865.
- After the War of 1812, William Rose Sr. and his brothers Joseph Rose Sr. and Benjamin F. Rose began to make surgical instruments in addition to edged tools, swords, and sword blades (their major output of the time) at Blockley Township, PA.
- I believe the New York shop probably specialized more in surgical instruments because of the large demand from the many doctors in the city.
- They also sold scissors and shears.
- I believe Benjamin F. Rose opened the shop in 1815 and ran it until 1817 before he opened his own surgical instrument shop in Philadelphia on 7th Street and operated that until c. 1840.
- We do not know who ran the New York office from 1817 to 1845.
- We know Peter Rose was listed as a surgical instrument maker in the New York directories (1845-1850). He was manager of the Rose New York office.
- We know that Joseph Rose Jr. was listed in New York directories (1850-1854). He was manager of the Rose New York offices.
- We know that while Joseph Rose Jr. was manager of the New York office, he made swords, sword blades, bowie knives, and surgical instruments.
- A naval presentation sword has his name on it.
- A silver-mounted bowie knife has his name on it ("Rose—New York").
- We know he sold sword blades to Harris (George) & Co., New York, NY (1850-1854).
- It is possible his brothers Rudolph F. Rose and John W. Rose also worked at the New York shop instead of the West Philadelphia shop run by William Rose Jr. (1850-1854).

- After William Rose Sr. died (1854), all three brothers (Joseph Jr., Rudolph F., and John W. Rose) formed a partnership in West Philadelphia called William Rose & Brothers.
- William Rose & Brothers was listed in city directories as cutlers (1854-1861) and trowel makers (1861-1890).
- We do not know who ran the New York office from 1854 to 1890.
- We know that William Rose & Sons, New York, displayed presentation swords at the New York Metropolitan Fair (1884). The fair was put on by the United States Sanitary Commission, a privately funded organization whose sole purpose was to make the life of Civil War soldiers easier while they were encamped away from home. The Sanitary Commission sponsored several of these fairs to raise money to buy supplies and special items from home to give to the soldiers.

THE ROSE FAMILY–GUN MAKERS OF NEW YORK

- This gun-making family was probably related to the Rose family cutlers of Pennsylvania.

JOSEPH ROSE (SR.)   NEW YORK, NY   Bc1764-1804
(Gunsmith)

J. (JOSEPH) ROSE (SR.) & SON (LODOWICK)   NEW YORK, NY   1804-1830

- Partner and son: Lodowick Rose (Born c. 1784; died 1848).
- Had a contract with the U.S. Office of Indian Trade for 36 tomahawks for $0.50 to $0.90 each (1806).

(Gunsmith, tomahawk maker)

LODOWICK ROSE   NEW YORK, NY   1830-1846

- Gun shop located at 80 Catherine Street.

(Gunsmith, rifle and pistol maker)

ROSE (LODOWICK) & HOPKINS (RUBAN)   NEW YORK, NY   1846-1848

- Gun shop located at 80 Catherine Street.
- Made percussion sporting and target rifles.

JOSEPH ROSE (JR.)   NEW YORK, NY   1848-1857

- Son of Lodowick Rose.
- Gun shop located at 80 Catherine Street.
- Employed seven gunsmiths.
- Produced 500 rifles and fouling pieces valued at $4,000 (1850).
- Some must have been silver-enlayed since he bought silver in 1849 and 1850.

JOSEPH ROSE & SON   NEW YORK, NY   1857-1860

(C) **MARK ROUNDS**   SACO, ME   1699-1715

- Armorer to the Maine district of the Massachusetts Bay Colony.

(A) **WILLIAM C. ROWLAND**   PHILADELPHIA, PA   1875-1937

- Locations:
    - 1235 Arch Street (1875-1910)
    - 1209 Arch Street (1910-1913)
    - 1026 Race Street (1913-1937)
- Also made military uniforms.

(A) **HAMILTON RUDDICK**   BOSTON, MA   1861-1868

- Locations:
    - 82 Sudbury Street (1861-1863)
    - 12 Hawkins Street (1863-1865)
    - 78 Saratog Street (1865-1868)

JOHN RUSSELL	**DEERFIELD, MA**	Bc1800-1832

(Jeweler, silversmith)

JOHN RUSSELL	**DEERFIELD, MA**	1832-1836

- Built a factory on the Green River called the Green River Works.
- Made cast steel socket chisels and butcher knives.
- The factory burned down (1836); built a new factory in Greenfield, MA.

JOHN RUSSELL	**GREENFIELD, MA**	1836-1868
(RUSSELL CUTLERY CO.)		

- Partners: Francis Russell, Henry Clapp (banker).
- New factory located on the Green River.
- Joseph Gardner was a knife shafter and later a sales agent for the company (1850-1858).
- Added steam power to run grinding wheels.
- Brought knife makers from Sheffield, England, to work in their factory.
- Production went from $60,000 to $700,000 annually.

JOHN RUSSELL CUTLERY CO.	**TURNER FALLS, MA**	1868-1933

- Built a new factory that is still on the Green River.
- Made famous "Barlow" pocket knives.
- Made hunting and bowie knives.
- Production was $721,000 (1870).
- Made an eagle-head pommel bowie knife with a gold, silver, and bronze hilt presented to President Theodore Roosevelt (March 4, 1907).
- Merged with the Harrington Cutlery Co. and became Russell, Harrington Cutlery Co. (1933).

(A) **HARRY SAFFORD**	**ZANESVILLE, OH**	1790-1815

- Made cavalry sabers for the War of 1812.

(N) **LEVI SAINT CYR**	**WINNEBAGO, NE**	Bc1875, 1875-1910

- Made nickel-plated brass pipe tomahawks (1895-1910).

HENRY SAUERBIER	**GERMANY**	Bc1830-1839
	(PROBABLY SOLINGEN, PRUSSIA)	

- Immigrated to Newark, NJ (1839).

HENRY SAUERBIER	**NEWARK, NJ**	1839-1848

- Probably apprenticed as a cutler (1845-1848).

HENRY SAUERBIER	**NEWARK, NJ**	1848-1851

- Listed in the Newark city directory as a cutler.
- Located at 101 Catherine Street (1848-1850), 333 Broad Street (1850-1851).
- Formed a partnership with cutlers Aaron Crawford and William Brown for one year (1851-1852). They used Crawford's shop at 7 Mechanic Lane.

CRAWFORD (AARON), BROWN	**NEWARK, NJ**	1851-1852
(WILLIAM) & SAUERBIER (HENRY)		

- Cutlery shop located at 7 Mechanic Lane.
- Partnership broke up (1852).
- Crawford opened his own cutlery shop at 212 Market Street.
- Brown had no listing in the city directory after 1852.
- Sauerbier opened his own cutlery shop at 162 Market Street.

H. (HENRY) SAUERBIER & CO.	**NEWARK, NJ**	1852-1866

- Cutlery shop located at 162 Market Street (1852-1855).
- For one year Sauerbier used the property next door at 158 Market Street as a tool factory (1854-1855).

- Advertised in the Newark city directory as a maker of tools for saddlers, harness makers, shoemakers, trunk makers, carriage trimmers, and mechanics (1854-1855).
- Cutlery shop located at 7 and 8 Mechanic Lane (1855-1861).
- Cutlery shop located at 24 and 26 Mechanic Lane (1861-1865).
- During the Civil War, made many high-quality swords and blades.
- Made M1840 (variation) cavalry trooper sabers.
- Made M1840 (variation) cavalry officer sabers.
- Had a U.S. contract for 100 M1850 foot officer swords ("U.S." cast into the guard).
- Made nonregulation M1850 staff and field officer swords.
- Made high-grade presentation M1850 staff and field officer swords with very unusual pommel caps, some incorporating precious stones and tin types.
- Sold swords to Shannon, Miller & Crane, New York, NY, and Schuyler, Hartley & Graham, New York, NY.
- Also sold high-quality blades to many silversmiths.
- In some cases Sauerbier used German blades imported from W.R. Kirschbaum of Solingen, Prussia.
- After the Civil War Sauerbier devoted all his time to tool making.

HENRY SAUERBIER   NEWARK, NJ   1866-1870
- Tool maker located at 24 and 26 Mechanic Lane.

H. (HENRY) SAUERBIER & SON   NEWARK, NJ   1870-1873
- Partner: Henry Sauerbier Jr.
- Set up shop at 34-38 Mechanic Lane (formerly Sayre & Beam Jewelers).

H. (HENRY) SAUERBIER & SONS   NEWARK, NJ   1873-1875
- Henry Sauerbier Sr. acted as financial director and tool designer.
- Sons and partners: Henry Sauerbier Jr. (sales and tool design), Theodore Sauerbier (factory superintendent).
- Had 75 employees (1874).
- Made $125,000 worth of tools (1874).
- Beginning in this period and continuing until the company closed in 1887, the Sauerbiers sold their tools nationally and internationally. Their tools were exported to Cuba, South America, Norway, and even Germany.
- *The Industrial Interest of Newark New Jersey* by William F. Ford (1874) shows Sauerbier making tools for saddlers, trunk makers, carriage trimmers, tanners, shoemakers, and curriers tools. He also made leather working machinery.

HENRY SAUERBIER'S SONS   NEWARK, NJ   1875-1880
- Located at 34-36-38-40 Mechanic Lane.
- Sons and partners: Henry Sauerbier Jr., Theodore Sauerbier.
- Henry Sauerbier Sr. still had input.
- Advertised as a maker of tools for saddlers, harness makers, trunk makers, carriage trimmers, shoemakers, and curriers. He also made Knox's leather fluting machine and rollers for patterning leather and hair crimpers. (1877).
- Henry Sauerbier Sr.'s son Julius began working at the factory during this time.

H. (HENRY) SAUERBIER   NEWARK, NJ   1880-1882
- Located at 34-36-38-40 Mechanic Lane.
- Sons and partners: Henry Sauerbier Jr., Theodore Sauerbier, Julius Sauerbier.
- Henry Sauerbier Sr. still had input.

HENRY SAUERBIER   NEWARK, NJ   1882-1884
- Located at 291 New Jersey Railroad Avenue.
- Sons and partners: Henry Sauerbier Jr., Theodore Sauerbier, Julius Sauerbier.
- Henry Sr. retired (1884).

HENRY SAUERBIER   NEWARK, NJ   1884-1887
- Brothers and partners: Henry Sauerbier Jr., Theodore Sauerbier.
- Located at 291 New Jersey Railroad Avenue.
- Henry Sauerbier Sr. died (1887).

JULIUS SAUERBIER   NEWARK, NJ   1884-1887
- Located at 291 New Jersey Railroad Avenue.
- Advertised as a maker of tools for saddlers, harness makers, carriage trimmers, tanners, shoemakers, and curriers, as well as leather working machinery (1885).

(See Aaron Crawford)
(See William Brown)

(N) **JOSEPH SCHILLING**   PHILADELPHIA, PA   1863-1894
- Locations:
    993 North 7th Street (1863-1865)
    238 New Street (1865-1874)
    234 New Street (1874-1894)
- Advertised as a sword maker, gilder, electroplater and brass finisher (sword hiltor).

JOSEPH & OTTO SCHILLING   PHILADELPHIA, PA   1894-1899
- Located at 234 New Street.

(N) **ALBERT SCHMID & CO.**   PROVIDENCE, RI   1867-1936
- Son of John M. Schmid.
- Located at 174 Westminster Street.
- General knife maker, including bowie knives.

(N) **JOHN M. SCHMID**   WATERVILLE, CT   B1836-1856
    JOHN M. SCHMID   PROVIDENCE, RI   1856-1867
- Located at 156 Westminster Street (1856-1867), 174 Westminster Street (1867-1879).
- Made razors, tableware, edged tools, and pocket and bowie knives.
- John M. Schmid retired (1867) and died (1879).

J.M. SCHMID & SON   PROVIDENCE, RI   1867-1936
- President: Albert Schmid (son of John M. Schmid).
- Employee: knife maker Frederick Paolantonio.

(Cutler)

(N) **PAUL SCHMIDT**   BALTIMORE, MD   1845-1865
- Located at 46 North Frederick Street.
- Made brass-hilted bowie knives.

(A) **JOHN LEONARD SCHREIBER**   CINCINNATI, OH   1845-1875
- Locations:
    482 Walnut Street (1845-1862)
    550 Vine Street (1862-1863)
    467 Walnut Street (1863-1875)
- Maker of door locks, printing presses, iron railings, fencing apparatus, fencing swords, and M1872 cavalry officer sabers.

SCHREIBER IRON WORKS   CINCINNATI, OH   1875-1950
- President: John Leonard Schreiber.
- Located at 467 Walnut Street.

(Blacksmith, cutler)

(N) **CASPAR C. SCHUBARTH**   PROVIDENCE, RI   1855-1868
- Gun shop located at 6 North Main Street (1855-1865), 84 Weybosset Street (1865-1868).
- Advertised as manufacturer and dealer in guns, pistols, and sporting apparatus.

- Had U.S. contract for 78,000 Model 1861 Springfield rifled muskets (1861-1862). Delivered 9,500 muskets.
- Advertised repairs of all kinds of firearms, swords, and surgical and dental instruments.

(A) **NATHAN SCOTHORN SR.** PITTSBURGH, PA 1750-1815
- Located on Front Street.

(A) **DANIEL SEARLES** BATON ROUGE, LA 1818-D1866
- Located on Philip Street (near America Street).
- Made exquisite silver-inlayed flintlock pistols and Kentucky flintlock rifles.
- Made several silver-mounted hunting knives for Rezin Pleasant Bowie, brother of James (Jim) Bowie (c. 1830). They were of the same style that Rezin gave his brother James in 1827 (maker unknown). Rezin Bowie gave them as gifts to his friends Lt. H.W. Fowler (U.S. Dragoons), E.D. White (Chief Justice of the Supreme Court), and a Mr. Stafford.
- They were standard hunting knives. The 9 1/4" x 1 1/2" blade had an almost straight back and a curved edge coming to a saber point. They had a cross guard but not the concave (clipped) point, which was on the knives that eventually became known as the "bowie knife."
- Made a silver-mounted hunting knife for James Bowie (c. 1830). Like his brother Rezin, James Bowie liked to give knives to friends. Searles knife was given by Bowie to a close friend, actor Edwin Forest. It had a 17" standard hunting knife blade with a straight back and a curved edge coming to a saber point. It did not have the cross guard or the concave (clipped) point, both of which were on the knives that eventually became known as the "bowie knife."
- The true "bowie knife" was first made by Henry Sheirley, Philadelphia, PA, for Rezin Pleasant Bowie (1832). Eventually Searles sold Sheirley bowie knives. (In 1840 he advertised rifles, pistols, and bowie knives in the *Baton Rouge Gazette*.)
- James Bowie selected bowie type fighting knives for the Texas troops (concave clipped point and a cross guard) in the Texas war for independence (c. 1835). The maker is unknown.
- Made a hunting knife for James Bowie (c. 1835). Bowie later gave it to his good friend Juan N. Sequin when Sequin left the Alamo (1836). It was silver-mounted, had an eagle-head pommel, a ball-ornamented D guard, and a 12" true bowie knife blade with a concave clipped point and cross guard.
- Rees Fitzpatrick (Baton Rouge, LA), silversmith and sword hiltor, did work for Searles. Some bowie knives (gold and silver mounted) are signed on the scabbard "Searles & F. Patrick" (Fitzpatrick) (1833-1838).

(Silversmith, cutler, whitesmith, blacksmith, knife, rifle and pistol maker)
(See Henry Sheirley)

(A) **WILLIAM SHANNON** STAUNTON, VA 1807-1808
- Located at 224 Shippen Street.

W. (WILLIAM) & H. (HUGH) SHANNON PHILADELPHIA, PA 1808-1823
- Located at 21 Passyunk Street (near 5th Street) (1808-1821), 293 S. 5th Street (1821-1823).

(A) **LEMUEL SHAW** PHILADELPHIA, PA 1790-1812
- Made 12 squaw axes for U.S. Office of Indian Trade (1811).

(N) **WILLIAM SHAW** GEORGETOWN, DC 1795-1815
- Made tomahawks for the U.S. Office of Indian Trade (1811).

(Blacksmith)

(A) **SHEBLE (SAMUEL) & FISHER (JOHN M.)** PHILADELPHIA, PA 1861-1870
- Made M1840 variation cavalry sabers.
- The blades had no false edge.

- Sold M1840 type cavalry saber blades to Horstmann Bros., Charles Hammond & Son, and P.S. Justice, all of Philadelphia, PA.

(A) HENRY SHEIRLEY (SCHIVELY) SR.　　PHILADELPHIA, PA　　1780-1813
- Located at 49 South 3rd Street.

(Cutler, surgical instrument maker)

HENRY SHEIRLEY (SCHIVELY) JR.　　PHILADELPHIA, PA　　1813-1840
- Son of Henry Sheirley Sr.
- Located at 45 South Chesnut Street (1813-1831), 75 Chesnut Street (1831-1840).
- Rezin Pleasant Bowie (James Bowie's brother) asked Sheirley to make him a hunting knife (1832).
- Bowie gave Sheirley a model knife, probably in the style of the one made by James Cliffe in 1812. Cliffe's knife had a 9 1/2″ blade and a cross guard to protect the hand. It had no concave (clipped) point.
- Sheirley made Rezin Pleasant Bowie a hunting knife with a cross guard to protect the hand and an 8″ blade. Sheirley, not Bowie, decided to make the blade with a stylish concave (clipped) point. This was the first bowie knife.
- Also made some additional knives, which he sold as "bowie knives." These were the first bowie knives sold to the public.

(Cutler, knife and surgical instrument maker)
(See James Cliffe)

(A) JOHN SHERTZ　　LANCASTER, PA　　1857-1865
- Located on Hazel Street.

(N) JOHN SHIELDS　　FORT MANDAN, ND　　1804-1806
- Hired as an armorer for the Lewis & Clark expedition (1804-1806).
- Lewis had Shields make scalping knives and Missouri War hatchets (tomahawks) while at Fort Mandan, Mercer County, ND, to be traded to local Indians.

(Armorer, blacksmith, gunsmith)

(N) JOHN SHUGART & CO.　　CHAMBERSBURG, PA　　1820-1828
- Owner: John Shugart.
- Factory located on Lemmos Street.
- Made edged tools, sickles, and knives.

JOHN SHUGART & CO.　　CHAMBERSBURG, PA　　1828-1866
- Owners: James Dunlap, George A. Maderia.
- Made bowie knives.
- Employee Jacob Banick won an award for best knives at the Franklin Institute Exposition (1828).
- Purchased by Huber & Co. (1866).

(Cutler, Edged tool and knife maker)
(See J. English, English & Huber)

(N) CHARLES SIPES　　BUFFALO, PA　　1790-D1831
　　　　ALLEGHENY CO.

- Musket and tomahawk maker.

(Blacksmith, gunsmith)

(N) JOHN SMALL　　NEW LISBON, OH　　B1772, 1787-D1825
- Had a gunsmith shop at Fort Quitanon.
- Made flintlock long rifles, flintlock pistols, and tomahawks.

- Used silver-inlayed designs such as knives and spears as decorations on his guns and tomahawks.
(Gunsmith, cutler)

(N) **JACOB SMITH**   BALTIMORE, MD   1785-1808
- Made tomahawks and scalping knives for local Indians.
(Cutler, blacksmith)

(N) **NOAH SMITHWICK**   SAN FELIPE, TX   B1808-1861
    NOAH SMITHWICK   SANTA ANA, TX   1861-1893
- Cutler and gun maker.
- Had a knife factory making bowie knives.

(N) **JACOB S. SNEVELY**   HARRISBURG, PA   1811-1824
    JACOB S. SNEVELY   PIQUA, OH   1824-1835
- Made Kentucky flintlock rifles and silver-mounted tomahawks.
(Gunsmith, silversmith)

(N) **J.P. SNOW & CO.**   HARTFORD, CT   1860-1880
- Located at 4 Central Row.
- Made folding dirk knives; knife, fork and spoon utensil sets; bowie knives; and steel pens.
- Had branches in Chicago and New York.

(C) **RALPH SNOW**   TROY, NY   1830-D1839

(A) **JOHN SNYDER**   TREDYFFRINE TWSP., PA   1800-1820
- Made belt axes (tomahawks) and belt knives.

(N) **O. (ORLANDO) B. SPRAQUE**   PRAIRIE DU CHIEN, WI   1861-1867
- Rifle maker.
- Also made pipe tomahawks for local Indians.
(Blacksmith)

(A) **WILLIAM STACKPOLE**   PITTSBURGH, PA   1790-1816
- Located on the corner of Pennsylvania Street and Cecils Alley.

(N) **MILES STANDISH**   FORT MICHILIMACKINAC   1800-1823
    MILES STANDISH   MONTREAL, CANADA   1823-1828
    MILES STANDISH   NEW YORK, NY   1828-D1868
- Made beaver and muskrat traps, American and Indian half-axes, and Indian tomahawks.
(Blacksmith, iron and steel worker)

(A) **NATHAN STARR & CO.**   MIDDLETOWN, CT   1798-1799
- Also called Starr (Nathan) & Sage (Francis) (partner).
- Had the first U.S. contract for horseman (cavalry) sabers with iron hussar hilts (1798).
- The contract showed 2,499 were purchased; most records show 2,000 (the 499 extra were probably blades only).
- Some Starr 1798 sword blades are found hilted with a brass hussar hilt instead of the iron hilt stipulated in the 1798 contract.

    NATHAN STARR SR.   MIDDLETOWN, CT   1799-1812
- Had a U.S. contract for cavalry sabers with iron reverse-P hilts (c. 1810).
- These swords had a deep, rather narrow fuller running along the top of the blade from the hilt cross guard

to about 4 1/2" from the tip. It had a unique leather scabbard with a curved metal strip along both edges from the mouthpiece to the drag (similar to the cavalry saber scabbard from the Rose 1807 contract). This was basically a hussar type scabbard, using the side metal strips to reinforce the scabbard, called a "caged scabbard." (He sold the same saber to state militias.)

NATHAN STARR (SR.) & SON　　　**MIDDLETOWN, CT**　　　1812-1837
- Built a sword factory in the Staddle Hill area of Middletown, CT (1813).
- It was 81′ x 33′ and three stories high.
- Sold sword blades to silversmith Christopher Griffing, NY.

(A) **THE STARR ARMS CO.**　　　**NEW YORK, NY**　　　1845-1867
- Treasurer: Everett Clapp.
- Had factories in Binghampton and Yonkers, NY.
- Advertised in the *Army-Navy Journal* (April 16, 1864).

Starr Arms Company, 267 Broadway, New York, NY
Manufacturers of Starr's patented breech-loading rifles and revolving pistols.
Dealers in Colt, Smith & Wesson, Sharp, Elliot, Moore, Deringer, and all other styles of revolvers and pistols.
Field and line officers supplied with all necessary articles for their equipment.
Navy and Marine officers supplied with swords, belts, passants, cap devices, etc.

(A, C) **FREDERICK STEINMAN**　　　**PHILADELPHIA, PA**　　　1784-1829
- Son of John Steinman.
- Worked at his father's gun shops (c. 1805-1829).

FREDERICK STEINMAN　　　**PHILADELPHIA, PA**　　　1829-1860
- Located on Elizabeth Street.

(A) **JOHN STEINMAN**　　　**PHILADELPHIA, PA**　　　1770-1804
　　JOHN STEINMAN　　　**RICHMOND, VA**　　　1804-1805
- Worked at the Virginia Manufactory in Richmond, VA, as a gun lock maker.

JOHN STEINMAN　　　**PHILADELPHIA, PA**　　　1805-1845
- Shop locations:
    - 85 Brown Street (1805-1808)
    - 442 North 3rd Street (1808-1811)
    - Germantown Rd. (1811-1818)
    - 17 Green Street (1818-1819)
    - 51 Green Street (1819-1822)
    - 59 Green Street (1822-1825)
    - 31 Green Street (1825-1829)
    - 22 Green Street (1829-1842)
    - Germantown Rd and 5th Street (1842-1845)
    - Mud Lane (1845)
- Son Frederick worked with him (c. 1805-1829).

(Gun maker, lock maker, blacksmith)

WINNER (JAMES), NIPPES　　　**PHILADELPHIA, PA**　　　1808-1815
(J. ABRAHAM, DANIEL, WILHELM) & STEINMAN (JOHN)
- A separate company was formed to manufacture M1808 muskets after obtaining a U.S. contract for 9,000 M1808 muskets at $10.75 a stand (1808).
- The muskets were made at the Nippes Mill Creek, PA, gun factory (Mill Creek Manufactory).
- Company headquarters located at 449 North 3rd Street, Philadelphia, PA.

(N) **SAMUEL STEVENS**　　　**PHILADELPHIA, PA**　　　1805-1815
- Located at 85 North 2nd Street (1805-1813), 99 North 2nd Street (1813-1815).

(Cutler)

(N) **GEORGE STEWART**   NORWICH, CT   1857-1860
- Made bowie knives with staghorn handles.

(Gunsmith, cutler, knife maker)

(C) **JOHN STRODE**   STAFFORD, VA   1760-1781
- Forge foreman at Hunters Iron Works and Rappahannock Forge (1775-1781).

JOHN STRODE   CULPEPER, VA   1781-1802

(N) **W. SWAIN**   FORT WAYNE, IN   1815-1825
- Made tomahawks for the U.S. Office of Indian Trade (1822).

(Blacksmith)

(N) **CONRAD SYLVIUS**   LANCASTER, PA   1857-1870
- Located on the corner of South Queen and Church Streets.

(Cutler)

(N) **STEVEN TAFT**   MILLBURY, MA   1861-1865
- Scythe and bowie knife maker.

(N) **EDWARD TASH**   CHARLESTON, SC   1780-D1798
- Located at 12 Queen Street (1780-1796), corner of Kinloch's Court and Queen Street (1796-1798).

TASH (EDWARD) & HENDERSON (DANIEL)   CHARLESTON, SC   1798
- Located at 24 Queen Street.
- Edward Tash died (1798).

(Cutler, gunsmith, blacksmith, knife maker)

DANIEL HENDERSON   CHARLESTON, SC   1798-1809
- Located at 24 Queen Street.

(N) **G.W. TAYLOR**   SAN FRANCISCO, CA   1860-1875
- Knife maker, including bowie knives.

(N) **JAMES TERRY**   FORT WAYNE, IN   1815-1825
- Sold tomahawks to the U.S. Office of Indian Trade (1822).

(Blacksmith)

(A) **J. (JACOB) TEUFEL**   PHILADELPHIA, PA   1850-1860
- Made bowie knives.

(N) **ISREAL THOMPSON**   YORK CO., PA   B1751-1793

(Cutler)

TIFFANY & CO.
(See Appendix F)

(A) **JOHN TODD**   NEW ORLEANS, LA   1830-1840
- Made bowie knives.
- There is no proof he made a knife for James (Jim) Bowie.

(Cutler)

(C) **JOHN TREAT** THOMASTON, ME 1745-1759
- Armorer for the Maine district of the Massachusetts Bay Colony.

(C) **JOSHUA TREAT** FORT POWNAL, ME 1770-1774
- Armorer for the Maine district of the Massachusetts Bay Colony.

(A, C) **JAMES TRISTIN** LONDON, ENGLAND B1774-1811
- Immigrated to Philadelphia, PA, and settled in Soho, PA (1811).

JAMES TRISTIN SOHO, PA 1811-1850
- Soho is near Pittsburgh, PA.
- In 1821 advertised as a smith manufacturing:
    - *Agricultural and gardening utensils*
    - *A variety of edged tools for various branches*
    - *Grates for chimneys*
    - *Shovels and touges of different descriptions*
    - *Scale beams*
    - *Screw blades and stocks*
    - *Turning lathes*
    - *Presses*
    - *Chasen*
    - *Composite sticks*
    - *Brass rules*
    - *Articles for printing offices*
    - *Ornamented pipe tomahawks*

(N) **EDWARD K. TRYON** PHILADELPHIA, PA Bc1827, 1841-D1909
- Son of George W. Tryon.
- Made muskets and muzzleloaders.
- Made bowie knives.

(N) **GEORGE W. TRYON** PHILADELPHIA, PA B1791-1810
- Apprenticed to gun maker Frederick W. Goetz (1805-1810).

TRYON (GEORGE W.) & GOETZ (FREDERICK W.) PHILADELPHIA, PA 1810-1811

GEORGE TRYON PHILADELPHIA, PA 1811-D1878
- Made muskets and Chambers repeating guns.
- Made bowie knives.
- Located at 134 North 2nd Street (1811-1833), 165 North 2nd Street (1833-1841).
- George W. Tryon retired (1841).

(N) **J. (JOHN) W. (WALTER) TUCKER & CO.** NEW YORK, NY 1800-1870
- Branch in San Francisco, CA.
- Made the silver-mounted sword presented to Maj. Gen. Joseph Hooker by the citizens of California (September 1862).

(Silversmith, sword hiltor)

(N) **ULSTER KNIFE CO.** ELLENVILLE, NY 1872-1900
- General knife maker, including bowie knives.

(N) **UNDERHILL BROTHERS** BOSTON, MA 1840-1866

	UNDERHILL EDGE TOOL CO.	BOSTON, MA	1866-1907

- Made edged tools and spike tomahawks.

UNDERHILL EDGE TOOL CO. NASHUA, NH 1907-1920

(A) **UNITED STATES ARMS & CUTLERY CO.** ROCHESTER, NY 1878-1880
- General knife maker, including bowie knives.

(A) **ABNER UPDEGRAFT** PITTSBURGH, PA 1800-1841
- Located at Fifth and Smithfield Streets.
- Made scalping knives and belt axes (tomahawks).

(C) **JACOB UPDEGRAFF** SCHUYLKILL CO., PA 1800-1810

(A) **WILLIAM UPDEGRAFF** PITTSBURGH, PA 1834-1872
- Made scalping knives and belt axes (tomahawks).

(N) **JOHN B. VAN EPS** NEW YORK, NY 1755-1775
- Made 100 belt axes at four shillings each for the British Indian Service to be provided to Indians friendly to the British (1770).

(Blacksmith)

(N) **J. (JONATHAN) VICKERS** CLEVELAND, OH B1801, 1821-1851
- Gun shop located on Main Street (next to Spangler's Tavern).
- Sold rifles and fowling pieces and repaired guns.
- Made silver-enlayed pipe tomahawks.

J. (JONATHAN) VICKERS MAUMEE CITY LUCUS CO., OH 1851-1860

J. (JONATHAN) VICKERS DELPHI, IN 1860-D1862

(Gunsmith, blacksmith)

(N) **COLONY OF VIRGINIA**
- The Virginia Company of London sent to the colony of Virginia 20 muskets, 40 swords and daggers, two barrels of powder, 600 weight of lead, 20 breastplates, 36 head pieces (helmets), and 500 weight of iron for repairs (1722).

(N) STATE OF VIRGINIA

Revolutionary War Sword Purchases

- In the spring of 1778, during the Revolutionary War, Jacques LeMaire, who came from France with the permission of the French court in 1777, offered his assistance to Virginia Governor Patrick Henry. Henry made him a captain and sent him back to France to buy war supplies. Mr. Loyeante, Virginia inspector general of artillery and military storekeeper, gave LeMaire state orders for the war materials.
- Upon arriving in Paris, Arthur Lee, one of Virginia's commercial agents already in France, sent Lemaire to Strasbourg, France, to purchase sabers and tools.
- On July 14, 1778, Lemaire contracted with Strasbourg dealers for swords, pick axes, hatchets, and shovels, costing 40,000 livres.
- LeMaire purchased two types of swords, both made at the Klingenthal manufactory.
  1) Approximately 600 "Grenadier of Virginia" short infantryman swords (hangers). After the Revolutionary War, only infantry sergeants carried swords, so these swords were later called sergeants or non-comm. swords.

2) Approximately 600 "Artillery of Virginia" short artillery man swords. After the Revolutionary War, only artillery sergeants carried swords, so these swords were later also called sergeants or non-comm. swords.
- The two short swords were very similar to the French 1767 infantry/artillery short sword, also called a "briguet."
- Lemaire also purchased approximately 600 "Dragoon of Virginia" cavalry (horseman) saber blades.
- "Klingenthal" was stamped on the back of both short sword blades and the dragoon blades.
- Features of the "Grenadier of Virginia" sword included:
    a) solid brass hussar hilt with grooved grips
    b) 27″ slightly curved flat blade with a heavy protruding false edge, similar to Turkish swords
    c) marked "Grenadier of Virginia" on the obverse and "Victory or Death" on the reverse of the blade
    d) leather scabbard with brass mounts
- Features of the "Artillery of Virginia" sword included:
    a) solid brass hussar hilt with grooved grips
    b) 24″ slightly curved flat blade with a heavy protruding false edge, similar to Turkish swords
    c) marked "Artillery of Virginia" on the obverse and "Victory or Death" on the reverse of the blade
    d) leather scabbard with brass mounts
- The "Dragoon of Virginia" saber blades were later mounted with split and divided hilts (both iron and brass are known). One had a bullet-shaped rounded pommel; one had a flat Phrygian helmet pommel. Both styles had leather-covered wooden grips wrapped with wire, and both had 36″ slightly curved blades (marked "Dragoon of Virginia" on the obverse and "Victory or Death" on the reverse of the blade. Both styles had leather scabbards with iron or brass mounts (depending if they had iron or brass hilts).
- The two short swords and the dragoon blades were shipped from the port of Brest, France, on May 10, 1779. They arrived in Virginia in August 1779. Many were issued immediately to state militia units. The balance of the short swords and dragoon blades were stored temporarily at the U.S. government New London arsenal. (Other Virginia state military supplies were also stored there). They were gradually moved to the Virginia Point of Fork Arsenal. A total of 557 short swords were transferred in July 1781 because the British were raiding near the U.S. New London Arsenal; the balance of the swords and the dragoon blades were transferred in 1783.
- I believe the blades were hilted and scabbards made at the Point of Fork Arsenal.
- In 1791, 1,214 "Grenadier of Virginia" and "Artillery of Virginia" swords and 25 horseman swords were on hand at the Point of Fork Arsenal. When the Point of Fork Arsenal was closed in 1801, 900 short swords were moved to Richmond, Virginia, and stored in the attic of the capital building (located just north of the Virginia Manufactory). Six hundred swords were in stock in 1806. A total of 187 "Grenadier of Virginia" swords were transferred to the Virginia manufactory in 1806. They were reissued as artillery non-comm. swords. The blade markings were removed and new belts and leather scabbards were made for the swords. Eighty were marked "7 VA REGT"; 107 were marked "4 VA REGT." All were issued to three artillery companies in Norfolk County, Virginia. Eventually the 413 remaining swords were transferred to the Virginia Manufactory. By 1808, all the French swords had been issued to militia units.

(See Virginia Manufactory)
(See New London Arsenal)
(See Point of Fork Arsenal)

(N) **J. (JAMES) WALKER**　　　　　FAYETTE CO., PA　　　　　1802-1810
　　J. (JAMES) WALKER　　　　　KNOX CO., OH　　　　　　1810-1830
- Sold tomahawks to the U.S. Office of Indian Trade (1819).

(Blacksmith, gunsmith)

(N) **SILAS A. WALKER**　　　　　BENNINGTON, VT　　　　　1850-1870
- Made approximately 170 bowie knives for the Bennington Rifles infantry regiment during the Civil War.

(Farmer, blacksmith)

(N) **WILLIAM WALKER**   SALT LAKE CITY, UT   1850-1860
- Made bowie knives, razors, and scissors.

(Cutler)

(A) **THOMAS WASHBORN**   RICHMOND, ME   1740-1742
- Armorer to the Maine district of the Massachusetts Bay Colony.

(A) **A. (ASA) H. (HOLMAN) WATERS & CO.**   MILLBURY, MA   1840-1887
- Benjamin Flagg bought gun and bayonet making machinery from Waters and opened his own gun factory in Millbury, MA (1849).
- Waters also sold pistol making machinery to William Glaze & Co., Columbia, SC (1851).

(N) **J. (JOHN) WATSON**   BALTIMORE, MD   1810-1818
- Made musket barrels and pipe tomahawks.

(Blacksmith)

(A, C) **EMMOR TREGO WEAVER**   PHILADELPHIA, PA   1808-D1860
- Made many silver-hilted infantry officer sabers with eagle-head pommels.
- Also made brass-hilted artillery officer sabers.

(N) **WEBER (HENRY) & STAHL (CHARLES)**   CINCINNATI, OH   1858-1863
- Made saber bayonets.

(Cutler)

(N) **J. (JACOB) WELSHANS (WELSHANTZ)**   YORK, PA   1775-1820
- Made brass pipe tomahawks.
- Made muskets for Pennsylvania Committee of Safety (1777-1780).

(Gun maker, brass founder)

(N) **STEPHEN WEST**   WOODWARD, MD   1775-1783
                                                                 FREDERICH CO.
- Sold muskets, bayonets, hunting swords (cutteau de Chase), and musket parts to the Maryland Committee of Safety during the Revolutionary War.
- Maryland Committee of Safety paid West 95 pounds and 11 shillings for gun locks and cutteau knives (March 19, 1776).
- Maryland Committee of Safety paid West for 200 gun locks and 200 bayonets (October 30, 1781).

(A) **THOMAS WHEAT**   WASHINGTON, DC   1811-1817
- Had contract with the U.S. Office of Indian Trade for 195 squaw axes (1811).

(C) **WHETCROFT & McFADON**   ANNAPOLIS, MD   1775-1777

(N) **RICHARD WHITEHOUSE**   FORT WAYNE, IN   1810-1830
- Made tomahawks for the U.S. Office of Indian Trade (1817).

(Blacksmith)

(A) **RUGGLES WHITING**   PHILADELPHIA, PA   1800-1815
- Located on the corner of Pennsylvania Street and Cecils Alley.

(Cutler)

(A) **JAMES W. WICKHAM**   PHILADELPHIA, PA   1790-1836
- Son of Marine T. Wickham.
- Partner in Wickham & Co. (1816-1836).

(A) **MARINE T. WICKHAM**   HARPERS FERRY, VA   1804-1811
- Armorer at the Harpers Ferry U.S. Arsenal.
- Helped design the U.S. M1812 musket and M1813 pistol.

    MARINE T. WICKHAM   PHILADELPHIA, PA   1811-1816
- Arms inspector and later chief inspector at the Schuylkill U.S. Arsenal.

    WICKHAM & CO.   PHILADELPHIA, PA   1816-1834
- Finished John Joseph Henry's 1815 U.S. contract for M1812 muskets. As part of the subcontract, Wickham was allowed to use space in Henry's gun factory to produce the muskets.
- Had a U.S. contract for 16,600 M1816 muskets (1816).
- Built an arms factory of his own at 94 Market Street, three doors above 3rd Street (1816-1836).
- Store and showroom locations:
    258 North 3rd Street at Noble Street (1816-1817)
    94 High Street (1817-1823)
    265 High Street (1823-1836)
- Made the prototype pattern for the M1832 foot artillery sword based on the guidelines of Col. George Bomford, Ordnance Dept. (based on the French M1816 foot artillery sword).
- Advertised as a military and fancy store and hardware merchant (1818).
- Advertised as an importer of cutlery, firearms, hardware and sporting goods including Sheffield files, iron dies and swedges, fowling pieces, pistols, sabers, swords, dirks, foils, guns, component parts, and fishing tackle (1829).
- Marine T. Wickham died (1834).

    WICKHAM & CO.   PHILADELPHIA, PA   1834-1836
- Located at 265 High Street.
- Partners: Martha Wickham (Marine's widow), James W. Wickham and William W. Wickham (Marine's son).

    WILLIAM W. WICKHAM   PHILADELPHIA, PA   1790-1836
- Son of Marine T. Wickham.
- Partner in Wickham & Co. (1816-1836).

(A) **FREDERICK WILHELM WIDMANN**   BRESLAU, PRUSSIA   B1789-1816
- Immigrated to Philadelphia, PA (1816).

    FREDERICK WILHELM WIDMANN   PHILADELPHIA, PA   1816-D1849
- Shop located at 115 North Front Street (1816-1828), 98 North Third Street (1828-1848).
- Offered a U.S. contract for M1840 lt. artillery sabers, but refused.
- Made many infantry and artillery officer swords with eagle-head pommels.

(A) **CAPT. THOMAS WILEY**   PHILADELPHIA, PA   1777
- Located on the corner of Market and 3rd Streets.

(N) **H. (HENRY) WILKINSON**   HARTFORD, CT   1850-1865
- Made bowie knives.

(A) **FREDERICK WILL**   SAN FRANCISCO, CA   1852-1860
- Located at 817 Kearny Street.

    WILL (FREDERICK) & KESMODEL (FRANK)   SAN FRANCISCO, CA   1860-1863
- Located at 904 Powell Street.
- Made bowie knives.

WILL (FREDERICK) & FINCK (JULIUS) SAN FRANCISCO, CA 1863-1934
- Located at 605 Jackson Street.
- Finck was a locksmith.
- Made ivory grip push daggers, bowie knives, and surgical instruments.

(Cutler)

(N) **ALEXANDER WILLARD** ST. LOUIS, MO 1790-1820
- Hired as a metalsmith for the Lewis and Clark expedition (1804-1806).
- Lewis had Willard make scalping knives and Missouri war hatchets (tomahawks), while at Fort Mandan, Mercer County, ND, to be traded to local Indians.

(Blacksmith)

(A) **WILLIAM WING** PHILADELPHIA, PA 1775-1778
    WILLIAM WING HARTFORD, CT 1778-1805
- Advertised in the *Hartford Courant* for workman for the purpose of gunsmithing such as locks, ramrods, bayonets, and other trimmings (September 3, 1798).
- Had a U.S. contract for M1797 boarding pikes (1797).
- Had a U.S. contract for navy pistols (1803).

(Pike, pistol, and musket maker)

(A) **FRANZ WOLF** COLUMBUS, OH 1834-1852
- Located on High Street (south of the county courthouse).

(N) **ABRAHAM WOLFERS** BALTIMORE, MD 1800-1825
- Located on fish market.

(Cutler)

(A) **W. (WILLIAM) A. WOODRUFF** MT. HOLLY SPRINGS, PA 1840-1860
- Maker of percussion rifles and shotguns and silver-mounted pipe tomahawks.

(N) **THOMAS WORLEY** MECKLENBURG, VA 1760-1776
                       BERKLEY CO.
    THOMAS WORLEY WASHINGTON CO., MD 1776-1783
- Partners: Henry and Philip Sheetz.
- Committee of Safety rifle maker.
- Had a U.S. contract for rifleman belt axes (tomahawks).

(Blacksmith, flintlock, military rifle maker, cutler)

(N) **THOMAS WORRELL** BALTIMORE, MD 1790-1810
- Made tomahawks for the U.S. Office of Indian Trade (1805).

(Blacksmith)

(N) **WILLIAM WRIGHTMAN** CHARLESTON, SC 1770-1810
- Advertised horseman swords, dirks, artillery swords and officer swords in the *Charleston Gazette* (1803).

(A) **JAMES YOULE** NEW YORK, NY 1775-1793
- Shop locations:
    5 Beckman Slip (1775-1787)
    179 Waters Street (1787-1792)
    50 Beckman Street (1792-1793)

- Advertised in the *New York Daily Advertiser* (February 1787):
    Silver mounted swords of all kinds, made and sold. Most elegant cutteaux with eagle, lion or dog head.
- Advertised in the *New York Daily Advertiser* (May 27, 1788)
    At the sign of the "cross-knives and gun"
    Makes all kinds of guns, swords, pistols, razors etc.
- Also made knives, small swords, and officer swords.

JAMES YOULE   BALTIMORE, MD   1793-1800
- Shop located on Forrest Street.

(N) **HENRY YOUNG**   EASTON, PA   1774-1786
- Brother of John Young Sr.
- Made flintlock Kentucky long rifles in a large one-story stone building on the main road near Chestnut Hill.
- Also made brass pipe tomahawks.

(N) **JOHN YOUNG SR.**   EASTON, PA   1755-1805
- Made brass-mounted pipe tomahawks.

WILLIAM W. YOUNG
(See John Cartwright)

CHAPTER 8

European Sword Makers and Dealers Who Exported Swords to Union Dealers during the Civil War

(A, C)
LOCATION/MAKER   **BLADE MARKING**

Solingen, Prussia (Germany)
Heinrich Boker
Carl Broch Jr.
Otto Curdts   Crossed swords
C.R. Kirschbaum   Knight's head
Abraham Kuller   Running bear
Frederick Potter (not Frederick Plucker Jr.)   Rabbit head

Nuremberg, Bavaria (Germany)
Johann Ludwig Werder

CHAPTER 9

U.S. Sword Dealers

(N) ABBATE (D.) & DE CARO (FRANK)   NEW YORK, NY   1901-1905
- Located at 169 Grand Street.

    FRANK DE CARO   NEW YORK, NY   1905-1911
- Sold M1872 cavalry officers swords.

(Military and naval goods)

(N) GEORGE T. ABBEY   UTICA, NY   B1823, 1845-1852
- Located at 6 Catherine Street.

    GEORGE T. ABBEY   CHICAGO, IL   1852-1880
- Shop located at 186 Lake Street (1852-1870), 155 Lake Street (1870-1880).
- Advertised in the *Chicago Tribune* (October 8, 1861):
  > *Swords, belts, sashes, etc.*
  > *Bowie knives and military goods*
  > *Gun materials*
  > *Sole agent for "Hazards" powder*
  > *All kinds of ammunition*
- Advertised in the *Chicago Tribune* (March 17, 1864): "*A large assortment of rifles, revolvers of all the best makers.*"
- Bought out Peacock (Joseph) & Thatcher (David C.) gun shop (1870).

(Military goods, guns, swords)

(N) A. (ALBERT) G. ALFORD & CO.   BALTIMORE, MD   1880-1905
- Locations:
  - 5 South Howard Street (1880-1883)
  - 116 W. Baltimore Street (1883-1884)
  - 116 and 129 W. Baltimore Street (1884-1885)
  - 129 W. Baltimore Street (1885-1886)
  - 221 E. Baltimore Street (1886-1905)
- Advertised guns, cutlery, military goods, arms, and sporting goods.

(N) **W. (WILLIAM) C. ALLEN & CO.** SAN FRANCISCO, CA 1853-1871
- Located at 136 Montgomery Street (1853-1856), 146 Clay Street (1856-1871).

(Jewelry, watches, military goods, cutlery and fancy goods)

(A) **HENRY V. ALLIEN** NEW YORK, NY 1870-1876
- Located at 734 Broadway.

HENRY V. ALLIEN NEW YORK, NY 1876-1948
- Located at 7 Bond Street.
- Sold M1860 staff and field officer swords.

(N) **ARMSTEAD (C. HUGHES)** BALTIMORE, MD 1840-1850
& MANNING (SAMUEL C.)
- Located at 2 Charles Street.

C. HUGHES ARMSTEAD BALTIMORE, MD 1845-1849
- Partner: Samuel C. Manning.
- Located at 235 Baltimore Street.
- Importer and dealer in hardware, cutlery, edged tools, guns, and saddlery.

(A) **ARMY NAVY COOP** NEW YORK, NY 1900-1922
- Owner: C.A. Devlin.
- Located at 245 West 42nd Street.
- Large military outfitter.
- Issued military goods catalogs.
- Sold M1902 sabers for all officers.

(N) **ARMY NAVY STORE** NEW YORK, NY 1915-1916
- Owner: Joseph A. Russell.
- Located at 1600 Broadway.

RUSSELL (JOSEPH A.) UNIFORM CO. NEW YORK, NY 1916-1922
- Located at 1600 Broadway.
- Bought Army-Navy Coop (1922).

RUSSELL (JOSEPH A.) INC. NEW YORK, NY 1922-1926
- Located at 245 West 42nd Street.

(Uniforms, military goods, equipment)

(A) **JOSEPH T. BAILEY (JR.) CO.** PHILADELPHIA, PA 1854-1878
- Located at 819 Chesnut Street.
- Made silver-mounted presentation swords given to a General King (1861) and Maj. Gen. George B. McClellan (1864).

BAILEY, BANKS, & BIDDLE PHILADELPHIA, PA 1878-1894
- Located at 819 Chesnut Street.
- Made a silver-mounted presentation sword given to Rear Admiral John W. Phillip (Spanish American War).

(N) **GEORGE BAKER** PROVIDENCE, RI 1821-1869
- Located at 61 Cheapside Street (1821-1844), 61 North Main Street (1844-1869).

(Military equipment, silversmith, jeweler)

(A) **JOHN A. BAKER** NEW YORK, NY 1847-1863
- Located at 63 Walker Street (near Broadway).
- John A. Baker died (1862).

L. (LAURA) S. BAKER	**NEW YORK, NY**	**1863-1864**

- John A. Baker's wife.
- Located at 63 Walker Street (near Broadway).
- Advertised in the *Army-Navy Journal* (February 13, 1864):
  > *Successor to John A. Baker*
  > *Manufacturer, importer and dealer in every description of military goods, consisting of caps, belts, swords, sashes, spurs, sword knots, shoulder straps, and cap ornaments and every variety of staff, field and line officers equipments.*
  > *Presentation swords of original design and of the most costly elegance.*
  > *Horse equipments complete, of various grades.*
  > *Bayonet scabbards, cartridge boxes, knapsacks always in stock.*

BAKER (LAURA S.) & McKENNEY (JAMES H. SR.)	**NEW YORK, NY**	**1864-1883**

- Located at 63 Walker Street (near Broadway) (1864-1865), 141 Grand Street (1865-1883).
- Advertised in the *Army-Navy Journal* (July 30, 1864):
  > *Manufacturers and dealers in all kinds of military goods—fatigue caps, presentation swords, sashes, belts, shoulder straps, and officers haversacks constantly on hand.*
- Advertised in the *Army-Navy Journal* (1881) as "manufacturers of the new regulation cork and felt helmets, military goods and equipment for officers of the Army, Navy and National guard."

(N) **THOMAS BAKER**	**CONCORD, NH**	**1815-1825**

- Advertised military goods, swords, jewelry, and watches (1820).

(Silversmith, sword hiltor, military goods dealer)

(A) **O. (OSCAR) S. BALDWIN**	**WILMINGTON, NC**	**1845-1865**

- City clothing store.
- Located at 38 Market Street.
- Sold clothing, uniforms, and furnishings.
- Advertised military goods, including swords, pistols, insignia, and buttons.

(A) **BALL (HENRY), BLACK (WILLIAM) & CO.**	**NEW YORK, NY**	**1851-1874**

- Moved from Silversmith listings in Volume I.
- Located on the corner of 5th Avenue and 28th Street (1851-1861), 565 and 567 Broadway (1861-1874).
- Advertised in the *Army-Navy Journal* (September 5, 1869):
  > *Manufacturers of military goods.*
  > *Fine presentation swords constantly on hand and made to order, which, in style of finish and elegance of design, are unsurpassed.*
  > *Regulation swords for the Army and Navy.*
  > *Epaulettes, sashes, belts, embroideries and regimental standards, national ensigns, guidons and flags of every style.*
  > *Designs furnished and orders promptly executed.*

(N) **BARNARD & McAINN**	**BALTIMORE, MD**	**1861-1865**

- Sold M1860 staff and field officer swords.

(Military goods)

(A) **S. (STEPHEN) O. BARNUM**	**BUFFALO, NY**	**1848-1865**

- Located at 211 Main Street.
- Advertised as a variety store and military goods supplier during the Civil War.

	S. (STEPHEN) O. BARNUM & SON	BUFFALO, NY	1865-1905

- Partner and son: Theodore Barnum.
- Located at 265 Main Street.

(N)	**JAMES D. BARONN**	WASHINGTON, DC	C1840-1865

- Baronn was agent for H. (Herman) Fersenheim at his Army-Navy Emporium (1861-1865).

	J. (JAMES) D. & B. (BERNARD) BARONN	WASHINGTON, DC	1865-1870

- Located at 220 Pennsylvania Avenue.
- Men's furnishing, army-navy equipment.

(A)	**JOSEPH BARTON**	STOCKBRIDGE, MA	B1764-1804
	JOSEPH BARTON	UTICA, NY	1804-1811

- Moved from Silversmith listing in Volume I.
- Advertised a large assortment of military equipment, including gilt and plated swords and pistols (1807).

	BARTON (JOSEPH) & PORTER (JOSEPH C.)	UTICA, NY	1811-1817
	JOSEPH BARTON	UTICA, NY	1817-1825
	BARTON (JOSEPH) & CLARK (WILLIAM BARTON)	UTICA, NY	1825-1829
	BARTON (JOSEPH) & SMITH (TRUMAN)	UTICA, NY	1829-1831
	BARTON (JOSEPH) & BUTLER (JAMES F.)	UTICA, NY	1831-1833

- Joseph Barton died (1833).

(Silversmith, goldsmith, military equipment, sword hiltor)
(See Joseph C. Porter)

(N)	**BAYLISS & HUTCHINS**	MONTPELIER, VT	1825-1833

- Advertised military goods, muskets, fowling pieces, and swords (1828).

(A)	**SAMUEL H. BECK**	NEW YORK, NY	1885-1899

- Located at 162 Elm Street (1885-1893), 62 Elm Street (1893-1899).

(Military goods)

(C)	**S. (SAMUEL) BERNSTEIN**	BROOKLYN, NY	1900-1920

(A)	**BENT (CHARLES SR.) & BUSH (FRANCIS SR.)**	BOSTON, MA	1849-1932

- Located at 30 Central Street (1849-1860), corner of Court and Washington Streets (1860-1932).
- Advertised in the *Army-Navy Journal* (August 21, 1864):

> *Military goods: Manufacturers, importers and dealers in every description of military goods, consisting of caps, swords, embroidery, belts, sashes, shoulder straps, spurs, sword knots, cap ornaments, and every variety of staff, field and line officers equipments. Officers of the Army and Navy visiting Boston are respectfully invited to call and examine our stock.*

(N)	**W. (WILLIAM) BINGHAM & CO.**	CLEVELAND, OH	1841-1945

- Gun and knife dealers (including bowie knives).

(C)	**JAMES BLACK**

- Now in Maker listing.

(A) **JOHN BLACK**   PHILADELPHIA, PA   1795-1811
- Located at 120 South Front Street.

    McMULLEN (JOHN) & BLACK   PHILADELPHIA, PA   1811-1850
    (JOHN)
- Located at 114 South Front Street.

(N) **V. (VIRGIL) H. BLACKINTON & CO.**   ATTLEBORO FALLS, MA   1852-1997
- Large maker of insignia, awards, medals, trophies, regalia, and metal trimmings for uniforms.
- Sold West Point cadet swords, M1902 sabers for all officers, and fraternal swords.

(A) **CALVIN T. BLAKE & CO.**   SAN FRANCISCO, CA   1860-1870
- Located at 136 Montgomery Street (1860-1863), 524 Montgomery Street (1863-1870).

(A, C) **BLODGET (HENRY T.) & BROWN**   NEW YORK, NY   1850-1868
    (CLARK S.) & CO.
- Branch of Blodget, Clarke & Brown of Boston, MA.
- Located at 83 Beckman Street.
- Imported 423 cavalry sabers and sold them to the U.S. government (1862).
- Agents for C. Roby & Co.

    HENRY T. BLODGET   NEW YORK, NY   1868-1870
- Located at 42 Warren Street (1868-1869), 273 Pearl Street (1870).

HERMAN BOKER & CO.
(See Maker listings)

(N) **BOSTON MILITARY SHOP**   BOSTON, MA   1815-1825
- Advertised swords, pistols, and military accessories (1824).

(N) **R.T. BOSWORTH**   AUGUSTA, ME   1855-1861
- Advertised military goods, uniforms, and swords.
- Sold out to Chisam & Cobb (1861).

(Military tailor, military goods)
(See Chisam & Cobb)

(A) **E. (ELIAS) R. BOWEN**   CHICAGO, IL   1853-1872
- Locations:
   8 South Clark Street (1853-1859)
   20 Clark Street at the corner of Lake Street (1859-1870)
   15 Centre Avenue (1870-1872)
- Glove dealer (1853-1861).
- Military goods dealer (1861-1872).
- Made gloves, military belts, and sashes.
- Advertised in the *Chicago Tribune* (October 8, 1861):
   A few officers sabers, sashes, shoulder straps and cap ornaments extra good and cheap just received. Belts and sashes manufactured at Bowens glove store, 20 Clark Street, over the U.S. Express office.
- Advertised in the *Chicago Tribune* (July 27, 1862):
   Military Notice: Officers of the 71st and all other new regiments will find it to their interest in purchasing outfits to call on E.R. Bowen, 20 Clark Street., upstairs over the U.S. Express office. Sword belts, sashes, shoulder straps, caps, bugles, pistols, cartridges and everything needed of the best quality and cheapest in market.

- Advertised in the *Army-Navy Journal* (July 30, 1864):
    Swords of all kinds.
    Revolvers of all kinds.
    Cartridges and rifles of all kinds.
    Belts, hats, gauntlets, shoulder straps, sashes, caps, flags, haversacks, etc.
    Presentation swords made to order.
    Buckskin gloves in great variety.
    Regalia goods.

(A) **BOWN (JAMES) & TETLEY (ABRAM)**   PITTSBURGH, PA   1848-1862
- Partner and son: John Tetley.
- Established a cutlery factory (1848).
- Advertised as cutlers and surgical and dental instrument makers as well as seller of "*an assortment of hardware, cutlery, guns, pistols and hunting equipage*" (1850). (Enterprise Works)
- Gradually got into the gun-making business.
- Advertised in the *Allegheny Pilot* (1855):
    Manufacturers of rifles, shotguns, etc.
    Dealers in every variety of firearms.
    He also keeps on hand a general variety of:
    Hardware
    Cutlery (including Bowie knives)
    Fishing tackle
    Percussion caps
    Powder, shot and balls
    Agents for the following:
    Sharps' rifles
    Colt's revolvers
    Volcanic pistols
    Allen's revolvers
    Ell's revolvers
    Allen's rifle pistols
- Bought the property at 136 Wood Street (40' x 90' gun barrel factory) from Noble & Little (1857).
- Renamed the factory complex the Enterprise Gun Works.
- James Bown bought out Abram and his son John Tetley (1862).

JAMES BOWN   PITTSBURGH, PA   1862-1871
- The Enterprise Gun Works, located at 136 Wood Street.
- Advertised as a manufacturer and importer of guns, pistols, hardware, gunsmiths material, and cutlery (including Bowie knives).
- Made brass-handled sword bayonets.

JAMES BOWN & SON (WILLIAM H.)   PITTSBURGH, PA   1871-1880
- Still the Enterprise Gun Works, now located at 136-138 Wood Street.

JAMES BOWN & SONS   PITTSBURGH, PA   1880-1885
- Partners and sons: William H. Bown, Edwin S. Bown, James W. Bown.
- Enterprise Gun Works, located at 136-138 Wood Street (1880-1882), 121 Wood Street (1882-1885).
- The company was purchased by W.S. Brown & August Hirth (1885).
- James Bown retired (1898).
- James Bown died (1901).

(See W.S. Brown & August Hirth)

(N) **SAMUEL BRADLEE**   BOSTON, MA   1806-1845
- Located at 142 Washington Street.

- Hardware and cutlery shop.
- Sold out to Martin L. Bradford (1845).

MARTIN L. BRADFORD & CO.   BOSTON, MA   1845-1856
- Located at 142 Washington Street.
- Importer and dealer in hardware, fishing tackle, cutlery, and gun powder.
- The cutlery included scissors, shears, razors, and pocket and bowie knives.

BRADFORD (MARTIN L.) & ANTHONY (NATHAN)   BOSTON, MA   1856-1881
- Bradford retired and Anthony died (1881).

(N) **WILLIAM BRADY**   HARRISBURG, PA   1863-1878
- Locations:
    62 Market Street (1863-1865)
    60 Market Street (1865-1867)
    302 Market Street (1867-1878)
- Advertised "*fine presentation swords made to order, fine watches, jewelry, silver and plate ware, military goods*" (1865).

(Silversmith, military goods, sword hiltor)

(A) **BENJAMIN FRANKLIN BROOKS**   UTICA, NY   1825-1828
- Moved from Makers listing.
- Located at 118 Genessee Street.

BLACKWELL (WILLIAM) & BROOKS (BENJAMIN FRANKLIN)   UTICA, NY   1828-1829

B. (BENJAMIN) F. (FRANKLIN) BROOKS & CO.   UTICA, NY   1829-1832
- Partner: Gaylord Griswold.

BROOKS (BENJAMIN FRANKLIN) & GRISWOLD (JACOB)   UTICA, NY   1832-1843

BROOKS (BENJAMIN FRANKLIN) & VAN VOORHIS (JOHN)   UTICA, NY   1843-1855

B. (BENJAMIN) F. (FRANKLIN) BROOKS & SON   UTICA, NY   1855-1858
- Son and partner: Charles V. Brooks.

BROOKS (BENJAMIN FRANKLIN) & HONE (JOHN)   UTICA, NY   1858-1865

(Goldsmith, silversmith, military and fancy goods, sword hiltor)

(A) **BROOKS BROS.**   NEW YORK, NY   1850-1945
- Located on Broadway at corner of Grand Avenue (1850-1868), Union Square (1868-1945).

(A) **SETH E. BROWN**   CONCORD, NH   B1821, 1843-D1884
- Located at 174 Main Street.

(A) **W. (WILLIAM) H. BROWN**   PITTSBURGH, PA   1836-1847
- Moved from Makers listing.
- Locations:
    126 Wood Street (1836-1838)
    7 Fifth Street (1838-1840)
    Corner of Diamond and Market Streets (1840-1847)

- Advertised double-barrel guns; single-barrel fowling pieces; holsters for dueling, belt, and pocket pistols; bowie and pocket knives; Dupont powder; percussion caps; shot and powder flasks and horns; game bags and pouches; fishing rods, canes, and tackle; Pennybackers rifle barrels; Rogers cutlery; table and pocket cutlery; edged tools of all kinds; Britannia and German silverware; and farm tools.

(A) **BROWN (W.S.) & HIRTH (AUGUST)** PITTSBURGH, PA 1885-1889
- Bought out James Bown & Sons (1885).
- Renamed it the Enterprise Gun and Machine Works.
- Located at 520 and 522 Wood Street.
- Catalog showed them as manufacturers and dealers in guns, rifles, revolvers, gun and rifle barrels, ammunition, gunsmith tools, gun parts, cutlery (including knives), fishing tackle, and sporting goods, (1886).

W.S. BROWN PITTSBURGH, PA 1889-1890
- Machine shop and factory located on Virgin Alley.

(A) **SAMUEL C. BUNTING JR.** PHILADELPHIA, PA 1861-1865
- Located at 232 Dock Street and 13 North 6th Street.

(A) **BURGER (JOHN) &** NEW YORK, NY 1901-1920
BAUMGARD (FERDINAND)
- Two locations at 105 Chambers Street and 89 Reade Street.

(Hardware dealer, military goods)

(N) **JOSEPH BURRITT** UTICA, NY B1795, 1815-1838
- Advertised jewelry, military, and fancy goods (1831).

JOSEPH BURRITT & SON UTICA, NY 1838-1862
- Son and partner: Joseph Curtiss Burritt (born 1817, died 1889).

JOSEPH CURTISS BURRITT UTICA, NY 1862-D1889

(Silversmith, jeweler, military and fancy goods)

(A) **EDWIN D. BURT & CO.** WASHINGTON, DC 1861-1865
- Two locations at the corner of Pennsylvania and 6th Streets and 27 Park Row.

(A) **JOHN A. BUSH** PEORIA & CHICAGO, IL 1862-1865
- Chicago location at 7 North Adams Street.

(N) **NATHANIEL BUTLER** SAVANNAH, GA B1760, 1780-1799
NATHANIEL BUTLER UTICA, NY 1799-1805
BUTLER (NATHANIEL) & UTICA, NY 1805-1807
OSBORN (JOHN)
N. (NATHANIEL) BUTLER UTICA, NY 1807
- Advertised military goods (1807).

BUTLER (NATHANIEL) & UTICA, NY 1807-1815
DEBENARD (CHARLES J.)
NATHANIEL BUTLER UTICA, NY 1815-D1829

(Silversmith, jeweler, military goods)

(A) **H. (HARVEY) R. CABERAY** CHICAGO, IL 1860-1907
- Locations:
    91 Lake Street (1860-1866)
    60 State Street (1866-1873)

98 E. Madison Street (1873-1876)
80 E. Madison Street (1876-1907)
- Advertised in the *Army-Navy Journal* (November 28, 1863):
    Manufacturers and dealers in military and navy goods.
    Swords, belts and sashes in great variety.
    Gold and silver embroidery of every description.
    Military goods of the finest quality.
    Presentation swords of original design made to order at the shortest notice.
    Watches and jewelry neatly repaired.

(A) **JOHN D. CALDWELL**   ZANESVILLE, OH   B1816, 1835-D1902
- Located at 233 W. 4th Street (1835-1891), 8 Masonic Temple Street (1891-1902).

(Tinner, Masonic goods, fencing supplies)

(N) **ROBERT CAMPBELL**   BALTIMORE, MD   B1799, 1819-1829
- Located at 126 Baltimore Street (1827-1829).

    R. (ROBERT) & A. (ANDREW)   BALTIMORE, MD   1829-1854
    CAMPBELL
- Locations:
    130 Baltimore Street (1829-1840)
    155 Baltimore Street (1840-1843)
    205 Baltimore Street (1843-1854)
- Advertised military goods, including swords (1846).

    R. (ROBERT) CAMPBELL & SONS   BALTIMORE, MD   1854-D1872
- Partners and sons: Robert Campbell Jr., John Campbell.
- Located at 205 Baltimore Street.

(Silversmith, watchmaker, jeweler, fancy goods, sword hiltor)

(A) **IRA C. CANFIELD JR.**   EAST HADDON, CT   B1808-1834
    WILLIAM B. CANFIELD   EAST HADDON, CT   B1809-1834
    CANFIELD (IRA C.) & BRO.   BALTIMORE, MD   1834-1860
    (WILLIAM B.)
- Locations:
    corner of Baltimore and Charles Streets (1834-1840, jewelers)
    corner of Baltimore and Charles Streets (1840-1845, jewelry, fancy and military goods)
    227 W. Baltimore Street (1845-1855, jewelry, fancy and military goods)
    229 W. Baltimore Street (1855-1860, jewelry, fancy and military goods)

    CANFIELD (IRA C.) & BRO.   BALTIMORE, MD   1860-1881
    (WILLIAM B.) & CO.
- Located at 229 W. Baltimore.
- Partners: Thomas Welch, Joseph B. Meredith, James Arminger.
- Issued catalogs during the Civil War.
- Advertised "military goods of every description," including swords, belts, sashes, spurs, buttons, lances, embroideries, haversacks, pistols, field and marine glasses, jewelry, and "presentation swords on hand and made to order" (1864).
- Advertised as importer of silverware and silverplate from Paris, Vienna, and London; American and Swiss watches; clocks; bronzes; porcelain; diamonds; jewelry; fans; umbrellas; leather goods; fancy goods; and medals and badges (1875).
- William B. Canfield died (1879).

IRA C. CANFIELD JR.	BALTIMORE, MD	1881-D1896

(N) **WILLIAM C. CARROLL & CO.**   CHICAGO, IL   1870-1890
- Partner: William Hoeleke.
- Located at 180 Michigan Avenue (Leland Hotel).
- Advertised in the *Army-Navy Journal* as a U.S. purchasing cooperative, military tailor, and general purveyor to the army (1881).

(N) **EDWARD W. CARRYL**   PHILADELPHIA, PA   1855-1863
- Locations:
    378 Chesnut Street (1855-1856)
    162 Chesnut Street (1856-1859)
    714 Chesnut Street (1859-1862)
    715 Chesnut Street (1862-1863)

E. (EDWARD) W. CARRYL & CO.   PHILADELPHIA, PA   1863-1865
- Partner: William E. Newhill.
- Located at 715 Chestnut Street.

(Military and fancy goods, silver-plated ware)

(N) **CARTER & SON**   NEW YORK, NY   1775-1783
- Sold U.S. mounted rifle officer swords during the Revolutionary War.

(A) **CHICAGO UNIFORM MFG. CO.**   CHICAGO, IL   1896-1900
- Located at 143 LaSalle Street.

CHICAGO UNIFORM & CAP CO.   CHICAGO, IL   1900-1915
- Located at 143 LaSalle Street.

(Uniforms, regalia, fraternal swords)

(A) **MOSES CHICK**   CONCORD, NH   1830-1860
- Located at 176 Main Street.

(N) **CHISAM & COBB**   AUGUSTA, ME   1861-1865
- Located at 147 Water Street.
- Bought out R.T. Bosworth (1861).

(Tailor, military goods, swords, uniforms)

(N) **C. (CHARLES) C. CHURCH**   BATAVIA, NY   1812-1832
- Advertised military goods and "yellow-mounted" (government term referring to brass or gold mounted) infantry, artillery and cavalry swords (1823).

(Goldsmith, silversmith, military goods, sword hiltor)

(A) **HENRY G. CLAGSTONE**   PHILADELPHIA, PA   1860-1864
- Located at 806 Chesnut Street.
- Advertised as a military goods dealer and manufacturer of corps badges, battle stripes, and presentation swords.

(N) **CLARK & ROGERS**   NEW ORLEANS, LA   1812-1815
- Sold presentation swords.

(Importer, silversmith, sword hiltor)

(N) **HERMAN COHN** BROOKLYN, NY 1896-1940
- Locations:
    69 Moore Street (1896-1899)
    242 Pearl Street (1899-1900)
    41 Sands Street (1900-1904)
    45 Sands Street (1904-1940)
- Military tailor and military goods.
- Sold M1902 saber for all officers and M1852 naval officer swords.
- President: Jerome M. Cohn (1930-1940).

(N) **FRANCES COLLINGWOOD SR.** ELMIRA, NY 1816-D1857
- Located on John Street.
  COLLINGWOOD BROS. ELMIRA, NY 1857-1865
- Brothers: Robert and Francis Collingwood Jr.
- Located at 13 Lake Street.

(Silversmith, watches, jewelry, military goods)

(A) **PELEG COLLINS** CINCINNATI, OH 1825-1828
- Located at 126 Main Street.
  COLLINS (PELEG) & SHIP (SAMUEL) CINCINNATI, OH 1829-1835
- Located on Sycamore Street.
  PELEG COLLINS CINCINNATI, OH 1836-1842
- Located at 53 Main Street.
  HAZAN (NATHAN L.) & COLLINS (PELEG) CINCINNATI, OH 1843-1847
- Located at 53 Main Street.
  PELEG COLLINS CINCINNATI, OH 1848-1850
- Located at 53 Main Street.

(A) **E. (ELIAS) COMBS & CO.** NEW YORK, NY 1844-1860
- Located at 244 Grand Street (1844-1855), 465 Broadway (1855-1860).

(A) **CONTINENTAL CLOTHING CO.** BOSTON, MA 1875-1920
- Located at 644 to 650 Washington Street (1875-1898), 651 Washington Street (at the corner of Boyleston Street) (1898-1900).

(N) **JOHN COOK & CO.** CHARLESTON, SC 1790-1796
- Located at 133 William Street.
- Moved to Boston, MA (1796).
  JOHN COOK BOSTON, MA 1796-1815

(Silversmith, military goods)

(A) **GARRETT COOPER** NEW YORK, NY 1833-1850
- Located at 139 Fulton Street (1833-1844), 162 Fulton Street (1844-1850).
  COOPER (GARRETT) & CAIRNS (JASPER) NEW YORK, NY 1850-1854
- Located at 198 Fulton Street (1850-1851), 40 Reade Street (1851-1854).

(Silversmith, sword hiltor, military ornaments)

(A) **JEREMIAH COOPER** BIRMINGHAM, ENGLAND Bc1780-1804
- Immigrated to New York, NY, with his father Thomas Cooper (1804).

JEREMIAH COOPER NEW YORK, NY 1804-D1831
- Son of Thomas Cooper.
- Locations:
    19 Partition Street (in father Thomas Cooper's shop) (1804-1809)
    67 Vesey Street (1809-1821)
    7 Maiden Lane (next to B&J Cooper at 6 Maiden Lane) (1821-1824)
    196 Broadway (1824-1828)
    192 Broadway (1828-1829)
    202 Broadway (1829-1831)
- Jeremiah Cooper died (1831) and was succeeded by his brother Joseph Cooper.

(Gun maker, military goods dealer, importer)
(See Joseph Cooper, Thomas Cooper)

(A, C) **THOMAS COOPER** BIRMINGHAM, ENGLAND Bc1760-1804
- Gun lock maker.
- Thomas Cooper and his sons Benjamin Cooper (born c. 1778), Joseph Cooper (born c. 1785), and Jeremiah Cooper (born c. 1780) immigrated to New York, NY (1804).

THOMAS COOPER NEW YORK, NY 1804-1809
- Gun shop located at 19 Partition Street.
- Thomas Cooper retired (1809) and died (1811).
- Succeeded by B&J Cooper and Jeremiah Cooper.

(A) **B. (BENJAMIN) & J. (JOSEPH) COOPER** NEW YORK, NY 1804-1831
- Sons of Thomas Cooper.
- Locations:
    19 Partition Street in father Thomas Cooper's shop (1804-1809)
    202 Broadway (1809-1811)
    19 Partition Street (1811-1812)
    6 Maiden Lane (1812-1831) (next to the gun shop of brother
        Jeremiah Cooper at 7 Maiden Lane, 1821-1824)
- Thomas Cooper retired (1809) and died (1811).
- They moved out of, but still owned, the 202 Broadway shop.
- Brother Jeremiah Cooper moved into the 202 Broadway shop (1829-1831).
- B&J Cooper contacted Nathan Starr of Middletown, CT, wanting to buy cavalry sabers (June 10, 1814).
- Starr replied that he could provide cavalry sabers at $7.50 each, broken down as blade for $3, guard for $1, and scabbard for $3.50 (June 22, 1814).
- John Joseph Henry of Philadelphia, PA, offered to sell B&J Cooper 500 secondhand horseman sabers at $5.50 each (1816).
- B&J Cooper bought swords from a relative, John Cooper of Birmingham, England, who was located on Bartholomew Street (1810-1820).
- Bought swords and sword parts from Nathan Starr.
- Advertised flintlock rifles, pistols, and sporting guns.
- Benjamin Cooper died (1831).
- B&J Cooper was succeeded by Joseph Cooper.

(Gun maker, military goods dealer, importer)
(See Joseph Cooper, Thomas Cooper)

(A) **JOSEPH COOPER** NEW YORK, NY 1831-1851
- Joseph Cooper's son Henry T. Cooper worked with him (1831-1840).
- Advertised as successor to B&J Cooper and Jeremiah Cooper (1831).

- Locations:
    202 Broadway (1831-1840)
    233 Broadway (1840-1845)
    187 Broadway (1845-1851)
- Joseph Cooper died (1851).
- Succeeded by his son Henry T. Cooper and grandson Albert Cooper.

(A) **HENRY T. COOPER** NEW YORK, NY Bc1810, 1831-1851
- Son of Joseph Cooper.
- Located at 202 Broadway (worked in his father Joseph's shop) (1831-1840), 178 Broadway (1840-1851).

HENRY T. & ALBERT COOPER NEW YORK, NY 1851-1857
- Partner and son: Albert Cooper.
- Advertised as successors to B&J Cooper and Joseph Cooper (1851).
- Henry T. Cooper died (1857).

COOPER (ALBERT) & POND (CHARLES H.) NEW YORK, NY 1857-1867
- Had U.S. contracts for 1,740 imported Enfield rifles and accouterments, kettles, and mess kits (1862).

COOPER (ALBERT) HARRIS (EDWIN S.) & HODGKINS (WALTER C.) NEW YORK, NY 1867-1874

(Gun maker, military goods dealer, importer)

(N) **JOHN J. COSTINETT** WASHINGTON, DC 1885-1933
- Advertised as a military tailor selling badges, pins, regalia, and swords.

(N) **WILLIAM CRAMMOND** PHILADELPHIA, PA 1805-1815
- Located at 218 Mulberry Street (1805-1812), 222 Mulberry Street (1812-1815).
- After the War of 1812, Callender Irving, U.S. Commissary of Military Supplies, authorized the sale of 400 discarded cavalry sabers with scabbards and belts (offered for sale by Marine T. Wickham, chief inspector at the U.S. Philadelphia Schuylkill Arsenal) to William Crammond (May 26, 1815).

(Military goods dealer)

(N) **SAMUEL CREUTZBERG** PHILADELPHIA, PA 1840-1850
- Located at 169 High Street.
- Cutler who sold swords.

(N) **J. CURLEY & BROTHERS** NEW YORK, NY 1861-1865
- Imported silver-enlayed folding knives with silver hilts from Sheffield, England.

(A) **H. (HENRY) N. DAGGETT** BOSTON, MA 1862
- Sold 5,031 cavalry sabers and 114 imported foot officer swords to the U.S. government (1862).
- Sold 68 musician's swords to the state of Massachusetts (1862).
- Repaired 49 cavalry swords and made scabbards for them for the state of Massachusetts (1862).
- The foot officer swords are acid-etched "H.N. Daggett" on the ricasso of the blade. The grips are rayskin and the scabbard is leather with plain brass mounts. The blade is etched and has a large "U.S."

(N) **PEYTON DANA** PROVIDENCE, RI B1785, 1803-D1849
- Advertised military goods, gilt-plated swords, and hangers (1809).

(Silversmith, military goods, sword hiltor)

(A, C) **ELIAS DAVIS** PHILADELPHIA, PA 1801-1804
- Located at 11 1/2 Union Street.

SAMUEL DAVIS	PHILADELPHIA, PA	1801-1804

- Located at 33 Marlboro Street.

DAVIS (SAMUEL & ELIAS) & BROWN (ROBERT JOHNSON)	BOSTON, MA	1804-1820

- Locations:
    - 53 Marlboro Street (military warehouse) (1804-1808)
    - 33 Marlboro Street (corner of Milk Street) (1808-1816)
    - 1 Marlboro Street (1816-1820)
- Advertised gilt- and silver-mounted cut and thrust swords.

DAVIS (SAMUEL) & WATSON (EDWARD E.) & CO.	BOSTON, MA	1820-1830

- Located at 1 Milk Street (corner of Marlboro Street).

T. (THOMAS) A. (ASPINWELL) DAVIS & CO.	BOSTON, MA	1830-1837

- Located at 1 Milk Street (corner of Marlboro Street).

DAVIS (THOMAS A.) & PALMER (JULIUS A.)	BOSTON, MA	1837-1846

- Located at 162 Washington Street.

PALMER (JULIUS A.) & BACHELDERS (JOSIAH G. & AUGUSTUS E.)	BOSTON, MA	1846-1881

- Located at 162 Washington Street.
- Advertised in the *Army-Navy Journal* (1862):
    > *Manufacturers and dealers in:*
    > *Fine swords*
    > *Sabres*
    > *Belts*
    > *Sashes*
    > *Armor*
    > *Rifles*
    > *Pistols*
    > *Rich embroidery*
    > *Sole agents for Ponds revolvers*
    > *Presentation swords ready made or made to order*
- Advertised in the *Army-Navy Journal* (December 12, 1863) as wholesale and retail dealers in swords, revolvers, embroideries, diamonds, watches, jewelry, and silverware.

PALMER (JACOB P.) & LEIGHTON (J.A.)	BOSTON, MA	1881-1890

(N) **ROBERT DAVIS SR. & JR.**	WARNER, NH	1800-1820
ROBERT DAVIS JR.	CONCORD, NH	1820-1826
DAVIS (ROBERT JR.) & EASTMAN (SETH)	CONCORD, NH	1826-1828

- Located opposite the State House.
- Advertised military goods, including training muskets, fowling pieces, rifles, horseman pistols, gilt and plated swords, watches, silverware, and Rogers cutlery. Also "military companies furnished with every article of equipment." (1826).

ROBERT DAVIS JR.	CONCORD, NH	1828-1856

(Silversmith, military goods, cutlery, sword hiltor)
(See Seth Eastman)

(A) **CHARLES M. DEANE**	PEORIA, IL	1855-1862

- Located at 18 Water Street.

(N) **MICHAEL S. DEBRUHL**	CHARLESTON, SC	1798-1815

- Located at 137 Queen Street.
- Advertised as a watchmaker, military goods dealer, and silversmith (1798).

(N) **P.P.F. DEGRAND** BOSTON, MA 1812-1820
- Advertised in the *New England Palladium and Commercial Advertiser* (August 11, 1815):
    Location over the Union Bank
    Has for sale:
      Wool, cotton, hemp, duct,
      Olive oil
      Pepper
      Log wood and bar wood
      1 long 4 pound cannon
      A quantity of shot
      38 Cutlasses
      29 Bayonets
      4 Pistols

(N) **RICHARD DENNIS** PHILADELPHIA, PA 1800-1815
- Located at 90 South 8th Street (1800-1810), 102 South 8th Street (1810-1815).
- Bought 50 cutlasses at $3.50 each and 20 boarding pikes at $1.80 each from John Joseph Henry, Philadelphia, PA (July 1812).

(A) **DETROIT REGALIA CO.** DETROIT, MI 1890-1900
- Located at 227 Jefferson Street.

(A, C) **DIEDERICK (FRANZ & FREDERICK) & CO.** NEW YORK, NY 1790-1815
- Was listed incorrectly as Landsmann Diedrick & Co. in Volume I.
- Company sales agent: John Roosevelt.
- Sent 98 imported German horseman sword blade samples to Tench Coxe at the U.S. Philadelphia Arsenal (October 1807). Coxe bought the blades.
- Coxe told George Ingels (U.S. Philadelphia Arsenal military storekeeper) to send the Diederick blades to William Strong of Philadelphia, PA, for mounting and to make scabbards at a price of $2.25 each (December 3, 1807).
- They were to have brass hilts, ebony grips, and leather scabbards.

(See William Strong)

(A) **WILHELM D. DIETRICH** NEW YORK, NY 1850-1865
- Located at 90 Fulton Street.

(A) **HORACE E. DIMICK** LEXINGTON, KY 1827-1850
- Cabinet maker, upholsterer.

  HORACE E. DIMICK ST. LOUIS, MO 1850-1852
- Opened a gun shop at 36 North Main.

  HORACE E. DIMICK & CO. ST. LOUIS, MO 1852-1873
- Locations:
    49 North Main Street (1852-1853)
    38 North Main Street (1853-1855)
    64 North 4th Street (1855-1859)
    97 North 4th Street (1859-1866)

402 North Main Street (1866-1870)
  315 Locust Street (1870-1873)
- Advertised Allen and Colt revolvers, shotguns, rifles, pistols, flasks, caps, powder, U.S. muskets, carbines and rifles, Sharp's rifles, bowie knives, and tomahawks.

(A) **WILLIAM J. DINSMORE**   BOSTON, MA   1887-1900
- Located at 521 Washington Street (1887-1896), 14 Bedford Street (1896-1900).

(N) **TIMOTHY DIX (SR. & JR.)**   BOSCAWEN, NH   1800-1812
    TIMOTHY DIX JR.   BOSCAWEN, NH   1812-1825
- Advertised military goods, muskets, bayonets, rifles, training muskets, fowling pieces, pistols small swords, cut and thrust swords, hangers, and dirks (1812).

(A) **GARVEY DONALDSON**   NEW YORK, NY   1885-1900
- Located at 442 West 20th Street.

(A) **DARIUS F. DRAKE**   BOSTON, MA   1861-1865
- Located at 95 Kilby Street.

(A) **G. (GEORGE) W. DREW**   CONCORD, NH   1861-1865
- Located at 184 Main Street.

(N) **F.D. DUTEIL**   NEW ORLEANS, LA   1835-1850
- Located on St. Philip Street.
- Had a presentation sword made to be presented to Zachary Scott (1846).

(Military goods dealer)

(A) **DYER (JOSEPH C.) & EDDY (JAMES)**   BOSTON, MA   1800-1806
- Located at 49 Marlborough Street.

    JOSEPH C. DYER   BOSTON, MA   1806-1818
- Located at 48 Marlborough Street.

(N) **SETH EASTMAN**   CONCORD, NH   B1801-1826
    DAVIS (ROBERT JR.) & EASTMAN (SETH)   CONCORD, NH   1826-1828
- Located opposite the State House.
- Advertised military goods, including training muskets, rifles, fowling pieces horseman pistols, gilt and plated swords, watches, silverware, Rogers cutlery, and "military companies furnished with every article of equipment" (1826).

    SETH EASTMAN   CONCORD, NH   1828-D1885
- Located opposite the Columbia Hotel.

(Silversmith, military goods, cutlery, sword hiltor)

(N) **EBNERS MILITARY SUPPLY HOUSE**   CHARLESTON, SC   1910-1919
- Located at 334 King Street.
- Advertised army and navy furnishings.

(A) **CHARLES A. EGGLESTON**   WASHINGTON, DC   1861-1865
- Located at 307 and 322 "E" Street.
- Advertised sutler supplies, officers' equipment, military clothing, and fancy goods.

(A) **EVANS (GEORGE) & HASSELL**   PHILADELPHIA, PA   1859-1866
     (WILLIAM S.)
- Located at 418 Arch Street.
- Advertised in the *Army-Navy Journal* (October 10, 1860): *"Swords, sashes, belts, passants and everything necessary for the complete outfit of Army and Navy officers. Banners, regimental and company flags."*
- Succeeded by Wilson & Hutchinson.

     WILSON (JAMES H.) & HUTCHINSON   PHILADELPHIA, PA   1866-1868
     (EDWARD E.)
- Located at 418 Arch Street.

     WILSON (JAMES H.) & STELLWAGON   PHILADELPHIA, PA   1868-1872
     (HENRY)
- Located at 1028 Chesnut Street.

(A) **JAMES EYLAND**   BIRMINGHAM, ENGLAND   B1795-1819
- Immigrated to Charleston, SC (1819).

     JAMES EYLAND   CHARLESTON, SC   1819-1820
- Located on King Street "at the sign of the drum."
- Advertised fine arts.

     JAMES EYLAND & CO.   CHARLESTON, SC   1820-1827
- Partners: William Carrington (Charleston, SC), W. & G. Chance (New York, NY, and Birmingham, England).
- Located at 330 King Street (1820-1824), 172 King Street at Wentworth Street (1824-1827).
- Advertised Sheffield plated goods (1820).

     JAMES EYLAND   CHARLESTON, SC   1827-1832
- Located at 172 King Street (at Wentworth Street).
- Went on a buying trip to Europe, including Britannia ware from Dixon & Co. (1830).

     EYLAND (JAMES) & HAYDEN (NATHANIEL)   CHARLESTON, SC   1832-1835
- Hayden was Eyland's accountant.
- Located at 172 King Street (at Wentworth Street) (1832-1835), 267 King Street (1835).
- James Eyland died of yellow fever (1835).
- Nathaniel Hayden purchased the stock of Eyland.

(Silverware, jewelry, military and fancy goods)
(See Nathaniel Hayden)

(A) **FARRANT (GEORGE W.) & LESTER**   NORFOLK, VA   1858-1865
     (JOHN T.)
- Located at 30 E. Main Street (1858-1859), 86 E. Main Street (1859-1865).

(A) **HERMAN FENSONHEIM**   WASHINGTON, DC   1861-1865
- Located at 456 Pennsylvania Avenue.
- Called Army-Navy Emporium.

(N) **RICHARD FISKE**   WORCESTER, MA   1841-1861
     FISKE (RICHARD) & GODDARD   WORCESTER, MA   1861-1862
     (CHARLES K.)
- Located at 195 Main Street.

     RICHARD FISKE   WORCESTER, MA   1862-1864
- Advertised as a dealer in watches, clocks, jewelry, silverware, and military equipment, including guns and pistols.

(A) **A.D. FITCH**   ST. PAUL, MN   1861-1865
- Located on 3rd Street (between St. Peter and Market Streets).

(N) **HENRY FLETCHER**   LEXINGTON, KY   1816-1830
    HENRY FLETCHER   LOUISVILLE, KY   1830-1859
- Located at 463 Main Street.

    FLETCHER (HENRY) & BENNETT (CHARLES) LOUISVILLE, KY   1859-1861
- Located at 463 Main Street.

    HENRY FLETCHER   LOUISVILLE, KY   1861-1865
- Located at 463 Main Street.

(Dealer in clocks, watches, jewelry, and military goods)

(A) **JOHN B. FLETCHER & CO.**   BOSTON, MA   1852-1855
- Located at 60 Milk Street.
- Advertised as dealer in hardware, silver-plated ware, jewelry, buttons, spectacles, and cutlery.

(A) **THOMAS FLETCHER**   BOSTON, MA   B1787-1808
    CHARLES FLETCHER   BOSTON, MA   B1790-1808
    FLETCHER (THOMAS & CHARLES) & GARDINER (BALDWIN & SIDNEY)   BOSTON, MA   1808-1811

- Advertised in the *Columbian Sentinel* (October 11, 1809) horseman sabers, cockades and eagles, hangers (short sabers), epaulettes, plates, tassels (gold and silver), breast plates, and shoulder straps.
- Locations:
    18 Marlboro Street (1808-1809)
    43 Marlboro Street (1809-1810)
    59 Cornhill Street (1810-1811)

    McFARLANE (JOHN), FLETCHER (THOMAS & CHARLES) & GARDINER (BALDWIN & SIDNEY)   BOSTON, MA   1811-1812

- Located at 59 Cornhill Street.
- Advertised in the Boston Patriot (May 5, 1811) military goods, including gold and silver tassels, epaulettes, Prussian binding, gold and silver lace, breast plates, cockades, gilt and plated swords, fencing foils, silk sashes, sword belts, cord, stocks, and pistols.

    FLETCHER (THOMAS & CHARLES) & GARDINER (BALDWIN & SIDNEY)   PHILADELPHIA, PA   1812-1828

- Located at 188 Chesnut Street (at 4th Street).
- Made gold- and silver-mounted swords for the state of Georgia for heroes of the War of 1812.

    THOMAS FLETCHER   PHILADELPHIA, PA   1828-1833

- Located at 188 Chesnut (at 4th Street).
- Sold the state of Maryland presentation swords for a Captain Ballard, Lieutenant Maya, and Lieutenant Cross (August 1828).
- Sold the state of Maryland presentation swords for a Col. Nathan Towson and Capt. John Gallagher (December 1833).

    FLETCHER (THOMAS) & BAILEY (THEODORE A.)   PHILADELPHIA, PA   1833-1838

- Located at 188 Chesnut (at 4th Street).

    FLETCHER (THOMAS) & BENNETT (JACOB)   PHILADELPHIA, PA   1838-1840

- Located at 188 Chesnut (at 4th Street).

    THOMAS FLETCHER   PHILADELPHIA, PA   1840-1866

- Locations:
    188 Chesnut Street (at 4th Street) (1840-1851)
    corner of 7th and Mulberry Street (1851-1855)

441 N. Broad Street (1855-1860)
4 Marsailles Street (1860-1866)
- Advertised as a maker of gold-mounted presentation swords.

(A) **GEORGE A. FLODING**   ATLANTA, GA   1875-1909
- Located at 155 Whitehall Street.

WILLIAM E. FLODING   ATLANTA, GA   1909-1920
- Located at 155 Whitehall Street.

THE FOLSOM FAMILY
MILITARY GOODS STORES

(A) **CHARLES FOLSOM**   NEW YORK, NY   1849-1902
- Locations:
    38 Maiden Lane (1849-1867)
    33 Maiden Lane (1867-1870)
    53 Chambers (1870-1881)
    103 Chambers (1881-1898)
    84 Chambers (1898-1902)
- Advertised in the *Army-Navy Journal* (October 22, 1864):
    To officers, sutlers, gunsmiths and the public generally. The closest buyers of all articles connected with guns, rifles, pistols, percussion caps, gunsmith's material, swords, belts, sashes, presentation articles, military, naval and fancy goods, etc. can get the best selections at the lowest prices, by purchasing through the subscriber, who from an experience of 15 years, is thoroughly posted and is now satisfactorily supplying some of the principal dealers in the country.
- Folsom purchased the gun business of J.W. Storrs (1870).

(A) **FOLSOM BROTHERS & CO**   CHICAGO, IL   1868-1870
- Located at 194 Lake Street.
- Partners: Henry and David Folsom.

(A) **FOLSOM BROTHERS (HENRY & DAVID)**   NEW ORLEANS, LA   1862-1870
- Located at 9 Old Levee Street.

(N) **HENRY FOLSOM & CO.**   MEMPHIS, TN   1859-1870
- Located at 345 Main Street.
- Advertised in the Memphis city directory military goods, guns, rifles, and pistols, as well as "presentation swords on hand or made to order" (1866).

(A) **HENRY FOLSOM**   ST. LOUIS, MO   1860-1870
- Located at 620-622 North Main Street (1860-1865), 77 Fourth Street (1866-1870).

(A) **GEORGE B. FOSTER**   BOSTON, MA   B1810, 1830-1843
- Located at 29 Tremont Row.

HARRIS (WILLIAM) & STANWOOD (HENRY B.)   BOSTON, MA   1843-1846
- Partner: George B. Foster.
- Located at 29 Tremont Row.

GEORGE B. FOSTER   BOSTON, MA   1846-D1887
- Located at 33 Tremont Street.

- Advertised in the *Army-Navy Journal* (October 10, 1863):
    Army and Navy Equipment
    Swords, pistols, belts, sashes, caps, straps, bugles, haversacks, laces, stars, buttons and all other articles wanted for the camp or ship by officers of the U.S. Army and Navy.
- During the Civil War advertised:
    Military articles and pistols
    Swords, belts, caps, sashes, straps and all the various articles wanted by officers of the Army and Navy at uniform low prices.

(A) **GEORGE F. FOSTER & CO**　　　　CHICAGO, IL　　　　1879-1892
- Located at 23 Washington Street (1879-1885), 172 Madison Street (1885-1892).

G.F. FOSTER SONS & CO.　　　　CHICAGO, IL　　　　1892-1904
- Located at 174 Madison Street.

B. (BENJAMIN) F. FOSTER UNIFORM & CAP CO.　　　　CHICAGO, IL　　　　1904-1915
- Located at 229 and 231 9th Street.

(N) **JAMES FOX**　　　　BALTIMORE, MD　　　　B1813, 1833-1875
- Located at 68 South Calvert Street (1833-1853), 64 South Calvert Street (1853-1875).

(Gunsmith, hardware, cutlery dealer)

(A) **JOHN SMITH FRAZER**　　　　NEW YORK, NY　　　　1830-1847
- Locations:
    85 Maiden Lane (1830-1836)
    168 Pearl Street (1836-1840)
    122 Broadway (1840-1846)
    118 Broadway (1846-1847)

(N) **ERNST FREDERICK**　　　　CHICAGO, IL　　　　1861-1865
- Located at 190 Lake Street.
- Advertised military goods in the *Chicago Tribune* during the Civil War.

(N) **GEORGE D. FRIES & JOHN H. FRIES**　　　　BALTIMORE, MD　　　　1853-1854
- Located at 66 Camdon Street.

GEORGE D. FRIES　　　　BALTIMORE, MD　　　　1854-1866
- Located at 34 Marion Street.

(Cutler, surgical instrument maker)

(A) **M.W. GALT & BROTHER**　　　　WASHINGTON, DC　　　　1847-1991
- Locations:
    254 Pennsylvania Avenue (1847-1861)
    354 Pennsylvania Avenue (1861-1874)
    1107 Pennsylvania Avenue (1871-1991)
- Advertised in the *Army-Navy Journal* (September 5, 1863):
    Rich military goods.
    Presentation swords.
    Fine embroideries.
    Army and Navy officers requisites of every description.
    Testimonials, in gold and silver, executed from original designs in the highest style of the art.

(A) **T. (THOMAS) D. GARD**   WORCESTER, MA   1861-1915
- Locations:
    205 3/4 Main Street (1861-1865)
    845 Main Street (1865-1873)
    3 Central Exchange Street (1873-1876)
    351 Main Street (1876-1880)
    345 Main Street (1880-1888)
    393 Main Street (1888-1892)
    310 Main Street (1892-1895)
    352 Main Street (1895-1915)

    THOMAS D. GARD INC.   WORCESTER, MA   1915-1920
- Located at 352 Main Street.

(Silversmith, jeweler, military goods)

(N) **J. (JAMES) R. GAUNT & SON**   NEW YORK, NY   1910-1912
- Partner and son: Charles F. Gaunt.
- Located at 79 5th Avenue.

    CHARLES F. GAUNT   NEW YORK, NY   1912-1939
- Locations:
    530 5th Avenue (1912-1920)
    717 W. 42nd Street (1920-1922)
    52 W. 46th Street (1922-1939)
- Advertised as metal worker and manufacturer of army and navy buttons, ornaments, insignia, military goods, presentation swords, honors, and decorations (1921).

(Silversmith, die sinker, military ornamentor, button maker, sword hiltor)

(A) **MORRIS J. GELHAAR**   KANSAS CITY, MO   1900-1910
- Located at 720 Walnut Street.

    GELHAAR (MORRIS J.) UNIFORM CO.   KANSAS CITY, MO   1910-1920

(A) **GELSTON (HUGH) & GOULD (JAMES)**   BALTIMORE, MD   1816-1823
- Located at the corner of Baltimore and St. Charles Streets.

    HUGH GELSTON   BALTIMORE, MD   1823-1833
- Located at the corner of Baltimore and St. Charles Streets.

(A, C) **GENERAL EMBROIDERY &**   NEW YORK, NY   1922-1997
    MILITARY SUPPLY CO. (GEMSCO)

(Manufacturer, importer, wholesaler, and distributor of army and navy equipment and insignia manufacturer)

(N) **ABBOT GERE & CO.**   COLUMBUS, OH   1830-1850
- Located at 61 High Street.
- Advertised as a hardware, cutlery, and military goods dealer.

(A) **GEORGE S. GETHEN**   PHILADELPHIA, PA   1886-1913
- Located at 1306 Arch Street.

    GEORGE S. GETHEN & CO.   PHILADELPHIA, PA   1913-1935
- Located at 1306 Arch Street (1913-1919), 237 5th Street (1919-1935).

(A) **WILLIAM GETHEN**   PHILADELPHIA, PA   1795-D1809
- Located at 170 Front Street.

JOHN WARD GETHEN	PHILADELPHIA, PA	1809-1836

- Locations:
    170 Front Street (1809-1821)
    106 South 10th Street (1821-1827)
    170 South 10th Street (1827-1832)
    112 Spruce Street (1832-1836)

JOHN WARD & ROBERT GETHEN	PHILADELPHIA, PA	1836-1849

- Located at 112 Spruce Street.

(A) **GEORGE H. GIBSON**	BOSTON, MA	1860-1875

- Sold M1872 artillery sabers.

(A) **A. (ALBERT) A. GILBERT**	PHILADELPHIA, PA	1861-1865

- Located at 715 Jayne Street.

(A) **EDWARD GILES**	NEW YORK, NY	1840-1864
PRICE (JOHN H.) GILES	NEW YORK, NY	1864-1865
(EDWARD) & UNDERHILL (JOHN T.)		
EDWARD GILES	NEW YORK, NY	1865-1866

- Located at 19 John Street.

(Silversmith, moulder, military goods)

(A) **CHARLES J. GODFREY**	NEW YORK, NY	1898-1904

- Bicycle shop located at 1019 1st Street (1898-1901).
- Sporting goods shop located at 5 Warren Street (1901-1904).
- Issued a war relics and souvenirs catalog that included U.S. regulation and fencing swords, guns, rifles, cutlery, and ammunition (1902).

(C) **JAMES M. GOODELL JR.**	CHICAGO, IL	1870

(A) **DANIEL T. GOODHUE**	PROVIDENCE, RI	1824-1861

- Locations:
    44 Cheapside Street (1824-1830)
    31 Westminster Street (1830-1847)
    87 Westminster Street (1847-1850)
    77 Westminster Street (1850-1861)

(N) **JOHN & WILLIAM GORDON**	BALTIMORE, MD	1796-1812

- Located at 70 Bowleys Wharf.

JOHN GORDON	BALTIMORE, MD	1812-1815

- Located at 72 Bowleys Wharf.
- Bought 20 cutlasses at $2.75 each from John Joseph Henry, Philadelphia, PA (July 1812).

(Military goods dealer)

(A) **JAMES GOULD**	BALTIMORE, MD	1822-D1874

- Locations:
    202 Baltimore Street (1822-1836)
    136 Baltimore Street (1836-1842)
    168 Baltimore Street (1842-1874)

GOULDING & CO.
(See W.R. Goulding in Makers listing)

(A) **RENE L. GRAVELLE**	PHILADELPHIA, PA	1812-1831

- Located at 12 North 2nd Street.

(N) **SAMUEL GRAVES**	AUBURN, NY	1790-1815
GRAVES (SAMUEL) & FITCH (JAMES)	AUBURN, NY	1815-1824
SAMUEL GRAVES	BATAVIA, NY	1824-1830

- Advertised as silversmith, military goods, swords, and fancy goods.

(A) **GRAY (GEORGE P.) &**	NEW YORK, NY	1861-1865
POTTER (AUGUSTUS W.)		

- Located at 115 Liberty Street.

(N) **S. (SAMUEL) P. GREELEY**	CONCORD, NH	1840-1850
S. (SAMUEL) P. GREELEY	MANCHESTER, NH	1850-1865

(Military equipment dealer)

(N) **BENJAMIN GREENWALD**	BALTIMORE, MD	1861-1865

- Located at 78 North Eutaw Street.

(Military goods)

(N) **CHARLES F. GREENWOOD**	NORFOLK, VA	B1828, 1851-1867

- Located at 27 E. Main Street.
- Advertised as silversmiths and jewelers selling clocks, plated ware, and military goods during the Civil War.

C. (CHARLES) F. GREENWOOD & BRO.	NORFOLK, VA	1867-D1904
(FREDERICK K.)		

- Located at 27 E. Main Street.

ARTHUR B. GRISWOLD
(See James N. Hyde in Confederate Makers listing)

(A) **JOSEPH C. GRUBB**	PHILADELPHIA, PA	1839-1861

- Located at 76 Market Street.
- Advertised as a hardware dealer.

JOSEPH C. GRUBB & CO.	PHILADELPHIA, PA	1861-1886

- Located at 236 Market Street (1861-1870), 712 Market Street (1870-1886).
- Advertised as importers of guns, pistols, swords and knives (1861-1866).
- Advertised as gun and pistol makers (1866-1880).
- Partners: John McLaughlin, Samuel Winchester (1867-1868).
- Advertised as a sporting goods store (1880-1886).

(N) **GEORGE H. GRUEBY**	PORTLAND, ME	1844-1849

- Located at 133 Middle Street.
- Advertised as silversmith and seller of watches, jewelry, and military goods.

(A) **J.H.F. HAHN**	BALTIMORE, MD	1904-1939

- Located at 25 South Calvert Street.

(A) **WILLIAM HAHN**	NEW YORK, NY	1858-1889

- Located at 224 E. 11th Street (1858-1870), 617 E. 11th Street (1870-1889).

- Imported and sold M1840 cavalry sabers and M1832 foot artillery swords.
- Made pocket pistols and sporting rifles with octagonal barrels.

(Gunsmith, shooting gallery operator)

(A) **IVORY A. HALL**	CONCORD, NH	B1795, 1825-D1880

- Located on the corner of Main and Franklin Streets.

(A) **M. HALL**	HILLDALE, MI	1880-1888

- Advertised regalia, military equipment, swords, flags, and firearms.

(A) **HANNIBAL G. HAMLIN**	CINCINNATI, OH	1833-1862

- Located at 63 W. 4th Street.

(A) **HARDING REGALIA & UNIFORM CO.**	BOSTON, MA	1913-1925

- Located at 22 School Street.

(A) **SMITH B. HARRINGTON**	BOSTON, MA	1915-1925

- Located at 370 Washington Street.

(N) **HENRY HARRINGTON**	WORCESTOR, MA	1819-1834
HENRY HARRINGTON	SOUTHBRIDGE, MA	1834-1841

- Gun and knife dealer.

(A) **C. (CLARENCE) A. HART**	PHILADELPHIA, PA	1871-1896

- Located at 131 North 3rd Street (1871-1877), 133 North 3rd Street (1877-1896).

(A) **FREDERICK F. HASSAM**	BOSTON, MA	1838-1856

- Located at Kilby Street.

KINGMAN (LEVI C.) & HASSAM (FREDERICK F.)	BOSTON, MA	1856-1861

- Located at 128 Washington Street.
- Advertised as cutlers and surgical instrument makers.
- Made bowie knives.

HASSAM BROTHERS	BOSTON, MA	1861-1868

- Located at 146 Washington Street.
- Partners: Frederick F. Hassam, Roswell Hassam.
- Knife makers, including bowie knives.
- Made bowie knives with stag antler handles.
- Made silver-mounted bowie knives with carved ivory grips.

FREDERICK F. HASSAM	BOSTON, MA	1868-1874

- Located on Green Street near Bowdoin Street.
- Importer and dealer in guns and military goods, especially during the Civil War.

(Cutler; surgical instrument and bowie knife maker)

(A) **HENRY HAUSMANN**	NEW ORLEANS, LA	1872-D1890

- Located at 186 Poydras Street.

T. (THERESA) HAUSMANN	NEW ORLEANS, LA	1890-1997

- Henry's widow.
- Locations:
    1818-1820 Poydras Street (1890-1895)

119 E. 18th Street (1895-1919)
117 E. 18th Street (1919-1997)
- Also a jewelry maker.

(A) **NATHANIEL N. HAYDEN**   CHARLESTON, SC   B1805-1832
- Worked as an accountant for James Eyland (1827-1832).

EYLAND (JAMES) & HAYDEN (NATHANIEL)   CHARLESTON, SC   1832-1835
- Located at 172 King Street (at Wentworth Street) (1832-1835), 267 King Street (1835).

(Silverware, jewelry, military goods store)

NATHANIEL HAYDEN   CHARLESTON, SC   1835-1838
- Located at 203 King Street.

HAYDEN (NATHANIEL & H. SIDNEY) & GREGG (WILLIAM) & CO.   CHARLESTON, SC   1838-1843
- Gregg owned a cotton mill in Chapel Hill, SC.
- Located at 250 King Street (at Hasel Street).

(Jewelry, silverware, and military goods store)

GREGG (WILLIAM) & HAYDEN (H. SIDNEY & AUGUSTUS H.)   CHARLESTON, SC   1843-1852
- Located at 250 King Street (at Hasel Street).

(Jewelry, silverware, and military goods store)

HAYDEN BROTHERS & CO   CHARLESTON, SC   1852-1855
- Partners: H. Sidney Hayden, Augustus H. Hayden.
- Located at 250 King Street (at Hasel Street).

HAYDEN (AUGUSTUS H.) & WHILDEN (WILLIAM G.)   CHARLESTON, SC   1855-1863
- Located at 250 King Street (at Hasel Street).
- A sales receipt of Hayden & Whilden (1861) shows the following:

> *Importers and dealers in:*
> *Watches*
> *Clocks*
> *Jewelry*
> *Silver and silver plated ware*
> *Japanned goods*
> *Lamps*
> *Gas fixtures*
> *House furnishings*
> *Fancy articles*
> *Military goods*
> *Cutlery, including swords*
> *Pistols*
> *Clocks and watches repaired*

AUGUSTUS H. HAYDEN   CHARLESTON, SC   1863-1866
- Located at 272 King Street (across the street from William G. Whilden at 250 King Street).

A. (AUGUSTUS) H. HAYDEN   CHARLESTON, SC   1866-1879
- Located at 255 King Street.

(Importer and dealer in watches, jewelry, military goods and crockery)
(See Whilliam G. Whilden)

(A)	PETER HAYDEN	NEW YORK, NY	1861-1865

- Located at 79 Beckman Street.

(A)	HAYS, ROSENTHAL & CO.	INDIANAPOLIS, IN	1865-1870

- Located at the corner of Illinois and Washington Streets.

(A)	W. (WILLIAM) & B. (BETSY) HAYWOOD	WASHINGTON, DC	1857-1880

- Located at 208 Broadway (1857-1875), 212 Broadway (1875-1880).

(A)	JOHN C. HAZLETON	WASHINGTON, DC	1861-1864

- Located at 384 Pennsylvania Street.

(A)	FRANCIS J. HEIBERGER	WASHINGTON, DC	1853-1857

- Employee of H.F. Louden & Co.

F. (FRANCIS) J. HEIBERGER	WASHINGTON, DC	1857-1862

- Located at 362 Pennsylvania Street.

HEIBERGER (FRANCIS J.) & KING (HENRY)	WASHINGTON, DC	1862-1865

- Located at 362 Pennsylvania Street.

F. (FRANCIS J.) HEIBERGER	WASHINGTON, DC	1865-1930

- Locations:
    362 Pennsylvania Street (1865-1870)
    615-617 Pennsylvania Street (1870-1878)
    535 15th Street (1878-1911)
    1419 "F" Street (1911-1924)
    1405 "F" Street (1924-1927)
    920 17th Street (1927-1930)

(Military tailor, military equipment)
(See H.F. Louden & Co.)

(N)	HEMMINGWAY (L.G.) & STEVENS (JAMES R.)	HARTFORD, CT	1858-1865

- Located at 284 Main Street.
- Sold M1850 staff and field officer swords.
- Advertised as silversmith and jeweler selling military goods and swords.

(See James R. Stevens)

(N)	GEORGE R.A. HESS	BALTIMORE, MD	B1826-1847
	KING (HENRY S.) & HESS (GEORGE R.A.)	BALTIMORE, MD	1847-1860

- Located at 307 W. Baltimore Street.

KING (HENRY S.) & HUPMAN (NICHOLAS A.)	BALTIMORE, MD	1860-1871
HENRY S. KING & SON (HENRY JR.)	BALTIMORE, MD	1871-1886

- Locations:
    303 W. Baltimore Street (1871-1881)
    53 South Sharp Street (1881-1883)
    53 Hopkins Place (1883-1886)

(Gunsmith, military goods dealer)
(See Henry S. King)

HIBBARD, SPENCER, BARTLET & CO.
(See Adolph F. Johnson)

(N) PHILLIP HILLEGAS	**CHARLESTON, SC**	**1820-1830**

- Located at 165 King Street.
- Military and fancy goods.

(A) JOSEPH J. HIRSCHBUHL	**LOUISVILLE, KY**	**1840-1858**

- Located at 75 E. 3rd Street.

HIRSCHBUHL (JOSEPH J.) & DOLFINGER (JACOB)	**LOUISVILLE, KY**	**1858-1864**

- Located at 233 Main Street.

(A, C) HODGSON (ROBERT & JOHN) & CO.	**BALTIMORE, MD**	**1790-1795**

- Located at 70 Hanover Street.

HODGSON (ROBERT & JOHN) & NEILSON (JOHN C.)	**BALTIMORE, MD**	**1795-1798**

- Located at 152 Baltimore Street.

HODGSON (ROBERT) & THOMPSON (HUGH)	**BALTIMORE, MD**	**1798-1815**

- Locations:
    - 72 Baltimore Street (1798-1800)
    - 10 North Gay Street (1800-1802)
    - 315 Baltimore Street (1802-1804)
    - 215 Cross Forrest Street (1804-1815)
- During the War of 1812, had U.S. contracts for flintlock pistols and rifles, infantry swords (hangers), and cavalry sabers (all imported).

(Hardware, gun and sword dealer)

(A) JOHN HOEY	**NEW YORK, NY**	**1861-1865**

- Company name: Hedden (Josiah) & Hoey (John).
- Sold the U.S. government 1,800 M1840 cavalry sabers and 5,000 muskets (both imported from Prussia).

(N) JOHN S. HOLLINS	**BALTIMORE, MD**	**1796-1812**

- Located at 39 South Gay Street.

HOLLINS (JOHN S.) & BLAIR (WILLIAM)	**BALTIMORE, MD**	**1812-1815**

- Located at 49 South Gay Street.
- Bought 150 cutlasses at $3.50 each from John Joseph Henry, Philadelphia, PA (July 1812).

(Military and fancy goods dealer)

(N) WILLIAM HOLLINS	**BALTIMORE, MD**	**1810-1820**

- Located at 44 South Gay Street.
- Bought 75 cutlasses at $3 each from John Joseph Henry, Philadelphia, PA (October 1813).
- Also took 150 cutlasses on consignment from Henry.

(Military goods dealer)

(C) FREDERICK J.A. HORR	**PHILADELPHIA, PA**	**1897-1940**

- Located at 1926 W. 18th Street (1914-1940).
- Advertised as military goods and naval equipment dealer.

(A) WILLIAM H. HORSTMANN	**PHILADELPHIA, PA**	**1817-1893**

- An 1838 Horstmann advertisement reads:
    WM. H. Horstmann
    No. 51 North Third Street., Philadelphia

Manufacturer and importer of:

Epaulettes	*Swords*
Wings	*Sword knots*
Contre Straps	*Military buttons*
Pompons	*Plumes*
Sashes	*Caps*
Hat bands	*Watch guards*
Cotton and worsted fringes	*Braids*
Coach lace	

- During the Civil War, Horstmann Bros. & Co. sold 13,440 M1840 cavalry sabers to the U.S. government. The first group of sabers delivered were made with blades Horstmann bought from Sheble & Fisher of Philadelphia, PA, and Emerson & Silver of Trenton, NJ.
- Purchased more than 5,000 M1840 cavalry saber blades from Emerson & Silver (1862). They were marked with a "keystone" mark because they were made at Emerson & Silver's Keystone tool works in Trenton, NJ.
- Sabers delivered later were made with German blades imported from Gebruder Weyersberg & William Clauberg of Solingen, Prussia.
- The last group of sabers delivered were not made by Horstmann. He imported them complete from Gebruder Weyersberg & William Clauberg.
- None of the Horstmann sabers had government stamps or inspector marks on the blades.
- Horstmann also sold tomahawks.
- Advertised in the *Army-Navy Journal* (August 27, 1864):

    Horstmann Brothers & Co., Philadelphia, PA
    Located at 5th and Cherry Streets
    Manufacturers of all kinds of military goods
    On hand and made to order:
    Presentation swords
    Staff, Field and Line Officers swords

Passants	*Sashes*	*Belts*
Hats	*Embroideries*	*Epaulettes*
Caps	*Spurs, etc.*	*Chapeaux*

    Navy and Marine officer swords
    Laces
    Belts
    Colts Army and Navy Revolvers
    Regimental and National Flags, guidons and standards

- Advertised in the *National Freemason* (November 1865):

    Horstman Bros. & Co.
    Manufacturers and importers of:
    Masonic, odd fellow, sons of temperance, American mechanics, Red men and other regalia.
    A full assortment of properties for societies, lodges, councils, chapters and commanderies of knights templer kept on hand or made to order.
    Military goods of every description.
    Flags and banners.
    Church embroideries, bouillon, spangles and material for vestments.
    Theatrical jewelry, decorations, armor and trimmings, etc., in large variety.
    5th and Cherry Streets, Philadelphia
    Military goods

Swords	*Hats*

Belts *Caps*
Sashes *Laces*
Epaulettes *Drums*
Shoulder Straps
Naval swords, belts, chapeaux, etc.

- Advertised in the *Army-Navy Journal* (July 30, 1870):
    Horstmann, Brothers & Co.
    5th and Cherry Streets—Philadelphia
    Horstmann Bros. & Allien
    540 Broadway, NY and 17 Rue Paradis Poissonniere Paris.
    Manufacturers and importers of military and naval goods.
    Orders by mail will receive our prompt attention.
    Cap ornaments, cords, gold loops, laces and cloth conforming to the New Naval regulations now ready.
    Full dress belts for all grades from admiral to midshipman now ready.
    Regalia, church and theatrical goods.
    Firemen's equipments.
    Railroad companies supplied with caps, buttons, etc. for the uniforming of employees.
    Fencing materials and boxing gloves.
    Silk, bunting and muslin flags, banners made to order.

- Advertised in the *Journal of the U.S. Cavalry Association* (1889):
    Horstmann Bros. & Co.
    5th & Cherry Streets
    Philadelphia
    Manufacturers of military equipments.
    We make a specialty of "Fine goods" in strict accordance with "The Regulations"
    Our shoulder straps, forage cap badges and embroideries generally are all made from the best materials in our own embroidery department.
    Our epaulette and shoulder knot department, as well as our leather, sword, helmet and cap departments, are complete in every detail, all being in charge of competent foremen with skilled workmen under our supervision. We therefore guarantee the quality and workmanship of our goods.
    Prices are as low as is consistent with our high standard of quality and workmanship.

(A) **BENJAMIN HOWELL** **BUFFALO, NY** **1835-1850**
- Located at 34 N. Main Street.

(N) **JOSEPH E. HOWELL** **PHILADELPHIA, PA** **1800-1810**
- Located at 219 Walnut Street.

HOWELL (JOSEPH E.) & SHAW (WILLIAM) **PHILADELPHIA, PA** **1810-1815**
- Located at 25 South Water Street.
- Bought 25 boarding pikes at $1.50 each and 16 boarding pikes at $1 each from John Joseph Henry, Philadelphia, PA (September 1812).

(Military and fancy goods dealer)

(A) **WILLIAM T. HOWELL & CO.** **PHILADELPHIA, PA** **1830-1835**
- Located at 167 Market Street.

(N) **H. & F.A. HUBER**		PHILADELPHIA, PA	1820-1866

- Dealer in knives, pipe tomahawks, and edged weapons.

(A) **HUNT (NEHEMIAH) & GOODWIN** **(E. STONE)**		WASHINGTON, DC	1861-1865

- Located at 390 Pennsylvania Avenue.

(N) **EDWARD H. HUTCHINS**		NORFOLK, VA	1890-1912
DEE & ESS INC.		NORFOLK, VA	1912-1918

- President: Edward H. Hutchins.
- Secretary and treasurer: Gaxton L. Myers.
- Located at 6 E. Hall Avenue.

EDWARD H. HUTCHINS		NORFOLK, VA	1918-1828

- Located at 103 Atlantic Street.
- Advertised as military tailor, selling military goods, army swords and regulation naval officers uniforms (1918).

(A) **GEORGE & ISAAC HUTTON**		ALBANY, NY	1799-1817

- Moved from Silversmith listing in Volume I.
- Located at 15 Court Street (1799-1815), 20 State Street (1815-1817).
- Sold swords during the War of 1812.
- George Hutton died (1816).

ISAAC HUTTON		ALBANY, NY	1817-1850
ISAAC HUTTON & CO.		ALBANY, NY	1850-1998

- Owned a purse factory.
- Sold military goods during the Civil War.

(Silversmith, silverware, merchant)

J.E. HYDE
(See Silversmith listings)

(A) **OTTO & REINHOLD IHLING**		GERMANY	B1848-c1854

- Immigrated to Milwaukee, WI (c. 1854).

OTTO & REINHOLD IHLING		MILWAUKEE, WI	c1854-1859

- Moved to Kalamazoo, MI (1859).

CHAPLIN (R) & IHLING **(REINHOLD & OTTO)**		KALAMAZOO, MI	1859-1869
IHLING BROS.		KALAMAZOO, MI	1869-1900

- Partners: Reinhold and Otto Ihling.
- Located at 2022 Fulford Street.

IHLING BROS. & EVERARD		KALAMAZOO, MI	1900-1936

- Located at 233-239 E. Main Street.
- Partners: Reinhold Ihling, Otto Ihling, H.H. Everard.
- Book printers and binders.
- Regalia, uniforms, military goods.

(N) **JAMES JACKS & CO.**		CHARLESTON, SC	1797-D1822

- Had a branch in Philadelphia, PA.

JAMES JACKS & CO.		PHILADELPHIA, PA	1797-D1822

- Advertised as a goldsmith, jeweler, watch maker, and importer of cutlery and military goods from London, England (1797-1800).

- Advertised silver- and gold-mounted dress swords, hangers, gilt- and steel-mounted horseman sabers, fencing foils, and dirks (1800-1822).

(A) S. JANOWITZ	WASHINGTON, DC	1861-1865

- Located at 248 Pennsylvania Street.

(A) J. (JOSEPH) A. JOEL & CO.	NEW YORK, NY	1840-1910

- Located at 88 Nassau Street.

(N) ADOLPH F. JOHNSON	CHICAGO, IL	1825-1857
JOHNSON (ADOLPH), SPENCER (WILLIAM E.) & CO.	CHICAGO, IL	1857-1859
WILLIAM E. SPENCER	CHICAGO, IL	1859-1874
WILLIAM E. SPENCER & CO.	CHICAGO, IL	1874-1880
HIBBARD (JOHN) & SPENCER (WILLIAM E.) CO.	CHICAGO, IL	1880-1883
HIBBARD (JOHN), SPENCER (WILLIAM E.) & BARTLET (GEORGE) CO.	CHICAGO, IL	1883-1963

- Located at 18 to 32 Lake Street.
- Published catalogs.
- Some goods marked "H.S.B. & Co."
- Large hardware, sporting goods, cutlery, and gun dealers.
- Sold bowie knives.
- Bought out by Cotter & Co. (1963).

(A) IVER JOHNSON SPORTING GOODS	BOSTON, MA	1915-1925

- Located at the corner of Washington and Cornhill Streets.
- Sold sporting goods, hunting knives, and bowie knives.

(A) T. ROGERS JOHNSON	SAN FRANCISCO, CA	1852-1880

- Located at 184 Montgomery Street.

(N) HIRAM JUDSON	SYRACUSE, NY	1824-1851

- Located on Water Street.

HIRAM & THOMAS JUDSON	SYRACUSE, NY	1851-1853

- Located on Genessee Street.

HIRAM JUDSON	SYRACUSE, NY	1853-1854

- Located on Genessee Street.

(Silversmith, watch maker, military goods)

(N) CHARLES F. KALKMAN	BALTIMORE, MD	1810-1812

- Located on South Gay Street (near Pratt Street).
- Bought 24 cutlasses at $3 each from John Joseph Henry, Philadelphia, PA (August 1812).

(Military and fancy goods)

(A) JAMES KELLY	PHILADELPHIA, PA	1850-1875

- Located on North 6th Street.

(N) CHARLES KENTGEN	NEW YORK, NY	1845-1873

- Importer of guns, pistols, and cutlery.

(A, C) KENYON HAT & FUR CO.	ROCHESTER, NY	1865-1868

- Sold M1860 (boys) cavalry sabers and staff and field officer swords.

(N) **HENRY S. KING**   BALTIMORE, MD   1827-1847
    KING (HENRY S.) & HESS   BALTIMORE, MD   1847-1860
    (GEORGE R.A.)
- Located at 307 Baltimore Street.
- Dealers in hardware, cutlery, and guns.

    KING (HENRY S.) & HUPMAN   BALTIMORE, MD   1860-1871
    (NICHOLAS A.)
- Located at 307 Baltimore Street.

    HENRY S. KING & SON   BALTIMORE, MD   1871-1886
- Locations:
    307 Baltimore Street (1871-1880)
    53 South Sharp Street (1880-1883)
    53 Hopkins Place (1883-1886)

(Gunsmith)
(See George R.A. Hess)

(N) **ALPHEUS D. KIRK**   NEW YORK, NY   1861-1875
- Located at 76 Fulton Street (1861-1864), 48 Fulton Street (1864-1875).

(Military tailor, military goods)

(A) **W. (WILLIAM) S. (STOKES) KIRK**   PHILADELPHIA, PA   1878-1978
- Locations:
    1514 North 6th Street (1878-1891)
    1016 Jefferson Street (1891-1893)
    1627 North 10th Street (1893-1978)
- A large company with many branches.
- Dealt in government surplus.
- Put out military equipment catalogs, which included swords.

(N) **C.V.N. KITTRIDGE**   MADISON, WI   1861-1865
- Advertised military goods, swords, and sutler's supplies

(A) **EATON KITTRIDGE**   ROCKINGHAM CO., NH   Bc1817-1847
    EATON KITTRIDGE   CINCINNATI, OH   1847-1852
- Partner and son: Benjamin Kittridge.

    B. (BENJAMIN) KITTRIDGE & CO.   CINCINNATI, OH   1852-1884
- Partner: Eaton Kittridge (retired in 1865).
- Partner and manager: Augustus A. Bennett (retired in 1884).
- Locations:
    134 Main Street (1852-1865)
    92 Main Street (1865-1867)
    140 Main Street (1867-1875)
    166 Main Street (1875-1884)
- Advertised guns and sporting apparatus, dueling pistols, pocket cutlery, bowie knives, and dirks (1852).

    B. KITTRIDGE ARMS CO.   CINCINNATI, OH   1884-1891
- Located at 166 Main Street.

(N) **J. (JOHN) C. (CHRISTIAN) E.**   SAN FRANCISCO, CA   B1817-1852
    (EBERHART) KLEPZIG
    J. (JOHN) C. (CHRISTIAN) E.   SAN FRANCISCO, CA   1852-1856

(EBERHART) KLEPZIG
- Located at 213 Washington Street.

BAUER (C.) & KLEPZIG (J.C.E.)	SAN FRANCISCO, CA	1856-1860

- Located at 212 Washington Street.

KLEPZIG (J.C.E.) & CO.	SAN FRANCISCO, CA	1860-D1878

- Locations:
    - 212 Washington Street (1860-1861)
    - 763 Washington Street (1861-1864)
    - 733 Washington Street (1864-1878)
- Manufacturer and dealer in shotguns, pistols, and swords.

(A) **H. (HENRY) KORN**	PHILADELPHIA, PA	1812-1860

- Locations:
    - 84 North 2nd Street (1812-1824)
    - 72 North 2nd Street (1824-1830)
    - 22 North 3rd Street (1830-1858)
    - 217 North 5th Street (1858-1860)

(N) **KREMENTZ (GEORGE) & CO.**	NEWARK, NJ	1864-1868
GRENUNG (ALFRED) & KREMENTZ (GEORGE)	NEWARK, NJ	1868-1874

- Located at 14 Oliver Street.

KREMENTZ (GEORGE) & CO.	NEWARK, NJ	1874-1880

- Partners: Julius Lebkeucher, Francis A. Lebkeucher.
- Located at 14 Oliver Street.

GEORGE KREMENTZ	NEWARK, NJ	1880-1890

- Located at 361-363 Mulberry Street.

(Silversmith, jewelry, military goods)

(A) **LAMBERT (JOSEPH H.) & WHITE (JAMES W.)**	PHILADELPHIA, PA	1854-1859

- Located at 103 N. 3rd Street.
- Advertised the following articles:
    Military caps and equipments
    Leather, felt, silk, cloth, bearskin and the new regulation caps
    Fatigue caps
    Fireman's hats
    Knapsacks
    Cartridge boxes
    Epaulets
    Knife, sword and bayonet scabbards
    Swords
    Canteens
    Belts and belt plates
    Pistol and body holsters
    Flags
    Drums
    Plumes
    Pompons
    Brushes and pickers

Web belting
Gun slings
Tents and tent poles
Haversacks
Tassels, cords, bindings
Gun cases
Shot bags
Fire buckets
Trunks
Valises
Carpet bags
Medical chests
Satchels

JOSEPH H. LAMBERT	PHILADELPHIA, PA	1859-1861

- Located at 103 North 3rd Street.

LAMBERT (JOSEPH H.) & MAST (JOHN)	PHILADELPHIA, PA	1861-1862

- Located at 532 Callowhill Road (1861), 527 Callowhill Road (1862).

J. (JOSEPH) H. LAMBERT	PHILADELPHIA, PA	1862-1882

- Locations:
    527 Callowhill Road (1862-1864)
    1317 Ogden Street (1864-1869)
    employee of Horstmann Bros., 5th and Cherry Streets (1869-1873)
    105 North 5th Avenue (1873-1882)

JOSEPH H. LAMBERT & SON	PHILADELPHIA, PA	1882-1925

- Located at 105 North 5th Avenue.

(A) **LARRABEE (CHARLES ROLLIN)** **& NORTH (ROBERT L.)**	CHICAGO, IL	1857-1885

- Located at 174 Lake Street.
- Advertised in the *Army-Navy Journal* (November 28, 1883):
    Military goods
    Fine gold embroidery
    Presentation, dress, and service swords and sabers
    Fine cutlery, pistols, infantry trimmings, buttons, etc.

J.P. LASSERRE
(See J.P. Lassure in Maker listings)

(A) **R. (RALPH) P. LATHROP**	ALBANY, NY	1857-1862

- Located at 57 State Street.

STEELE (J.) & LATHROP (RALPH P.)	ALBANY, NY	1862-1867

- Located at 57 State Street.

(N) **J.H. LAW**	NEW YORK, NY	1775-1783

- Sold small swords and fencing foils.

(A) **SAMUEL P. LEIGHTON**	BOSTON, MA	1877-1890

- Located at 7 Temple Street.

BOSTON REGALIA CO.	BOSTON, MA	1890-1925

- President: Samuel P. Leighton.
- Located at 7 Temple Place.

(A) **H. (HENRY) G. LEISENRING**   PHILADELPHIA, PA   1859-1871
- Located at 222 Gold Street (1859-1864), 237-239 Dock Street (1864-1871).
- Had U.S. contract for 20,000 cavalry sabers at $7 each (1861).
- Built three factories to make the sabers, per a letter to Lt. T.J. Treadwell, ordnance officer, U.S. Frankford Arsenal.
- Delivered 25,433 sabers to the U.S. Frankford Arsenal near Philadelphia, PA (4,199 rejected; 21,234 accepted).
- No sabers are known with his name on them.

(A) **LEMON (JAMES INNES) & KENDRICK (WILLIAM)**   LOUISVILLE, KY   1832-1858
- Located at the corner of Main and Wall Streets.

    JAMES INNES LEMON & CO.   LOUISVILLE, KY   1858-1861
- Located at 535 Main Street.

    LEMON (JAMES INNES) & SON   LOUISVILLE, KY   1861-D1869
- Located at 279 Main Street (1861-1864), 73 Main Street (1864-1869).

(N) **H. (HEYMAN) LEON & CO.**   NEW YORK, NY   1861-1863
- Located at 20 Day Street.

    HEYMAN LEON & CO.   NEW YORK, NY   1863-1865
- Located at 49 Warren Street.
- Leon Heyman died (1865).

    THEDA HEYMAN   NEW YORK, NY   1865-1867
- Widow of Leon Heyman.
- Located at 16 College Road.
- Importer of English and German guns, pistols, and cutlery.

(A) **LEWECK (G.) & CAHN (T.)**   NEW YORK, NY   1855-1870
- Located at 283 Grand Street.

    G. LEWECK   NEW YORK, NY   1870-1877
- Located at 283 Grand Street.

(A) **EDWARD J. LEWIS**   BROOKLYN, NY   1851-1865
- Located at 111 High Street.

(A) **J. (JOHN) A. L'HOMMEDIEU**   MOBILE, AL   1834-D1867
- Locations:
  - 21 Dauphin Street (1834-1842)
  - Water and St. Francis Streets (1842-1855)
  - 54 Dauphin Street (1855-1867)
  - 30 Dauphin Street (1867)

(A) **CHARLES LIBEAU**   CINCINNATI, OH   1827-1829
- Located at 127 Main Street.

    VALENTINE G. & CHARLES LIBEAU   CINCINNATI, OH   1829-1831
- Located at 3rd and Main Street.

    CHARLES LIBEAU   CINCINNATI, OH   1831-D1862
- Located at 30 North 5th Street.

(A) **ROSE LIPP REGALIA & CO.**	BOSTON, MA	1910-1925

- Located at 74 Boyleston Street (1910-1914), 175 Tremont Street (1914-1925).

(A) **JOSEPH M. LITCHFIELD**	SAN FRANCISCO, CA	1849-1869
PURDY (ISREAL B.) & SON (CHARLES)	SAN FRANCISCO, CA	1869-1872

- Employee: Joseph M. Litchfield.
- Isreal retired (1872).

PURDY (CHARLES) & LITCHFIELD (JOSEPH M.)	SAN FRANCISCO, CA	1872-1874

- Located at 500-502 Washington Street.

J. (JOSEPH) M. LITCHFIELD	SAN FRANCISCO, CA	1874-1981

- Locations:
    - 500-502 Washington Street (1874-1878)
    - 415 Montgomery Street (1878-1886)
    - 12 Post Street (1886-1901)
    - 513 Golden Gate Avenue (1901-1981)

(N) **THEODORE C. LOCKERMAN**	PHILADELPHIA, PA	1869-D1880

- Locations:
    - 812 Arch Street (1869-1870)
    - 807 Arch Street (1870-1871)
    - 411 Arch Street (1871-1872)
    - 51 South 4th Street (1872-1873)
    - 318 York Street (1873-1880)

(Military goods and regalia, including swords)

(A) **C. (CHARLES) L. LOCKWOOD & CO.**	WASHINGTON, DC	1861-1867

- Located at 324 Pennsylvania Avenue.

LOCKWOOD (CHARLES L.), HUFTY (FRANCIS) & TAYLOR (R.H.)	WASHINGTON, DC	1867-1875

- Located at 324 Pennsylvania Avenue.

R.H. TAYLOR & FRANCIS HUFTY	WASHINGTON, DC	1875-1886

- Located at 324 Pennsylvania Avenue.

(Military outfitters)

(A) **L. (LORING) F. LOMBARD**	NEW YORK, NY	1861-1865

(A) **H.F. LOUDAN & CO.**	WASHINGTON, DC	1853-D1857

- Located at 362 Pennsylvania Avenue.
- Employee: Francis J. Heiberger.
- H.F. Loudan died (1857).

(A) **JOHN J. LOW**	BOSTON, MA	B1800-1822
PUTNAM (EDWARD) & LOW (JOHN J.)	BOSTON, MA	1822-1825

- Located at 35 Cornhill Street.

JOHN J. LOW	BOSTON, MA	1825-1838

- Located at 12 to 18 Washington Street.
- Advertised in the *Columbian Centinal* (1825):
    For sale from Liverpool England

*8 packages containing swords from Paris France,
Army swords, chapeaus, belts, chains, buttons and Navy swords.*

JONES (JOHN B.), LOW   **BOSTON, MA**   **1838-1840**
(JOHN J.) & BALL (S.S.)
- Located at 123 Washington Street.
- Advertised in the *Boston Atlas* (1840):
    *For sale, imported from Paris, France
    Army swords, chapeaus, belts, chains, buttons & Navy swords.*

(N) **J. (JOHN) P. LOWER**   **PHILADELPHIA, PA**   **B1833, 1851-1872**
     J. (JOHN) P. LOWER   **DENVER, CO**   **1872-D1915**
- Located at 281 Blake Street.
- Sold guns, Deringer pistols, and knives (including bowie knives).
    J.P. LOWER'S SONS   **DENVER, CO**   **1915-1920**
- Located at 1729 Champa Street.

(A) **JAMES LUCKEY**   **NEW YORK, NY**   **1875-1890**
- Two locations at 133 Grand Street and 19 Crosby Street.

(A) **EDMUND A. LUDLOW**   **FULTON, NY**   **1840-1856**
- Located at 153 Water Street.

(N) **LYNCH & KELLY**   **UTICA, NY**   **1865-1875**
- Sold fraternal swords.

(A) **MICHAEL MAGEE**   **PHILADELPHIA, PA**   **1800-1823**
     MICHAEL MAGEE   **PHILADELPHIA, PA**   **1823-1840**
- Located at 18 Decatur Street.
    MAGEE (MICHAEL) & CO.   **PHILADELPHIA, PA**   **1840-1859**
- Partners: N.B. Kneass, John B. George.
    MAGEE (MICHAEL) & KNEASS (N.B.)   **PHILADELPHIA, PA**   **1859-1865**
- Had a branch in New Orleans.
    MICHAEL MAGEE & CO.   **PHILADELPHIA, PA**   **1865-1872**
    MAGEE (MICHAEL) & GEORGE   **NEW ORLEANS, LA**   **1859-1865**
    (JOHN B.)
- Manager: John B. George.
- Assistant Manager: George Horton.

(N) **CHARLES H. MALLORY**   **NEW YORK, NY**   **1860-1916**
- Warehouse located at 56 South Street.
- Shop and office located at 153 Maiden Lane.
- Bought eight Roman swords and 14 cavalry swords from Schuyler, Hartley & Graham, New York (1868).
    E. (EDWARD) A. MALLORY & SONS INC.   **NEW YORK, NY**   **1916-1920**
- Located at 234 5^(th) Avenue.
- President: Charles H. Mallory.

(Military goods dealer)

(N) **JAMES MANNING & CO.**   **NEW YORK, NY**   **1795-1797**
- Located at 61 Front Street.
    JAMES MANNING   **NEW YORK, NY**   **1797-1808**
- Located at 23 Albany.

MANNING (JAMES) & RICHMOND (THOMAS)	NEW YORK, NY	1808-1815

- Merchant and military goods importer.
- Sold military goods and swords to local militia units.

(A) **SEREPHIM MASI**   WASHINGTON, DC   1822-1827
- Located at Pennsylvania Avenue (between 9th and 10th Streets).

(Jeweler)

    F. (FERDINAND) MASI & CO.   WASHINGTON, DC   1827-1834
- Located at Pennsylvania Avenue (between 9th and 10th Streets).
- Partner: Serephim Masi.

(Military and fancy store)

    S. (SEREPHIM) MASI   WASHINGTON, DC   1827-1834
- Located at Pennsylvania Avenue (between 4th and 6th Streets).

(Jeweler)

    F. FERDINAND) & S. (SEREPHIM) MASI   WASHINGTON, DC   1834-1855
- Located at Pennsylvania Avenue (between 4th and 6th Streets).

(Jeweler, military and fancy store)

(A) **MASONIC FURNISHINGS & CO.**   NEW YORK, NY   1870-1875
- Located at 52 Bleeker Street.

(N) **JOHN H. McALPINE**   ST. LOUIS, MO   1860-1866
- Located at 52 Olive Street.

    J. (JOHN) H. McALPINE   ST. LOUIS, MO   1866-1880
- Located at 316 Olive Street.

(Military tailor, uniforms, military goods)

(A) **J. (JOHN) B. McFADDEN**   PITTSBURGH, PA   1830-1850
- Located at 85 Market Street.

    JOHN B. McFADDEN & SON (JAMES B.)   PITTSBURGH, PA   1850-1865
- Located at 95 Market Street.

(N) **JOHN McFARLANE**   SALEM, MA   1790-1796
    JOHN McFARLANE   BOSTON, MA   1796-1811
    McFARLANE (JOHN), FLETCHER (THOMAS & CHARLES) & GARDINER (BALDWIN & SIDNEY)   BOSTON, MA   1811-1812

(Silversmith, military goods, sword hiltor)
(See Thomas Fletcher)

(N) **J. (JOHN) & H. (HORACE) MEACHAM**   ALBANY, NY   1812-1827
- Located at 104 State Street (1812-1820), 84 State Street (1820-1827).

    MEACHAM (JOHN & HORACE) & POND (S.B.)   ALBANY, NY   1827-1832
- Located at 84 State Street.

    MEACHAM & CO.   ALBANY, NY   1832-1860
- Partners: Horace Meacham, son Roswell S. Meacham.

- Located at 84 State Street (1832-1848), 7 Pear Street (1848-1860).
- Advertised military goods, including pistols, 200 infantry officer swords, and 200 artillery and cavalry officer swords (1831).

(Importer and dealer in military goods, swords, and musical instruments)

(A) MEAD (EDWARD EDMUND)   ST. LOUIS, MO   1831-1842
     & ADRIANCE (EDWIN)
- Located at the corner of Pine and 1st Streets.

     EDWARD EDMUND MEAD   ST. LOUIS, MO   1842-1864
- Located at 82 Market Street (1842-1852), Main and Pine Street (1852-1864).

(Dealer in military and fancy goods, clocks, watches, jewelry, cutlery)

(A) J. (JAMES) AMBROSE MERRILL   PORTLAND, ME   1830-1851
     JAMES APPLETON & CO.   PORTLAND, ME   1851-1853
- Partner: James Ambrose Merrill.

     MERRILL J. (JAMES AMBROSE)   PORTLAND, ME   1853-1856
     & QUIMBY (M.)
- Located at 129-131 Middle Street.

     J. AMBROSE MERRILL   PORTLAND, ME   1856-1869
- Located at 129-131 Middle Street (1856-1860), 139 Middle Street (1860-1869).

     J. MERRILL & CO.   PORTLAND, ME   1869-1965
- Locations:
    139 Middle Street (1869-1873)
    299 Middle Street (1873-1889)
    503 Congress Street (1889-1965)

(A) JAMES H. MERRILL   WASHINGTON, DC   B1816-1840
     JAMES H. MERRILL   BALTIMORE, MD   1840-1856
- Located on the corner of South and Pratt Streets (1840-1845), 65 South Street (1845-1856).

     MERRILL (JAMES H.),   BALTIMORE, MD   1856-1861
     LATROBE (FERDINAND C. & JOHN H.B.)
     & THOMAS (PHILIP E. & LEWEN W.)
- Located at 6 Hanover Street.

     MERRILL (JAMES H.),   BALTIMORE, MD   1861-1869
     THOMAS (PHILIP E. & LEWEN W.) & CO.
- Called Merrill Patent Fire Arm Mfg. Co.
- Located at 239 W. Baltimore Street.
- Had U.S. government contract for 14,495 Merrill carbines and 583 Merrill rifles (January 1861 to June 1866).
- Also made Starr Deringers with four barrels.

(N) MERWIN (JOSEPH) & CO.   WASHINGTON, DC   1861-1865
- Located at 354 Pennsylvania Avenue.

(Military outfitters)

(A) JOHN C. METCALF   NEW YORK, NY   1843-1845
- Located at 37 Ferry (at the corner of Cliff Street) (1843-1844), 36 Maiden Lane (1844-1845).

     METCALF (JOHN C.) & SMITH (THOMAS)   NEW YORK, NY   1845-1846
- Located at 36 Maiden Lane.

(A) **J. (JAMES) MEYER**   NEW YORK, NY   1861-1865
- Located at 408 Broadway.

(A) **N. (NATHAN) S. MEYER**   NEW YORK, NY   1875-1920
- Located at 79 5th Avenue.

N.S. MEYER INC.   NEW YORK, NY   1920-1998
- Locations:
  - 103 5th Avenue (1920-1924)
  - 43 Elgin Street (1924-1934)
  - 419 4th Avenue (1934-1998)

(A) **S. (SIMON) N. MEYER**   WASHINGTON, DC   1871-1902
- Locations:
  - 405 and 621 4 1/2 Street (1871-1875)
  - 525 4 1/2 Street (1875-1877)
  - 922 7th Street (1877-1898)
  - 1141 Pennsylvania Avenue (1898-1900)
  - 1411 Pennsylvania Avenue (1900-1902)

MEYER (SIMON N.) MILITARY SHOP   WASHINGTON, DC   1902-1930
- Locations:
  - 1231 Pennsylvania Avenue (1902-1909)
  - 1327 "F" Street (1909-1916)
  - 1339 "F" Street (1916-1930)

(N) **JULIUS MEYER**   OMAHA, NE   1830-1840
- Located at 170 Farnham Street (at the corner of 11th Street).
- Dealer in Indian items such as tomahawks, bow and arrows, moccasins, clothing, beadwork, and wigwams.

(A) **MILITARY STORES & SPONGE FACTORY**   PHILADELPHIA, PA   1795-1800
- Located at 14 Chesnut Street.

(A) **MILLER (JOHN) & CO**   NEW YORK, NY   1863-1868
- Located at 9 Maiden Street.
- Advertised in the *Army-Navy Journal* (July 30, 1864):
  > *Manufacturers and importers of military goods*
  > *Offer to the trade and military public generally a full stock of:*
  > *Foreign and American swords (gold and gilt)*
  > *Presentation swords*

Passants	*Embroideries*	*Laces*
Belts	*Sashes*	*Cords*
Hats	*Plumes*	*Sword knots*
Caps	*Chevrons*	*Gauntlets*
Gloves	*Money belts*	*Field glasses*
Drum flasks	*Haversacks*	*Traveling bags*
Metallic ornaments	*Revolvers*	*Metallic straps*

MILLER (JOHN) & WILSON (ERASTUS E.)   NEW YORK, NY   1868-1871
- Located at 25 St. John Street.
- John Miller died (1871).

(N) **JOHN P. MILNOR**   BALTIMORE, MD   1860-1865
- Located at 347 Lexington Street (1860-1863), 117 Baltimore Street (1863-1865).
- Advertised military goods of every description, including pistols and swords.

(A) **PETER MINTZER**   PHILADELPHIA, PA   1818-1840
- Located at 83 North 3rd Street.

(Military goods, brass button maker, sword dealer)

     WILLIAM G. MINTZER   PHILADELPHIA, PA   1840-1869
- Son of Peter Mintzer.
- Located at 83 North Street (1840-1857), 131 North 3rd Street (1857-1869).

(Military goods, sword dealer)

(A) **CHARLES H. MOELLER**   ST. LOUIS, MO   1850-1865
- Located at 7 North 4th Street.
- Advertised as a fancy and variety store and seller of toys and military goods.

(N) **N. (NICHOLAS) C.D. MOLLER & CO.**   NEW YORK, NY   1831-1836
- Located at 69 Pearl Street (1831-1834), 52 South Street (1834-1836).

     MOLLER (NICHOLAS C.D.) &   NEW YORK, NY   1836-1838
     OPPENHEIMER (JOHN)
- Located at 52 South Street (1836-1837), 207 Water Street (1837-1838).
- Sold M1832 foot artillery short swords.

(Merchants and military goods)

(A) **MORGAN (JAMES G.), PUHL**   DETROIT, MI   1892-1903
     (EMIL P.) & MORRIS (CHARLES P.)
- Located at 102 Woodward Avenue (1892-1902), 47-49 Grand River Road (1902-1903).

(A) **ALEXANDER C. (CHASER) MORIN**   PHILADELPHIA, PA   1810-1874
- Located at 91 North 3rd Street (1810-1845), 618 Market Street (1845-1874).
- Morin died (1878).

(A) **JOHN MORIN**   PHILADELPHIA, PA   1790-D1833
- Located at 77 North 3rd Street.

(A) **I.M. MOSS & BROTHERS**   PHILADELPHIA, PA   1855-1860
- Located at 125 4th Street.

(N) **H. (HENRY) J. MULLAN & CO.**   NEW ORLEANS, LA   1866-1883
- Two locations at 52 Canal Street and 69 and 71 Common Street.
- Advertised as importer and dealer in hardware, cutlery, guns, and pistols.

(N) **ASA MUNGER**   HERKIMER, NY   B1778, 1798-1818
     ASA MUNGER   AUBURN, NY   1818-1826
     MUNGER (ASA) & BENEDICT (J.H.)   AUBURN, NY   1826-1838
- Advertised military goods; gilt and plated watches; steel-, silver-, and brass-mounted swords, horseman pistols, pocket pistols, flutes, and fifes (1830).

     A. (ASA) MUNGER & SON   AUBURN, NY   1838-1846

(Silversmith, watchmaker, sword hiltor, military goods)

(N) **SYLVESTER MUNGER**   ONONDAGA, NY   1820-1824

MUNGER (SYLVESTER) & DODGE (ABRAHAM JR.)	ITHACA, NY	1824-1830
MUNGER (SYLVESTER) & PRATT (DANIEL)	ITHACA, NY	1830-1835

- Advertised jewelry, military, and fancy goods (1831).
- Located on Owego Street.

SYLVESTER MUNGER	ITHACA, NY	1835-1839
JAMES E. MUNGER	ITHACA, NY	1839-1845

(Silversmith, military and fancy goods)

(A) **GEORGE MYERS** — ST. LOUIS, MO — 1845-1856
- Located at 23 Vine Street.

(A) **CHARLES NAYLOR** — PHILADELPHIA, PA — 1870-1923
- Located at 110 North 5th Street.

(A) **NEWBOULD (JOHN A.) & RUSSELL (A. THOMAS)** — NEW YORK, NY — 1843-1845
- Located at 140 Fulton Street.
- Advertised imported hardware, cutlery, guns, and pistols (1844).

(A) **WASHINGTON NOEL** — LOUISVILLE, KY — 1830-D1838
- Located at Main Street (between 3rd and 4th Streets).

(A) **NOELL (LOUIS) & OELBERMANN (EMIL)** — NEW YORK, NY — 1861-1865
- Located at 54 Barclay Street (1861-1862), 105 Reade Street (1862-1865).

(A) **DANIEL NORCROSS & CO.** — SAN FRANCISCO, CA — 1849-1890
- Located at 6 Post Street.

(A) **OAK HALL CLOTHING** — BOSTON, MA — 1861-1913
- Trade name of George W. Simmons.

(See George W. Simmons)

(A) **FREDERICK OAKES** — HARTFORD, CT — 1820-1842
- Located at 132 Main Street (1820-1838), 194 Main Street (1838-1842).

FREDERICK & WILLIAM OAKES — HARTFORD, CT — 1842-1848
- Located at 184-194 Main Street.

FREDERICK OAKES & SON — HARTFORD, CT — 1848-D1855
- Located at 184-194 Main Street.

(A) **CHARLES OAKFORD & SONS** — PHILADELPHIA, PA — 1862-1865
- Advertised during the Civil War:
    The fashionable hatters, Nos. 834 and 836 Chesnut Street under the Continental Hotel, have now in store a superb assortment of fine military trappings for army and navy officers, hats, caps, swords, belts, saches, etc. to which we invite the attention of our military readers.

(N) **CHARLES N. OEHM** — BALTIMORE, MD — 1858-1867
- Located at 150 Light Street.

CHARLES N. OEHM & CO. — BALTIMORE, MD — 1867-1868
- Located at 150 Light Street.

CHARLES N. OEHM & BRO. (FRANZ F.)	BALTIMORE, MD	1868-1875

- Located at 150 Light Street.

C. (CHARLES) N. OEHM	BALTIMORE, MD	1875-1878

- Located at 150 Light Street.

C. (CHARLES) N. OEHM & SON (CHARLES H.)	BALTIMORE, MD	1878-1887

- Located at 230 Pratt (1878-1886), 55 and 123 Hanover Street and 230 Pratt Street (1886-1887)

OELM (CHARLES N. & CHARLES H.) & CO.	BALTIMORE, MD	1887-1912

- Called the Acme Hall Clothing Company.
- Locations:
    5 W. Baltimore Street (1887-1889)
    5 and 7 W. Baltimore Street (1889-1896)
    1 to 7 W. Baltimore Street (1896-1900)
    5 and 7 W. Baltimore Street (1900-1904)
    16 W. Lexington Street (1904-1910)
    110 E. Baltimore Street (1910-1912)
- Charles N. Oelm left the company (1909).
- During the Civil War, advertised Army-Navy officer swords, buttons, uniforms, and "equipment for the armed forces."

(A) **SAMUEL W. OWENS**	WASHINGTON, D.C.	1864-1869

- Located at 212 Pennsylvania Avenue.

OWENS (SAMUEL W.) & PUGH (JOHN)	WASHINGTON, D.C.	1869-1875

- Located at 212 Pennsylvania Avenue.

(N) **WILLIAM G. PADDOCK**	ALBANY, NY	1855-1881

- Clerk at R.H. Scott Co. (1877-1881).

WILLIAM G. PADDOCK	ALBANY, NY	1881-1885

- Bought out R.H. Scott Co.
- Located at 60 State Street.
- Advertised guns, military goods, swords, and regalia.

(A) **JOHN PARKES**	NEW YORK, NY	1850-1868

- Locations:
    198 Fulton Street (1850-1858)
    178 Fulton Street (1858-1864)
    188 Fulton Street (1864-1868)

(A) **TIMOTHY P. PARSON & SONS**	ST. LOUIS, MO	1866-1883

- Sons: Timothy T., John, and William J. Parson.

TIMOTHY T. & JOHN PARSON	ST. LOUIS, MO	1883-1897
TIMOTHY T. PARSON	ST. LOUIS, MO	1897-1910

(A) **B. PASQUALE CO.**	SAN FRANCISCO, CA	1879-1980

- Located at 115-117 Post Street (1908-1980).

(N) **THOMAS PASSMORE & CO.**	PHILADELPHIA, PA	1805-1810

- Located at 172 High Street.

(Tin manufacturer)

THOMAS PASSMORE   PHILADELPHIA, PA   1810-1811
- Located at 34 South Frost.

(Iron dealer)

PASSMORE (THOMAS) & SPERRY   PHILADELPHIA, PA   1811-1815
(FREDERICK W.)
- Located at 34 South Frost.
- Commercial merchants and auctioneers.
- John Joseph Henry (Philadelphia, PA) consigned 450 cutlasses at $3.50 each to Passmore & Sperry (1812).
- Frederick W. Sperry was a merchant located at 101 South Front.

(N) **J&E PHILLIPS**   BOSTON, MA   1810-1826
- Located at 2 Kilby Street, Phillips Building.
- Advertised in the *Columbian Centinal* cutlery, pocket knives, hardware, iron wire, and brass ware from England (November 25, 1812).

(A) **E.C. PHILLIPS**   BOSTON, MA   1900-1919
- Located at 202-203 Masonic Street.

(A) **A. (ADOLPHUS) J. PLATE**   SAN FRANCISCO, CA   1849-1863
- Located at 103 Commercial Street (1849-1859), 507 Commercial Street (1859-1863).

A. (ADOLPHUS) J. PLATE & CO.   SAN FRANCISCO, CA   1863-1885
- Locations:
    411 Sansome Street (1863-1867)
    510 Sacramento Street (1867-1879)
    325 Montgomery Street (1879-1882)
    418 and 420 Market Street (1882-1883)
    101 Powell Street (1883-1885)
- Employed Charles Schlotterback as a gunsmith.
- Listed in the city directory as an importer of guns, swords, trimmings and sporting materials (1863).
- Advertised in the *Army-Navy Journal* as manufacturers and importers of helmets, caps, chapeaux, belts, swords, and trimmings (1880).
- Partners: William B. Cottrell, John Wolfe, son Henry J. Plate

(A) **E.M. PLATT**   BOSTON, MA   1875-1897
- Located at 139 Court Street.

(Hatter, military goods)

(N) **JOHN R. PLATT**   NEW YORK, NY   1861-1865
- Located at 79 Murrey.

(Merchant and importer of bowie knives, military goods, and glassware)

(N) **ROBERT PLUMACHER**   NEW YORK, NY   1889-1896
- Located at 227 E. 74th Street (1889-1895), 314 E. 75th Street (1895-1896)

ROBERT PLUMACHER & SONS   NEW YORK, NY   1896-1930
- Sons: August and Robert Jr.
- Locations:
    314 E. 75th Street (1896-1897)
    341 E. 59th Street (1897-1910)
    344 E. 59th Street (1910-1930)

(Silversmith, plater, sword hiltor, military goods)

(N) **MATTHEW PLUMSTEAD**   BATH, ME   1820-1830
- Located on Washington Street.
- Advertised sword belts, swords, helmets, harnesses, and military equipment.

MATTHEW PLUMSTEAD   PORTLAND, ME   1830-1840

(A) **EDWARD POLE**   PHILADELPHIA, PA   1760-1800
- Located at 34-36 Dock Street.

(Auctioneer, military accouterment supplier)

(A) **ABNER W. POLLARD**   BOSTON, MA   1833-1863
- Locations:
    - 6 Ann Street (1833-1834)
    - 34 Merchant Street (1834-1835)
    - 36 Merchant Street (1835-1837)
    - 31 Merchant Street (1837-1847)
    - 6 Court Street (1847-1863)
- An Abner W. Pollard business card shows the following:

    A.W. Pollard merchant tailor
    Manufacturers of costumes and regalia
    Also dealer in;
    - *Military cloths and trimmings*
    - *U.S. Regulation swords*
    - *Epaulets*
    - *Saches*
    - *Laces, stars and emblems*
    - *Regalia*
    - *Theatrical costuming articles*
    - *Theatrical battle swords*
    - *Fencing foils and masks*
    - *Banner silks, fringes and tassels*
    - *U.S. Flags and decorations*
    - *Jewels for all the "orders"*
    - *Masonic books*
    - *Masonic carpets*

A. (ABNER) W. POLLARD & CO.   BOSTON, MA   1863-1866
- Located at 6 Court Street.
- Advertised in the *Army-Navy Journal* (July 30, 1864):

    Military and Navy equipments on hand and made to order to elegant style, consisting of:

Swords	*Epaulettes*	*Cords*
Sashes	*Gauntlets*	*Laces*
Belts	*Shoulder Straps*	*Buttons*
Spurs	*Embroideries*	*Binding*

    Silk and bunting, flags, guidons and standards
    Masonic and odd fellows regalia
    Military and masonic books

POLLARD (ABNER) & LEIGHTON (SAMUEL P.)   BOSTON, MA   1866-1875
- Located at 6 Court Street (1866-1867), 104 Tremont Street (1867-1875).

POLLARD (ABNER) & ALFORD (FREDERICK)   BOSTON, MA   1875-1890

- Locations:
    - 22 West Street (1875-1879)
    - 58 Temple Street (1879-1888)
    - 65 Franklin Street (1888-1889)
    - 10 Temple Street (1889-1890)

(A) **JOHN PONDIR**　　　　　　　　　　　　PHILADELPHIA, PA　　　　　　1861-1865
- Located at 1134 Callowhill.

(Importer and merchant)

(A) **NATHANIEL C. POOR**　　　　　　　　BOSTON, MA　　　　　　　　　B1808-1837

NATHANIEL C. POOR &　　　　　　　　　BOSTON, MA　　　　　　　　　1837-1838
STEPHEN S. STONE
- Located at 98 Washington Street.

NATHANIEL C. POOR　　　　　　　　　　BOSTON, MA　　　　　　　　　1838-1840
- Located at 98 Washington Street.

LOWS (R.) BALL (S.S.) & CO.　　　　　　BOSTON, MA　　　　　　　　　1840-1846
- Partner: Nathaniel C. Poor.
- Located at 123 Washington Street.

JONES (JOHN B.), BALL (S.S.)　　　　　　BOSTON, MA　　　　　　　　　1846-1856
& POOR (NATHANIEL C.)
- Located at 226 Washington Street.

NATHANIEL C. POOR　　　　　　　　　　BOSTON, MA　　　　　　　　　1856-D1895

(N) **CHARLES POORE**　　　　　　　　　　NEW YORK, NY　　　　　　　　1810-1820
- New York sales agent for sword maker Nathan Starr, Middleton, CT.
- Consigned 184 Nathan Starr cavalry sabers with iron hilts and scabbards to George H. Beck, master of the schooner *Dash* (April 5, 1815). Beck was to sell the sabers in Cartegenia, Colombia (seaport).
- Starr told Poore that if the sabers sold well, he could provide large quantities at $8 each or cheaper cavalry sabers at $6 each.
- Poore wrote Starr, saying that Beck needed more cavalry sabers (early July 1815).
- Starr wrote Poore that he could furnish Beck 500 cavalry sabers at $6 each or small swords at $3 each (July 20, 1815).

(A) **JOSEPH S. PORTER**　　　　　　　　　UTICA, NY　　　　　　　　　　1817-1842
- Located at 46 Genessee Street.

(N) **POULTNEY (THOMAS) & TRIMBLE**　　BALTIMORE, MD　　　　　　　1860-1876
　　(DAVID B.)
- Located at 200 W. Baltimore Street.

(Gunsmith, hardware, fishing tackle, cutlery dealer)

(N) **EDGAR PRAY**　　　　　　　　　　　　NEW YORK, NY　　　　　　　　1840-1845
- Located at 56 Frankfort (same address as Henry A. Dingee).

(Military store and military equipment, including swords)

(N) **PRENTISS (JOHN M.) & CARTER**　　　BALTIMORE, MD　　　　　　　1812-1815
　　(ROBERT)
- Located at 13 Boyley's Wharf.
- Advertised military goods including swords (1814).

(A) **GEORGE RAPHAEL**   PHILADELPHIA, PA   1849-1862
- Located at 109 South Front Street.

    GEORGE RAPHAEL & CO.   PHILADELPHIA, PA   1862-1865
- Located at 109 South Front Street.

(A) **RAYMOLD (WILLIAM A.) & WHITLOCK (BENJAMIN M.)**   NEW YORK, NY   1881-1891
- Located at 39 W. 14th Street (1881-1886), 99 W. 4th Street (1886-1891).

(A) **JOSEPH RAYNES & CO.**   LOWELL, MA   1835-1865
- Located at 43 Central Street. ("Tyler's block")
- Advertised in the *Army-Navy Journal* as follows:

    Swords, belts, sashes, etc.—the largest assortment in Lowell.
    We can show you swords of a half a dozen different makers including the Chelmsford sword manufactured by C. Roby & Co. West Chelmsford.
    We have all kinds of military goods direct from the manufacturers and can sell at the lowest cash prices.

(A) **LANE (THOMAS) & READ (WILLIAM)**   BOSTON, MA   1825-1849
- Locations:
    17 Dock Square (1825-1828)
    24 Merchants Row (1828-1831)
    6 Market Street (1831-1849)

    WILLIAM READ   BOSTON, MA   1850-1854
- Located at 6 Market Street.

    WILLIAM READ & SON   BOSTON, MA   1855-1868
- Located at 6 Market Street.

    WILLIAM READ & SONS   BOSTON, MA   1869-1910
- Located at 17 Dock Square (1869-1888), 107 Washington Street (1888-1910).

(A) **REDDING (N.W.) & CO.**   NEW YORK, NY   1859-1923
- Locations:
    212 Broadway (1859-1885)
    200 Fifth Street (1885-1891)
    721 Broadway (1891-1923)

(N) **R.M.J. REED**   PHILADELPHIA, PA   1882-1945
- Locations:
    918-922 Chestnut Street (1882-1897)
    1412-1414 Chestnut Street (1897-1906)
    1426 Chestnut Street (1906-1945)

(A) **JACOB REED'S SONS**   PHILADELPHIA, PA   1877-1882
- Located at 2nd and Spruce Street.

(N) **F.G. REINEMAN**   PITTSBURGH, PA   1882-1900
- Locations:
    54 6th Street (1862-1884)
    52 6th Street (1884-1896)
    214 6th Street (1896-1900)
- Advertised regalia, including swords and military, police, and fireman's goods (1896).

(A) H. (HARMON) G. REYNOLDS	SPRINGFIELD, IL	1860-1870

- Located at 25 South Street.

(N) **WALTER A. RHODES**   **NEW YORK, NY**   1903-1907
- Located at 43-45 E. 19th Street (1903-1906), 27 E. 21st Street (1906-1907).

RHODES UNIFORM CO.   **NEW YORK, NY**   1907-1908
- President: Walter A. Rhodes.
- Located at 27 E. 21st Street.
- Sold M1902 saber for all officers.

(Uniforms and military goods)

(N) **HENRY RICE**   **BOSTON, MA**   1810-1820
- Located at 2 Union Street.
- Advertised cutlery, pocket knives, pocket holster, pistols, saddlery, hardware, and tools in the *Columbian Centinal* (November 25, 1812).

(A) **RICHARDS (STEPHEN), UPSON (GEORGE) & CO.**   **NEW YORK, NY**   1808-1816
- Located at 145 Pearl Street.

(A) **JAMES A. RIDABOCK & CO.**   **NEW YORK, NY**   1888-1966
- Showroom located at 141 Grand Avenue.
- Factory locations:
    141 Grand Avenue (1888-1899)
    112 W. 4th Street (1899-1909)
    149-151 W. 36th Street (1909-1928)
    251 6th Street (1928-1931)
    65-67 Madison Avenue (1931-1966)
- In a 1931 Ridabock & Co. catalog, the following merchandise is listed:

    Manufacturers and importers of the finest quality presentation swords and sabers.
    Imported presentation swords by the best sword factory in Europe
    Manufacturers of
        Privates helmets—artillery, cavalry and infantry
        Fatigue caps
        Artillery and cavalry sabers
        Sabers belts
        Webbing and leather infantry equipment
        Gun slings
        Shoulder knots and epaulettes
        Chevrons
        Metal shoulder scales
        Leggings
        Knapsacks, haversacks and canteens
        Bearskin shakos
        Fur body and cloth covered dress hats
        Worsted pompons
        Feather, horse and buffalo hair plumes
        Army duck helmets
        Steel bayonet scabbards
        Roman, Lancer and Dragoon helmets

Regimental and bunting flags
Gold and silver lace and cords

(A) **RUFUS R. RIKER**   MONTPELIER, VT   1840-1850
- Advertised *"Will furnish military goods of every description for militia companies"* (1843).

(N) **H. (HORACE) H. (HALL) ROWELL**   COLUMBIA, CA   B1830, 1856-1870
    H.H. ROWELL   SAWMILL FLAT, CA   1870-1875
    H.H. ROWELL   SONOMA, CA   1875-1909
- Sold military goods, including bowie knives.

(A) **BENJAMIN RUSSELL**   BALTIMORE, MD   1861-1865
- Located at 293 W. Baltimore Street.

(A) **GUSTAVUS S. SACCHI**   NEW YORK, NY   1860-1882
- Located at 45 William Street.

(A) **AMOS SANBORN**   LOWELL, MA   1860-1875
- Located at 25 Central Street.

(A) **JACOB SARGEANT**   HARTFORD, CT   B1761, 1795-D1843
- Moved from Silversmith listing.
- Located on Main Street.
- Advertised as jeweler, watch and clock maker, and seller of military goods, including swords and hangers (short swords) (1810-1811).

(A) **WILLIAM J. SAVAGE**   COLUMBUS, OH   1845-1880
- Located at 83 High Street (1845-1860), 197 South 3rd Street (1860-1880).

(A) **WILLIAM SAYERS**   NEW YORK, NY   1840-1853
- Located at 58 Hudson Street.
    SAYERS (WILLIAM) & LENT (JAMES H.)   NEW YORK, NY   1853-1856
- Located at 143 Fulton Street.
    WILLIAM SAYERS   NEW YORK, NY   1856-1858
- Located at 143 Fulton Street.

(N) **SCHAEFFER (RINEHART) & LONEY (FRANCIS B.)**   BALTIMORE, MD   1847-1868
- Located at 1 and 3 Hanover Street.

(Gunsmith, importer of hardware, guns, and cutlery)

(A) **G. (GRAHAM) A. & E. (ERNEST) SCHEIDT**   NEW YORK, NY   1858-1862
- Located at 2 and 4 Platt Street.

(A) **PHILLIP & LEWIS SCHIFFLIN**   NEW YORK, NY   1861-1863
- Located at 95 William Street.
    GEORGE P. SCHIFFLIN   NEW YORK, NY   1863-1865
- Located at 95 William Street.

(A) **CHARLES F. SCHMIDT** NEW YORK, NY 1861-1885
- Located at 38 Beaver Street.

ADDITIONAL FACTS IN THE HISTORY OF
SCHUYLER, HARTLEY, & GRAHAM, NEW YORK, NY

JACOB RUTSEN SCHUYLER
- Born in Belleville, NY (1815).
- Joined Young (Henry), Smith (William H.) & Co. New York, NY (1838-1843) and Young & Smith (1843-1846).
- Became a partner in Young & Smith (1846) and William H. Smith & Co. (1846-1854).
- Became a partner in Schuyler (Jacob Rutsen), Hartley (Marcellus) & Graham (Malcohm) (1854-1878).
- Schuyler retired (1878).
- Jacob Rutsen Schuyler died (February 5, 1887).

MARCELLUS HARTLEY
- Born in New York, NY (1828).
- Joined Francis Tomes & Son (1847-1854).
- Became head of their sporting guns department.
- Became partner in Schuyler, Hartley, & Graham. Handled the gun business (1854-1878).
- During the Civil War (1861-1865), Hartley was a U.S. government agent purchasing arms and munitions in Europe as a brigadier general.
- Partner in Hartley & Graham (1878-1899).
- Opened his own company, called Hartley & Co. (1899-1902).
- Marcellus Hartley died (January 19, 1902).

MALCOLM GRAHAM
- Born in New York, NY (1832).
- Became a partner in Young & Smith (1846) and William H. Smith & Co. (1846-1854).
- Became a partner in Schuyler, Hartley & Graham (1854-1878).
- A partner in Hartley & Graham (1878-1899).
- Malcolm Graham died (December 19, 1899).

SCHUYLER (JACOB RUTSEN), NEW YORK, NY 1854-1878
HARTLEY (MARCELLUS) & GRAHAM (MALCOLM)
- Advertised in the *Army-Navy Journal* (September 5, 1863):
    Located at 19 Maiden Lane.
    Importers, manufacturers and dealers in rifles, guns and every description of military and naval goods.
    Enfield rifles and all of celebrated American and Foreign makes.
    U.S. Regulation swords
    Sashes, belts, epaulettes, spurs, laces, braid
    Sword knots, military trimmings, etc.
    Presentation swords of original designs constantly on hand and made to order
    A full assortment of field glasses
    Horse equipments of every description
- Advertised as importers and manufacturers of military goods, guns and pistols, and fancy goods in the Schuyler, Hartley & Graham 1864 catalog (largest Civil War catalog). The catalog listed the following items:
1) *Rich presentation swords for army officers, including general officers, field and line officers and cavalry officers*
2) *U.S. regulation swords for all branches*
3) *Masonic swords*

4) *Sword knots*
5) *Sword belts*
6) *Gauntlets*
7) *Belt plates*
8) *Chapeaux, hats and caps*
9) *Plated numbers and letters*
10) *Hat cords*
11) *Knapsacks*
12) *Cartridge box, belt, bayonet sheath sets*
13) *Overcoat and bed pack slings*
14) *Shoulder knots*
15) *Ornaments within crescents of epaulettes*
16) *Ornaments on strap of epaulettes*
17) *Epaulettes*
18) *Shoulder straps*
19) *Embroidered ornaments*
20) *Hat and cap ornaments*
21) *Sleeve rank trimmings*
22) *Army Corps badges*
23) *Cord, lace and binding*
24) *Buttons*
25) *Candlesticks*
26) *Camp knives*
27) *Canteens and flasks*
28) *Spurs*
29) *Head pieces and tassels for flag pole*
30) *Sashes*
31) *Fencing swords and masks*
32) *Bugles*
33) *Aiguilettes*
34) *Saddles, with all accessories*
35) *Sabretashes*
36) *Bridles*
37) *Bits*
38) *Drums*
39) *Field glasses*
40) *Medals*
41) *Fine sword blades from Solingen, Prussia*
42) *Damascus blades*
43) *Sword cases*
44) *Overcoat throgs, braid and cord*
45) *Masonic goods, tassels and fringes*
46) *Shotguns*
   William Greener—laminated steel
   Lefaucheux—breech loading
   Poultrey & Sneider—breech loading
   Sharps
   Colt
47) *Shotgun cartridges*
48) *Rifles*

    Sharps—octagon and round barrel
    Enfield with sword bayonet
    United States flint lock musket—socket bayonet
    United States percussion musket—socket bayonet
    United States Mississippi
    Ballard—breech loading
    Henry—repeating
    Spencer's—breech loading
    Smith's—breech loading
    French Flobert
    Colts—revolving
    F. Wesson—breech loading

49) *Rifle ammunition*
50) *Carbines*
    Sharps—rifled, with sabre bayonet
    Burnside—breech loading
    Joslyn
    Maynard—breech loading
    Spencers—breech loading
    Smiths—breech loading
    Colt
    Gallager—breech loading
51) *Carbine ammunition*
52) *Pocket Flasks*
53) *Pistol belts*
54) *Pistol holsters*
55) *Pistols*
    Colt revolving—new model
    Colt pocket—revolving
    Colt navy—revolving
    Colt holster—revolving
    Colt revolving—old model
    Colt pocket—revolving
    Colt belt—Army-Navy, revolving
    Colt holster—revolving
    Colt saloon—single shot
    Colt breech—single shot
    Smith & Wesson breech loading—revolving
    Moore—single shot
    Sharps patent—revolving barrel
    Remington Navy and Army—revolving
    Lefaucheax—revolving
    Rider—revolving
    Moore—revolving
    Bacon—revolving
    Elliot—4 barrel breech loading
    Starr—4 barrel breech loading
    Adams—revolving
    Slocum—revolving
    Tranter—revolving

Rupenter—barrel revolving
Allen—revolving
Lefaucheaux—barrel revolving
Deringer—pocket
Lefaucheaux—2 barrel breech loading
Pond—revolving

56) Pistol ammunition

- Schuyler, Hartley & Graham had a military goods depot at 41 Broadway, New York, NY (May 20, 1868-April 24, 1873).
- The depot purchased, warehoused, and shipped military goods.
- It also shipped to many foreign countries, including Japan, China, Liberia, France, Mexico, Columbia, Bolivia, Chile, Peru, Venezuela, Costa Rica, Cuba, Dominican Republic, Ecuador, Haiti, Honduras, and El Salvador.
- Sent eight Roman swords (short artillery swords) and 14 cavalry swords to C.H. Mallory & Co., New York, NY (June 29, 1868).
- Sent a steel-hilted saber (sample) to Yokohama, Japan (September 30, 1868).
- Sent 50 iron-hilt cutlasses and 100 Roman swords (short artillery swords) to Cuba (January 23, 1869).
- Sent 150 German-made heavy cavalry sabers to Argentina (December 1, 1871).
- Advertised in the *Army-Navy Journal* (April 21, 1869): *19 Maiden Lane, NY*
    Importers and dealers in military goods, society, church, and theatrical goods, embroideries, laces, breech loading guns and pistols.
- A Schuyler, Hartley & Graham trade card from 1873 reads:
    Importers and manufacturers of guns, rifles, pistols and sporting articles
    19 Maiden Lane and 22 John Street—New York
    Colts and Smith & Wesson's revolvers
    Metallic cartridges
    Deringer and breech loading pistols
    Eley's wads and cartridges
    Dixon's and Hawkeley's flasks and pouches
    Genuine French G.D. percussion caps
    Fine guns and rifles manufactured and imported to order
- A Schuyler, Hartley & Graham trade card from 1875 reads:
    Military goods, guns, pistols, cutlery, plated wares, jewelry, fancy goods, druggists sundries.

(A) **R. (RICHARD) H. &** ALBANY, NY 1842-1871
W. (WILLIAM) J. SCOTT

- Locations:
    60 State Street (1842-1845)
    3 Beaver Street (1845-1850)
    9 Beaver Street (1850-1862)
    60 State Street (1862-1871)
- Advertised as a gunsmith, selling military goods, cap ornaments, pistols, guns, drums, shot, buttons, and swords (1855).

R. (RICHARD) H. SCOTT ALBANY, NY 1871-1881

- Locations:
    60 State Street (1871-1878)
    8 James Street (1878-1880)
    78 State Street (1880-1881)

(N) **WILLIAM D. SCOTT** LOUISVILLE, KY 1820-1832
RICHARD E. SMITH LOUISVILLE, KY 1832-1841

- Employee: William D. Scott.
- Located at the corner of Main and 4th Streets.

SCOTT (WILLIAM D.) & KILLS (JOHN)   LOUISVILLE, KY   1841-1843
- Located at the corner of Main and Wall Streets.

W. (WILLIAM D.) SCOTT   LOUISVILLE, KY   1843-1848
- Located at Main and Wall Streets.

W. (WILLIAM) D. SCOTT & CO.   LOUISVILLE, KY   1848-1851
- Located at 489 Main Street.
- Partner: T.H. Scott.
- Advertised watches, jewelry, silver and plated ware, military goods, fancy goods, and cutlery.

(A) **SEEBASS BROTHERS**   NEW YORK, NY   1861-1865
- Partners: Oscar and Emil Seebass.
- Locations:
    540 Pearl Street (1861-1863)
    294 Broadway near Reade Street (1863-1864)
    17 Maiden Lane (1864-1865)
- Advertised in the *Army-Navy Journal* (September 17 1864):
    New York manufactory of military goods
    The cheapest place for

Swords	*Embroideries*
Belts	*Sashes*
Hat cords	*Metal goods of every description*

    We manufacture our own goods.

(A) **L. (LEOPOLD) SELDNER & CO.**   WASHINGTON, D.C.   1862-1865
- Located at 344 Pennsylvania Avenue.

(N) **FRANK SELIGER**   NEW YORK, NY   1861-1876
- Locations:
    167 William Street (1861-1862)
    39 Beckman Street (1862-1863)
    175 William Street (1863-1869)
    45 Ann Street (1869-1876)

FRANK SELIGER & SON   NEW YORK, NY   1876-1890
- Partner and son: Frank Seliger Jr.
- Locations:
    53 Ann Street (1876-1877)
    389 Broome Street (1877-1881)
    207 Centre Street (1881-1890)
- Advertised ornaments, all kinds of swords, regalia, brass finishing, fire gilding, and silver plating (1881)

FRANK SELIGER JR.   NEW YORK, NY   1890-1892
- Located at 389 Broome Street.

(Silversmith, metal worker, sword hiltor, military ornaments)

(A) **SHANNON (LIVINGSTON A.), MILLER (WALSINGHAM A.) & CRANE (HAROLD L.)**   NEW YORK, NY   1867-1896
- Located at 32 Maiden Lane (1867-1869), 46 Maiden Lane (1869-1896).
- Advertised in the *Army-Navy Journal* (1881) military goods, swords, belts, shoulder straps, epaulettes, chapeaux, fatigue and dress hats, caps, banners, flags, gold and silver trimmings, laces, and fringes.

MILLER (WALSINGHAM A.)	NEW YORK, NY	1896-1899

- Located at 768 Broadway.

(A) **W. (WILLIAM) J. SHAFFER**   HARRISBURG, PA   1861-1865
- Located at Market Square.

(N) **SHEPHARD & BOYD**
(see Silversmith listings)

(A) **SAMUEL SHIPP**   CINCINNATI, OH   1819-1828
- Located at 27 Main Street.

    COLLINS (PELEG) & SHIPP (SAMUEL)   CINCINNATI, OH   1829-1834
- Located at 44 Main Street.

(A) **GEORGE W. SIMMONS**   BOSTON, MA   1835-1895
- Trade name: Oak Hall Clothing.

(A) **GEORGE W. SIMONS & CO.**   PHILADELPHIA, PA   1840-1864
- Located in Sansom Street Hall, Sansom Street, above 6th Street.
- Advertised in the *Army-Navy Journal* (October 10, 1863):
  > *Sword Manufactory*
  > *Manufacturers of fine swords of every description and dealers in every variety of military goods, sashes, belts, sword knots, badges.*
  > *Staff, field and line officers swords for infantry and cavalry; also navy swords.*
  > *All our swords tested and manufactured with celebrated imported blades.*
  > *(Blades from Solingen and J. Harrison of London)*
  > *Also, all the home fabricant's blades, including Collins (Samuel) and Co. and Emerson & Silver.*

(A) **A. (ABRAHAM) SINK (SR.)**   PHILADELPHIA, PA   1785-D1831
- Located at 21 Market Street.
- Military and music store.
- Advertised (1825):
  > *A. Sink's Military and Music Store*
  > *21 Market Street (2 doors above Front Street.)*
  > *1) Holster and pocket pistols*
  > *2) Silver, steel, gilt, plated and brass mounted swords and dirks*
  > *3) Sword and dirk blades (very unusual to sell blades)*
  > *4) Sword and dirk belts*
  > *5) Silk, cotton and worsted saches*
  > *6) Gold, silver, gilt and plated epaulets*
  > *7) Lace, cord and threads*
  > *8) Gilt and plated swords*
  > *9) Real gilt and plated military buttons*
  > *10) Military spurs*
  > *11) Military feathers*
  > *12) Cockades and eagles*
  > *13) Gold and silver spangles*
  > *Also every other article in the military line (wholesale and retail)*

    ABRAHAM SINK (JR.)   PHILADELPHIA, PA   1831-D1836
- Located on High Street.
(Hardware and military goods store)

ANN SINK	PHILADELPHIA, PA	1836-1840

- Widow of Abraham Sink Jr.
- Located at 200 South 4th Street.

(A) **HENRY H. SINKLER**	PHILADELPHIA, PA	1878-1890

- Located at 609 Callowhill Street.
- Advertised in Philadelphia city directory as a military goods supply shop.

(A) **ALEXANDER SLOAN**	PHILADELPHIA, PA	1869-1922

- Located at 225 Market Street.

(N) **BERNARD SLOAN**	NEW YORK, NY	1903-1918
SLOAN'S MILITARY SHOP	NEW YORK, NY	1918-1919

- Located at 217 W. 55th Street.
- Partners: Bernard Sloan, Nathan Kuppelson.

(Military goods, military tailors)

(A) **WARRINGTON C. SLOAT**	MOBILE, AL	1819-1838
SMITH (CHASE) & SLOAT (WARRINGTON L.)	MOBILE, AL	1838-1839

- Located at 24 Dauphin Street.

WARRINGTON L. SLOAT	MOBILE, AL	1839-1842

- Located at 24 Dauphin Street.

(A) **SMITH (JAMES S.) & SHIERS (ANDREW M.)**	NEW YORK, NY	1834-1838
JAMES E. SMITH	NEW YORK, NY	1838-1860
SMITH (JAMES S.) & SONS	NEW YORK, NY	1860-1863
SMITH (JAMES S.) & SPAULDING (GEORGE)	NEW YORK, NY	1863-1864
JAMES S. SMITH & CO.	NEW YORK, NY	1864-1891

- Two locations at 15 Dutch Street and 564 Broadway.
- Advertised in the *Army-Navy Journal* (September 17, 1864):

> *James S. Smith & Co.*
> *New York, NY—Beaufort, SC—Vicksburg, MS*
> *Manufacturers and dealers in military goods*
> *Swords, belts, sashes, shoulder straps, cords, spurs, caps, hats,*
> *and in fact everything for the officers of the Army and Navy.*
> *Medals, checks, stamping and press work done at short notice.*
> *Sole manufacturers of James S. Smith's patent metallic shoulder straps.*

(N) **NORMAND SMITH**	HARTFORD, CT	B1772, 1795-1818

- Advertised horseman's pistols, swords, holsters, saddles, and harnesses in the *Hartford Courant* (September 3, 1798).

(Military goods dealer)

(A) **STADERMAN (JOHN C.) & SHAPTER (JAMES D.)**	NEW YORK, NY	1863-1864

- Located at 292 Broadway (at corner of Reade Street).

JOHN C. STADERMANN	NEW YORK, NY	1864-1878

- Located at 292 Broadway at corner of Reade Street.
- Advertised in the *Army-Navy Journal* (September 17, 1864):
  Importers and manufacturers of military goods
  Sashes
  Genuine Solingen swords
  Extra fine presentation swords
  Extra fine presentation belts
  Hat and cap ornaments
  Plumes
  Military buttons
  Gold epaulettes
  Gold embroideries
  Shoulder straps
  Hat cords
  Haversacks
  Fine silver-plated swords

(N)	WILLIAM P. STANTON	ROCHESTER, NY	B1794-1826
	W. (WILLIAM) P. & H. (HENRY) STANTON	ROCHESTER, NY	1826-1844
	STANTON (WILLIAM P.) & BROTHER (HENRY)	ROCHESTER, NY	1844-1850
	WILLIAM P. STANTON	ROCHESTER, NY	1850-D1878

- Advertised as dealers in watches, jewelry, military goods, cutlery, and fancy goods.

(Silversmith, sword hiltor)

(N)	HENRY STANTON	ROCHESTER, NY	B1803-1826
	W. (WILLIAM) P. & H. (HENRY) STANTON	ROCHESTER, NY	1826-1844
	STANTON (WILLIAM P.) & BROTHER (HENRY)	ROCHESTER, NY	1844-1850
	HENRY STANTON	ROCHESTER, NY	1850-D1872

- Advertised as dealers in watches, jewelry, military goods, cutlery, and fancy goods.

(Silversmith, sword hiltor)

(A)	HENRY B. STANWOOD	BOSTON, MA	B1818-1838
	HARRIS (WILLIAM) & STANWOOD (HENRY B.) & CO.	BOSTON, MA	1838-1852

- Located at 29 Tremont Row (1838-1846), 253 Washington Street (1846-1852).

	HENRY B. STANWOOD & CO.	BOSTON, MA	1852-1861

- Partner: George D. Low.
- Located at 226 Washington Street.

	SHREVE (BENJAMIN), STANWOOD (HENRY B.) & CO.	BOSTON, MA	1861-1869

- Located at 226 Washington Street.
- Advertised during the Civil War:
  Army and Navy equipment consisting of swords, belts, sashes, epaulettes, buttons, laces, caps, shoulder straps, camp chests, etc. Presentation swords and all other articles usually kept by military dealers.

(A)	THOMAS STEPHENSON	BUFFALO, NY	1835-1839

- Located at 200 Main Street.

(A)	**JAMES R. STEVENS**	HARTFORD, CT	1856-1858
	HEMMINGWAY (L.G.) & STEVENS (JAMES R.)	HARTFORD, CT	1858-1865

- Located at 284 Main Street.

	JAMES R. STEVENS	HARTFORD, CT	1865-1867
	STEVENS (JAMES R.) & ROGERS (ROBERT T.)	HARTFORD, CT	1867-1873

- Located at 284 Main Street.

	JAMES R. STEVENS & CO.	HARTFORD, CT	1873-1875

- Located at 280 Main Street.
- Sold M1850 staff and field officer swords.

(Masonic and military goods, watches, jewelry)

(N)	**MORTIMER STILWELL**	ROCHESTER, NY	1844-1865

- Locations:
    5 State Street (1844-1846)
    2 Exchange Street (1846-1863)
    51 Buffalo Street (1863-1865)

(Dealer in watches, jewelry, silverware, and military goods of all kinds)

(N)	**JOHN H. (HATTER) STILZ**	PHILADELPHIA, PA	1884-1887
	LOUIS E. STILZ & BROTHER (JOHN H.)	PHILADELPHIA, PA	1887-1936

- Locations:
    212 North 9th Street (1887-1889)
    151 North 4th Street (1889-1893)
    155 North 4th Street (1893-1936)
- Hatters, regalia, military goods.
- Invoices showed them as hatters and manufacturers of society and military goods (1889), including *"uniforms for all societies, chapeaux, helmets, caps, baldrics, uniform hats, gloves, valises, banners, regalia, belts, badges, flags, cuffs, and swords."*
- Had a U.S. contract for guidons (1901).

	L. (LOUIS) E. STILZ BROS. INC.	PHILADELPHIA, PA	1936-1940

- President: Louis E. Stilz Jr.

(A)	**HENRY STORMS**	NEW YORK, NY	1815-1842

(Saddler)

	HENRY STORMS & CO.	NEW YORK, NY	1842-1848

- Located at 34 Fulton Street.
- Partners and sons: Henry J. Storms, Christian S. Storms.
- Henry Storms was also commissary general of the state of New York.
- Advertised saddles, military goods, muskets, cutlasses, ammunition, and horse equipment (1846).

	C. (CHRISTIAN) S. (SCHAEFFER) STORMS	NEW YORK, NY	1848-1854

- Located at 53 Fulton Street.
- Partner: Henry J. Storms.
- Christian S. Storms went to St. Louis, MO (1854-1862).

	HENRY J. STORMS	NEW YORK, NY	1854-1862

- Located at 95 Fulton Street.

	HENRY J. & C. (CHRISTIAN) S. STORMS	NEW YORK, NY	1862-1871

(A)	**STORRS (CHARLES) & DAVIES (THOMAS)**	UTICA, NY	1829-1830

- Located at 30 Genessee Street.

(N) **A. STOWELL**   BALTIMORE, MD   1861-1865
- Located at 147 and 178 W. Baltimore Street.
- Advertised army and navy military goods and importer.

(A) **WILLIAM B. STRONG**   WASHINGTON, DC   1861-1863
- Located at 225 Pennsylvania Avenue.

(A) **W. (WILLIAM) J. SYMS & BRO. (SAMUEL R.)**   NEW YORK, NY   1860-1863
- Located at 300 Broadway.
- Advertised in the *Army-Navy Journal* as importers and manufacturers of military goods, including presentation swords, guns, pistols and revolvers (1863).

(N) **N. TAYLOR & CO.**   NEW YORK, NY   1812-1815
- Wrote to and requested swords from Nathan Starr, Middleton, CT (August 2, 1814). Starr sent three sample swords to N. Taylor:
    - cavalry saber—can provide several hundred at $3.50 each
    - cavalry saber—can provide 1,000 at $5.00 each
    - small sword—can provide 400-500 at $5.00 each

(N) **GEORGE S. THURBER**   CHICAGO, IL   1869-1875
- Located at 119 Randolph Street.
- Advertised as an importer and dealer in military and theatrical goods.

(A) **C.F.G. TISDALL**   NEW YORK, NY   1855-1860
- Located at 335 Broadway.

(A) **G. (GILBERT) R. TOBEY**   NEW YORK, NY   1861-1865
- Located at 86 John Street.

(A) **TOMES (FRANCIS JR.), SON (BENJAMIN) & MELVAIN (ROBERT C.)**   NEW YORK, NY   1859-1864
- Located at 6 Maiden Lane.

TOMES (FRANCIS JR. & CHARLES H.), MELVAIN (ROBERT C.) & CO.   NEW YORK, NY   1864-1874
- Advertised in the *Army-Navy Journal* (September 17, 1864):
    Dealers in everything necessary for the uniform of Army and Navy officers

    | *Swords* | *Sashes* | *Belts* |
    | *Shoulder straps* | *Epaulets* | *Laces* |
    | *Buttons* | *Fatigue caps* | |

    A large assortment of firearms, cutlery, double and single barrel shotguns, sporting ammunition.
    Sole agents for "Heiffers" celebrated army razors,
    Westley Richards fowling pieces and rifles,
    Eley's percussion caps for revolvers.
    Publishers of the "Uniform of U.S. Navy"
- Advertised in the *Army-Navy Journal* on (April 16, 1870):
    Importers

Have constantly on hand swords, sashes, embroideries, epaulets, full dress regulation army hats, navy laces, etc.

(N) **G.W. TUCKERMAN**   PORTSMOUTH, NH   1800-1820
- Located on Congress Street.

- Advertised in the *New Hampshire Patriot* (1812):
  > *Military goods, including plated and gilt mounted cut and*
  > *thrust swords; hangers, horseman swords and sword blades.*

(N) **W. (WILSON) & G. (GARLAND) TUCKERMAN BOSTON, MA**   1810-1820
- Both worked at the Virginia Manufactory as forgers (1802).
- Located at 61 State Street.
- Advertised in the *Columbian Centinel* (1812):
  > *Iron and brass barreled pistols, cutlery, saddlers, gunflints, shot belts, powder flasks,*
  > *assorted hardware and tools from Birmingham and Sheffield England.*

(A) **TUNNEL CITY REGALIA CO.**   FORT HURON, MI   1881-1898
- Located at 502 to 508 Huron Street.

(N) **B. TURK & BRO. CO.**   NEW YORK, NY   1914-1918
- Located at 1107 Broadway.
- Military store with branches in Columbus, OH, Cincinnati, OH, and Burlington, VT.
- Sold M1902 saber for all officers (the swords were German made).

(C) **P. (PHILIP) H. TUSKA**   NEW YORK, NY   1861-1865
- U.S. contract for 2,779 cavalry sabers.

(N) **THOMAS TYRER**   RICHMOND, VA   1845-1855
- Located at 60 Main Street.
- Partner and son: Thomas H. Tyrer.
- Advertised as importer and manufacturer of guns, pistols, rifles, military equipment, and swords (1845).

(N) **J.H. TYSON**   YORK, PA   1790-1810
- Located on North Beaver Street.
- Sold infantry officer swords with blued and engraved blades.

(Gun maker, gun and sword dealer)

(A) **J. (JOSHUA) M. VARIAN & SON**   NEW YORK, NY   1864-1874
- Located at 70 and 72 Bowery (near Canal Street).
- Advertised in the *Army-Navy Journal* as a clothing and furnishings warehouse (April 16, 1870). Also advertised:
  > *Military clothing for the Army, Navy and National Guard constantly*
  > *on hand, epaulets, swords, shoulder straps, belts, embroideries, etc.*

(A) **B. (BOYD) A. & A. (ALVIN) S. WADHAMS**   CHICAGO, IL   1868-1871
- Located at 101 Madison Street (1868-1869), 463 Madison Street (1869-1871).

A. (ALVIN) S. WADHAMS & CO.   CHICAGO, IL   1871-1874
- Located at 190-192 South Clark Street.

WADHAMS (ALVIN S.) & ROUNDY (DANIEL CURTIS)   CHICAGO, IL   1874-1880
- Located at 190-192 South Clark Street.

DANIEL C. (CURTIS) ROUNDY & SON   CHICAGO, IL   1880-1892
- Located at 190-192 South Clark Street.

ROUNDY REGALIA   CHICAGO, IL   1892-1925
- Locations:

190 South Clark Street (1892-1906)
187 South Clark Street (1906-1910)
111 South Clark Street (1910-1915)
312 South Clark Street (1915-1925)

(N) **JOSEPH & DANIEL WALDO**   BOSTON, MA   1750-1760
- Sold silver-hilted small swords.

(Merchant, importer)

(A) **WALL (WILLIAM),**   WASHINGTON, DC   1863-1875
    STEPHENS (THOMAS K.) & CO.
- Located at 322 Pennsylvania Avenue (between 9th and 10th Streets).
- Advertised in the *Army-Navy Journal* (October 10, 1863):
  > *Have always on hand a large stock of military and naval clothing;*
  > *also swords, shoulder straps, sashes, belts, epaulets, laces, etc.*

(N) **WASHINGTON G. WALLACE**   VALLEY FORGE, PA   1860-1865
- Advertised military goods.

(A) **MOSES A. WALLACH**   BOSTON, MA   B1756-1800
    MOSES A. WALLACH   BOSTON, MA   1800-1809
- Located at 54 Essex Street.
- Advertised in the *Boston Gazette* (May 26, 1800):
  > *Attention—to be sold at Wallach's Armoury, near the glass house, the following articles:*
  > *Fencing foils*
  > *Cut and thrust gilt eagle head pommel swords with ivory*
  > *handles and blades enclosed in gold also with a silver plated hilt*
  > *Gilt hangers with ivory handles*
  > *Common hangers with ivory handles*
  > *Yellow (brass) small swords*
  > *Steel small swords*
  > *White (silver or pewter) small swords*

    MOSES A. WALLACH   BOSTON, MA   1809-1820
- Located at 54 Essex Street.

(Armoury)

    MOSES A. WALLACH   BOSTON, MA   1820-D1836
- Located on Columbia Street.

(Armoury)

(A) **WARNOCK & CO.**   NEW YORK, NY   1838-1866
- Located at 519 Broadway.

    WARNOCK UNIFORM CO.   NEW YORK, NY   1866-1945
- Located at 19 and 21 West 31st Street (between Broadway and 5th Avenue).

(A) **M. (MARMADUKE) D. WAUD & CO.**   BOSTON, MA   1861-1865
- Located at 193 Washington Street.
- Advertised on in the *Army-Navy Journal* (October 10, 1863):
  > *M.D. Waud & Co.*
  > *Invites the attention of the military public to their complete assortment of all articles,*
  > *including an entire outfit for Army or Navy officers.*

The only store in this city exclusively for the sale of military goods, camp sets, army valises, camp cots and stools.
Presentation swords of all description on hand or made to order.

Swords	*Sword belts*	*Sashes*
Epaulettes	*Passants*	*Sword-knots*
Embroideries	*Haversacks*	*Caps*
Cap ornaments	*Ammunition*	*Holsters*
Pistols	*Cartridges*	

Everything necessary for the complete outfit of Army and Navy officers.

(A, C) **GEORGE I. WELLES**　　　　　　　　　**BOSTON, MA**　　　　　　　　　B1784-1807
　　　ALFRED & GEORGE I. WELLES　　　**BOSTON, MA**　　　　　　　　　1807-1809
- Moved from Silversmith listing.
- Advertised in the *Columbian Centinel* swords, epaulets, lace, bindings, and cords imported from Europe (May 20, 1809).

　　　GEORGE I. WELLES & CO.　　　　　**BOSTON, MA**　　　　　　　　　1809-1827
- Partners: Alfred Welles, Hugh Gelston.
- Advertised in the *Columbian Centinel* (September 1809):
  > *Military goods at reduced prices*
  > *No. 55 Cornhill, for sale*
  > *A complete assortment of Military goods consisting of:*
  > *Gilt and Plated cut and thrust swords*
  > *Gilt and Plated sabres*
  > *Gilt and Plated dirks*
  > *Gold, silver, gilt and plated epaulets*
  > *Counter straps*
  > *Sword knots*
  > *Bindings*
  > *Laces*
  > *Cords*
  > *Tassels*
  > *Silk saches*
  > *Morocco belts*
  > *Cockades*
  > *All kind of plumes*
  > *Cased dueling pistols*
  > *Sets of horseman's pistols*

(N) **CHARLES WELLS**　　　　　　　　　　**NEW YORK, NY**　　　　　　　　1850-1856
- Located at 7 Platt Street (1851-1853), 45 Gold Street (1853-1856).

(Merchant, hardware, military goods)

(A) **LEMUEL WELLS**　　　　　　　　　　　**NEW YORK, NY**　　　　　　　　1770-1794
- Located on Broadway (1770-1791), 2 Queen Street (1791-1793).

　　　L. (LEMUEL) & H. (HORACE) WELLS　**NEW YORK, NY**　　　　　　　　1794-1799
- Located at 158 Pearl Street.

　　　LEMUEL WELLS & CO.　　　　　　　**NEW YORK, NY**　　　　　　　　1799-1808
- Located at 158 Pearl Street.
- Hardware and military goods store.

　　　LEMUEL WELLS　　　　　　　　　　**NEW YORK, NY**　　　　　　　　1808-1816
- Located at 158 Pearl Street.

(C) THE WENDELL CO.	MINNEAPOLIS, MN	1875

(C) WESTERN UNIFORM CO.   CHICAGO, IL   1870-1881
- Sold fraternal swords and regalia.

(N) WILLIAM G. WHILDEN   CHARLESTON, SC   1835-1855
     HAYDEN (AUGUSTUS H.) & WHILDEN (WILLIAM G.)   CHARLESTON, SC   1855-1863
- Located at 250 King Street (at Hasel Street).
- Silverware, watch, clocks, jewelry, and military and fancy store.

     WILLIAM G. WHILDEN   CHARLESTON, SC   1863-1870
- Located at 250 King Street (across from Augustus H. Hayden's store at 272 King Street).

     W. (WILLIAM) E. WHILDEN & CO.   CHARLESTON, SC   1870-1900
- Located at 250 King Street.
- Silverware, clock, watch, jewelry, and crockery store.

(A) WHITE (ELIZABETH) & LOUGHRAN (MICHAEL)   NEW YORK, NY   1858-1868
- Located at 110 William Court.

     JAMES E. WHITE & CO.   NEW YORK, NY   1868-1870
- Located at 61 Fulton Street.

     WHITE (JAMES E.) & CO.   NEW YORK, NY   1870-1875
- Located at 61 Fulton Street.

(A) HENRY K. WHITE   NEW YORK, NY   1840-1874
- Located at 3 Water Street.

(A) RAYMOLD (WILLIAM A.) & WHITLOCK (BENJAMIN M.)   NEW YORK, NY   1881-1891
- Located at 39 W. 14th Street.

     B. (BENJAMIN) M. WHITLOCK   NEW YORK, NY   1891-1895
- Located at 99-101 4th Avenue.

(A) WHITMORE (M.) & WOLFF (C.H.) & CO.   PITTSBURGH, PA   1841-1854
- Located at 60 Wood Street.

     WHITMORE (M.), WOLFF (C.H.) & DUFF (GEORGE J.)   PITTSBURGH, PA   1854-1872

(A) WILLETT (JAMES P.) & RUAFF (CHARLES)   WASHINGTON, DC   1880-1884
- Located at 905 Pennsylvania Avenue.

(A) DANIEL H. WILSON & CO.   BOSTON, MA   1868-1890
- Located at 5 Temple Place.

(N) GERARD WILSON   BALTIMORE, MD   1810-1820
- Located at 47 South Gay Street.
- Bought 50 cutlasses at $3.50 each from John Joseph Henry Philadelphia, PA (July 1812).

(Merchant, military goods)

(A) WILLIAM H. WILSON   PHILADELPHIA, PA   1850-1857
- Located on the corner of 5th and Cherry Streets (across from William H. Horstmann & Sons).

WILLIAM H. WILSON & SON (ROBERT)   PHILADELPHIA, PA   1857-1866
- Located at 341 Jarvis Street.

(A) **WILLIAM W. WILSON**   PITTSBURGH, PA   1835-1865
- Located at 67 Market Street (corner of 4th Street).

WILSON & HUTCHINSON
(See Evans & Hassell)

WILSON & STELLWAGON
(See Evans & Hassell)

(A) **WILLIAM P. WILSTACH & CO.**   PHILADELPHIA, PA   1861-1865
- Located at 38 North 3rd Street.
- President: Edwin M. Sellers.
- Had an 1861 U.S. contract for 1,000 cavalry sabers (delivered 937) and 1,000 non-comm. swords. They were not imported; they were made in Philadelphia.

(N) **ELIJAH WITHINGTON**   BOSTON, MA   1810-1820
- Located at 54 State Street.
- Advertised *"dupont gunpowder, shot, musket and pistol bullets, buck shot, musket and pistol flints, powder horns, cannonball and grape shot, cannon and cannonade"* (December 9, 1812).

(Military goods dealer)

(A) **WOLFE (CHRISTOPHER) & CLARKE (WILLIAM)**   NEW YORK, NY   1833-1841
- Located at 193 Pearl Street.

WOLFE (CHRISTOPHER), CLARKE (WILLIAM) & GILLESPIE (DAVID)   NEW YORK, NY   1841-1856
- Located at 193 Pearl Street.

WOLFE (CHRISTOPHER), DASH (JOHN B.) & FISHER (GEORGE)   NEW YORK, NY   1856-1881
- Located at 38 Warren Street.

(N) **LEMUEL S. WOOD**   WASHINGTON, DC   1861-1865
- Located at 450 Pennsylvania.
- Advertised as a military outfitter.

(N) **ALFRED WOODHAM**   NEW YORK, NY   1854-1869
- Located at 160 Fulton Street.
- Advertised as gun, pistol, and cutlery importer and dealer.
- Sold bowie and pocket knives.

(A) **ENOS WOODRUFF**   CINCINNATI, OH   1800-1860
- Sold silver-plated tomahawks.

(A) **ENOCH WOODS**   CHICAGO, IL   1861-1870
- Successor to Charles A. Eaton.
- Located at 180 Lake Street.
- Advertised as awholesale and retail dealer in guns, sporting apparatus, fishing tackle, pistols, bowie knives, military goods, powder, and shot.

CHAPTER 10

U.S. Silversmiths Who Mounted Swords

(N) **GEORGE AITKIN (AIKEN)**　　　　　　BALTIMORE, MD　　　　B1765, 1782-D1832
- Located at 1 South Calvert Street.

(A) **JOHN AITKIN (AIKEN)**　　　　　　　PHILADELPHIA, PA　　　　1785-1814
- Located at 76 North 2nd Street (1785-1813), Broad Street (near Chesnut Street) (1813-1814).

(C) **WILLIAM AITKIN (AIKEN)**　　　　　BALTIMORE, MD　　　　　1800-1825

(A) **SAMUEL ALFORD**　　　　　　　　　PHILADELPHIA, PA　　　　1758-D1762
- Located on Lombard Street.

(A) **THOMAS ALFORD**　　　　　　　　　PHILADELPHIA, PA　　　　1740-1765
- Located on Front Street (between Chesnut and Market Streets).

(A) **JOSEPH ANTHONY JR.**　　　　　　　PHILADELPHIA, PA　　　B1763, 1780-1810
- Located at Market Street (1780-1790), 94 High Street (1790-1810).
  JOSEPH ANTHONY & SONS　　　　　PHILADELPHIA, PA　　　　1810-D1814
- Located at 5 Chesnut Street.
- Sold two gilt-mounted small swords to Andrew Jackson (1803).
- Advertised as a goldsmith, silversmith, and seller of an assortment of cutlery and hardware (October 4, 1783).

(A) **JOHN BAILEY (BAYLEY)**
(See Makers listing)

(A) **WILLIAM BALL SR.**　　　　　　　　PHILADELPHIA, PA　　　B1729, 1750-1761
- Shop located on Front Street (1750-1761).
- Moved to Birmingham, England.
  WILLIAM BALL SR.　　　　　　　　　BIRMINGHAM, ENGLAND　　1761-1765
- Moved back to Philadelphia, PA, with his son William Ball Jr. (1765).

WILLIAM BALL SR.	**PHILADELPHIA, PA**	1765-D1810

- Shop located on Front Street (next to the London coffee shop) (1765-1775), north side of Market Street (between Front and 2nd Streets) (1775-1810).
- Advertised as a warehouse of gold, silver, pewter, copper, and brass wares (1775).
- William Ball Sr. died (1810).

(A) **WILLIAM BALL JR.**	**BIRMINGHAM, ENGLAND**	B1763-1765

- Immigrated to Philadelphia, PA, with his father William Ball Sr. (1765).

WILLIAM BALL JR.	**PHILADELPHIA, PA**	1765-1785

- In his father's shop.

JOHNSON (ISREAL H.) & BALL (WILLIAM JR.)	**BALTIMORE, MD**	1785-1790
WILLIAM BALL JR.	**BALTIMORE, MD**	1790-1812

- Locations:
    - Market Street (between South and Calvert Street) (1790-1793)
    - corner of Market Street and Tripolet Alley (1793-1796)
    - 62 Baltimore Street (1796-1799)
    - 60 Baltimore Street (1799-1812)
- Advertised silver-mounted swords and epaulets (1794).

BALL (WILLIAM JR.) & HEALD (JOHN S.)	**BALTIMORE, MD**	1812-1815

- Located at 60 Baltimore Street.
- William Ball Jr. died (1815).

(A) **STANDISH BARRY**	**BALTIMORE, MD**	B1763-1783

- Apprenticed to David Evans (1780-1783).

STANDISH BARRY	**BALTIMORE, MD**	1783-1784

- Shop located on Market Street (three doors below Calvert Street).

(Silversmith, engraver, watch and clock maker)

RICE (JOSEPH) & BARRY (STANDISH)	**BALTIMORE, MD**	1784-1787

- Located on Market Street (1784-1785), corner of Market and Calvert Street (1785-1787).
- Advertised engraving of copper plates, seals, medals, etc.
- Gold and silver work.

STANDISH BARRY	**BALTIMORE, MD**	1787-D1844

- Locations:
    - corner of Market and Calvert Street (1787-1796)
    - 92 Baltimore Street (1796-1800)
    - 20 North Gay Street (1800-1844)
- Made infantry officer swords with eagle-head pommels.

(Also goldsmith, engraver, clock and watch maker, merchant)

(N) **FRANCIS BASSETT**	**CHARLESTON, MA**	1678-1715
FRANCIS BASSETT	**ALBANY, NY**	1715-1765

- Made silver-hilted infantry officers swords with eagle-head pommels.

FRANCIS BASSETT	**NEW YORK, NY**	1765-1774

(N) **MORTON BEDFORD**	**BALTIMORE, MD**	1780-1810

- Located at 10 Water Street.

(Also goldsmith)

(N) **JEAN BAPTISTE BENOIT**	**BALTIMORE, MD**	1780-1820

- Located at 29 Charles Street.

(Also goldsmith)

(A)	BEST (SAMUEL) & DETERLY (JACOB)	CINCINNATI, OH	1806-1817
	SAMUEL BEST	CINCINNATI, OH	1817-D1859

(N) **BIGELOW BROS.**   BOSTON, MA   1840-1845
- Partners: Alanson Bigelow, John Bigelow, Abraham O. Bigelow.

      BIGELOW BROS. & KENNARD (JOHN)   BOSTON, MA   1845-1852
      BIGELOW, KENNARD & CO.   BOSTON, MA   1852-1911
- Located at 219 Washington Street.
- Designed and manufactured a presentation sword for Adm. Frank Wilder.

      BIGELOW, KENNARD & CO. INC.   BOSTON, MA   1911-1976
- Located at 511 Washington Street.

(A) **WILLIAM BOLTON (BOULTON)**   PHILADELPHIA, PA   1797-1810
- Located at 18 South 6th Street.

      BOLTON (WILLIAM) & HORN (HENRY)   PHILADELPHIA, PA   1810-1813
- Located at 18 South 6th Street.

      WILLIAM BOLTON   PHILADELPHIA, PA   1813-1815
- Located on Boltons Court.

(A) **EPHRIAM BRASHER**   NEW YORK, NY   B1744, 1766-1789
- Coin maker (made gold doubloons).
- Made silver-mounted infantry officer swords with dog-head pommels and split-and-divided hilts.

(A) **NICOLAS BROOKS**
(See Makers listings)

(N) **JOHN EDEN BROWN**   BALTIMORE, MD   1810-1816
- Located on Liberty Street.

(A) **R. (ROBERT) J. (JOHNSON)**   BOSTON, MA   1821-1833
     BROWN CO.
- Made silver- and brass-hilted infantry officer sabers with eagle-head pommels and hussar hilts.

(A) **BROWN (LIBERTY) & SEALE (WILLIAM)**   PHILADELPHIA, PA   1809-1811
- Located at 70 South Front Street.

      LIBERTY BROWN   PHILADELPHIA, PA   1811-1819
- Located at 119 Chesnut Street.

(A) **BENJAMIN BURT**   BOSTON, MA   B1727, 1750-D1805
- Located at 5th Street.

(A) **JOHN BURT**   BOSTON, MA   B1691, 1711-D1745
- Made silver-hilted court swords.

(N) **BENJAMIN BUSSEY**   DEDHAM, MA   B1757, 1777-1842
(Goldsmith)

(N) **THOMAS D. BUSSEY**   BALTIMORE, MD   B1773, 1792-D1804
- Located at 140 Baltimore Street.

(Also goldsmith)

(A) JAMES E. (EMOTT) CALDWELL	POUGHKEEPSIE, PA	B1801-1839
BENNETT (JAMES M.) & CALDWELL (JAMES E.)	PHILADELPHIA, PA	1839-1848

- Located at 140 Chesnut Street.

J. (JAMES) E. (EMOTT) CALDWELL & CO.	PHILADELPHIA, PA	1848-1998

- Locations:
    163 Chesnut Street (1848-1861)
    822 Chesnut Street (1861-1867)
    902 Chesnut Street (1867-1998)

(N) CHRISTOPHER CAMPBELL	NEW YORK, NY	1790-1815

- Made silver-hilted infantry officer swords with eagle-head pommels.

(N) THOMAS CAMPBELL	NEW YORK, NY	1770-1800
THOMAS CAMPBELL	RALEIGH, NC	1800-1828
THOMAS CAMPBELL	PHILADELPHIA, PA	1828-1833

(A) MICHAEL CARIO	LONDON, ENGLAND	Bc1688-1728

- Immigrated to New York, NY (1728).

MICHAEL CARIO	NEW YORK, NY	1728-1734
MICHAEL CARIO	PHILADELPHIA, PA	1734-Dc1748

- Advertised in the *American Weekly Journal* as goldsmith and engraver (1736).

(A) WILLIAM I. CARIO SR.	LONDON, ENGLAND	Bc1708-1728

- Immigrated to New York, NY (1728).
- Probably Michael Cario's son.

WILLIAM I. CARIO SR.	NEW YORK, NY	1728-1734
WILLIAM I. CARIO SR.	BOSTON, MA	1734-Dc1760

- Advertised in the *Boston Gazette* "fine sword blades sold and mounted" (October 23, 1738 and October 30, 1738).

WILLIAM I. CARIO JR.	BOSTON, MA	B1734-1760

- Apprenticed with his father William Cario Sr. (c. 1748-1752).
- Worked in his father's shop (c. 1752-1760).
- William I. Cario Sr. died (c. 1760).

WILLIAM I. CARIO JR.	PORTSMOUTH, NH	1760-1790
WILLIAM I. CARIO JR.	NEW MARKET, NH	1790-1808
WILLIAM I. CARIO JR.	NEWSFIELDS, NH	1808-D1809

(A) JOHN CARMAN	PHILADELPHIA, PA	1751-1772

- Located on the corner of 2nd and Chesnut Streets.
- Advertised in the *Pennsylvania Journal*, "makes and sells all sorts of gold, silver and jewelry work, including sword hilts" (August 1, 1771).

(N) THOMAS CARSON	ALBANY, NY	1790-1810
CARSON (THOMAS) & HALL (GREEN)	ALBANY, NY	1810-1828

- Made silver-hilted naval officer sabers.

THOMAS CARSON	ALBANY, NY	1828-1850

(See Green Hall)

(A) **R. CASHWELL**
(See Makers listing)

(N) **THOMAS CHADWICK** PHILADELPHIA, PA 1800-1814
- Located at 36 Coates Alley (1800-1811), 12 North Front Street (1811-1814).
  THOMAS CHADWICK & JOHN HEIMS ALBANY, NY 1814-1825
- Made silver-hilted navy officer swords with D-guards.

(N) **SIMON CHAUDRON** PHILADELPHIA, PA 1780-1798
  CHAUDRON (SIMON) & RASCH (ANTHONY) PHILADELPHIA, PA 1798-1808
  S. (SIMON) CHAUDRON & CO. PHILADELPHIA, PA 1808-1820
- Located at 12 South 2nd Street.
- Made silver-mounted knives and dirks.
(See Anthony Rasch)

(A) **EBENEZER CHITTENDEN** EAST GUILFORD, CT B1726-1762
- Apprentice: Abel Buell (1757-1762).
  BUELL (ABEL) & CHITTENDEN EAST GUILFORD, CT 1762
  (EBENEZER)
  EBENEZER CHITTENDEN EAST GUILFORD, CT 1762-1770
  EBENEZER CHITTENDEN NEW HAVEN, CT 1770-D1783
(Also goldsmith, gunsmith)

(N) **EPHRAIM COBB** BOSTON, MA B1708-1735
- Apprenticed to Moody Russell, Barnstable, MA (1728-1735).
  EPHRAIM COBB PLYMOUTH, MA 1735-D1775

(N) **RICHARD CUTLER (SR.)** NEW HAVEN, CT B1736-1765
  CUTLER (RICHARD) (SR.) NEW HAVEN, CT 1765-1770
  SILLIMAN (HEZEKIAH), WARD (AMBROSE) & CO.
  RICHARD CUTLER (SR.) NEW HAVEN, CT 1770-1800
  RICHARD CUTLER (SR.) & SONS NEW HAVEN, CT 1800-1817
- Sons and partners: Richard Cutler Jr. (B1774-D1811), William Cutler (B1785-D1817).
- Richard Cutler Sr. died (1810).
(See Ambrose Ward)
(See Hezekiah Silliman)
(Also goldsmith)

(N) **JONATHAN DAVENPORT** BALTIMORE, MD 1789-1793
- Located at 102 Baltimore Street.
  JONATHAN DAVENPORT PHILADELPHIA, PA 1793-D1801
(Also goldsmith)

(A) **SERIL DODGE** PROVIDENCE, RI 1784-D1802
- Made silver-hilted officer hangers with eagle-head pommels.

(A) **DANIEL DUPUY SR.** PHILADELPHIA, PA 1749-1783
- Located at 4 South 2nd Street (1749-1772), 2nd Street (1772-1783).
(Also goldsmith, clock and watch maker)

(A) **DANIEL DUPUY JR.**   PHILADELPHIA, PA   1805-D1826
- Located at 16 South 2nd Street.

(A) **JOHN DUPUY**   PHILADELPHIA, PA   1805-D1838
- Located at 16 South 2nd Street.

(C) **JOHN FOSTER**   MARTINSBURG, VA   1826-1835

(A) **WILLIAM GIFFING JR.**   GENEVA, NY   1795-1809
    GIFFING (WILLIAM JR.) &   GENEVA, NY   1809-1815
    SWEENEY (JOHN)
    CHRISTOPHER GIFFING   NEW YORK, NY   1815-1816
- Located at 40 Chapel Street (carpenter George Giffing also at that address).

    GIFFING (CHRISTOPHER) &   NEW YORK, NY   1816-1817
    HEBARD (JOHN J.)
- Located at 64 Partition Street.

    CHRISTOPHER GIFFING   NEW YORK, NY   1817-1835
- Located at 40 Chapel Street.
- Made officers sabers with reverse-P hilts, checkered ivory grips, and blades made by Nathan Starr of Middletown, CT.
- Made naval officer sabers with eagle-head pommels and reverse-P hilts.

(A) **JOHN WARD GILMAN**   EXETER, NH   B1774, 1792-D1823
- Made silver-hilted hunting swords with lion-head pommels.

(N) **ALEXANDER S. GORDON**   NEW YORK, NY   1795-1803
    A. (ALEXANDER S.) & J. (JAMES) GORDON   NEW YORK, NY   1803-1820
- Made silver-hilted infantry officer swords with bird-head pommels.

(A) **CHARLES HALL**   LANCASTER, PA   B1742, 1755-D1795
- Located at North Queen Street.

(A) **DAVID HALL SR.**   PHILADELPHIA, PA   1765-1777
- Located at 2nd Street (near Chesnut Street).

(N) **GREEN HALL**   NEW YORK, NY   B1782-1810
    CARSON (THOMAS) & HALL (GREEN)   ALBANY, NY   1810-1826
- Made silver-hilted naval officer sabers.

    HALL (GREEN) & BROWER   ALBANY, NY   1826-1840
    (S. DOUGLAS) & CO.
- Partner: John D. Hewson (B1815-D1852).

    HALL (GREEN), HEWSON   ALBANY, NY   1840-1845
    (JOHN D.) & CO.
- Partners: S. Douglas Brower, Thomas V.Z. Merrifield (B1817-D1845).

    HALL (GREEN) & HEWSON (JOHN D.)   ALBANY, NY   1845-1847
- Partner: S. Douglas Brower.

    HALL (GREEN), HEWSON   ALBANY, NY   1847-1852
    (JOHN D.) & BROWER (S. DOUGLAS)
- John D. Hewson died (1852).

    HALL (GREEN) & BROWER   ALBANY, NY   1852-1854

(S. DOUGLAS) **(C) GREEN HALL** (Also goldsmith)	ALBANY, NY	1854-D1863
(C) THOMAS HARPER	CHARLESTON, SC	1773-1782

(A) PHILIP HARTMAN   PHILADELPHIA, PA   1810-1815
- Located at 27 South 2nd Street.
- Bought 12 sword blades at $2.75 each and nine sword scabbards and hilts at $6.50 each from John Joseph Henry, Philadelphia, PA (May 1813).

(A) DANIEL HENCHMAN   BOSTON, MA   B1736-1762
- Made officer hangers with stylized eagle-head pommels.

(C) EPAPHRAS HINSDALE   NEWARK, NJ   B1869, 1881-D1910

(C) HORACE SEYMOUR HINSDALE   NEWARK, NJ   B1782-1810

(A) HORN (HENRY) & KNEASS (WILLIAM)   PHILADELPHIA, PA   1813-1837
- Located at 16 South 6th Street.

(N) JAMES HOWELL   PHILADELPHIA, PA   1802-1810
- Located at 50 South Front Street.

JAMES HOWELL & CO.   PHILADELPHIA, PA   1810-1815
- Located at 50 South Front Street.

RICHARD HUMPHREYS   PHILADELPHIA, PA   B1749-D1831
- Located on Front Street (near the drawbridge).

(N) THOMAS B. HUMPHREYS   PHILADELPHIA, PA   1785-1829
- Shop located at 11 Knights Court (1805-1829).

THOMAS B. HUMPHREYS	BALTIMORE, MD	1829-1831
THOMAS B. HUMPHREYS	RICHMOND, VA	1831-1845
THOMAS B. HUMPHREYS & SON	RICHMOND, VA	1845-1850

- Son and partner: Thomas F. Humphreys.

(N) J. (JAMES) E. HYDE   NEW YORK, NY   1790-1810
CLEVELAND (SAMUEL) & HYDE (JAMES E.)   NEW YORK, NY   1810-1820
- Made silver-hilted infantry officer swords with stylized eagle-head pommels and straight, blued, and gilded blades.

(A) GEORGE W. JACOBS   BALTIMORE, MD   B1775, 1802-1836
- Located on Eutaw Street.

GEORGE W. JACOBS   PHILADELPHIA, PA   1836-D1846

(N) JEAN BAPTISTE JAMIN   BALTIMORE, MD   1780-1810
- Located at 15 North Gay Street.

(A) REUBAN JOHNSON   RICHMOND, VA   1815-D1820
- Located on Main Street (between 12th and 13th Streets).

(A) WILLIAM KENDRICK		LOUISVILLE, KY	B1810-1830
HARRIS (JOHN C.) & KENDRICK (WILLIAM)		LOUISVILLE, KY	1830-1832
LEMON (JAMES INNES) & KENDRICK (WILLIAM)		LOUISVILLE, KY	1832-1843
WILLIAM KENDRICK		LOUISVILLE, KY	1843-1880

- Located at 71 North 3rd Street (1843-1864), 225 North 3rd Street (1864-1880).

(Fancy goods, military goods, watches, silverware, jewelry, Masonic goods)

(A) ROBERT KEYWORTH — WASHINGTON, DC — 1822-1858

- Located on Main Street (between 9th and 10th Streets).

(Also watch maker, jeweler)

(N) J. (JOHN) H. KINZIE — DETROIT, MI — 1773-D1828

- Made silver- and bronze-inlayed pipe tomahawks.

(N) SAMUEL KIRK — BALTIMORE, MD — B1793-1813
KIRK (SAMUEL) & SMITH (JOHN) — BALTIMORE, MD — 1813-1846
SAMUEL KIRK & SON — BALTIMORE, MD — 1846-1861

- Son and partner: Henry Child Kirk.

SAMUEL KIRK & SONS — BALTIMORE, MD — 1861-1896

- Sons and partners: Henry Child Kirk, Charles D. Kirk, Clarence E. Kirk.
- Located at 187 North Calvert Street.
- Samuel died (1872).

SAMUEL KIRK & SONS CO. — BALTIMORE, MD — 1896-1924
SAMUEL KIRK & SONS INC. — BALTIMORE, MD — 1924-1979

(Also goldsmith)

(A) CHRISTIAN KNEASS — PHILADELPHIA, PA — 1811-1837

- Located at 25 Carters Alley (1811-1813), 152 North 9th Street (1813-1837).

(Also silver plater, engraver)

(A) WILLIAM KNEASS — PHILADELPHIA, PA — 1792-1813

- Located at 3 Chancery.

HORN (HENRY) & KNEASS (WILLIAM) — PHILADELPHIA, PA — 1813-1837

- Located at 16 South 6th Street.

(Also silver plater, engraver)

(A) KRIDER (PETER L.) & BIDDLE (SAMUEL) — PHILADELPHIA, PA — 1860-1878

- Located on the corner of 8th and Jayne Streets.

(A) JACOB KUCHER — PHILADELPHIA, PA — 1805-1835

- Located at 87 New Street (1805-1813), North 8th Street (1813-1835).

(N) HENRY KUNSMAN — FREDERICKSBURG, VA — 1800-1819
HENRY KUNSMAN — RICHMOND, VA — 1819-1823
HENRY KUNSMAN — RALEIGH, NC — 1823-1824

- Advertised swords for sale in the *Raleigh Register* (July 23, 1824).

JOHN Y. SAVAGE & HENRY KUNSMAN — SALISBURY, NC — 1824-1825

(Also watch maker, jeweler)
(See John Y. Savage)

(A)	**PIERRE LAMOTHE**	NEW ORLEANS, LA	1809-1822

- Made silver-mounted hunting knives.

(A)	**PETER LERRETT (LERET)**	CARLISLE, PA	1775-1787
	PETER LERRETT	BALTIMORE, MD	1787-1802

- Located at 114 Baltimore Street.

(Also goldsmith, jeweler)

(A)	**LEWIS (HARVEY) & SMITH (JOSEPH D.)**	PHILADELPHIA, PA	1805-1810

- Located at 2 South 2nd Street.

	HARVEY LEWIS	PHILADELPHIA, PA	1810-D1835

- Located at 2 South 2nd Street (near High Street) (1810-1813), 143 Chesnut Street (1813-1835).
- Made swords for naval heroes of the War of 1812, commissioned by the state of Maryland. One was for Lt. George W. Rodgers of the frigate *Wasp*.

(A)	**JOSEPH LUKEY**	PITTSBURGH, PA	1790-D1822

- Located at Diamond Alley between Wood and Market Streets.

	MRS. JOSEPH LUKEY	PITTSBURGH, PA	1822-1840

- Located at 5th Street between Wood and Market Streets.

(A)	**JOHN LYNCH**	BALTIMORE, MD	B1761, 1786-D1848

- Locations:
    Franklin Street (1786-1807)
    Franklin Street at Strawberry Alley (1807-1822)
    7 Franklin Street (1822-1848)
- Made swords with eagle-head pommels and split-and-divided hilts.
- Made silver-hilted foot officer and artillery officer swords.

(Also clock maker, watch maker, jeweler)

(N)	**THOMAS MADDOCK JR.**	PHILADELPHIA, PA	1861-1866

- Located at 814 Chesnut Street (1861-1862), 610 Sansom Street (1862-1866).

(Also jeweler)

(N)	**L. (LEMUEL) MANNERBACK**	READING, PA	1810-1820

(N)	**WILLIAM MANNERBACK**	READING, PA	1820-1835

- Made silver-hilted hunting swords.

(A)	**MARQUAND (ISAAC), PAULDING (CORNELIUS) & PENFIELD (JOSIAH)**	SAVANNAH, GA	1812-1815

- Advertised as importers and dealers in swords and military goods and jewelers.

(A)	**JOHN McMULLEN**	PHILADELPHIA, PA	B1765-1796
	ERWIN (HENRY) & McMULLEN (JOHN)	PHILADELPHIA, PA	1796-1805
	JOHN McMULLEN	PHILADELPHIA, PA	1805-1811

- Located at 120 South Front Street.

	McMULLEN (JOHN) & BLACK (JOHN)	PHILADELPHIA, PA	1811-1817

- Located at 14 South Front Street.

(Also goldsmith, jeweler)

(A) EDMUND MILNE		PHILADELPHIA, PA	B1724, 1757-D1820

- Located on 2nd Street at Market Street.

(N) SAMUEL MINOTT		BOSTON, MA	B1732-1750
MINOTT (SAMUEL) & SIMPKINS (WILLIAM)		BOSTON, MA	1750-1760
MINOTT (SAMUEL) & AUSTIN (JOSIAH JOHN)		BOSTON, MA	1760-1769
SAMUEL MINOTT		BOSTON, MA	1769-D1803

(A) PETER MOOD (SR.)		CHARLESTON, SC	B1766-1816
PETER MOOD (SR.) & SON (JOHN I.)		CHARLESTON, SC	1816-1819

- Advertised as swordsmiths and silversmiths, silver- or gilt-hilted sabers with scabbards (1816-1819).
- Made silver-hilted infantry officer sabers with lion-head pommels.

PETER MOOD (SR.) & SONS (JOHN I. & PETER JR.)		CHARLESTON, SC	1819-1821

- Peter Mood Sr. died (1821).

P. (PETER JR.) MOOD & CO.		CHARLESTON, SC	1821-1834

- Partners: John Evan and John I. Mood.

J. (JOHN I.) & P. (PETER JR.) MOOD		CHARLESTON, SC	1834-1841
JOHN I. MOOD		CHARLESTON, SC	1841-D1864
PETER MOOD JR.		CHARLESTON, SC	1841-D1876

(N) DAVID MOSELEY		BOSTON, MA	B1753-1775

- Apprenticed to Paul Revere Jr. (1770-1775).

DAVID MOSELEY		BOSTON, MA	1775-D1812

- Made silver-hilted small swords.

(A) EBENEZER S. MOULTON		NEWBURYPORT, MA	B1768-1796
EBENEZER S. MOULTON		BOSTON, MA	1796-1821

- Locations:
    42 Cornhill Street (1796-1800)
    11 Cornhill Street (1800-1804)
    57 Cornhill Street (1804-1805)
    3 South Row (1805-1821)

EBENEZER S. MOULTON		NEWBURYPORT, MA	1821-D1824

(Also goldsmith, jeweler)

(A) JOHN MYERS		PHILADELPHIA, PA	B1756, 1785-1810

- Located at 13 2nd Street (1785-1793), 71 North 2nd Street (1793-1810).
- Made light horse sabers with split-and-divided hilts.
- Advertised: *"Gentleman of the Army and Navy may be supplied with swords and dirks of every description. Silver and gilt mounted plain or eagle-head pommels."*

(Also goldsmith, jeweler)

(A) JONATHAN OTIS		SANDWICH, MA	B1723-1738
JONATHAN OTIS		BOSTON, MA	1738-1743

- Apprenticed to silversmith Edward Winslow.

JONATHAN OTIS		BOSTON, MA	1743-1775

(N) **DANIEL PARKER**   BOSTON, MA   B1726, 1746-D1785
- Advertised in the *Boston Gazette* (1761-1765):
  For sale an assortment of stones, tools and other necessities for goldsmiths and jewelers. Best sword blades. Silver hilted gentleman's swords.

(N) **JOHN TYNG PEABODY**   ENFIELD, CT   B1756-1787
    JOHN TYNG PEABODY   WILMINGTON, NC   1787-D1822
- Advertised in the *Wilmington Gazette* (November 15, 1798): *"For sale 2 or 3 silver mounted swords."*

(Also clock maker, watch maker, cutler)

(A) **MALTBY PELLETREAU**   NEW YORK, NY   1815-1818
- Located on Broadway.

    CLARK (CURTIS H.) &   NEW YORK, NY   1818-1821
    PELLETREAU (MALTBY)
- Located at 88 Broadway.

    CLARK (CURTIS H. & GREGORY),   NEW YORK, NY   1821-1824
    PELLETREAU (MALTBY) & UPSON (GEORGE)
- Located at 170 Broadway.

(A) **HORACE PORTER & CO.**   BOSTON, MA   1827-1833
- Located at 75 Washington Street.

(N) **ANTHONY RASCH (ROUSH)**   PHILADELPHIA, PA   1780-1798
    CHAUDRON (SIMON) &   PHILADELPHIA, PA   1798-1808
    RASCH (ANTHONY)
    ANTHONY RASCH   PHILADELPHIA, PA   1808-1818
- Located at 4 Watkins Alley.

    RASCH (ANTHONY) & WILLIG   PHILADELPHIA, PA   1818-1819
    (WILLICK) (GEORGE JR.)
    ANTHONY RASCH & CO.   PHILADELPHIA, PA   1819-1821
    ANTHONY RASCH   NEW ORLEANS, LA   1821-1851
- Made silver-mounted knives and dirks.

THE REVERE FAMILY OF BOSTON

1. **APOLLOS RIVOIRE**   SAINTE-FOY   B1702-1715
                                                     LA GRANDE, FRANCE

- Immigrated to Boston, MA (1715).
- Changed name to Paul Revere.

    PAUL REVERE I   BOSTON, MA   1715-1722
- Apprenticed to John Coney (1715-1722).
- Coney was a cutler, silversmith, goldsmith, and sword hiltor.

    PAUL REVERE I   BOSTON, MA   1722-D1754
- Located at town dock (1722-1730) at North End (1730-1754).
- Father of Paul Revere Sr. II (B1734-D1818), Thomas Revere Sr. (B1739-D1779), John Revere Sr. I (B1741-D1801).
- Son Paul Revere Sr. II apprenticed with him (1747-1752) and then worked with him (1752-1754).
- Paul Revere I died (1754).
- Probably made silver-hilted swords since he apprenticed to silversmith and sword hiltor John Coney.

THE REVERE FAMILY OF BOSTON

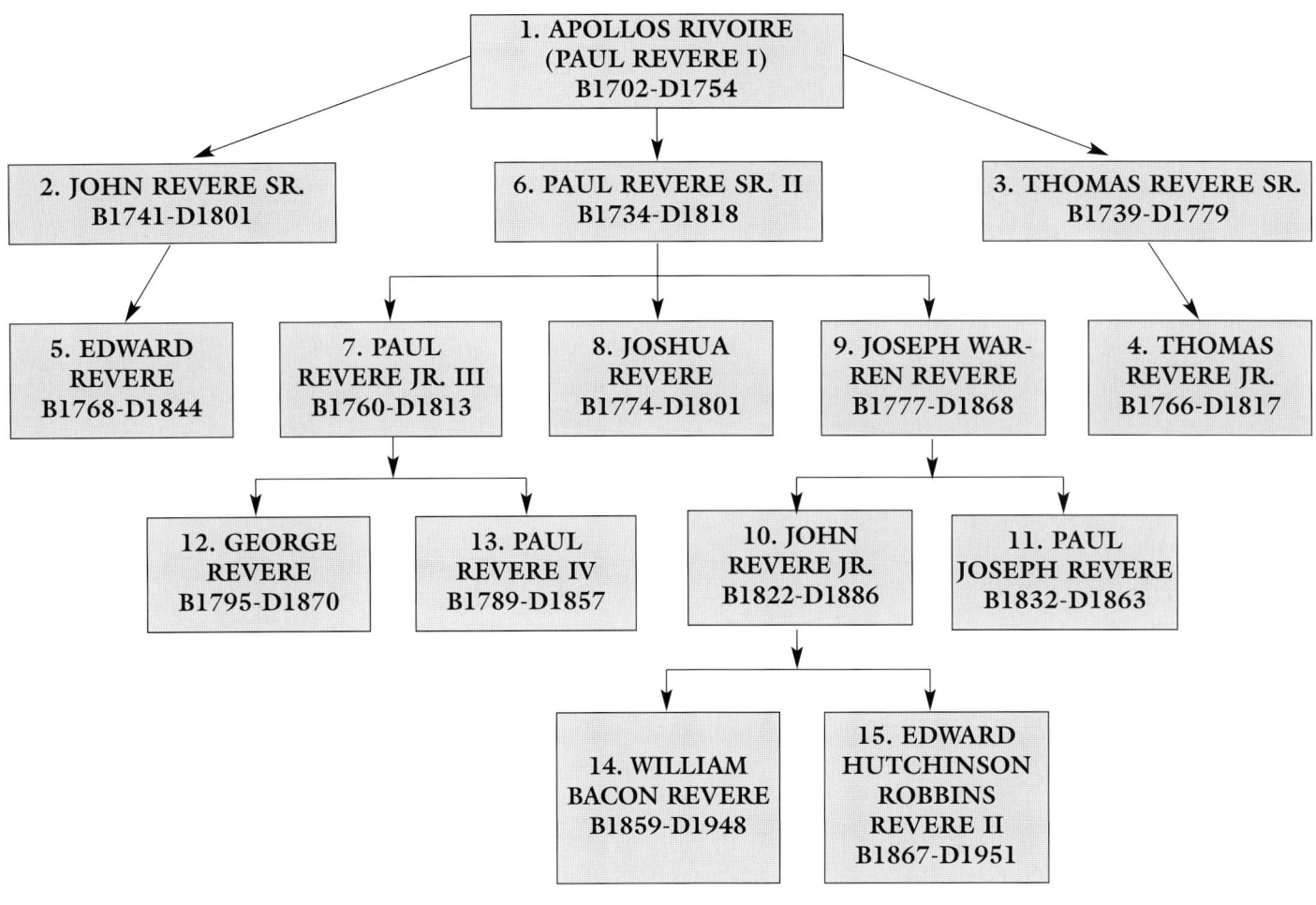

2. JOHN REVERE SR. I BOSTON, MA B1741-D1801
- Son of Paul Revere I.
- Worked as a tailor.
- Father of Edward Revere (B1766-D1844).

3. THOMAS REVERE SR. BOSTON, MA B1739-1759
- Son of Paul Revere I.
- Apprenticed under his brother Paul Revere Sr. II as a silversmith (c. 1754-1759) instead of his father, who died in 1754.

THOMAS REVERE SR. BOSTON, MA 1759-D1779
- Father of Thomas Revere Jr. (B1766-D1817).
- Operated a silversmith shop.
- Probably made silver-hilted swords.
- Member of Col. Thomas Craft's Massachusetts Artillery regiment (1775-1776).
- His brother Paul Revere Sr. II was also in the regiment.
- Thomas Revere Sr. died (1779).

4. THOMAS REVERE JR. BOSTON, MA B1766-1788
- Son of Thomas Revere Sr. (B1739-D1779).
- Apprenticed with his uncle Paul Revere Sr. II (1783-1788).

THOMAS REVERE JR.	BOSTON, MA	1788-D1817

- Opened several silversmith shops.
- Locations:
    - Newbury Street (1788-1798)
    - Orange Street (1798-1802)
    - Back Street (1802-1803)
    - Hull Street (1803-1817)
- Thomas Revere Jr. died (1817).
- Probably made silver-hilted swords since he apprenticed under Paul Revere Sr. II, who hilted swords.

5. EDWARD REVERE	BOSTON, MA	B1768-1788

- Son of John Revere Sr. (B1741-D1801).
- Apprenticed under his uncle Paul Revere Sr. II as a silversmith and goldsmith (1783-1788).

EDWARD REVERE	BOSTON, MA	1788-1811

- Locations:
    - Ship Street (1788-1800, goldsmith)
    - 30 Prince Street (1800-1804, silversmith)
    - 50 Middle Street (1805-1809, silversmith)
    - Showhill Street (1810, silversmith)
- Moved to Reading, MA (1811).

EDWARD REVERE	READING, MA	1811-1816

- Silversmith shop.

EDWARD REVERE	BOSTON, MA	1816-1818

- Located on North Street (goldsmith).
- Moved back to Reading, MA (1818).

EDWARD REVERE	READING, MA	1818-1821
EDWARD REVERE	BOSTON, MA	1821-D1844

- Locations:
    - Charter Street (1821-1822, goldsmith)
    - 28 Back Street (1823-1825, silversmith)
    - 68 Salem Street (1826-1828, silversmith)
    - 70 Salem Street (1829, silversmith)
    - 10 Lynn Street (1830, silversmith)
    - 56 Salem Street (1831-1844, silversmith)
- Probably made silver-hilted swords since he apprenticed under Paul Revere Sr. II, who hilted swords.

6. PAUL REVERE SR. II	BOSTON, MA	B1734-1754

- Son of Paul Revere I.
- Father of Paul Revere III (B1760-D1813), Joshua Revere (B1774-D1801), and Joseph Warren Revere (B1777-D1868).
- Apprenticed with father Paul Revere I (1747-1752).
- Worked in father's shop at North End (1752-1754).
- His father died in 1754.

PAUL REVERE SR. II	BOSTON, MA	1754-1765

- Opened a silversmith shop at the head of Clarkes Wharf.
- Made silver-hilted swords as shown in his silver design book.
- Also made standard items such as cups, mugs, spoons, pitchers, tankards, etc.
- His brother Thomas Revere Sr. apprenticed with him (c. 1754-1759).
- As a lieutenant in the British Army, he participated in the expedition against the French at Crown Point on Lake Champlain (1756).

PAUL REVERE SR. II	BOSTON, MA	1765-1775

- Opened a silversmith shop at 50 Cornhill Street.

- Began engraving on copper plates (1765).
- His well-known engravings included "The Boston Massacre" (1770) and "The British Landing in Boston Harbor" (1768).
- Also made copper plates for printing pictures in books.
- Joined the "Sons of Liberty," a secret patriotic society formed when the British passed the Stamp Act (1765).
- Advertised in the *Boston Gazette* as a maker of replacement teeth. Learned from an English dentist in Boston (1768).
- Became a Free Mason and Master of St. Andrews Lodge (1770).
- Made Masonic jewelry.
- Had brother-in-law David Mosely as a silversmith apprentice (1770-1772).
- Son Paul Revere III apprenticed with him (1773-1775).
- Took part, with his son Paul Revere III, in the Boston Tea Party (December 16, 1773).
- Designated courier to the Continental Congress by the Massachusetts Provincial Assembly (1774).
- Had an apprentice, David Moseley (1770-1775).
- Made his famous ride to Lexington, MA, to warn fellow patriots, including John Hancock and Samuel Adams, that the British were on the march (April 18, 1775).
- Since he couldn't return to Boston (British knew he was a patriot and knew of his ride), he stayed in Charleston, MA.

PAUL REVERE SR. II   **CHARLESTOWN, MA**   1775-1776

- Stayed with his family in Charleston for almost one year until the British left Boston.
- Engraved the plates for the first issue of Continental currency (1775).
- The Continental Congress sent him to Philadelphia, PA, to inspect a powder mill (1775).
- Learned the process for making gun powder while at the mill.

PAUL REVERE SR. II   **BOSTON, MA**   1776-1796

- Still had a goldsmith and silversmith shop at 50 Cornhill.
- Bought land in Canton, MA, and set up a powder mill to supply gun powder to the Continental Army (1776).
- Sent by George Washington to repair cannon at Castle William in Boston Harber, which the British had badly damaged before they left. He designed and had built new carriages for the cannon (mid-1776).
- Under orders from the Continental Congress, superintended the casting of brass cannon for the Continental Army (winter 1776). Would later open his own brass foundry and make bells and cannon (1792).
- Given the rank of lieutenant colonel in the Massachusetts militia and commanded an artillery regiment.
- His brother Thomas Revere served in his regiment.
- His son Paul Revere III was a captain and adjutant in his artillery regiment.
- Given command of Castle William in Boston Harbor (winter 1778).
- Took part in the Penobscot River expedition against the British on the Castine Peninsula (1779).
- Son Joshua and nephews Thomas Jr. and Edward Revere apprenticed with him (1783-1788).
- Son Joseph Warren Revere apprenticed with him (1791-1796).

PAUL REVERE SR. II   **BOSTON, MA**   1783-1792

- Opened a large retail hardware store on Essex Street (1783-1792).

PAUL REVERE SR. II   **BOSTON, MA**   1789-1792

- Opened a brass and copper foundry at 13 Lynn Street (Revere Brass & Copper Co.).

PAUL REVERE SR. II & SONS   **BOSTON, MA**   1792-1804

- Brought his sons Joshua and Paul III into the Revere Brass & Copper Co.
- Began casting church bells at the shop (40' x 46') on 13 Lynn Street (1792).
- Son Joshua worked at the foundry until he died (1792-D1801).
- Son Paul III worked at the foundry from 1792 until 1800, when he opened his own silversmith and goldsmith shop (succeeding father Paul Revere Sr. II at Ann Street).
- Invented a process for making malleable copper.
- Invented a process for rolling sheet copper (1796).

- Supplied all the brass and copper work for the U.S. ironside frigate *Constitution* (1796).
- Provided bolts, spikes, etc., of malleable copper and a brass ships bell.

PAUL REVERE SR. II & SON **BOSTON, MA** 1796-1798
- Partner and son: Joseph Warren Revere.
- Moved his goldsmith and silversmith shop from 50 Cornhill to Ann Street.
- Leased the shop (18′ x 18′) from a Mary Landon.

PAUL (SR. II) & J. (JOSEPH) **BOSTON, MA** 1798-1800
W. (WARREN) REVERE
- Goldsmith and silversmith shop.
- Located on Ann Street.
- Son Paul Revere III succeeded Paul Revere Sr. II at this shop (1800).

REVERE (PAUL SR. II) & SON **CANTON, MA** 1800-1818
- Partner and son: Joseph Warren Revere.
- Bought a rolling and slitting mill on the Naponset River in Canton, MA, from Leonard (Jonathan) & Kinsley (Adam) (1799).
- Converted it to a copper rolling mill called the Paul Revere Copper Manufactory.
- Joseph Warren Revere worked at Canton from 1800-1804, then moved back to Boston and joined his father in the bell and cannon foundry's main office.
- Canton employed 20 workers.
- The Canton copper rolling mill became part of the Revere Brass & Copper Co. at 13 Lynn Street, Boston, MA.
- Supplied copper plate for the Boston state house (1802).
- Supplied copper plates (sheathing) for the hull of the U.S. ironside frigate *Constitution* ("Old Iron Sides") and other ships (1803).
- Made copper plates for two boilers on Robert Fulton's Hudson River steamboat (1808).
- Turned over Revere Brass & Copper Co. to his son Joseph Warren Revere and retired (1811).
- Paul Revere Sr. II died and his son Joseph Warren became owner (1818).
- Became the Joseph W. Revere Copper Manufactory, as part of the Joseph W. Revere Brass & Copper Co.

REVERE (PAUL SR. II) & SON **BOSTON, MA** 1800-1805
- Partner and son: Joseph Warren Revere.
- Revere Brass & Copper Co.
- Bell and cannon founders at 13 Lynn Street.
- Copper rolling mill located in Canton, MA.
- A business card (c. 1804) reads:

Revere and Son
Foundry at the north part of Boston
Cast bells and brass cannons of all size
All kinds of composition work
Manufacturers of sheets, bolts, spikes, nails, etc. from malleable copper
(Cold rolled)
(Cash for old brass and copper)

PAUL REVERE (SR. II) & SON **BOSTON, MA** 1805-1811
- Partner and son: Joseph Warren Revere.
- Revere Brass & Copper Co.
- Bell founders at 13 Lynn Street (discontinued cannon making).
- Copper-rolling mill located in Canton, MA.

PAUL REVERE (SR. II) & SON **BOSTON, MA** 1811-1818
- Partner and son: Joseph Warren Revere.
- Revere Brass & Copper Co.
- Bell founders at Charter Street (temporary office in their home).

- Copper-rolling mill located in Canton, MA.
- Paul Revere Sr. II retired (1811) (his son Paul III came down with consumption and moved into his house on Charter Street in 1810).
- Turned over the complete business to his son, Joseph Warren Revere, who was made company president.
- The office and brass foundry at 13 Lynn Street was closed.
- A brass foundry and rolling mill was opened at Stoughton, MA (had trip hammers).
- New offices were opened in Boston at the following locations:
    10 Kilby Street (1811-1816)
    14 Water Street (1816-1818)
    11 Kilby Street (1818)
- With the War of 1812 came a demand for arms, so Revere began making cannon again.
- Paul Revere Sr. II died and his son Joseph Warren Revere took over the Brass & Copper Company (1818).

(Paul Revere Sr. II was a goldsmith, silversmith, sword hiltor, gun powder maker, artificial tooth maker, rolled sheet copper maker, engraver on copper plate, brass bell maker, brass cannon maker, and copper and brass hardware maker)
(See Joseph W. Revere Brass & Copper Co.)

7. PAUL REVERE JR. III　　　　　BOSTON, MA　　　　　B1760-1792
- Son of Paul Revere Sr. II (B1774-D1818).
- Father of George Revere (B1795-D1870) and Paul Revere IV (B1789-D1857).
- Apprenticed at father's shop (1773-1775).
- Took part with his father in the Boston Tea Party (December 16, 1773).
- Served as first lieutenant in Col. Thomas Craft's Massachusetts artillery regiment.
- Served as captain and adjutant in his father's Massachusetts artillery regiment.
- Worked in father's goldsmith and silversmith shop at 50 Cornhill (1783-1792).

PAUL REVERE SR. II & SONS　　　　　BOSTON, MA　　　　　1792-1800
- Brass and copper foundry at 13 Lynn Street.
- Paul Revere III and brother Joshua Revere worked at the shop.
- Joshua died (1801).
- Paul Revere III opened his own goldsmith shop (1810).

PAUL REVERE JR. III　　　　　BOSTON, MA　　　　　1800-D1813
- Succeeded his father and brother Joseph Warren Revere when they left the silversmith business on Ann Street to concentrate on the brass and copper business.
- Goldsmith and silversmith shop locations:
    Ann Street (1800-1805)
    Fish Street (1805-1807)
    Henchman Lane (1807-1810)
- Son Paul Revere IV apprenticed with him (1804-1810).
- Came down with consumption (tuberculosis) and moved into his father's house on Charter Street (1810).
- Paul Revere III died (1813).
- Probably made silver-hilted swords.

(Goldsmith, silversmith, brass and copper founder)

8. JOSHUA REVERE　　　　　BOSTON, MA　　　　　B1774-1792
- Son of Paul Revere Sr. II.
- Apprenticed at father Paul Revere Sr. II goldsmith and silversmith shop at 50 Cornhill (1788-1792).

PAUL REVERE SR. II & SONS　　　　　BOSTON, MA　　　　　1792-1800
- Brass and copper foundry on Lynn Street.
- Sons Joshua Revere and Paul Revere III both worked at the shop.
- Joshua Revere died (1801).
- Paul Revere III left to open his own silversmith shop, succeeding his father at the Ann Street shop (1800).

9. JOSEPH WARREN REVERE   BOSTON, MA   B1777-1796
- Son of Paul Revere Sr. II (B1734-D1818).
- Father of John Revere Jr. (B1822-D1886), Paul Joseph Revere (B1832-D1863), Edward Hutchinson Robbins Revere I (B1827-D1868) (not a silversmith).
- Apprenticed as silversmith at his father's shop at 50 Cornhill (1791-1796).

PAUL REVERE SR. II & SON   BOSTON, MA   1796-1798
(JOSEPH WARREN)
- Goldsmith and silversmith shop on Ann Street.

PAUL (SR. II) & J. (JOSEPH)   BOSTON, MA   1798-1800
W. (WARREN) REVERE
- Goldsmith and silversmith shop on Ann Street.
- Paul Revere III succeeded them (1800).

REVERE (PAUL SR. II) & SON   CANTON, MA   1800-1818
(JOSEPH WARREN)
- Copper-rolling mill (Revere Copper Manufactory).
- Joseph Warren Revere worked there (1800-1804).

REVERE (PAUL SR. II) & SON   BOSTON, MA   1800-1805
(JOSEPH WARREN)
- Bell and cannon founders at 13 Lynn Street.
- Still had the copper manufactory in Canton.
- Son Joseph Warren joined Paul Revere Sr. from Canton (1804).

PAUL REVERE (JR. II) & SON   BOSTON, MA   1805-1811
(JOSEPH WARREN)
- Bell founders at 13 Lynn Street (discontinued cannon).
- Still had the copper manufactory in Canton.

PAUL REVERE (SR. II) & SON   BOSTON, MA   1811-1818
(JOSEPH WARREN)
- After his son Paul Revere III came down with consumption in 1810, Paul Revere Sr. II retired and turned over the Brass & Copper Co. to Joseph Warren Revere (1811).
- The office and foundry at 13 Lynn Street was closed.
- Temporary offices were located at the Revere home on Charter Street.
- New Boston office locations:
    10 Kilby Street (1811-1816)
    14 Water Street (1816-1818)
    11 Kilby Street (1818)
- Copper manufactory located in Canton, MA.
- Opened a brass foundry and rolling mill at Stoughton, MA (with trip hammers).
- Began operating as bell and cannon founders again (went back to cannon making for the War of 1812).
- Joseph Warren's nephew George Revere apprenticed under him (1811-1816).
- Paul Revere Sr. II died and Joseph Warren Revere took over the company (1818).

JOSEPH W. (WARREN) REVERE   BOSTON, MA   1818-1828
- Joseph W. Revere Brass & Copper Co.
- Bell manufacturer and copper dealer.
- Joseph W. Revere Copper Manufactory located in Canton, MA.
- Brass foundry and rolling mill located in Stoughton, MA (closed 1828)
- Boston offices locations:
    Liberty Square (1818-1821)
    Water Street at corner of Adams (1821-1825)
    75 Kilby Street (1825-1828)

REVERE COPPER CO.   BOSTON, MA   1828-1845
- President: Joseph Warren Revere.

- Treasurer: James Davis Jr.
- Copper and brass works located in Canton, MA.
- Boston office locations:
  - 22 Fayette Place (1828-1830, home)
  - 122 Tremont Street (1830-1832, home)
  - North Battery Wharf (1832-1845)
- Joseph Warren's son John Revere Jr. joined as company clerk (1843-1845).

REVERE COPPER CO.   **BOSTON, MA**   1845-1861

- President: Joseph Warren Revere, North Battery Wharf office.
- Treasurer: James Davis Jr., North Battery Wharf office.
- Sales agent: John Revere, new sales office at 97 State.
- Joseph Warren's son Paul Joseph joined the company (1856-1861), then joined the army and was killed during the Civil War (1863).
- Copper & Brass Works located in Canton, MA.
- Canton superintendent: Frederick Walker Lincohn.
- Company offices at North Battery Wharf were consolidated with the new sales office at 97 State Street (1861).

REVERE COPPER CO.   **BOSTON, MA**   1861-1867

- President: Joseph Warren Revere.
- Treasurer: James Davis Jr.
- Sales agent: John Revere Jr.
- Company offices located at 97 State Street.
- Copper & Brass Works located in Canton, MA.
- Canton superintendent: Frederick Walker Lincohn.
- Made cannon during the Civil War.
- Joseph Warren Revere died (1867).
- Frederic Walker Lincohn became company president.

(Joseph Warren Revere was a goldsmith, silversmith, brass bell and cannon founder, and copper founder. Rolled sheet brass and copper products. Probably made silver-hilted swords while a silversmith.)

10. JOHN REVERE JR.   **BOSTON, MA**   B1822-1845

- Son of Joseph Warren Revere (B1777-D1867).
- Father of William Bacon Revere (B1859-D1948), Edward Hutchinson Robbins Revere II (B1867-D1951).
- Attended Harvard University (1837-1841).
- Employed at A&C Cunningham, Boston, MA (1841-1843).
- Joined Revere Copper Co. as clerk (1843-1845).

REVERE COPPER CO.   **BOSTON, MA**   1845-1861

- President at North Battery Wharf office: Joseph Warren Revere.
- Treasurer at North Battery Wharf office: James Davis Jr.
- Sales agent at 97 State Street: John Revere Jr.
- Company office at North Battery Wharf consolidated with the sales office at 97 State Street (1861).

REVERE COPPER CO.   **BOSTON, MA**   1861-1867

- President: Joseph Warren Revere.
- Treasurer: James Davis Jr.
- Sales agent: John Revere Jr.
- Company manufacturing and sales office located at 97 State Street.
- Copper & Brass Works located in Canton, MA.
- Made cannon during the Civil War.
- Joseph Warren Revere died (1867).

REVERE COPPER CO. BOSTON, MA 1867-1871
- New manufacturing and sales office located at 47 Kilby Street.
- Copper and brass works located in Canton, MA.
- President: Frederic Walker Lincohn.
- Treasurer: S.T. Show.
- Sales agent: John Revere Jr.
- Frederick Walker Lincohn died (1871).
- James Davis Jr. was made a partner.

REVERE COPPER & CO. BOSTON, MA 1871-1881
- Manufacturing and sales office located at 47 Kilby Street.
- Copper and brass works located in Canton, MA.
- President: James Davis Jr.
- Treasurer: John Revere Jr.
- Sales agent: S.T. Show.
- James Davis Jr. died (1881).

REVERE COPPER CO. BOSTON, MA 1881-1886
- Manufacturing and sales office located in 47 Kilby Street.
- Copper and brass works: Canton, MS.
- President: John Revere Jr.
- Treasurer: William Bacon Revere (son of John Revere Jr.).
- Sales agent: S.T. Snow.
- John Revere Jr. died (1886).

REVERE COPPER CO. BOSTON, MA 1886-1900
- Manufacturing and sales office located at 47 Kilby Street.
- Copper and brass works located in Canton, MA.
- President: Henry Winsor.
- Sales agent: Edward Hutchinson Robbins Revere II (son of John Revere Jr.).
- Superintendent at the Canton works: William Bacon Revere.
- Revere Copper Co. merged with Taunton Copper Co. and New Bedford Copper Co. (1900).

TAUNTON, NEW BEDFORD COPPER CO. BOSTON, MA 1900-1928
- President: E. (Edward) H. (Hutchinson) R. (Robbins) Revere II.
- Merged with five other copper and brass companies (1928).

REVERE COPPER & BRASS INC. BOSTON, MA 1928-1998
- Edward Hutchinson Robbins Revere II was on the board of directors.

11. PAUL JOSEPH REVERE BOSTON, MA B1832-D1863
- Son of Joseph Warren Revere.
- Graduated from Harvard University (1852).
- Worked with father at Revere Copper Company offices at 97 State Street (1856-1861).
- Served in Civil War in 20th infantry regiment of Massachusetts.
- Captured at Richmond (1861).
- Exchanged in 1862.
- Died at Gettysburg (1863).

12. GEORGE REVERE BOSTON, MA B1795-1816
- Son of Paul Revere III (B1760-D1813).
- Apprenticed under uncle Joseph Warren Revere (Revere & Son) as a brass founder (1811-1816).

GEORGE REVERE BOSTON, MA 1816-1828
- Listed in Boston city directory as a plate worker.
- Locations:

    55 Hanover Street (1816-1817)
    9 Union Street (1817-1823)
    14 Exchange Street (1823-1825)
    Poplar Street (1825-1826, home)
    Spring Street (1826-1828, home)

RICE (JOHN H.) & REVERE (GEORGE)   BOSTON, MA   1828-1841

- Locations:
    3 Faneuil Hall (1828-1832)
    3 and 7 Faneuil Hall (1832-1839)
    31 Union Street (1839-1841)
- Advertised in Boston city directory as maker of sheet tin, sheet iron ware, stoves and grates, and seller of brass, "Britannia lamps of every description," and cast iron work.
- George Revere died in Somerville, MA (1870).

13. PAUL REVERE (IV)   BOSTON, MA   B1789-1821

- Son of Paul Revere III.
- Apprenticed and worked with his father as a silversmith (1804-1810).
- His father died of consumption (tuberculosis) (1813).
- Worked for uncle Joseph Warren Revere as a bell and cannon founder (1811-1818) and bell manufacturer and copper dealer (1818-1821).

REVERE (PAUL IV) & BLACK (WILLIAM)   BOSTON, MA   1821-1822

- Brass founders located at 3 Battery Street (at the corner of March Street).

PAUL REVERE (IV) & CO.   BOSTON, MA   1822-1823

- Partners: William Blake, John W. Sullivan.
- Brass founders located at 3 Battery Street (at the corner of March Street).

PAUL REVERE (IV)   BRIDGEWATER, MA   1823-D1857

- Brass founder.
- Paul Revere IV died (1857).

(N)   **JOSEPH RICE**   BALTIMORE, MD   B1761-1785
       RICE (JOSEPH) & BARRY (STANDISH)   BALTIMORE, MD   1785-1788

- Located on Market Street (below Calvert Street).

       RICE (JOSEPH) & RUTTER (RICHARD)   BALTIMORE, MD   1788-1796
       JOSEPH RICE   SAVANNAH, GA   1796-1801
       JOSEPH RICE   AUGUSTA, GA   1802-D1808

(Also engraver)

(A)   **SAMUEL S. RICHARDS**   PHILADELPHIA, PA   1800-1818

- Located at 136 South Front Street.

(Also goldsmith)

(A)   **GEORGE W. RIGGS**   MONTGOMERY CO., VT   B1777-1805
       GEORGE W. RIGGS   GEORGETOWN, VT   1805-1812
       GEORGE W. RIGGS   BALTIMORE, MD   1812-1815

- Located at 74 Baltimore Street.
- Jewelry and fancy store.
- Made silver-mounted officer swords with bird-head pommels and ivory grips.

       RIGGS (GEORGE W.) & GRIFFITH (HENRY)   BALTIMORE, MD   1815-1819

- Located at 74 Baltimore Street.

GEORGE W. RIGGS	BALTIMORE, MD	1819-D1864

- Located at 260 Baltimore Street.

(N) **JOHN ROSS**	BALTIMORE, MD	B1756, 1780-D1798

- Located at 65 Harrison Street.

(N) **RICHARD RUTTER**	BALTIMORE, MD	1768-1788
RICE (JOSEPH) & RUTTER (RICHARD)	BALTIMORE, MD	1788-1796
RICHARD RUTTER	BALTIMORE, MD	1796-1798

- Located at 87 Baltimore Street.

(N) **JOHN Y. SAVAGE**	RALEIGH, NC	1800-1819
JOHN Y. SAVAGE & JOHN C. STEDMAN	RALEIGH, NC	1819-1824
JOHN Y. SAVAGE & HENRY KUNSMAN	SALISBURY, NC	1824-1825
JOHN Y. SAVAGE	NEW YORK, NY	1825-1839

(Also watch maker, jeweler)
(See Henry Kunsman)
(See John C. Stedman)

(A) **ROBERT SHEPHERD**	ALBANY, NY	B1781-1800
SHEPHERD (ROBERT) & BOYD (WILLIAM)	ALBANY, NY	1800-1810

- Made silver-hilted swords with eagle-head and bird-head pommels.
- Sold swords to Lemuel Wells & Co., New York, NY.

ROBERT SHEPHERD	ALBANY, NY	1810-1822

(N) **HEZEKIAH SILLIMAN**	NEW HAVEN, CT	B1738-1765
CUTLER (RICHARD), SILLIMAN (HEREKIAH), & WARD (AMBROSE)	NEW HAVEN, CT	1765-1770
HEZEKIAH SILLIMAN	NEW HAVEN, CT	1770-D1804

(See Richard Cutler)
(See Ambrose Ward)

(A) **THOMAS SPARROW JR.**	PHILADELPHIA, PA	B1746-1765

- Apprenticed with his father Thomas Sparrow Sr. (c. 1760-1765).
- Advertised the following (1765):
  - *Makes all sorts of gold and silver work*
  - *Doctors instruments of all sorts*
  - *Masons medals*
  - *Engraving plates*
  - *Guns and pistols mounted with silver*
  - *Letters and cyphers*
  - *All kinds of stones*
  - *Barometers*
  - *Whip and cane heads*
  - *Seals of all sorts*
  - *Silver spurs*
  - *Coat and jacket buttons*
  - *Shoe and knee buckles*

Gorgets
Silver table ware, dishes, pots, etc.
Candle sticks
Chased, pierced, gadrooned and plain sword hilts
Garter and belts buckles

THOMAS SPARROW JR.   ANNAPOLIS, MD   1765-1784
- Located on South East Street (near St. Ann's church).

(A) **JAMES SPENCER**   ANNAPOLIS, MD   1765-1784
- Located on East Street.
- Advertised "chased, pierced, gadrooned and plain sword hilts" (1765).

(N) **JOHN C. STEDMAN**   RALEIGH, NC   1800-1818
    JOHN Y. SAVAGE & JOHN STEDMAN   RALEIGH, NC   1818-1824
    JOHN C. STEDMAN   RALEIGH, NC   1824-D1833

(See John Y. Savage)
(Also watch maker, jeweler)

(N) **JAMES STEEL**   BALTIMORE, MD   1812-1815

(N) **JOHN STEEL**   ANNAPOLIS, MD   1700-D1722

(N) **SAMUEL STEELE**   BALTIMORE, MD   1829-1850

(A) **ROBERT SWAN (SWAINE)**   PHILADELPHIA, PA   1799-1831
- Located at 77 South 2nd Street.

(N) **WILLIAM SWAN (SWAINE)**   WORCESTER, MA   B1715, 1735-D1774

(A) **JOHN SYNG**   PHILADELPHIA, PA   1734-1772
- Located on Market Street.

(A) **PHILIP SYNG JR.**   PHILADELPHIA, PA   1720-1771
- Made silver-hilted swords for army officers during the French and Indian War (1756-1763).

(N) **ANDREW TYLER**   BOSTON, MA   B1692, 1712-D1747

(A) **PETER VAN DYKE**   NEW YORK, NY   B1664, 1684-D1751
- Made silver-hilted court swords.

(N) **AMBROSE WARD**   BRIDGEPORT, CT   B1735-1765
- Made silver-hilted infantry officer swords with eagle-head pommels.
    CUTLER (RICHARD), SILLIMAN   NEW HAVEN, CT   1765-1770
    (HEREKIAH), & WARD (AMBROSE) & CO.
    AMBROSE WARD   NEW HAVEN, CT   1770-D1808

(See Richard Cutler)
(See Hezekiah Silliman)

(N) **ANDREW ELLICOTT WARNER (SR.)**   HARTFORD CO., MD   B1786-1798
- Moved to Baltimore with his father Cuthbert Warner and brother Thomas Warner (1798).

CUTHBERT WARNER	BALTIMORE, MD	1798-1805

- Andrew Ellicott Warner Sr. apprenticed with his father (c. 1800-1805).

T. (THOMAS) & A. (ANDREW) E. (ELLICOTT) WARNER SR.	BALTIMORE, MD	1805-1812

- Located at 5 North Gay Street.

ANDREW ELLICOTT WARNER (SR.)	BALTIMORE, MD	1812-D1870

- Son Andrew Ellicott Warren Jr. apprenticed and worked with him (c. 1830-1870).
- Located at 5 North Gay Street.
- Made silver-hilted short swords (hangers and hunting swords) with bird-head and eagle-head pommels.

(Also watch maker)

(N) **ANDREW ELLICOTT WARNER JR.**	BALTIMORE, MD	Bc1815-1870

- Apprenticed and worked in his father's shop at 5 North Gay Street (c. 1830-1870).

ANDREW ELLICOTT WARNER JR.	BALTIMORE, MD	1870-1893

- Located at 135 W. Baltimore Street.
- Retired (1893).

(Also watch maker)

(N) **CUTHBERT WARNER**	BUCKS CO., PA	B1760-1783
CUTHBERT WARNER	HARTFORD COUNTY, MD	1783-1798

- Father of Andrew Ellicott Warner and Thomas Warner.
- Moved to Baltimore with sons Thomas and Andrew Ellicott Warner (1798).

CUTHBERT WARNER	BALTIMORE, MD	1798-D1838

- Thomas Warner apprenticed with him (c. 1798-1805).
- Andrew Ellicott Warner apprenticed with him (c. 1800-1805).

(Also watch maker)

(N) **JOSEPH WARNER**	PHILADELPHIA, PA	1800-1850

- Located at 22 Greenleaf Ct. (1800-1813), 2 Greenleaf Ct. (1813-1850).

(C) **JOSEPH P. WARNER**	BALTIMORE, MD	B1811, 1830-1837
JOSEPH P. WARNER	PHILADELPHIA, PA	1837-1839
JOSEPH P. WARNER	BALTIMORE, MD	1839-D1862

(N) **THOMAS WARNER**	HARTFORD CO., MD	B1780-1798

- Moved to Baltimore with father Cuthbert Warner and brother Andrew Ellicott Warner (1798).

CUTHBERT WARNER	BALTIMORE, MD	1798-1805

- Thomas Warner apprenticed with his father (c. 1798-1805).

T. (THOMAS) & A. (ANDREW) E. (ELLICOTT) WARNER	BALTIMORE, MD	1805-1812

- Located at 5 North Gay Street.

THOMAS WARNER	BALTIMORE, MD	1812-D1828

- Located on East Street (between North Gay and Holliday Streets).

(Also watch maker)

(A) **GEORGE I. WELLES**	HEBRON, CT	B1784-1807
ALFRED & GEORGE I. WELLES	BOSTON, MA	1807-1812

- Located at 55 Cornhill Street.

WELLES (ALFRED & GEORGE I.) & WILLIAMS (DEODAT)	BOSTON, MA	1812-1815

- Located at 55 Cornhill Street.
  GEORGE I. WELLES & CO.   BOSTON, MA   1815-D1827
- Located on Somerset Street.
- Partners: Alfred Welles, Horace Porter, Hugh Gelston.

(A) **ALFRED WELLES**   HEBRON, CT   B1783-1805
    ALFRED WELLES   BOSTON, MA   1805-1807
    ALFRED & GEORGE I. WELLES   BOSTON, MA   1807-1812
- Located at 55 Cornhill Street.
  WELLES (ALFRED & GEORGE I.) & WILLIAMS (DEODAT)   BOSTON, MA   1812-1815
- Located at 55 Cornhill Street.
  GEORGE I. WELLES & CO.   BOSTON, MA   1815-1827
- Located on Somerset Street.
- Partners: Alfred Welles, Horace Porter, Hugh Gelston.
  WELLES (ALFRED) & GELSTON (HUGH)   BOSTON, MA   1827-1829
- Located at 69 Washington Street.
  ALFRED WELLES & CO.   BOSTON, MA   1829-D1860
- Located at 69 Washington Street.

(A) **ALVAN WILCOX**   NORWICH, CT   B1783-1805
    HART (JUDAH) & WILCOX (ALVAN)   NORWICH, CT   1805-1807
    ALVAN WILCOX   NEWARK, NJ   1807-1819
    ALVAN WILCOX   FAYETTEVILLE, NC   1819-1823
    ALVAN WILCOX   NEW HAVEN, CT   1823-D1870
- Made silver-hilted infantry officer swords with pillow pommels and straight blued and gilded blades.

(A) **DEODAT WILLIAMS**   HARTFORD, CT   D1756, 1776-1812
- Advertised plated ware, jewelry and "a great variety of rich and elegant military goods" (1812).
  WELLES (ALFRED & GEORGE I.) & WILLIAMS (DEODAT)   BOSTON, MA   1812-1815
- Located at 55 Comhill Street.
  DEODAT WILLIAMS   BOSTON, MA   1815-D1816

(N) **WILLIAM A. WILLIAMS**   ALEXANDRIA, VA   B1787, 1809-D1846

(A) **SAMUEL WILLIAMSON**   PHILADELPHIA, PA   1800-D1843
- Located at 118 South Front Street.

(N) **GEORGE WILLIG JR. (WILLICK)**   PHILADELPHIA, PA   B1800-1818
    RASCH (ANTHONY) & WILLIG (GEORGE JR.)   PHILADELPHIA, PA   1818-1819
    GEORGE WILLIG JR.   PHILADELPHIA, PA   1819-1830
- Made silver-mounted knives and dirks.

(N) **JAMES WILLIG**   BALTIMORE, MD   B1798, 1818-1831

(A) **WILTBERGER (CHRISTIAN JR.) & ALEXANDER (SAMUEL)**   PHILADELPHIA, PA   1793-1797
- Located at 33 South 2nd Street.

CHRISTIAN WILTBERGER JR.	**PHILADELPHIA, PA**	1797-1815

- Located at 16 Sassafras Street. (1797-1800), 13 North 2nd Street (1800-1815).

CHRISTIAN WILTBERGER JR.	**WASHINGTON, DC**	1815-D1851

(A) **EDWARD WINSLOW**   **BOSTON, MA**   B1669, 1690-D1753
- Apprentice: Jonathan Otis (1738-1743).

(A) **HUGH WISHART**   **NEW YORK, NY**   B1766, 1784-1818
- Located at 62 Wall Street and 98 Market Street (1784-1810), 60 Maiden Lane (1810-1818).

HUGH & DANIEL WISHART   **NEW YORK, NY**   1818-1840
- Located at 45 Maiden Lane.
- Hugh Wishart died (1840).

DANIEL WISHART   **NEW YORK, NY**   1840-D1845
- Located at 45 Maiden Lane.
- Daniel Wishart died (1845).

(A) **GENERAL GEORGE WOLF**   **PHILADELPHIA, PA**   1828-1856
- Made silver-hilted infantry officer short sabers with eagle-head pommels and reverse-P knuckle bows.

(A) **JOSEPH WYATT**   **PHILADELPHIA, PA**   1791-1798
- Made silver-hilted infantry officer short sabers with eagle-head pommels.

CHAPTER 11
Confederate Sword Makers

(A) **BOYLE (EDWARD), GAMBLE**   RICHMOND, VA   1861-1865
    (THOMAS) & McFEE (EDWARD P.)
- Located on South 6th Street (one block from the Richmond Armory–old Virginia Manufactory).

(A) **BURGER (PETER) & BRO. (HENRY R.)**   RICHMOND, VA   1861-1865
- Sword factory located at the Petersburg Railroad Bridge.

(A) **C.B. CHURCHILL & CO.**   NATCHEZ, MS   1861-1862
- Moved to Shelby County, AL (October 1862).
    C.B. CHURCHILL & CO.   SHELBY CO., AL   1862-1865
- Operated an iron foundry.
- Made edged weapons.

(A) **JAMES CONNING**   MOBILE, AL   1840-1846
- Advertised as a dealer, importer, and repairer of silver (fancy) goods of all descriptions. (Silversmith, jeweler)

    JAMES CONNING   MOBILE, AL   1846-1861
- Advertised a wide variety of goods for the "gentleman soldier" (Mexican War, 1846-1848).
- Served as a sergeant in the Washington light infantry.
- Advertised a complete line of military goods, including swords, firearms, and buttons.
- Advertised in the *Mobile Daily Register* (September 14, 1859):
  > *Just Received:*
  > *State regulation fatigue caps.*
  > *Can get A.V.C. (Alabama Volunteer Cavalry) or M.V.C.*
  > *(Mobile Volunteer Cavalry) in the front.*
  > *50 gross buttons (A.V.C. or M.V.C.)*
  > *10000 U.S. Musket caps*
  > *100 Colt's Navy revolvers*

Also swords, epaulettes and military accoutrements of every description.
I have on hand a full assortment of military goods of every description, such as adopted by the state (Alabama) and U.S. regulations and can furnish General and regimental officers with everything they require.

Chapeaux	*Caps*	*Swords*
Belts	*Silk sashes*	*Sword knots*
Epaulettes	*Arquilettes*	*Shoulder straps*
Buttons	*Gold and gilt stars*	*Laces*

Volunteer companies will be furnished with all their equipments at short notice.
James Conning
Military Emporium
Mobile, AL

- A James Conning & Co. receipt (1861) reads:

    Importer of:

Jewelry	*Watches*
Cutlery	*Silver and plated ware*
Guns	*Pistols*
Military goods	*Fancy goods*
"Eley's" wire cartridges	*Caps and wads*

    Repairing clocks, watches and jewelry.
    At the sign of the Golden Eagle and watch.

(A) **COOK (FERDINAND W.C.) & BROTHER (FRANCIS L.)** ATHENS, GA   1863-1864
- Used Swedish iron.
- Had a Confederate contract for 30,000 Enfield-type saber bayonets with sheaths and frogs at $3 each.
- Made infantry rifles, light artillery and cavalry carbines (musketoon), cavalry horseshoes, agricultural machinery (Sorghum Mills), and bayonets and repaired small arms.

(A) **ABRAHAM HENRY DEWITT**   COLUMBUS, GA   1847-1862
- Sent a sample infantry non-comm. sword to Governor Pickens of South Carolina (October 1861).
- Governor Pickens sent the sword sample and a letter introducing Dewitt to his chief ordnance officer, Edward Manigault, asking Manigault to inspect the sword and decide if any were needed by the state (November 8, 1861).

(N) **DICKSON (WILLIAM) & NELSON (OWEN O.) CO.**   TUSCUMBIA, AL   1861-1862
- President: attorney Owen O. Nelson (B1823-D1892).
- Partners: planter William Dickson (B1798-D1880), armorer Lewis H. Sadler (B1818-D1887).
- Had an Alabama contract for 500 Mississippi rifles with bayonets at $33 each (January 1862).
- Started to build an arms factory near the Memphis and Charleston railroad line in Franklin County, AL (Dickson, AL), 20 miles west of Tuscumbia, AL (1862). The factory was never completed.

DICKSON (WILLIAM) & NELSON (OWEN O.)   ROME, GA   1862
- Rented space in the O.B. Eve Carriage Plant, Rome, GA (summer 1862).
- The plant burned down (August 28, 1862). Moved to Adairsville, GA.

DICKSON (WILLIAM) & NELSON (OWEN O.)   ADAIRSVILLE, GA   1862-1864
- Obtained space at the old railroad shops of the Tennessee and Georgia railroad (the railroad ran between Chattanooga and Atlanta) (September 1862).

- Bought rolled gun iron and bayonet iron from Shelby Iron Works, Selma, AL.
- Reportedly made bowie knives and swords.
- Moved to Dawson, GA (March 1864).

DICKSON (WILLIAM) & NELSON (OWEN O.)   DAWSON, GA   1864-1866

- Bought 25 acres of land from W.H. Bailey near the Dawson Railroad depot.
- Set up a gun shop called the Shakanoosa Arms Manufacturing Co.
- Superintendent: Frank Benjamin.
- Had an iron foundry.
- The company went out of business (1866).

DAWSON MFG. CO.   DAWSON, GA   1866-1885

- President: Owen O. Nelson.
- Made railroad passenger and freight cars.
- Had a lumber mill, iron foundry, and machine shop.

(A) **A. & B. DOUGLAS**   BEECH, MO   1860-1861
     A. & B. DOUGLAS   COLUMBIA, SC   1861-1862

- Advertised as B. Douglas Arms Co. in the *Daily Southern Guardian* (1862) as follows:
Companies now being equipped, can be supplied with, swords, sabers, spurs and bits etc. at the A.&B. Douglas & Co. Sword factory/old foundry/Washington Street.

(A, C) **AGRIDER H. DUFILHO SR.**   PARIS, FRANCE   B1833-1853

- Immigrated to New Orleans, LA (1853).

     A. (AGRIDER) H. DUFILHO SR.   NEW ORLEANS, LA   1853-D1907

- Locations:
  - 86 Custom House (1853-1857)
  - 96 Custom House (1857-1860)
  - 21 Royal Street (1860-1907)
- In addition to swords, made silver-mounted push daggers and bowie knives.
- Advertised on Civil War receipts as manufacturer of fine cutlery and surgical instruments and repairer of cutlery.

(A) **THE FARISH CARTER COTTON MILL**   COLUMBUS, GA   1849-1865

- Had six stories and a basement.
- Made yarn and cloth.
- The mill closed (late 1860).
- Five companies rented space in the now-vacant mill (January 1861).
  - Basement: A.H. Dewitt. Sword factory. Left in early 1862.
  - First floor: A.D. Brown (Jr. and Sr.). Wood products factory; made mill shuttles, canteens, and sword handles.
  - Second floor: Brands & Korner. Drums, fifes, India rubber cloth, and oil cloth (sword-handle covering).
  - Third floor: E.S. Greenwood & W.C. Gray. Rope factory (sword grip windings).
  - Fourth floor: L. Haiman & Son. Sword factory. Left in late 1861.
  - No information is known about the occupants of the fifth and sixth floors.
- The mill was burned down by the cavalry corps of Union Gen. James C. Wilsons (April 19, 1865).

(A) **REES FITZPATRICK**   CINCINNATI, OH   B1809-1833
     REES FITZPATRICK   BATON ROUGE, LA   1833-1838

- Purchased a house behind cutler Daniel Searles' house on St. Louis Street (near America Street). Daniel Searles was a sword, dirk, and bowie knife maker.
- Fitzpatrick did not make a bowie knife for Col. James Bowie as reported, but he did work with Daniel Searles.
- Searles made knives for Rezin Pleasant Bowie and Col. James Bowie.

- Some bowie knives are signed "Searles & F. Patrick" (Fitzpatrick).
- Fitzpatrick did the silver and gold work on some of Searles' bowie knives.
- Fitzpatrick also made quality silver-hilted bowie knives, some with horse-head pommels.

REES FITZPATRICK	NATCHEZ, MS	1838-D1868
L. (LOUIS) A. FITZPATRICK	NATCHEZ, MS	1868-1885

- Son of Rees Fitzpatrick.
- Located at 521 Main Street.

(See Daniel Searles)

(A, C) **B. (BENJAMIN) FLAGG** MILLBURY, MA 1851-1852
- Was a partner in William Glaze & Co., Columbia, SC, while they filled a large South Carolina contract (1851-1852) for pistols, muskets, and rifles.

(See William Glaze)

(A) **LOUIS B. FROELICH** BAVARIA, GERMANY B1819-c1857
- Immigrated to London, England (c. 1857).

LOUIS B. FROELICH LONDON, ENGLAND c1857-1861
- Worked on steam engines for ships.
- Immigrated to New York, NY (c. 1860), and from there to Wilmington, NC (early 1861).

LOUIS B. FROELICH NEW HANOVER CO. WILMINGTON, NC 1861

- Worked for Loeb & Swartzman, dealers in coal, wood, and groceries. They decided to open a button manufactory when the Civil War began.
- Froelich managed the button factory.
- Advertised in the *Daily Journal* (June and July 1861):

    Loeb & Swartzman as the Wilmington N.C. Button Manufactory under the direction of Mr. L. Froelich, a thoroughly educated mechanic. We are able to turn out, at the quickest notice, all sizes of uniform buttons.

- Froelich formed a partnership with a Col. Benjamin Estran, who had arrived in Wilmington in early 1861 from Richmond, VA (fall 1861).

ESTRAN (BENJAMIN) & FROELICH (LOUIS B.) SWORD FACTORY WILMINGTON, NC 1861-1862

- Also called the Wilmington Sword Factory and the Confederate Arms Factory.
- Before the partnership with Froelich, Estran had proposed to North Carolina Governor Henry T. Clark that he could train a company in the use of the cavalry lance (June 1861). Governor Clark wrote to Confederate General Anderson that he could raise such a company if Anderson approved. Such "lancer" regiments were formed in Texas (1st, 2nd, and 3rd Lancer regiments).
- No record of a North Carolina lancer unit is known. Estran & Froelich did sell lance heads to North Carolina and the Confederate ordnance offices.
- They obtained North Carolina arms contracts for:
    400 cavalry sabers (only 102 accepted)
    Approximately 900 sword (saber) bayonets with sheaths and attachment rings
    Approximately 200 foot artillery swords
    Some light artillery sabers (probably samples only)
    Approximately 200 lances (heads)
    Some naval cutlasses (probably samples only)
- Estran was the promoter of the contracts, passing himself off as a Confederate colonel of cavalry.
- Froelich supervised the making of the edged weapons in their factory.

A list of documented Estran & Froelich products paid for by the North Carolina ordnance office in Raleigh, NC (December 1861-March 1862)

226 sword (saber) bayonets @ 10.50 each
102 cavalry sabers with belts @ 24 each (contract for 400; 298 were rejected)
151 artillery swords (foot artillery short swords) @ 12 each
4 artillery swords (probably sample sergeant swords) @ 35 each
300 saber (sword) bayonets @ 12 each
50 attachments (bayonet rings) @ .90 each
192 lances (cavalry lance heads) @ 5 each
1 artillery cutlass (probably sample naval cutlass) @ 12 each
232 saber (sword) bayonets with sheaths and rings (attachment) @ 10.50 each

- In a letter to Confederate Secretary of War Judah P. Benjamin (March 11, 1862), North Carolina Governor Henry T. Clark stated that three-quarters of the Estran & Froelich cavalry sabers were worthless (only 102 of the 400 cavalry sabers made were accepted).

A list of documented Estran & Froelich products paid for by the Confederate ordnance office in Richmond, VA (December 1861-March 1862)

128 lances (cavalry lance heads) @ 7 each (November 16, 1861)
270 lance boots (cavalry lance head sheaths) @ .72 each (November 16, 1861)

- Estran & Froelich advertised in the *Daily Journal* (January 1862) for mechanics who can "execute round wood" (sword grips) and that they paid highest prices for old iron, copper, brass, and pewter.
- Advertised for coal @ .01 per pound (February 1862).
- A notice in the *Daily Journal* shows Estran & Froelich dissolving their partnership (March 12, 1862).
- Estran was exposed as a fraud in an article in the *Daily Richmond Examiner*, which quoted from an article in the *New York Herald* (1863).
- The *New York Herald* article said that Estran was a Hungarian who served in European wars, came to Richmond to open a military school, was appointed a military inspector by the Confederacy, and then was appointed a colonel in the Confederate cavalry. (Estran had written a book called *War Pictures from the South*, in which he called himself a Confederate hero.)
- The *Daily Journal* article revealed that Estran was, in reality, an unemployed valet who was known in Richmond before the war as a thief and vagabond, did not repay his debts, and had deserted his wife and family in Richmond. His wife was supporting him.
- His real name was Benjamin Raussey, and he was not a Confederate cavalry officer or inspector, nor had he fought in European wars or opened a military school.
- Froelich purchased a 2.5-acre lot from Asa Southerland in Kenansville, Duplin County, NC, for $900 (September 1862). It was the old James Kenan plantation at the western edge of town. It probably had sheds, barns, and a blacksmith shop or iron forge used on the old plantation.

CONFEDERATE STATES ARMORY **DUPLIN CO. KENANSVILLE, NC** 1862-1864

- Owner: Louis B. Froelich.
- Employee: Charles Bissinger.
- Froelich added a leather shop and steam-powered edged weapon machinery.
- Finished up his North Carolina contract for 900 sword (saber) bayonets.

A list of documented Froelich products paid for by the North Carolina ordnance office in Raleigh, NC (September 1862-July 1863)

153 saber (sword) bayonets @ 13 each.

- Sent a sample sergeants (non-comm.) sword to the Confederate ordnance department (1863). No contract was awarded.

A list of documented Froelich products paid for by the Confederate ordnance office in Richmond, VA (September 1862-July 1863)
    2 brass kettles @ 70 each
    99 saber (cavalry) belts @ 3 each
    34 saber (cavalry) belts @ 4 each
    102 saber (sword) bayonets with scabbards @ 10.50 each
    200 sets of infantry accouterments @ 13 a set

(The infantry accouterment set included a cartridge box, (percussion) cap pouch, cartridge box belt, waist belt, and bayonet scabbard.)

- On the evening of July 4, 1863, a battalion of Union cavalry under a Major Jacobs attached to Col. George W. Lewis's 3rd New York cavalry raided Kenansville, NC. They captured some Confederate cavalry troopers, their horses and equipment, and destroyed an armory, knapsack factory, 2,500 sabers, saber bayonets, and bowie knives, and a large quantity of tools, saddles, machinery, and food stores at Froelich's armory complex. The complete installation was not destroyed because it got dark and Major Jacobs was forced to move the next day to Warsaw, NC, because of a large Confederate force camped at nearby Magnolia, NC.

A list of documented Froelich products paid for by the Confederate ordnance office after the Union raid
    80 pounds of candles (November 12, 1863)
    1 sergeant (artillery non-comm.) sword with belt (sample) @ 35 (November 24, 1863)

- Froelich took in Mr. Jacob W.N. Cornehlson as a partner and formed Louis B. Froelich & Co. (January 1, 1864). Cornehlson paid $29,930.62 for his partnership.

LOUIS B. FROELICH & CO.   **KENANSVILLE, NC**   **1864-1865**

- Still called the Confederate States Armory during the Civil War.

A list of documented Froelich products paid for by the Confederate ordnance office in (1864)
    200 knapsacks @ 6 each (January 4, 1864)
    23 sword (saber) bayonets @ 10.50 each (January 25, 1864)
    436 cavalry sabers @ 28 each (January 25, 1864)
    133 saber (sword) bayonets @ 10 each (January 25, 1864)
    645 cavalry sabers @ 28 each (May 2, 1864)
    293 knapsacks @ 6 each (May 2, 1864)
    97 cavalry sabers @ 28 each (May 6, 1864)
    30 axes @ 12 each (December 31, 1864)

- The *Wilmington Journal* published a list (not a complete list) of Froelich's products furnished to the Confederacy from 1861 to 1864 (April 28, 1864):
  18 sets of surgical instruments
  800 gross buttons
  1,700 sets of infantry accoutrements
  300 saber belts
  500 knapsacks
  3,700 lances (cavalry lance heads)
  6,500 saber bayonets
  11,700 cavalry sabers

                600 naval cutlasses
                800 artillery cutlasses
- Froelich actually made the following products for the Confederacy:
        Cavalry sabers
        Cavalry saber belts
        Saber (sword) bayonets
        Foot artillery swords
        Naval cutlasses
        Foot officer sabers
        Bowie knives
        Lances (cavalry lance heads)
        Lance boots (cavalry lance head sheaths)
        Saddles
        Knapsacks
        Infantry accouterment sets
        Buttons
        Brass kettles
        Axes
        Surgical instruments sets
        Horseshoes

LOUIS B. FROELICH & CO.	**KENANSVILLE, NC**	**1865-1869**

- Made edged tools and leather goods.
- Listed as a horticulturist (farmer) in the city directory (1870).

(A)	**MIDDLETON GLAZE**	**CHESTER CO., SC**	**1780-1812**
	GLAZE (MIDDLETON) & PRESCOTT (JOHN)	**CHESTER CO., SC**	**1812-1816**
	GLAZE (MIDDLETON) & BOATWRIGHT (JAMES)	**CHESTER CO., SC**	**1816-1838**
	GLAZE (MIDDLETON) & BOATWRIGHT (JAMES)	**COLUMBIA, SC**	**1838-1851**

- Built a gun factory on the northeast corner of Laurel and Lincoln Streets in an area called Arsenal Hill (the South Carolina state arsenal was located there).

(A)	**WILLIAM GLAZE**	**CHESTER CO., SC**	**B1815-1838**

- Son of Middleton Glaze.

VEAL (JOHN SR.) & GLAZE (WILLIAM)	**COLUMBIA, SC**	**1838-1841**

(Silversmith, jeweler, clock and watch sales and repair, military goods)

WILLIAM GLAZE	**COLUMBIA, SC**	**1841-1848**

- Sold military goods, hardware, clocks and watches, silver tableware (forks and spoons), silver mugs, silver-plated goods, a variety of firearms, swords, gun powder, military goods, andirons, fireplace equipment, castors, candlesticks, spectacles, flower vases, and mantel ornaments.

(Silversmith, jeweler, clock and watch sales and repair)

GLAZE (WILLIAM) & RADCLIFFE (THOMAS W.)	**COLUMBIA, SC**	**1848-1851**
WILLIAM GLAZE & CO.	**COLUMBIA, SC**	**1851-1860**

- Called the Palmetto Armory.
- Partners: Benjamin Flagg (1851-1852), James Boatwright (died in 1857).
- Obtained a South Carolina contract (April 15, 1851), negotiated with Maj. James H. Trapier of the South Carolina ordnance department for:

1,000 M1841 rifles @ 15.50 each
6,000 M1842 muskets with bayonets @ 14.50 each
1,000 pair of M1842 pistols @ 14.50 each
1,000 M1840 cavalry sabers with scabbards @ 6.50 each
1,000 M1840 light artillery sabers with scabbards @ 6.50 each

- By November 1852, 2,500 muskets had been completed.
- George A. Shields joined the company (1851).
- Shields became foreman and later a partner (1865).
- The factory was located in the old Glaze & Boatwright factory at the northeast corner of Laurel and Lincoln Streets.
- Glaze added another three-story factory building with a bell tower and a 64′ x 154′ wing on the first floor.
- Employed machinists, iron workers, stockers, and burnishers.

WILLIAM GLAZE & CO.　　　　　　　　　　**COLUMBIA, SC**　　　　　　　　　　1860-1865

- Now called the Palmetto Iron Works.
- George A. Shields now foreman operating the foundry.
- Rifled and refurbished for the South Carolina ordnance department 3,720 rifled muskets that Glaze originally made and sold to the state of South Carolina in 1852 (mid 1861).
- Sold the state of Georgia 5,000 sword bayonets @ 6.50 each.
- Advertised with Thomas W. Radcliffe (former partner, 1848-1851) in the *Richmond Daily Examiner* and *Macon Telegraph* (June 6, 1861) for contributions to form a new arms company to be called the Confederate States Armory and Foundry Company (capital necessary: $1,000,000).
- The company was to fabricate artillery of all types, rifles, pistols, swords, bayonets, rockets, and munitions of war.
- Thomas E. McNeil was to be superintendent and agent.
- The company was never formed.
- Pistol-making machinery was purchased from A.H. Waters & Co., Millbury, MA (not brought to the company by Benjamin Flagg).
- Advertised in the Columbia, SC, city directory as an iron founder and machinist (1860).
- Offered to make the South Carolina ordnance department 24-lb. shot, 10-inch shells, heavy cannon, heavy mortars, 30 to 50 rifled muskets a day, and more than 50 pistols a day (December 4, 1860). No contract was negotiated.
- Offered to make the South Carolina ordnance department 25-30 guns a day for two years (February 26, 1861), requesting a $25,000 advance. No contract was negotiated.
- Obtained a Confederate contract for 5,000 rifled muskets (June 10, 1863).
- During the Civil War made 150,000 minnie balls as well as 10 inch bombshells, picks, and shovels for the Confederate ordnance department. Also made rollers for the powder mills at Raleigh and Columbia, SC.

GLAZE (WILLIAM) &　　　　　　　　　　**COLUMBIA, SC**　　　　　　　　　　1865-1866
SHEILDS (GEORGE A.)

- Still called the Palmetto Iron Works.
- Sheilds was now a junior partner.

SHIELDS (GEORGE A.) &　　　　　　　　　　**COLUMBIA, SC**　　　　　　　　　　1866-1868
GLAZE (WILLIAM)

- Still called the Palmetto Iron Works.
- Sheilds now senior partner.
- William Glaze declared himself bankrupt with the U.S. District Court (April 6, 1868).
- Sold his armory to partner George Sheilds and went back to the silversmith, cutlery, jewelry, and military goods business.
- Shields converted the armory into a cotton mill machinery factory.
- Shields died (1911) and his wife carried on the business until she died (1927).

WILLIAM GLAZE　　　　　　　　　　**COLUMBIA, SC**　　　　　　　　　　1868-D1883

- Located at 126 Richardson Street.

- Advertised jewelry, cutlery, watches, fishing tackle, silver and plated ware, eyeglasses, clocks, guns, and military goods.
- R.N. Richbourg joined the company (1873).
- Richbourg became manager (1882).
- William Glaze died (1883).

(Silversmith, jeweler, military goods, cutlery shop)

R.N. RICHBOURG   **COLUMBIA, SC**   1883-1930

(A) **JOHN D. GRAY**   **LONDON, ENGLAND**   c1825-1845

- Immigrated to Charleston, SC (1845).

JOHN D. GRAY & CO.   **CHARLESTON, SC**   1845-1850

- Started a railroad construction company.
- Built the first railroad line in South Carolina.
- Received a Georgia contract to build a railroad line between Dalton, GA (northwest Georgia) and Chattanooga, TN (southeast Tennessee) (1848). Completed in late 1849.
- Built his home along the railroad near Dalton, GA (late 1849).
- Built a furniture factory, grain mill, and lime kiln (1850s).
- Also owned and operated a wheat farm.
- A town grew up around his holdings, which became Graysville, GA.

JOHN D. GRAY & CO.   **GRAYSVILLE, GA**   1850-1864

- Furniture factory located on Whitehall Street.
- Contracted with the owners of the Muscogee Railroad to complete a rail line between Columbus, GA, east to Butler, GA (early 1850).
- Built an iron foundry and gun factory in Columbus, GA (early 1861).
- Also built his permanent home there (1861).
- Converted his Graysville furniture factory to a military wood products factory (1861).
- The products produced were gun stocks (Confederate contract and for use on his own firearms made at Columbus), 2,000 wooden (cedar) buckets (Virginia contract), 2,000 wooden canteens (Tennessee contract), 1,000 wooden tent poles, and slides and buttons (contract with White & Co., Dalton, GA).
- Graysville factory foremen included:
    - K.A. Buzzell
    - W.C. Davidson
    - J.D. Douglas
    - C.F. Miller
    - W.J. Page
    - J.H. Webb
    - P.L. Webb
- The factory was burned down by Gen. William T. Sherman's army (1864). Gray moved to Columbus, GA.

JOHN D. GRAY   **COLUMBUS, GA**   1861-1865

- Iron foundry and gun factory was called the Columbus Armory.
- Located on the Chattahoochee River at the foot of Franklin Street on Broad Street.
- Promised to make 500 to 600 guns a month in a letter to Col. Josiah Gorgas, chief of the Confederate ordnance department.
- Gray's contracts are as follows:
    - Confederate contract for 200 Mississippi rifles
    - Confederate contract for 1,000 carbines
    - Confederate contract for up to 20,000 Enfield rifles
    - Alabama contract for 177 Mississippi rifles
    - Georgia contract for 600 bowie knives
    - Georgia contract for 1,445 pikes
    - Georgia contract for 2,000 cavalry sabers

- For a short time, the Columbus Armory was leased by the Confederate government (c. 1863-1864).
- Advertised for laborers, carpenters, and blacksmiths and began to produce iron ware to sell to the public, including pots, fry pans kettles, andivons, ovens, skillets, axes, shovels, chains, ploughs, and sugarmills.
- The Columbus Armory was burned down by Union Gen. James C. Wilson's cavalry corps (April 19, 1865).

(A) ARTHUR BREEZE GRISWOLD		POUGHKEEPSIE, NY	B1829-1847
ARTHUR BREEZE GRISWOLD		NEW ORLEANS, LA	1847-1860

- Joined Hyde & Goodrich (1860).

HYDE (AUGUSTUS L.) & GRISWOLD (ARTHUR BREEZE)	NEW ORLEANS, LA	1860-1861
THOMAS (HENRY JR.) & GRISWOLD (ARTHUR BREEZE)	NEW ORLEANS, LA	1861-1865
ARTHUR BREEZE GRISWOLD & CO.	NEW ORLEANS, LA	1865-1866

- Located at 119 Canal Street.
- Partners: son George P. Griswold, Albert L. (Little) Abbott, Henry Ginder.

A. (ARTHUR) B. (BREEZE) GRISWOLD & CO.	NEW ORLEANS, LA	1866-1906

- Locations:
    - 119 Canal Street (1866-1895)
    - 701 Canal Street (1895-1897)
    - 728 Canal Street (1897-1906)
- Arthur Breeze Griswold died (1877).
- Son George P. Griswold took over the company.

(Silversmith, jeweler, military goods, imported revolvers)

A.B. GRISWOLD & CO. LTD.	NEW ORLEANS, LA	1906-1946

- Located at 728 Canal Street.
- President: George P. Griswold.

(A) L. (LOUIS) HAIMAN & BROTHER	COLUMBUS, GA	1860-1865

- Rented the upper floor of the Columbus Iron Works located on the corner of Thomas and Short Streets (next to the Haiman Armory) and set up a sword factory (Confederate States Sword Factory).
- Began making swords (1861).
- Their first sword was presented to Col. Peyton H. Colquitt.
- The first shipment of cavalry sabers (Confederate contract for 8,000 sabers) was shipped to a Captain Wagner, superintendent of the arsenal at Montgomery, AL, for Clanton's Alabama Cavalry Regiment.
- L. (Louis) Haiman & Bro. bought the Muscogee foundry and machine shop from the Columbus Iron Works and converted it to a pistol factory, which they called the Columbus Firearms Manufacturing Co. (April 1, 1862).
- Had a Confederate contract for 10,000 navy revolvers (August 26, 1862).
- Factory located at the corner of 14th and Oglethorpe Streets.
- Also bought the Muscogee Iron Works.
- The Muscogee Iron Works became part of the Columbus Firearms Manufacturing Co. complex.
- Located on the corner Franklin and Oglethorpe Streets.
- Advertised swords *"at reasonable prices for officers and sergeants, finished in the best quality for sale at the Confederate States Sword Factory of Columbus, GA. We can furnish officers swords with belts for $25 or $22 if four were ordered in one lot. Our swords are tested according to the rules laid down by the* Manual of War.*"*
- Elijah Haiman traveled to Europe to purchase materials, including Solingen, Prussia, sword blades.
- L. Haiman & Bro. also made brass plates for belts and cartridge boxes, leather bayonet mountings, camp stove parts, shotgun bayonets, rifle bayonets, wagon covers, mess plates, and tin cups.

(A) **HILLMAN BROTHERS**   **MEMPHIS, TN**   **1859-1861**
- Manufactured iron castings, nails, and pig iron (1859-1860).
- Located at 56 Front Street.

    HILLMAN BROTHERS   **MEMPHIS, TN**   **1861-1863**
- Located at 49 Front Row (at Court Street).
- Received a Confederate contract for 25,000 Mississippi rifle bayonets and 10,000 shotgun bayonets (August 1861).

(A) **JAMES N. (NEVINE) HYDE**   **NEW YORK, NY**   **1780-1798**
    HYDE (JAMES N.) & NEVINS (RUFUS)   **NEW YORK, NY**   **1798-1810**
    JAMES N. HYDE   **NEW YORK, NY**   **1810-1837**
- Opened a branch store in New Orleans (1814).

(Jeweler, merchant)

    JAMES N. HYDE   **NEW YORK, NY**   **1837-1860**
- Manager and partner: son Augustus L. Hyde.
- Merchant and fancy goods.
- Closed his New York store and sold his interest in the New Orleans branch to his son Augustus L. Hyde (1860).
- Augustus L. Hyde moved to New Orleans to run that store.
- James N. Hyde died (1867).

    JAMES N. HYDE   **NEW ORLEANS, LA**   **1814-1832**
- Located at 58 Chartres Street (1814-1822), 132 Chartres Street "at the sign of the Golden Pelican" (1822-1832).
- Jeweler and merchant until 1822; then added military goods.
- Bought guns and military goods from Henry & Francis Tomes, New York.
- Advertised plated and gilt sabers, cut and thrust swords, dirks, pocket knives, silverware, hardware, cutlery, and fancy goods (1822).
- Another 1822 advertisement lists for sale the following: cutlery, knives, swords and dirks, holsters, belt and pocket pistols, epaulets, military caps and hats, watches, buttons, jewelry, silver and plated ware, needles, belts, and lamps.

    HYDE (JAMES N.) & GOODRICH   **NEW ORLEANS, LA**   **1832-1861**
    (CHARLES W.)
- Located at 15 Chartres Street at St. Louis Street.
- Partners: James Nevine Hyde, Charles Whiting Goodrich, William M. Goodrich (Charles' son).
- Arthur Breeze Griswold joined as a clerk (1847).
- Edward G. Hyde (James' son) joined (1848), left (1852).
- Charles Whiting Goodrich died (1849).
- Albert L. (Little) Abbott joined as jeweler (1852).
- Henry Ginder joined as jeweler (1852).
- Henry Thomas Jr. joined as jeweler (1852).
- Sold English Tranter revolvers, Deringer pistols and pepperboxes, and Scoville Mfg. Co. buttons.
- A Hyde & Goodrich receipt shows them as dealers in diamonds, watches, silverware, fine jewelry, fine guns, and military goods.
- A Hyde & Goodrich advertisement shows them as importers of guns, pistols, fancy goods, watches, diamonds, fine jewelry, all kinds of silverware, and swords. Located "at the sign of the Golden Pelican."
- Advertised (July 21, 1861):

        Hyde & Goodrich
        We are now manufacturing in this city
        Regulation line officers swords of good quality
        Having filled most of our advance orders, we can now furnish to customers a reliable article at a reasonable price.
        Also sargeants swords and belts, plates, sashes, stars, etc.

- James Nevine Hyde closed his New York store and sold his interest in the New Orleans store to his son Augustus L. Hyde, manager of New York store (1860).
- Augustus than moved to New Orleans to run that store.
- Charles W. Goodrich died (1861).
- Company name changed to Hyde & Griswold (1861).

HYDE (AUGUSTUS L.) & GRISWOLD (ARTHUR BREEZE) NEW ORLEANS, LA 1861

- Partners: Augustus L. Hyde, Arthur Breeze Griswold, William M. Goodrich, Henry Thomas Jr., Albert L. (Little) Abbott, Henry Ginder.
- Factory and foundry located at Canal and Royal Streets.
- Augustus L. Hyde retired and a new company was formed (Thomas, Griswold & Co.) (1861).

THOMAS (HENRY JR.), GRISWOLD (ARTHUR BREEZE) & CO. NEW ORLEANS, LA 1861-1865

- Initials: T.G. & Co.
- Partners: Henry Thomas Jr., Arthur Breeze Griswold, William M. Goodrich, Albert L. (Little) Abbott, Henry Ginder.
- Factory and foundry located at Canal and Royal Streets.
- Advertised line officer swords, sergeant swords, belts, plates, sashes, and Scoville Mfg. Co. buttons (1861).
- Offered to make cavalry lances and infantry pikes for Gen. A. Sidney Johnson of Bowling Green, KY (1862).
- Advertised in the *New Orleans Picayune* for two machinists, two gunsmiths, plus forgers and finishers (1862).
- The advertisement showed a new factory location at 15 3rd Street (top floor) between Bacchus and Dryades Streets.
- Sold 1,100 lances and pikes to J.E. Merriman & Co., Memphis, TN (1862).
- Had a North Carolina contract with Gen. Mansfield Lovell for cavalry sabers (used imported blades). They were shipped to South Carolina military store keeper Richard Lambert.
- Also made naval cutlasses for the gunboats defending the western rivers.

(See Arthur Breeze Griswold)

(N) GEORGE KANE BALTIMORE, MD 1861

- Kane was the Baltimore police marshal.
- On April 19, 1866, the U.S. 6th Massachusetts Infantry entered Baltimore. Local Confederate sympathizers rioted. Mayor Brown, a Confederate sympathizer, ordered Kane to have iron infantry pikes made so that Baltimore citizens could defend themselves against the northern troops.
- Kane contracted with the following companies:
    3,285 iron spears (pikes heads) from A.W. Denmead & Son (iron foundry at North and Monument Streets)
    5,000 pikes from Ross Winan (locomotive maker at corner of Parkin and Hollins Streets) (made 2,000)
    300 pikes from Hayward, Bartlet & Co. (stove factory, with warehouse and foundry at Pratt and Scott Streets; office 24 Light Street)
    415 pikes from George Page & Co. (hardware and naval stores and machine shop)
        (9,000 total pikes and pike heads)
- When Union Gen. Benjamin F. Butler was sent to Baltimore to quell the riots, his troops captured 115 boxes of spears (pike heads) and 60 boxes of pikes (found at a warehouse at Gay and 2nd Streets).

(A) V.J. KARNES NASHVILLE, TN 1856-1866

- Located at 54 No. College Street.

(N) G. (GEORGE) A. (ADDISON) KELLY GREENE CO., TN B1832-1841

- Son of Jacob Kelly.
- The Kelly family moved to Bradley County, TN (1849).

G. (GEORGE) A. KELLY	BRADLEY CO., TN	1841-1849

- The Kelly family moved to Grandecore, LA (1849).

G. (GEORGE) A. KELLY	GRANDECORE, LA	1849-1850

- The Kelly family moved to Natchitoches, LA (1850).

G. (GEORGE) A. KELLY	NATCHITOCHES, LA	1850-1854

- The family worked a farm.
- Worked with his brother Jacob Jr. on a river steamboat and as wood shingle maker.
- When Jacob Jr. died (1854), his brother-in-law M. (Mathias) S. (Samuel) Lum requested George move to Marion County, TX, near Four Mile Branch (a small village four miles from Jefferson, TX).

G. (GEORGE) A. (ADDISON) KELLY & M. (MATHIAS) S. (SAMUEL) LUM	FOUR MILE BRANCH MARION CO., TX	1854-1860

- Became partners in a bell shop (foundry).
- Made cow and horse bells.
- Kelly continued the bell shop after Lum died (1862).
- Married Lucy Ann Stewart (1855).
- Lucy's brother John A. Stewart was partner with Zachariah Lockett.
- Stewart and Lockett made sandy land plows nearby at their blacksmith shop and iron foundry.
- Kelly bought out Lockett's interest for $50 (1860).

KELLY (GEORGE ADDISON) & STEWART (JOHN A.)	FOUR MILE BRANCH MARION CO., TX	1860-1861

- John A. Stewart died (1861) and Kelly bought his interest from his widow for $572.

G. (GEORGE) A. (ADDISON) KELLY	FOUR MILE BRANCH MARION CO., TX	1861-1862

- Built a larger plow factory called the Kelly Plow Co.
- Made a cast iron plow he called "The Confederate."
- Also began making iron products, including gin segments, gudgeons, andirons, stoves, country holloware (such as kettles and pots), waffle irons, tea kettles, and kitchen utensils.
- Made cannon balls and iron products for the Confederacy during the Civil War.
- A Confederate infantry officer sword marked "G.A. Kelly" is known.
- Drafted as a private in Company A, 19th Regiment, Texas infantry, but the Confederate government told him to stay home and continue making iron products.
- Organized and was captain of a home guard infantry regiment.
- Built a larger foundry and began to produce an improved Hall & Spear plow and a small Pony plow (1865).
- Built a blast furnace and turned out his own pig iron two miles west (1869).
- Began to produce the famous "blue" (painted) plow (1875).
- Four Mile Branch began to be called Kellyville (incorporated in 1887).
- The Kelly factory and foundry complex was severely damaged by fire (1880).
- Kelly had no insurance, so he borrowed money and built a new factory.
- The new company directors reorganized and squeezed Kelly out.
- Kelly moved to Longview, TX, and built a new plow factory (1882).

THE KELLY PLOW CO	LONGVIEW, TX	1882-1970

- Kelly continued to enlarge and added a full line of tilling implement.
- G.A. Kelly died and his sons Robert Marvin Kelly and LeGrande D. Kelly took over (1909).
- Began to make planters, cultivators, harrows, and tractor equipment and parts.
- The company closed (1970).

(A) PETER KIND	COLUMBIA, SC	1850-1861

- Located at his home on the west side of Pulaski Street between Richland and Lumber Streets.
- Advertised in the Columbia, SC, city directory as a brass moulder (1860).
- Made brass sword mountings for Kraft, Goldsmith & Kraft (Columbia, SC).

(A) **PETER W. KRAFT**   COLUMBIA, SC   1855-1862
- Located at 184 Richardson (now Main Street).
- Gun maker who advertised as a maker of custom double guns, rifles, and pistol and dealer in sportsman's apparatus.

    H. (HENRY) F. KRAFT   COLUMBIA, SC   1855-1862
- Located at 184 Richardson (now Main Street).
- Gold and silver plater and master etcher.

    KRAFT (PETER W.), GOLDSMITH (LIPMANN) & KRAFT (HENRY F.)   COLUMBIA, SC   1862-1865
- Located at 184 Richardson Street.
- Henry F. Kraft etched many of their sword blades.
- Made cavalry broadswords with two-branch brass hilts and 36 7/8" double-edged, triple-fullered straight blades 1 7/16" wide.
- Made a cavalry broadsword with brass cruciform hilt and 34 3/4" double-edged, triple-fullered straight blade 1 1/2" wide for Col. Wade Hampton's Legion (Charleston, SC).
- Hampton took his troops to Richmond, VA, and trained the cavalry in the use of broadswords.
- Made the broadsword presented to Col. Wade Hampton by Bradley J. Johnson and Matthew Galbraith.
- Made cavalry officer broadswords with brass three-branch hilts and 38" double-edged, triple-fullered straight blades.
- All broadswords were made with old blades imported from Solingen, Prussia, sword maker Schimmelbusch (Carl) & Joest (Abraham) (1804-1839).

(A) **THOMAS LEECH & CO.**   MEMPHIS, TN   1857-1862
- Advertised in the *Memphis Daily Appeal* (October 1861):

    Memphis Novelty Works
    Thomas Leech & Co.
    Corner Main & McCall Streets
    Memphis, Tennessee
    Manufacturers of army cutlery and brass castings of all kinds.
    We are now prepared to receive and fill orders for the following articles!
    Infantry swords
    Cavalry swords and sabers
    Artillery cutlasses and knives
    Bowie knives of every description
    Bayonets for shot guns and rifles
    Artillery
    Stirrups and spurs of the latest patterns
    Bullet moulds of all kinds
    Brass mountings for gunsmiths
    Brass mountings for saddlery
    Special attention paid to repair of printing presses and light machinery
    Machine blacksmithing

    THOMAS S. LEECH & CO.   COLUMBUS, MS   1862-1863
- Also known as Leech & Rigden.
- Purchased a one-acre factory site next to the Confederate Briarfield Armory.
- Submitted a sample 36-caliber, iron-framed, six-shot revolver to Col. W.S. Downer, superintendent of the Richmond, VA, Confederate armory.
- Downer recommended to Colonel Gorgas (chief of ordnance) that pistols be purchased from Leech & Rigdon (January 21, 1883).

THOMAS S. LEECH & CO. GREENSBORO, GA 1863-1864
- Established a pistol factory in the old Greensboro steam factory (four-story brick building).
- Secured a Confederate contract from Col. Gorgas for 1,500 Navy revolvers after sending in a sample from Columbus, MS (March 6, 1863).
- Advertised the sale of their sword-making machinery now that they no longer made swords (April 1863).
- Rigdon sold out his interest in the company to Thomas S. Leech (January 1, 1864).
- Rigdon than formed a company in Augusta, GA, with Jesse A. Ansley called Rigdon (Charles H. and W.) & Ansley (Jesse A.).

(A) W. (WILLIAM) J. (JOHN) McELROY MACON, GA 1845-1860
- Tin shop and coppersmith located on 3rd Street.

W. (WILLIAM) J. (JOHN) McELROY MACON, GA 1860
- McElroy formed several temporary partnerships before the Civil War began that lasted only one year (1860).
- He was in partnership with:
1) James B. Thompson, pistol maker from Watkins, NY. Dissolved as war was imminent.
2) Alexander S. Reynolds, brass founder. Reynolds went to work for the Macon Armory.
3) Cornelius D. Wall, machinist. Wall went to work for the Macon Armory.
4) John R. Hunt, brass moulder from North Carolina. Hunt joined the Confederate army.

W. (WILLIAM) J. (JOHN) McELROY & CO. MACON, GA 1860-1870
- Had separate facilities for his blacksmith shop, tin shop, and polishing and grinding shops (1860).
- Advertised in the *Macon Telegraph* (September 1861):
  Brass founders
  Swords and knives of all descriptions
  (Made to order at short notice)
  Brass mountings for swords, knives and guns
  Light ornamental castings of all kinds at the old stand
  Third Street—Macon, GA
- Son Henry McElroy born (1860).
- Also made spurs, bits, cap letters, and all types of military hardware of tin, copper, and brass.
- Was a major and colonel in the 50th Georgia militia (1862).
- Joined the Macon Guards (Co. B) militia unit (1864).

(N) MEKIN 1861-1865
- A Confederate foot artillery sword with "Mekin" stamped on the guard is known.

(N) MEYER & LINZ LOUISVILLE, KY 1861-1865
- The Louisville, KY, city directory lists a "Mike Linz—Carpenter" and a "Charles Meyer—Blacksmith" (1865) Both crafts needed to make sword handles and blades.
- There is also a Charles H.L. Meyer hardware dealer at 409 West Market Street.
- A Confederate cavalry saber with the name "Meyer & Linz, Louisville, KY" on the ricasso has been found.

(C) NASHVILLE PLOW WORKS NASHVILLE, TN 1861-1865
- Owners: Thomas A. Sharp, James M. Hamilton.

HAMILTON (JAMES M.) & CUNNINGHAM (GEORGE W.) NASHVILLE, TN 1865-1895
- Mr. George W. Cunningham was probably a relation of Mr. L.T. Cunningham of the College Hill Iron Works & Armory (Nashville, TN).

(C) BLAISE PRADEL JR.	NEW ORLEANS, LA	1868-D1884
(A, C) THOMAS W. RADCLIFFE	COLUMBIA, SC	B1807-1827

- Apprenticed to William Gregg, Columbia, SC (1822-1827).

T. (THOMAS) W. RADCLIFFE & WILLIAM GREGG	COLUMBIA, SC	1827-1833
T. (THOMAS) W. RADCLIFFE	CAMDEN, SC	1833-1848
GLAZE (WILLIAM) & RADCLIFFE (THOMAS W.)	COLUMBIA, SC	1848-1851
T. (THOMAS) W. RADCLIFFE & CO.	COLUMBIA, SC	1851-1856
RADCLIFFE (THOMAS W.) & GUIGNARD (JAMES SAUNDERS)	COLUMBIA, SC	1856-1859

- Located at 166 Richardson Street.

T. (THOMAS) W. RADCLIFFE & CO.	COLUMBIA, SC	1859-D1870

- Located at 166 Richardson.
- Partners: Son Lewis J. Radcliffe (clerk), son Thomas W. Radcliffe Jr. (watchmaker), Richard Davis (bookkeeper).
- William Glaze and Thomas W. Radcliffe advertised in the *Richmond Daily Examiner* and *Macon Telegraph* requesting contributions to form the Confederate States Armory and Foundry Co. (June 6, 1861).
- They needed $1,000,000 to "fabricate artillery of all types, rifles, pistols, swords, bayonets, rockets and munitions of war."
- Thomas E. McNeil was to be acting superintendent and agent.
- The company was never formed.

(See William Glaze)

(N) THOMAS RIGGINS	McMINN CO., TN	B1821-1840

- A gunsmith apprentice (c. 1835-1840).
- Opened his own gun shop (c. 1840).

THOMAS RIGGINS	McMINN CO., TN	1840-1862

- Made sporting rifles for a Tennessee volunteer cavalry unit called the "East Tennessee Squirrel Shooters."
- Joined Colonel Vaughn's 3rd Tennessee infantry regiment (1861).

THOMAS RIGGINS	KNOXVILLE, TN	1862-1863

- Riggins worked at the Knoxville Arsenal (formerly the Maxwell, Briggs & Co. machine shop and iron foundry), which made bridge parts, iron products, steam engines, and steam boilers.
- Became superintendent of 60 armorers at the arsenal.
- Designated as "Armorer of the South" by the Confederate ordnance department.
- Supervised the conversion of sporting and country flintlock rifles to military percussion rifles and large-bore cavalry carbines.
- The arsenal had 100 armorers.
- U.S. Gen. Ambrose Burnside entered Knoxville (September 2, 1863).
- Burnside seized the arsenal (October 21, 1863) and burnt it down (November 23, 1863).
- Two thousand pikes were found in the arsenal.
- Some say Riggins moved to Athens, GA, after Knoxville was taken by Burnside and worked at the Cook & Brother Armory. A company called Riggens & Cook (R&C) was supposedly formed. There is no documentation of this move or company.

(N) SHELBY COUNTY IRON MANUFACTURING CO.	COLUMBIANA, AL	c1840-1862
SHELBY IRON CO.	SELMA, AL	1862-1929

- Had an iron rolling mill.
- During the Civil War, Shelby Iron Co. rolled iron into the proper thickness and cut it into the proper diameter for use in firearms and swords.

- Sold 21,472 pounds of 4" x 3/8" gun iron @ $0.15/lb. to the Dickson Nelson Co., Tuscumbia, AL, and C.B. Churchill Co., Nathchez, MS (1862).
- Also made gunboat armor.

(A, C) **ARMAND SOUBIE**　　　　　　　　　　NEW ORLEANS, LA　　　　　　　1834-1862
- Locations:
    24 Toulouse Street (1834-1850)
    160 Chartres Street (1850-1858)
    460 Chartres Street (1858-1862)

(C) **JOHN N. STATION**　　　　　　　　　　SCOTTSVILLE, VA　　　　　　　1861-1865

(C) **TREDEGAR IRON WORKS**　　　　　　　RICHMOND, VA　　　　　　　1838-1869
- Located on the south side of the Kanawah Canal, a tributary of the James River that ran through Richmond, VA.

(A) **JOHN VEAL (SR.)**　　　　　　　　　　COLUMBIA, SC　　　　　　　Bc1805-1825
　　JOHN VEAL (SR.)　　　　　　　　　　COLUMBIA, SC　　　　　　　1825-1827
- Watch repair and silversmith shop located at 5 Brick Range.
　　JOHN VEAL (SR.)　　　　　　　　　　COLUMBIA, SC　　　　　　　1827-1838
- Moved across the street to 2 Brick Range.
- Rented a brick building from John Block.
　　VEAL (JOHN SR.) & GLAZE (WILLIAM)　COLUMBIA, SC　　　　　　　1838-1841
- Shop located at 2 Brick Range.
(Silversmith, jeweler, clock and watch repair, silverware)
　　JOHN VEAL (SR.)　　　　　　　　　　COLUMBIA, SC　　　　　　　1841-1857
- Shop located at 2 Brick Range.
- Partner and son: John Veal Jr. (jeweler).
- Advertised as a dealer in watches, clocks, jewelry, silverware, guns, pistols, and military goods.
- John Veal retired and sold his business to Samuel Townsend (1857).
　　JOHN VEAL CO.　　　　　　　　　　　COLUMBIA, SC　　　　　　　1857-1865
- Owner: Samuel Townsend.
- Located at 120 Richardson (now Main Street).
- John Veal died at the age of 92 (c. 1897).

(N) **ROSS WINAN**　　　　　　　　　　　　BALTIMORE, MD　　　　　　　C1830-1863
- Advertised as a machinist and locomotive manufacturer (1850).
- Was the largest locomotive engine and railroad car maker in the U.S. (1861).
- Located at the corner of Parkin and Hollins Streets.
- Contracted with Baltimore police marshal George Kane to make 5,000 pikes (April 1861) for use by the citizens of Baltimore to defend themselves against the northern troops entering the city (Kane was a Confederate sympathizer) and actually made 2,000.
- Produced a steam-powered armored cannon (invented by Charles S. Dickerson in 1859) mounted on a large horse-drawn carriage. It could fire 200 balls a minute.
- Police Marshall Kane stole the cannon, abducted Dickerson, and tried to flee to Richmond, VA (he disguised the gun as farm machinery). Union troops captured him and the cannon and freed Dickenson.
- Winan made rifles, muskets, and cannon balls for the north during the Civil War.

(N) **W.P. WOODSON**　　　　　　　　　　　HONEY GROVE　　　　　　　1850-1865
　　　　　　　　　　　　　　　　　　　　　FANNIN CO., TX
- An item in the *Northern Standard* (December 21, 1861) read:

At Honey Grove in Fannin County (Texas), we were shown. Last week, Swords, and Bowie knives, the manufacture of Mr. W.P. Woodson of that place, which are conclusive evidence, that the necessities of the present crisis, will be met in a great degree by home production. These weapons were of very serviceable shape, well tempered, neatly finished, with good handles—the sword with a double guard to the hilt—the knife with a single guard—both with leather scabbards. The swords are sold at $20.00—the knives at $10.00. Mr. Woodson had carried on a blacksmith shop heretofore, and had made plain sheath knives, but never anything like these weapons, until necessity stimulated the effort. Most of the officer's in Maxey's Regiment have swords made by Mr. Woodson.

- The "Maxey" referred to in the advertisement is Col. Samuel Bell Maxie, Paris, TX, 9th Regiment, Texas Infantry.

(A, C) **M. ZIMMERMAN**	NEW ORLEANS, LA	1816-1856

- Father of J.F. Zimmerman and C.H. Zimmerman.
- Located at 140 Bourbon Street (home).

ZIMMERMAN (M.) & SON (C.H.)	NEW ORLEANS, LA	1856-1858

- Located at 93 Canal Street.

M. ZIMMERMAN & SON (C.H.)	NEW ORLEANS, LA	1858-1865

- Located at 96 Canal Street.

C.H. ZIMMERMAN & CO.	NEW ORLEANS, LA	1865-1871

- Son of M. Zimmerman.
- Located at 94 and 96 Canal Street.

(Silversmith, watch maker, sword blade engraver, jeweler)

(A) **J.F. ZIMMERMAN**	NEW ORLEANS, LA	1836-1865

- Son of M. Zimmerman.
- Etched some blades for A.H. Dufilho of New Orleans during the Civil War.
- Peter Zimmerman was probably his son.

(Silversmith, watch maker, sword blade engraver, jeweler)

CHAPTER 12

European Sword Makers and Dealers Who Exported Swords to Confederate Dealers during the Civil War

(A) GERMAN FIRMS

    Carl Broch Jr. (Solingen, Prussia)
    Wilhelm Clauberg (Solingen, Prussia)
    Otto Curdts (Solingen, Prussia)
    Carl Joseph Falkenberg (Solingen, Prussia)
    C.R. Kirschbaum (Solingen, Prussia)
    W.R. Kirschbaum (Solingen, Prussia)
    Paul D. Luneschloss (Solingen, Prussia)
    Schnitzler & Kirschbaum (Solingen, Prussia)
    Johann Ludwig Werder (Nuremberg, Bavaria)

ENGLISH FIRMS

    Firmin & Sons (London)
    Isaac, Campbell, & Co. (London)
    Robert Mole & Son (Birmingham)
    Joseph Rogers & Sons (Sheffield)
    Henry Wilkinson (London)

FRENCH FIRMS
    F.P. Devisme (Paris)

CHAPTER 13
Confederate Sword Dealers

(A) **ALLEN (JOHN M.) & DIAL (JOHN C.)**　　　**COLUMBIA, SC**　　　1860-1865
- Partner and sales agent: George L. Dial.
- Located at 192 Richardson Street (now Main Street).
- Advertised in the Columbia city directory as a hardware store (1860).
- Advertised wholesale/retail rifles, pistols, and swords and agricultural implements (1860).
- Advertised rifles and pistols for mounted men (1861).

(A) **JOHN STILES BIRD**　　　**CHARLESTON, SC**　　　B1794, 1822-1852
- Locations:
    - Broad Street (1822-1832)
    - 172 King Street (1832-1836)
    - 223 King Street (1836-1840)
    - 231 King Street (1840-1849)
    - 225 King Street (1849-1852)

J. (JOHN) S. (STILES) BIRD & CO.　　　**CHARLESTON, SC**　　　1852-1860
- Son and partner: Charlton H. Bird.
- Located at 225 King Street.

CHARLTON H. BIRD　　　**CHARLESTON, SC**　　　1860-1887
- Located at 225 King Street.

(N) **FRANCIS C. CLARK**　　　　　　　　　　　　　　　　AUGUSTA, GA　　　1802-1822
　　F. (FRANCIS C.) CLARK & CO.　　　　　　　　　　AUGUSTA, GA　　　1822-1830
　　F. (FRANCIS C.) & H. (HORACE) CLARK　　　　　AUGUSTA, GA　　　1830-1840
　　CLARK (FRANCIS C. & HORACE)　　　　　　　　　AUGUSTA, GA　　　1840-1859
　　& RACKETT (GEORGE) & CO.
- George Rackett died (1852).
- J.S. Clark joined (1852).

- Located at 206 Broad at McIntosh Street.

    J.S. CLARK & CO.   AUGUSTA, GA   1859-1865
- Located at 206 Broad Street (at McIntosh Street).
- Advertised watches, jewelry, silverware, cutlery, guns, pistols, and fancy goods

(N) **FREDERICK H. CLARK**   MEMPHIS, TN   1840-1855
      CLARK (FREDERICK H.) & CO.   MEMPHIS, TN   1855-1865
- Partners: James S. Wilkins, Thomas Hill, Stephen Remington.
- Located at corner of Main and Madison Streets.
- Advertised as a jeweler and silversmith and seller of guns and fancy goods.

(A) **COURTNEY (WILLIAM C.) & TENNENT**   CHARLESTON, SC   1852-1865
     (GILBERT B.)
- Advertised as a hardware and cutlery dealer and importer (1860).
- Gilbert B. Tennent operated company offices at 10 Lansdown Terrace in Leaminton, England. He purchased naval officers swords and cutlasses from Robert Mole & Son of Birmingham, England, as well as other supplies and goods to sell in Charleston, SC.
- Sold large quantities of military equipment to the Confederate navy.

(N) **COL. CHARLES DE MORSE**   CLARKSVILLE, TX   1860-1863
                                                            RED RIVER CO.
- Organized the 29th Regiment, Texas Cavalry.
- Owner and editor of the *Northern Standard* newspaper.
- Advertised in his newspaper (February 10, 1860):

                                     Regalia Trimmings
                             A lot of laces, fringes, stars.
              Tassels, Odd Fellows emblems, etc., for sale at standard office

- Advertised in his newspaper (September 22, 1860):

                               Military Sashes and Swords
           A few extra fine silk sashes and Swords for sale. Apply at standard office.

- Advertised in his newspaper (October 26, 1861):

                                     Sword and Belt!
           A handsome, gilt scabbard, Regulation sword, Ames manufacture,
              with neat home made belt for sale. Inquire at standard office.

(Masonic regalia and sword dealer)

(N) **GERHARD DIERCKS**   COLUMBIA, SC   1855-1861
- An employee of George Bruns (jeweler, silversmith).

     GERHARD DIERCKS   COLUMBIA, SC   1861-1865
- Shop located at 182 Richardson Street (now Main Street).
- Advertised as a silversmith, jeweler, watch maker, and seller of military goods (probably swords) (1861).

     PHOENIX IRON WORKS   COLUMBIA, SC   1865-D1886
- Owner: Gerhard Diercks (died 1886).

(A) **J. (JACOB) F. EISENMEAN & CO.**   COLUMBIA, SC   1850-1865
- Partner: G. (George) V. Antwerp.
- Located at 150 Richardson Street (now Main Street).
- Sold swords during the Civil War.

(Military tailor)

(A) ENGLISH (JAMES A.), ALEXANDRIA, VA 1855-1865
CASTLEMAN (CHARLES M.) & CO.
- Iron forge located on King Street.
- Partner: Charles Baldwin.
- Sold coach and saddlery hardware; bar iron; and cast, shear, and blister steel.
- Advertised as importer and dealer in hardware, English and German guns, and cutlery (swords).

(N) FISHER (EDWARD H.) & AGNEW (JOHN) COLUMBIA, SC 1856-1865
- Located at southeast corner of Richardson (now Main Street) and Plain Streets.
- Shown in the Columbia city directory as hardware and cutlery store (1860).
- Sold swords during the Civil War.

(N) H. (HENRY) FRANKO NEW ORLEANS, LA 1858-1865
- Located on Poydras Street.
(Silversmith, watch maker, jewelry, military goods)

(N) F. (FREDERICK) G. GLASSICK MEMPHIS, TN 1865-1866
- Located at 352 Front Street.
- Advertised in the Memphis city directory as manufacturers and dealers in guns, rifles, pistols, ammunition, fancy goods, cutlery, and musical instruments.

(N) T. (THOMAS F.) & H. (HENRY C.) GUION NEW ORLEANS, LA 1838-1840
- Located on the corner of Charles and Common Streets.

THOMAS F. GUION NEW ORLEANS, LA 1840-1869
- Located at 20 St. Charles Street.
- During the Civil War advertised fancy goods, gentleman's furnishings, variety store, guns, rifles, swords, and sporting goods.

(A, C) ETHELBERT HALFMANN DUIJ, PRUSSIA B1809-1830
- Immigrated to Philadelphia, PA (1830).

ETHELBERT HALFMANN PHILADELPHIA, PA 1830-D1863
- Clothing shop and factory located at 327 Market Street.
- Son L.W. Halfmann born (1842).
- Opened a second store in Montgomery, AL (1858).

ETHELBERT HALFMANN MONTGOMERY, AL 1858-1861
- Clothier located at 7 Court Square.
- The shop was called Halfmann's One Price Clothing Emporium.
- Advertised shirts, hats, and "everything necessary to furnish a gentlemans wardrobe" and "All clothing sold at this establishment is manufactured by the proprietor in Philadelphia."
- Formed a partnership with another clothier, Taylor (William B.) & Torrey (Samuel) located near him at 6 Court Square (1861).

HALFMANN (ETHELBERT) & TAYLOR MONTGOMERY, AL 1861-1862
(WILLIAM B.)
- Partner: Samuel Torrey.
- Located at 6 and 7 Court Square.
- Became a military goods dealer.
- Imported M1854 British foot officer swords from Isaac (Saul), Cambell (S.) & Co., London, England.
- Sold buttons to the state of Alabama. There are no records showing whether the buttons were made by Halfmann & Taylor or imported. They were marked "Halfmann & Taylor Montgomery, AL" on the back.
- The buttons came with six different designs on the face:

1) "A.V.C." (Alabama Volunteer Corps) over an eagle with a crest in the center of the eagle
2) "M.V.C." (Mobile Volunteer Corps) over an eagle with a crest in the center of the eagle
3) Alabama state map over the word "cadet" over an eagle with a crest in the center of the eagle
4) "C.S.A." on a shield in the center of an eagle
5) Gothic "A"
6) Script "A.C.I & R."

E. (ETHELBERT) HALFMANN MONTGOMERY, AL 1862-D1863
- Sold 37 1/2 dozen silver-plated buttons to the Confederate quartermaster (Maj. J.L. Calhoun), Montgomery, AL (August 28, 1862).
- Sold Calhoun four gross of military buttons at $40 per gross (December 18, 1862).

(A) **C. (CHARLES) HALL** NORFOLK, VA 1852-1865
- Located at 1 E. Main Street.

(N) **M.A. LYONS** RICHMOND, VA 1850-1852
- Located at 131 Broad Street.

McDONALD (EDWARD) & LYONS (ASHER S.) RICHMOND, VA 1852-1855
- Located at 7 Exchange Place.
- Called Regalia & Banner Emporium.

EDWARD McDONALD RICHMOND, VA 1855-1875
- Located at Locust Alley (1855-1860), 9th Street (between Main and Cary Streets) (1860-1875).
- Sold military goods during the Civil War.
- Edward McDonald died (1875).

McDONALD & CO. RICHMOND, VA 1875-1880
- Owner: Rachel McDonald (Edward's widow).

(N) **J. (JAMES) E. MERRIMAN & CO.** MEMPHIS, TN 1855-1863
- Bought 1,100 cavalry lances and infantry pikes from Thomas, Griswold of New Orleans, LA (1862).

(Silversmith, military goods, watchmaker, jeweler, cutlery dealer)

(N) **P. (PETER) T. MOORE** RICHMOND, VA 1858-1875
- Located at 24 Pearl Street at 14th Street.
- Advertised in Richmond city directory as importer and dealer in foreign and domestic hardware, cutlery, guns, and edged tools (1860).

(A) **J. (JULIUS) A. PALMER** ALEXANDRIA, VA 1861-1865
- Located on King Street.

(A) **W.W. WALKER** COLUMBIA, SC 1850-1865
- Located at 186 Richardson Street (now Main Street).
- Advertised in the Columbia city directory as a military tailor (1860).
- Sold swords during the Civil War.

(N) **SAMUEL WILMOT JR.** SAVANNAH, GA 1860-1870
- Located at Whitaker and Julian Streets.
- Advertised as a dealer in clocks, jewelry, silverware, guns, pistols, rifles, and military and fancy goods (1860).

(N) **WOLF (GEORGE) & DURRINGER (JOSEPH)** LOUISVILLE, KY 1859-1872

(Jeweler, watchmaker, guns, pistols, military goods)

CHAPTER 14

Bibliography and List of Reference Material on Edged Weapons Makers and Dealers

City and County Directories

Baltimore, Maryland, city directories, 1796 (by William Thompson & James L. Walker), 1814 (by James Lakin)

Boston, Massachusetts, city directories, 1789-1881 (thanks to John Dorsey and John Devine, Boston Public Library researchers)

Business Directory of Ulster Co., NY
1871-1872
by Hamilton Child

Columbia, South Carolina, city directory, 1860

Newark, New Jersey, city directories, 1839-1885

Philadelphia, Pennsylvania, city directories, 1809, 1811, 1813, 1862-1863

Wilmington, North Carolina, city directories, 1860-1861

Books and Pamphlets

A Sure Defense: The Bowie Knife Book
by Kenneth J. Burton, 1988

American Arms and Arms Makers
by Robert E. Gardner, 1938

American Knives: The First History and Collectors Guide
by Harold L. Peterson, 1958

American Presentation Swords
by Jay P. Altmayer, 1958

American Swords and Sword Makers
by Richard H. Bezdek, 1994

Bowie Knives of the Ben Palmer Collection
by Ben Palmer, W.F. Moran, and Jim Phillips, 1992

Collins Machetes and Bowie, 1845-1965
by Daniel Edward Henry, 1995

Directory of American Military Goods Dealers and Makers (1785-1915)
Revised and enlarged edition
by Bruce S. Bazelon and William F. McGuinn, 1995

French Swords for Virginia 1779
by Giles Cromwell, 1995

Gazetteer of New York State
by J.H. French, 1860

The History of North Smithfield, RI (Forestdale)
by Walter A. Nebiker, 1929

The History of the Town of Smithfield, RI (Forestdale)
by Thomas Steers, 1881

The History of Ulster Co. New York
by Nathaniel B. Sylvester, 1880

Indian Tomahawks & Frontiersmen Belt Axes
by Daniel D. Hartzler & James A. Knowles, 1995

The Industrial Interests of Newark, NJ
by William F. Ford, 1874

"John D. Gray and His Columbus Armory Carbine"
Militaria, Newsletter of the AOPA Ltd., Vol. 1, #2
by AOPA and George Greene

Maryland Silversmith (1715-1830)
by Pleasants and Sill, 1930

New England Cutlery
by Philip R. Pankiewicz, 1990

Oyez, Oyez: An Account of the First 110 Years of Landers, Frary & Clark Co.
by Barbara Ann Duggan, 1953

Paul Revere information pamphlet
by the John Hancock Mutual Life Insurance Co., 1930

Steel Canvas—The Art of American Arms
by R.L. Wilson, 1995

Swords and Sword Makers of the War of 1812
by Richard H. Bezdek, 1997

Tiffany Silver
by Charles H. Carpenter Jr. and Mary Grace Carpenter, 1978

United States Ordnance, Vol. II: Ordnance Correspondence Relative to Muskets, Rifles, Pistols, and Swords
by James E. Hicks, 1940

Magazine Articles

"Armourer John Miles at Moose Fort"
by Michael D. Woods
The Beaver, April/May 1986

"The Confederate Bowie Knife"
by C.S. Harris
National Knife Magazine, July 1984

"Halfmann & Taylor"
by Cecil Anderson
North South Trader, Vol. II, No. 4, 1975

"Hyde & Goodrich, et al"
by Cecil W. Anderson
The North South Trader, Vol. VI, No. 4. May/June 1979

"The John Fraser Tomahawk"
by William H. Guthman
Man at Arms, September/October 1994

"The John Miles Virginia Sabers"
by Richard A. Johnson
Man At Arms, March/April 1994

"The Revere Family"
by Donald M. Nielsen
The New England Historical and Genealogical Register, Vol. CXLV

"Rochus Heinisch: American Cutler"
by W.R. Williamson
Gun Report, March 1972

"Schuyler, Hartley & Graham: A Review of Some Exciting Documents"
by Herbert G. Houze
Man At Arms, March/April 1995

"The Starr-Wolcott Carbines"
by Edward A. Hull
Man At Arms Magazine, May/June 1984

"Thomas Riggins: Oldest Gunmaker"
by G. Elsworth Brown
The Confederate Veteran, Vol. XIX, July 1911

Institutions

The Hagley Library and Museum, Wilmington, DE
(The John Joseph Henry Philadelphia Day Book, 1811-1816)

Longview Texas Public Library
Nova J. Motley, Genealogy/Local History
(Kelly Plow Co. information)

Meriden, CT, Public Library
Jan Franco, Librarian
(Landers, Frary Co. information)

New Britian, CT, Public Library
Arlene C. Palmer, Curator
(Landers, Frary & Clark information)

The New Jersey Historical Society
Bob Grand, David J. Franz
(Henry Sauerbier information)

Newark, NJ, Public Library (Business Information Center)
Dale E. Colston, Librarian; Robert Blackwell, New Jersey Division
(Henry Sauerbier information)

Articles from The American Society of Arms Collectors Bulletins

"The Dickson Nelson Company (Alabama Civil War Gun Maker)"
by Douglas Jones
The American Society of Arms Collectors Bulletin, Spring 1989

"The Edged Weapons of Keenansville, North Carolina"
by Frederick Edmunds
The American Society of Arms Collectors Bulletin, Bulletin #54, 1986

"Jacob Hurd and the Boston Small Sword"
by John D. Hamilton
The American Society of Arms Collectors Bulletin #70, 1994

"Louis Froelich: Immigrant Sword Maker"
by John J. Frawner Jr.
The American Society of Arms Collectors Bulletin #66, 1992

"U.S. Cavalry Sabers"
by Richard Johnson
The American Society of Arms Collectors Bulletin, Spring 1982

Arms Maker Catalogs

The Ames Sword Company catalog, 1881
The Starr Arms Company catalog, 1864
(carbines and revolvers)

Military Manuals

Craigs Swords Exercise, Drill & Evolutions for the Cavalry
Baltimore, 1812

Sword Exercise of the Cavalry
by Robert Hewes
Boston, 1812

Articles from the Pennsylvania Antique Gun Collectors Assoc. Inc., *Monthly Bugle* (Kurt Stein, editor)

"A Non-commissioned Officer's Sword of the War of 1812 (W. Rose)"
by Robert H. McCauley Jr., August 1970

"Homely Beauty (Philadelphia Balled Hilt Cavalry Saber)"
by Kurt Stein, September 1991

"Horstmann Philadelphia"
by Kurt Stein, September 1982

"J. Henry Philadelphia—Sword Maker?"
by Kurt Stein, October 1971

"Lovely Rose (M1807 cavalry saber)"
by Donald F. Eismann, August 1982

"Rose Revisited"
by Milton Heinzer, August 1990

"Militia Dragoon Saber"
by James P. Sweeney, January 1988

"Notes on the Rose Saber M1812"
by Kurt Stein, March 1977

"Rose Unmarked"
by Kurt Stein, May 1990

"The Saber Contracts of 1798"
by Samuel Asbell, July 1971

"Some Notes on the Rose Family"
by Kurt Stein, October 1977

APPENDIX A

U.S. Cavalry Sword Makers

Jacob Allen	New York, NY	1773-1783
Oliver Allen	Norwich, CT	1790-1816
William Allen	New York, NY	1754-1826
N. (Nathan) P. Ames	Chicopee Falls, MA	1829-1834
Ames Mfg. Co.	Cabotsville, MA	1834-1881
Ames Sword Co.	Chicopee, MA	1881-1928
James Anderson	Williamsburg, VA	1760-1780
James Anderson	New York, NY	1770-1800
John Bailey	New York, NY	1784-1794
Melchior Baker & Albert Gallatin	Fayette Co., PA	1781-1801
S. (Samuel) Beck	Philadelphia, PA	1775-1783
James Bent	Canton, MA	1809-1842
Hendrick Bosch	New York, NY	1650-1701
John Bouchette	Philadelphia, PA	1810-1820
Charles Oliver Bruff	New York, NY	1765-1776
Buell & Greenleaf	Hartford, CT	1799
Abel Buell	Hartford, CT	1799-1825
W.T. Clement	Northampton, MA	1857-1865
Collins & Co.	Hartford, CT	1826-1966
Henry Deringer	Philadelphia, PA	1808-1868
Henry Disston	Philadelphia, PA	1833-1998
Gilbert Dubois	Napanock, NY	1840-1867
Dunbar & Leonard	Canton, MA	1813-1816
Joseph Elliott	Baltimore, MD	1769-1782
Emerson & Silver	Trenton, NJ	1860-1865
Jacob Funk	Muskingum Co., OH	1790-1816
Robert Gamble	Richmond, VA	1780-1810

Glaze & Prescott	Chester Co., SC	1812-1816
William Glaze	Columbia, SC	1851-1883
John Goodman Sr.	Philadelphia, PA	1758-1805
Charles Hammond & Son	Philadelphia, PA	1862-1864
George Heighberger	Philadelphia, PA	1760-1790
Henderson-Ames	Kalamazoo, MI	1893-1923
Daniel Henkels	Philadelphia, PA	1806-1817
John Joseph Henry	Philadelphia, PA	1807-1822
The Hope Furnace	Scituate, RI	1765-1812
Ezekial Hopkins	Scituate, RI	1740-1765
Horstmann Bros.	Philadelphia, PA	1854-1893
James Hunter (Rappahonnock Forge)	Stafford Co., VA	1775-1782
Joseph Jenks Sr.	Lynn, MA	1642-1660
Joseph Jenks Jr.	Pawtucket Falls, RI	1650-1680
Philip S. Justice	Philadelphia, PA	1837-1859
John Keller (Kehler)	Lancaster, PA	1780-1820
John Godfried Knecht	Baltimore, MD	1795-1820
Landers, Frary & Clark	New Britain, CT	1865-1965
H.G. Leisenring	Philadelphia, PA	1859-1871
Samuel Leonard	Canton, MA	1775-1854
The M.C. Lilley & Co.	Columbus, OH	1892-1931
The Lilley-Ames Co.	Columbus, OH	1931-1951
William Low	Ovid, NY	1793-1818
Mansfield & Lamb	Slaterville, RI	1820-1861
William McKnight	Pittsburgh, PA	1815-1820
John Miles	Philadelphia, PA	1801-1818
D. (David) J. Millard	Clayville, NY	1849-1875
Samuel Miller	Boston, MA	1725-1745
Abraham Nippes	Philadelphia, PA	1813-1856
J. Abraham Nippes	Philadelphia, PA	1808-1813
Daniel Nowell	Philadelphia, PA	1790-1815
Abiel Pease	Enfield, CT	1780-1828
Daniel Pettibone	Boston, MA	1811-1815
John Pim	Boston, MA	1705-1730
James Potter	New York, NY	1755-1786
Lewis Prahl	Blockley Twsp., PA	1750-1784
Lewis Prahl	Philadelphia, PA	1784-1809
Providence Tool Co.	Providence, RI	1846-1885
Leonard & James Reiche (Rickey)	Philadelphia, PA	1790-1812
C. (Christopher) Roby	West Chelmsford, MA	1853-1867
Thomas Rode	Pittsburgh, PA	1800-1815
Joseph Rose Sr.	Blockley Twsp., PA	1778-1819
William Rose	Blockley Twsp., PA	1800-1810
William Rose Sr. (Companies)	Blockley Twsp., PA	1783-1854
William Rose & Sons	New York, NY	1815-1890
Elijah Ross	Zanesville, OH	1804-1864
William Rowland Sr.	Philadelphia, PA	1803-1875
Hamilton Ruddick	Boston, MA	1861-1868
Harry Safford	Zanesville, OH	1780-1815
Henry Sauerbier	Newark, NJ	1853-1874

Sheble & Fisher	Philadelphia, PA	1861-1870
Jeremiah Snow Sr.	Springfield, MA	1760-1783
Nathan Starr Sr.	Middletown, CT	1755-1821
Nathan Starr Jr.	Middletown, CT	1784-1852
Nathan Starr & Co.	Middletown, CT	1798-1799
William Strong	Philadelphia, PA	1789-1810
James Winner	Philadelphia, PA	1803-1815
Josiah Wood	Philadelphia, PA	1775-1783
William Wrightman	Charleston, SC	1770-1810

APPENDIX B

U.S. Naval Cutlass Makers

Ames Mfg. Co.	Chicopee, MA	1848-1881
James Anderson	New York, NY	1770-1800
Jacob S. Baker	Philadelphia, PA	1796-1860
John Chaloner	Philadelphia, PA	1775-1783
Francis Clark	Reading, PA	1775-1783
Benjamin Comstock	Providence, RI	1775-1783
Isaac Cox	Philadelphia, PA	1775-1783
Henry Deringer	Philadelphia, PA	1808-1868
Robert Dingee Sr.	New York, NY	1806-1843
Capt. Furham	Philadelphia, PA	1775-1783
Richard Gridley	Sharon, MA	1775-1796
Daniel Henkels	Philadelphia, PA	1808-1817
John Joseph Henry	Philadelphia, PA	1807-1822
Andrew Hodge	Philadelphia, PA	1775-1783
Samuel Holmes	Philadelphia, PA	1775-1783
Samuel Howell	Philadelphia, PA	1755-1800
Leonard, Kinsley & Dana	Canton, MA	1816
The Lilley-Ames Co.	Columbus, OH	1931-1951
Nicholas Low	Philadelphia, PA	1775-1783
Mayweg & Nippes	Philadelphia, PA	1814-1815
Elizabeth Miller	Boston, MA	1775-1783
Samuel Miller	Boston, MA	1725-1745
Samuel Morris	Philadelphia, PA	1775-1783
John Nicholson Sr.	Philadelphia, PA	1754-1799
J. Abraham Nippes	Philadelphia, PA	1808-1813
John Phillips	Philadelphia, PA	1775-1783
Hamilton Ruddick	Boston, MA	1861-1868

Joseph Sims	Philadelphia, PA	1775-1783
Nathan Starr Sr.	Middletown, CT	1755-1821
Francis Tillgham	Philadelphia, PA	1775-1783
Simon Walker	Baltimore, MD	1775-1805
James Wallace	Philadelphia, PA	1775-1783
Josiah Wood	Philadelphia, PA	1775-1783

APPENDIX C

U.S. Bowie Knife Makers

Ezekial Adams	Webster, NH	1860-1868
American Flask & Co.	New York, NY	1857-1900
American Knife Co.	Reynolds Bridge, CT	1849-1963
Ames Mfg. Co.	Chicopee, MA	1848-1881
Ames Sword Co.	Chicopee, MA	1881-1928
L.W. Babbitt	Cleveland, OH	1832-1838
William Bacon	New York, NY	1825-1845
Bay State Hardware Co.	Northhampton, MA	1863-1871
John & Amos Belknap	St. Johnsbury, VT	1879-1887
Belknap Hardware Co.	Louisville, KY	1830-1850
Samuel Bell	Knoxville, TN	1830-1845
Charles E. Billings	Hartford, CT	1855-1862
James Black	Washington, AR	1829-1872
C.J. Blittersdorf	Philadelphia, PA	1780-1865
Bown & Tetley	Pittsburgh, PA	1848-1862
Bridgeport Gun Implement Co.	Bridgeport, CT	1900-1910
Bridgeport Knife Co.	Bridgeport, CT	1870-1900
Brown & Son	Newcastle, PA	1861-1865
Buck Bros.	Worcester, MA	1853-1893
Burkinshaw Knife Co.	Pepperell, MA	1853-1923
Canton Cutlery Co.	Canton, OH	1880-1930
John Cartwright	Pittsburgh, PA	1830-1858
Case Bros.	Little Valley, NY	1880-1890
Cattaraugus Cutlery Co.	Little Valley, NY	1880-1960
Central City Knife Co.	Phoenix, NY	1880-1920
John D. Chevalier	New York, NY	1835-1870
Daniel Clarke	Philadelphia, PA	1820-1858

Clement, Hawkes Mfg. Co.	Northhampton, MA	1866-1882
Collins & Co.	Hartford, CT	1826-1966
W.M. Cotton	Leominster, MA	1820-1850
Emerson & Silver	Trenton, NJ	1860-1865
Empire Knife Co.	West Winslead, CT	1840-1850
John English	Philadelphia, PA	1800-1820
English & Huber	Philadelphia, PA	1820-1845
E. Estep & Sons	Pittsburgh, PA	1844-1856
Joseph Fenton	Franklin, OH	1840-1865
Rees Fitzpatrick	Baton Rouge, LA	1831-1838
William R. Goulding	New York, NY	1850-1855
William Greaves & Sons	Philadelphia, PA	1845-1865
Griffiths & Siebert	Cincinnati, OH	1852-1854
John A. Griffiths	Cincinnati, OH	1854-1866
Charles Halback	Baltimore, MD	1835-1856
Harrington Cutlery Co.	Southbridge, MA	1850-1933
Hassam Bros.	Boston, MA	1861-1868
M.J. Hayes & Son	San Francisco, CA	1887-1901
Rochus Heinisch Sr.	Newark, NJ	1825-1865
Otto Helmold	Pittsburgh, PA	1859-1872
Anton Heninger	New Haven, CT	1861-1865
Hibbard, Spencer, Bartlett & Co.	Chicago, IL	1880-1910
Andrew G. Hicks	Cleveland, OH	1830-1851
Holley Mfg. Co.	Lukeville, CT	1854-1936
Rudolph Hug	Cincinnati, OH	1801-1865
Alfred Hunter	Newark, NJ	1840-1865
Hyde & Jacobs	Southbridge, MA	1875-1881
Samuel Jackson	Baltimore, MD	1831-1895
Kingman & Hassam	Boston, MA	1861-1868
Pierre Lamothe	New Orleans, LA	1809-1822
Lamson & Goodnow	Shelburne Falls, MA	1837-1996
Landers, Frary & Clark	New Britain, CT	1865-1965
Joseph Manning	New York, NY	1820-1845
Marks & Rees	Cincinnati, OH	1815-1840
Hugh McConnell	San Francisco, CA	1850-1863
Charles McDonald	Richmond, IN	1861-1865
Meridan Cutlery Co.	Meridan, CT	1855-1865
Miller Bros. Cutlery Co.	Meridan, CT	1886-1925
Sheldon Nash	Cincinnati, OH	1853-1865
New York Knife Co.	Walden, NY	1853-1870
Northfield Knife Co.	Northfield, CT	1858-1919
Daniel Pease	Blue Hill, NY	1860-1869
Michael Price	San Francisco, CA	1840-1888
Charles C. Reinhardt & Co.	Philadelphia, PA	1850-1865
Reinhardt & Brother	Philadelphia, PA	1865-1872
F. Richter	Boston, MA	1840-1850
C. Roby & Co.	West Chelmsford, MA	1853-1867
J.B. Rogers	York, ME	1801-1865
David Ropes	Saccarapa, ME	1832-1846
Joseph Rose Jr.	New York, NY	1850-1854

J. Russell Cutlery Co.	Turner Falls, PA	1836-1933
Albert Schmid & Co.	Providence, RI	1867-1936
John M. Schmid	Providence, RI	1856-1979
Paul Schmidt	Baltimore, MD	1845-1865
Daniel Searles	Baton Rouge, LA	1818-1860
Searles & Fitzpatrick	Baton Rouge, LA	1833-1838
Henry Sheirley Sr.	Philadelphia, PA	1813-1840
John Shugart & Co.	Chambersburg, PA	1828-1866
Noah Smithwick	San Felipe, TX	1827-1861
Noah Smithwick	Santa Ana, TX	1861-1893
J.P. Snow & Co.	Hartford, CT	1860-1865
George Stewart	Norwick, CT	1857-1868
Steven Taft	Millbury, MA	1861-1865
G.W. Taylor	San Francisco, CA	1860-1875
J. (Jacob) Teufel	Philadelphia, PA	1850-1860
John Todd	New Orleans, LA	1830-1840
Edward K. Tryon	Philadelphia, PA	1827-1904
George W. Tryon	Philadelphia, PA	1791-1878
Ulster Knife Co.	Ellenville, KY	1872-1900
United States Arms & Cutlery Co.	Rochester, NY	1878-1886
Walden Knife Co.	Walden, NY	1870-1927
Silas A. Walker	Bennington, VT	1850-1870
William Walker	Salt Lake City, UT	1850-1860
H. (Henry) Wilkinson	Hartford, CT	1850-1865
Will & Finck	San Francisco, CA	1863-1934
Will & Kesmodel	San Francisco, CA	1860-1863
Franz Wolf	Columbus, OH	1834-1852

APPENDIX D

U.S. Tomahawk & Belt Axe Makers

Samuel Abbot	Fort Michilimackinac, MI	1839-1845
Ezekial Adams	Webster, NH	1860-1868
R. (Robert) Adams	Baltimore, MD	1790-1810
Joseph Albot	New York, NY	1755-1765
J.B. Allere	Chicago, IL	1810-1840
N.P. Ames	Cabotville, MA	1834-1848
Ames Mfg. Co.	Chicopee, MA	1848-1881
James Anderson	Williamsburg, PA	1760-1780
Peter C. Angstadt	Berks Co., OH	1800-1810
Peter C. Angstadt	Montgomery Co., OH	1810-1850
Jean Baptiste Amvot	Fort Michilimackinac, MI	1742-1750
Ettienne Ballard	Detroit, MI	1775-1783
Frances Baxler	Baltimore, MD	1800-1810
Christian Beck III	Several locations	1807-1830
John Book	Lancaster Co., PA	1785-1790
Squire Boone	Roman Co., NC	1744-1790
Squire Boone	Harvardsville, KY	1790-1815
John Bordeau	Ft. Laramie, Dakota	1730-1750
Ryer Bowen Sr.	Pittsburgh, PA	1756-1800
Ryer Bowen Jr.	Pittsburgh, PA	1780-1819
Ryer Bowen Jr.	Whiting, PA	1819-1828
William Bowen	Pittsburgh, PA	1736-1770
Isaac Brabant	Purysburgh, SC	1750-1760
James (Jim) Bridger	Fort Bridger, WY	1843-1853
R. Broderick	Piqua, OH	1815-1825
J.M. Brown	Green Bay, WI	1815-1830
William Burnett	Green Bay, WI	1815-1830

Name	Location	Dates
Thomas Burney	Ohio Frontier	1740-1750
Thomas Burney	Pickawillany, Ohio Frontier	1750-1752
Thomas Burney	West Moreland Co., PA	1752-1755
Richard & William Butler	Fort Pitt (Pittsburgh, PA)	1765-1770
Thomas Butler Sr.	Carlisle & Lancaster Co., PA	1740-1791
John Campbell	Fort Michilimackinac, MI	1820-1830
William Campbell	Frederick Co., VA	1766-1780
William Campbell	Annapolis, MD	1780-1781
John F. Casell	Baltimore, MD	1838-1848
James Chambers	Lancaster Co., PA	1750-1763
Lefevre Chaparo	Detroit, MI	1775-1783
William Clinton	Philadelphia, PA	1750-1770
Moses Coats (Coates)	East Caln, Chester Co., PA	1785-1796
Collins & Co.	Hartford, CT	1826-1966
John Concklin	Baltimore, MD	1790-1800
C. Cowan	Pittsburgh, PA	1800-1819
Peter Cremar	Pittsburgh, PA	1758-1770
Peter Cronin	Pittsburgh, PA	1758-1770
William H. Cummings	Philadelphia, PA	1820-1855
Robert Cunie	West Augusta, VA	1775-1783
Henry Deringer	Philadelphia, PA	1808-1868
John Dodd	Pon Pon, British Province of SC	1750-1755
Louis Duplesis	Oviatenon, IN	1775-1783
J. Durant	Philadelphia, PA	1775-1783
Francois Dyelle	Ohio Territory	1775-1783
John Endsor	Baltimore, MD	1790-1800
Joseph English	Philadelphia, PA	1830-1840
Daniel Evans	Philadelphia, PA	1753-1783
Joseph Feinour	Lancaster Co., PA	1775-1783
Augustine Feltcan	Fort Michilimackinac, MI	1775-1783
Jesse Fishpaw	Baltimore, MD	1800-1815
Gilbert Forbes	New York, NY	1750-1775
Foster & Murray	Pittsburgh, PA	1800-1814
John Fraser	Turtle Creek, PA	1753-1754
J. Gallarno	Green Bay, WI	1785-1800
Richard Ghiselin (Gisling)	Philadelphia, PA	1700-1720
Jacob Glasser	Baltimore, MD	1800-1815
John Godfried	Frederick Co., MD	1791-1816
Goulding & Ford	New York, NY	1855-1866
Carlos Gove	Several locations	1835-1900
William A. Hall	Chicago, IL	1820-1840
Charles Hammond	Philadelphia, PA & Boston, MA	1830-1864
Isaac Harrow	Trenton, NJ	1710-1740
J. Hayes	Fort Pitt (Pittsburgh, PA)	1760-1770
John Hendricks	Albany, NY & Philadelphia, PA	1735-1798
F. Hoff	Lancaster Co., PA	1800-1815
Frederick Hoffman	Philadelphia, PA	1750-1820

Cornelius Howard	Annapolis, MD	1750-1800
Jacob Irvin	Natchitoches, LA	1820-1830
Richard Jellere	Baltimore, MD	1800-1820
Joseph Jenks Jr.	Pawtucket Falls, RI	1650-1680
Reynaldo Johnson	Philadelphia, PA & Aquasco, MD	1800-1815
Samuel Johnson	Chicago, IL	1810-1830
Joseph Jourdain	Several locations	1780-1866
Rudolph Koch	Fort Michilimackinac, MI	1765-1775
Agustin Lafay	Detroit, MI	1770-1780
J.P. Lassure (Lasserre)	New Orleans, LA	1841-1844
John Lewis	Detroit, MI	1820-1840
Nicodemus Lloyd	Philadelphia, PA	1790-1820
F. (Francois) Lusignant	Fort Wayne, IN	1810-1830
A. Madison	New York, NY	1820-1830
John Malony	Baltimore, MD	1785-1800
Joseph Manning	New York, NY & Medina, OH	1820-1845
George McGunnegle	Pittsburgh, PA & Cumberland Co., PA	1787-1820
George Meldrum	Fort Michilimackinac, MI	1775-1783
John Peter Menta	Baltimore, MD	1790-1800
Soloman Mignevon	Philadelphia, PA	1820-1840
Nathaniel Miller	Woodstock Co., CT	1750-1770
Benjamin Moore	Sutton, MA	1800-1815
A.D. Newton	LaPointe, WI	1825-1850
A.D. Newton	DePere, WI	1850-1857
William Opy	Philadelphia, PA	1740-1770
Sergeant John Ordway	Fort Mandan, ND	1804-1806
Leber & Sylvestre Papin	St. Louis, MO	1825-1835
William Parke	Hudson Bay, Canada	1770-1796
Joseph Thomas & William Parkinson	Yogogania Co., VA	1770-c1783
Thomas Pearson	Philadelphia, PA	1677-1690
Daniel Pease	Blue Hill, NY	1860-1869
William Perkins	Philadelphia, PA	1775-1790
Daniel Pettibone	Boston, MA	1811-1815
J. (Joseph) Petty	LaCrosse, WI	1835-1857
Daniel Pose	Baltimore, MD	1790-1800
William Printup	New York, NY	1750-1770
Pierre Provinsable	Saginaw, MI	1810-1830
John D. Reed	Baltimore, MD	1800-1815
William Rightman	Charleston, SC	1775-1783
E. (Elisha) Rogers	Utica, NY	1815-1835
J. Rose & Son	New York, NY	1804-1820
Levi Saint Cyr	Winnebago, NE	1895-1910
Lemuel Shaw	Philadelphia, PA	1790-1812
William Shaw	Georgetown, DC	1795-1815
John Shields	Shenendoah Co., VA	1790-1810
Charles Sipes	Buffalo, Allegheny Co., PA	1790-D1831

John Small	New Lisbon, OH	1787-D1825
Jacob Smith	Baltimore, MD	1785-1800
Jacob S. Snevely	Harrisburg, PA & Piqua, OH	1811-1835
John Snyder	Tredyffrine Twsp., PA	1800-1820
O.B. Sprague	Prairie du Chien, WI	1861-1867
William Stackpole	Pittsburgh, PA	1790-1816
Miles Standish	Fort Michilimackinac, MI	1800-1823
Miles Standish	Montreal, Canada	1823-1828
Miles Standish	New York, NY	1828-D1868
W. Swain	Fort Wayne, IN	1815-1825
James Terry	Fort Wayne, IN	1815-1825
James Tristin	Soho, PA	1811-1850
Underhill Brothers	Boston, MA	1840-1866
Abner Updegraff	Pittsburgh, PA	1800-1841
William Updegraff	Pittsburgh, PA	1834-1872
John B. Van Eps	New York, NY	1755-1775
J. (Jonathon) Vickers	Cleveland, OH	1821-1851
J. (James) Walker	Knox Co., OH	1810-1830
J. (John) Watson	Baltimore, MD	1810-1818
J. (Jacob) Welshans	York, PA	1775-1820
Thomas Wheat	Washington, DC	1811-1817
Richard Whitehouse	Fort Wayne, IN	1810-1830
Alexander Willard	St. Louis, MO	1790-1820
W.A. Woodruff	Mt. Holly Springs, PA	1840-1860
Thomas Worley	Washington Co., MD	1776-1783
Thomas Worrell	Baltimore, MD	1790-1810
Henry Young	Easton, PA	1774-1786
John Young Sr.	Easton, PA	1755-1805
Nathaniel M. Young	Fairfield Co., OH	1803-1813

APPENDIX E

U.S. Pike Makers

Cromel Barney	Philadelphia, PA	1775-1810 (Naval)
Benicia Arsenal	Benicia, CA	1845-1865 (Naval)
Charles Blair & Charles Hart	Collinsville, CT	1857
Boston Navy Yard	Boston, MA	1799-1930 (Naval)
Abel Buell	Hartford, CT	1799-1825
John Coler	Philadelphia, PA	1797-1805
John Coney	Boston, MA	1675-1722
Claudius M. Cox	Philadelphia, PA	1790-1820 (Naval)
Henry Deringer	Philadelphia, PA	1808-1868 (Naval)
Thomas Farr	Charleston, SC	1775-1783 (Naval)
Henry Foxell	Baltimore, MD	1779-1800 (Naval)
Robert Gill	Baltimore, MD	1779-1799 (Naval)
John Harris	York, PA	1775-1808 (Naval)
Abasueres Hendricks	New Amsterdam, Long Island	1675-1727
James Hendricks	Philadelphia, PA	1746-1800
John Joseph Henry	Philadelphia, PA	1807-1822 (Naval)
J. Burley Hill	Boston, MA	1816 (Naval)
Frederick Hoffman	Philadelphia, PA	1750-1820 (Naval)
Jacob Howell	Philadelphia, PA	1775-1783
Henry Johns	Philadelphia, PA	1775-1783
David Kelly	Baltimore, MD	1795-1805 (Naval)
Benjamin King	Baltimore, MD	1775-1805 (Naval)
Benjamin Lincohn	Baltimore, MD	1775-1805 (Naval)
John Martin	Baltimore, MD	1775-1805 (Naval)
M. Melcher	Baltimore, MD	1775-1805 (Naval)
Theophilus Munson	New Haven, CT	1700-1747
New York Naval Yard	New York, NY	1812-1815 (Naval)

William Nevin	Annapolis, MD	1775-1783
James Ormsbee	Baltimore, MD	1775-1805
Stephen Paschall	Philadelphia, PA	1750-1783
Pensacola Navy Yard	Pensacola, FL	1820 (Naval)
Daniel Pettibone	Boston, MA	1811-1815
Lewis Prahl	Blockley Twsp., PA	1750-1784
William Smeeton	Baltimore, MD	1775-1805 (Naval)
Nathan Starr Sr.	Middletown, CT	1755-1821 (Naval)
Simon Walker	Baltimore, MD	1775-1805 (Naval)
Washington Navy Yard	Washington, DC	1799-1993 (Naval)
Samuel Wheeler	Philadelphia, PA	1744-1790 (Naval)
William Wing	Philadelphia, PA	1775-1805 (Naval)
Josiah Wood	Philadelphia, PA	1775-1783 (Naval)
John Yager	Trenton, NY	1775-1783 (Naval)

APPENDIX F
Tiffany & Co.

1) A BRIEF HISTORY OF TIFFANY & CO.

Tiffany Company Names

TIFFANY (CHARLES LEWIS) & YOUNG (JOHN B.)	NEW YORK, NY 259 Broadway	1837-1841
TIFFANY (CHARLES LEWIS), YOUNG (JOHN B) & ELLIS (JABEZ LEWIS)	NEW YORK, NY 259, 260, 271 Broadway	1841-1848
TIFFANY & CO.	NEW YORK, NY 550 and 552 Broadway	1848-1870
	NEW YORK, NY Union Square	1870-1905
	NEW YORK, NY 5th Ave. and 37th St.	1905-1940
	NEW YORK, NY 5th Ave. and 57th St.	1940-1997

Tiffany European Offices

TIFFANY (CHARLES LEWIS), REED (GIDEON F.T.) & CO. TIFFANY & CO	PARIS, FRANCE 79 Rue Richelieu	1850-1868
TIFFANY & CO	PARIS, FRANCE	1868
TIFFANY & CO	LONDON, ENGLAND	1868

General Information

- Charles Lewis Tiffany was born in Connecticut (1812).
- He apprenticed as a silversmith and opened his first shop (1837).
- Tiffany contracted with the New York Silversmith John Chandler Moore to make hollowware (1851).
- Moore's son, Edward C. Moore, was manager of Silver Products Manufacturing for Tiffany and design director (1862-1891).
- Tiffany & Co. merged with the John C. Moore Company (1868).
- Known sword designers for Tiffany & Co. included Edward Chandler Moore, George Paulding Farnham, and Eugene Julius Soligny.
- Tiffany & Co. showed presentation swords at the 1893 Columbian Exposition in Chicago.
- Tiffany & Co. sold all its military stocks to Shannon, Miller, & Co. (1866) but continued to sell presentation revolvers and presentation swords until the early 1900s.

Tiffany & Co. Civil War Blade and Sword Purchases

- Bought sword belt plates from Gaylord Mfg. Co.
- Bought blades from D.J. Millard.
- Bought blades and swords from Collins & Co.
- Bought blades from Ames Mfg. Co.
- Imported blades from France, England, and Germany.
- Imported Damascus steel blades from Solingen, Germany.
- Imported blades from Schnitzer & Kirschbaum, Solingen, Germany.
- Imported M1850 staff and field officer swords and blades from Paul D. Lunesehloss, Solingen, Germany.
- Imported M1850 foot officer swords.
- Bought the building at 552 Broadway and set up a military store (1861).
- Made many one-of-a-kind silver-mounted presentation swords, especially during the Civil War.

Tiffany & Co. at the New York Metropolitan Fair

- Tiffany & Co. displayed presentation swords at the New York Metropolitan Fair.
- The fair opened on April 4, 1864.
- It was to benefit the United States Sanitary Commission.
- A museum was set up displaying military antiques from the Revolutionary War, War of 1812, and Mexican War.
- A large display of Civil War military goods was set up. It included 12 presentation sword makers and dealers.
- Tiffany & Co. donated two presentation swords (one army and one navy), worth $1,000 each, to the fair.
- They were to be presented to two Civil War heroes. Anyone could vote for his hero by paying $1 for a ballot. Gen. Ulysses Simpson Grant was presented with the army sword; Commodore Rowan won the navy sword. Almost $100,000 was raised by the voting.

2) **TIFFANY & CO. CIVIL WARS ARMS CONTRACTS**

- U.S. contracts for 12,454 imported cavalry sabers (1861-1863), including the following:
    Iron-hilted M1840-style sabers from Paul L. Luneschloss (PDL), Solingen, Germany.
    Iron-hilted British M1821 sabers from Robert Mole & Sons (R.M. & S.B.), Birmingham, England.
    Iron hilted British M1821-style sabers from Schnitzler & Kirschbaum (S&K), Solingen, Germany.
- U.S. contract for 6,815 imported non-comm. swords (1861-1862).
- U.S. contract for 145 short artillery swords (1861-1862).
- U.S. contract for 10 pioneer swords with sawback blades (1861).
- U.S. contract for Enfield rifles.

- U.S. contract for Leflaucheau carbines.
- U.S. contract for Leflaucheau revolvers.

3) TIFFANY & CO. ADVERTISEMENTS

- The following merchandise was advertised by Tiffany & Co. in its Civil War Presentation Sword Catalog:
    1) *Manufactures and importers of all kinds of military wares*
    2) *Enfield, Birmingham & Liege fire arms of every quality*
    3) *Sharpe's and Westley Richard's Breech loading rifles*
    4) *Pistols by Colt, Tranter, Adams, Lafaucheux, Smith & Wesson, Divisme, Bacon Mfg. Co. & other fabricants*
    5) *Choice fowling pieces*
    6) *Chapeaux*
    7) *Cap ornaments*
    8) *Epaulets, shoulder-straps and aiquillettes and all the details of a uniform*
    9) *Knapsacks*
    10) *Cartridge boxes*
    11) *Canteens*
    12) *Tiffany & Co. are sole agents and manufacturers of the Rockwell combination union camp chest*
    13) *Regimental standards, national ensigns, guidons, swallow tails and all styles of flags (embroidered or painted from original designs or made to order)*
    14) *Special attention paid to the manufacture of articles of military Presentation Swords, Standards, etc. The artistic resources of the house giving it particular advantages in this respect*
    15) *Swords, Sabres and Cutlasses*

        Rich staff & dress army & navy swords including the choicest blades of English Manufacture identical with those made by Wilkinson of London, worn by the officers of the British Army and most approved by experienced Europeans authorities; The elegantly wrought blades of Solingen on the Rhine, in fiber and finish the recognized modern type of the celebrated Damascus Steel.

        The excellent and serviceable blades of Collins of Hartford besides those of other domestic fabricants. The mounting of these blades, in all cases executed within the establishment, will be found to comprise all requisite styles of ornamentation, the scabbards being of silver, silver-gilt, bronze, plain or fire-gilt, silver plated, burnished steel, rich leather etc. with bands of plain chased or embossed gilt or solid silver, the grips or guards of the same variety of materials and finish, and of either regulation pattern or original design.

        Presentation swords

Cavalry sabres	*Infantry swords*	*Straight swords for Generals*
4 Basic types	*4 Basic types*	*6 Basic types*

- On April 12, 1862. Tiffany & Co. advertised in Frank Leslie's illustrated newspaper as follows:

    SWORDS FOR PRESENTATION
    Tiffany & Co.
    Nos. 550 and 552 Broadway, New York
    And No. 79 Rue Richelieu, Paris
    Importers and manufacturers of all kinds of military wares.
    Solicit the attention of civic and military associations, commands or national or state service, patriotic clubs and individuals to their large stock of rich staff and dress army and navy swords. Their assortment includes;

    THE CHOICEST BLADES OF ENGLISH MANUFACTURE
    Identical with those made for Wilkinson of London, worn by the officers of the British Army, and most approved by experienced authorities.

THE ELEGANTLY WROUGHT BLADES OF SOLINGEN ON THE RHINE
In fibre and finish, the recognized modern type of the celebrated damascus steel.

THE EXCELLENT AND SERVICEABLE BLADES OF COLLINS OF HARTFORD
Besides those of the other domestic fabricants

The mounting of these blades in all cases, executed within the establishment, will be found to comprise all requisite styles of ornamentation. The scabbards being of Silver, Silver gilt, Bronze, Plain or Fine gilt, Silver-plated, Barnished steel, rich leather; and with bands of plain, chased, embossed gilt or solid silver. The grips and guards of the same variety and material and finish, and of either regulation pattern or original design.

Should an article of extraordinary elegance of a richness and costliness, not represented in stock, be required for presentation, the capabilities of the establishment for the manufacture of the choicest works of gold and silver and its general artistic resources are unusual guarantee of its satisfactory and speedy production. In answer to orders, designs and estimates will be promptly forwarded.

Individuals purchasing swords of Tiffany & Co. are informed that every blade is subjected to tests even more severe than those enjoined by government, before it is placed on sale. The testing block being in the establishment, and in the command of all who prefer immediate proof of the excellence of their blades.

- On August 29, 1863, Tiffany & Co. advertised in the *Army-Navy Journal* as follows:

    Presentation swords
    Depot of General Equipment

    Comprising everything pertaining to the personnel or camp furniture of the soldier officers studying the necessities of active service, or the perfection of uniform and materials will do well to examine this large collection of foreign and domestic arms, uniforms and miscellaneous trappings.

- Tiffany & Co. advertised presentation revolvers and swords in its Bluebook catalog (1890-1909).

4) **A LIST OF TIFFANY & CO. PRESENTATION SWORDS**

Mexican War

GENERAL SCHUYLER HAMILTON, 1848
"By his fellow citizens of New York in recognition of his services in the Mexican War"

Civil War

MAJOR GENERAL JOHN C. ROBINSON, July 4, 1863
"By his friends and the city of New York for gallantry at Gettysburg"

MAJOR GENERAL ANDREW JACKSON SMITH, September 19, 1864
"By the commissioned officers 3rd Div. 16 AC and citizen friends for gallantry at Vicksburg"

BRIGADIER GENERAL DANIEL E. SICKLES, 1861
"By his friend upon the formation of the Excelsior Brigade"
(Supposedly presented by Abraham Lincoln)

MAJOR GENERAL LEWIS MERRILL, 1862
"By the loyal men of Northwest Missouri"

CAPTAIN DAVID C. LOEWENSTINE, 1864
"By his friends in Memphis"

BRIGADIER GENERAL WILLIAM VANDEVER, March 7, 1863
"By his friends in St. Louis, Missouri"

GENERAL STEWART VAN VLIET, January 1863
No dedication

GENERAL J.H. HOBERT WARD, May 1863
"By the officers & privates of the old 38 regiment N.Y.S.V."

BRIGADIER GENERAL SAMUEL WYLIE CRAWFORD, 1864
"3rd Div. 5th Corp., A token of regard from his staff"

MAJOR GENERAL JAMES G. BLUNT, date unknown
"From L. & M.C."

MAJOR GENERAL H. W. HALLECK, 1862
"By the ladies of St. Louis"

MAJOR GENERAL AMBROSE E. BURNSIDE, 1862
"By the state of Rhode Island"

BRIGADIER GENERAL J.J. STEVENS, 1862
"By the non-commissioned officers & privates of the 79th Highland Guard N.Y.S.M. at Beufort S.C."

BRIGADIER GENERAL WILLIAM A. PILE, date unknown
"By the non-commissioned officers and privates of the 58th U.S. Infantry Cold. after the capture of Ft. Blakely, Alabama"

COLONEL RUSH C. HAWKINS (HAWKINS ZOUAVES), 1863
"By his fellow citizens of New York"

CAPTAIN PERCIVAL DRAYTON U.S.N., 1863
"By his fellow citizens of New York"

BRIGADIER GENERAL T.E.G. RANSOM, 1863
"By the officers of his brigade"

LT. COLONEL HENRY C. HODGE USA, 1863
"By his friend Capt. John Wright"

BRIGADIER GENERAL A.G. EDWARDS, November 26, 1862
"From his friends"

COLONEL HUGH W. McNEIL (1st PENN RIFLES), February 18, 1862
"By Co. D The Raftsman Guards"

MAJOR GENERAL RANDOLPH B. MARCY, 1861
No dedication

BRIGADIER GENERAL GODFREY WEITZEL, October 1863
"By the enlisted men of the 75th Regiment N.Y. Volunteers"

MAJOR GENERAL JOHN McALLISTER SCHOFIELD, 1864
No dedication

ADMIRAL DAVID G. FARRAGUT, April 23, 1864
"By the members of the Union League Club as a token of their appreciation of his gallant services rendered in defence of his county–New York"

GENERAL WILLIAM TECUMSEH SHERMAN, 1862
"By the Congress of the United States in recognition of his services during the battle of Shiloh"

MAJOR GENERAL WINFIELD SCOTT HANCOCK, 1864
"Presented at the Mississippi Valley Sanitary Fair, St. Louis"

GENERAL ULYSSES SIMPSON GRANT, 1864
"Presented at the Metropolitan Fair in New York, United States Sanitary Commission"

BRIGADIER GENERAL MICHAEL CORCORAN, 1862
"By the city of New York in recognition of his love for and zealous devotion to the cause of the Union, etc."

BRIGADIER GENERAL H.E. DAVIES, September 16, 1863
"Upon his promotion to Brigadier General"

MAJOR GENERAL J.C. FREMONT, November 21, 1862
"The Pathfinder of the West by the citizens of St. Louis"

CAPTAIN JOHN J. TIDBALL, January 14, 1864
"By the non-commissioned officers and privates of Co. A 2nd U.S. Artillery"

COLONEL JOHN TILLSON, July 17, 1862
"By the members of the staff"

CAPTAIN F. MEMMERT, 1862
"By the members of Co. H 5th regt. Maryland volunteer infantry"

LT. COLONEL C.M. FERREL, 1862
"By the Enlisted men of the 29th Illinois volunteers"

COMMODORE ROWAN, 1864
"Presented at the 1864 Metropolitan Fair in New York–United States Sanitary Commission"

COLONEL THEODORE B. GATES, August 25, 1863
"20th NY Militia by the citizens of Ulster Co."

Indian Wars

GENERAL NELSON A. MILES, September 4, 1887
"By the people of Arizona"
(For the capture of Geronimo)

Spanish-American War

COMMANDER RICHARD WAINWRIGHT, USN, 1898
"For his victory in the war with Spain off Santiago Cuba, etc."

ADMIRAL ROBLEY D. EVANS, 1898
"By the state of Iowa for the hero of the Battle of Santiago, Cuba"

COLONEL LAWRENCE D. TYSON, 1898
"By the officers of the 6th US Infantry as a token of their personal esteem, etc."

CAPTAIN JOHN W. PHILIP, commander of the battleship *Texas*, 1898
"By the Sunday school children of Texas in recognition of his bravery, etc."

REAR ADMIRAL GEORGE DEWEY, USN, 1899
"The gift of the nation in memory of the victory at Manila Bay, etc."

BRIGADIER GENERAL FUNSTON, 1898
"By the people of Kansas"

World War I

ADMIRAL DAVID FOOTE SELLERS, USN, June 8, 1934
"Commander in Chief–U.S. Fleet, by the members of the World War crew of U.S.S. *Wisconsin*"

FRENCH MARSHAL FOCH, 1915

Tiffany & Co. Presentation Sword Original Designer Sketches
1) Silversmith Design Drawings

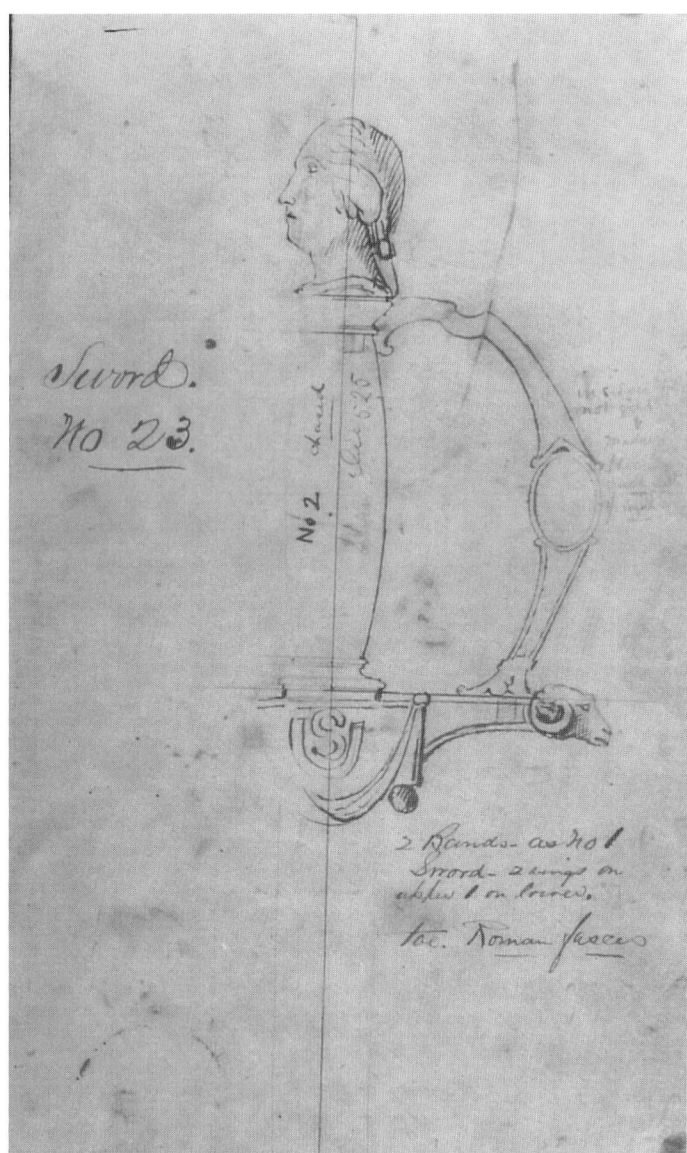

Silversmith design drawing of the sword presented to Brig. Gen. Godfrey Weitzel in 1862. (Tharpe Collection of American Military History, photo courtesy of Donald R. Tharpe, © Donald R. Tharpe)

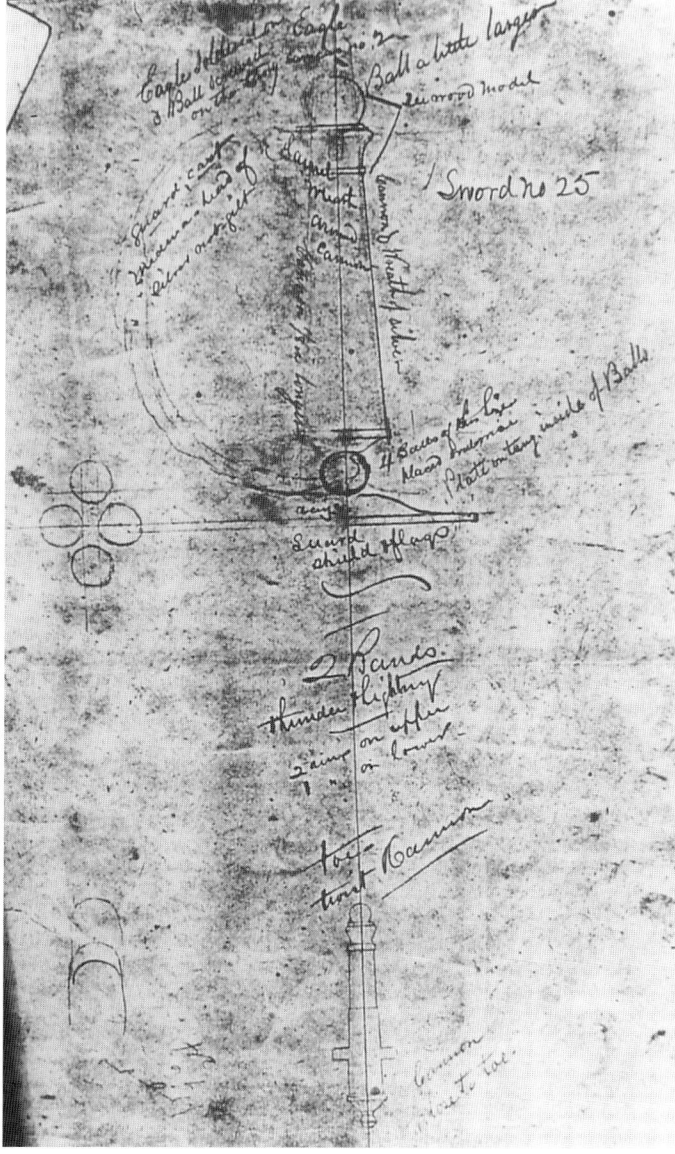

Silversmith design drawing of the sword presented to Gen. John C. Robinson in July 1865. (Tharpe Collection of American Military History, photo courtesy of Donald R. Tharpe, © Donald R. Tharpe)

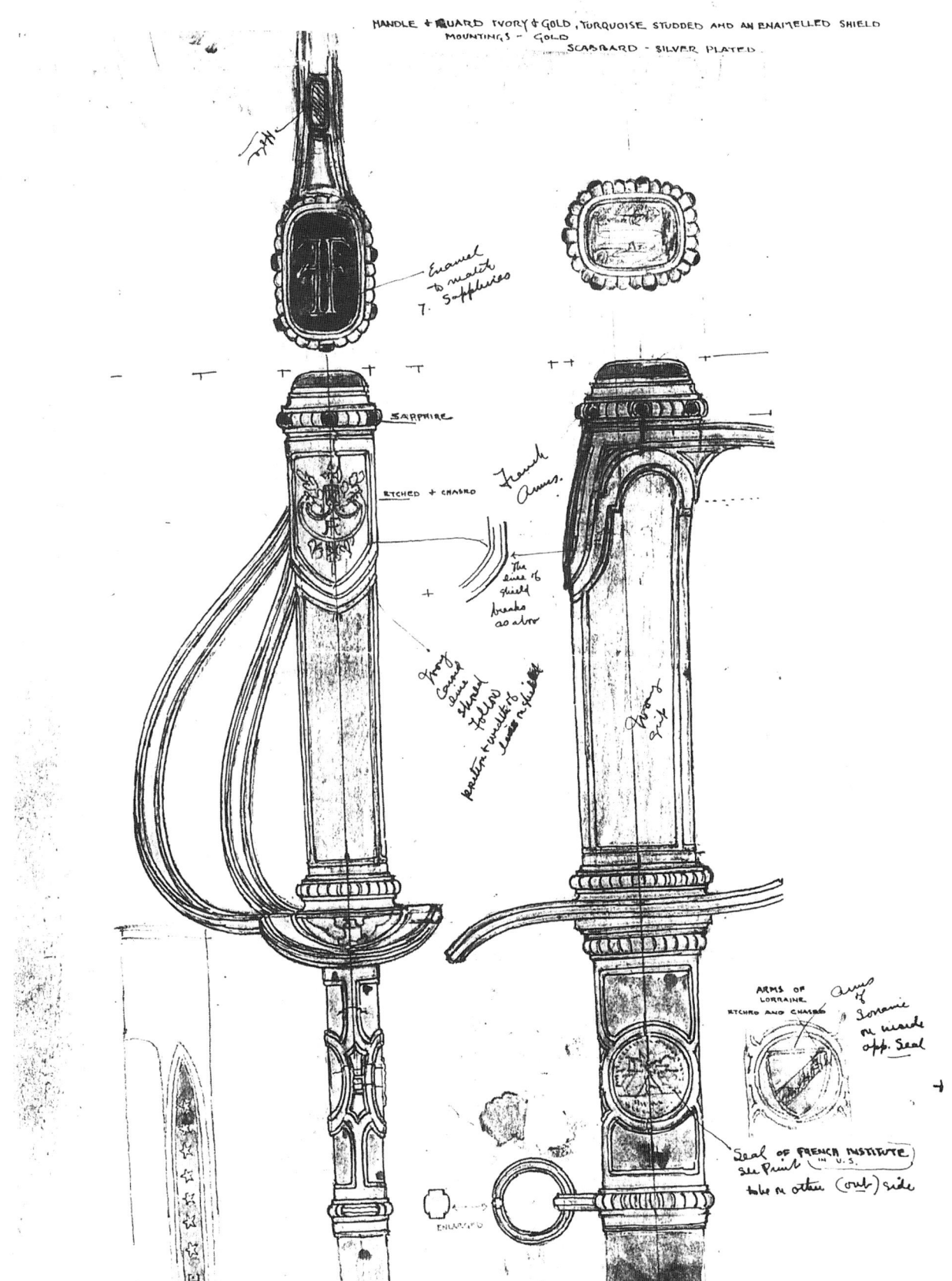

Silversmith design drawing of the sword presented to French Marshal Ferdinand Foch, commander of the Allied armies during World War I, in 1921. (© Tiffany & Co., from the archives)

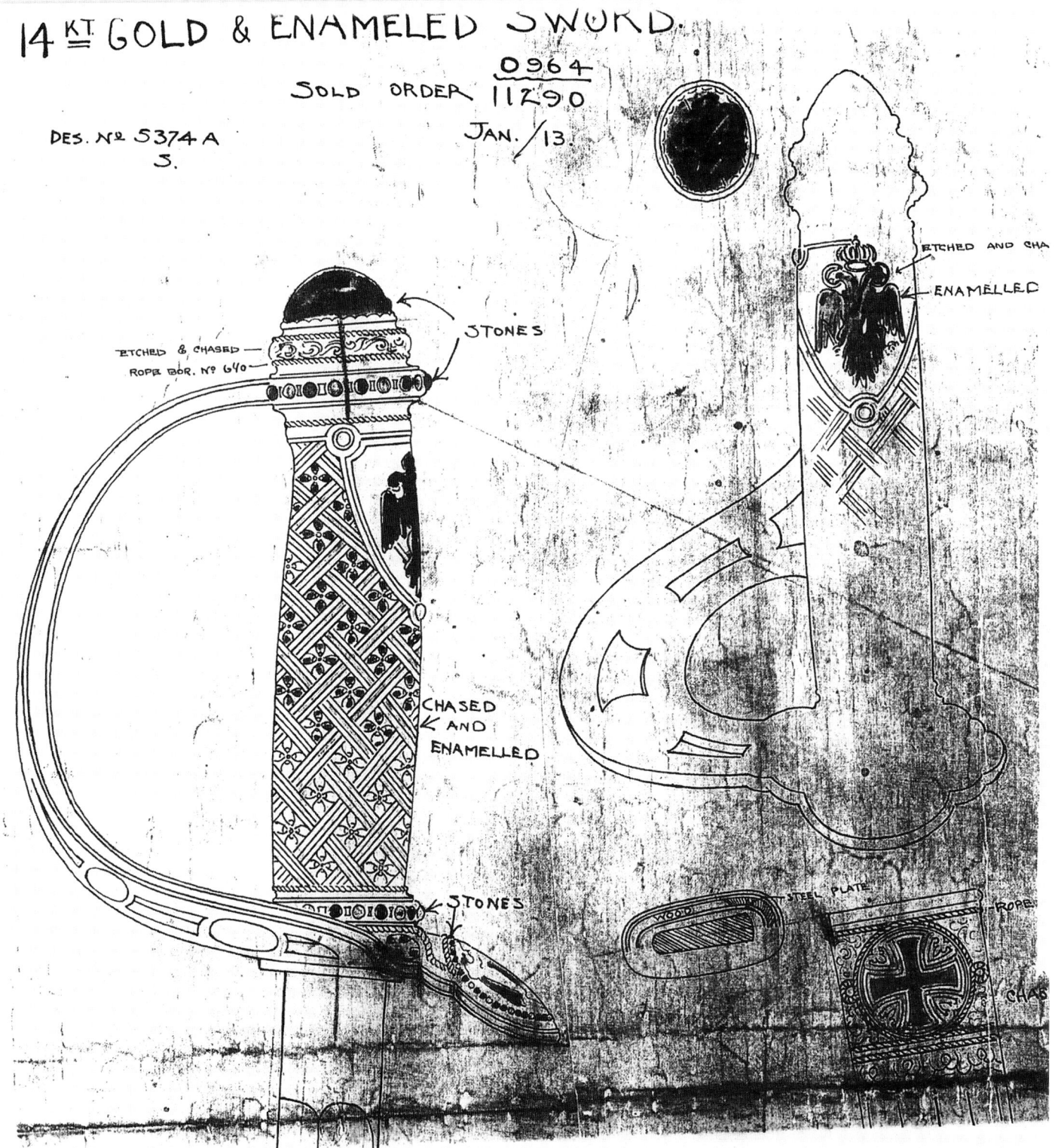

Silversmith design drawing showing the positioning of the stones, etching, and enameling as well as the requested design. (© Tiffany & Co., from the archives)

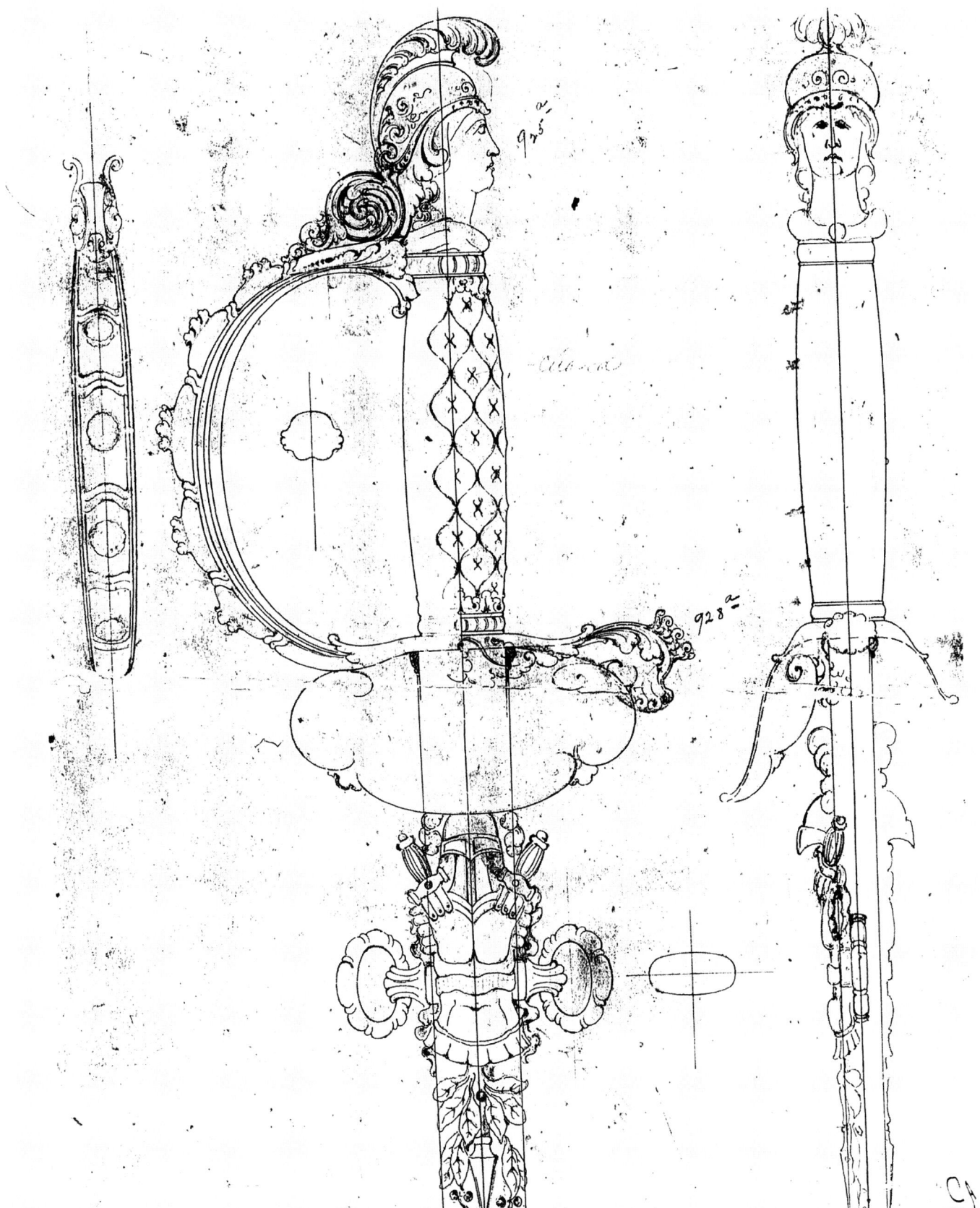

Silversmith design drawing of a presentation sword. (© Tiffany & Co., from the archives)

2) Presentation Sword Drawings

Presentation sword drawing by Tiffany & Co. silversmith Eugene Julius Soligny, September 1862. (© Tiffany & Co., from the archives)

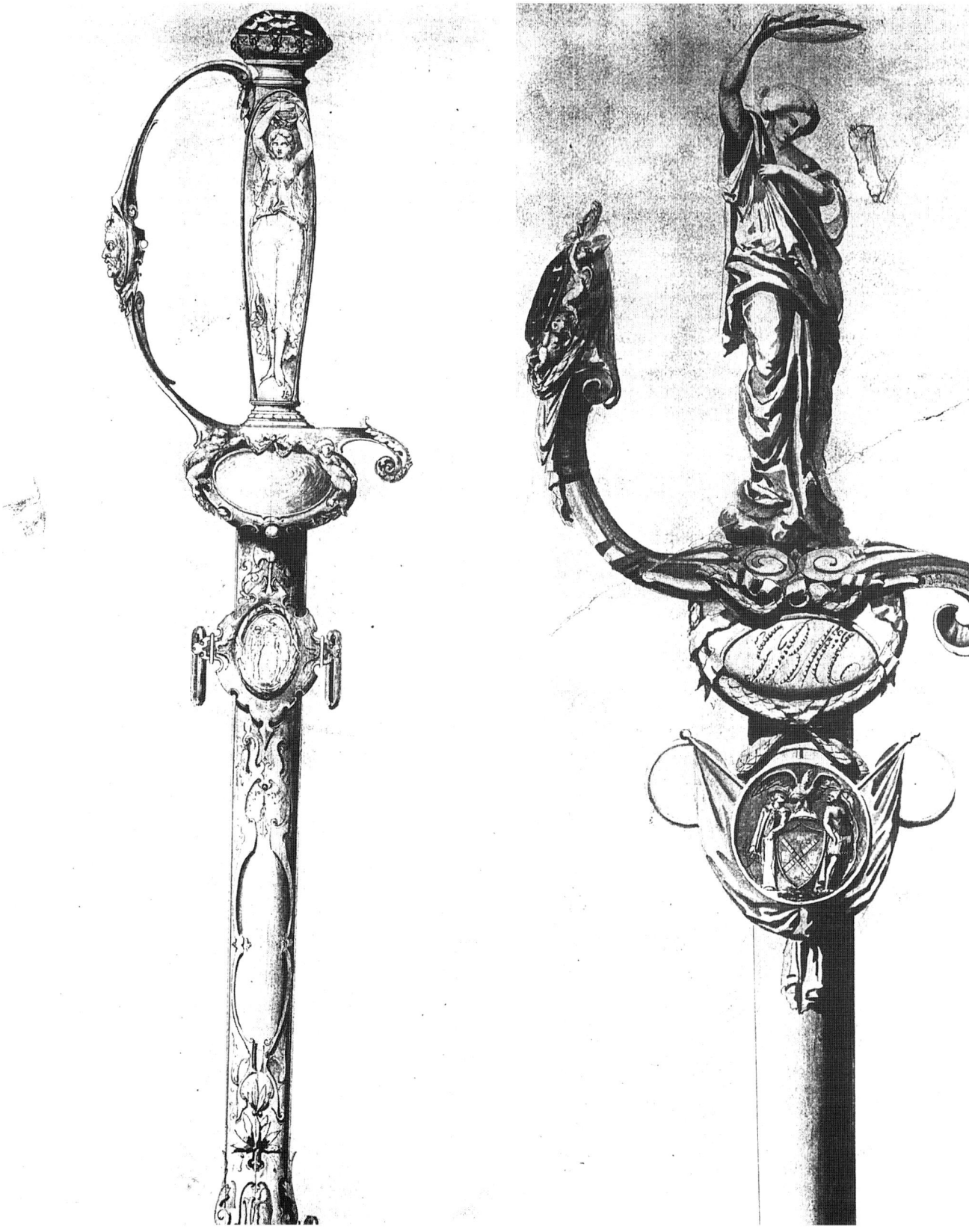

Presentation sword drawing by Tiffany & Co. silversmith Edward C. Moore, assisted by Eugene Julius Soligny. (© Tiffany & Co., from the archives)

Presentation sword drawing by Tiffany & Co. silversmith Eugene Julius Soligny (signed on the finial). (© Tiffany & Co., from the archives)

3) Presentation Sword Illustrations from the Tiffany & Co. Sword Design Book of Silversmith Edward C. Moore

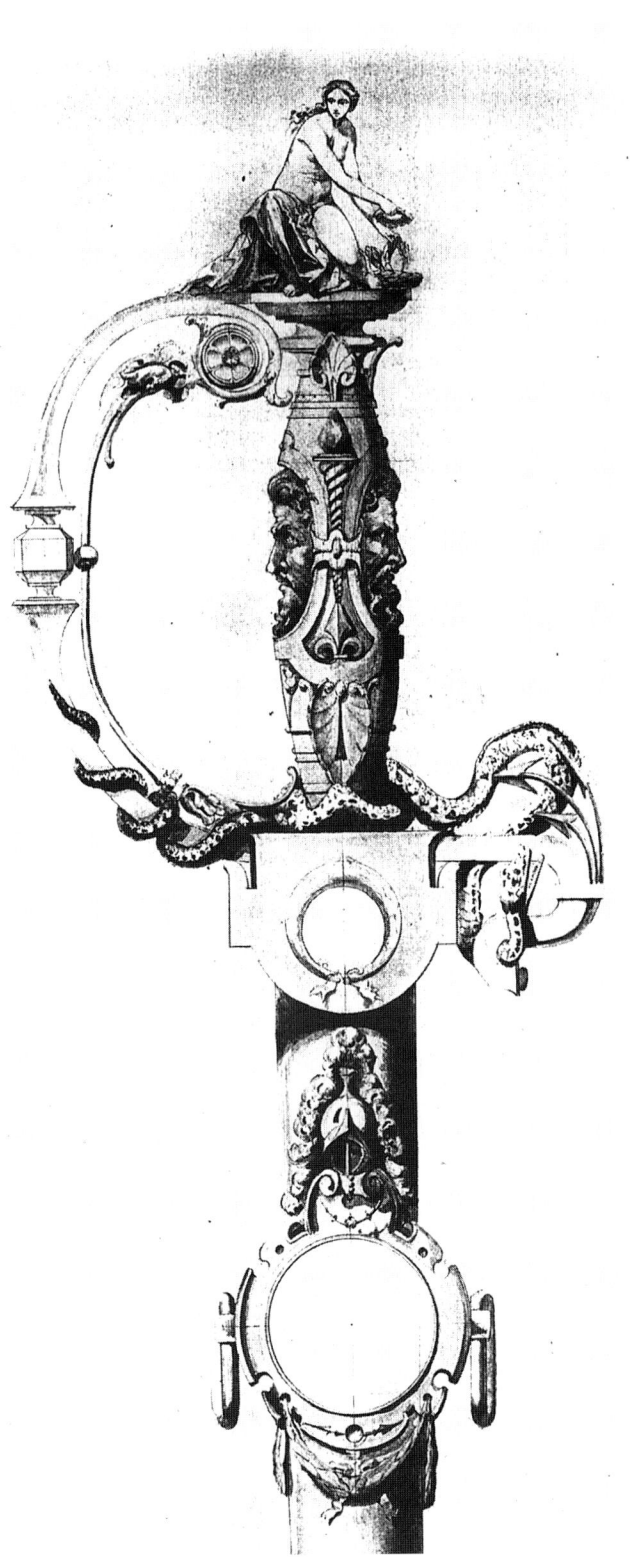

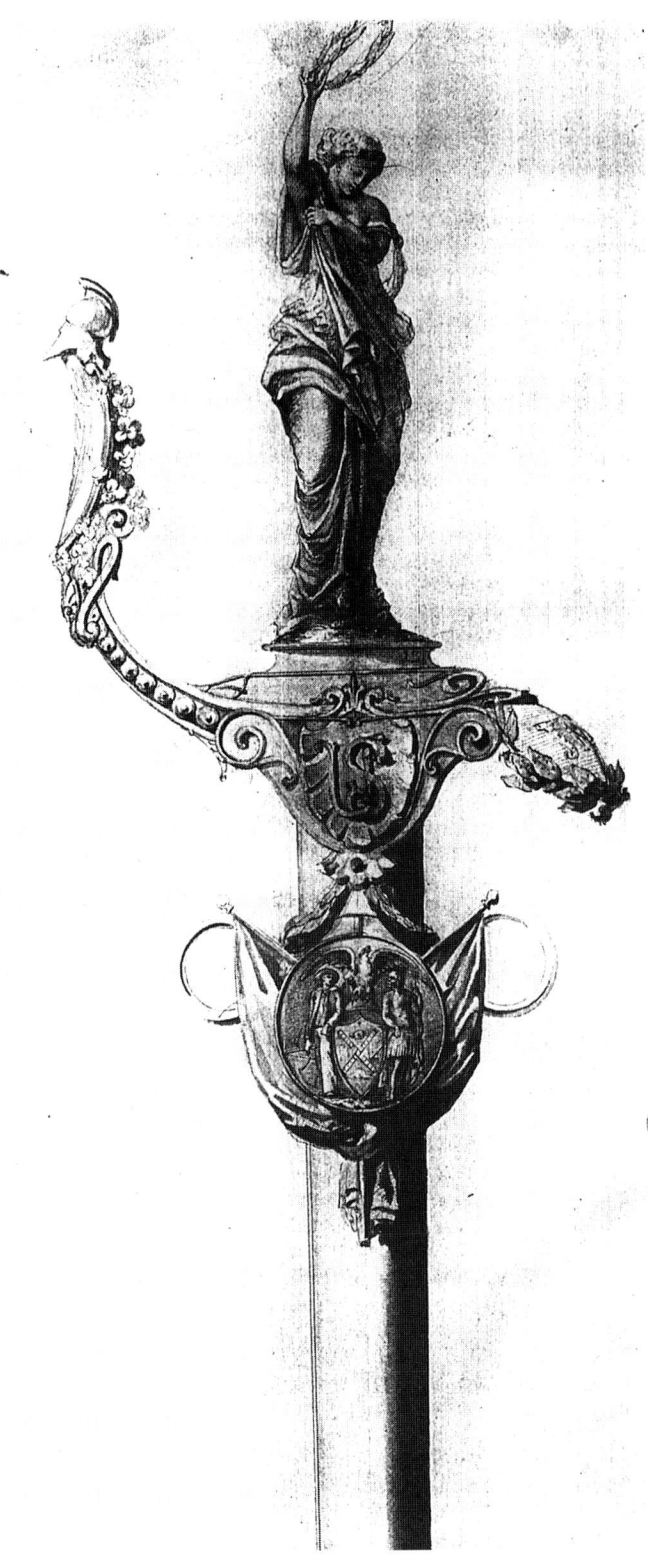

Presentation sword illustration (design #19) from the Tiffany & Co. sword design book of silversmith Edward C. Moore. (© Tiffany & Co., from the archives)

Presentation sword illustration with sailor and Indian on crest (design #20) from the Tiffany & Co. sword design book of silversmith Edward C. Moore. (© Tiffany & Co., from the archives)

Presentation sword illustration with Civil War Zouave infantryman on grip (design #22) from the Tiffany & Co. sword design book of silversmith Edward C. Moore. (© Tiffany & Co., from the archives)

Civil War naval presentation sword illustration with *Monitor* and *Merrimac* on shield (design #36) from the Tiffany & Co. sword design book of silversmith Edward C. Moore. (© Tiffany & Co., from the archives)

TIFFANY & CO. PHOTOGRAPHS

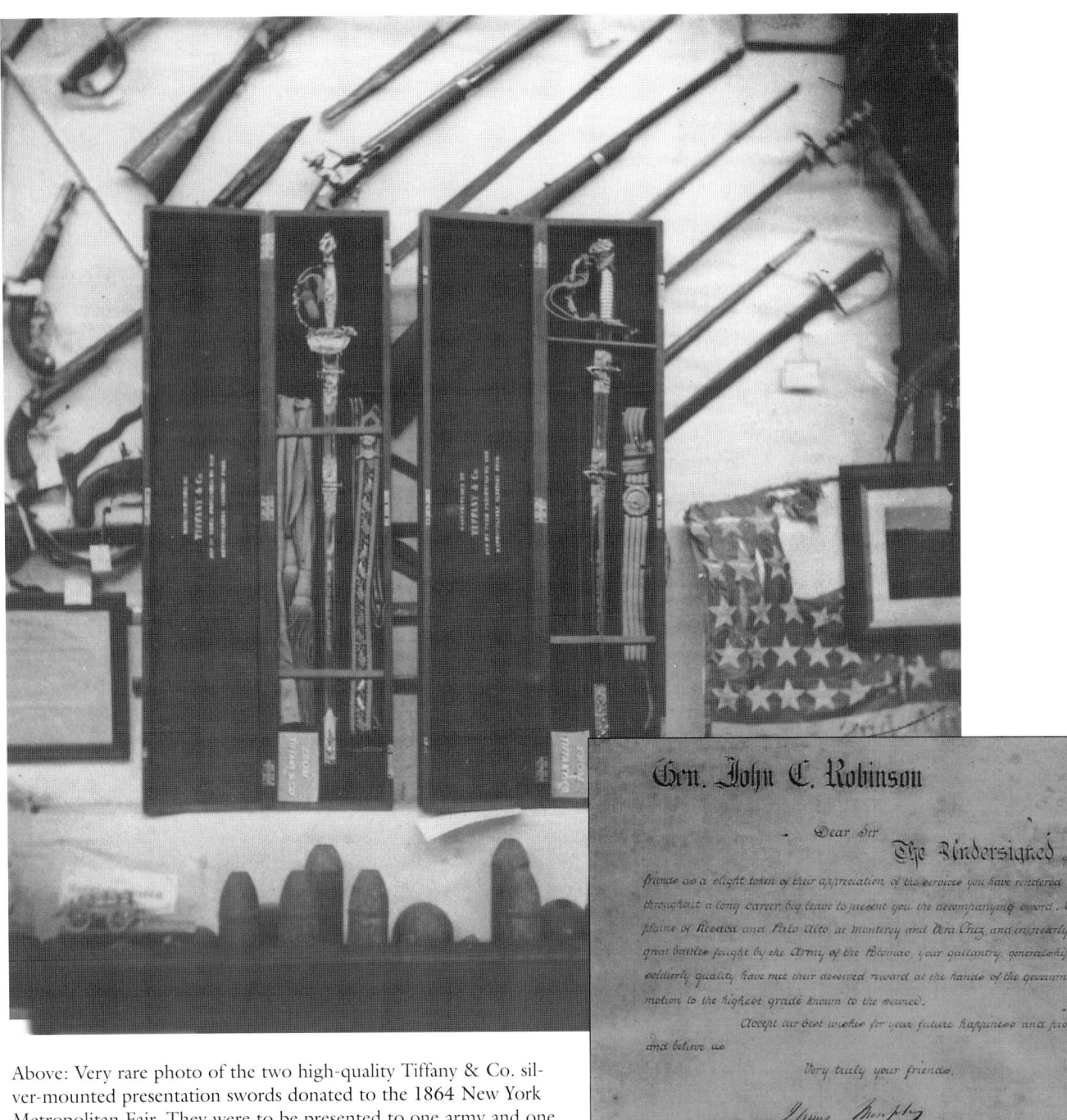

Above: Very rare photo of the two high-quality Tiffany & Co. silver-mounted presentation swords donated to the 1864 New York Metropolitan Fair. They were to be presented to one army and one navy hero of the Civil War. Patrons of the fair were allowed to vote for their heroes at the cost of $1 per ballot. All proceeds went to the U.S. Sanitary Commission. Ulysses S. Grant was voted to receive the army sword; a Commodore Rowan won the navy sword. The cases are enscribed: "Manufactured by Tiffany & Co. and by them presented to the Metropolitan Sanitary Fair." (Courtesy of Don Ball)

Right: Written sword presentation to Gen. John C. Robinson, July 4, 1865. Signed by C. (Charles) L. (Lewis) Tiffany and others. (Photo courtesy of Donald R. Tharpe, Tharpe Collection of American Military History, © Donald R. Tharpe)

Tiffany & Co. Blade Markings

Above: Tiffany & Co. sword blade marking. Blade made by Collins & Co., Hartford, CT. (James Cocalas collection)

Far left: Tiffany & Co. sword blade marking. Blade made by Collins & Co., Hartford, CT.

Left: Tiffany & Co. sword blade marking. Blade made by Collins & Co., Hartford, CT, dated 1862. (Kevin T. Hoffman collection)

Tiffany & Co. blade marking on a sword presented to Lt. William S. Marble by the veterans of Company H, 7th Corps. Note also the Tiffany & Co. marking on the scabbard. (Kevin T. Hoffman collection)

Tiffany & Co. sword blade marking. Blade made by Collins & Co., Hartford, CT.

Tiffany & Co. sword blade marking. (Susan Di Camillo collection; photo by Paul J. DeSarbo)

Tiffany & Co. Enlisted Man's Cavalry Sabers

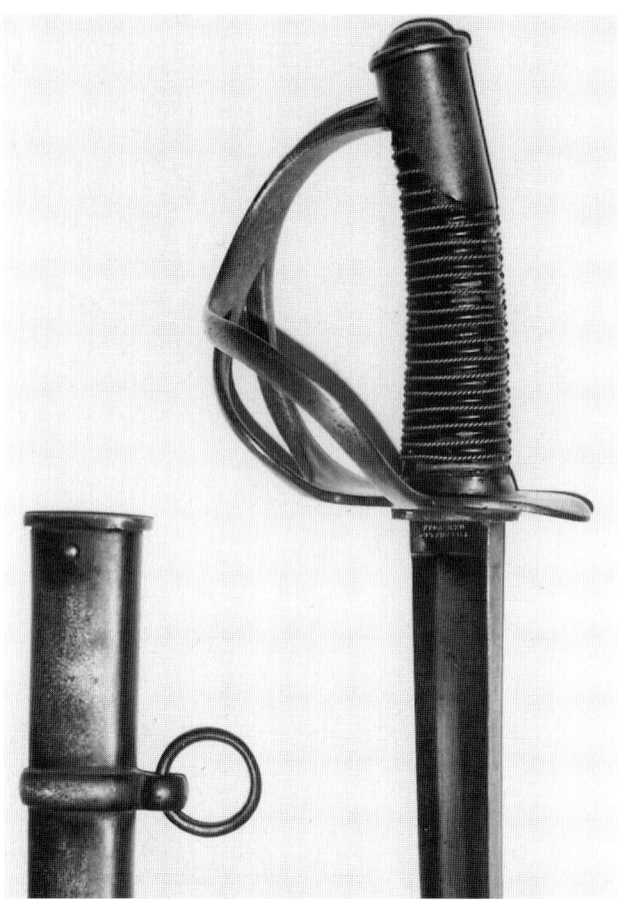

Model 1840 nonregulation iron-hilted cavalry saber made by Paul D. Luneschloss, Solingen, Germany, and imported for the Civil War by Tiffany & Co., c. 1861-1862. (Author's collection)

Nonregulation iron-hilted Civil War cavalry saber made by Robert Mole & Son, Birmingham, England, and imported by Tiffany & Co., c. 1861-1862. (Author's collection)

Tiffany & Co. Cavalry Officer Saber

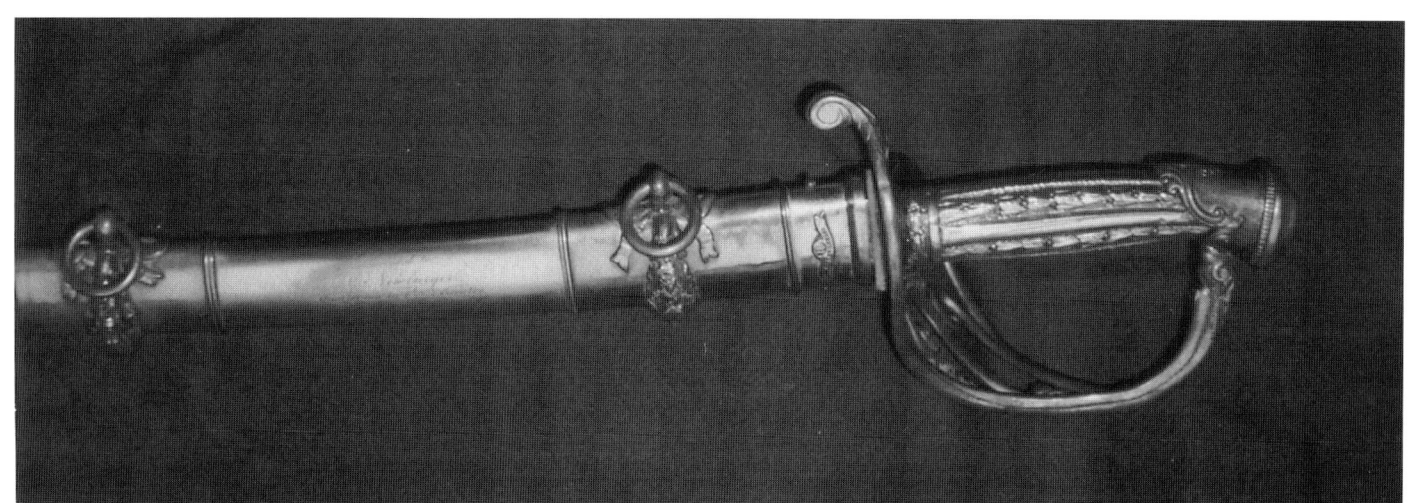

Presentation-grade Model 1860 cavalry officer saber with silver grip, brass hilt, and silver- and brass-mounted scabbard.

Tiffany & Co. Foot Officer Swords

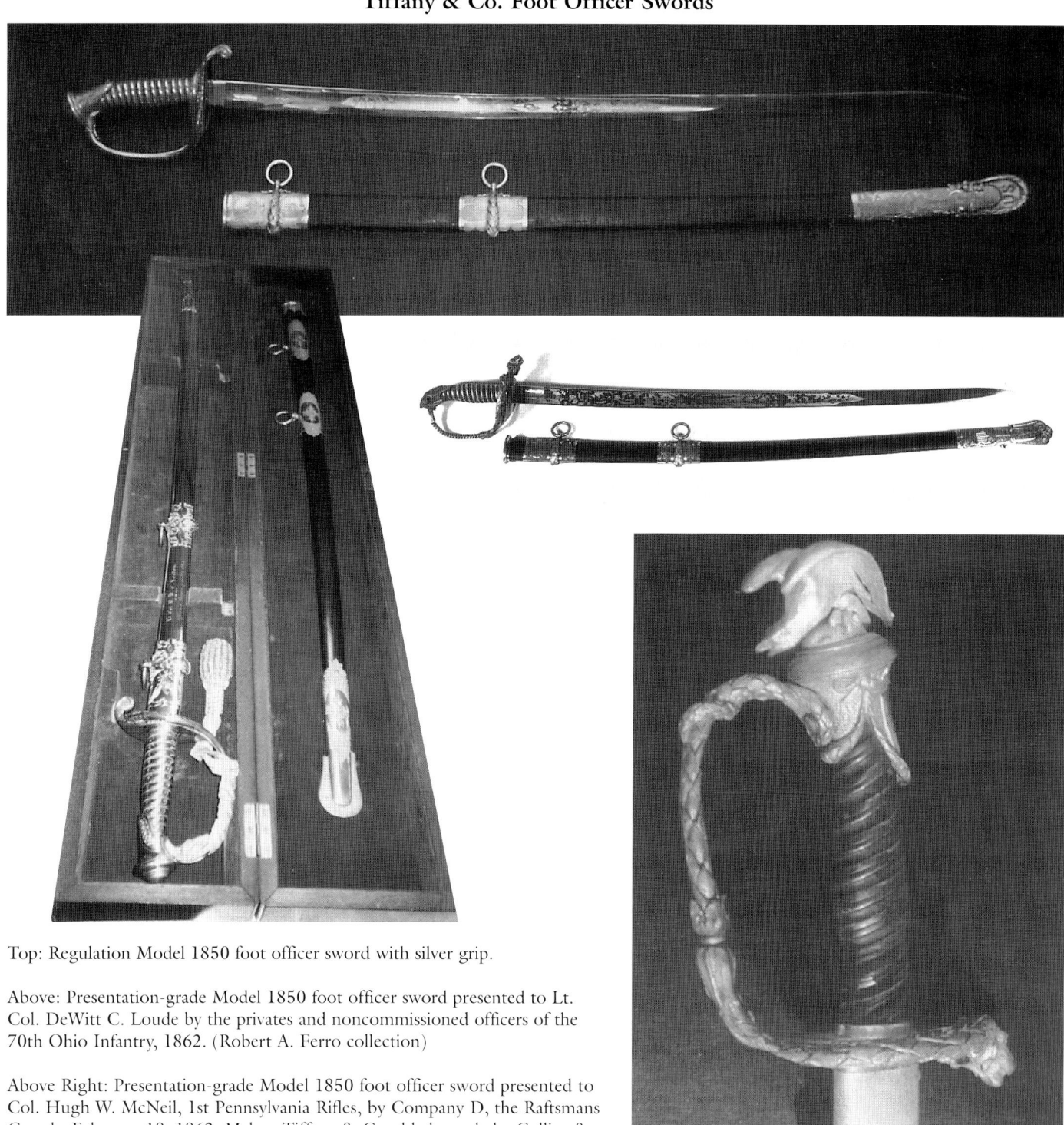

Top: Regulation Model 1850 foot officer sword with silver grip.

Above: Presentation-grade Model 1850 foot officer sword presented to Lt. Col. DeWitt C. Loude by the privates and noncommissioned officers of the 70th Ohio Infantry, 1862. (Robert A. Ferro collection)

Above Right: Presentation-grade Model 1850 foot officer sword presented to Col. Hugh W. McNeil, 1st Pennsylvania Rifles, by Company D, the Raftsmans Guards, February 18, 1862. Maker: Tiffany & Co.; blade made by Collins & Co. (Courtesy of the State Museum of Pennsylvania, Pennsylvania Historical Museum Commission)

Right: Presentation-grade Model 1850 foot officer sword presented to Capt. John J. Tidball on January 14, 1864, by the privates and noncommissioned officers of Company A, 2nd U.S. Artillery. (Courtesy of Gordon A. Blaker)

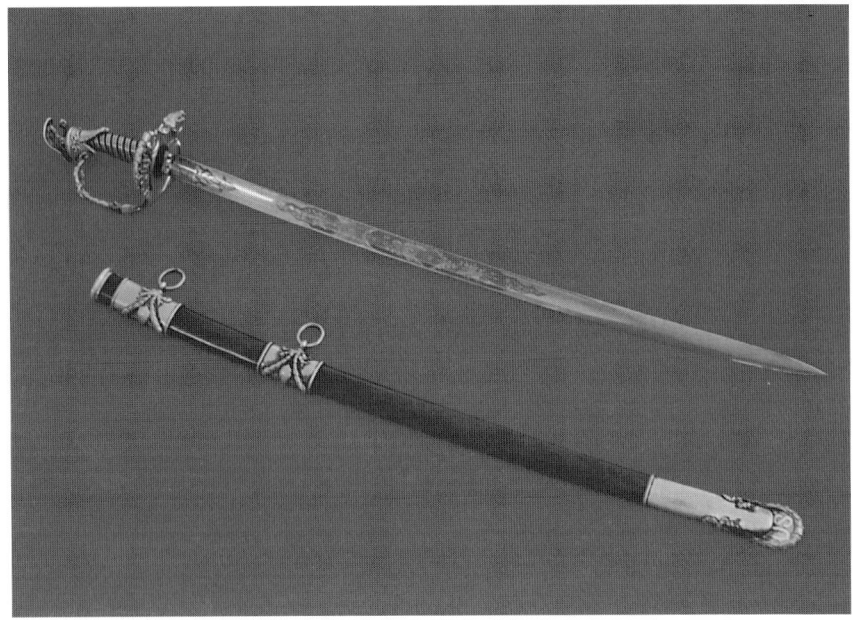

Above: Presentation-grade Model 1850 foot officer sword presented to Col. Henry C. Deming by the city council of Hartford, CT, 1862. Mounted by Tiffany & Co. with a Collins & Co. blade.

Right: Close-up of hilt on the Deming sword.

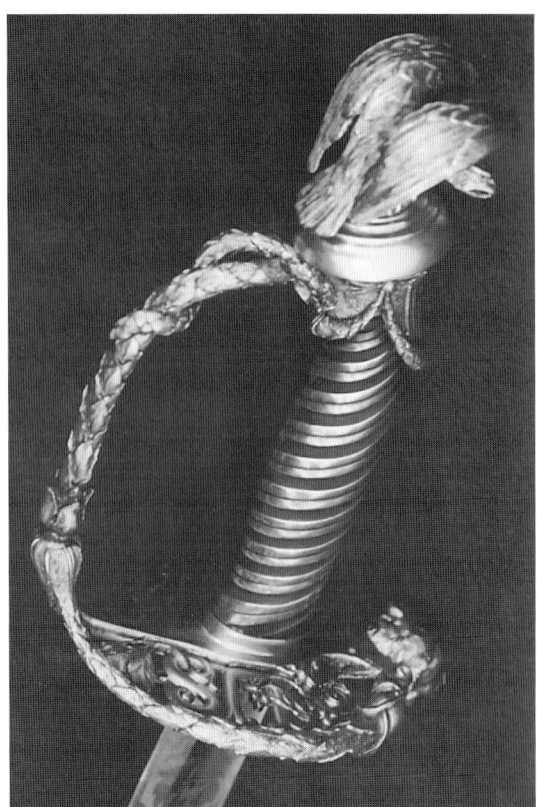

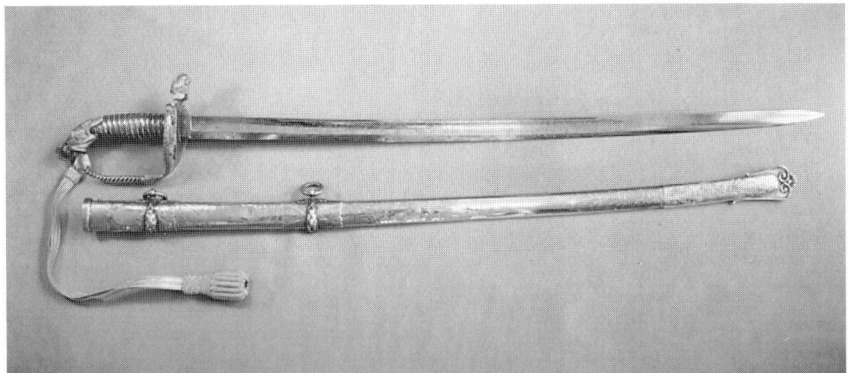

Left: Presentation-grade Model 1850 foot officer sword presented to Lt. Col. Henry C. Hodges by his friend Capt. John T. Wright, 136th Reg. New York Volunteers, Quartermaster Company, January 18, 1863. Tiffany & Co. mounted the sword; blade by Collins & Co. (CDR John Retzaff collection)

Below left: Close-up of hilt on Hodges sword.

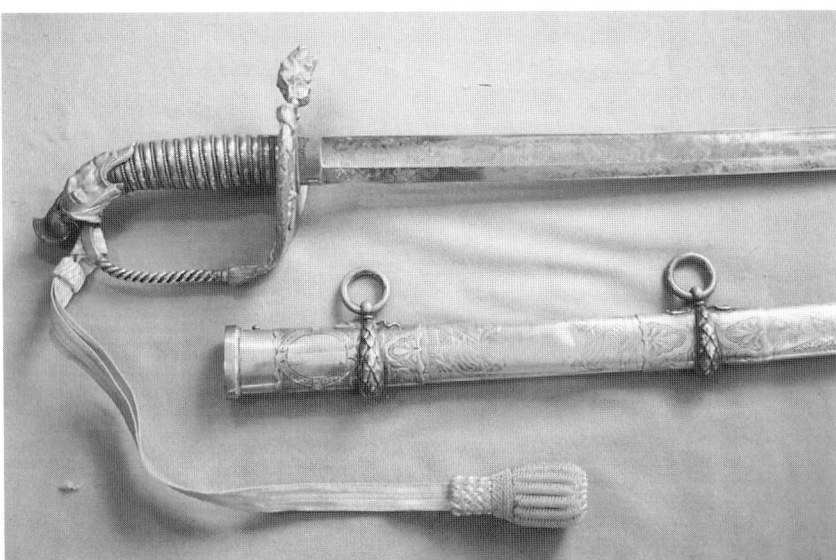

Tiffany & Co. Staff and Field Officer Swords

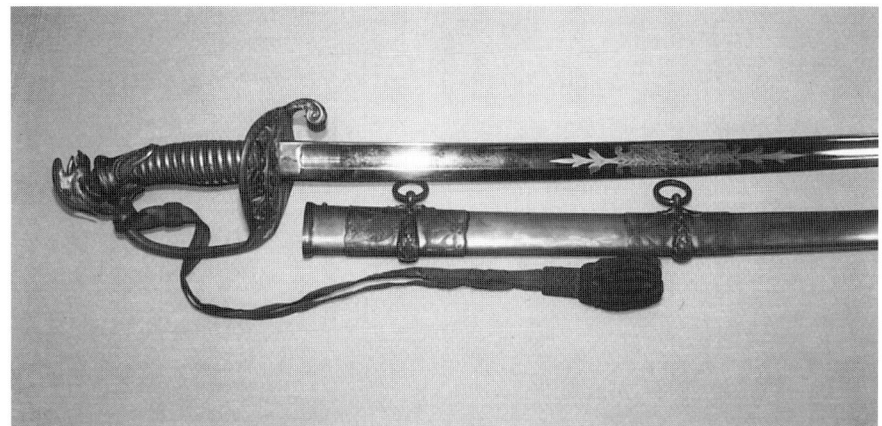

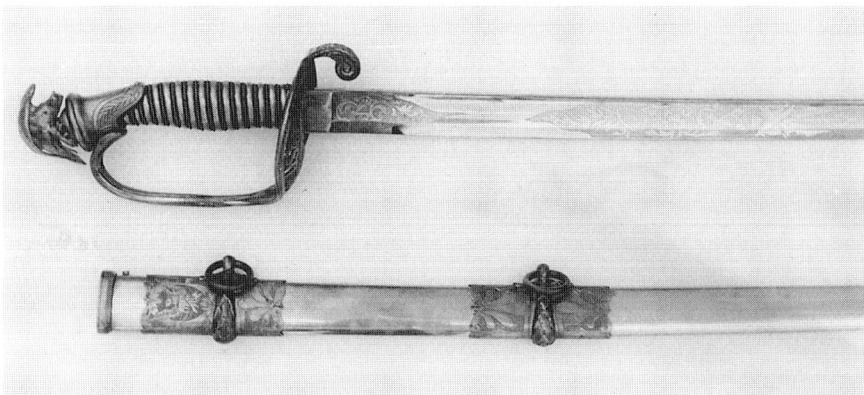

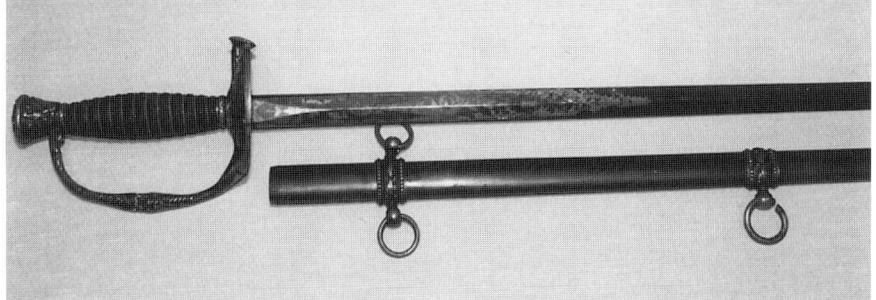

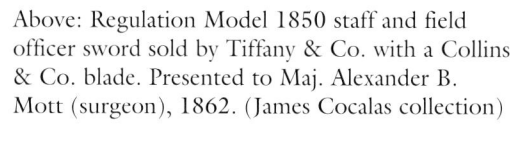

Above: Regulation Model 1850 staff and field officer sword sold by Tiffany & Co. with a Collins & Co. blade. Presented to Maj. Alexander B. Mott (surgeon), 1862. (James Cocalas collection)

Top: Presentation-grade Model 1850 staff and field officer sword presented to Lt. William S. Marble by the veterans of Company H, 7th Corps. (Kevin T. Hoffman collection)

Middle: Presentation-grade Model 1850 silver-mounted staff and field officer sword. (Courtesy of Don Ball)

Bottom: Regulation Model 1860 staff and field officer sword. (Kevin T. Hoffman collection)

Tiffany & Co. Naval Officer Swords

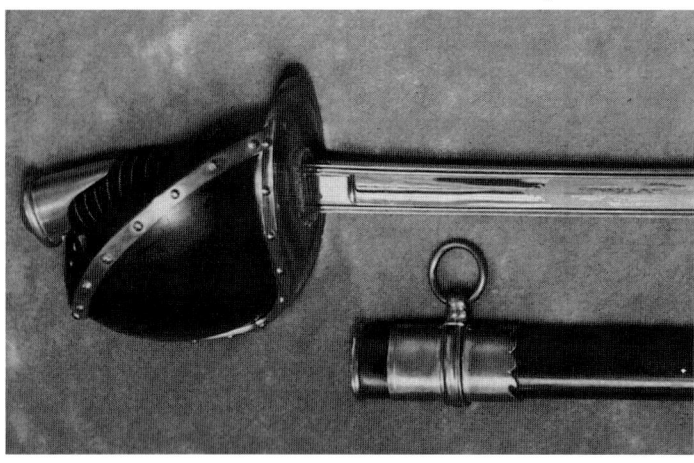

Custom-designed silver-mounted naval officer sword with a cutlass-style hilt. (Susan Di Camillo collection; photo by Paul J. DeSarbo)

Regulation Model 1852 naval officer sword. (Kevin T. Hoffman collection)

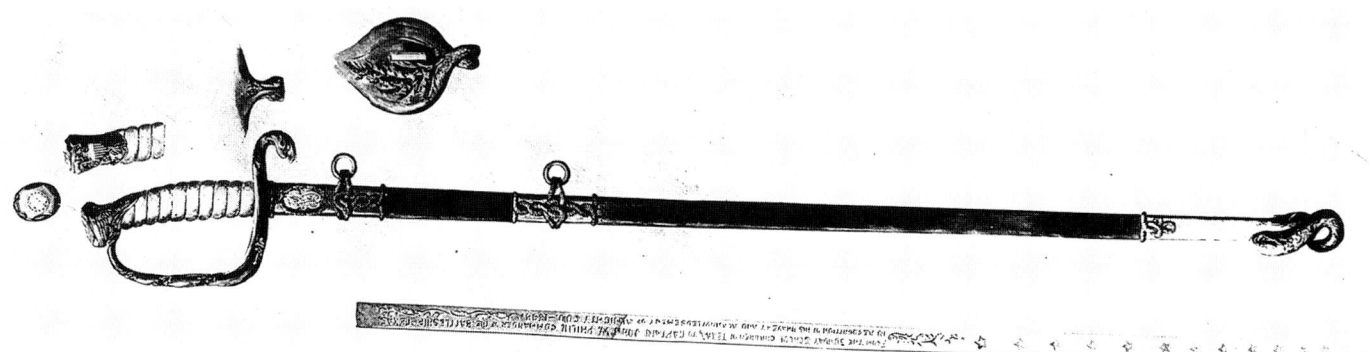

Above: Presentation-grade Model 1852 naval officer sword "from the Sunday school children of Texas to Captain John W. Philips, U.S.N., Commander of the Battleship Texas. In recognition of his bravery and acknowledgement of Almighty God, 1898." (© Tiffany & Co., from the archives)

Right: Presentation-grade Model 1852 naval officer sword presented to Adm. George Dewey, U.S.N., in memory of the victory at Manila Bay, May 1, 1898. Designer: Paulding Farnham. (© Tiffany & Co., from the archives)

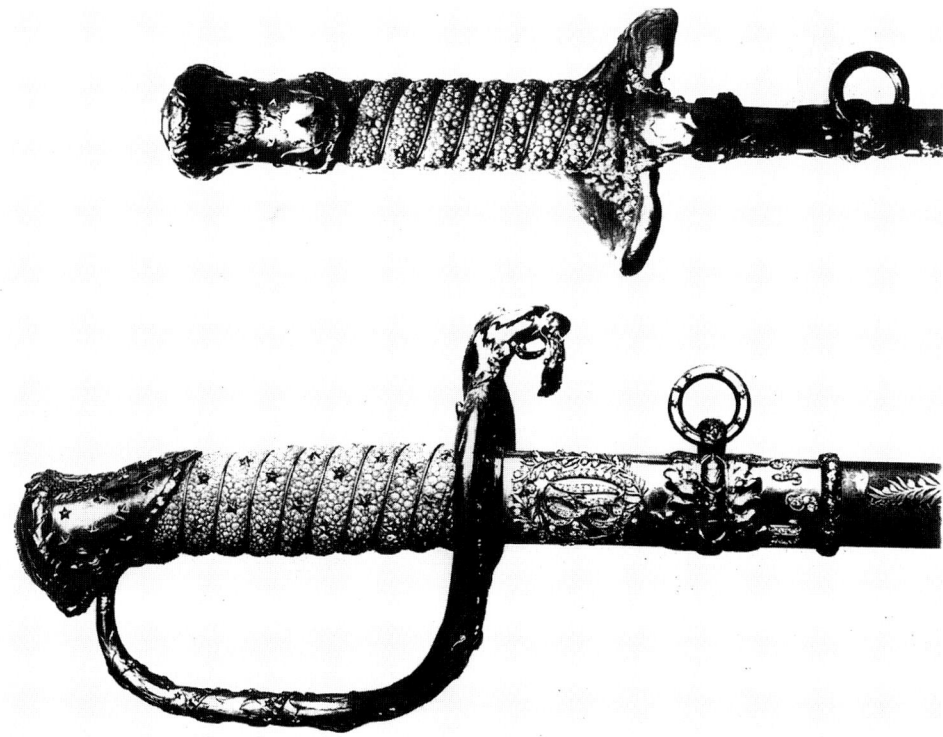

Tiffany & Co. Custom Made Presentation Swords

Above: Sword presented to Capt. Schuyler Hamilton by General Winfield Scott, November 1848. Hamilton was Scott's aide to camp after the Mexican War. (Photo courtesy of Donald R. Tharpe, Tharpe Collection of American Military History, © Donald R. Tharpe)

Above right: Close-up of the presentation plaque on the Hamilton sword.

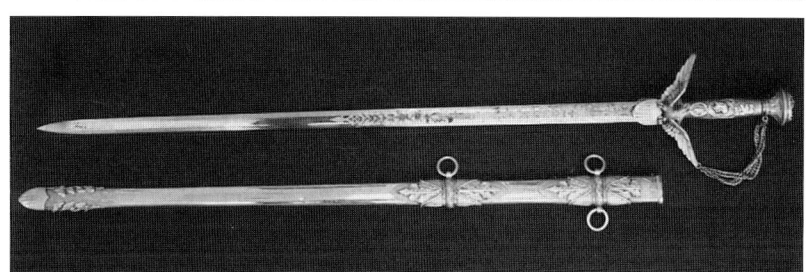

Right: Presentation sword shown in Tiffany's Civil War catalog as item #9 under "Straight Swords for Generals."

Middle: Sword presented to Col. John Fitzroy deCourcy by the officers and soldiers of the 16th Ohio Volunteers. Colonel deCourcy was a former British Army officer and mercenary who offered his services to the Union forces during the U.S. Civil War. He was made a commander of a newly formed volunteer regiment. The sword was design #19 by Tiffany silversmith Edward C. Moore.

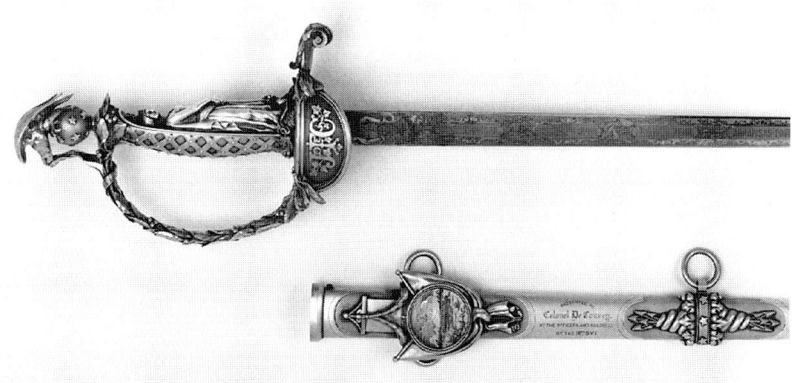

Bottom: The deCourcy sword in its case.

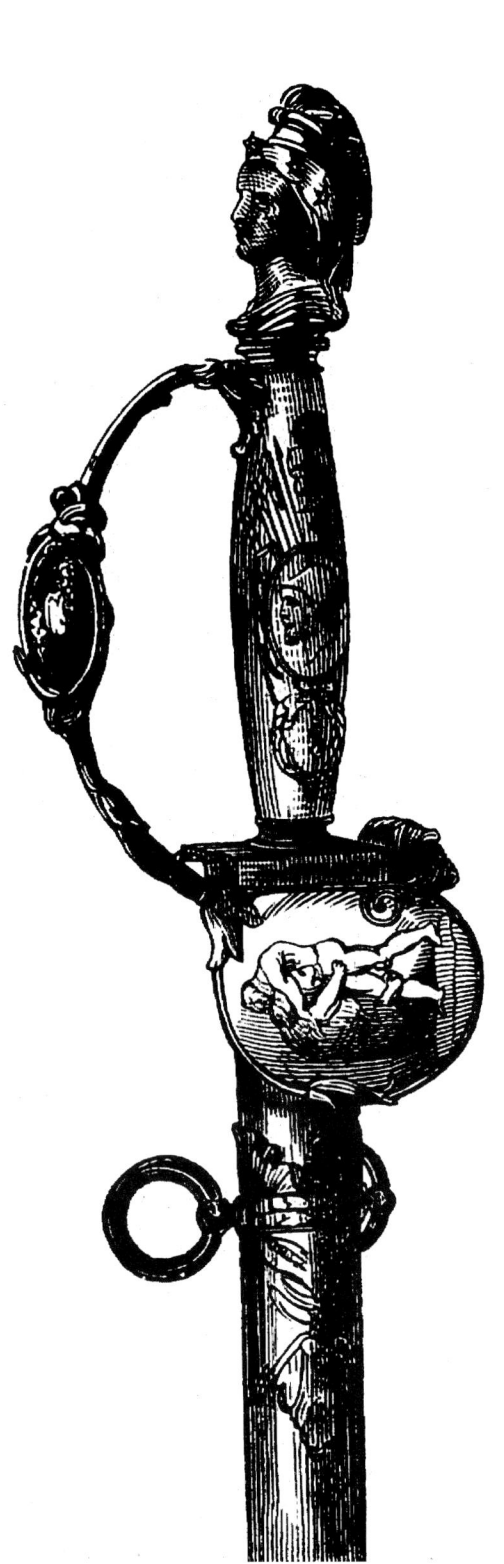

Sword presented to Maj. Gen. Henry W. Halleck by the Union Ladies of St. Louis in 1862. Illustration from Tiffany & Co. Civil War catalog. (© Tiffany & Co., from the archives)

Sword with silver-statue hilt presented by the state of Rhode Island to Maj. Gen. Ambrose Everett Burnside "in testimony of the brilliant victory achieved at Roanoke Island on the 8th day of February 1862." Illustration from Tiffany & Co. Civil War catalog. (© Tiffany & Co., from the archives)

Sword with silver-statue hilt presented to Maj. Gen. John Charles Fremont, "the Pathfinder," by the men of the west, 1862. Fremont was the commander of the U.S. Department of the West. Illustration from Tiffany & Co. Civil War catalog. (© Tiffany & Co., from the archives)

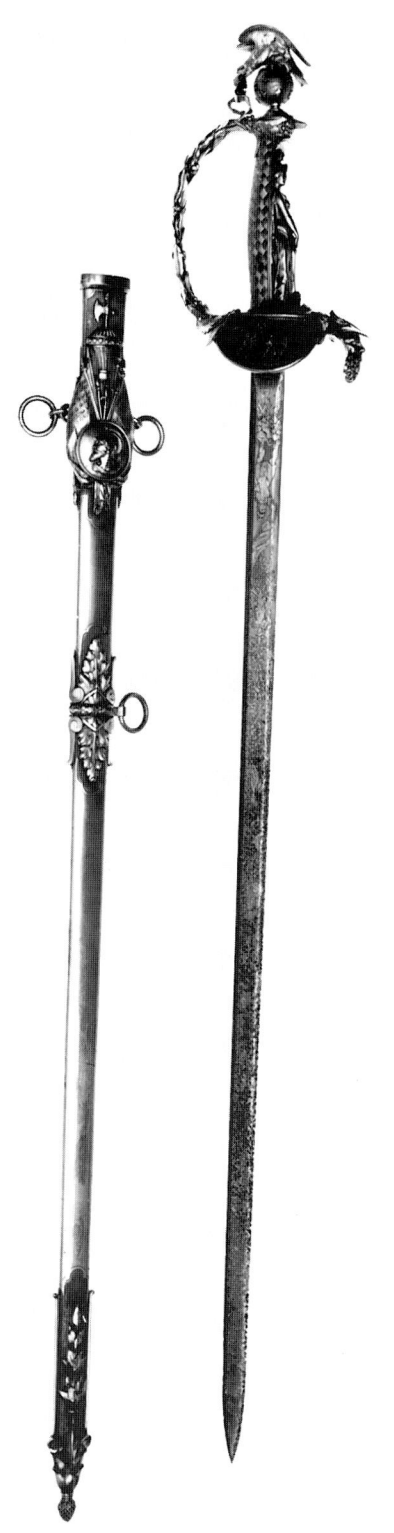

Sword presented to Gen. William Tecumseh Sherman in recognition of his service during the Battle of Shiloh, April 13, 1862. (The Smithsonian Institution collection)

Close-up of the hilt on the Sherman sword.

255

TIFFANY & CO.

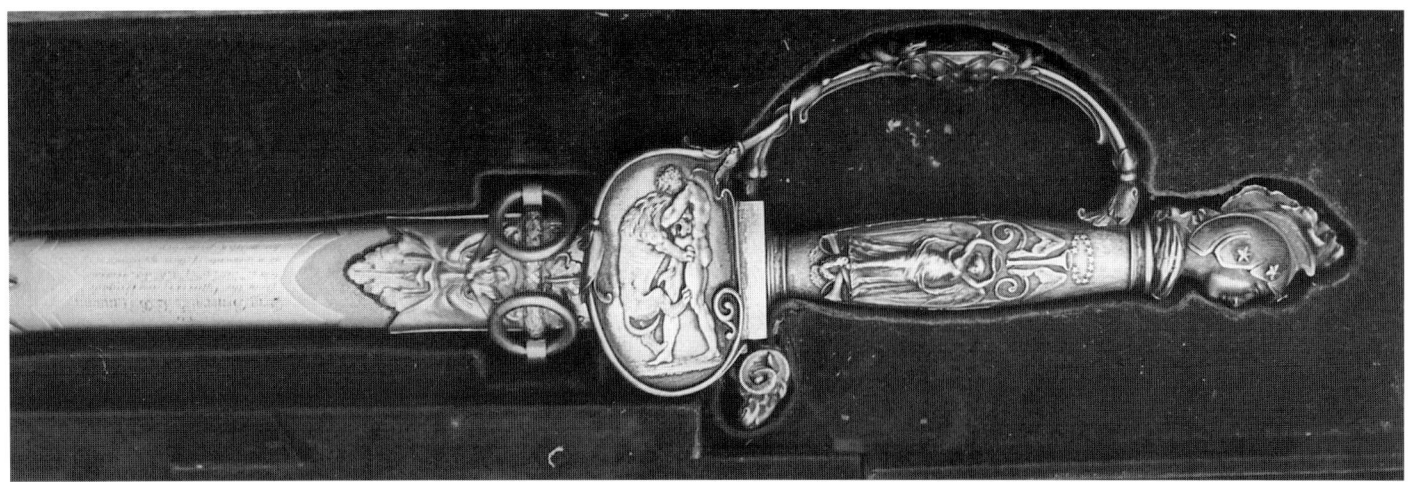

Sword presented to Brig. Gen. T.E.G. Ranson by the officers of his brigade, 1863. (Courtesy of Don Ball)

Sword presented to Gen. John C. Robinson by his "personal friends, New York," July 4, 1865. (Photo courtesy of Donald R. Tharpe, Tharpe Collection of American Military History, © Donald R. Tharpe)

Close-up of hilt on Robinson sword.

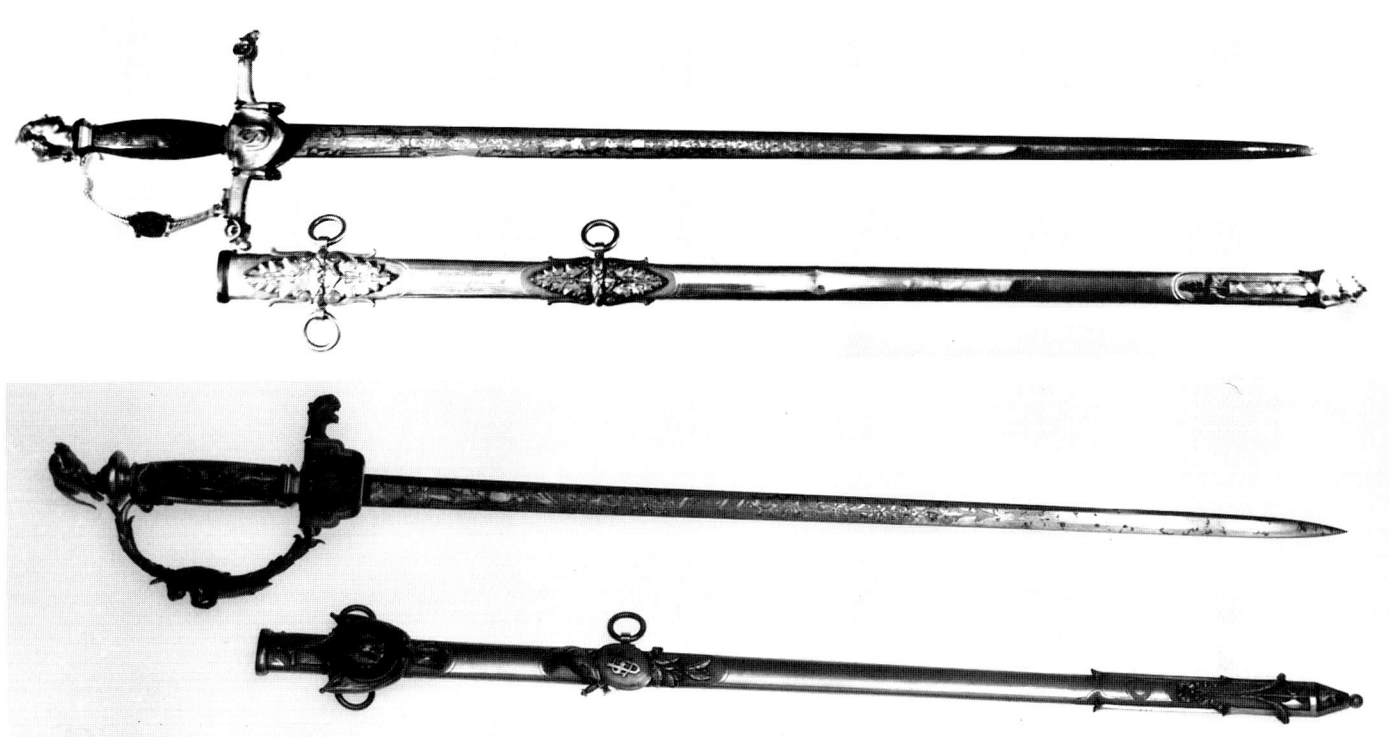

Top: Sword presented to Maj. Gen. John M. Schofield by the citizens of St. Louis, MO, January 30, 1864. (West Point Museum collection)

Above: Sword voted to be awarded to Maj. Gen. Winfield Scott Hancock at the Mississippi Valley Sanitary Fair, St. Louis, June 4, 1864. (The Smithsonian Institution collection)

Far left: Close-up of the hilt on the Hancock sword showing a female victory figure on the knuckle bow and an eagle on the pommel.

Left: Sword presented to Brig. Gen. Godfrey Weitzel from the enlisted men of the 75th Reg., New York Volunteers, October 1863. (Photo courtesy of Donald R. Tharpe, Tharpe Collection of American Military History, © Donald R. Tharpe)

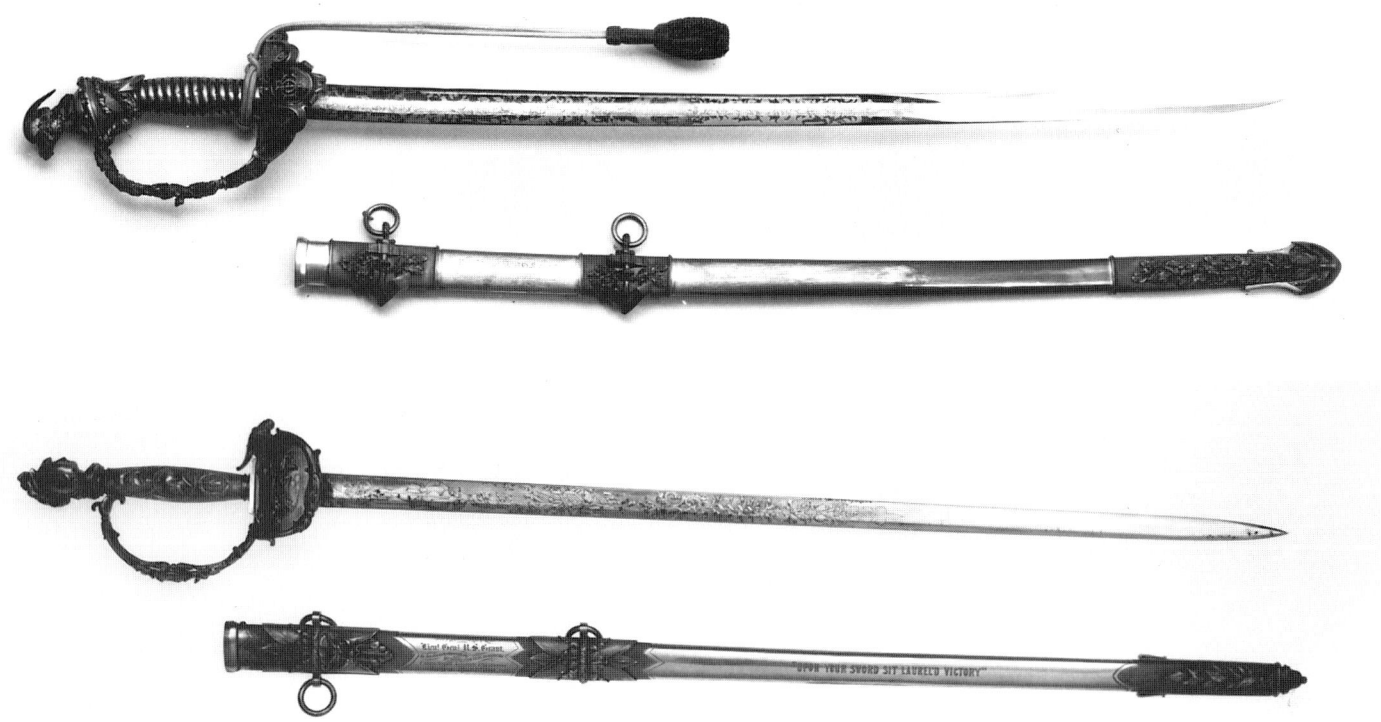

Top: Sword presented to Adm. David G. Farragut by the Union League Club of New York, 1864. Maker: Tiffany & Co. on a Collins & Co. blade. (The Smithsonian Institution collection)

Above: Sword donated to the New York Metropolitan Fair by Tiffany & Co. Voted to be awarded to Gen. Ulysses Simpson Grant, April 23, 1864. (The Smithsonian Institution collection)

Right: Close-up of the hilt on the Farragut sword.

Far right: Close-up of the hilt on the Grant sword.

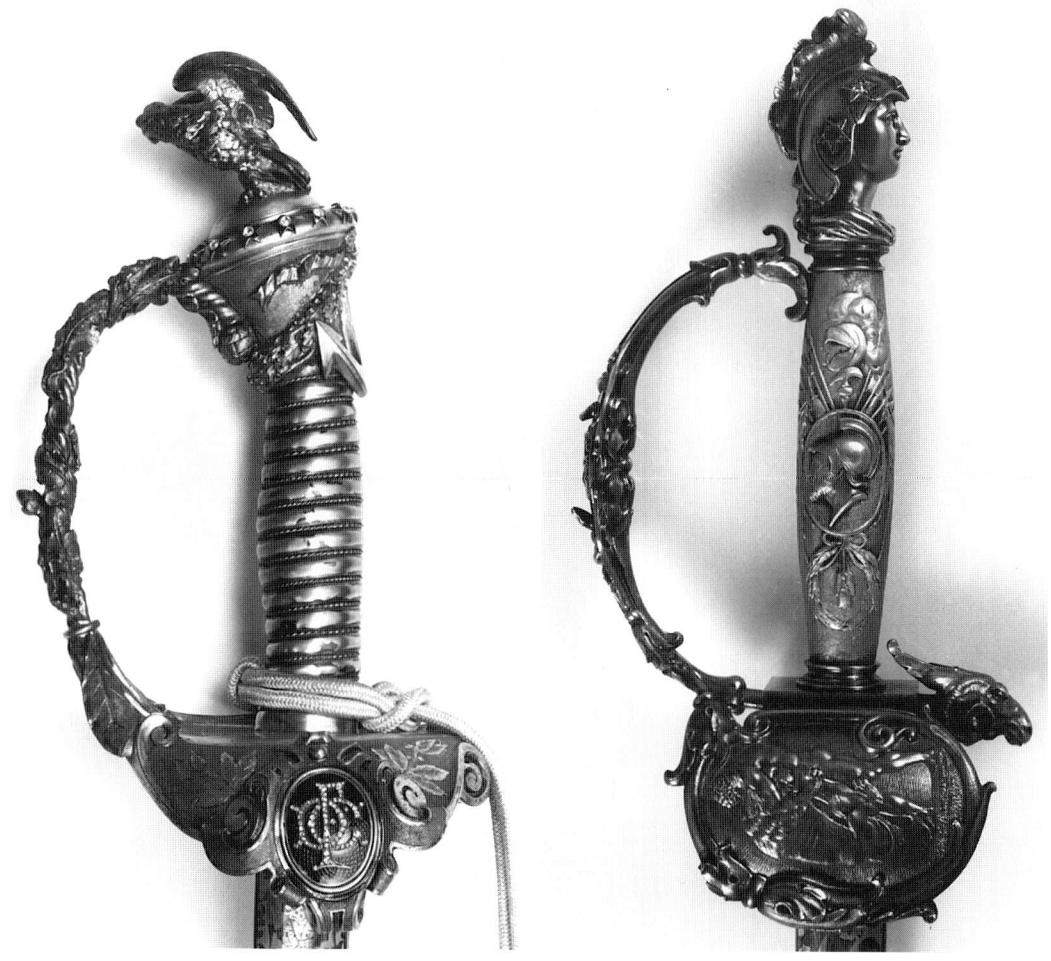

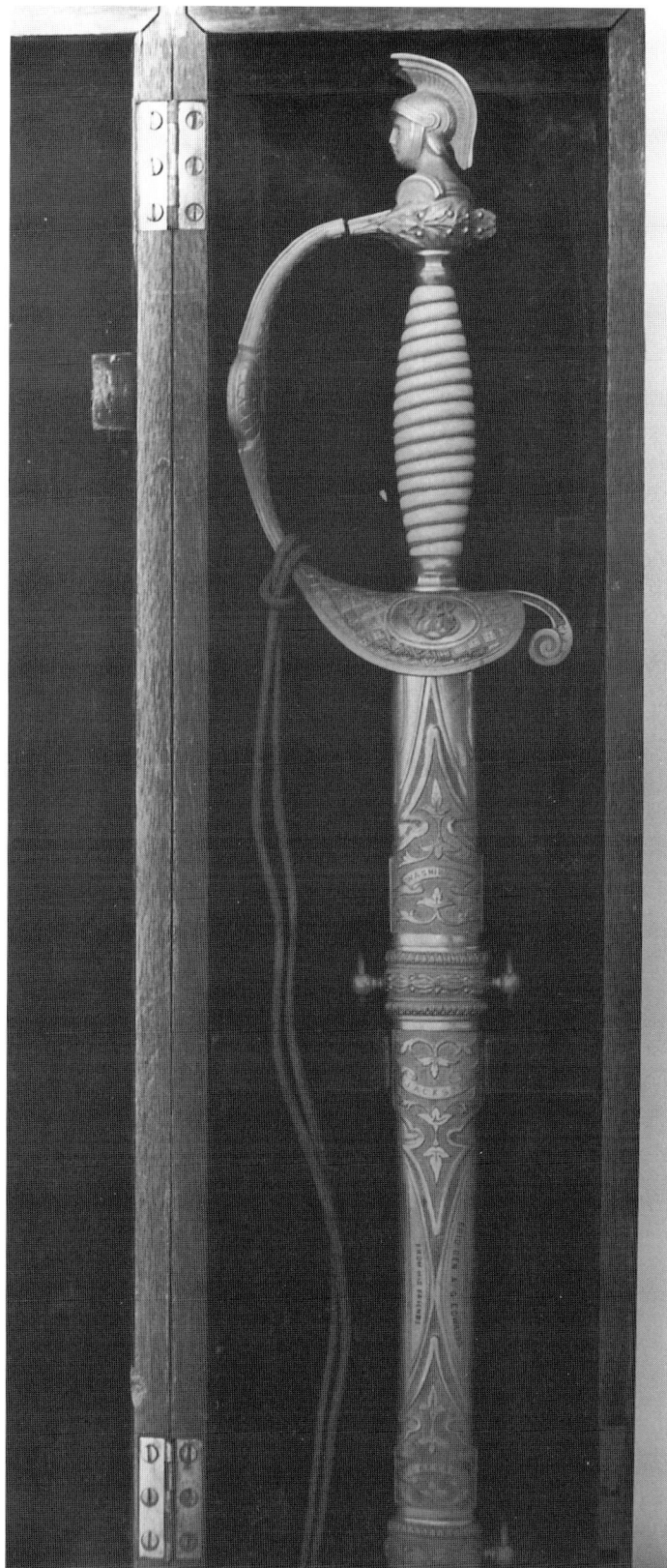

High-quality cased sword presented to Gen. A.E. Edwards from his friends, November 20, 1862. (Courtesy of Don Ball)

Sword presented to Lt. Col. C.M. Ferrel by the enlisted men of the 29th Illinois Volunteers. (Courtesy of David V. Stroud; Don Ball collection)

U.S. Sword Photos

Enlisted Men's Cavalry Sabers

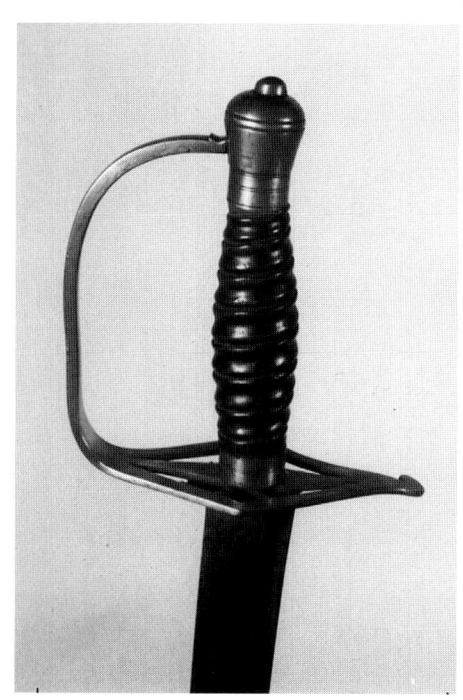

Revolutionary War horseman's saber. (George C. Neumann collection)

Revolutionary War horseman's saber. (George C. Neumann collection)

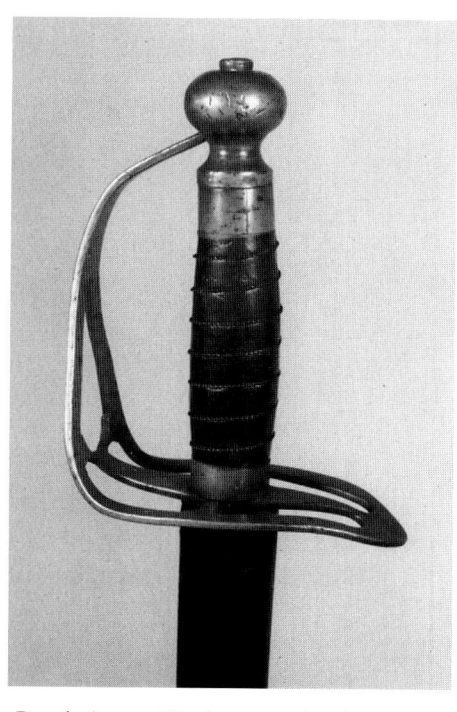

Revolutionary War horseman's saber. (George C. Neumann collection)

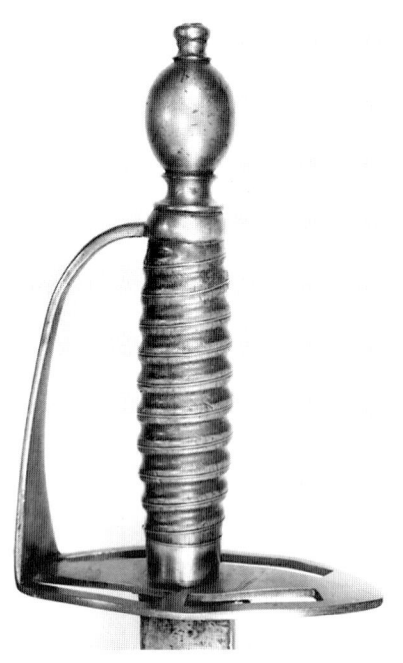

Revolutionary War horseman's saber, c. 1770-1785, with 33 5/8″ blade, triple fullers, and brass hilt. (George C. Neumann collection)

Revolutionary War horseman's saber with lion-head pommel. (George C. Neumann collection)

Revolutionary War horseman's saber with very unusual brass basket hilt, 35 1/4″ straight blade with center fuller, walnut grip, and heart-shaped counterguard. (Jerry Waszak collection)

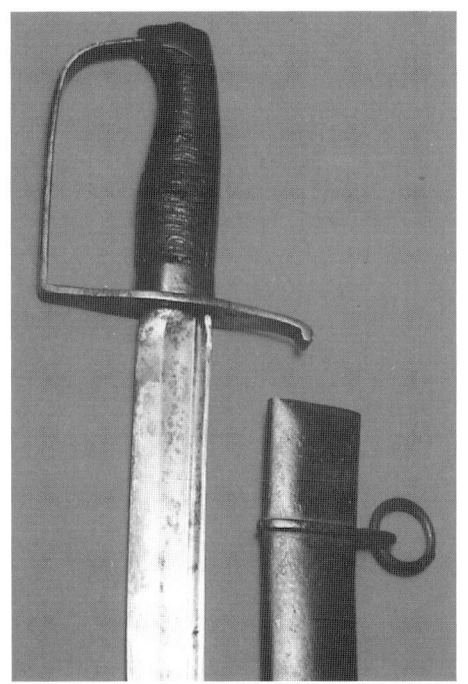

Cavalry saber with hussar hilt made by Daniel McClintoch, c. 1790. (Author's collection)

Cavalry saber with hussar hilt made by John Miles for the 1801 state of Virginia contract. (Author's collection)

One of only 22 cavalry sabers made by James Winner (marked on blade) for the U.S. 1810 contract. Scabbard made by J. Abraham Nippes in 1811. (Leonard Garigliano photo)

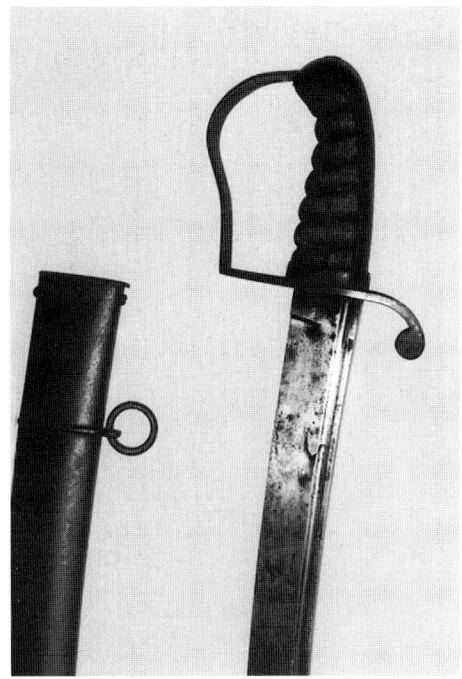 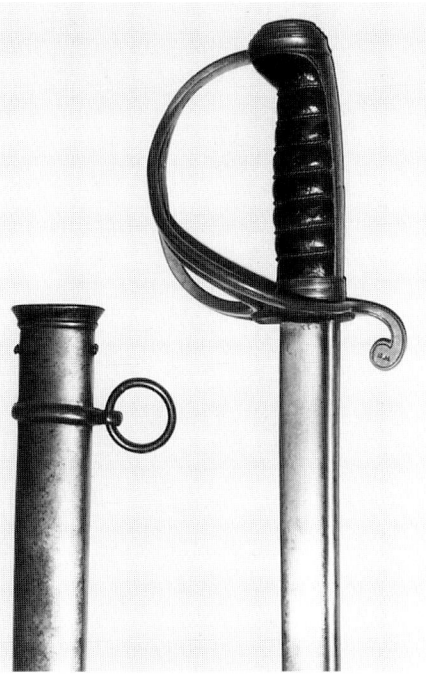 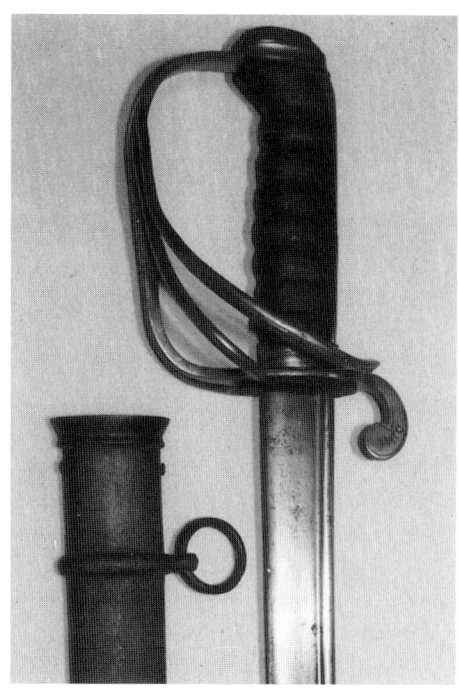

War of 1812 cavalry saber with 33 1/8" blade and balled grip. The hilt shape and dimensions are the same as his U.S. 1810 contract. Note the standard style scabbard. Maker: James Winner. (Author's collection)

One of the 6,100 U.S. Model 1833 dragoon sabers made between 1834 and 1839 by Nathan P. Ames. (Author's collection)

Very rare U.S. Model 1833 dragoon saber with steel scabbard sold to the state of North Carolina. "N.C." marked on quillion. Maker: Ames Manufacturing Company. (Kevin T. Hoffman collection)

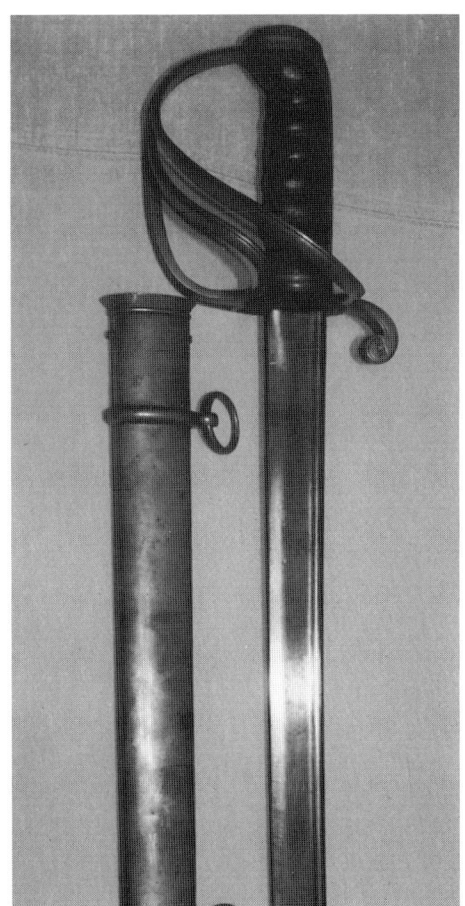

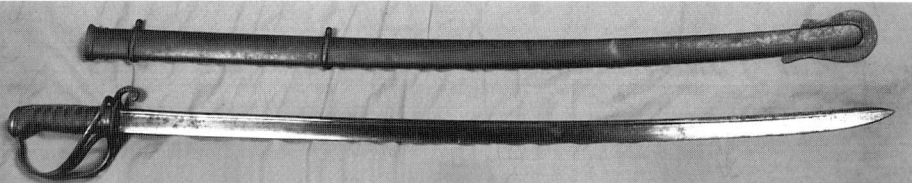

Top: One of 280 Model 1833 Texas dragoon sabers (same as U.S. Model 1833 sabers) sold to the Republic of Texas in 1846. Has a leather grip and "Texas Dragoons" etched on the blade. Maker: Ames Manufacturing Co. (Bob M. Owens collection)

Above: Close-up of blade etching on Texas dragoon saber.

Left: Very rare Model 1833 dragoon saber with brass scabbard sold to the state of Massachusetts. "M.S." marked on the quillion. Maker: Ames Manufacturing Company. (Kevin T. Hoffman collection)

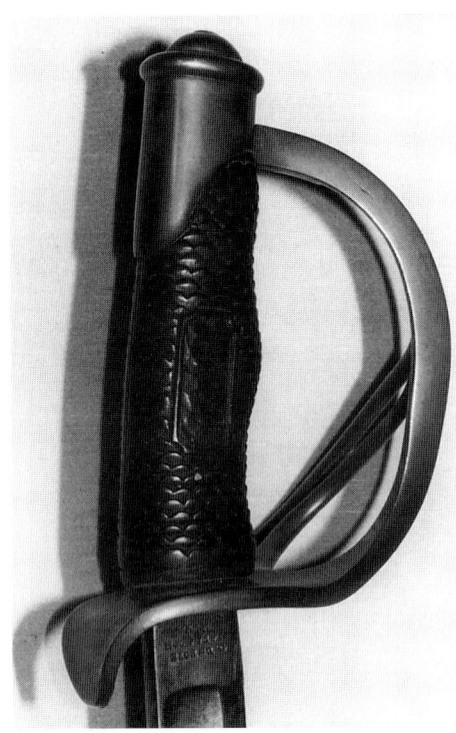

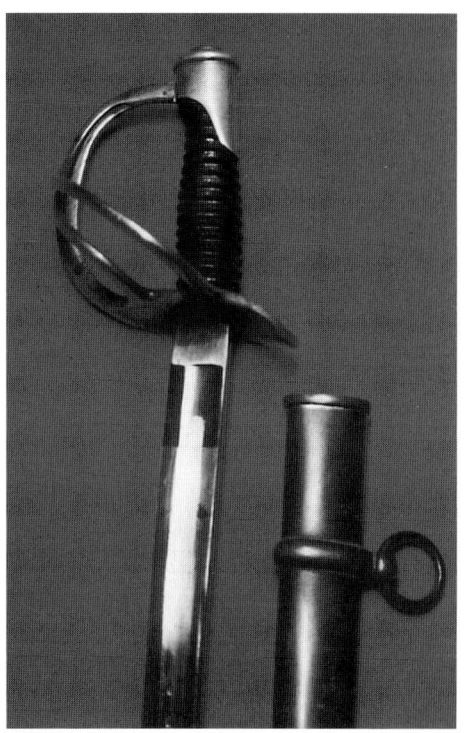

Very rare variation of the Model 1860 U.S. cavalry saber with a hard-rubber fish-scale grip. Made by G. (Gilbert) Dubois of Napanoch, NY. (Kevin T. Hoffman collection)

Close-up of blade markings on the Dubois cavalry saber.

Civil War Model 1840 variation cavalry saber, 1862, with a flat back M1840 blade and thicker M1860 type grip. Maker: Samuel Collins & Co. (Author's collection)

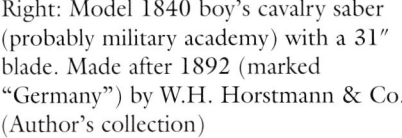

Right: Model 1840 boy's cavalry saber (probably military academy) with a 31″ blade. Made after 1892 (marked "Germany") by W.H. Horstmann & Co. (Author's collection)

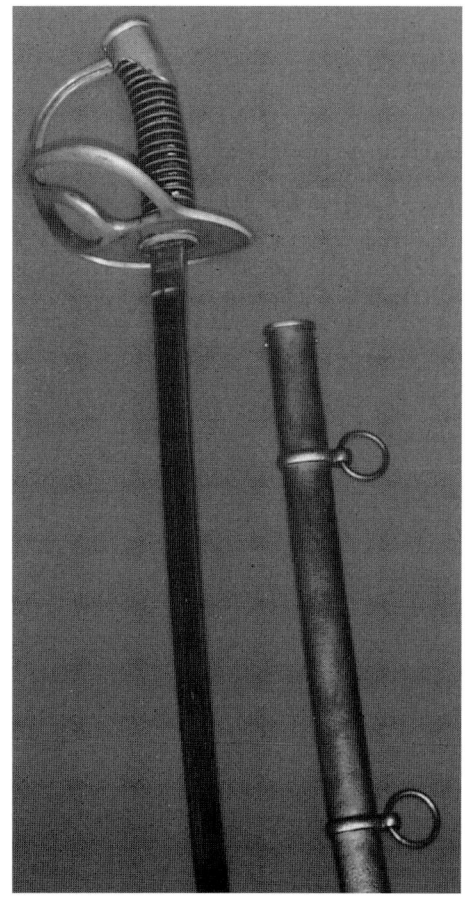

Enlisted Men's Cavalry Practice Swords

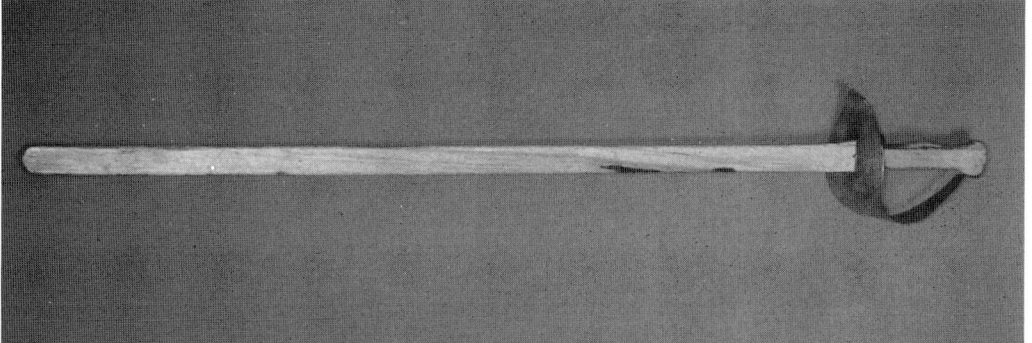

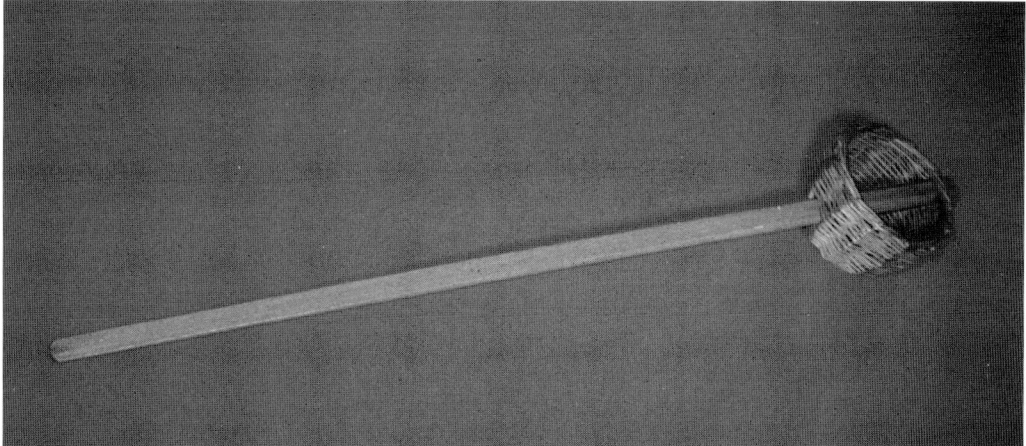

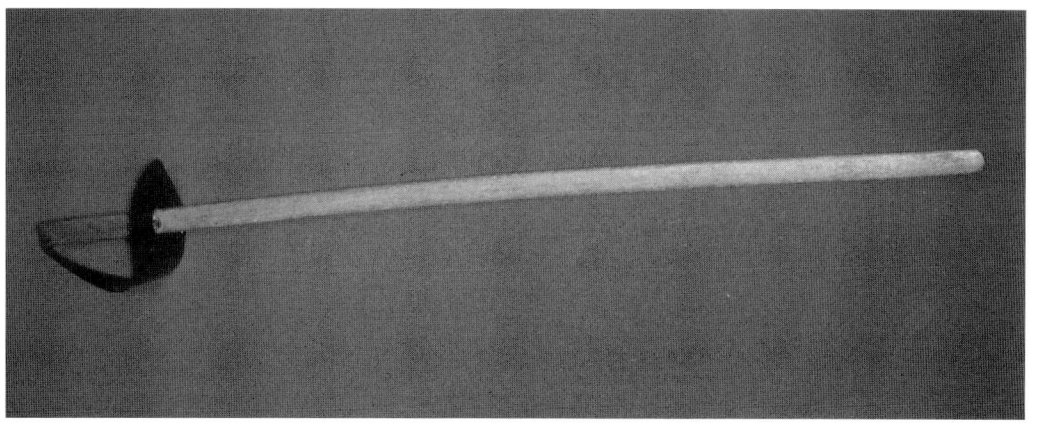

Top: Model 1891 cavalry practice saber made by the Rock Island Arsenal, 1908. Note the rounded pommel and bulge in the grip. (Author's collection)

Second from top: Model 1891 cavalry single stick practice sword, 1904, regulation variation, with wickered handguard and tapered blade. (Author's collection)

Third from top: Model 1913 cavalry practice sword with variation wicker hand guard and straight grip made by the Rock Island Arsenal. (Author's collection)

Bottom: Model 1913 cavalry practice sword with steel hand guard and straight grip made by the Rock Island Arsenal. (Author's collection)

Cavalry Officer Swords

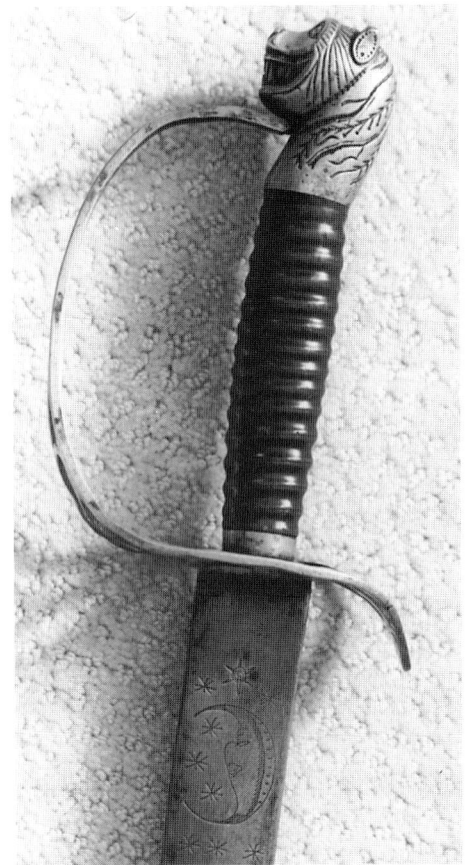

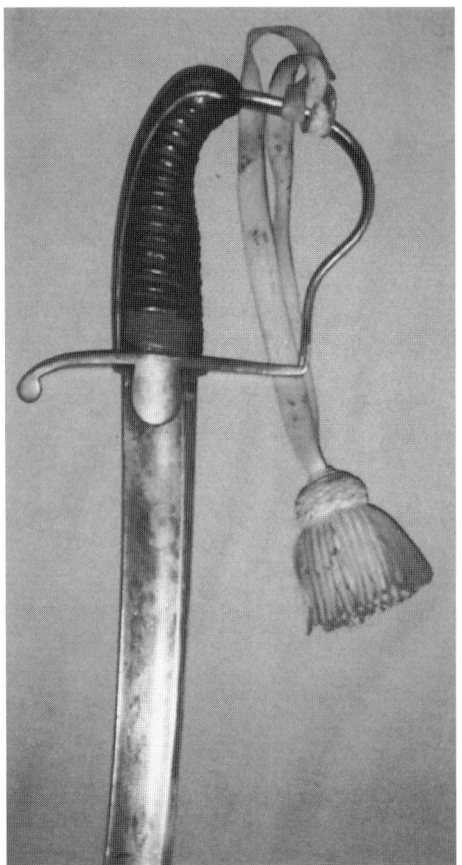

Top left: Cavalry officer saber, c. 1770-1780, with split-and-divided brass hilt and lion-head pommel. (Courtesy of American Ordnance Preservation Association Ltd.)

Top middle: Rare Federal period cavalry officer saber, c. 1795-1815, with brass hilt, bone grip, unusual hand guard, and huge 37 1/2" blade. Imported by Lemuel Wells & Co., New York, NY, from Thomas Gill, Birmingham, England. (C. Philip Johnson Jr. collection)

Top right: War of 1812 cavalry officer sword with 33" blade and clipped point. The fuller runs all the way to the tip. Probably made by Woolley of Birmingham, England. (Grafton H. Cook II collection)

Right: Extremely rare War of 1812 silver-hilted cavalry officer saber with 32 5/8" blade. The sword was made by silversmith Joseph Lownes, Philadelphia, PA; the blade was made by Joseph Rose, Blockley Township, PA. (Roger T. Gelbuda collection)

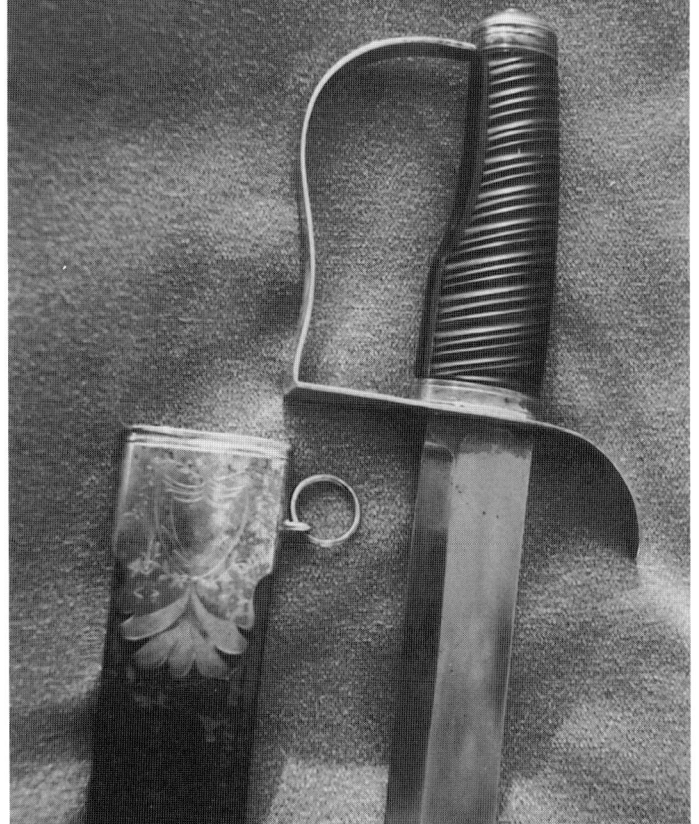

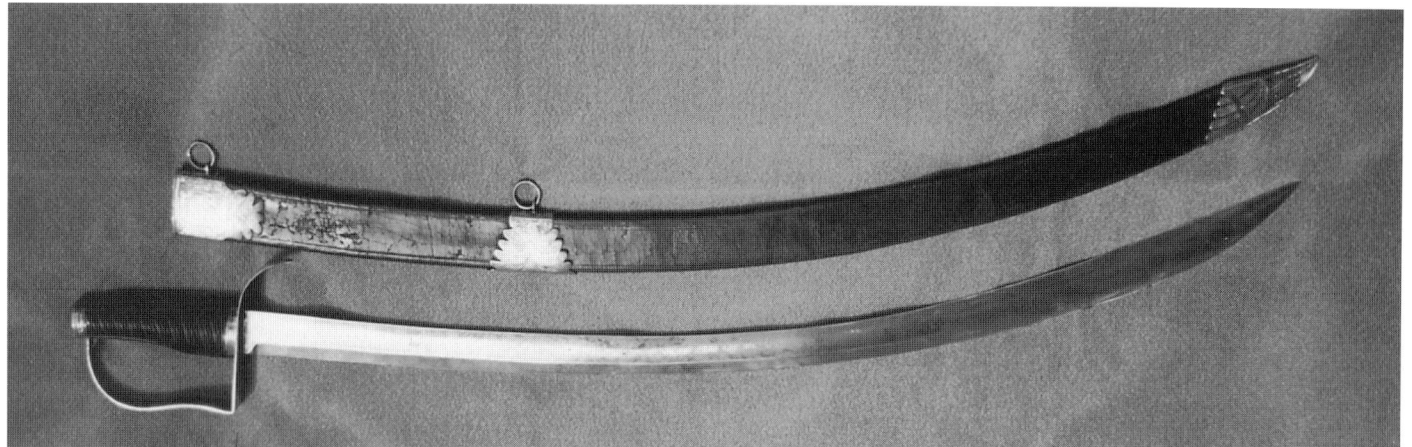

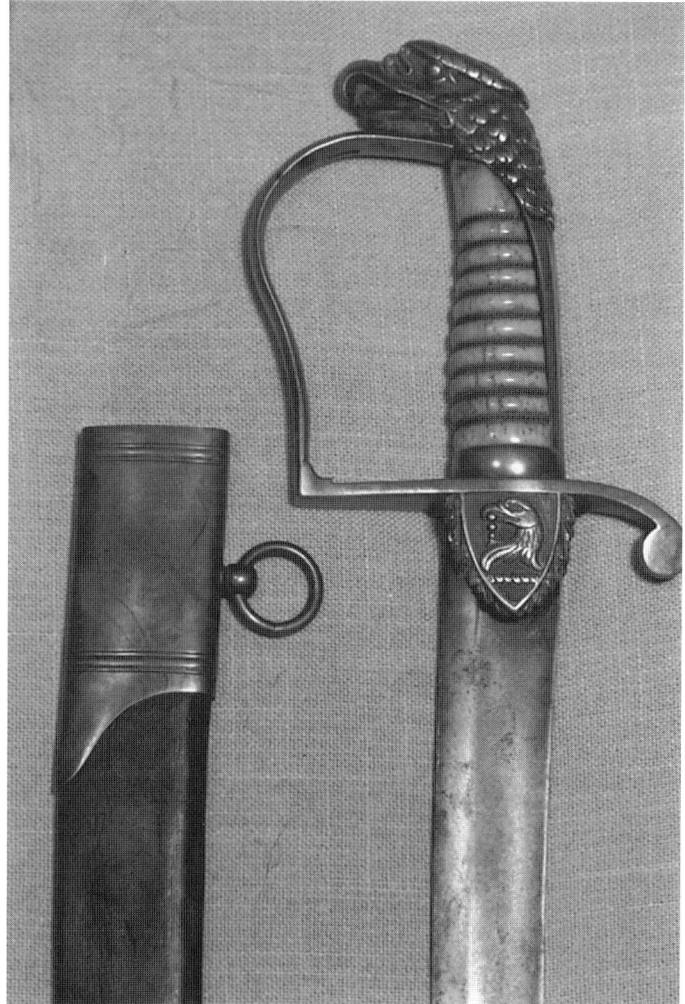

Top: Full-length view of the Joseph Lownes War of 1812 cavalry officer saber. (Roger T. Gelbuda collection)

Above left: Cavalry officer saber, c. 1810-1815, with brass hilt, eagle-head pommel, and 30 1/2″ blade. A very unusual eagle head is cast into the langet. The blade is marked "Louisville Light Horse." (Jan H. Zajac collection)

Above right: U.S. Model 1833 dragoon officer saber with fish skin grip wrappings. The engraved blade reads, "Presented to Capt. Smith P. Bankhead" in 1847. Captain Bankhead later became a Confederate general. Maker: Ames Manufacturing Co. (Kevin T. Hoffman collection)

Right: Close-up of inscription on the U.S. Model 1833 dragoon officer saber.

Second from top: U.S. Model 1833 dragoon officer saber with hanger, fish skin grip wrappings, and engraved blade. Maker: Ames Manufacturing Co. (Kevin T. Hoffman collection)

Third from top: U.S. Model 1833 dragoon officer saber sold to the state of South Carolina with engraved blade, fish skin grip wrappings, and engraved brass scabbard showing a palmetto tree. Made by the Ames Manufacturing Co. (Kevin T. Hoffman collection)

Bottom: Very rare Texas dragoon officer saber (same as U.S. Model 1833) with fish skin grip wrappings and Texas star etched on blade. One of 18 sold to the Republic of Texas in 1846. Maker: Ames Manufacturing Co. (Bob M. Owens collection)

Below: Close-up of blade etching on Texas dragoon officer saber.

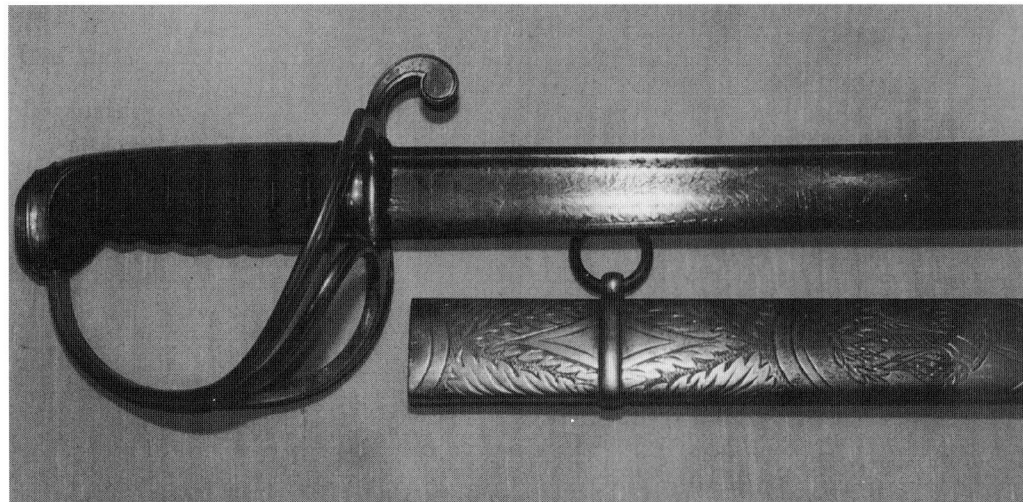

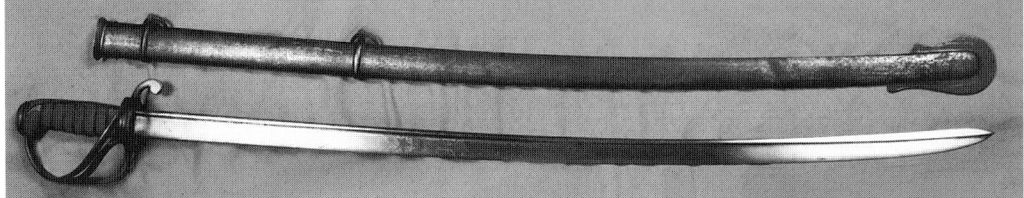

 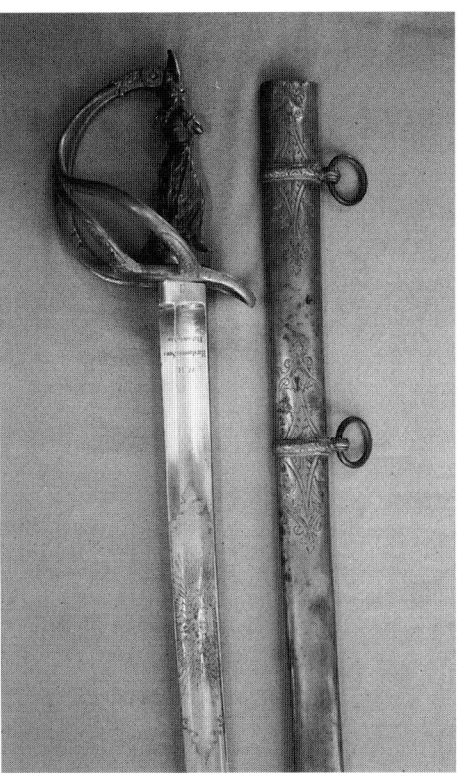 

Custom-hilted Model 1833 dragoon officer saber with eagle-head pommel, fish skin grip wrappings, and engraved blade. Sold to the state of South Carolina. Palmetto trees are engraved on the scabbard mounts. Maker: Ames Manufacturing Co. (Kevin T. Hoffman collection)

Very rare presentation-grade Model 1840 Civil War cavalry officer saber with elaborately etched 35″ blade, brass hilt guard and scabbard, and bronze hilt of a female warrior. The sword was made by W.H. Horstman & Sons, the blade by Gebruder Weyersberg, Solingen, Prussia. (CDR John Retzaff collection)

Close-up of the female warrior statue hilt.

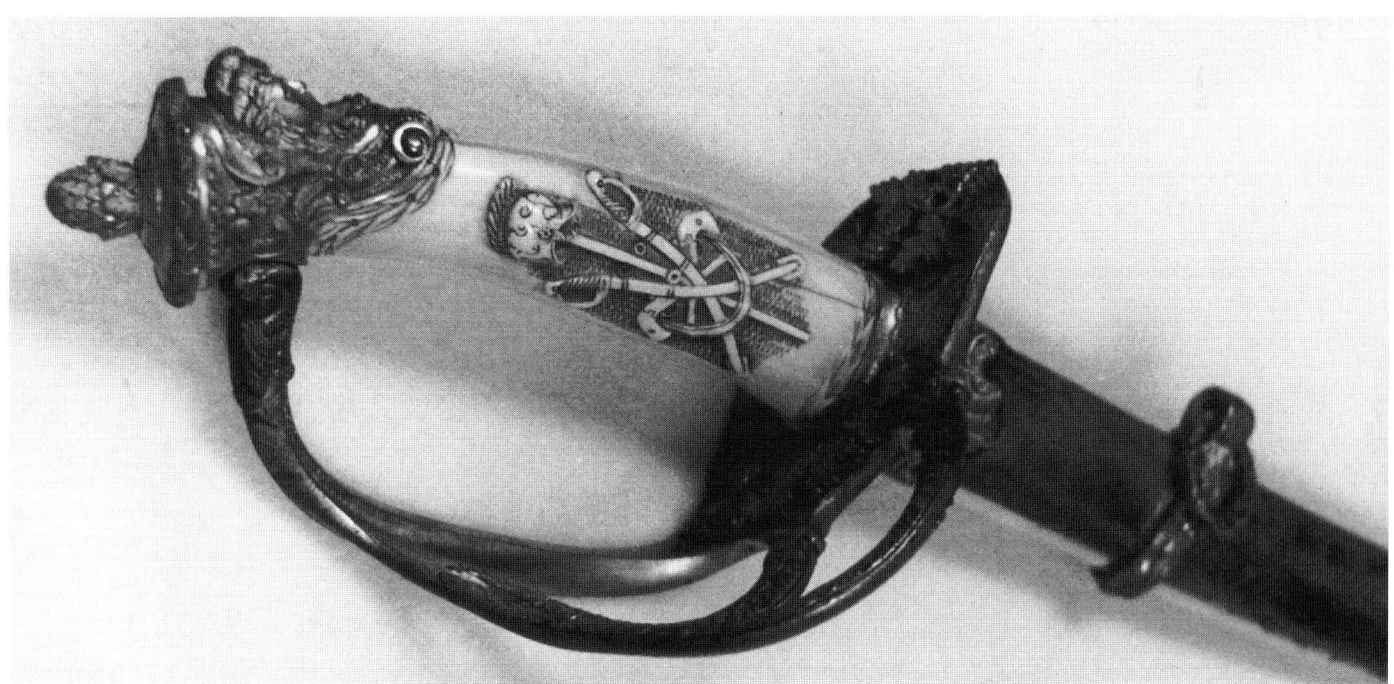

Model 1840 presentation-grade Civil War cavalry officer saber with carved ivory grip. (Courtesy of Don Ball)

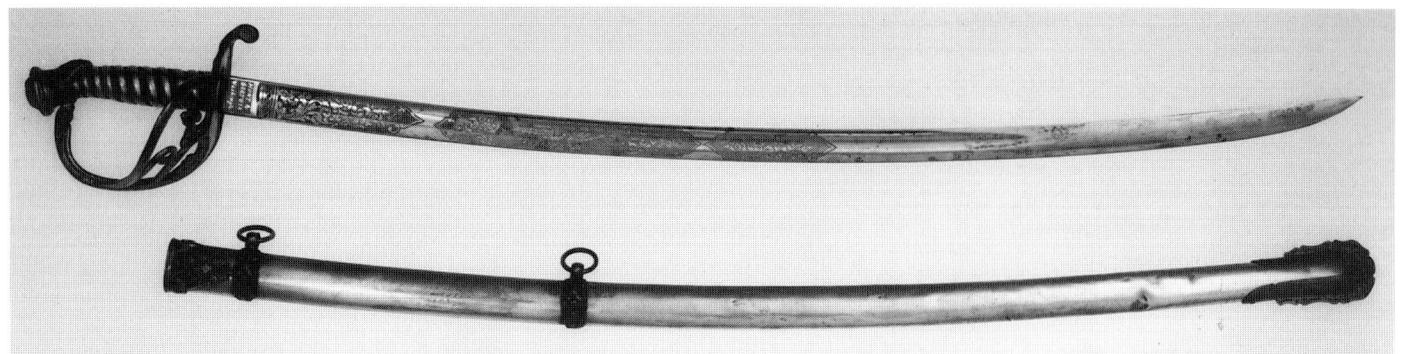

Above: Model 1860 Civil War presentation-grade cavalry officer saber originally presented to C.W. Bryant, 1st New York Volunteer Cavalry (retailer: Hunt & Goodwin, Washington, D.C.). On March 10, 1864, this sword was captured by Confederate Lt. A.E. Richards and presented to Lt. Col. John Singleton Mosby ("the Grey Ghost"). In September of 1864, the sword was recaptured by the 13th New York Cavalry under Col. H.S. Gansevoort. (Courtesy of David V. Stroud, the Smithsonian Institution Collection)

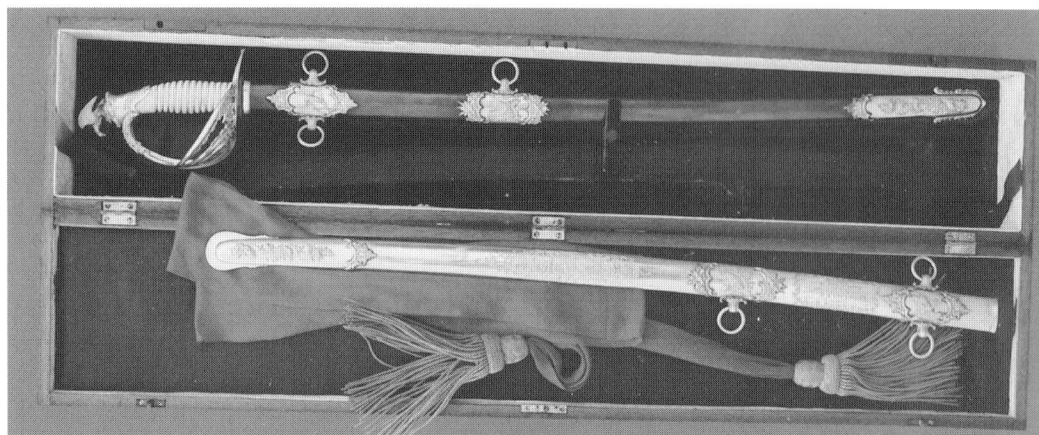

Top right: Model 1860 presentation-grade cavalry officer saber in its original case presented to Lt. Col. Clark B. Baldwin, 1st Regiment, Massachusetts Volunteers, by his friends in South Boston, March 4, 1863. Maker: Ames Manufacturing Co.

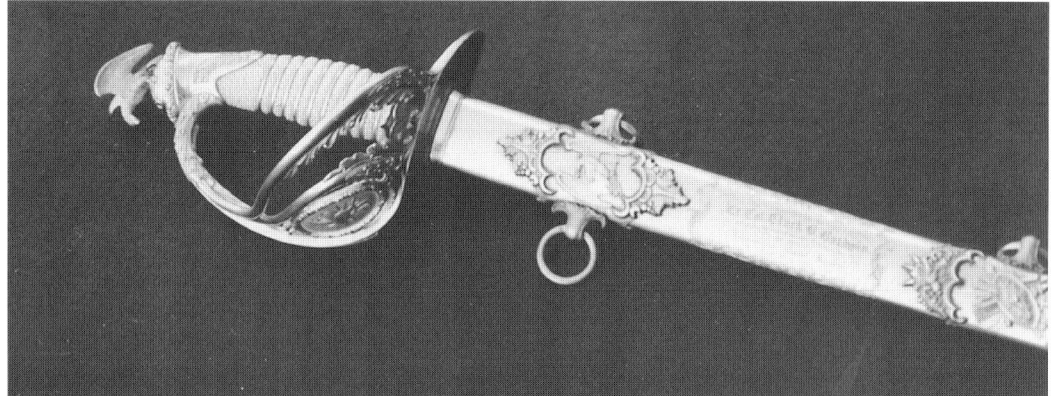

Middle: Close-up of the hilt, upper scabbard, and inscription on the Baldwin sword.

Right: Model 1872 presentation-grade cavalry officer saber presented to Col. Myron H. McCord by his Arizona friends in 1898. Maker: M.C. Lilley & Co. (Arizona Historical Society collection)

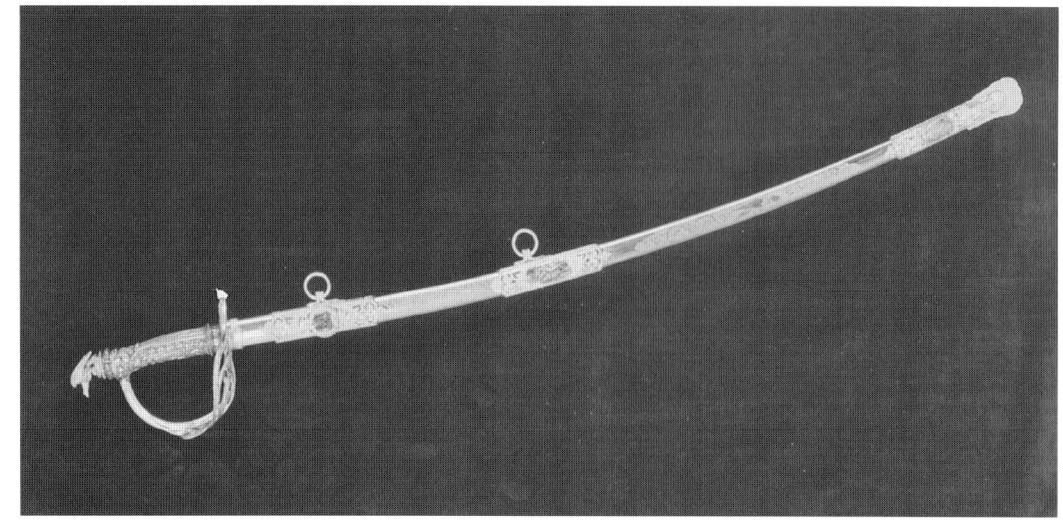

Close-up of the hilt on the McCord sword.

Right: Model 1872 presentation-grade cavalry officer saber. (Susan Di Camillo collection; photo by Paul J. DeSarbo)

Below: Model 1872 presentation-grade cavalry officer saber won by Lt. Col. James Moran, 69th Regiment, NGSNY, in the "most popular National Guard contest," 1889. (Susan Di Camillo collection; photo by Paul J. DeSarbo)

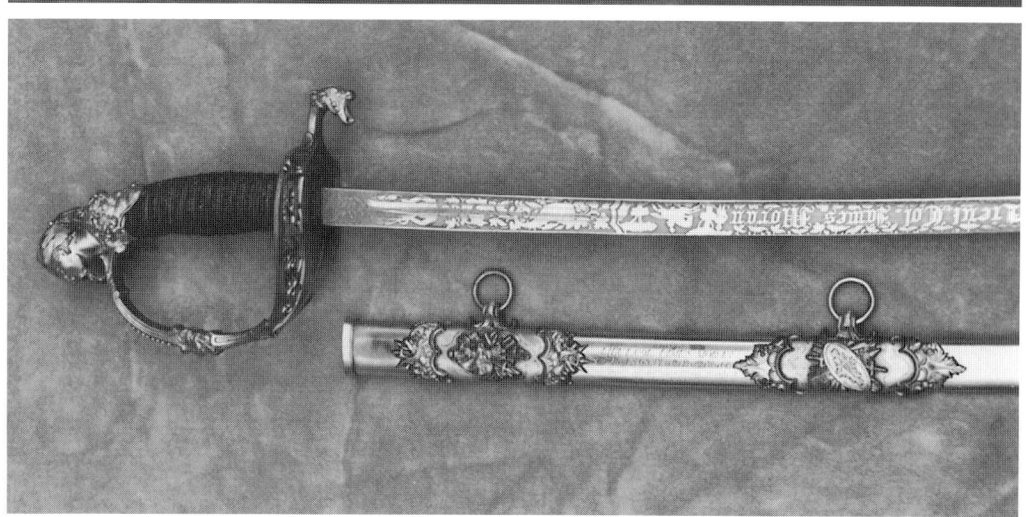

Enlisted Man's Mounted Artillery Saber

Artillery Noncommissioned Officer Sword

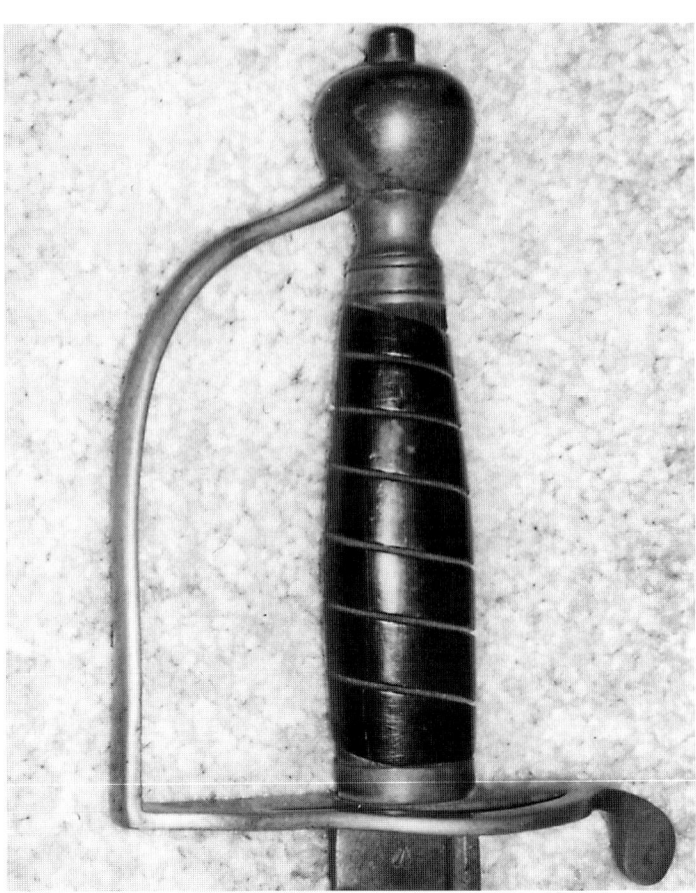

Model 1872 nonregulation mounted artillery trooper saber. (Author's collection)

Very rare U.S. 1812 contract artillery non-comm. sword with brass hussar hilt, ebony grip, and 27″ blade made by William Rose. (C. Philip Johnson Jr. collection)

Mounted Artillery Officer Sabers

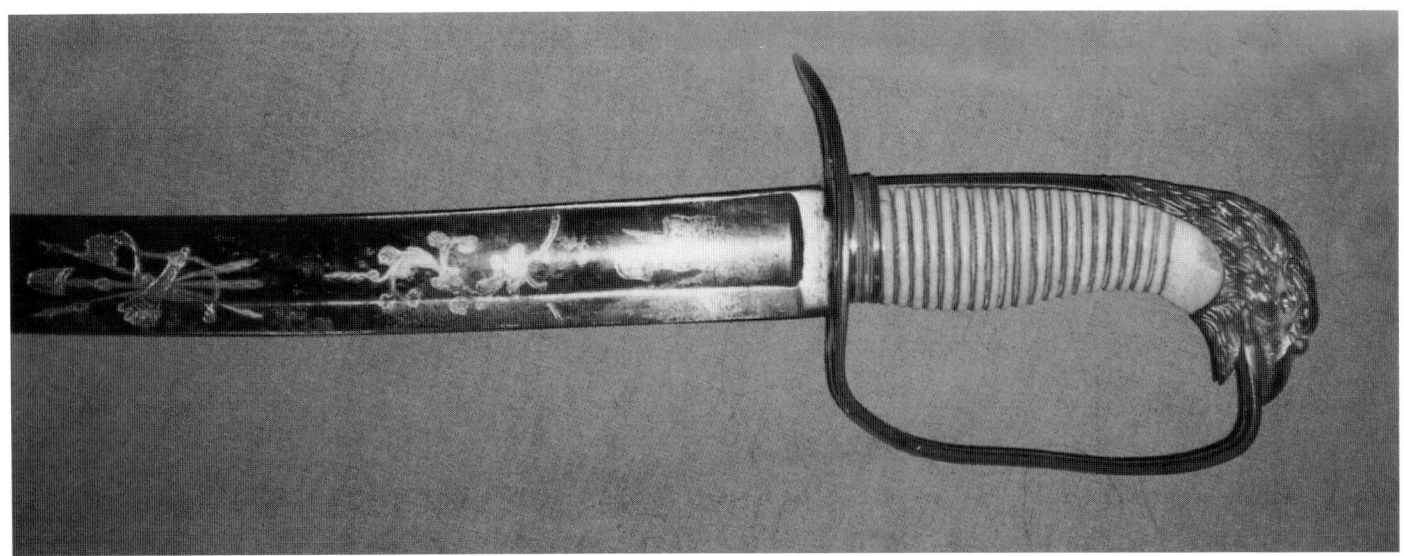

Mounted artillery officer saber, c. 1795-1800, with eagle-head pommel, gilted brass hilt, and ivory grips. (Grafton H. Cook II collection)

 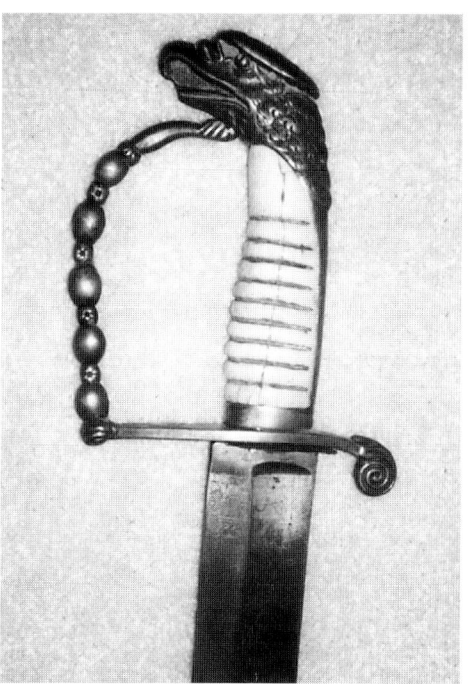 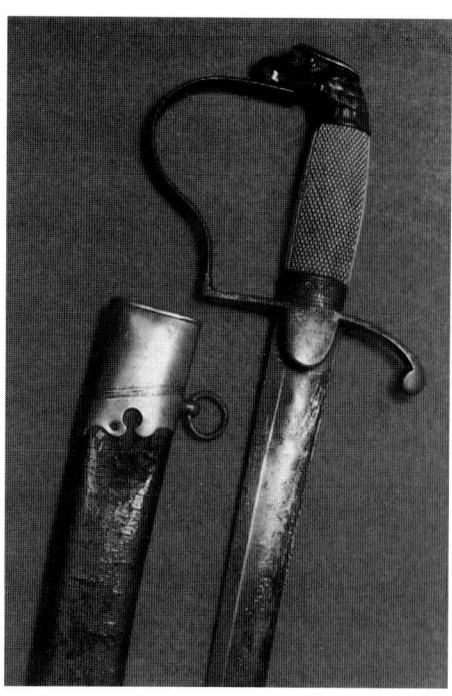

Mounted artillery officer saber with very rare brass parrot-beaked eagle-head pommel, arrowhead langets, bone chevron-pattern grips, and 32 1/2" blade, c. 1805. (Jan H. Zajac collection)

Mounted artillery officer, c. 1805-1810, with brass eagle-head pommel, unusual beaded knuckle bow, and 31" blued and etched blade. (C. Philip Johnson Jr. collection)

Mounted artillery officer saber, c. 1810-1820, with checkered ivory grips. (Courtesy of Leonard Garigliano)

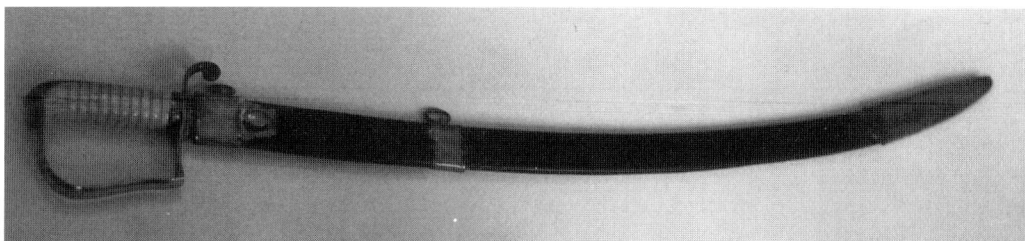

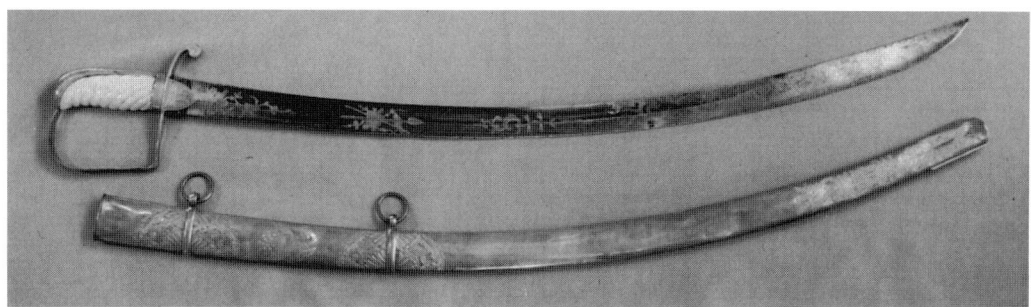

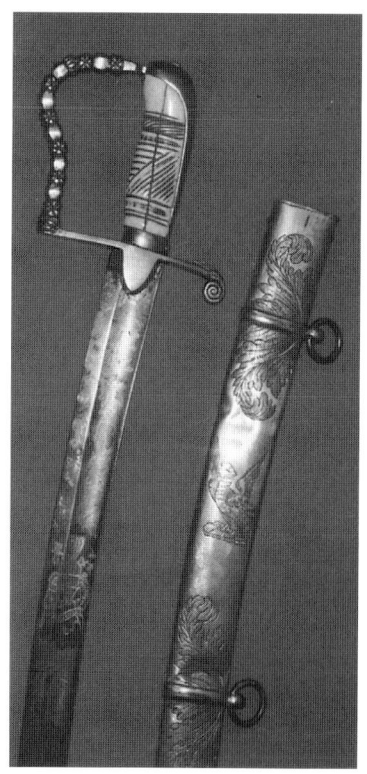

Top: Mounted artillery officer saber, c. 1805-1815, with brass hilt and scabbard mounts, bone grip, and decorated blade worn by Capt. Daniel Bissell during the War of 1812. By the end of the war, Bissell was a brigadier general. (Courtesy of Bissell House Museum, St. Louis, MO)

Above: High-grade mounted artillery officer saber, 1810, with unusual carved bone grip, brass hilt and scabbard, blued and gold-gilt 29 1/2" blade, and hussar-type bird-head pommel. (CDR John Retzaff collection)

Right: War of 1812 mounted artillery officer saber, c. 1810-1820, with bone grip, unusual beaded brass knuckle bow, and etched brass scabbard. (Grafton H. Cook II collection)

Top: War of 1812 mounted artillery officer presentation sword, c. 1810-1820. (Courtesy of Don Ball)

Second from top: High-grade War of 1812 mounted artillery officer saber, c. 1810-1820, with carved bone grip, brass hilt and scabbard, and 30″ blued and gold-gilt blade. (CDR John Retzaff collection)

Third from top: High-grade War of 1812 mounted artillery officer saber, c. 1810-1820, with ivory grip, blued and gilt blade, heavily etched brass scabbard, and brass hilt with sea serpent knuckle bow. (CDR John Retzaff collection)

Bottom: War of 1812 light artillery officer saber with brass hilt and scabbard mounts, checkered bone grip, 33″ blued and etched blade, and very rare horse-head pommel. (C. Philip Johnson Jr. collection)

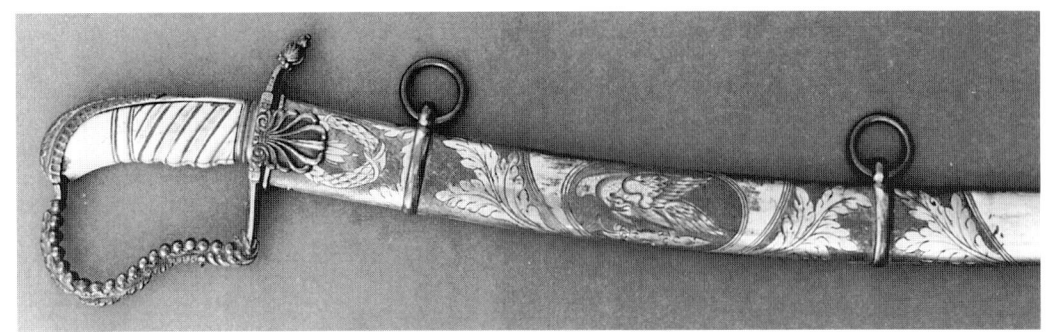
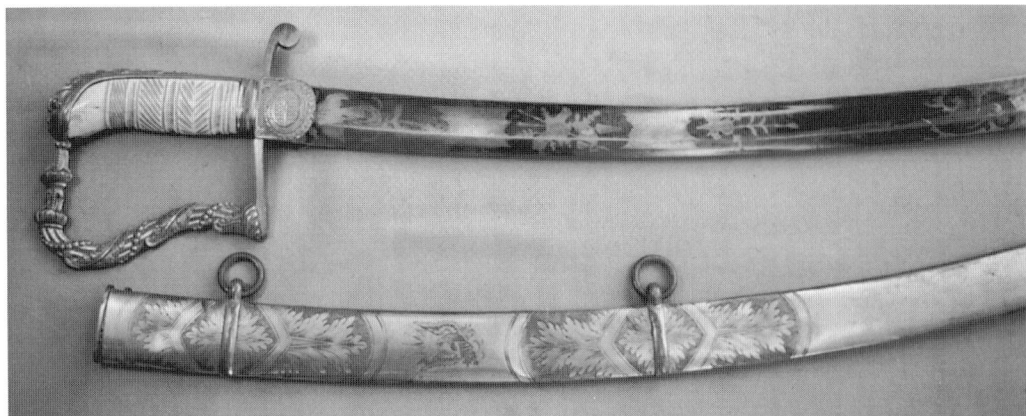
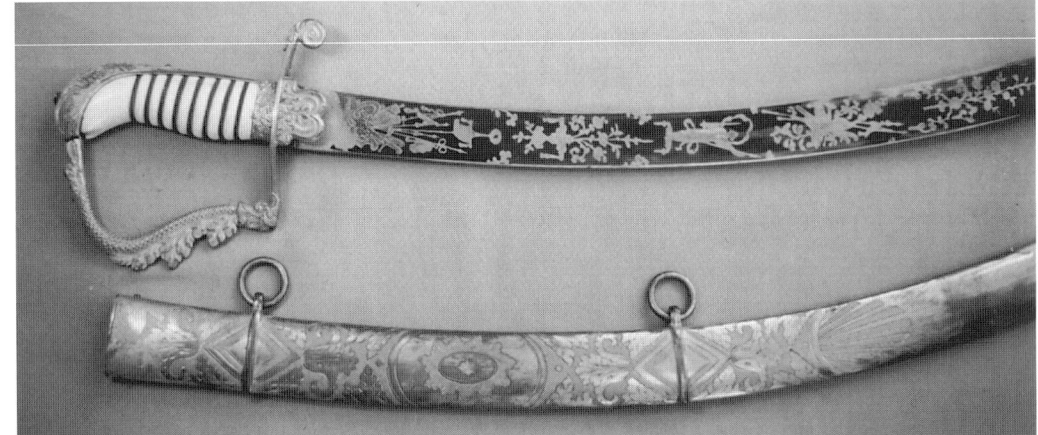
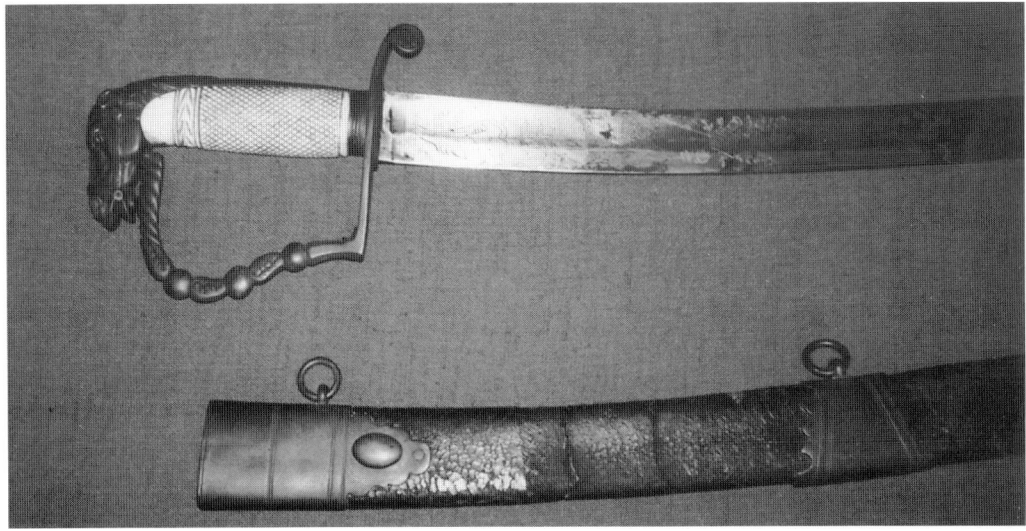

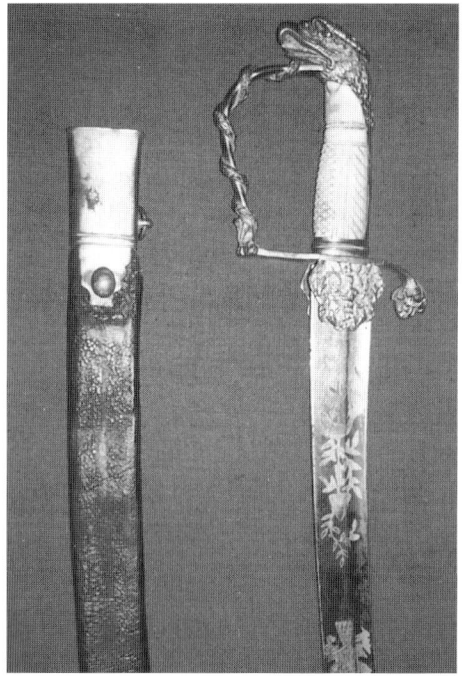
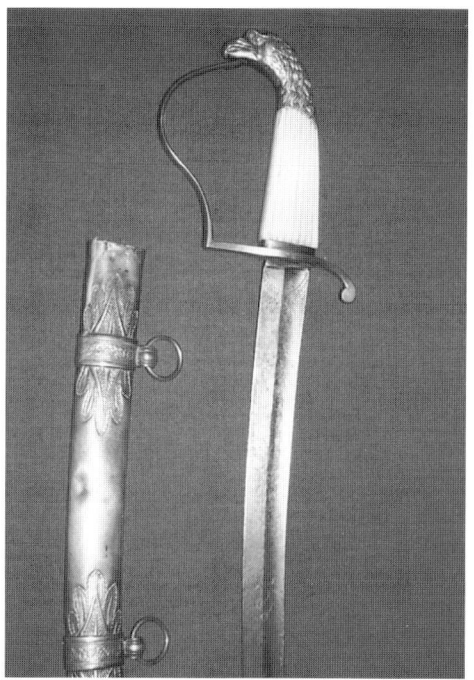
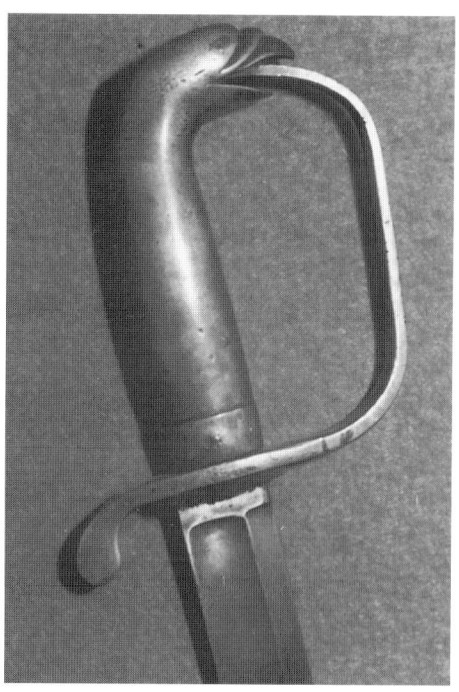

War of 1812 light artillery officer saber with eagle-head pommel, checkered ivory grip, 30 3/4″ blued and fire-gilded etched blade, and brass hilt and scabbard mounts. "E Pluribus Unum" is etched on the blade. (C. Philip Johnson Jr. collection)

Very unusual German-made U.S. light artillery officer sword, c. 1820, with eagle-head pommel, rectangular reeded ivory grip, brass hilt and scabbard, and 31″ etched blade. Maker: Schnitzler & Kirschbaum, Solingen, Prussia. (C. Philip Johnson Jr. collection)

Mounted artillery officer saber, c. 1830, with solid brass eagle-head hilt made by F.W. Widmann. (Courtesy of Leonard Garigliano)

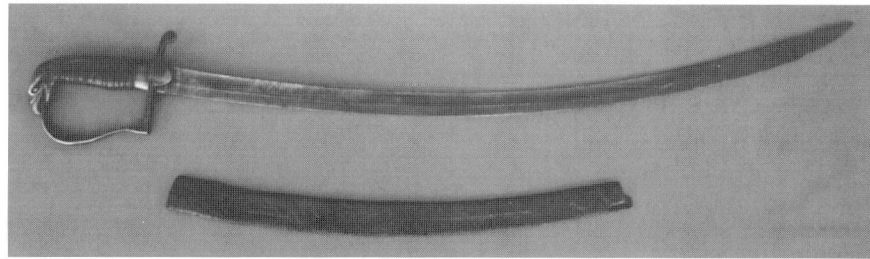

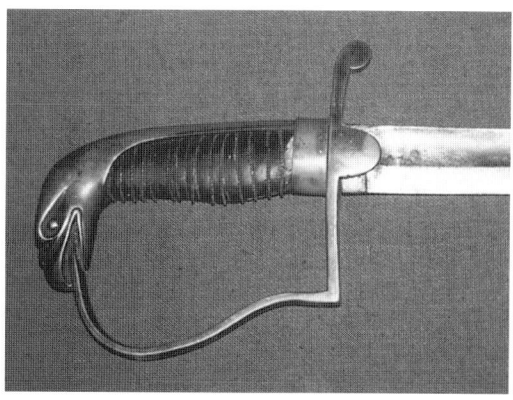

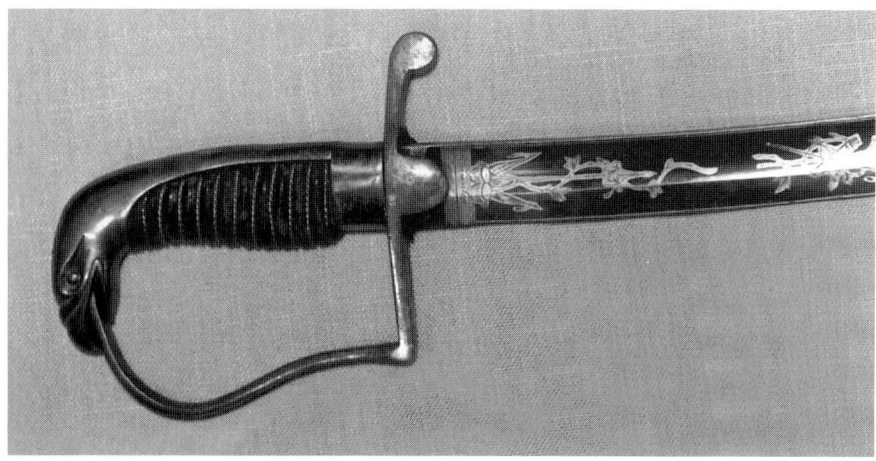

Above: Very rare light artillery officer saber, c. 1835, with stylized eagle-head pommel and etched 32 1/4″ blade. Maker: F.W. Widmann. (C. Philip Johnson Jr. collection)

Above left: Full-length view of F.W. Widmann light artillery officer saber. (C. Philip Johnson Jr. collection)

Left: Mounted artillery officer saber, c. 1850, with brass hilt made by W.H. Horstmann & Sons from a F.W. Widmann design. (Jan H. Zajac collection)

Artillery Officer Swords

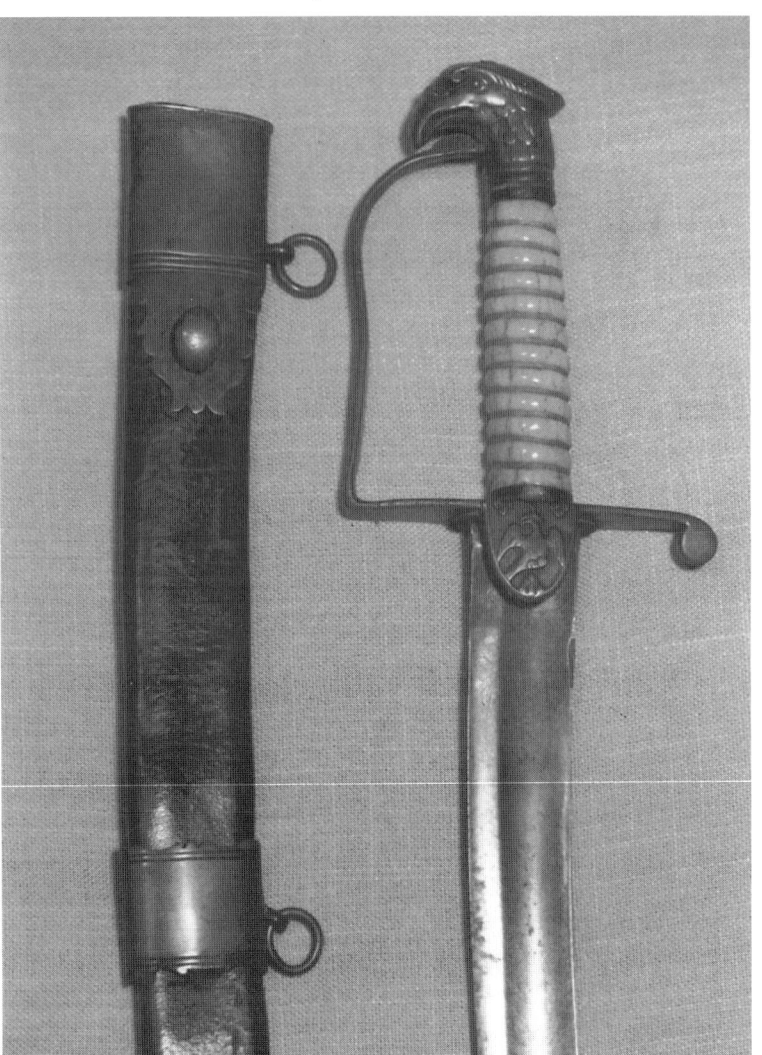

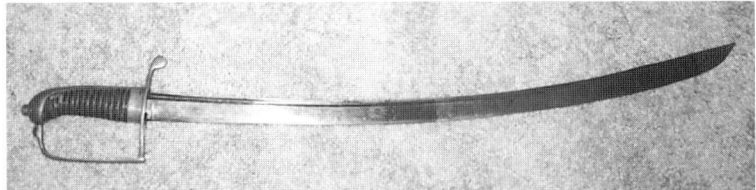

Top: Artillery officer saber, c. 1795-1805, with unusual brass eagle-head pommel, spiral bone grip, and 28" blade. (Jan H. Zajac collection)

Above: Early artillery officer saber, c. 1805-1810, with 27" etched and blued blade (unmarked). (C. Philip Johnson Jr. collection)

Presentation-grade Model 1872 mounted artillery officer saber presented to Lt. D. Murphy, Battery C, Utah Volunteers. (Susan Di Camillo collection; photo by Paul J. DeSarbo)

Artillery officer saber, c. 1810-1815, with very rare horse-head pommel, ivory grip with 35 strands of brass wire, and 29 1/2" etched blade. (Jan H. Zajac collection)

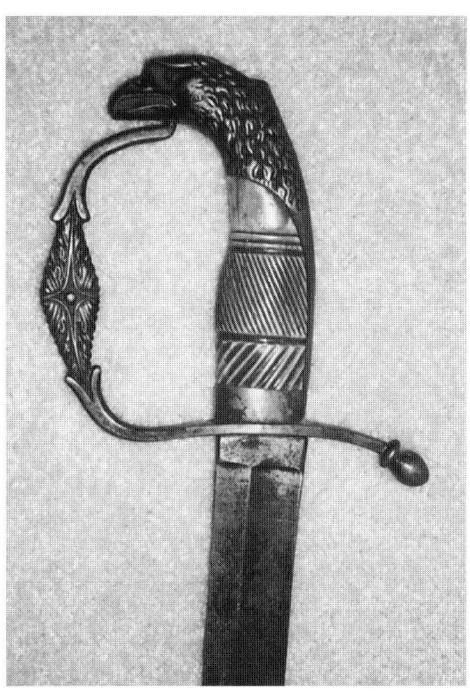
Artillery officer short saber, c. 1810-1820, with brass eagle-head pommel, ivory grip, and 30 1/2" etched blade made by A. (Antoine) Berger, St. Etienne, France. (C. Philip Johnson Jr. collection)

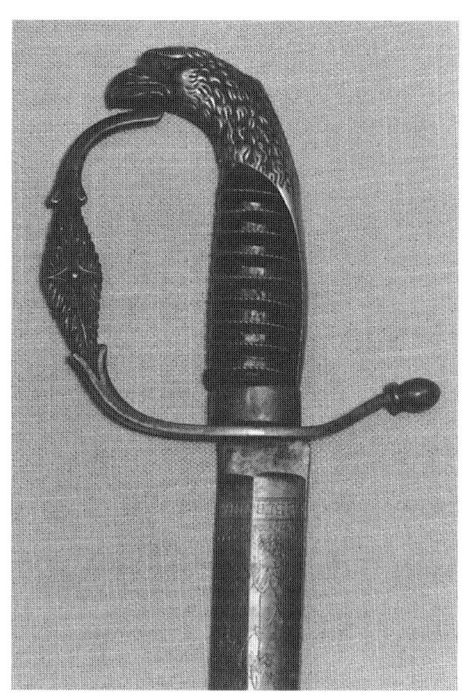
Artillery officer saber, c. 1810-1820, with brass eagle-head pommel with a backstrap, leather grips, and 29" blade. Maker: A. (Antoine) Berger, St. Etienne, France. (Jan H. Zajac collection)

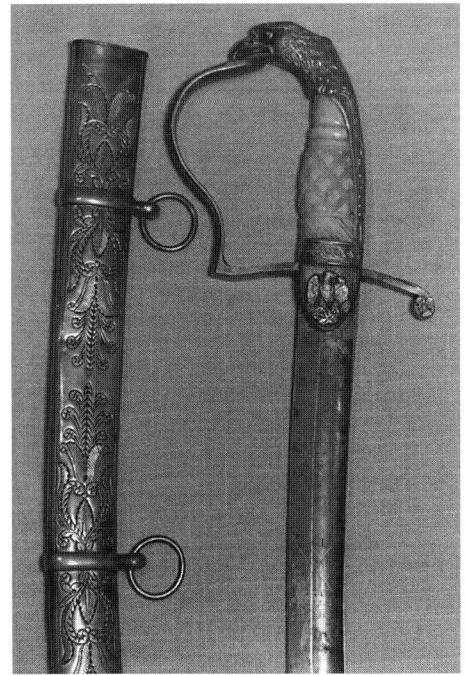
Artillery officer saber, c. 1810-1820, with brass eagle-head pommel and ivory grip. Made for the American market by famous French cutler A. (Antoine) Berger, St. Etienne, France. (Jan H. Zajac collection)

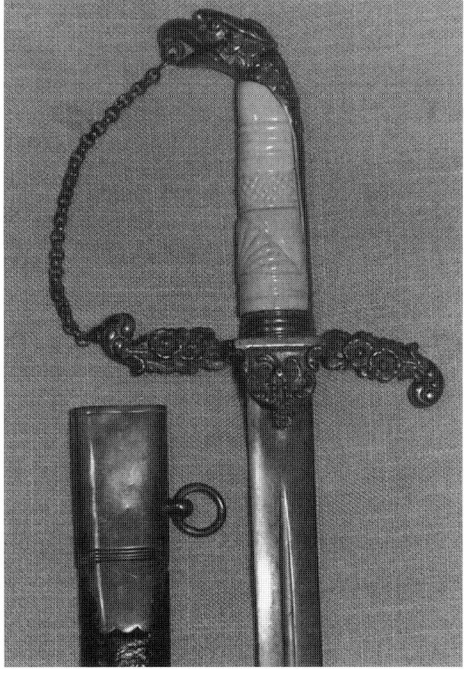
Artillery officer saber, c. 1820-1835, with gilt copper eagle-head pommel and 31" double-edged blade. (Jan H. Zajac collection)

Artillery officer saber, c. 1820-1835, with brass eagle-head pommel sold by dealer A. (Adam) W. Spies, New York, NY. (Jan H. Zajac collection)

Right: Artillery officer saber, c. 1820-1835, with brass eagle-head pommel sold by A.W. Spies. (Jan H. Zajac collection)

Far right: Artillery officer saber, c. 1820-1835, with screaming eagle pommel and rare gilt copper hilt and scabbard. (Jan H. Zajac collection)

Middle: Presentation-grade artillery officer saber, c. 1820-1835, with eagle-head pommel, brass hilt and scabbard, and blued and gold washed blade.

Bottom right: Artillery officer saber, c. 1835-1850, with eagle-head pommel, mother of pearl grip, brass hilt and scabbard, and blued and gilt etched blade. A rare sword from Schnitzler & Kirschbaum, Solingen, Prussia. (CDR John Retzaff collection)

Below: Artillery officer saber, c. 1835-1850, with eagle-head pommel, pearl grips, and brass hilt and scabbard. (Thomas L. Jones collection; photo by Thomas L. Jones)

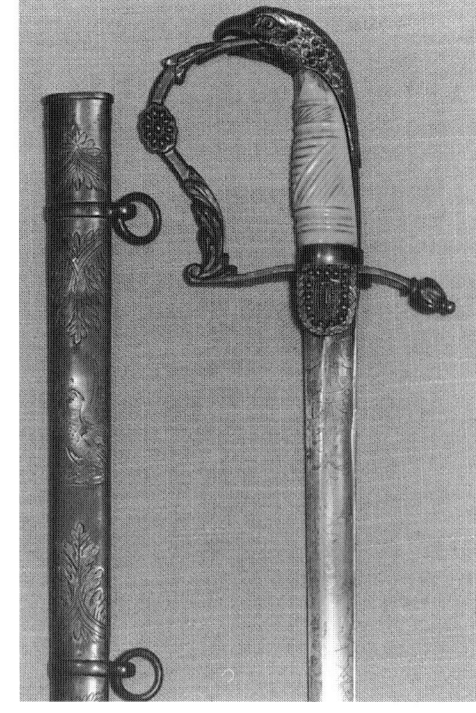

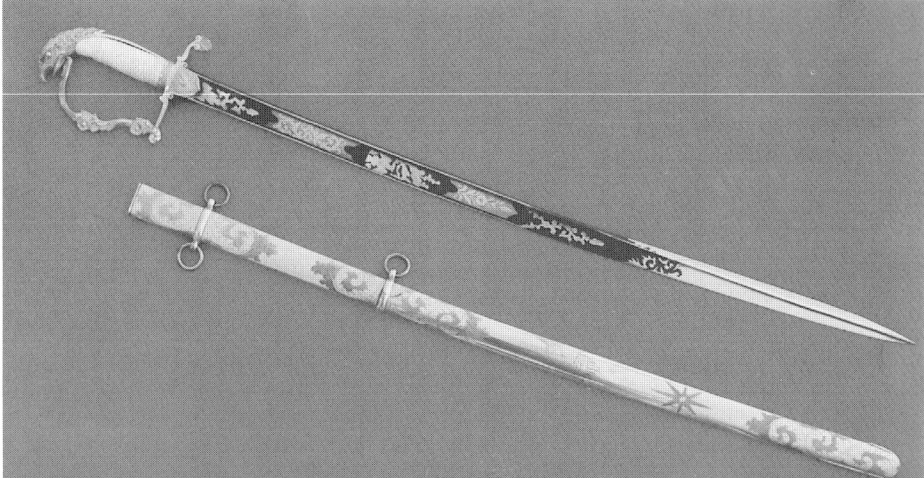
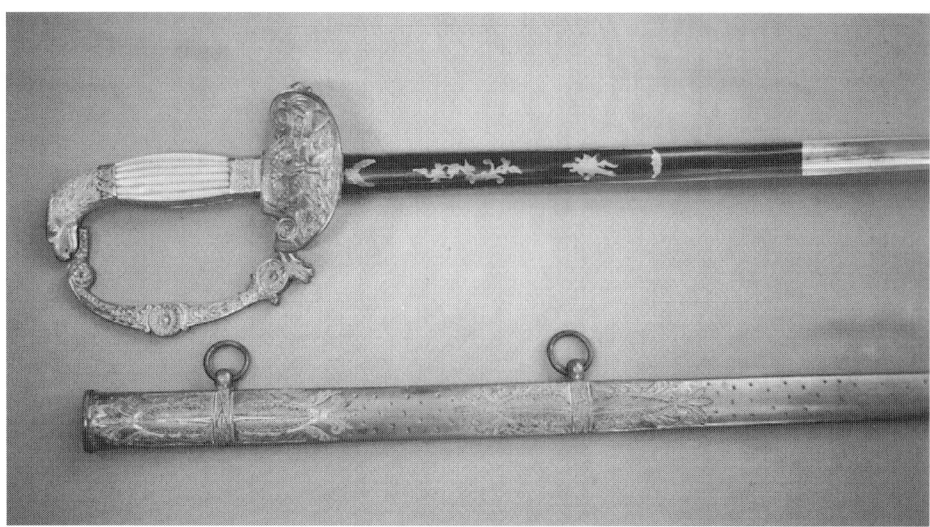

Infantry Noncommissioned Officer Sword

Infantry Officer's Hunting Sabers

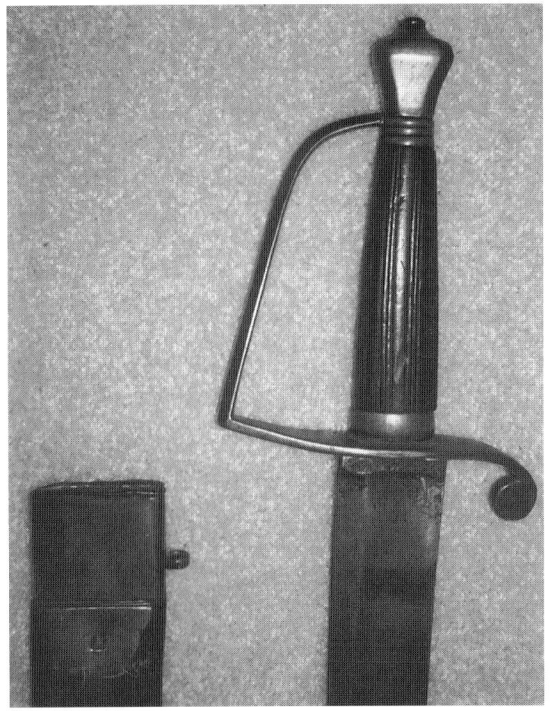

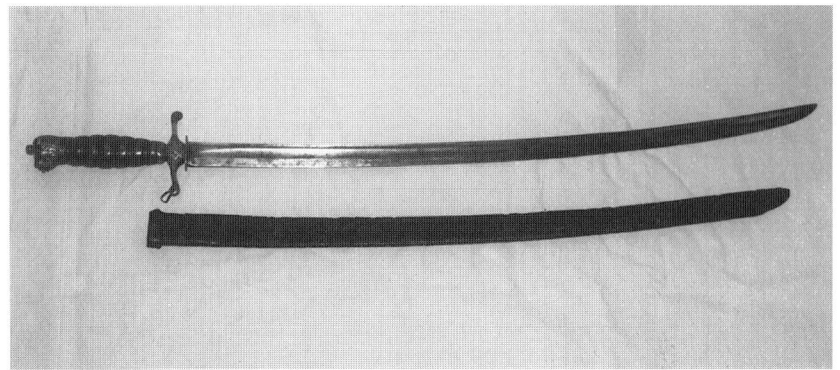

Infantry non-comm. officer sword, c. 1790-1810, with horn grip, iron hilt, and 28 1/2" blade. Sold by Lemuel Wells & Co., New York, NY. (C. Philip Johnson Jr. collection)

Top: Revolutionary War officer's hunting saber with very rare fully carved green ivory lion-head hilt. (Grafton H. Cook II collection)

Above: Revolutionary War infantry officer's hunting saber. (Kentucky Historical Society Military History Museum collection)

Infantry Officer Swords

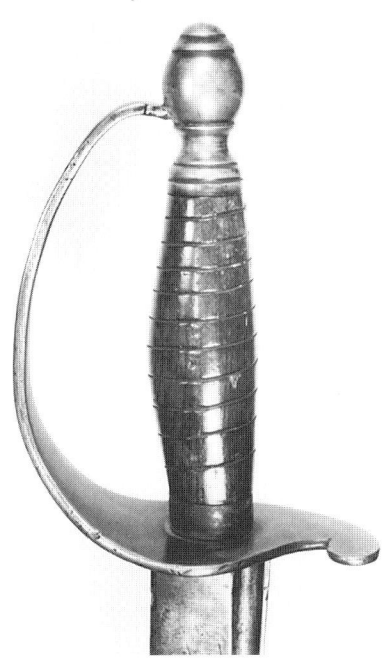

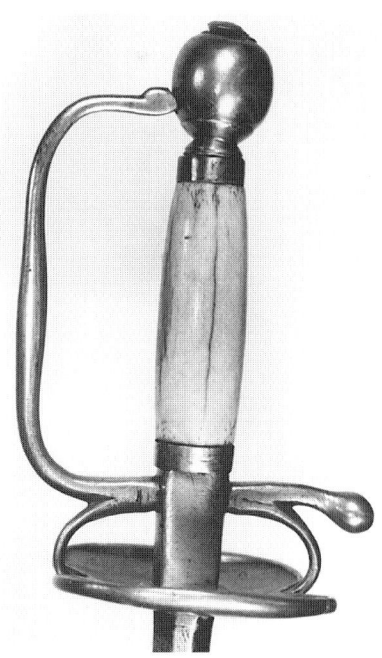

Revolutionary War infantry officer short saber with brass wagon wheel hilt, bone grip, and 27 5/8" blade. (George C. Neumann collection)

Revolutionary War infantry officer short saber with brass hilt, wooden grip, and 26 1/2" blade. (George C. Neumann collection)

Revolutionary War infantry officer small sword with brass hilt, ivory grip, and 30" blade. (George C. Neumann collection)

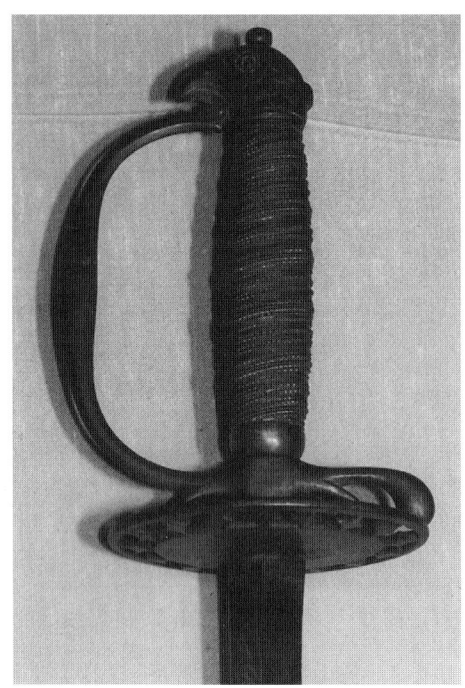

Early infantry officer small sword, c. 1785-1795, with disk guard, steel hilt, and eagle-head pommel. (Kevin T. Hoffman collection)

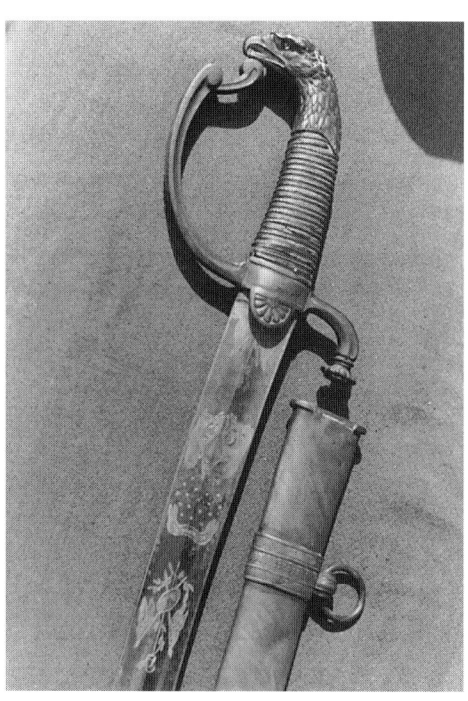

Infantry officer short saber, c. 1805, with eagle-head pommel made by Jean LePage, Paris, France. (Courtesy of Leonard Garigliano)

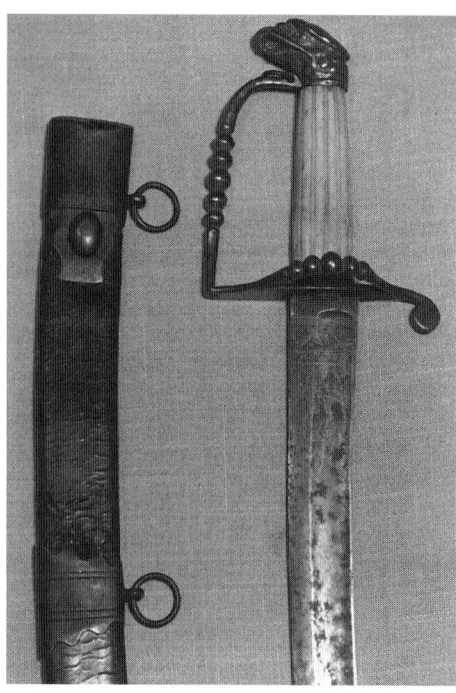

Infantry officer short saber, c. 1805-1810, with English-style beaded hilt (silver over brass), reeded bone grips, and wide saber blade. Maker: Robert Johnson Brown, Boston, MA. (Jan H. Zajac collection)

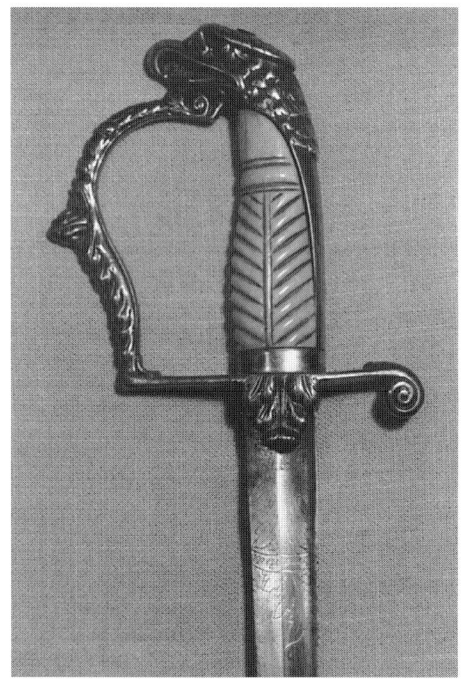

Infantry officer short saber, c. 1815-1820, with eagle-head pommel, silver hilt, and curved blade. (Jan H. Zajac collection)

Infantry officer short saber, c. 1815-1820, with eagle-head pommel and unusual beaded knuckle bow. (C. Philip Johnson Jr. collection)

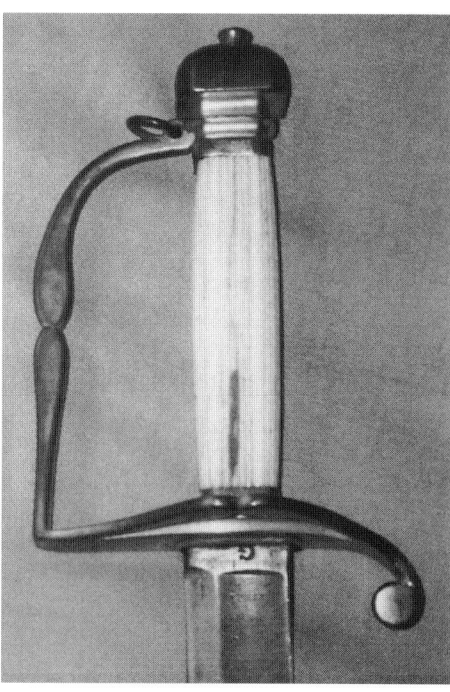

Infantry officer sword, c. 1825, with brass pillow hilt, ivory grip, and 32 1/4" blade. Maker: Thomas Gill, Birmingham, England. (Grafton H. Cook II collection)

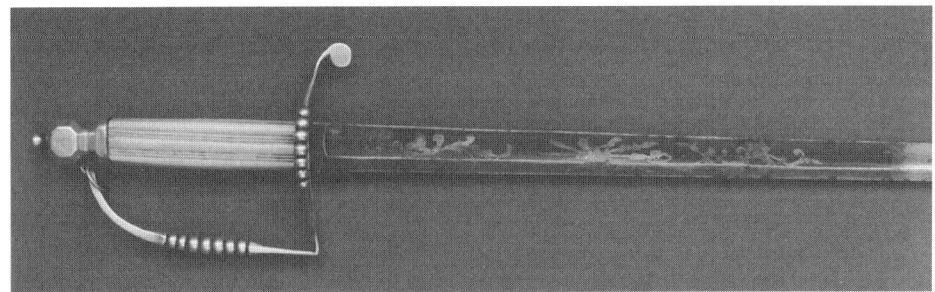

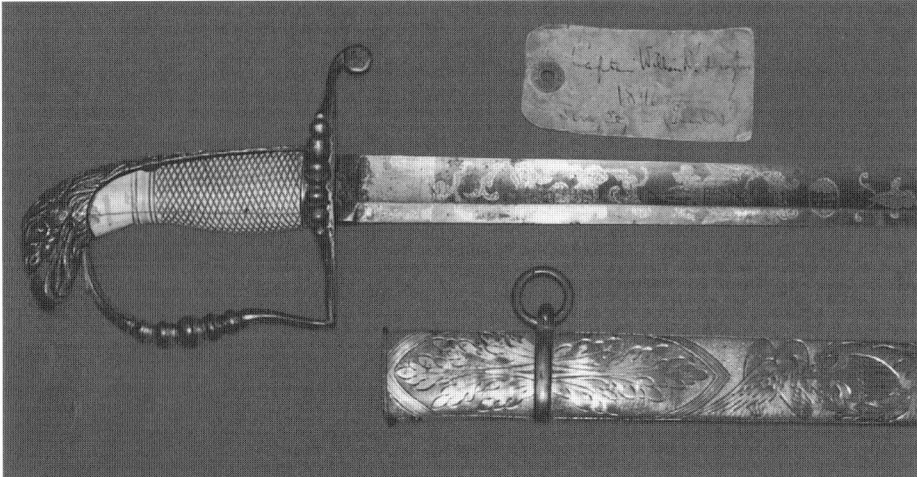

Top: Infantry officer sword, c. 1825, with bone grip and beaded knuckle bow and cross guard. (Courtesy of Leonard Garigliano)

Middle: Infantry officer sword, c. 1825, with eagle-head pommel, checkered bone grip, beaded knuckle bow and cross guard, and blued and gilted blade. This sword was sold by Lemuel Wells, New York, NY, and carried by Capt. William R. Drayton, Jersey City Guards. (Thomas L. Jones collection; photo by Thomas L. Jones)

Bottom left: Presentation-grade Model 1840 sword for company-grade infantry officers. Presented to Brigadier General Francis E. Patterson by his brigade, 1st Division, P. Vol., on February 22, 1862. (Kevin T. Hoffman collection)

Bottom right: Presentation-grade Model 1840 sword with silver hilt for company-grade infantry officers. Presented to Governor Andrews in 1862. Blade made by Collins & Co. (Courtesy of Don Ball)

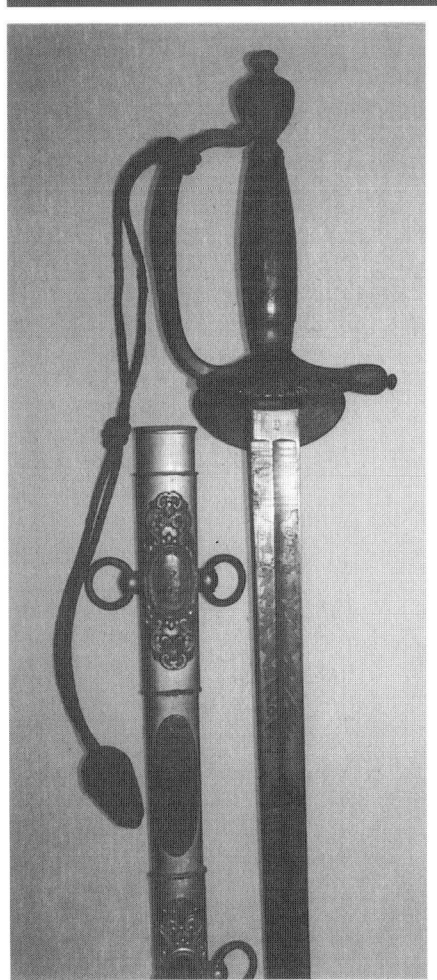

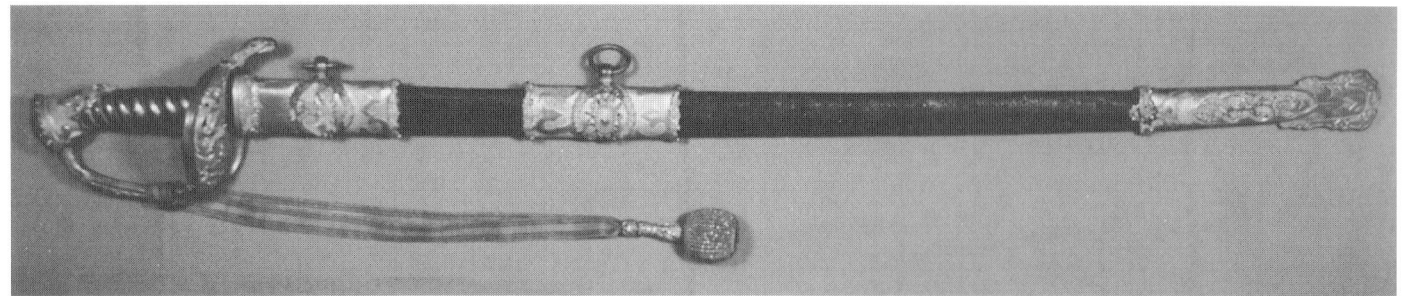

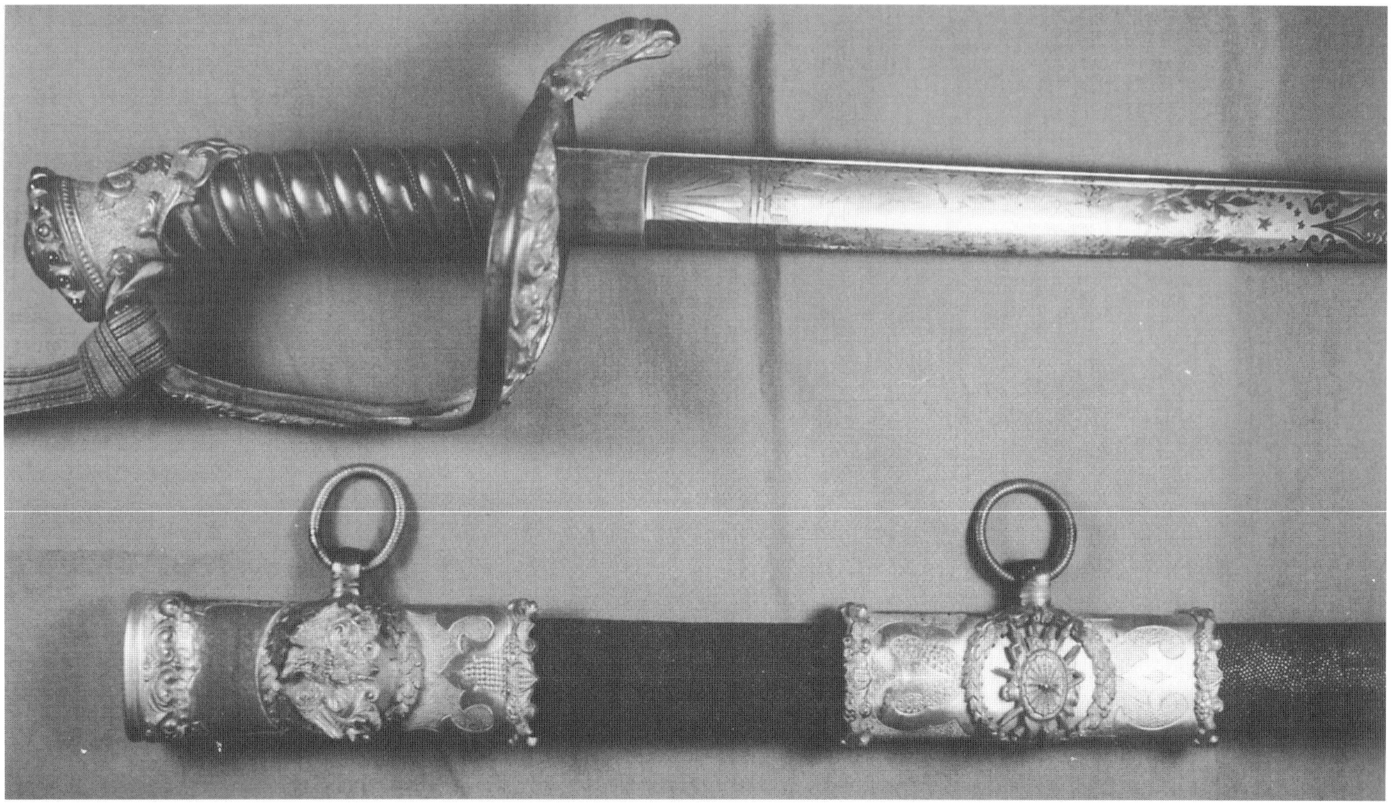

Top: Rare presentation-grade Model 1850 foot officer (infantry) sword with silver grip and spread eagle mounting on the scabbard. Presented to Henry Clark of Buffalo, 1st lieutenant, U.S. Army, by the employees of the New York Central Railroad Co. (Courtesy of R.H. Kirchhoff)

Above: Close-up of the Clark sword's hilt and upper scabbard.

Staff and Field Officer (Infantry and Artillery) Swords

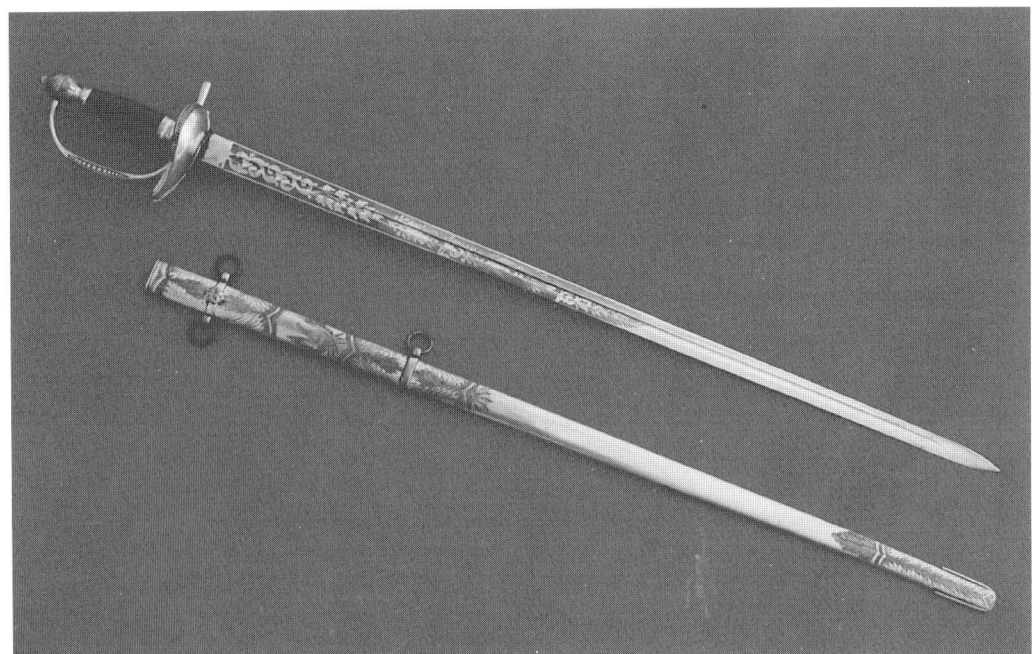

Top: Model 1832 general staff officer sword with gilt brass hilt and scabbard. Maker: N.P. Ames.

Middle: Presentation-grade Model 1850 staff and field officer sword with extra fine engraved blade and unusual three-ring gilt brass scabbard with silver mountings that has been hand chased and engraved. Presented to Capt. Robert Brodie, Company A, 35th KY, from his company. Maker: Ames Manufacturing Co. (R.H. Kirchhoff collection)

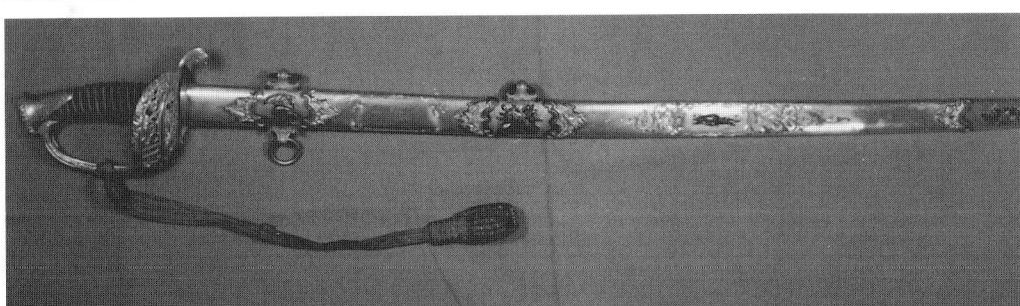

Bottom: Close-up of the Brodie sword's hilt and inscribed scabbard.

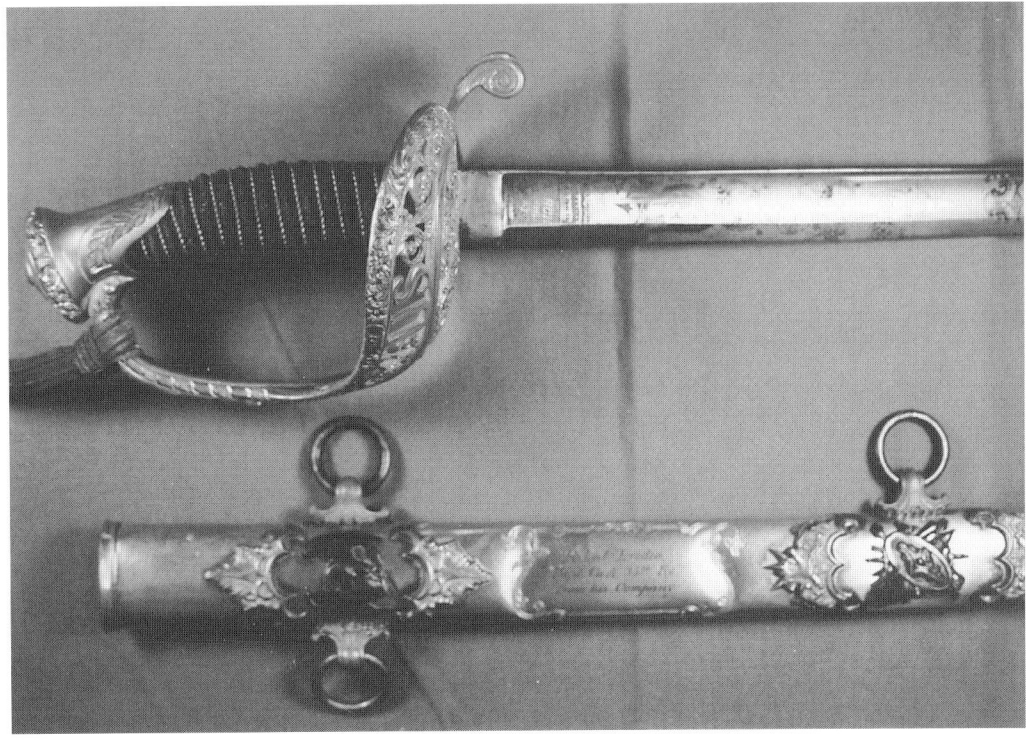

  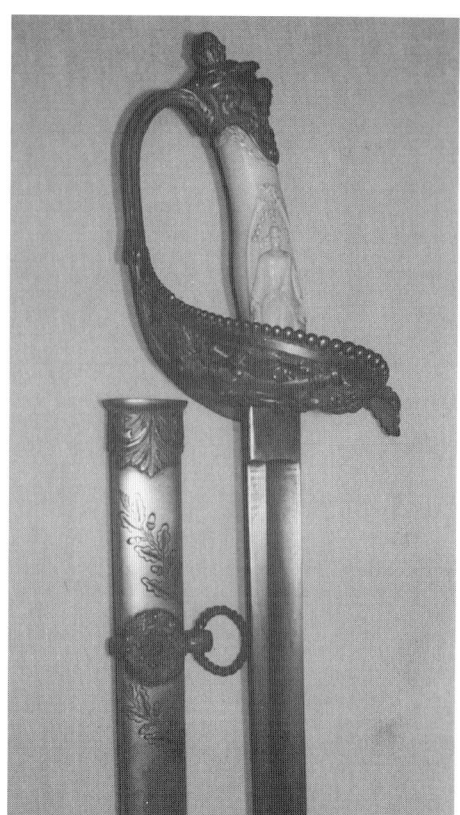

Top left: Model 1850 staff and field officer silver-hilted presentation-grade sword given to Lt. Charles W. Gibbs, 44th New York Infantry, on October 1, 1862, by his friends in Albany, NY. Lieutenant Gibbs fought at Gettysburg at the battle for Little Round Top. (Kevin T. Hoffman collection)

Top middle: High-grade silver- and gold-mounted Model 1850 presentation staff and field officer sword presented to General Powell C. Clayton, 5th Kansas, by the citizens of Pine Bluff, AR, for his gallant defense of that place on October 25, 1863. (Kevin T. Hoffman collection)

Top right: Model 1850 staff and field officer presentation-grade sword with unusual carved ivory grips and enameled scabbard. (Kevin T. Hoffman collection)

Right: Close-up of the carved ivory grip on Model 1850 staff and field officer sword.

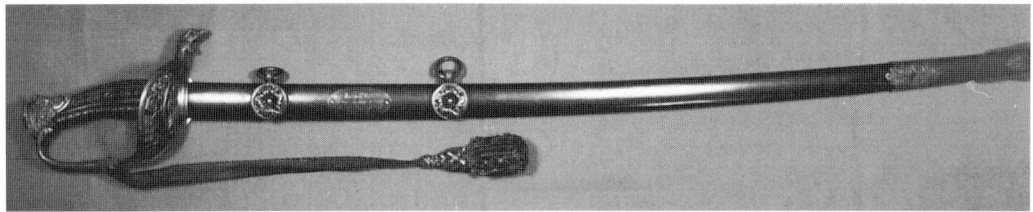

Top: Presentation-grade Model 1850 staff and field officer sword with brass-mounted hilt and scabbard and unusual silver grip. Presented to Capt. Matthew Donovan from the members of Company D, 16th Regiment, Massachusetts Volunteers, on October 16, 1864. Maker: Wilhelm Clauberg, Solingen, Prussia. (Courtesy of R.H. Kirchhoff)

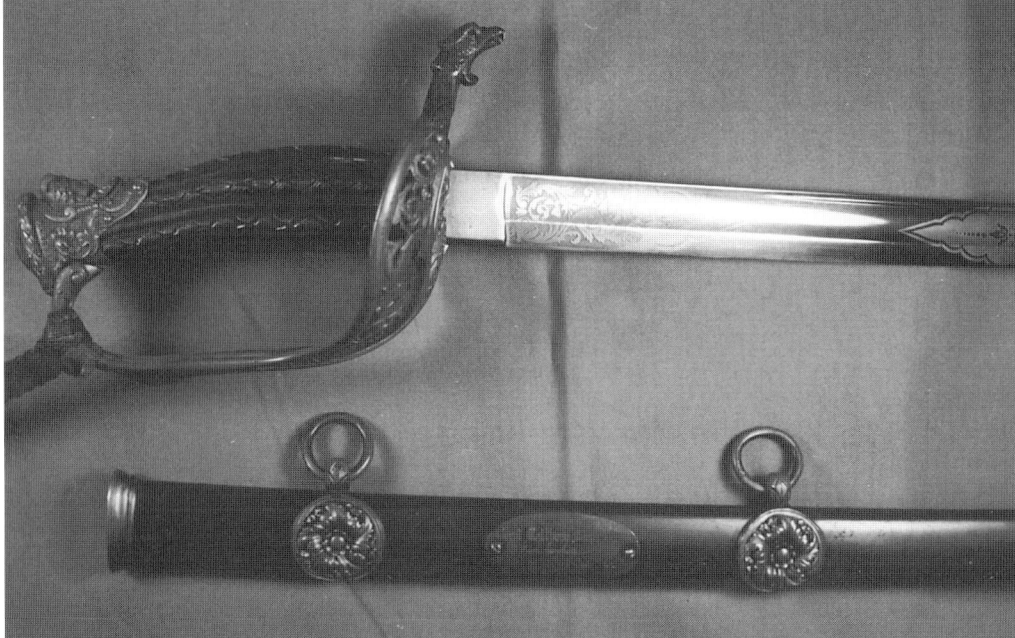

Middle: Close-up of the Donovan sword's hilt.

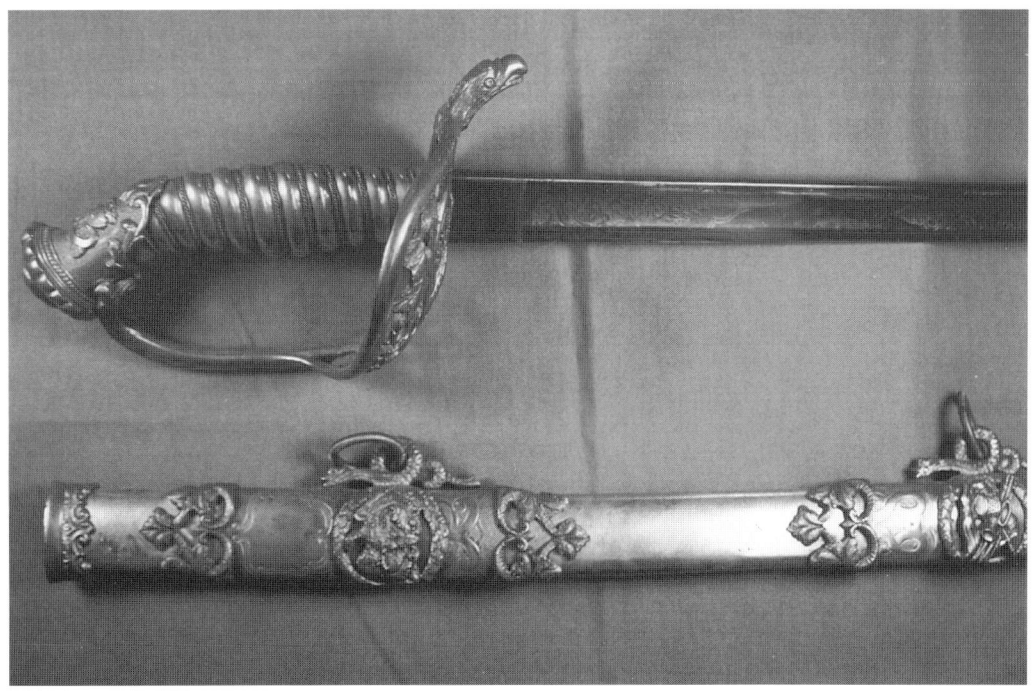

Bottom: Presentation-grade Model 1850 staff and field officer sword with silver grip and eagle finial. Presented to AJT. George F. Young from the officers and men of the 152nd Indiana Volunteers. Maker: Wilhelm Clauberg, Solingen, Prussia. (Courtesy of R.H. Kirchhoff)

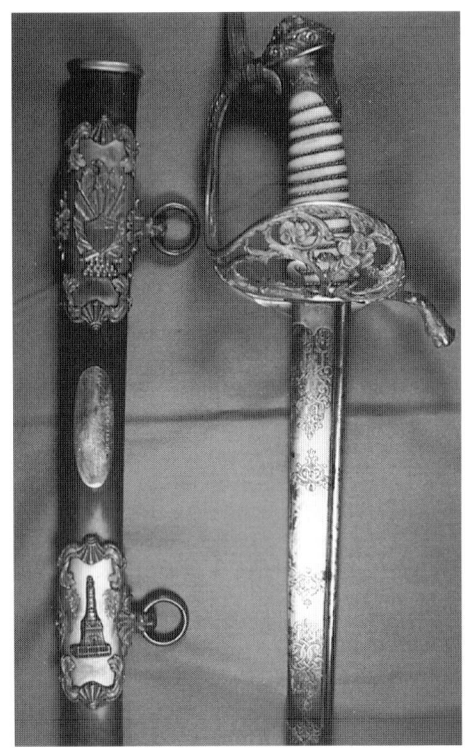
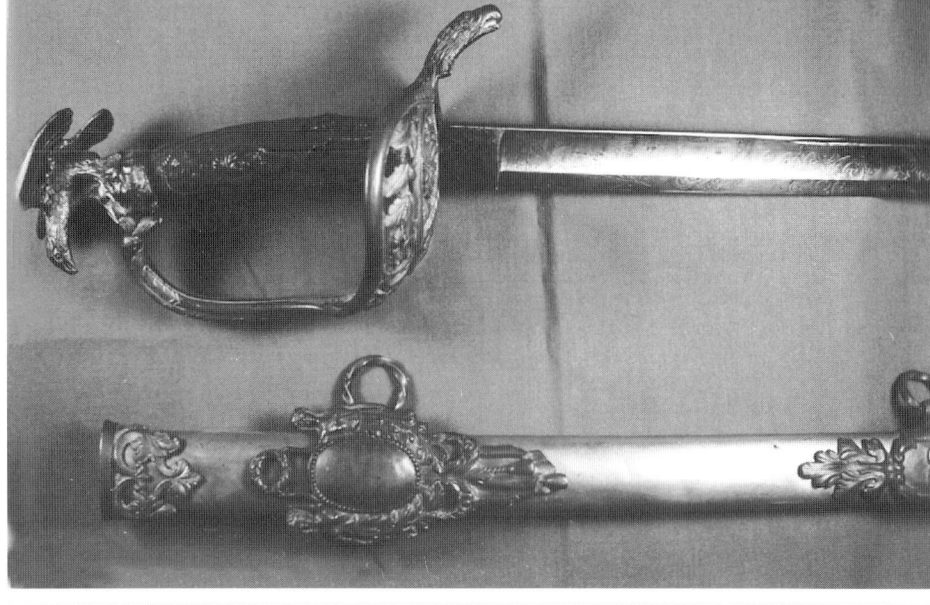
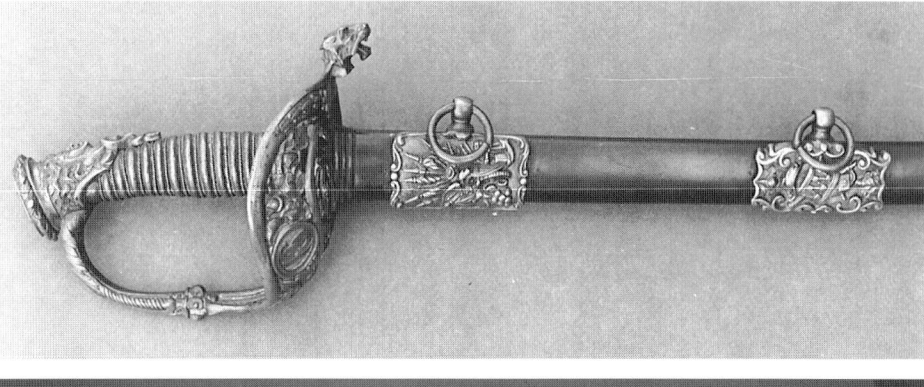
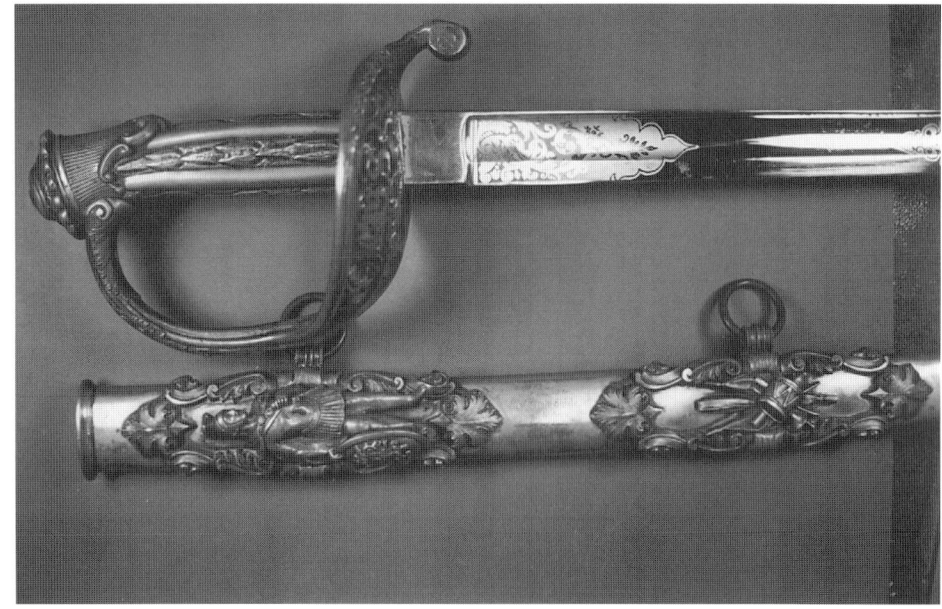

Above: Presentation-grade Model 1850 staff and field officer sword with ivory, wire-wrapped grip, Damascus, gold-inlaid, and engraved blade, and silver Baltimore monument on the scabbard. Presented to Col. James M. Anderson by the commissioned officers of the 53rd Regiment, MVI, on June 5, 1854. Moehle & Greshoff of Baltimore, MD, was either the maker or the dealer. (Courtesy of R.H. Kirchhoff)

Top right: High-grade Model 1850 staff and field officer presentation sword with statue cast into the grip. Presented to Lt. Col. Werner W. Bjerq by the officers of the 147th Illinois Volunteers on February 20, 1865. Maker: Wilhelm Clauberg, Solingen, Prussia. (Courtesy of R.H. Kirchhoff)

Middle: Model 1850 staff and field officer presentation-grade sword with lion-head finial and silver grip and mounting. Mounted by Ball, Black, & Co., New York, NY. (Courtesy of Don Ball)

Bottom: Presentation-grade Model 1850 staff and field officer sword with silver grip and soldier cast on the scabbard. Presented to Lt. Joseph Shiele by the members of Company E, 2nd New York Artillery. Maker: Wilhelm Clauberg, Solingen, Prussia. (Courtesy of R.H. Kirchhoff)

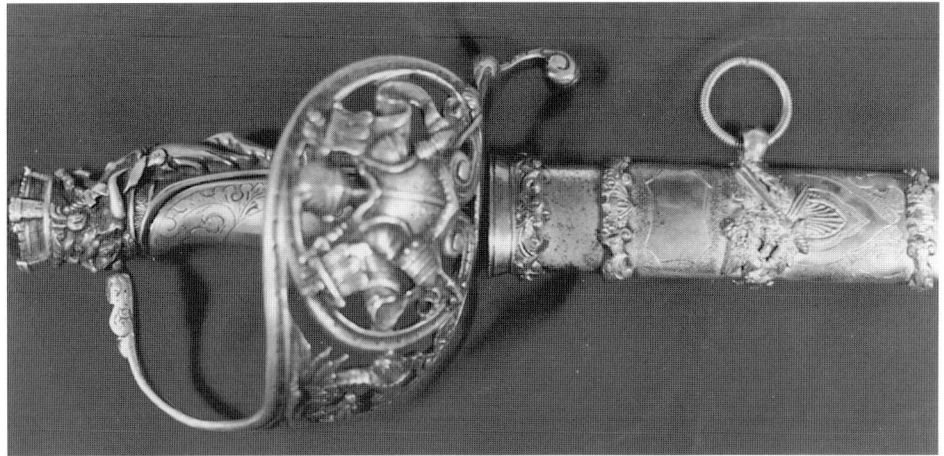

Top: Presentation-grade Civil War nonregulation staff and field officer sword. (Courtesy of Robert S. Porter)

Second from top: Very rare Model 1850 nonregulation staff and field officer sword with a very unusual Damascus blade with spear point, a gilt gold panel at the top of the blade, and a spread eagle on the shell guard. Maker (engraved on the blade): P.D. Luneschloss, Solingen, Prussia. Dealer: Schuyler, Hartley, & Graham, New York, NY. (C. Philip Johnson Jr. collection)

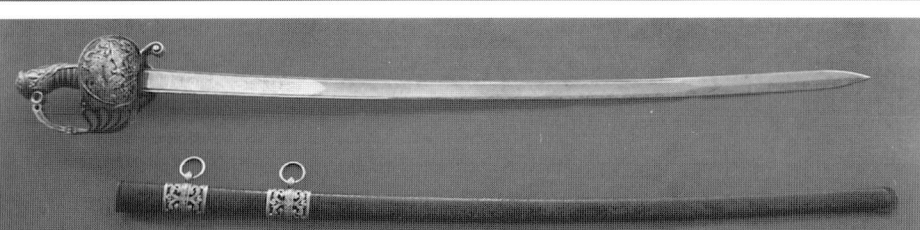

Third from top: Close-up of the hilt on the Luneschloss sword.

Bottom: Presentation-grade Model 1850 nonregulation staff and field officer sword with gem-mounted hilt and scabbard, blued and gilded blade, and silver statue of a female warrior with sword as part of the hilt. (Courtesy of George Juno)

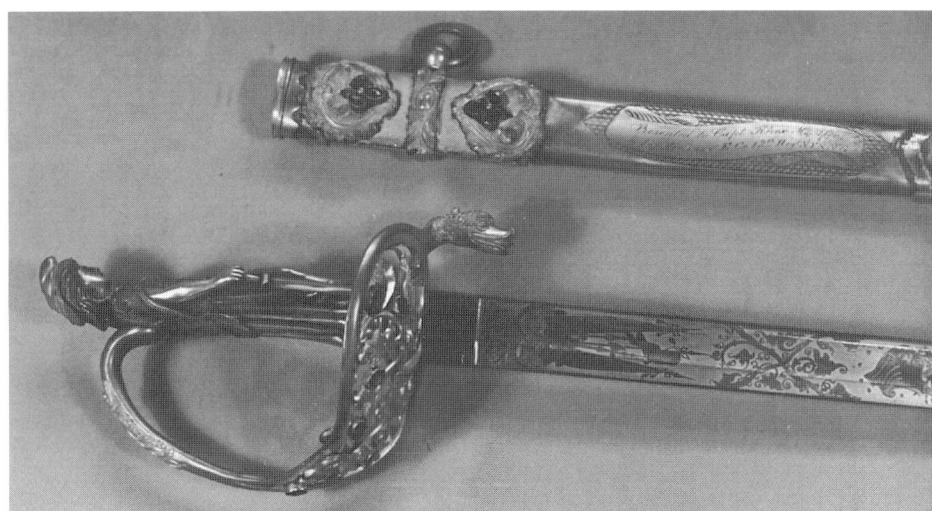

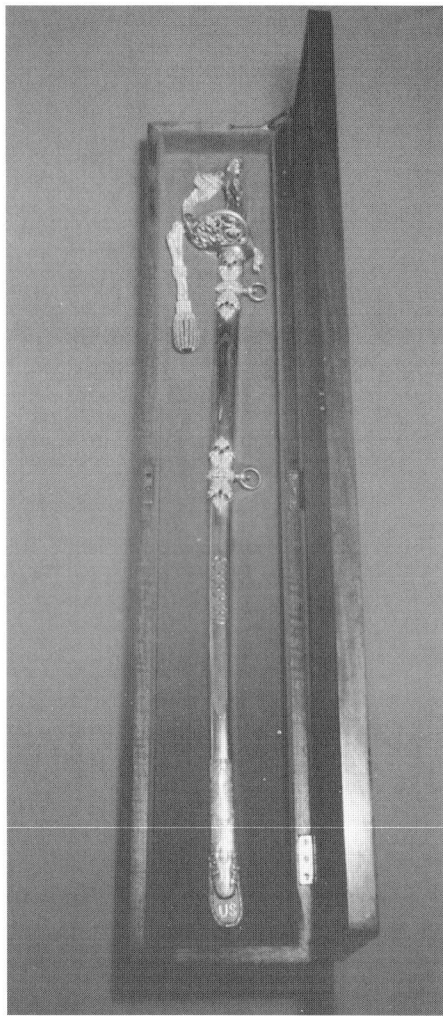
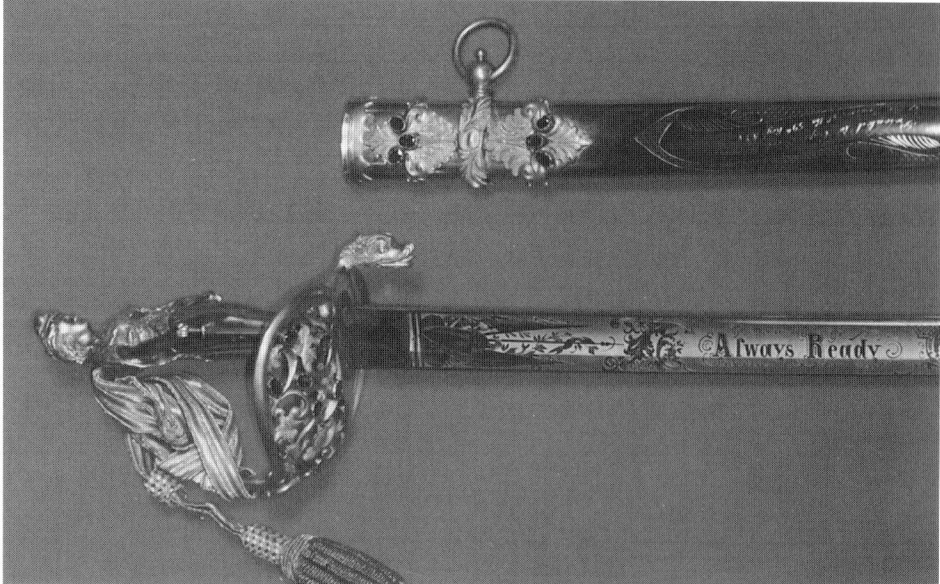
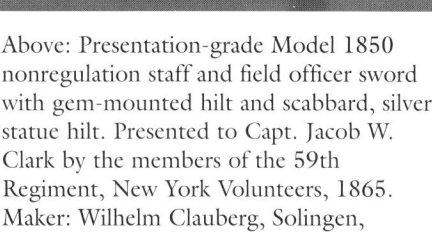

Above: Presentation-grade Model 1850 nonregulation staff and field officer sword with gem-mounted hilt and scabbard, silver statue hilt. Presented to Capt. Jacob W. Clark by the members of the 59th Regiment, New York Volunteers, 1865. Maker: Wilhelm Clauberg, Solingen, Prussia. (Robert A. Ferro collection)

Top right: Close-up of the silver statue hilt on the Clark sword.

Far right: Very high quality presentation-grade Model 1850 nonregulation staff and field officer sword with a gem-mounted bronze statue hilt and scabbard mounts, gold-inlaid etched blade, and engraved scabbard. Presented to Maj. M.A. Stearns from the commissioned and noncommissioned officers of the 2nd Vetran Cavalry, December 17, 1863. Dealer: Schuyler, Hartley, & Graham (shown on page 38 of their 1864 catalog). (James Schomberger collection)

Above: Presentation-grade Model 1860 Civil War staff and field officer sword with fabulous spread eagle and shield on shell guard and a fine Damascus blade. Made at the famous French sword factory at Klingenthal, Alsace. (Jan H. Zajac collection)

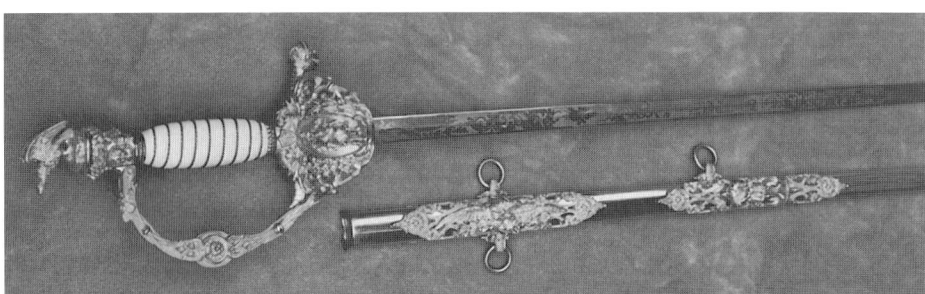

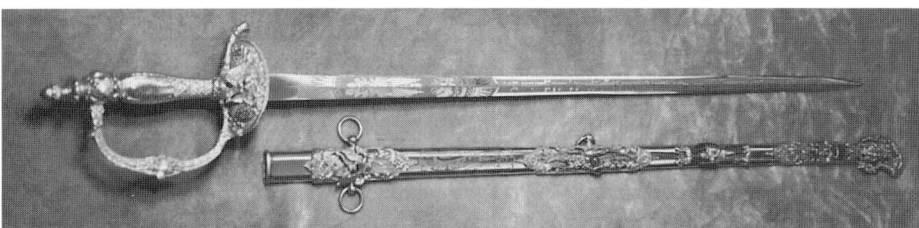

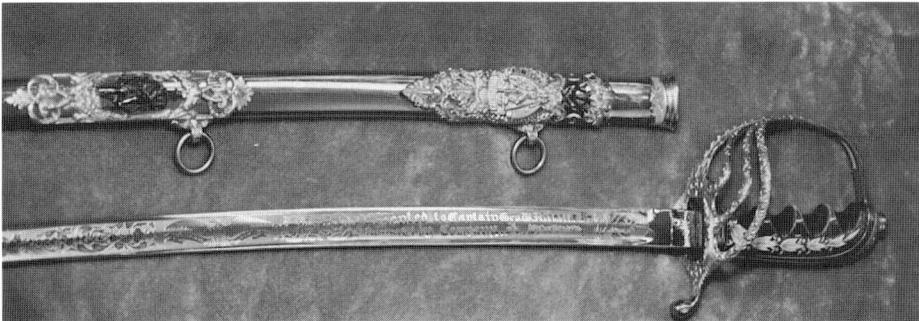

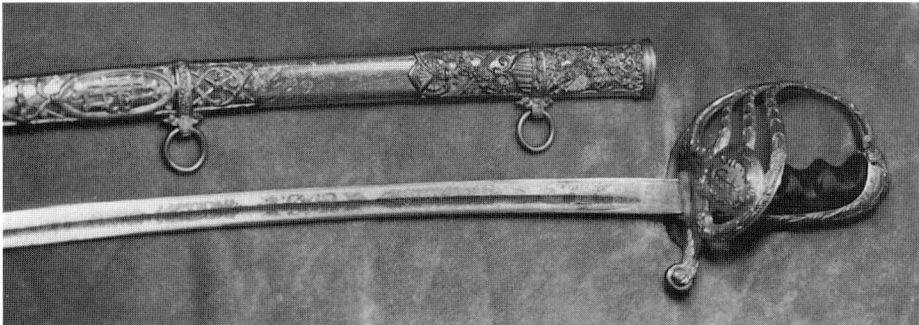

Above: Presentation-grade Model 1860 staff and field officer sword with engraved silver grip presented to Brig. Gen. Joshua T. Owen by the officers of his brigade, 1863. (Courtesy of the American Ordnance Preservation Association Ltd.)

Top: Close-up of the General Owen sword showing the scabbard plaque and blued and gold-washed blade.

Second from top: Presentation-grade Model 1860 staff and field officer sword with a rare winged eagle on the pommel. Presented to Col. E.P. Clark. Maker: C.E. Ward. (Susan Di Camillo collection; photo by Paul J. DeSarbo)

Third from top: High-quality presentation-grade Model 1860 staff and field officer sword showing four generations of the Grisholm family officers who served in the Civil War, Spanish-American War, World War I, and World War II on the blade. (Susan Di Camillo collection; photo by Paul J. DeSarbo)

Fourth from top: Silver-mounted presentation-grade Model 1902 saber for all officers. The crest of the Virginia Military Institute and the seal of the state of Virginia are on the scabbard. (Susan Di Camillo collection; photo by Paul J. DeSarbo)

Above: Silver-mounted presentation-grade Model 1902 saber for all officers with the state seal of Rhode Island on the hilt. (Susan Di Camillo collection; photo by Paul J. DeSarbo)

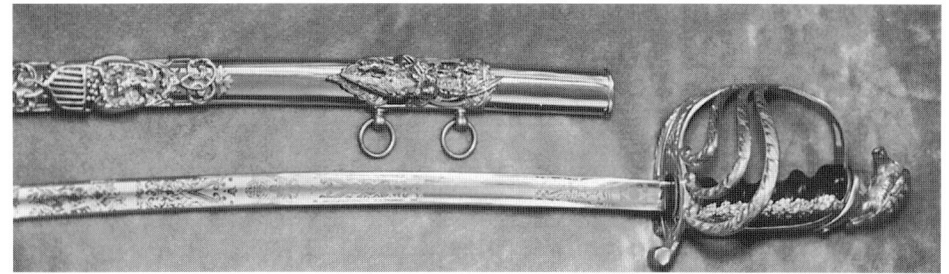

Left: Presentation grade Model 1902 saber for all officers made by C.E. Ward. (Susan Di Camillo collection; photo by Paul J. DeSarbo)

Enlisted Man's Naval Cutlasses

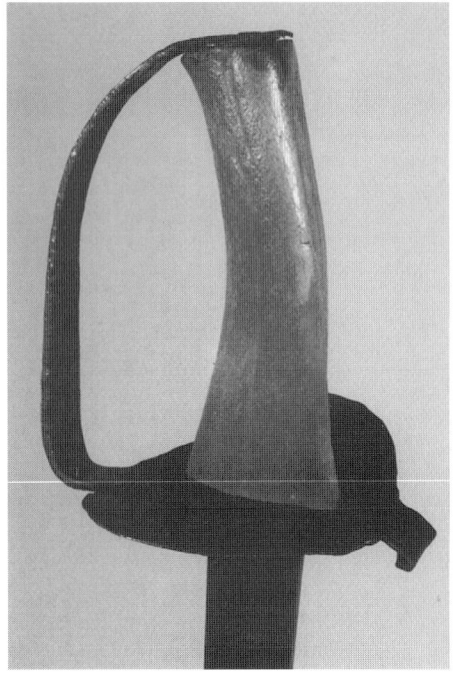

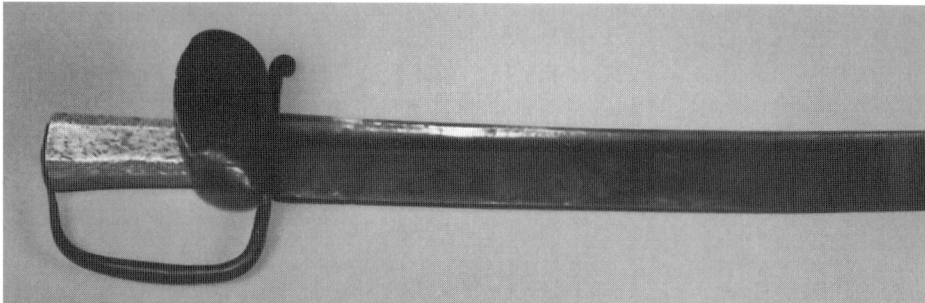

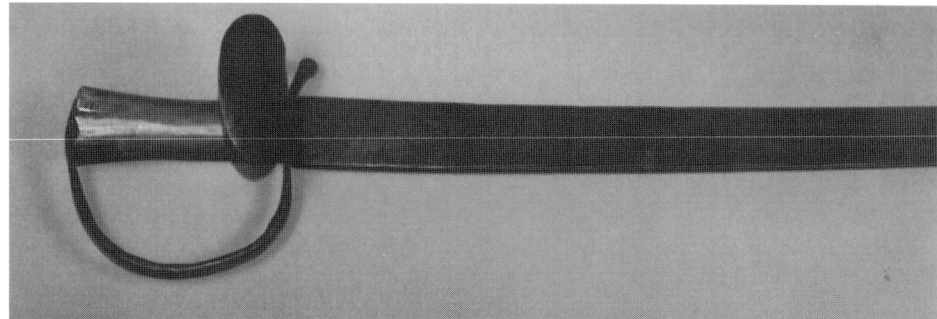

Above: American naval cutlass, c. 1760-1780. (George C. Neumann collection)

Above right: American naval cutlass, c. 1760-1780. (Peter Tuite collection)

Middle: American naval cutlass, c. 1760-1780. (Peter Tuite collection)

Bottom: Naval cutlass probably used by a U.S. privateer. Probably made in Solingen, Prussia, c. 1805-1815. (Peter Tuite collection)

Enlisted Man's Naval Practice Cutlass

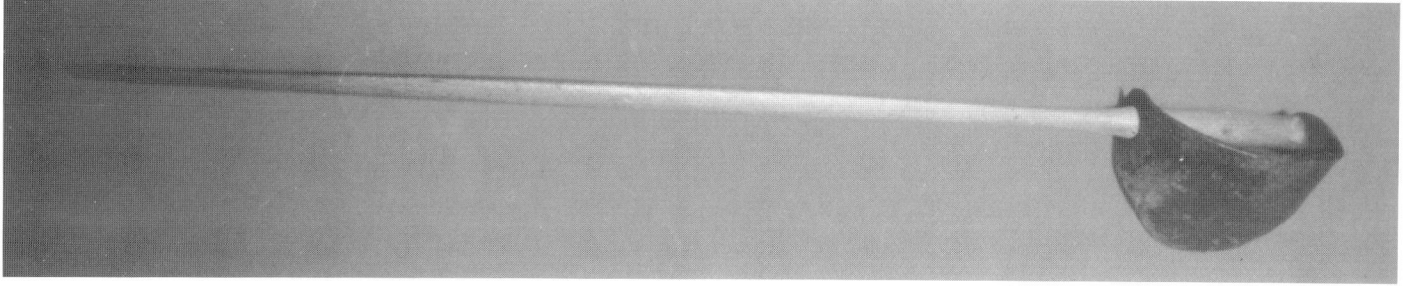

Civil War naval practice cutlass (single stick) with leather hand guard. The wooden blade widens in the middle. (Author's collection)

Naval Officer Swords

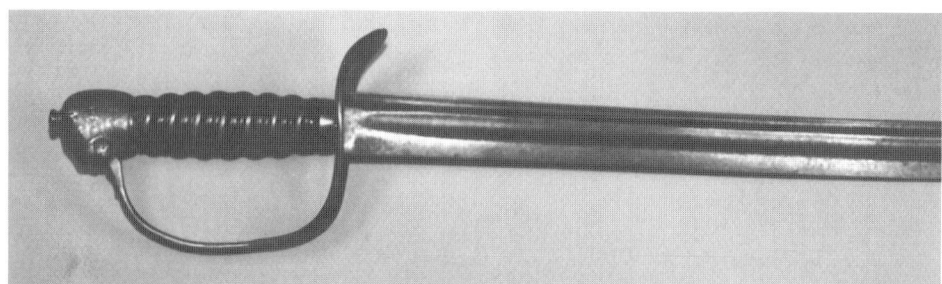

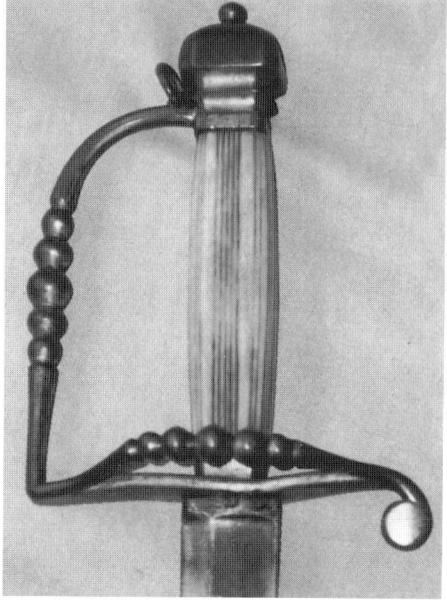

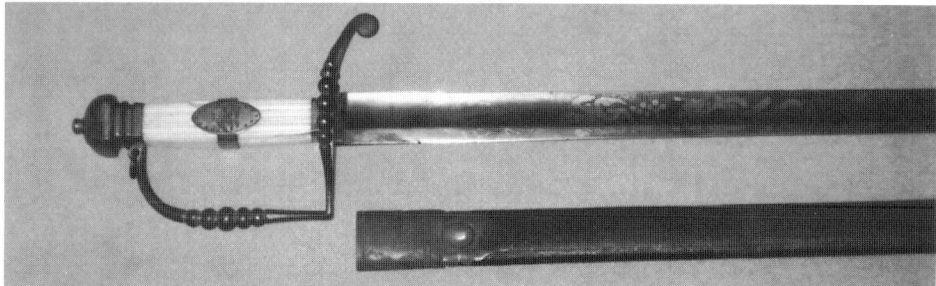

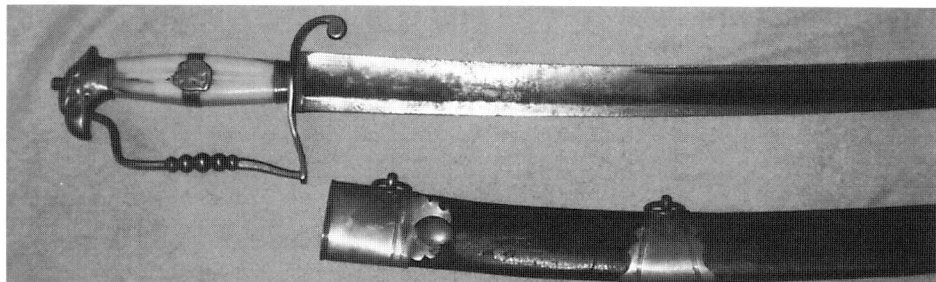

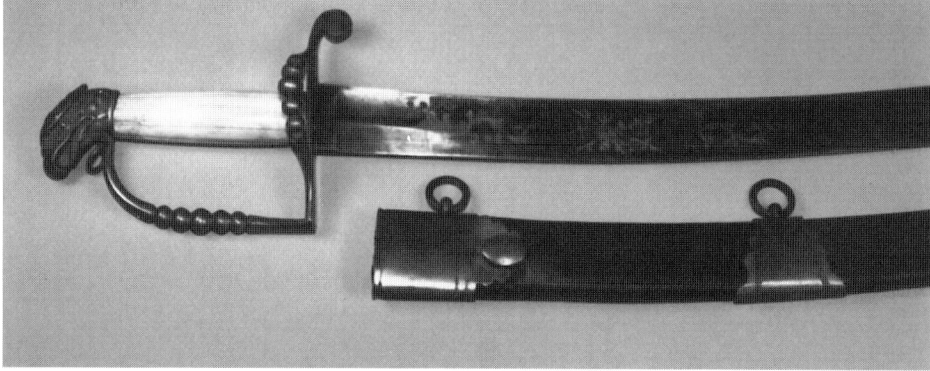

Above: Naval officer sword, c. 1800, with pillow pommel, brass hilt, ivory grip, and eagle on 32″ blade. Made in England for the American market. (Grafton H. Cook II collection)

Top left: Naval officer sword, c. 1795, with split-and-divided guard and lion-head pommel. (Peter Tuite collection)

Second from top: Naval officer sword, c. 1800, with pillow pommel, five-ball knuckle bow and guard, and eagle and anchor on grip medalion. (Peter Tuite collection)

Third from top: Naval officer sword, c. 1805, with eagle-head pommel and eagle and anchor on grip medalion. Maker: George Armitage. (Peter Tuite collection)

Bottom: Naval officer sword, c. 1815-1820, with eagle-head pommel. (Peter Tuite collection)

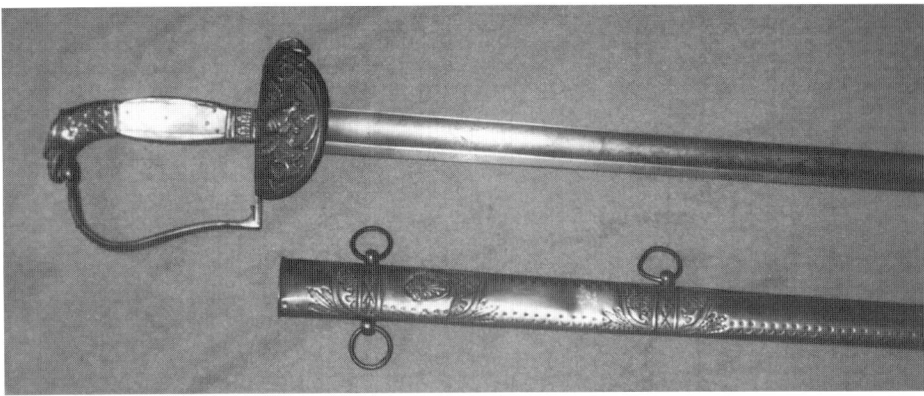

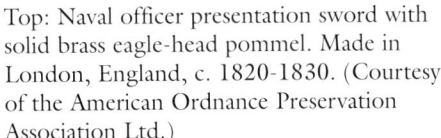

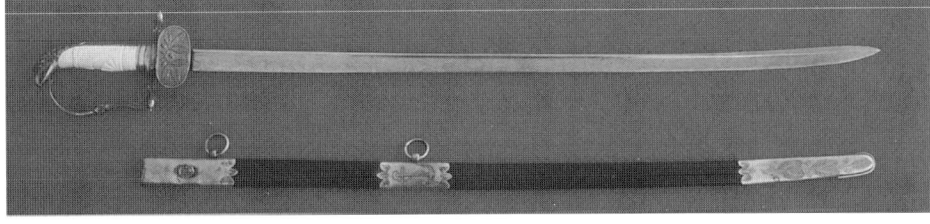

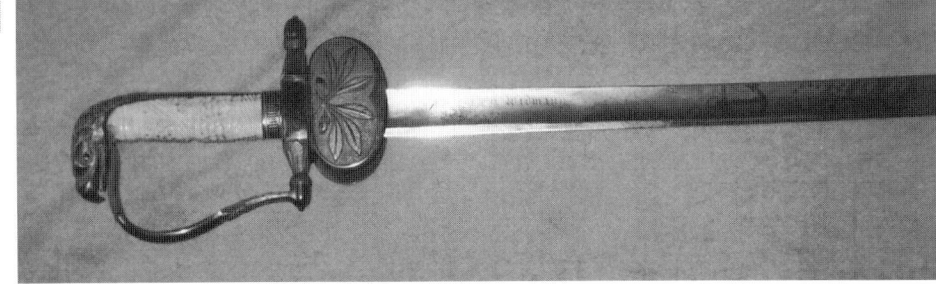

Top: Naval officer presentation sword with solid brass eagle-head pommel. Made in London, England, c. 1820-1830. (Courtesy of the American Ordnance Preservation Association Ltd.)

Above: Naval officer sword, c. 1830-1840, with silver over brass eagle-head pommel. (Jan H. Zajac collection)

Top: Naval officer sword, c. 1830-1840, with eagle-head pommel. Maker: P.D. Luneschloss, Solingen, Prussia. (Peter Tuite collection)

Second from top: Naval officer sword, c. 1830-1840, with Indian princess pommel, spread eagle on an anchor on the shell guard, and engraved blade and scabbard. (Peter Tuite collection)

Third from top: Model 1841 naval officer sword with quill-back blade made by the Ames Manufacturing Co.

Fourth from top: Model 1841 variation naval officer sword with large eagle-head pommel and engraved blade with a large fuller. Maker: F.W. Widmann. (Peter Tuite collection)

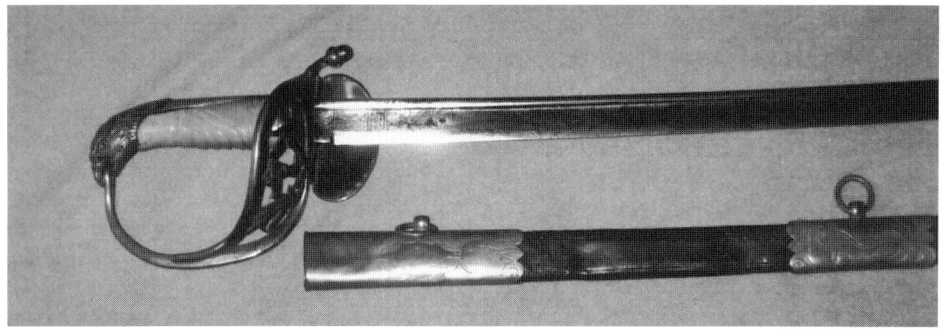

Top: Naval officer sword, c. 1845, with eagle-head pommel and carved ivory grip. Dealer: William Horstmann & Sons. (Peter Tuite collection)

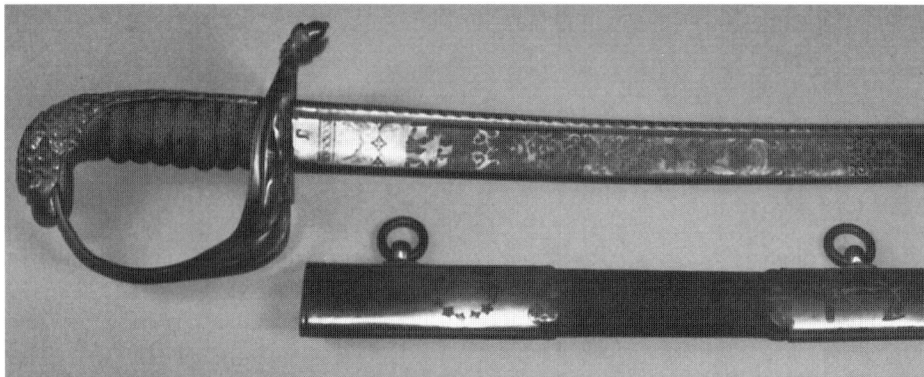

Second from top: High-grade naval officer sword, c. 1845, with eagle-head pommel and very rare Damascus pattern-welded blade (blued and gilt). Scabbard mounts are decorated with a star circle and anchor. (Peter Tuite collection)

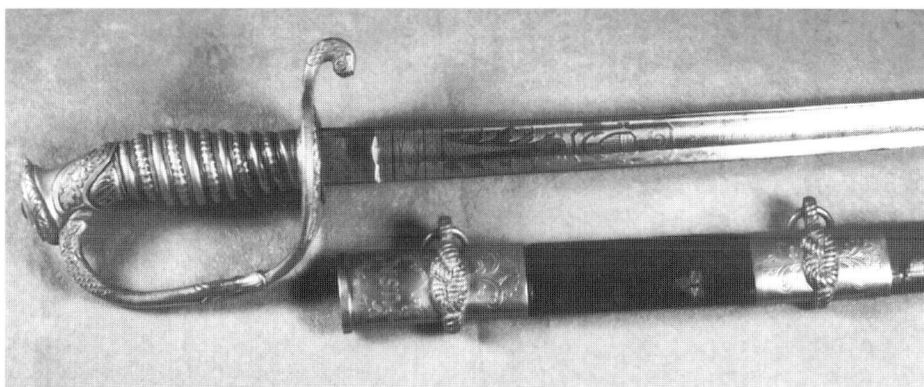

Third from top: Presentation-grade Model 1852, naval officer sword. Made in Solingen, Prussia, and imported by William Price & Co., New York, NY.

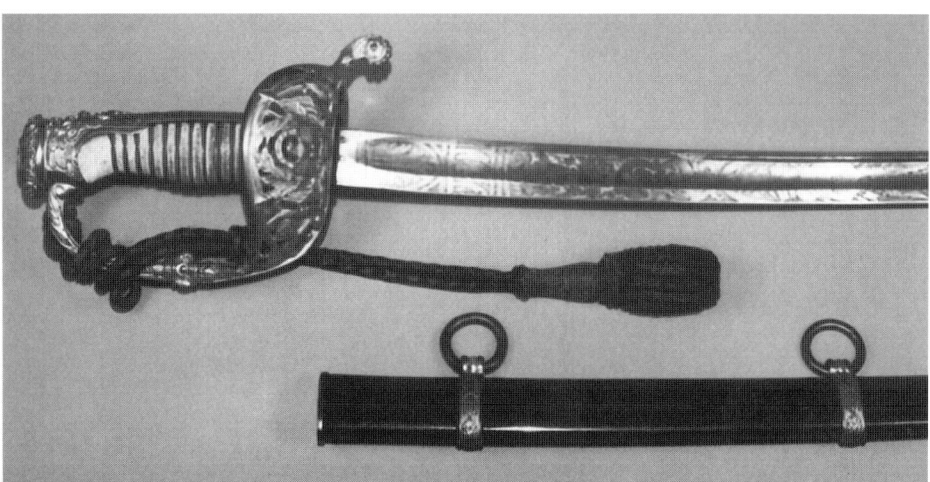

Bottom: Very rare Civil War naval officer nonregulation presentation sword made in Klingenthal, Alsace. (Peter Tuite)

Top: Civil War nonregulation naval officer sword marked "V. Labuna—Napoli, 1864." The hilt has an eagle on an anchor. (Kevin T. Hoffman collection)

Second from top: Civil War nonregulation naval officer sword with eagle-head pommel and Gothic hilt. Maker: Lees & Son, London, England. (Kevin T. Hoffman collection)

Third from top: Model 1852 Civil War presentation naval officer sword presented to Capt. Charles Wilkes, captain of U.S.S. *San Jacinto*. Maker: Shreve, Stanwood, Boston, MA. (Courtesy of David V. Stroud, Smithsonian Institution Collection)

Bottom: Model 1852 presentation-grade naval officer sword presented to F. Schultz by the petty officers of the U.S.S. *New Hampshire*. (Susan Di Camillo collection; photo by Paul J. DeSarbo)

Below: High-grade Model 1852 presentation naval officer sword, c. 1910. Maker: C.E. Ward. (Susan Di Camillo collection; photo by Paul J. DeSarbo)

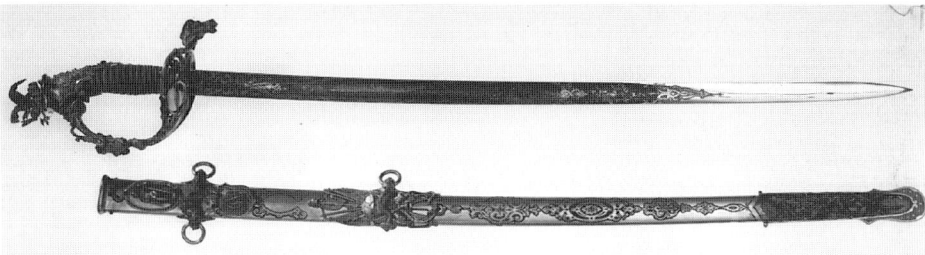

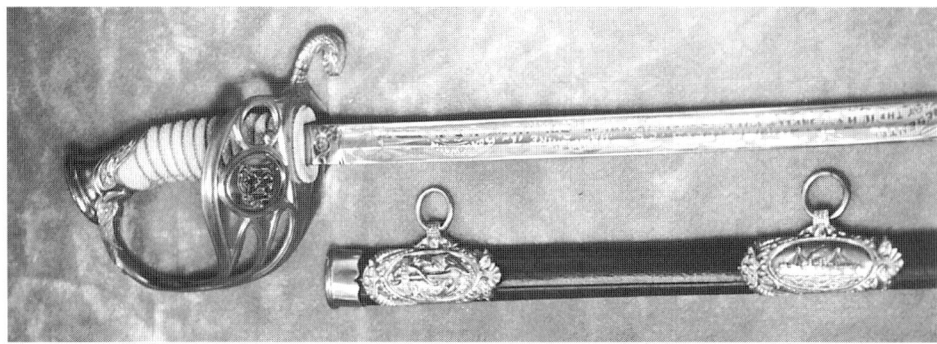

Revenue Cutter Service Officer Swords

Marine Corps Swords

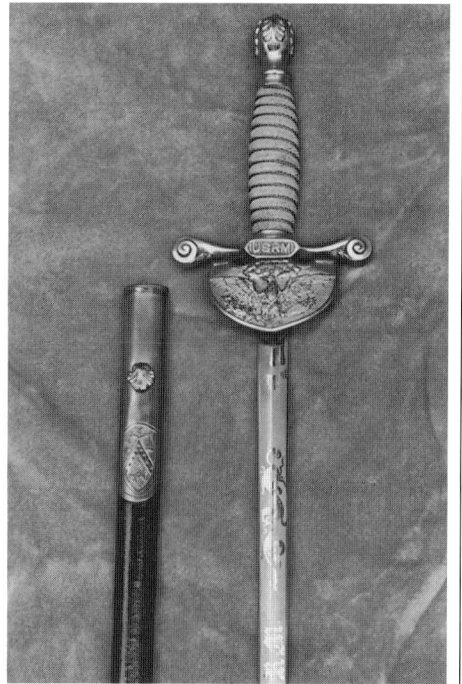

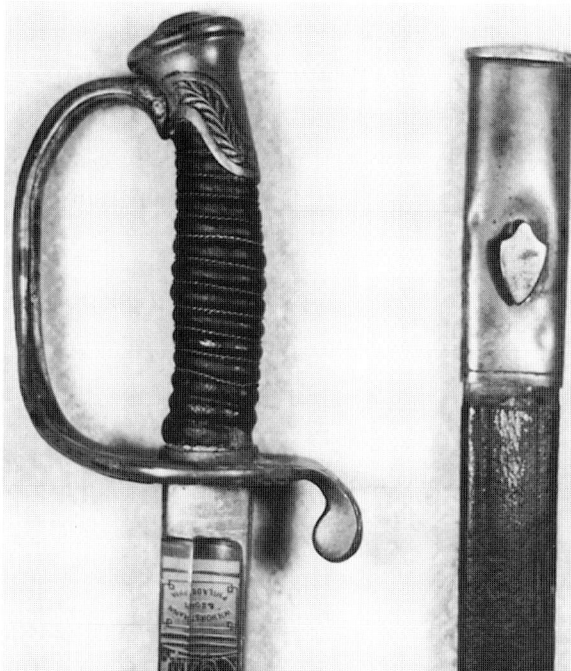

Left: Marine Corps Regulation of 1859 non-comm. officer sword. Maker: W.H. Horstmann & Sons. (C. Philip Johnson Jr. collection; photo by Bob Joseph)

Second from top: Blade marking on Marine Corps non-comm. sword.

Third from top: Very rare Marine Corps Civil War musician's sword. (Kevin T. Hoffman collection)

Bottom: Blade marking on Marine Corps musician's sword.

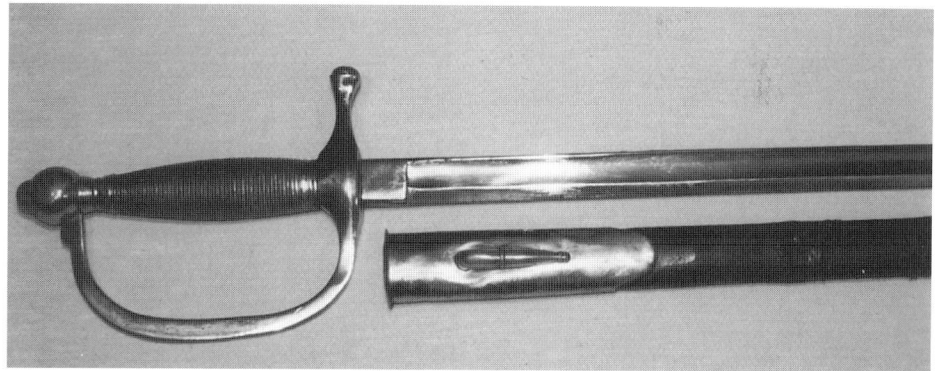

Top: Model 1834 Revenue Cutter Service officer sword made by the Ames Sword Co. (Susan Di Camillo collection; photo by Paul J. DeSarbo)

Above: Model 1834 Revenue Cutter Service officer sword made by W.H. Horstmann & Sons. (Kevin T. Hoffman collection)

295

U.S. Sword Photos

Right: Early Marine Corps officer saber, c. 1804-1820, with crude eagle-head pommel and solid brass hilt. (Kevin T. Hoffman collection)

Bottom right: Regulation of 1875 presentation-grade Marine Corps officer saber with brass Mameluke hilt. Maker: W.H. Horstmann & Sons. (Kevin T. Hoffman collection)

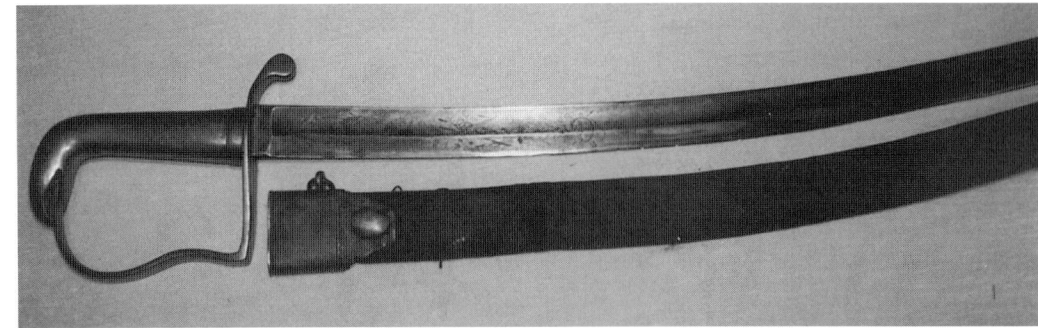

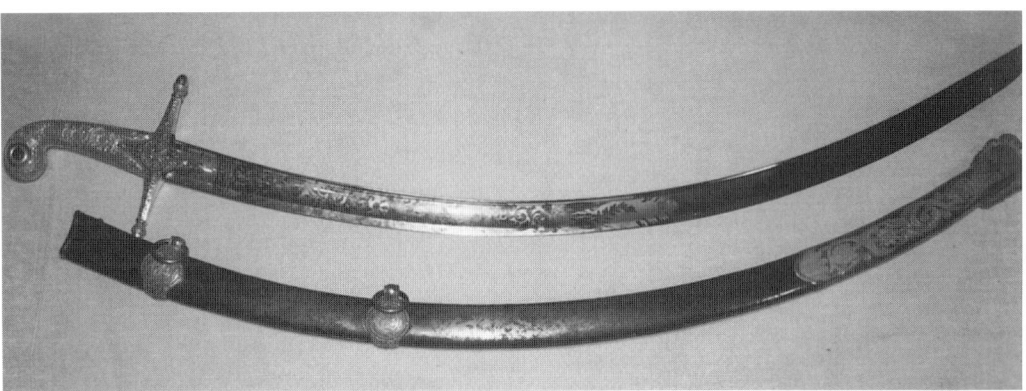

Diplomat's Swords

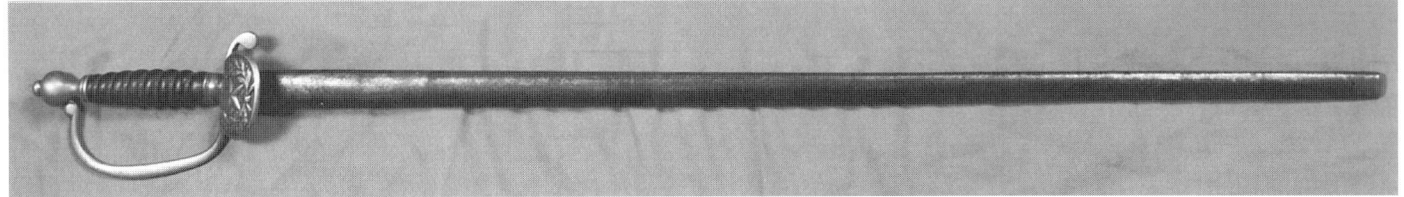

Republic of Texas diplomat's sword with Texas seal on langet and 25 1/4″ blade. (Bob M. Owens collection)

Close-up of hilt of Republic of Texas diplomat's sword.

Diplomat's sword, c. 1860, with gilt brass hilt, straight fullered 29 3/4″ blade. Made by the famous French sword maker Coulaux & Cie., Klingenthal, Alsace. (Jan H. Zajac collection)

Diplomat's sword, c. 1820, with brass pommel, wire grip, straight 26″ blade, and the great seal of the United States on the shell guard. A very rare style. (Jan H. Zajac collection)

Medical Officer Swords

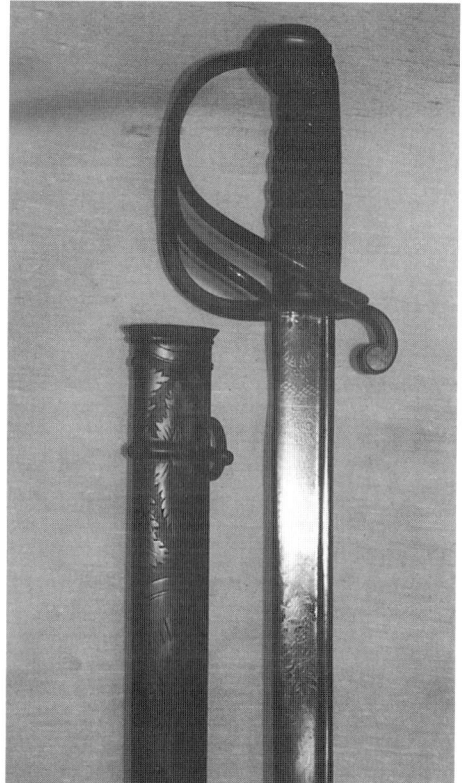

Only known example of the Model 1833 dragoon saber for medical officers. It is shorter than the Model 1833 dragoon saber, and a large medical caduceus is engraved on the blade. (Kevin T. Hoffman collection)

Close-up of the scabbard for the Model 1833 dragoon medical officer saber.

Model 1840 medical officer sword. (Alan Jay Rice collection)

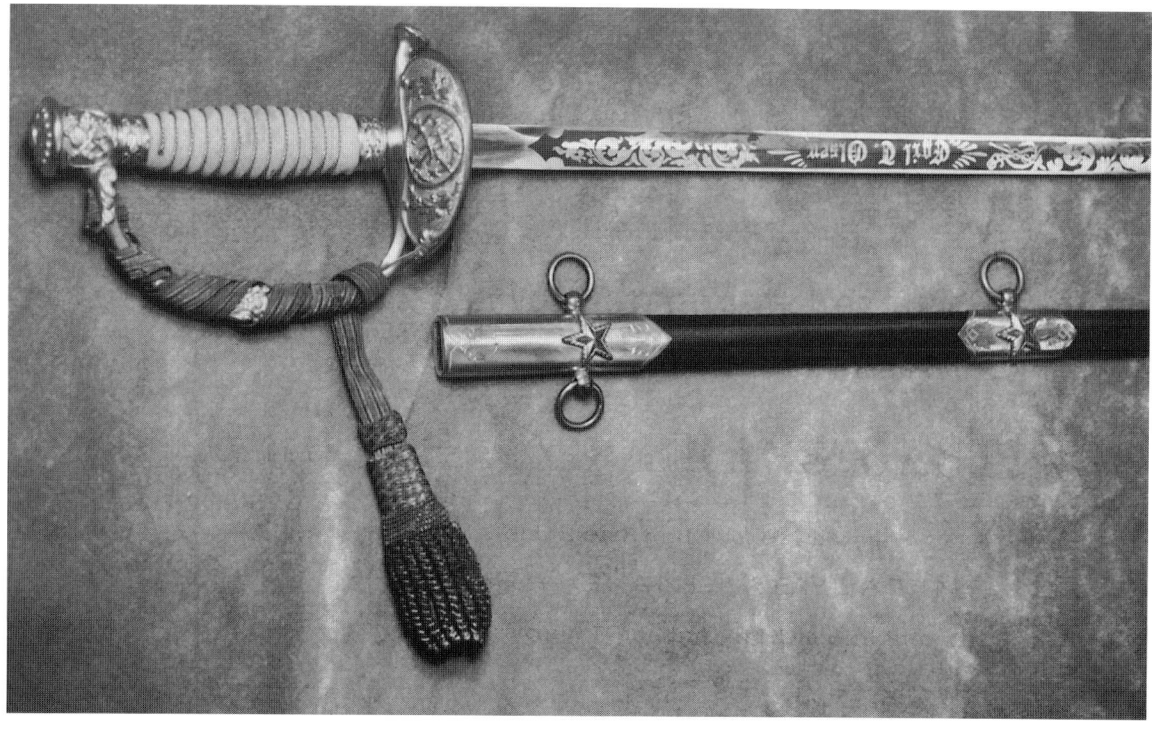

Model 1871 Marine Corps hospital service officer sword. (Susan Di Camillo collection; photo by Paul J. DeSarbo)

Engineer Officer Swords

Right: Model 1839 topographical engineer's sword owned by Col. George Thom. Maker: Ames Manufacturing Co. (Arizona Historical Society collection)

Bottom right: Very rare Model 1840 engineer officer sword with brass hilt and scabbard. (Kevin T. Hoffman collection)

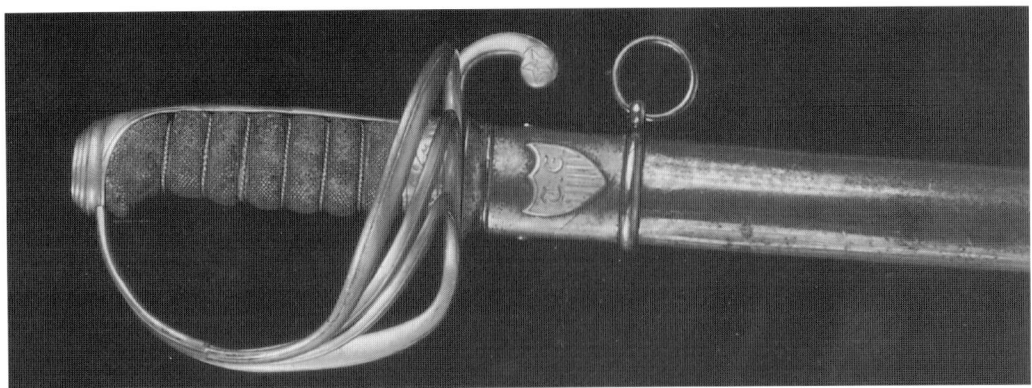

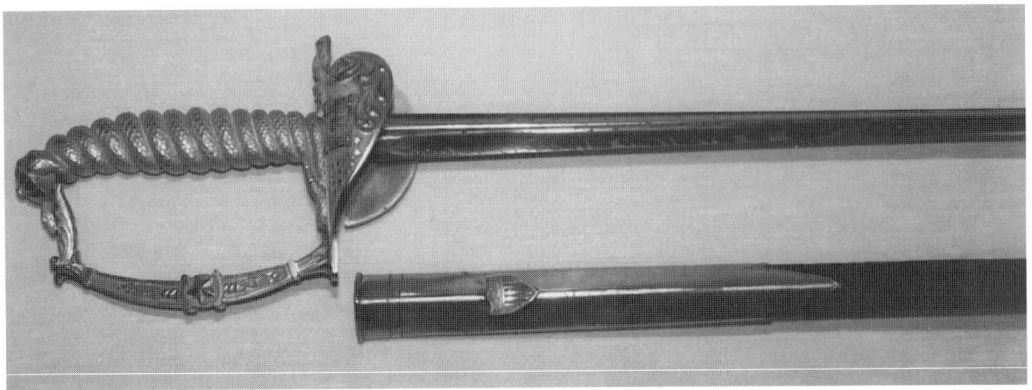

Custom Made Presentation Swords

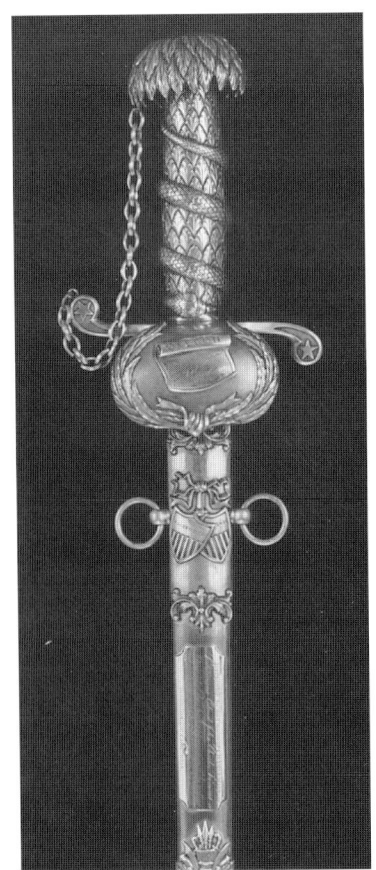

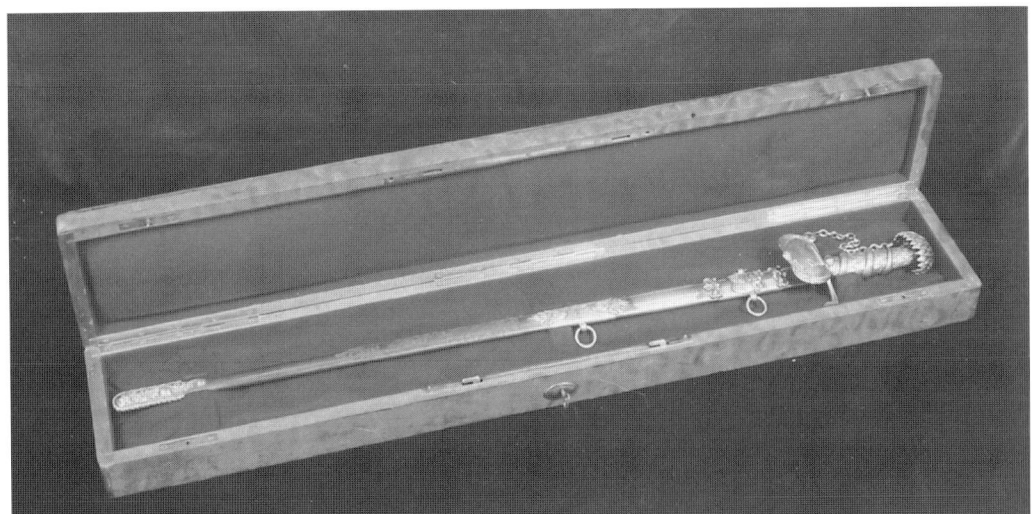

Far left: Sword presented by the citizens of Charleston, SC, to Lt. Col. John Charles Fremont, "a memorial of their high appreciation of the gallantry and science he has displayed in his services in Oregon and California." Maker: Ames Manufacturing Co. (Arizona Historical Society collection)

Above: The Fremont sword in its display box.

Left: Sword guard on the Fremont sword showing a map of Oregon.

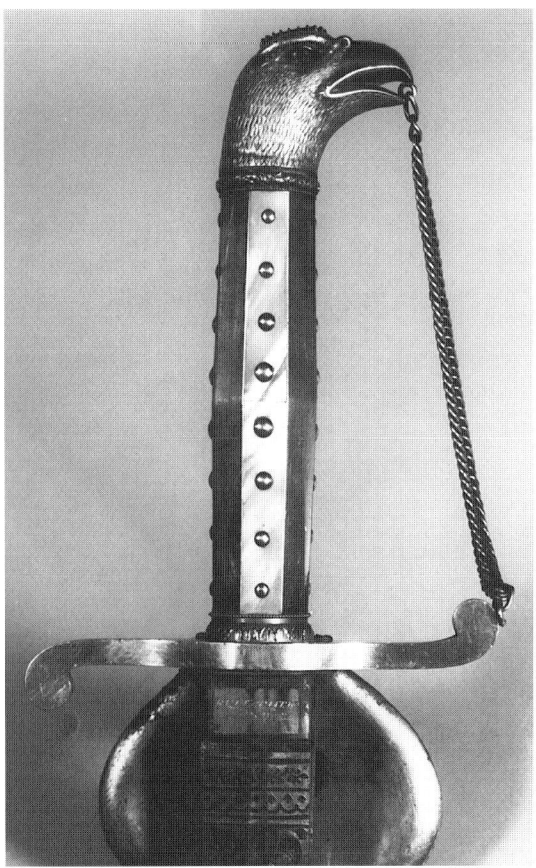

Far left: Sword presented to Maj. Gen. John Anthony Quitman by the citizens of Adams County, April 11, 1848 for his service in the Mexican War. Maker: Rees Fitzpatrick. (Old Capital Museum of Mississippi History collection)

Left: Sword presented to Brig. Gen. David G. Twiggs by President James Polk for his gallantry in storming Monterey during the Mexican War. Maker: Ames Manufacturing Co. (Kevin T. Hoffman collection)

Middle: Sword presented to Maj. Earl Van Dorn by the state of Mississippi "in testimony of her appreciation of the gallantry of her native son in the many battles" (Indian Wars), February 3, 1860. Maker: Rees Fitzpatrick. (Old Capital Museum of Mississippi History collection)

Bottom: Sword presented to Gen. Joseph B. Carr from his friends, September 7, 1862. (Courtesy of the American Ordnance Preservation Assocation Ltd.)

Far right: Presentation-grade Civil War militia officer sword with mother-of-pearl grip. Maker: Ames Manufacturing Co. (Courtesy of Don Ball)

Right: Presentation-grade Civil War militia officer sword made by the Ames Manufacturing Co. (Courtesy of Don Ball)

Bottom: Sword presented to Brig. Gen. G.B. Tyler by a few officers of the 1st and 3rd Brigades, 8th Army Corps, for service in the Civil War. (Kevin T. Hoffman collection)

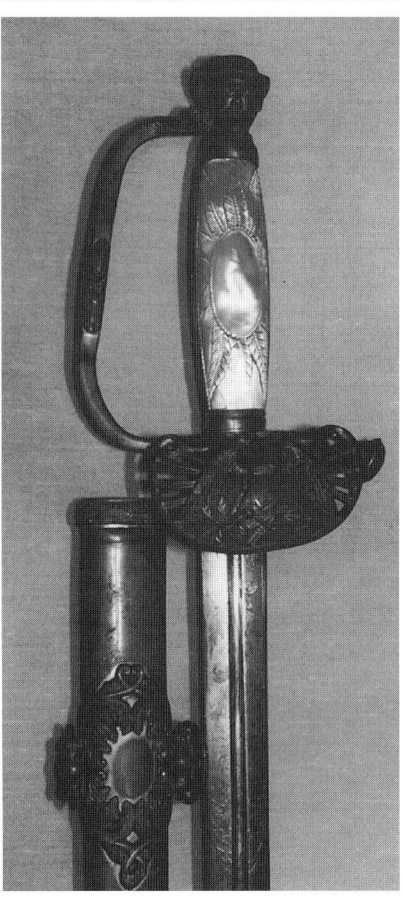

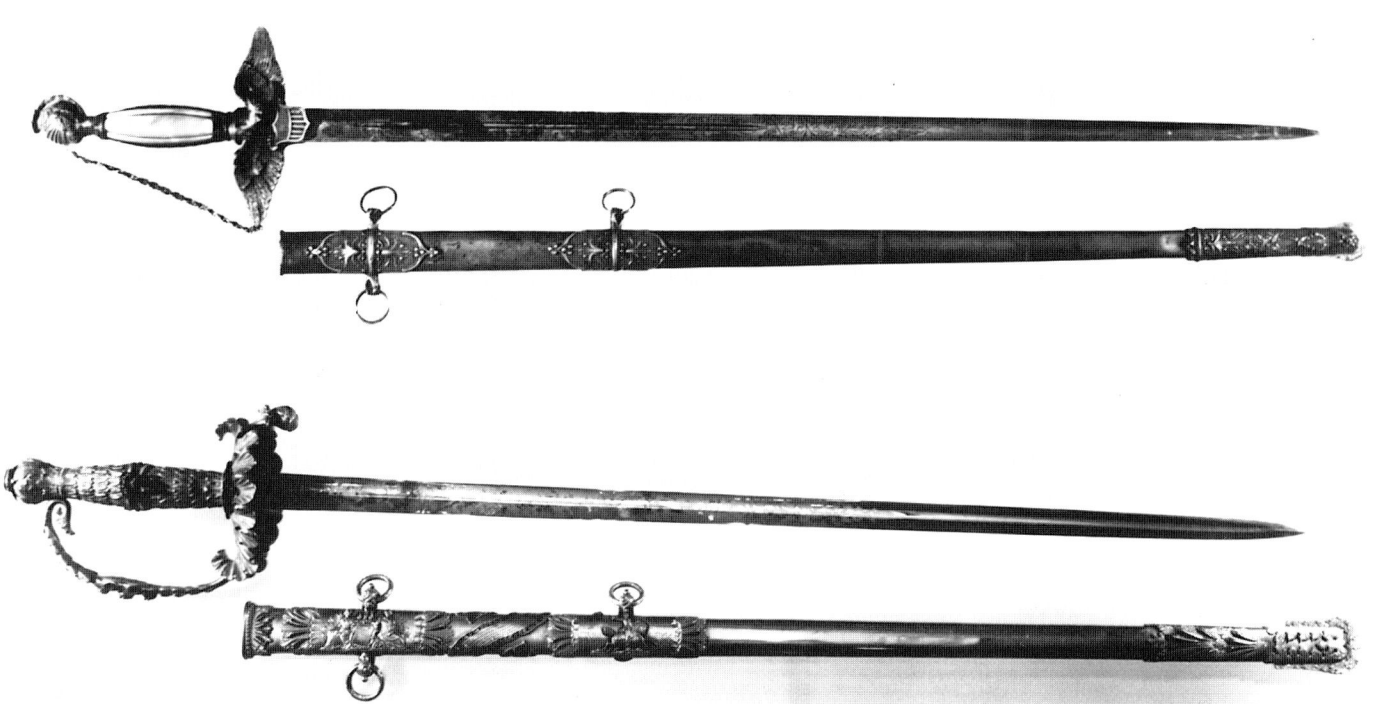

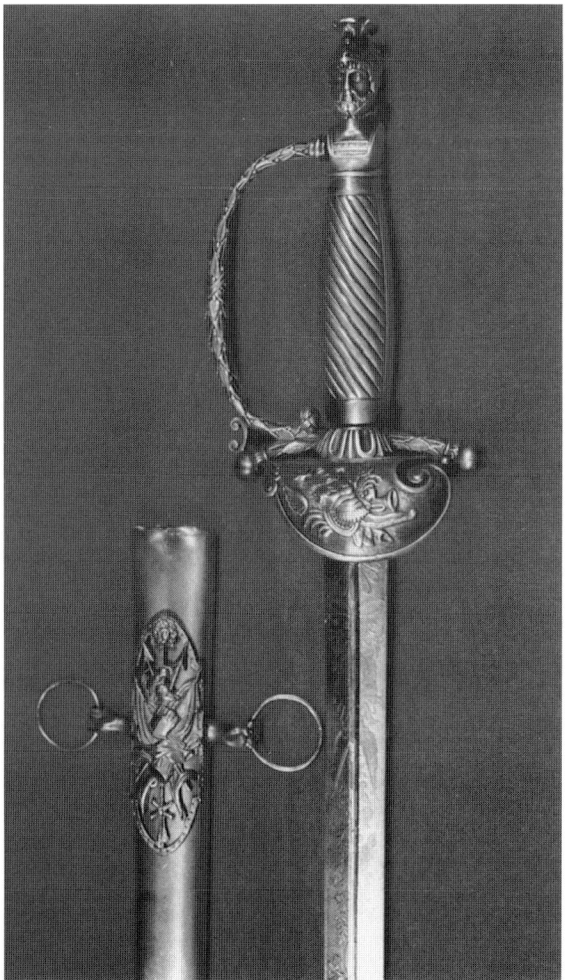

Top: Sword presented to Brig. Gen. Alex McDowell McCook, 2nd Division, from his friend Brig. Gen. Lovell H. Rousseau, for his service in the Civil War. Maker: Ames Manufacturing Co. (West Point Museum collection)

Above: Sword presented to Gen. Charles F. Smith in 1862. Blade made by Collins & Co. Mounted by George W. Simons & Co. (West Point Museum collection)

Left: Sword presented to Adjutant General Lazarus Noble by the officers of the 17th Regiment, Indiana Volunteer Militia, for service in the Civil War. (Thomas L. Jones collection; photo by Thomas L. Jones)

Confederate Sword Photos

Enlisted Men's Cavalry Sabers

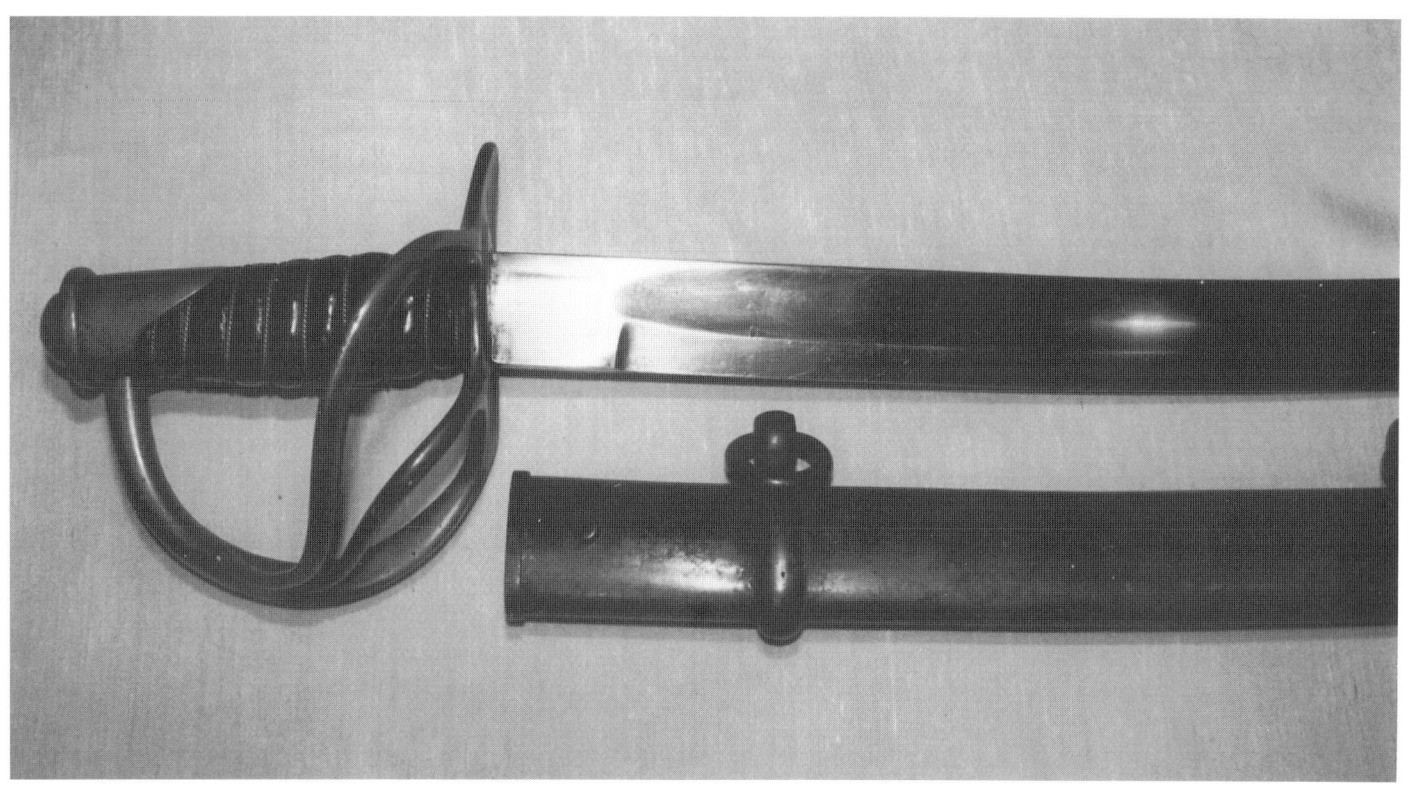

Rare cavalry saber made by unknown maker Meyer & Linz, Louisville, KY. (Kevin T. Hoffman collection)

Left: Maker's mark on Myer & Linz cavalry saber.

Right: Cavalry saber with very unusual straight blade. Maker: Leech & Rigdon, Memphis Novelty Works. (Bob M. Owens collection)

Bottom right: Cavalry saber made by Thomas, Griswold, & Co. (Bob M. Owens collection)

Cavalry Officer Sabers

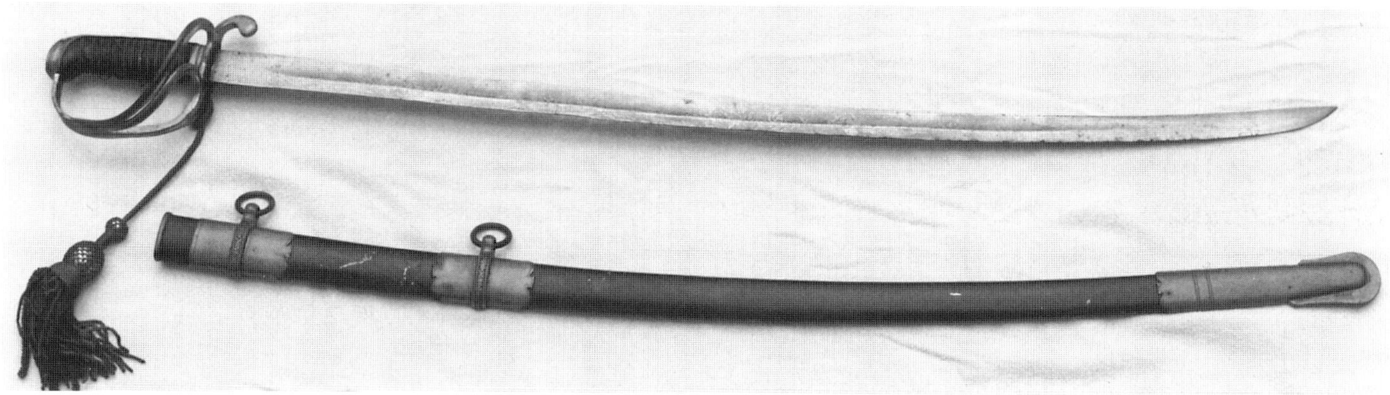

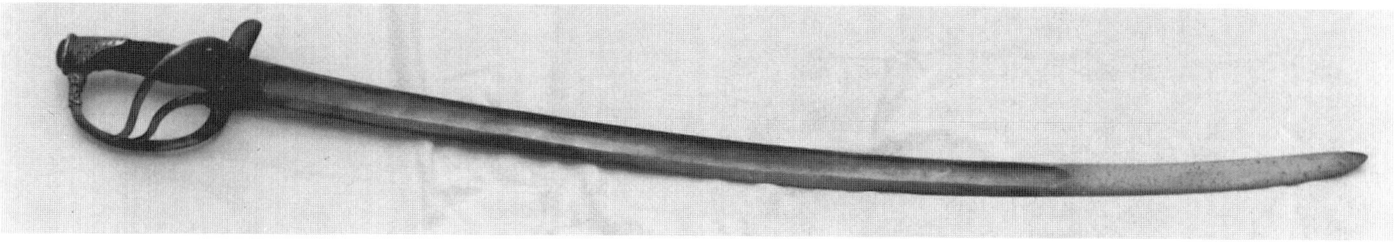

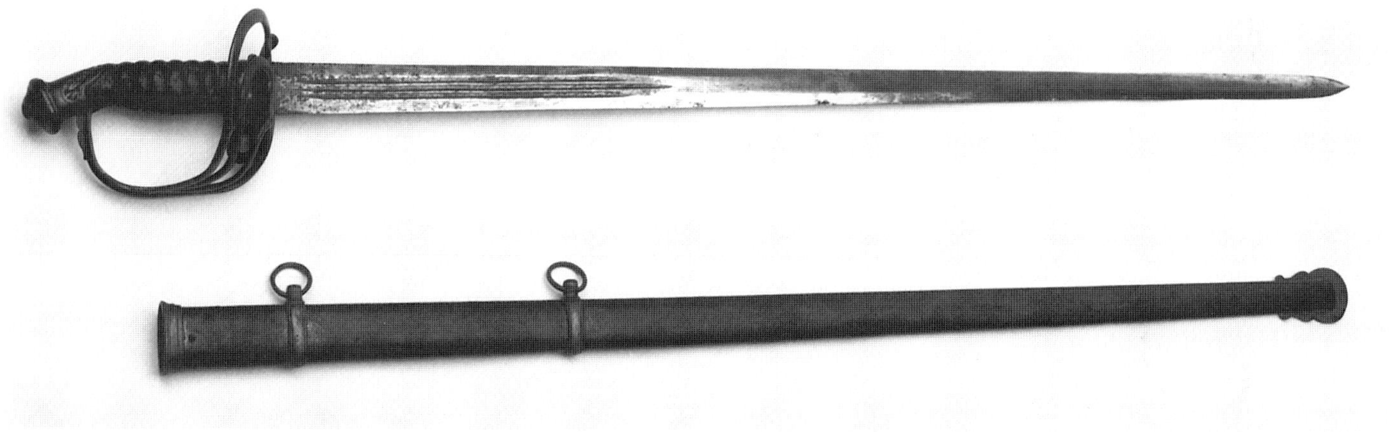

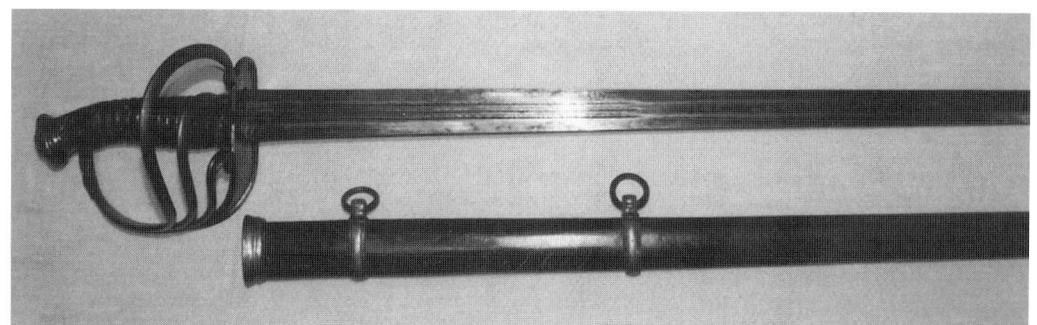

Above: Cavalry officer broadsword presented by Gen. Wade Hampton to his Legion officers. Made by Kraft, Goldsmith, & Kraft, which used imported blades made by Schimmelbusch & Joest, Solingen, Prussia. (Kevin T. Hoffman collection)

Top: Cavalry officer saber made by Louis Haiman & Bro. (Bob M. Owens collection)

Second from top: Cavalry officer saber made by Thomas, Griswold, & Co. (Bob M. Owens collection)

Third from top: Cavalry broadsword owned by Gen. Wade Hampton (Hampton's Legion). Made by Kraft, Goldsmith, & Kraft, which used imported blades made by Schimmelbusch & Joest, Solingen, Prussia. (Museum of the Confederacy collection; photo by Katherine Wetzel)

Enlisted Man's Foot Artillery Sword

Enlisted man's foot artillery sword marked "Mekin" on the guard. (Kevin T. Hoffman collection)

Mounted Artillery Officer Saber

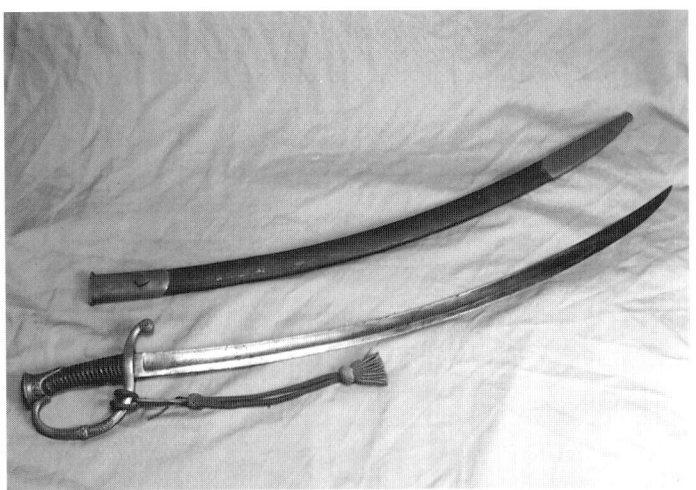

Mounted artillery officer saber made by A.H. Dewitt. (Bob M. Owens collection)

Foot Officer Swords

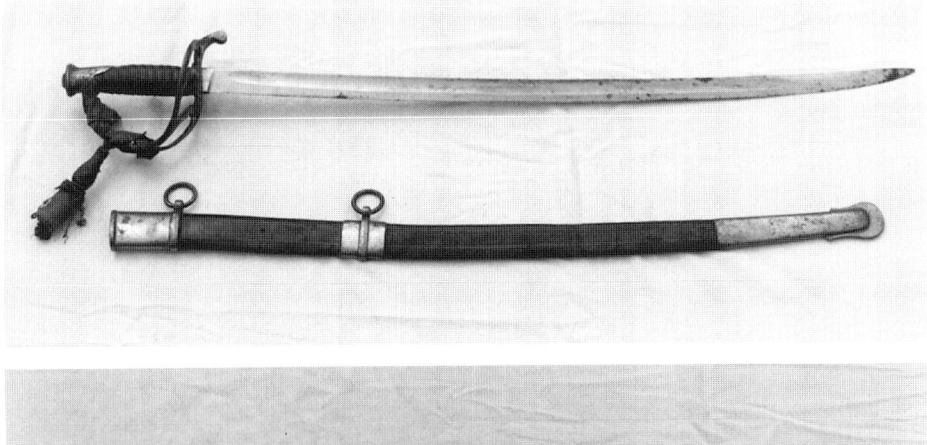

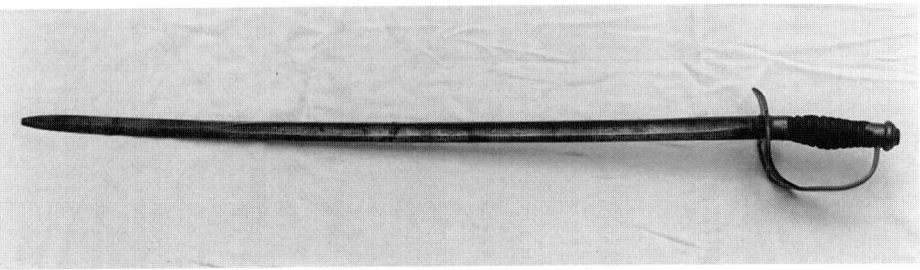

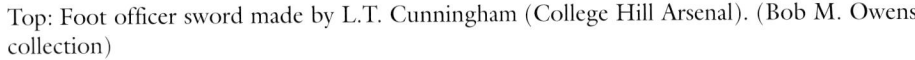

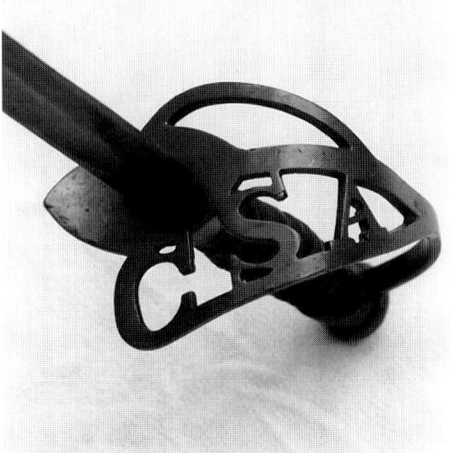

Top: Foot officer sword made by L.T. Cunningham (College Hill Arsenal). (Bob M. Owens collection)

Top right: Close-up of hilt on the College Hill Arsenal foot officer sword.

Above: Foot officer sword made by Louis Froelich. (Bob M. Owens collection)

Right: Close-up of hilt on the Froelich foot officer sword.

Top: Foot officer sword made by Leech & Rigdon (Memphis Novelty Works). (Bob M. Owens collection)

Second from top: Close-up of hilt on Leech & Rigdon foot officer sword showing "C.S." on the guard.

Third from top: Foot officer sword made by A.H. Dewitt. (Bob M. Owens collection)

Bottom: Close-up of hilt on Dewitt foot officer sword.

Right: Foot officer sword made by Blaise Pradel Jr. (marked on blade). (Bob M. Owens collection)

Below: Presentation-grade foot officer sword with ivory grips. (Courtesy of Don Ball)

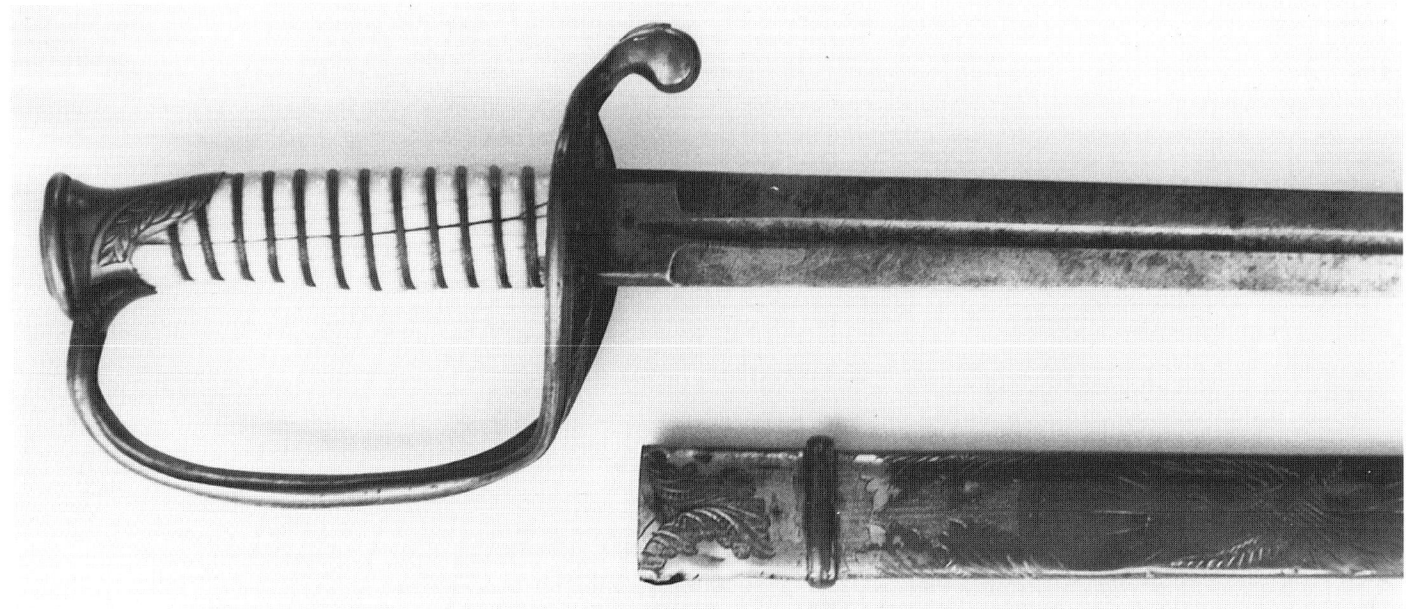

Staff and Field Officer Swords

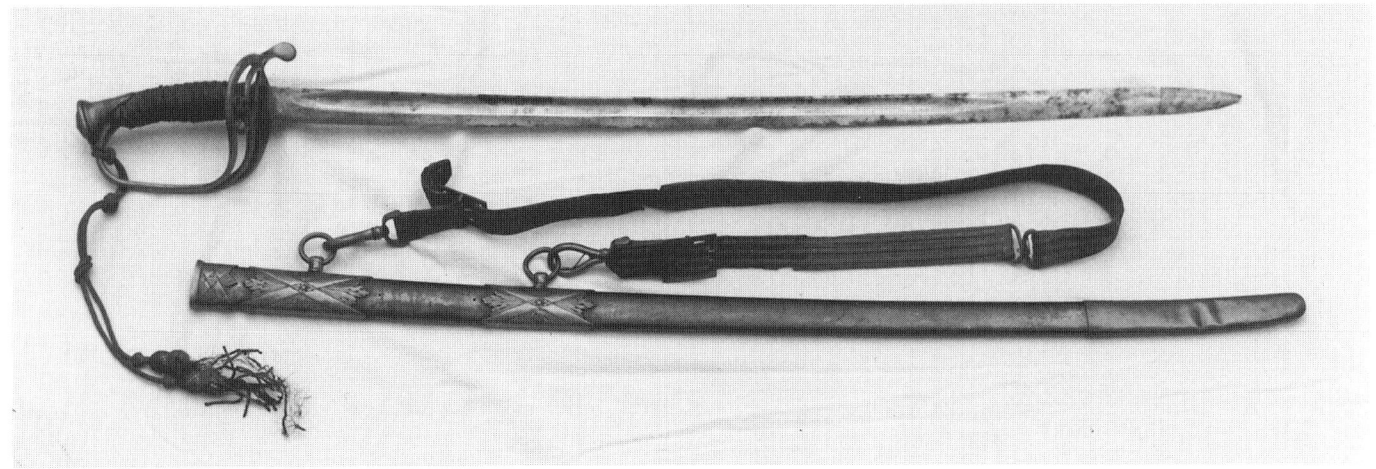

Staff and field officer sword made by Leech & Rigdon (Memphis Novelty Works). (Bob M. Owens collection)

Staff and field officer sword (hilt #1). Maker: Leech & Rigdon. (Bob M. Owens collection)

Staff and field officer sword (hilt #2). Maker: Leech & Rigdon. (Bob M. Owens collection)

Staff and field officer sword (hilt #3). Maker: Leech & Rigdon. (Bob M. Owens collection)

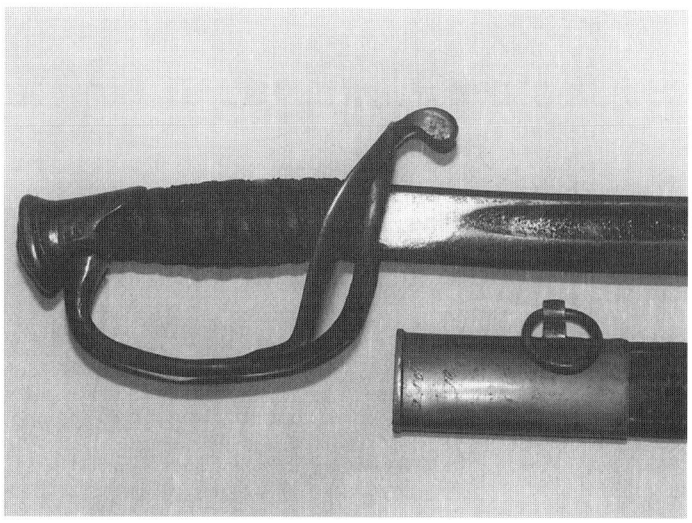
Staff and field officer sword made by Leech & Rigdon (branch added to a foot officer sword). (Kevin T. Hoffman collection)

Staff and field officer sword with two extra branches, attributed to Agrider H. Dufilho Sr. (Kevin T. Hoffman collection)

Staff and field officer sword presented to Capt. William J. Dabney by G.A.L., W.A.A., F.W.D., C.C.D., and J.C. "as a token of regard," 1862. Maker: Boyle & Gamble. (Kevin T. Hoffman collection)

Staff and field officer sword presented to Brig. Gen. Daniel Marsh Frost, Trans Mississippi Department, March 3, 1862. Maker: Boyle & Gamble. (Kevin T. Hoffman collection)

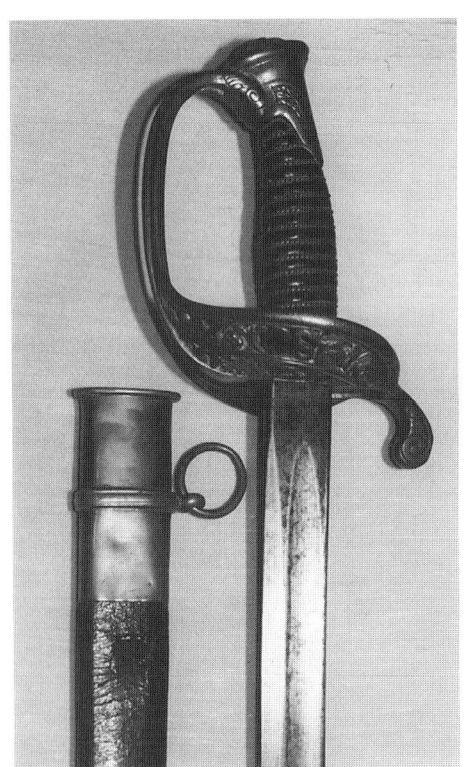

Staff and field officer sword made by James Conning. (Kevin T. Hoffman collection)

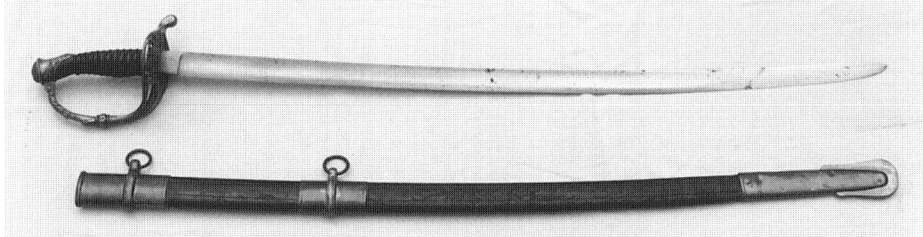

Above: Staff and field officer sword made by Thomas, Griswold, & Co. (Bob M. Owens collection)

Right: Close-up of hilt on Thomas, Griswold, & Co. staff and field officer sword showing very unusual C.S. in script.

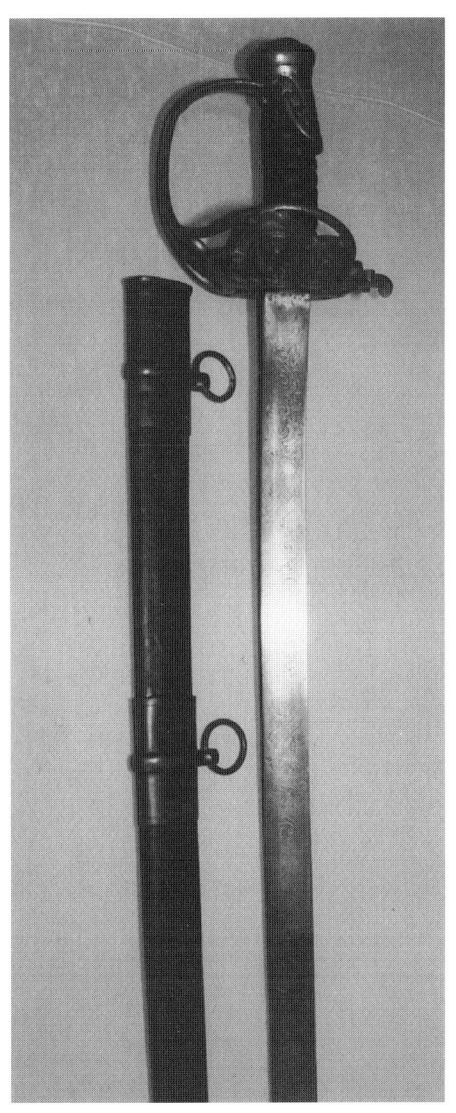

Far left: Staff and field officer sword attributed to Blaise Pradel Jr. with the Louisiana seal on the guard. (Kevin T. Hoffman collection)

Left: Front view of hilt on Pradel staff and field officer sword.

Below left: Staff and field officer sword presented to Capt. A. Hart by his friends, February 22, 1862. Maker: Thomas, Griswold, & Co. (Bob M. Owens collection)

Below: Staff and field officer sword presented to W.U. Garrard, 31st Alabama Volunteers. Maker: Louis Haiman & Co. (Kevin T. Hoffman collection)

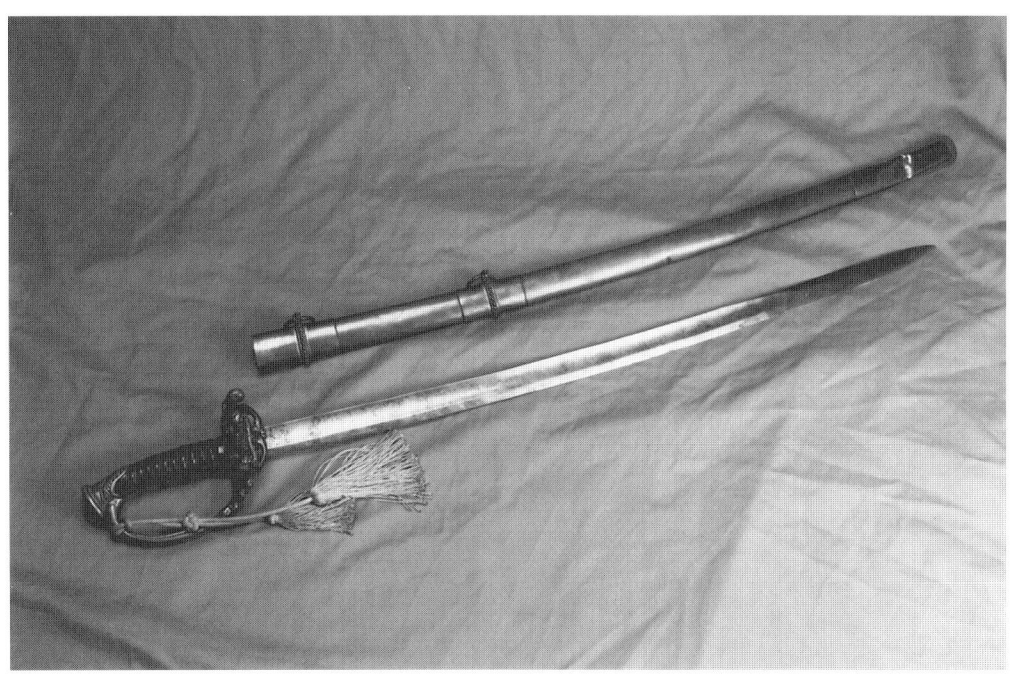

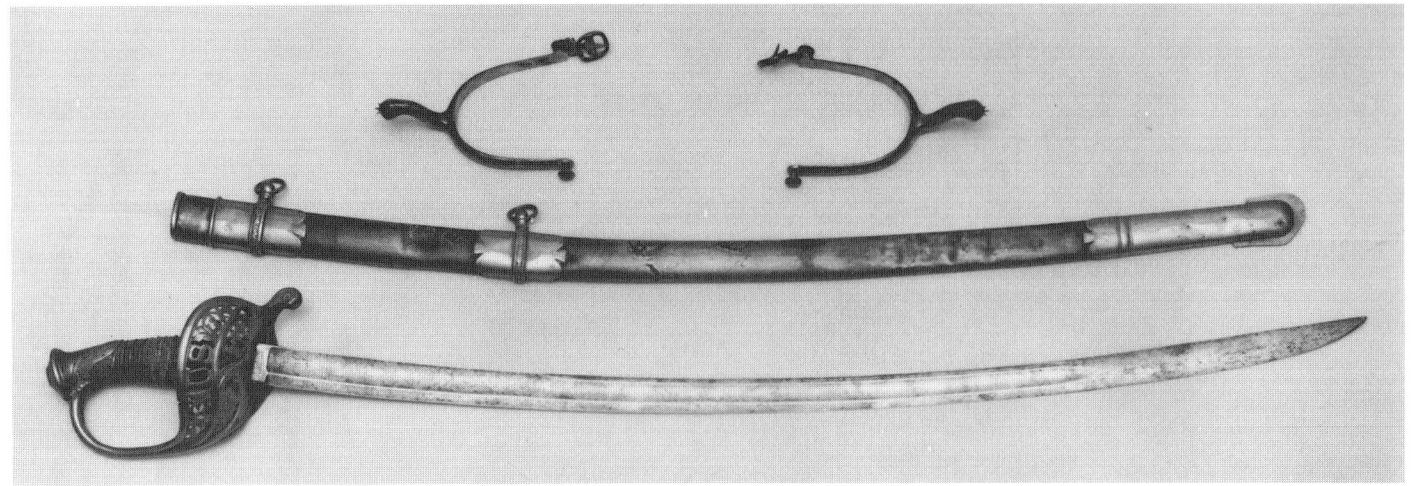

Model 1850 staff and field officer sword and spurs of Gen. Thomas Jonathan "Stonewall" Jackson. (Courtesy of David V. Stroud, the Museum of the Confederacy collection)

Enlisted Men's Naval Cutlasses

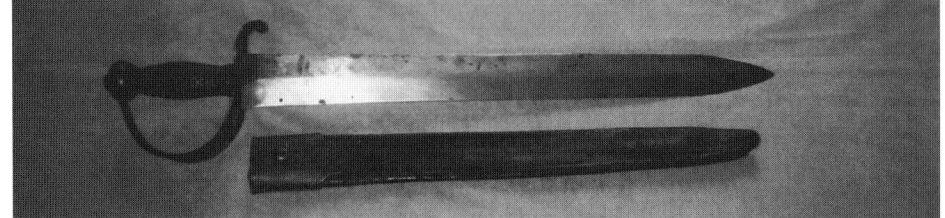

Above: Very rare Confederate naval cutlass. Maker: Cook & Brother. (Kevin T. Hoffman collection)

Above right: Close-up of maker mark on Cook & Brother naval cutlass hilt.

Right: Naval cutlass made by Union Car Works. (Bob M. Owens collection)

Bottom: Naval cutlass with a very rare scabbard. Maker: Cook & Brother. (Peter Tuite collection)

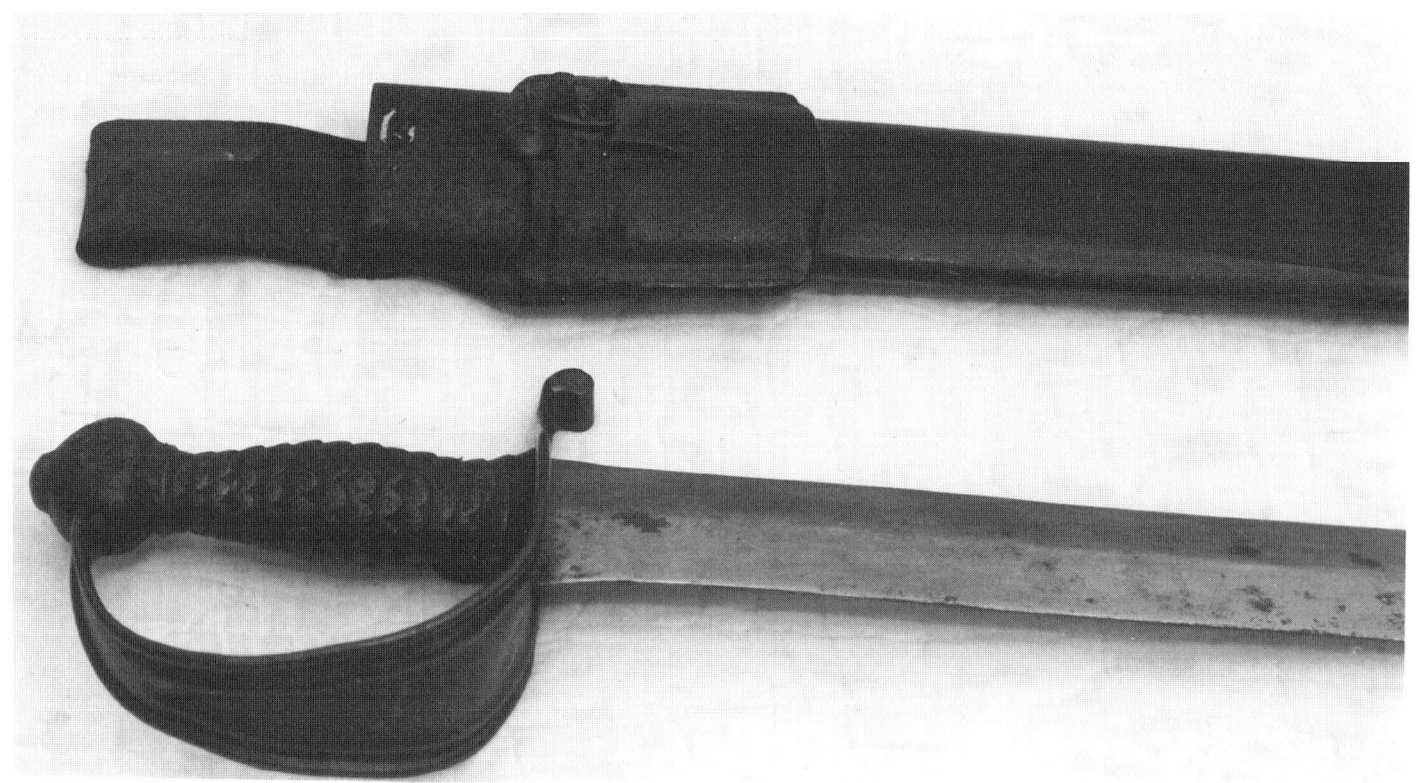

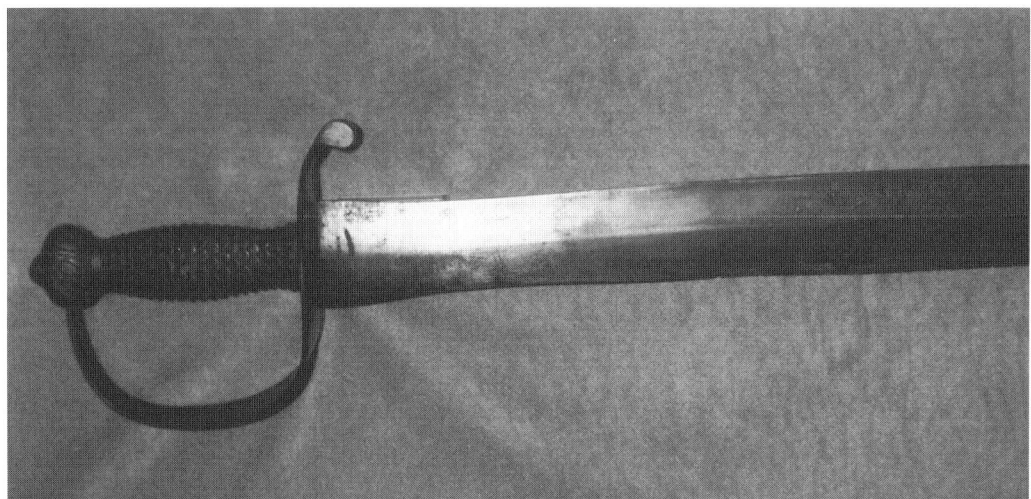

Top: Unmarked naval cutlass with wood scabbard, tin scabbard mounts, cast brass grip and pommel, and sheet brass guard and knuckle bow. (Bob M. Owens collection)

Middle: Naval cutlass made by Thomas, Griswold, & Co. (Peter Tuite collection)

Bottom: Very rare naval cutlass made by Robert Mole & Son, Birmingham, England, using a Model 1853 British cavalry saber hilt. Imported by Courtney & Tennent, Charleston, SC. (Peter Tuite collection)

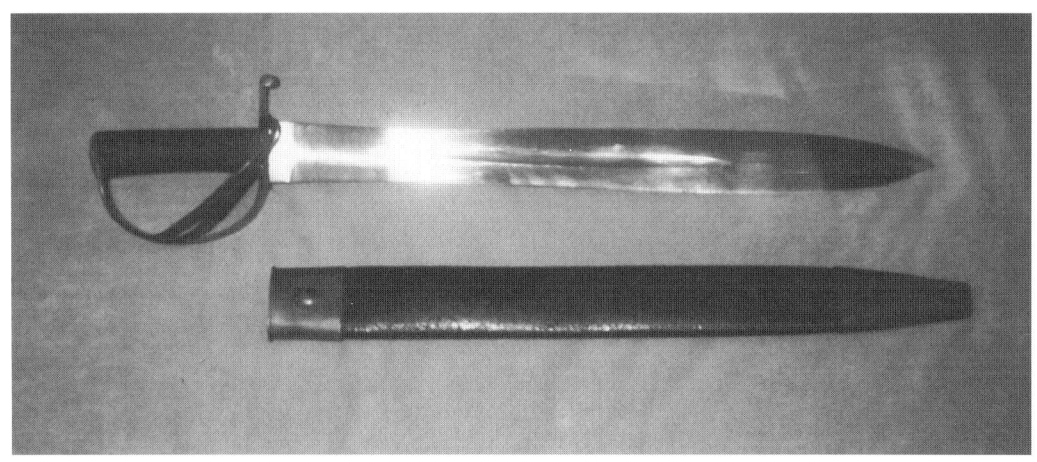

Naval Officer Swords

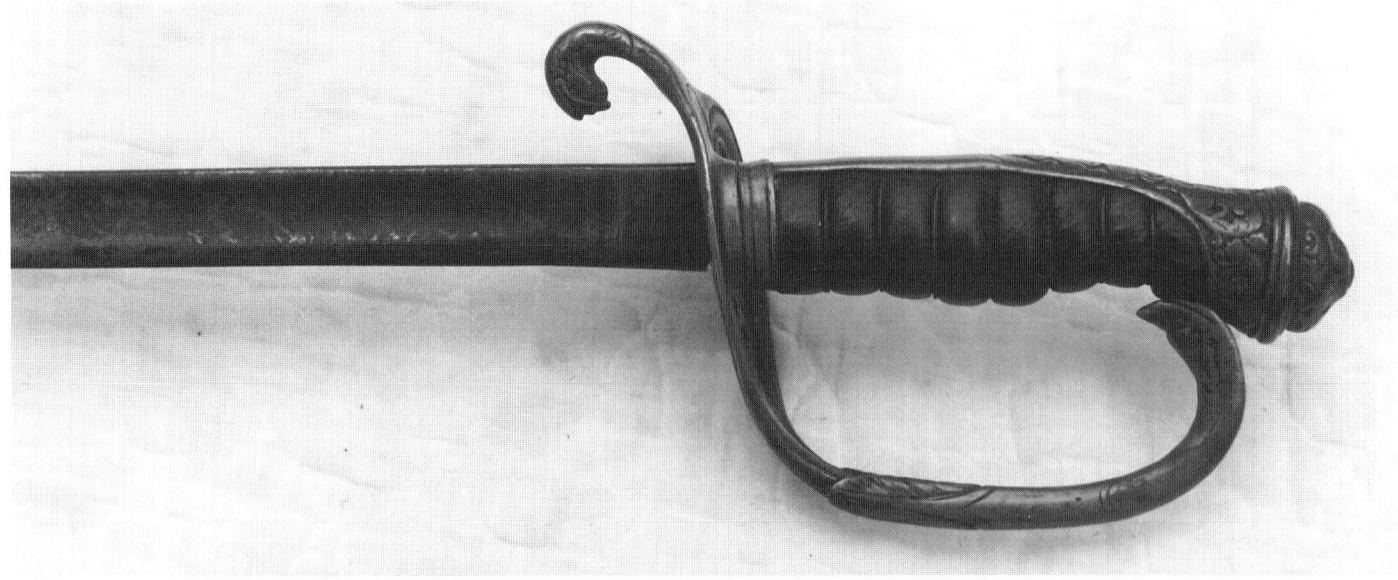

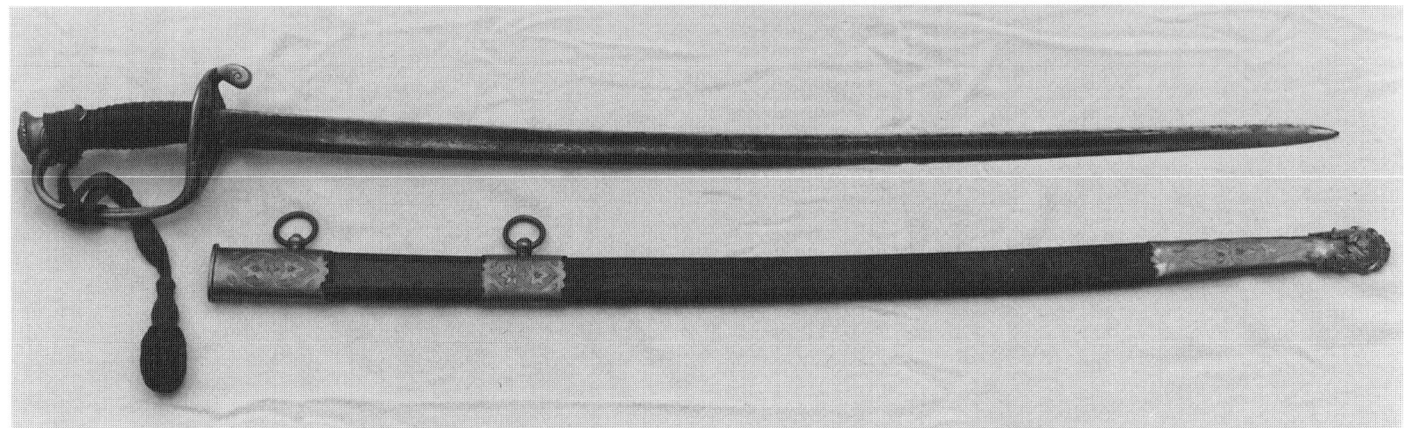

Top: Naval officer sword made by F. Heyer. (Bob M. Owens collection)

Above: Unmarked naval officer sword with silver-plated hilt. (Bob M. Owens collection)

Right: Close-up of hilt on silver-plated naval officer sword.

Musician's Sword

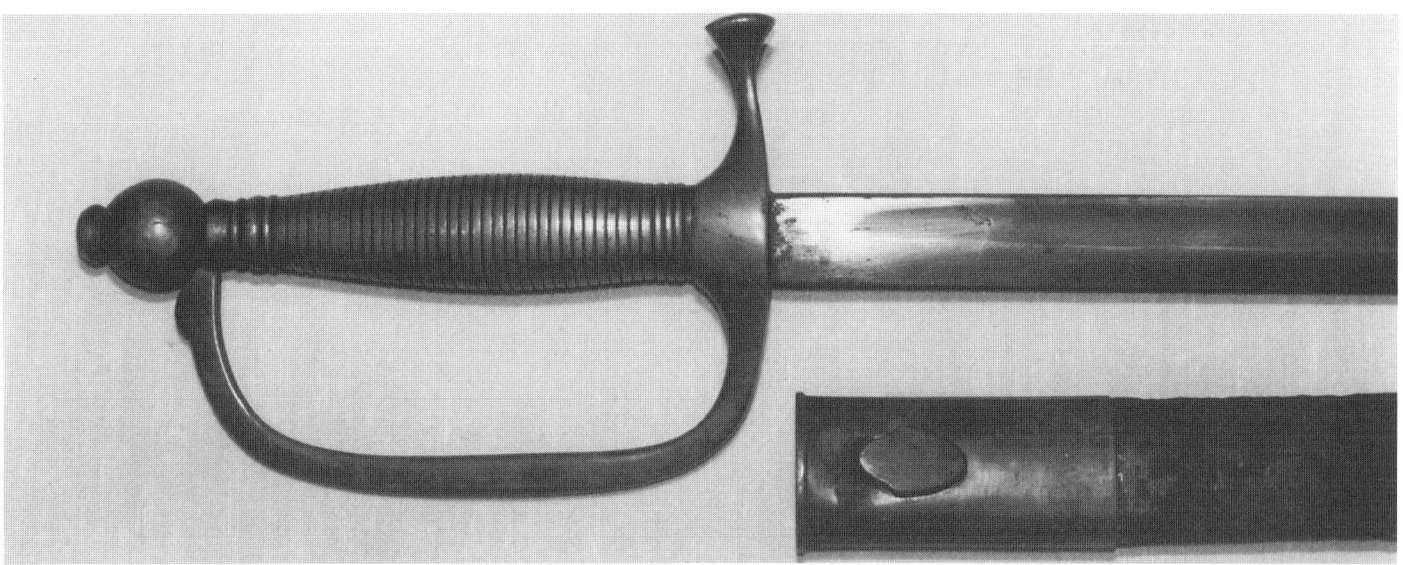

Musician's sword marked "M. Moore—Drummer. Company K, 13th Reg., N.H. Vol." (Kevin T. Hoffman collection)

Custom-Made Presentation Swords

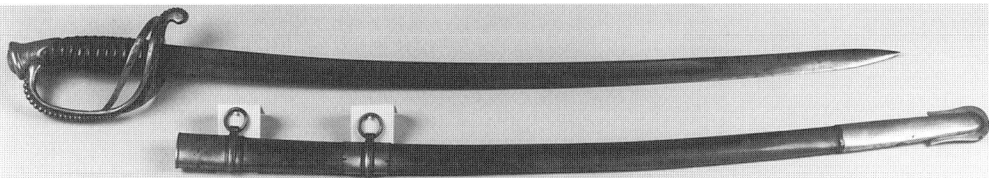

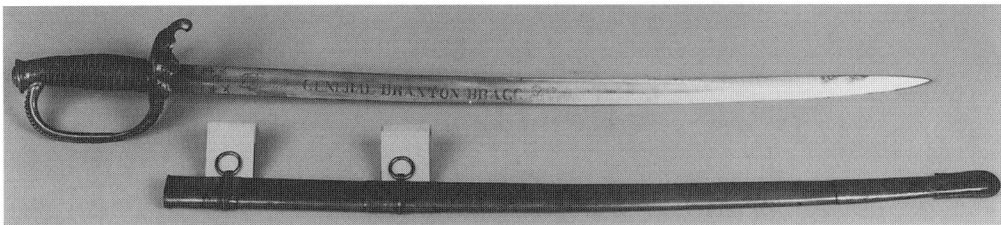

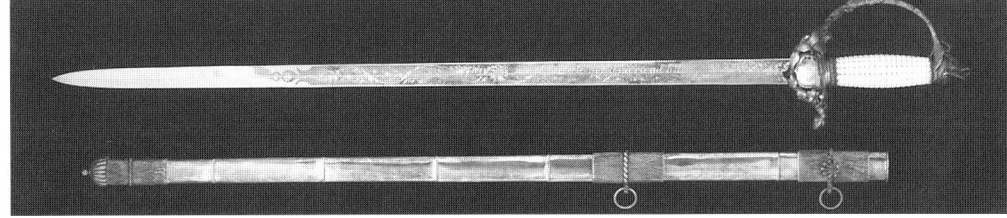

Top: Presentation sword of Gen. Samuel Garland Jr. presented by the Lynchburg, VA, Home Guard in 1860. (Virginia Military Institiue collection. *From Echoes of Glory: Arms and Equipment of the Confederacy,* copyright 1991, Time Life Books Inc. Photo by Larry Sherer, High Impact Photography.)

Second from top: Sword of Gen. Daniel W. Adams, presented to him in July 1861. Maker: Leech & Rigdon. (Confederate Memorial Hall collection; photo by Claude A. Levet)

Third from top: Sword of Gen. Braxton Bragg, presented to him by the men of his personal guard (Louisiana cavalry). Maker: L. Bissonnet, Mobile, AL. (Confederate Memorial Hall collection; photo by Claude A. Levet)

Bottom: Sword presented to Gen. Sterling Price by the city of New Orleans, 1862. The guard has a hemp stalk, cotton boll, tobacco leaf, and grapes. The grip (an ear of corn) is ivory. (The Museum of the Confederacy collection; photo by Katherine Wetzel)

Sword Illustrations from Old Military Dealer Catalogs

Schuyler, Hartley, & Graham's 1864 Catalog
(Courtesy of Norm Flayderman)

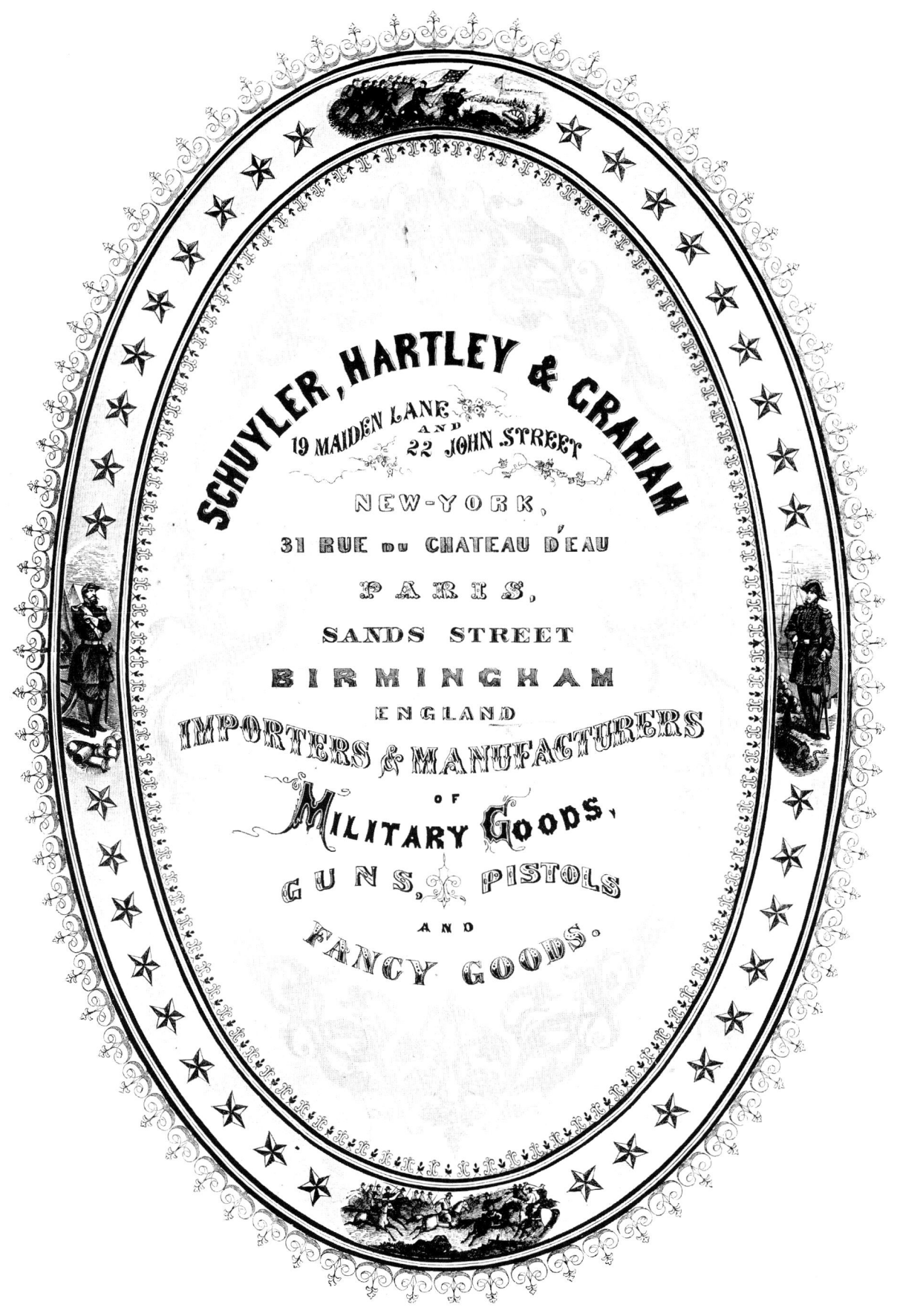

ILLUSTRATED CATALOGUE

OF

ARMS AND MILITARY GOODS:

CONTAINING

REGULATIONS FOR THE UNIFORM

OF THE

Army, Navy, Marine and Revenue Corps

OF THE

UNITED STATES.

New York:
PUBLISHED BY SCHUYLER, HARTLEY & GRAHAM,
MILITARY FURNISHERS,
19 MAIDEN LANE AND 22 JOHN STREET.
1864.

ILLUSTRATED CATALOGUE OF MILITARY GOODS.

Rich Presentation Swords—Solid Silver Scabbard.

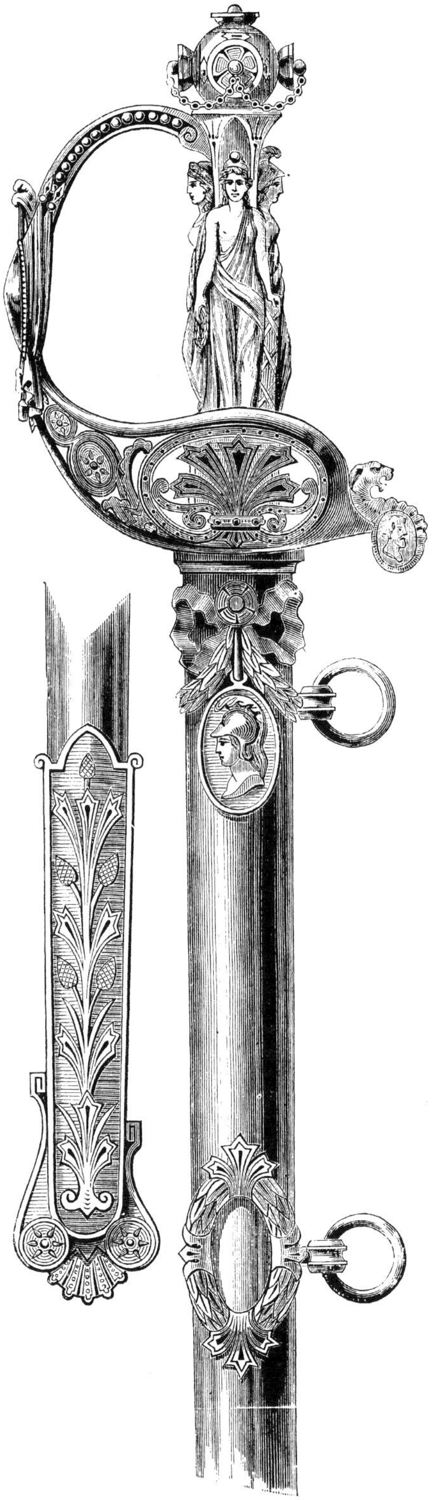

No. 1—For General Officers. 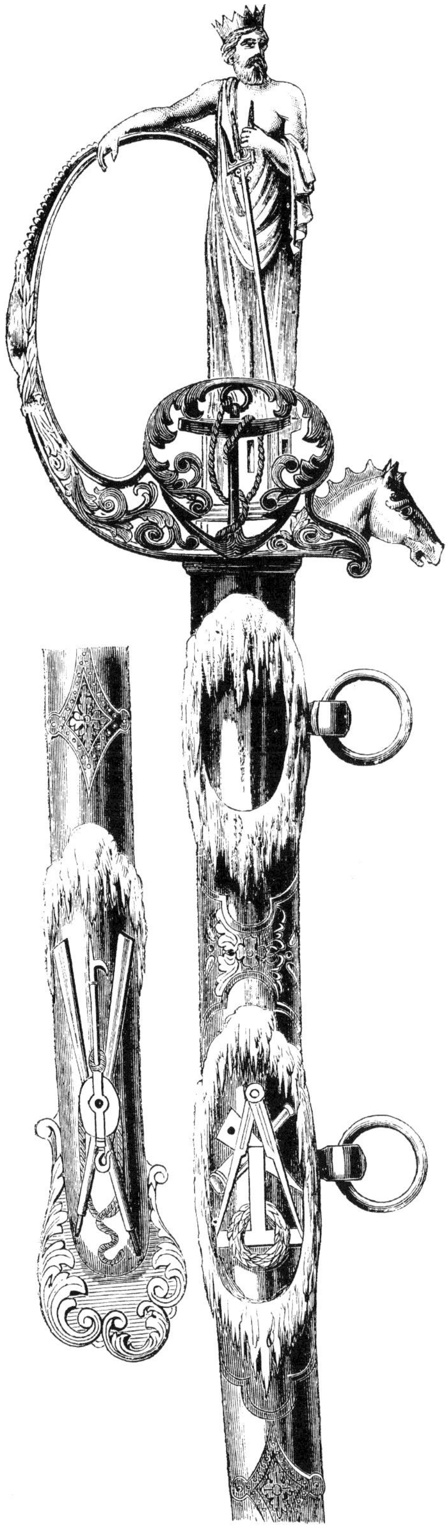   **No. 2—For Navy Officers.**

Rich Presentation Swords.

No. 3—For Cavalry.　　　No. 4—For General Officers.

Rich Presentation Swords for Field & Line Officers.

No. 9. No. 10.

ILLUSTRATED CATALOGUE OF MILITARY GOODS.

Rich Presentation Sabres for Cavalry Officers.

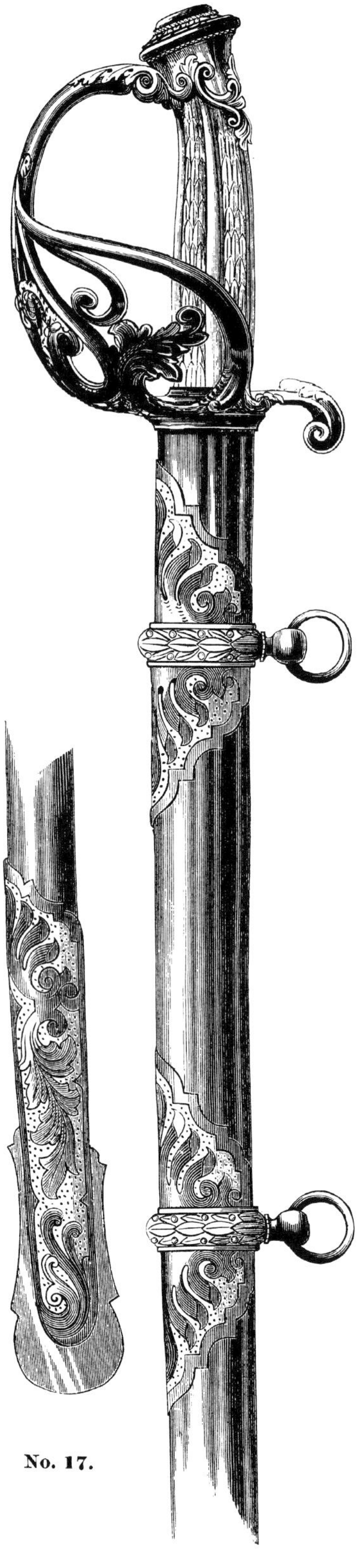

No. 17.    No. 18.

ILLUSTRATED CATALOGUE OF MILITARY GOODS. 39

U. S. Regulation Swords.

No. 21.
For General Officers.

No. 22.
Fancy Gilt Scabbard for General Officers.

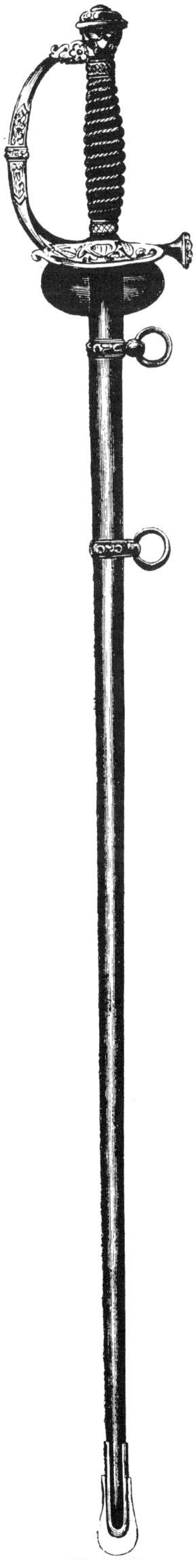

No. 23.
Bronze Scabbard & Gilt Mountings, for General and Staff Officers.

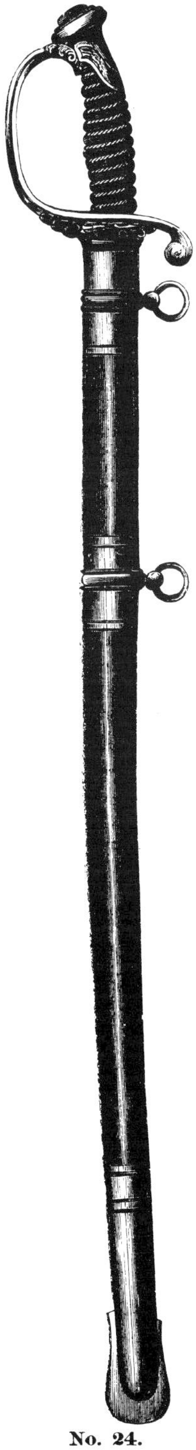

No. 24.
Leather Scabbard, for Line Officers.

ILLUSTRATED CATALOGUE OF MILITARY GOODS.

Steel Scabbard Swords.

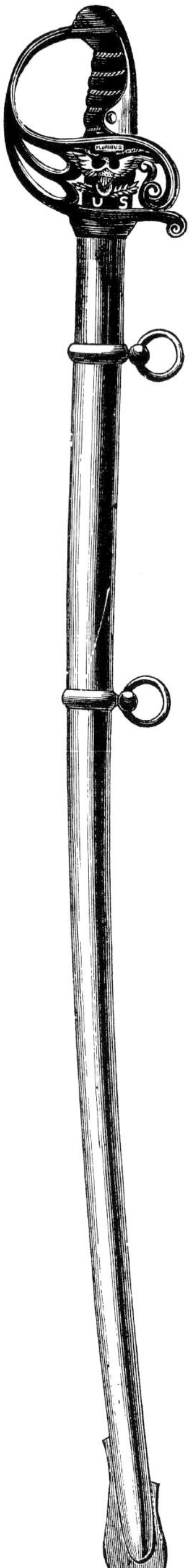

No. 29. Steel Scabbard & Steel Eagle hilt.

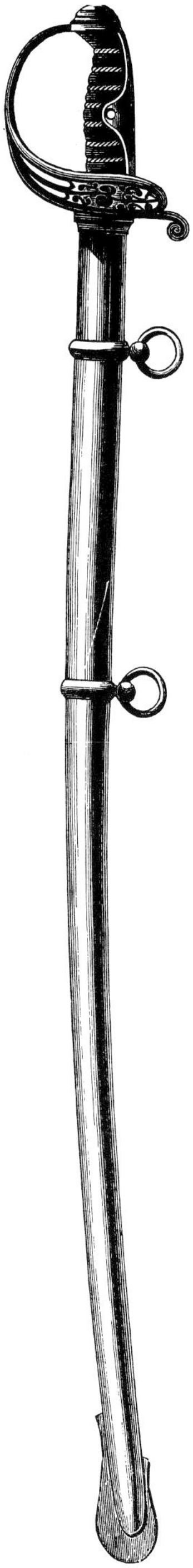

No. 30. Steel Scabbard, Steel Scroll hilt.

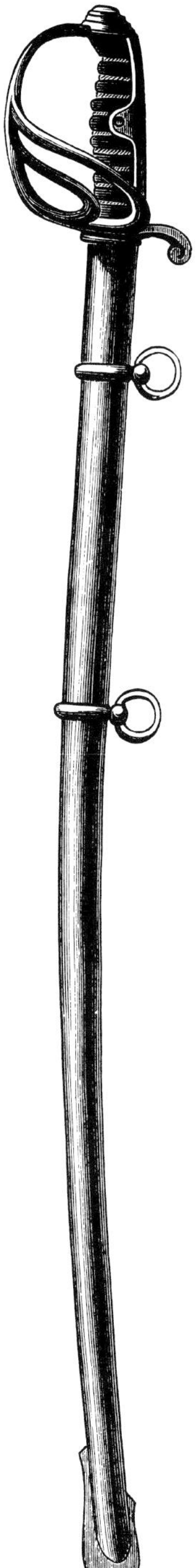

No. 31. Steel Scabbard, Steel Cavalry hilt.

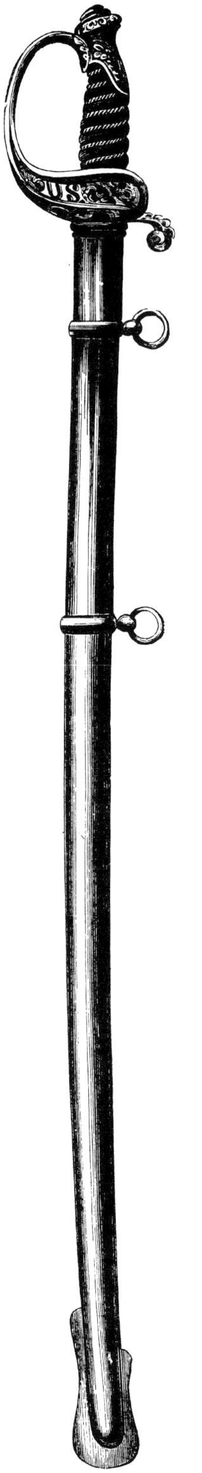

No. 32. Steel Scabbard, Gilt hilt.

No. 33. Cent Garde, Steel Scabbard, Gilt hilt, Blade thirty-seven inches—Straight.

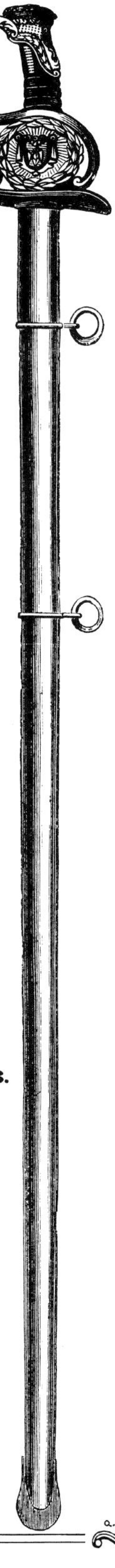

Horstmann Bros. & Co. 1877 Catalog
(Jacques Noel Jacobsen Jr., © Pioneer Press)

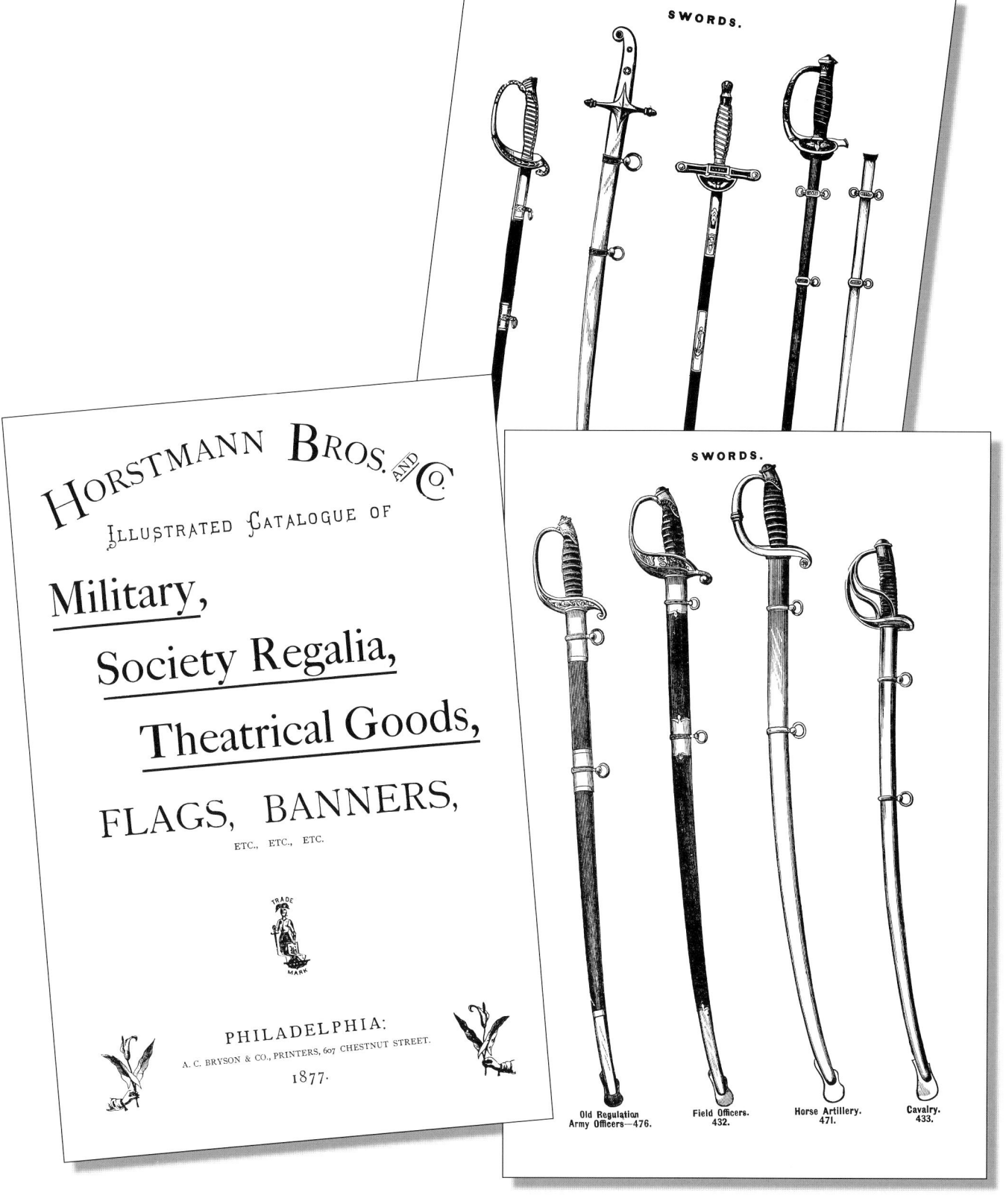

Sword Illustrations from Old Military Dealer Catalogs

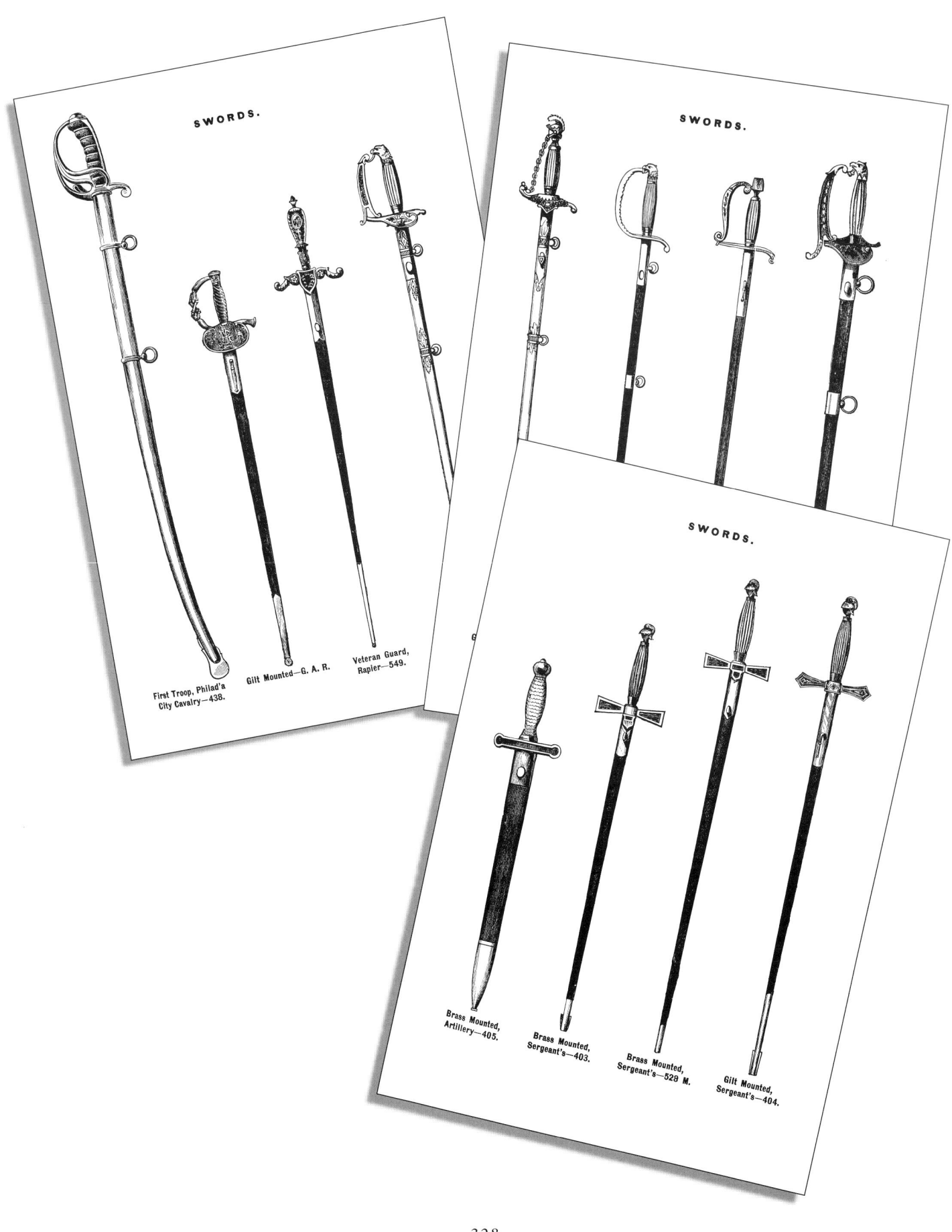

WORKS ESTABLISHED 1828.

ILLUSTRATED CATALOGUE AND PRICE LIST
OF THE
AMES SWORD COMPANY,
CHICOPEE, MASS., U. S. A.

DESIGNERS AND MANUFACTURERS OF

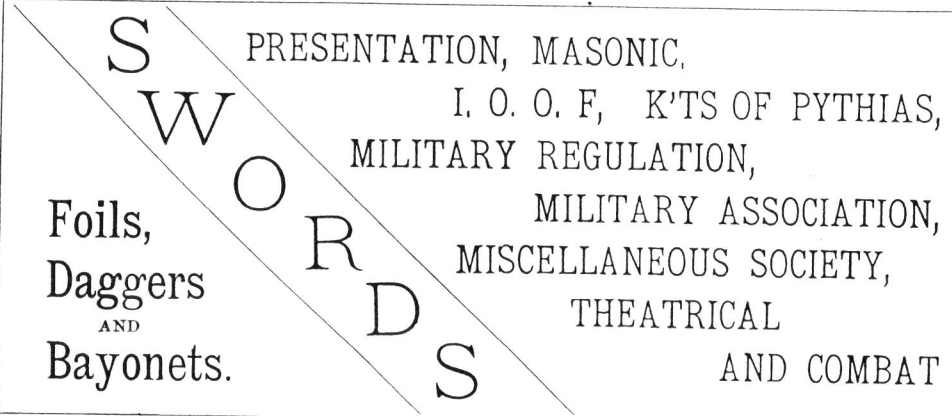

SWORDS — PRESENTATION, MASONIC, I. O. O. F, K'TS OF PYTHIAS, MILITARY REGULATION, MILITARY ASSOCIATION, MISCELLANEOUS SOCIETY, THEATRICAL AND COMBAT

Foils, Daggers AND Bayonets.

ALSO

Sword Belts and Mountings,
LINK AND BARREL CHAINS.

Baldric Stars, Fasteners and Hangers.

Commandery, Chapter and Regalia Jewels.

Rod Tops, Society Badges, Stone Hammers, Etc.

BRONZE AND BRASS CASTINGS.

Gold, Silver and Nickel Plating,

REPAIRING AND REPLATING,

Engraving, Modeling and Die Sinking.

MILITARY REGULATION.

505 **506** **507** **508**

No. **505**—Line Officer; Gilt Mountings, Nickel Plated Steel Scabbard; Fish Skin Grip; Spring and Fall Guard; Etched Diamond Blade,... Gilt, $15.00

No. **506**—Presentation; Embossed Gilt Mountings, Nickel Plated Steel Scabbard; Silver Grip; Spring and Fall Guard; Gold Etched Diamond Blade,... Gilt, 25.00

No. **507**—Presentation; Embossed Gilt Mountings, Nickel Plated Steel Scabbard; Silver Grip; Spring and Fall Guard; Gold Etched Diamond Blade,... Gilt, 30.00

No. **508**—Presentation; Embossed Gilt Mountings, Nickel Plated Steel Scabbard; Silver Grip; Spring and Fall Guard; Gold Etched Diamond Blade,... Gilt, 35.00

MILITARY REGULATION.

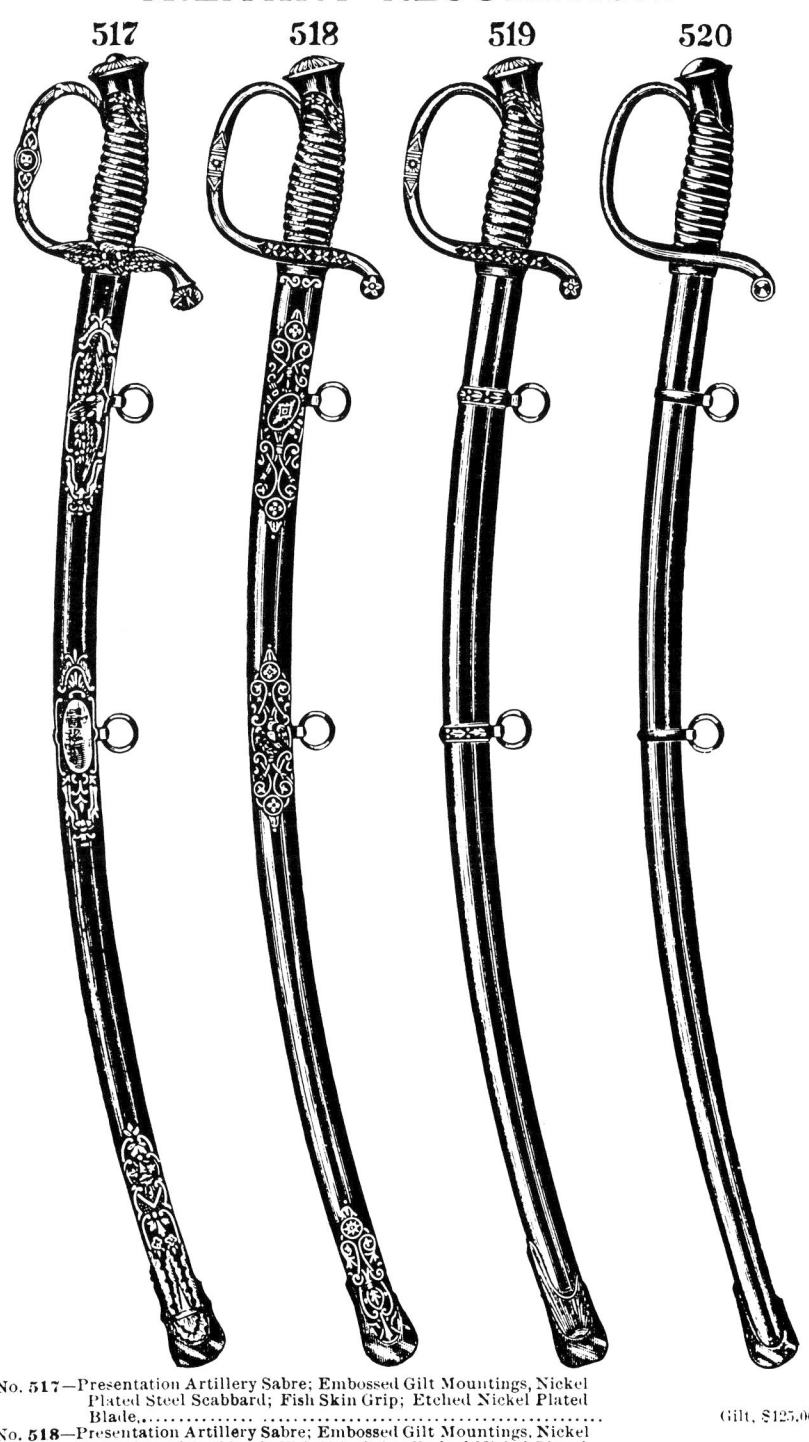

No. 517—Presentation Artillery Sabre; Embossed Gilt Mountings, Nickel Plated Steel Scabbard; Fish Skin Grip; Etched Nickel Plated Blade,... Gilt, $125.00

No. 518—Presentation Artillery Sabre; Embossed Gilt Mountings, Nickel Plated Steel Scabbard; Fish Skin Grip; Etched Nickel Plated Blade,... Gilt, 75.00

No. 519—New Regulation Officer's Artillery Sabre; Gilt Mountings, Nickel Plated Steel Scabbard; Fish Skin Grip; Etched Nickel Plated Blade,... Gilt, 18.00

No. 520—New Regulation Private's Artillery Sabre; Steel Scabbard; Twist Grip; Plain Blade,................................... Brass, $9.00

—148—

MILITARY REGULATION.

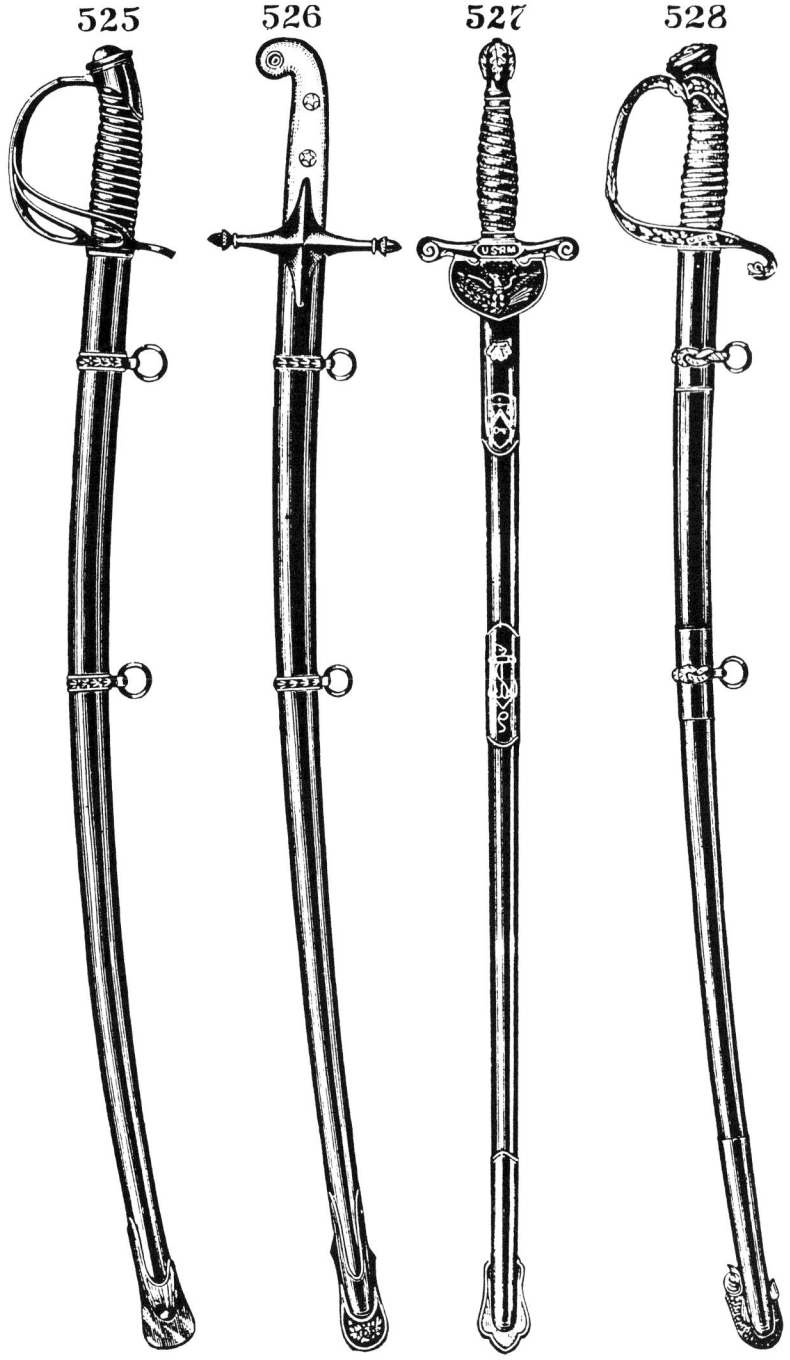

No. 525—Cavalry Sabre; Gilt Mountings, Nickel Plated Steel Scabbard;
    Twist Grip; Etched Blade,.. Gilt, $16.00
No. 526—New Regulation Marine; Gilt Mountings, Nickel Plated Steel
    Scabbard; Ivory Mameluke Grip; Etched Blade,............... Gilt, 35.00
No. 527—U. S. Revenue and Marine; Engraved Mountings, Black Leather
    Scabbard; Fish Skin Grip; Etched Diamond Blade,............ Gilt, 18.00
No. 528—Regulation Navy; Gilt Mountings, Black Leather Scabbard;
    Fish Skin Grip; Etched Blade,.. Gilt, 13.00

—152—

MILITARY REGULATION.

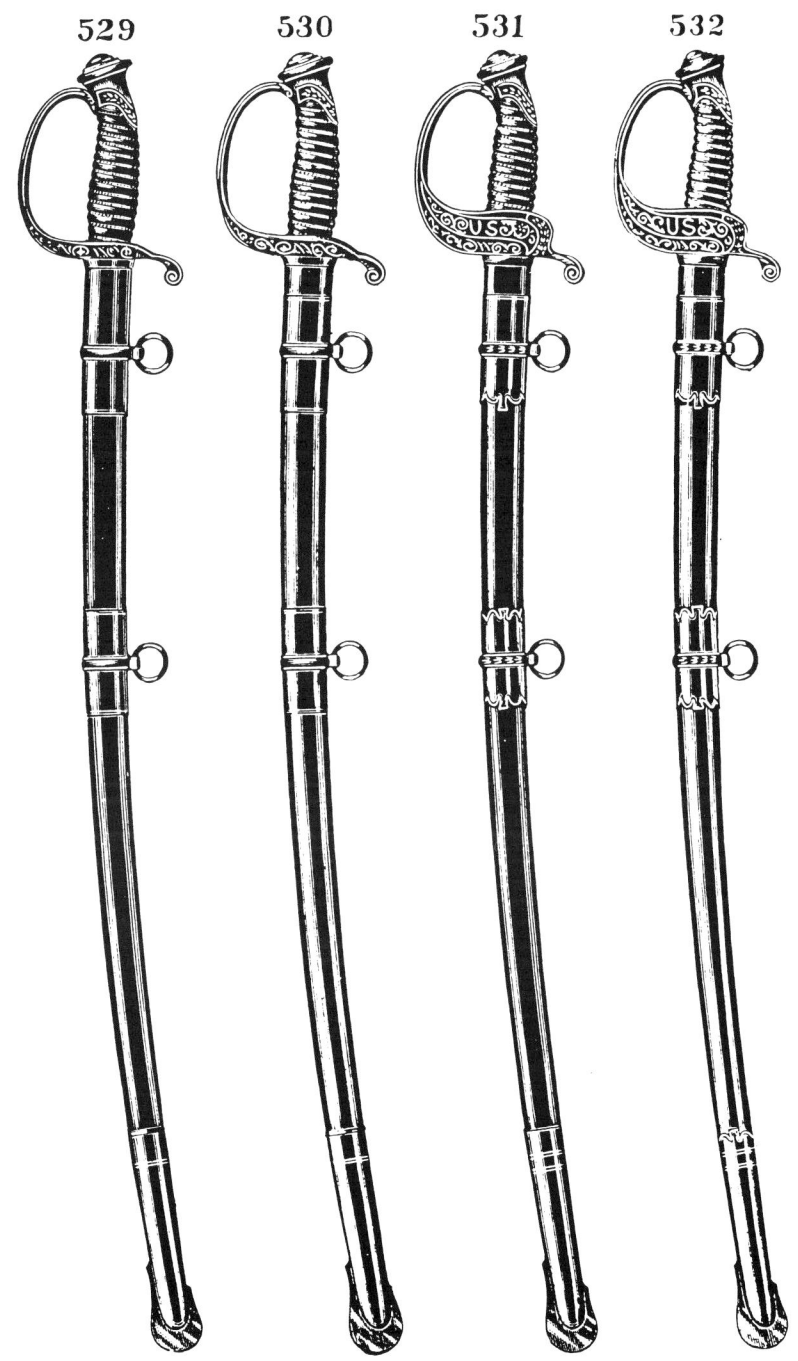

No. 529—Old Regulation Line Officer; Gilt Mountings, Black Leather Scabbard; Fish Skin Grip; Etched Blade, ... Gilt, $13.00
No. 530—Old Regulation Line Officer; Gilt Mountings, Nickel Plated Steel Scabbard; Fish Skin Grip; Etched Blade, ... Gilt, 18.00
No. 531—Old Regulation Field Officer; Gilt Mountings, Bronze Scabbard; Fish Skin Grip; Etched Blade, ... Gilt, 18.00
No. 532—Old Regulation Field Officer; Gilt Mountings, Nickel Plated Steel Scabbard; Fish Skin Grip; Etched Blade, ... Gilt, 18.00

—154—

MILITARY REGULATION.

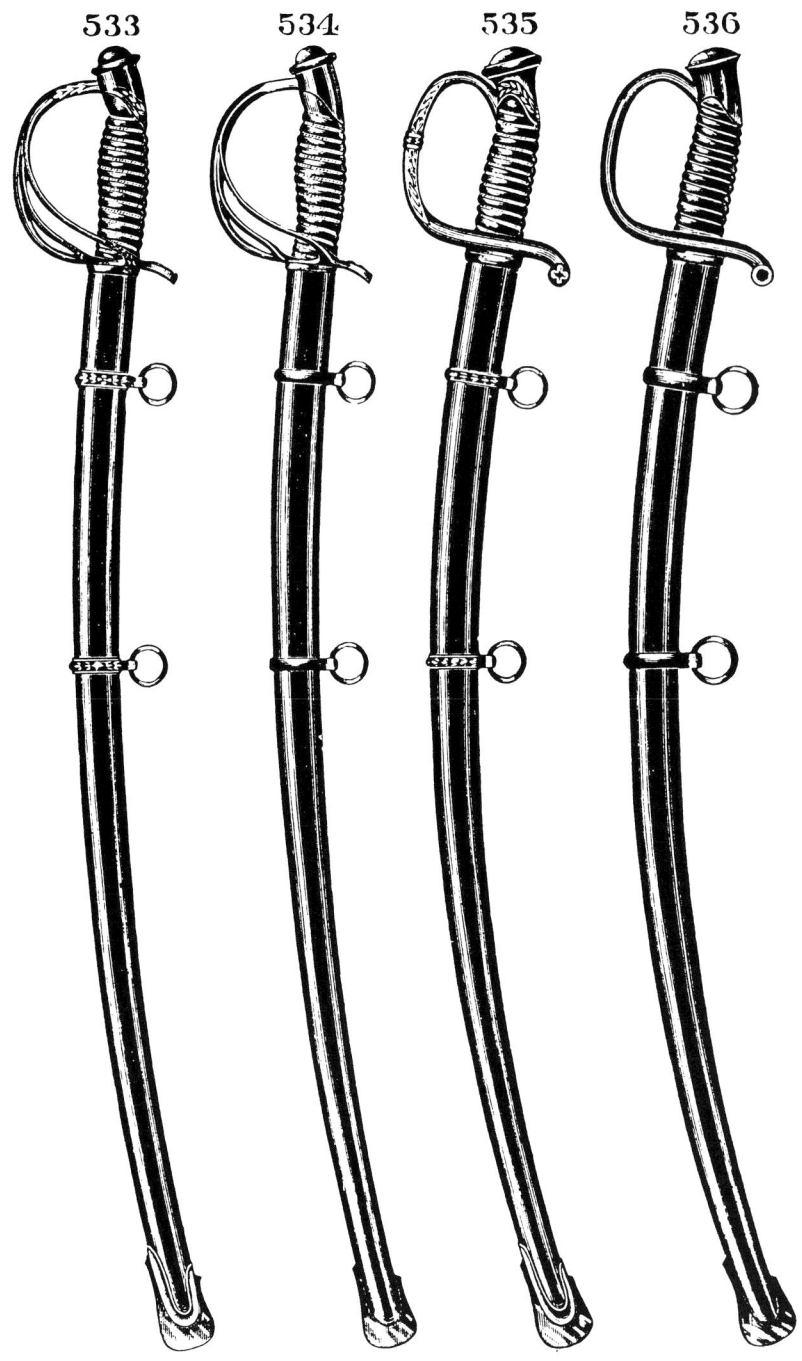

No. 533—Old Regulation Cavalry Officer's Sabre; Gilt Mountings, Nickel
    Plated Steel Scabbard; Fish Skin Grip; Etched Blade, ... Gilt, $18.00
No. 534—Old Regulation Cavalry Private's Sabre; Steel Scabbard; Twist
    Grip; Plain Blade,..Brass, $9.00
No. 535—Old Regulation Artillery Officer's Sabre; Gilt Mountings, Nickel
    Plated Steel Scabbard; Fish Skin Grip; Etched Blade,......... Gilt, 18.00
No. 536—Old Regulation Artillery Private's Sabre; Steel Scabbard;
    Twist Grip; Plain Blade,......................................Brass, 9.00

—156—

MILITARY REGULATION.

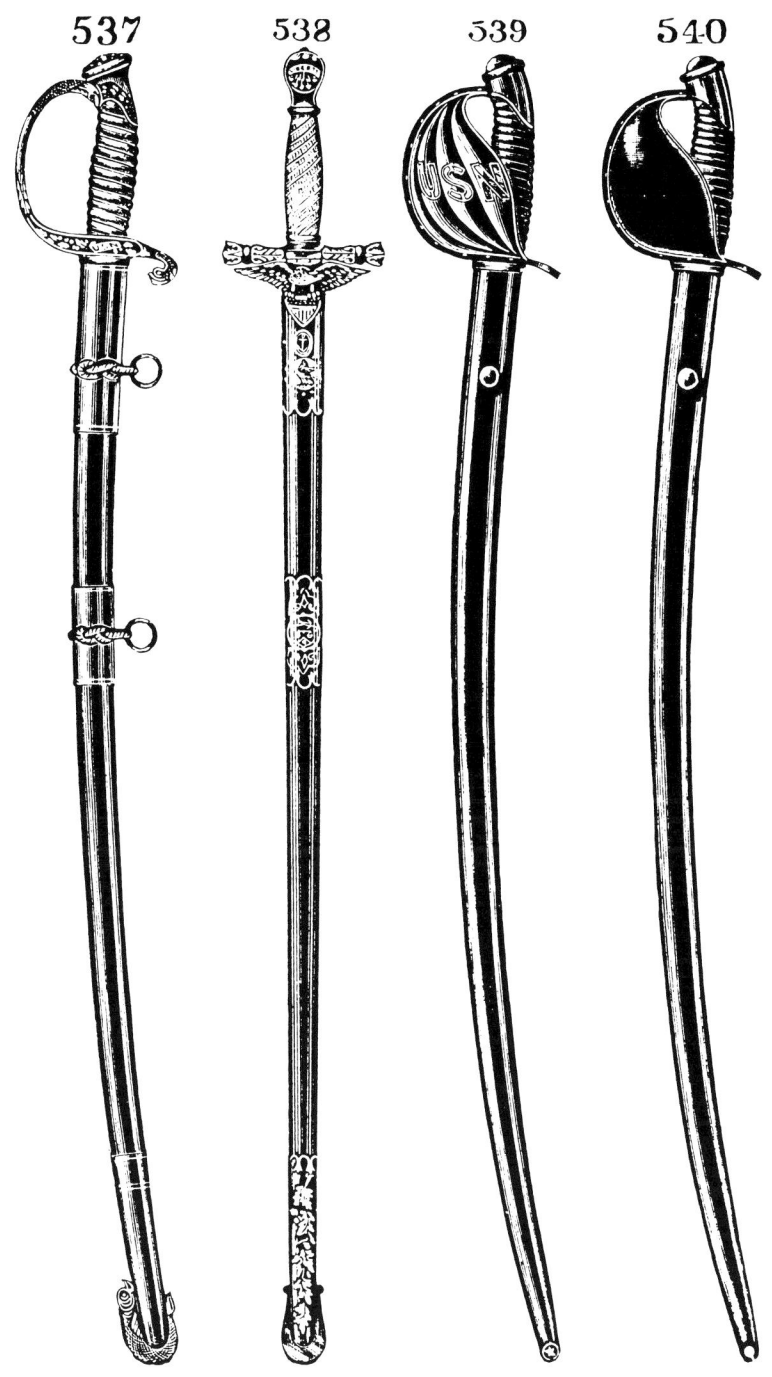

No. 537—Old Regulation Navy; Gilt Mountings, Black Leather Scabbard;
  Fish Skin Grip; Etched Blade,... Gilt, $13.00
No. 538—Old Regulation Revenue and Marine; Engraved Mountings,
  Black Leather Scabbard; Silver Grip; Etched Diamond Blade,.. Gilt, 20.00
No. 539—Officer's Navy Cutlass; Black Leather Scabbard; Black Twist
  Grip; Plain Blade,... Gilt, 18.00
No. 540—Navy Cutlass; Black Leather Scabbard; Black Twist Grip;
  Plain Blade,..Bronze, $12.00

—158—

MILITARY REGULATION.

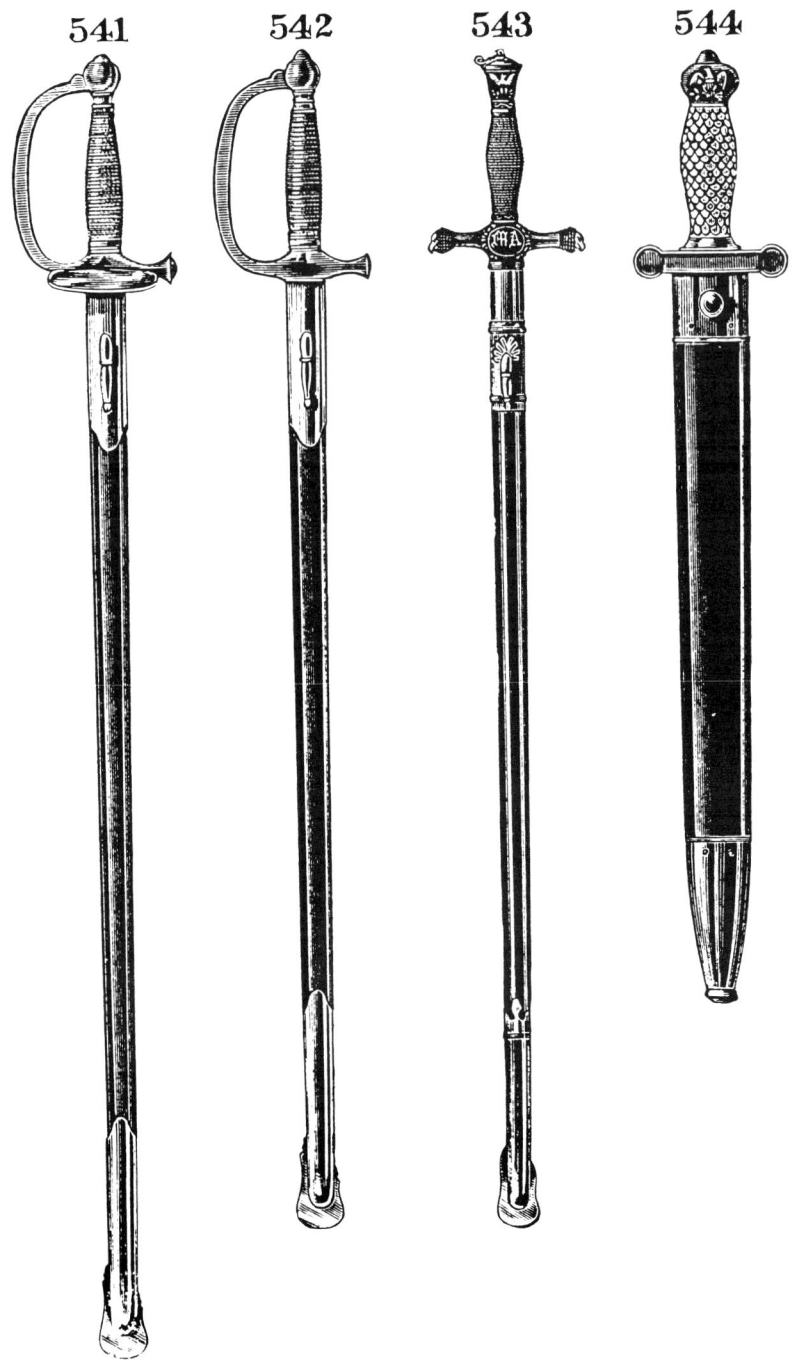

No. 541—Non-Commission; Mounted Black Leather Scabbard.; Metal Grip; Plain Blade, ... Brass, $6.75 Plated, $8.00 Gilt, $10.00
No. 542—Musicians; Mounted Black Leather Scabbard; Metal Grip; Plain Blade, ... Brass, 6.00 Plated, 7.50 Gilt, 9.00
No. 543—Mounted Nickel Plated Steel Scabbard; Silver Grip; Etched Diamond Blade, ... Gilt, 15.00
No. 544—Foot Artillery; Mounted Black Leather Scabbard; Metal Grip; Grooved Blade, ... Brass, 6.00

—160—

James A. Ridabock & Co. 1888 Catalog
(Author's collection)

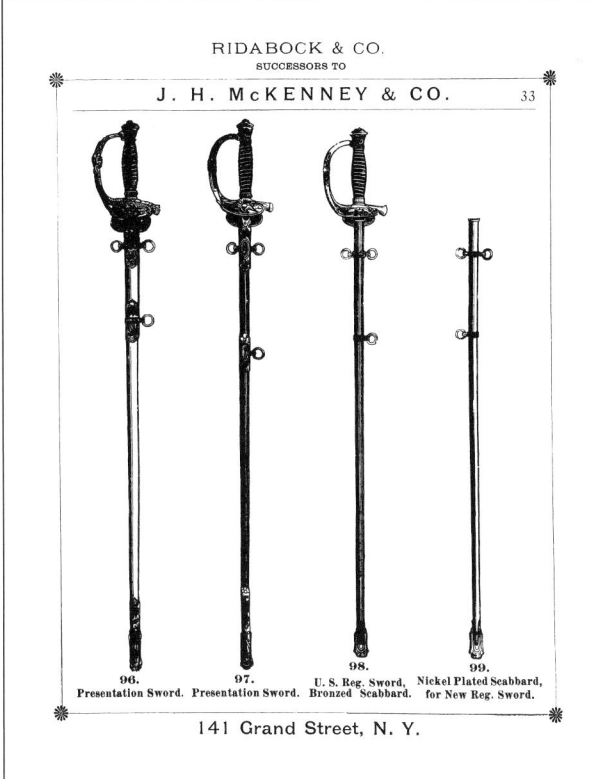

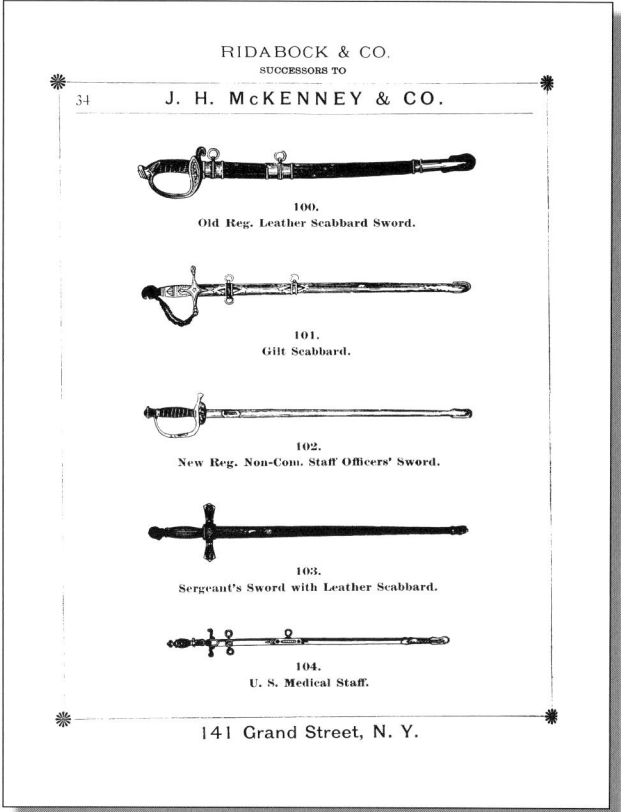

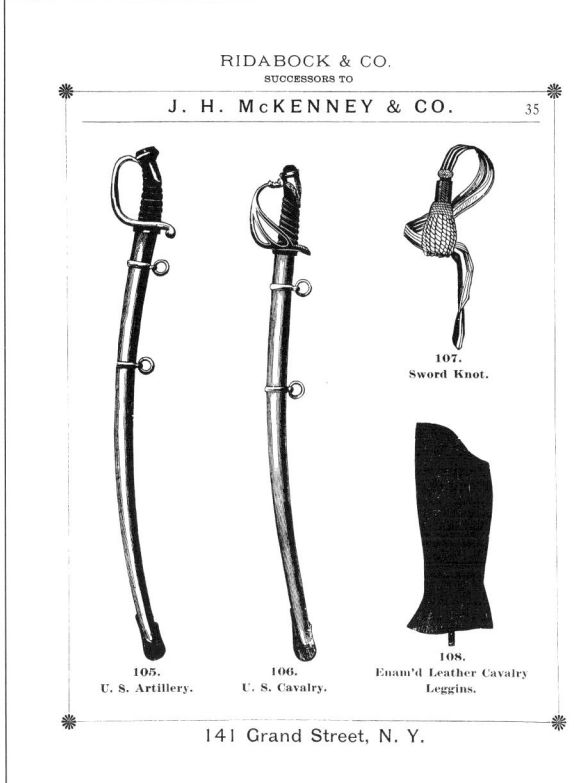

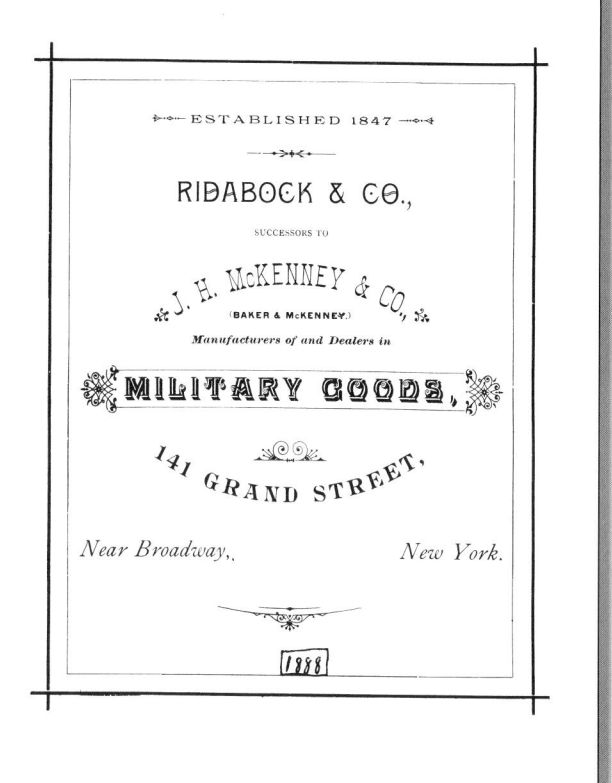

W.A. Raymold 1895 Catalog
(Jacques Noel Jacobsen Jr., © Pioneer Press)

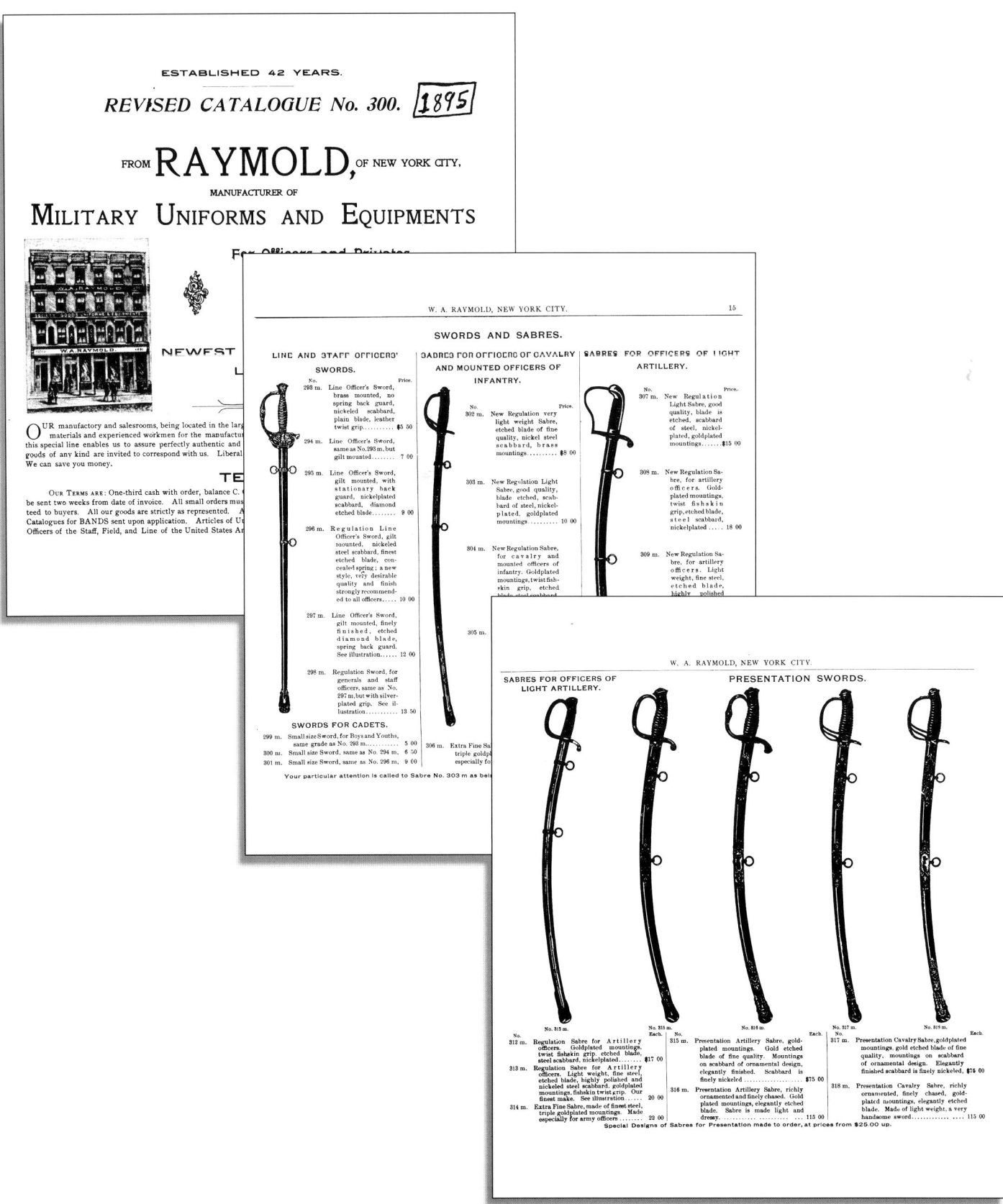

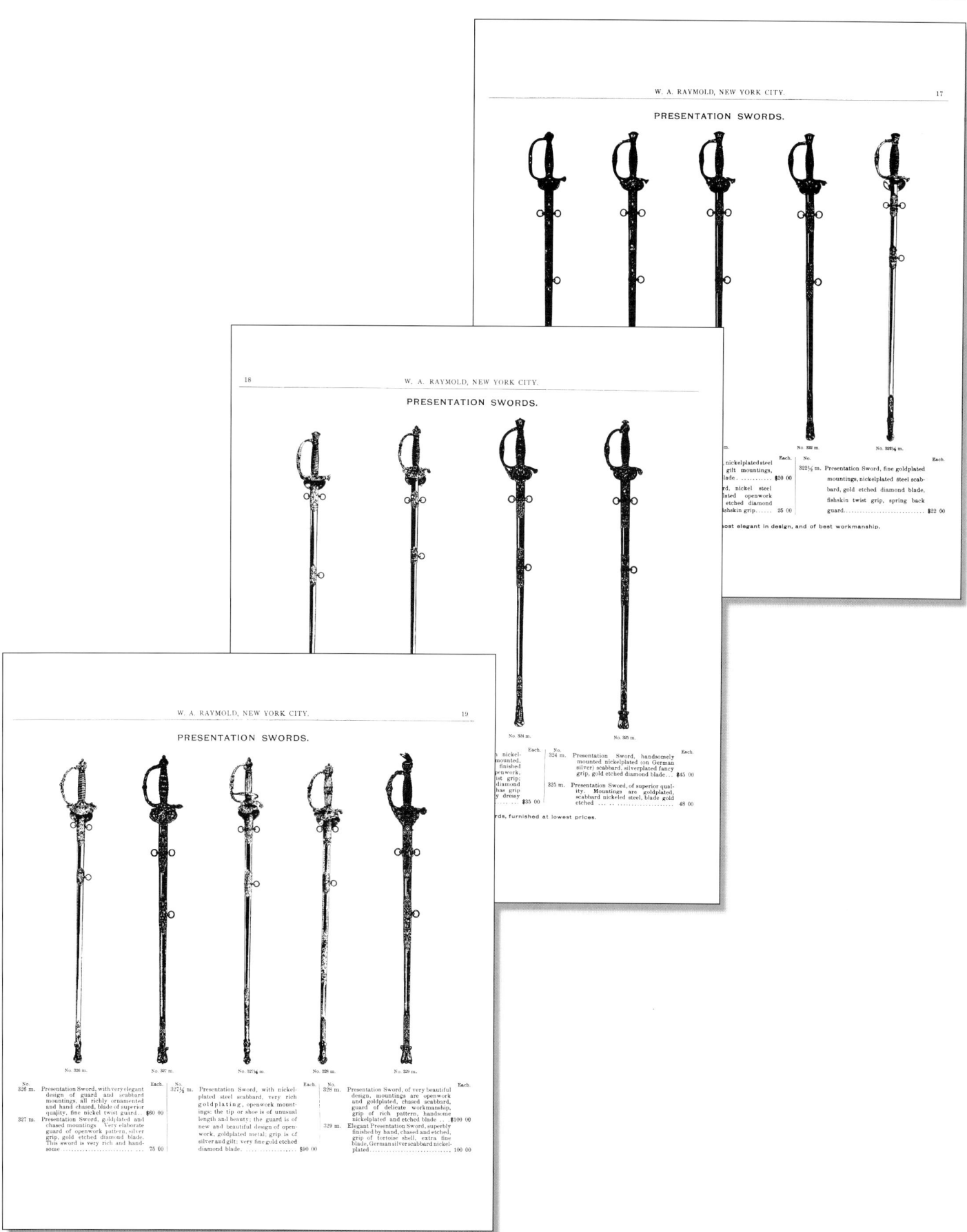

Joseph W. Warnock Uniform Co. 1901 Catalog
(Author's collection)

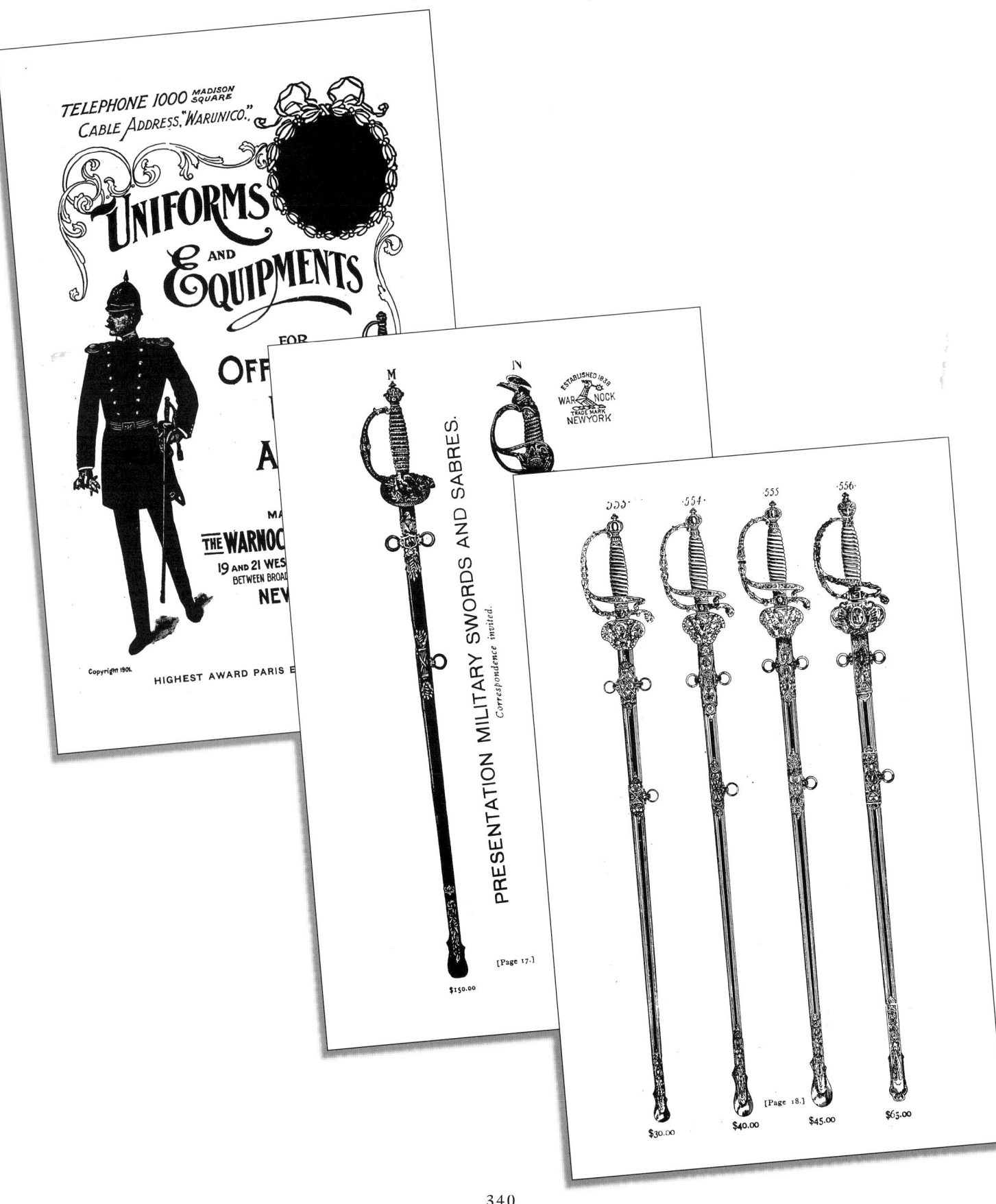

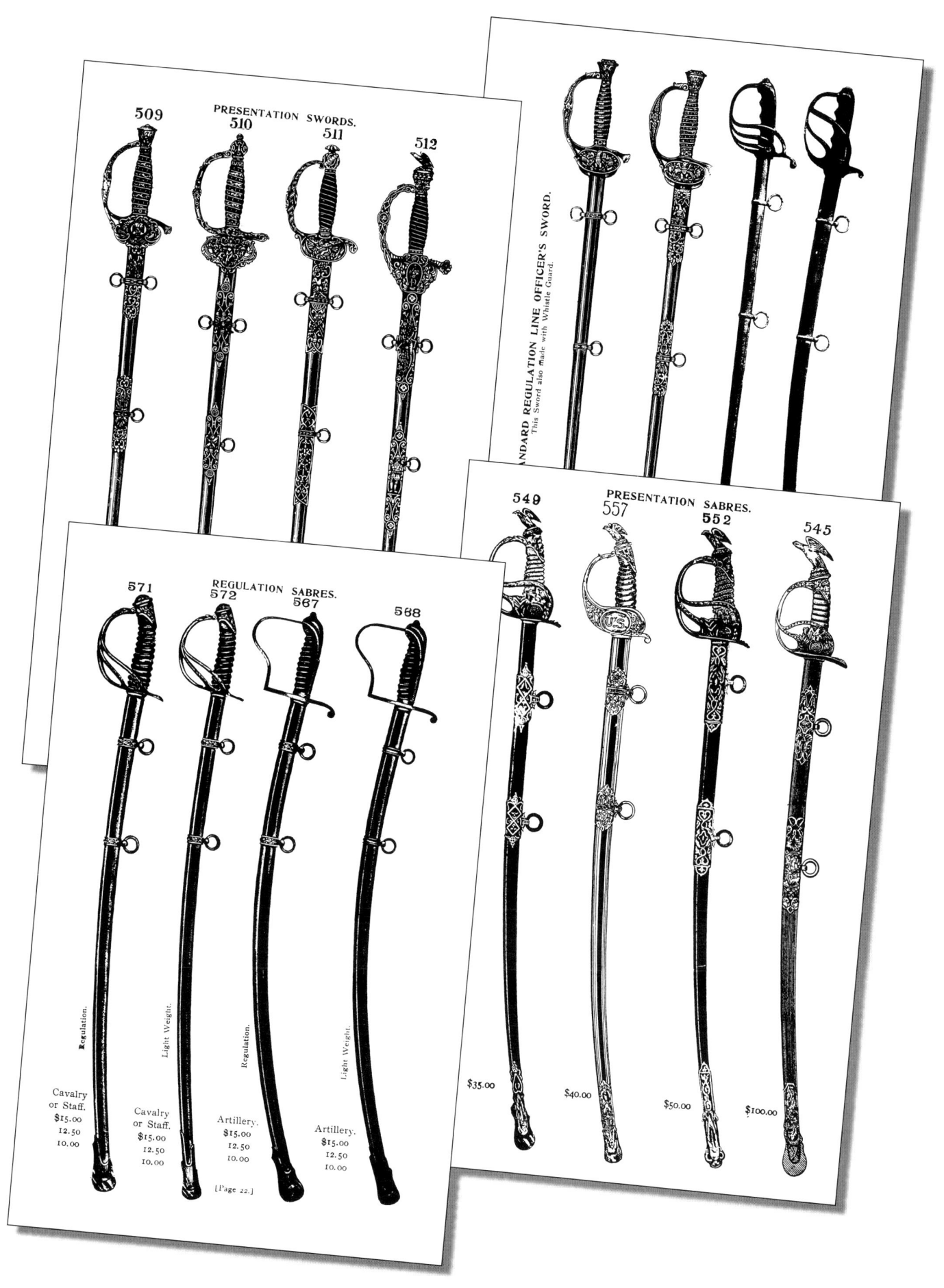

SWORD ILLUSTRATIONS FROM OLD MILITARY DEALER CATALOGS

M.C. Lilley & Co. 1919 Catalog
(Author's collection)

ESTABLISHED 1865

Presentation Sabres and Swords

For Officers of the Army, Navy and Marine Corps

Catalog No. 235

The M. C. Lilley & Co.
Sword Manufacturers
Columbus, Ohio

Copyright, 1919, by The M. C. Lilley & Co., Columbus, Ohio

Presentation Army Officer's Sabre No. 220

Extra heavy gold plating; hand chased and engraved; sterling silver monogram; gold etched and ornamented steel blade; nickel plated steel scabbard; genuine horn grip.

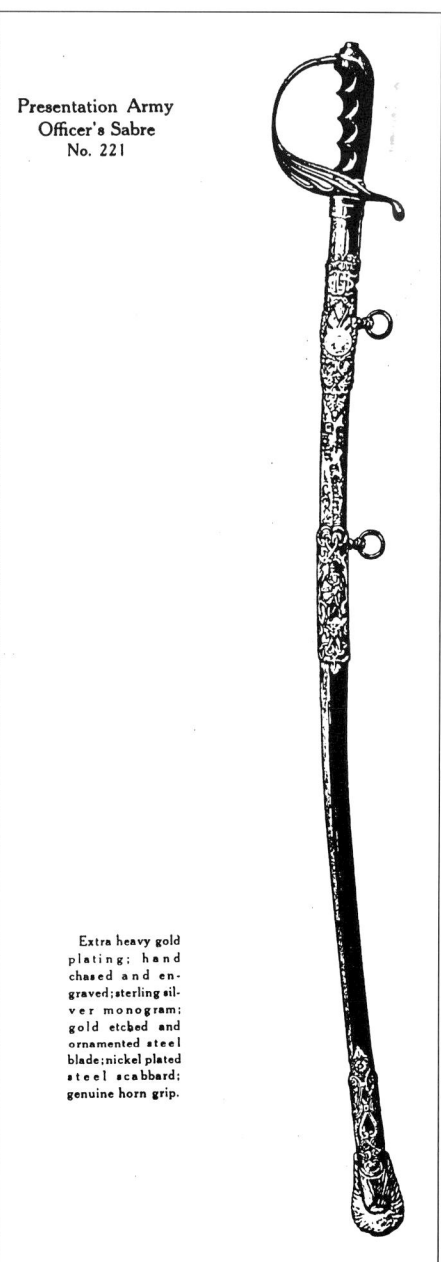

Presentation Army Officer's Sabre No. 221

Extra heavy gold plating; hand chased and engraved; sterling silver monogram; gold etched and ornamented steel blade; nickel plated steel scabbard; genuine horn grip.

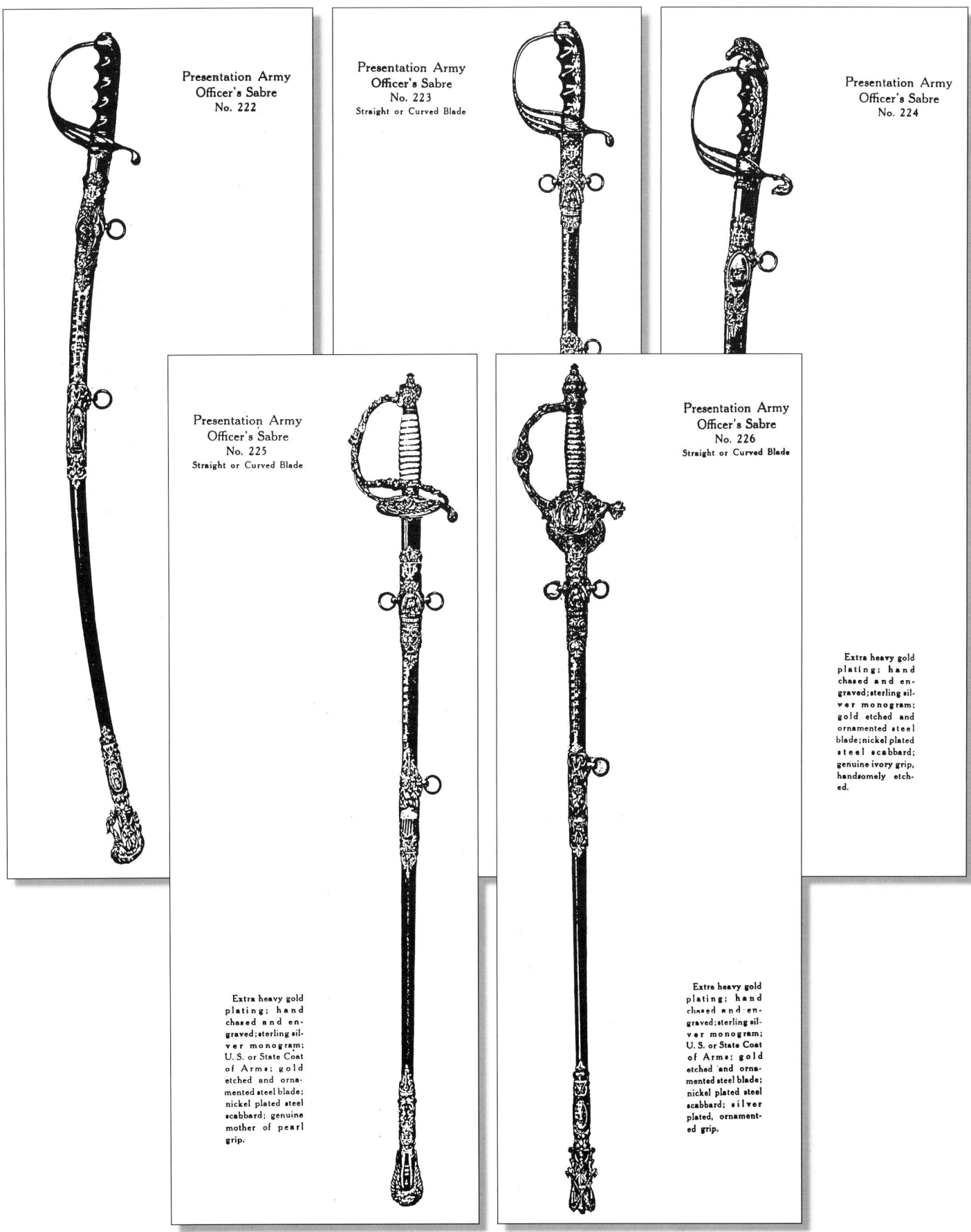

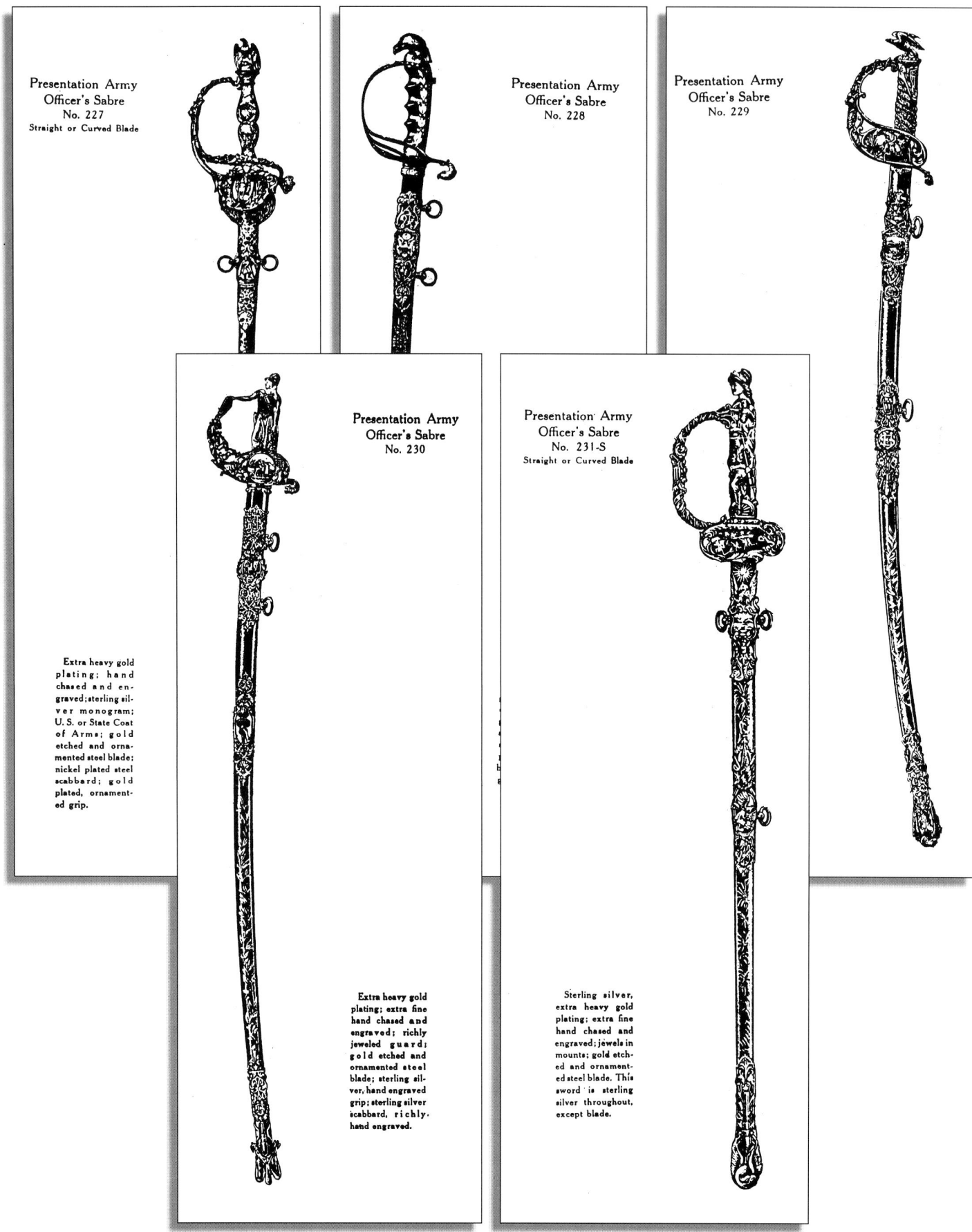

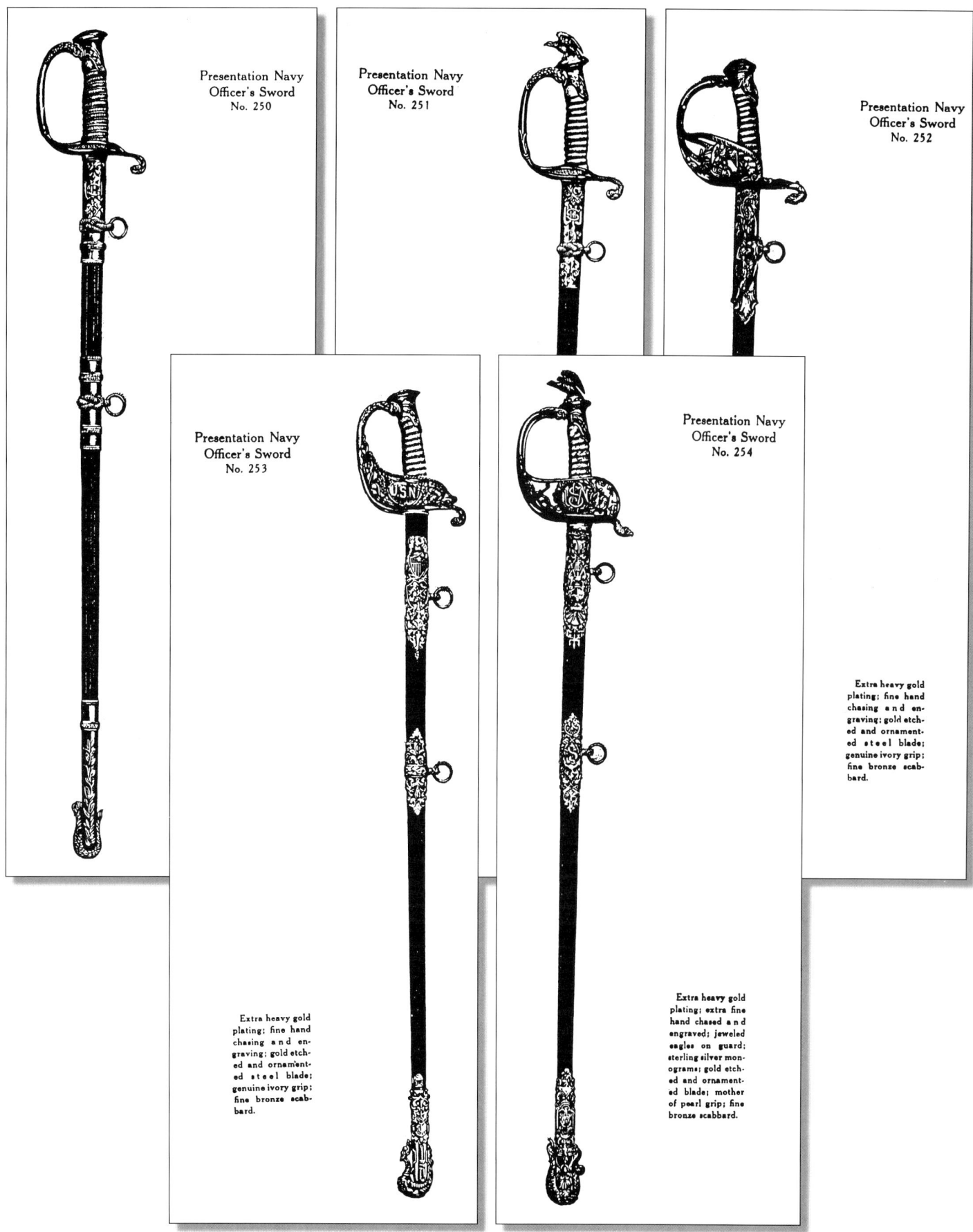

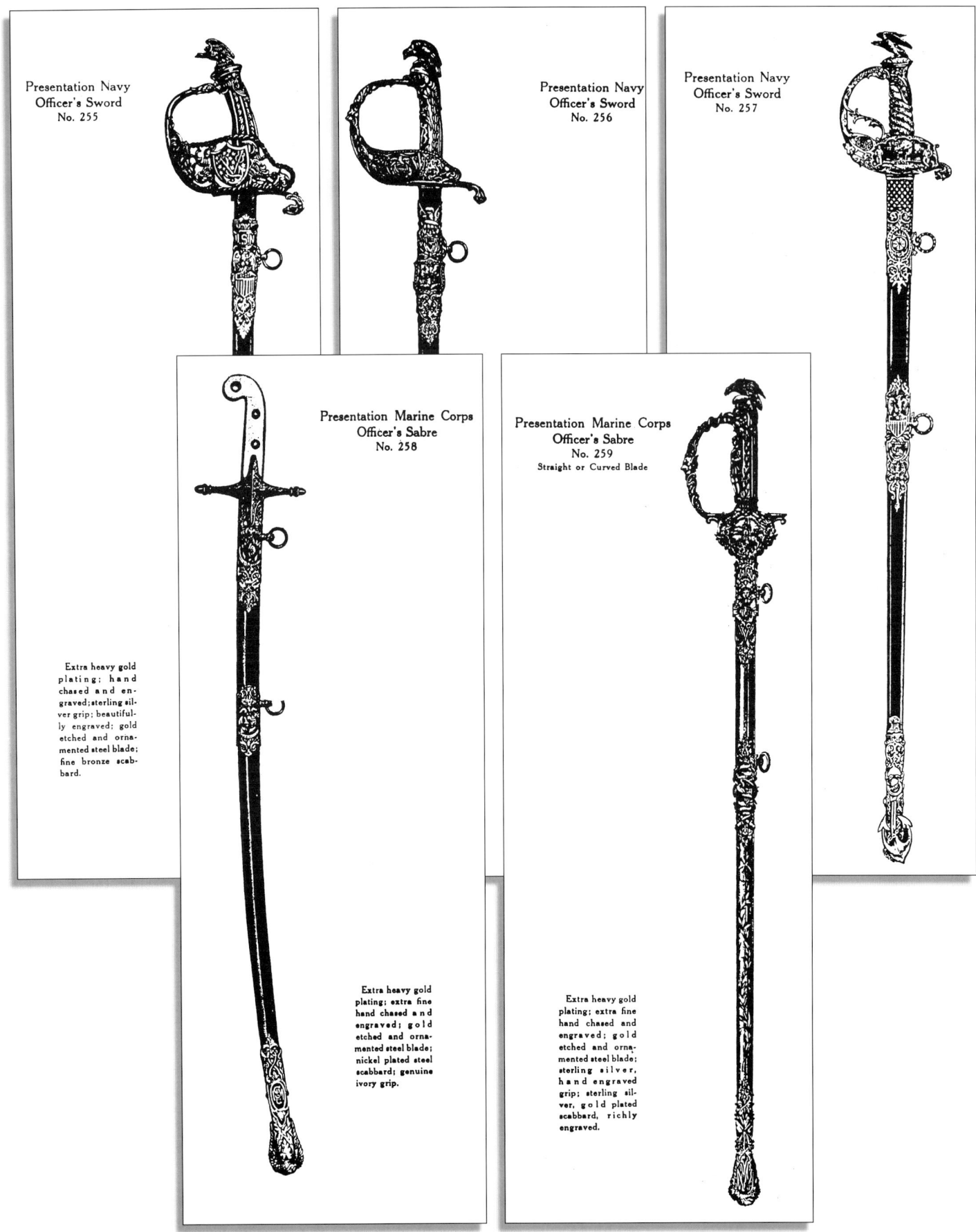

James A. Ridabock & Co. 1931 Spring Catalog
(Author's collection)

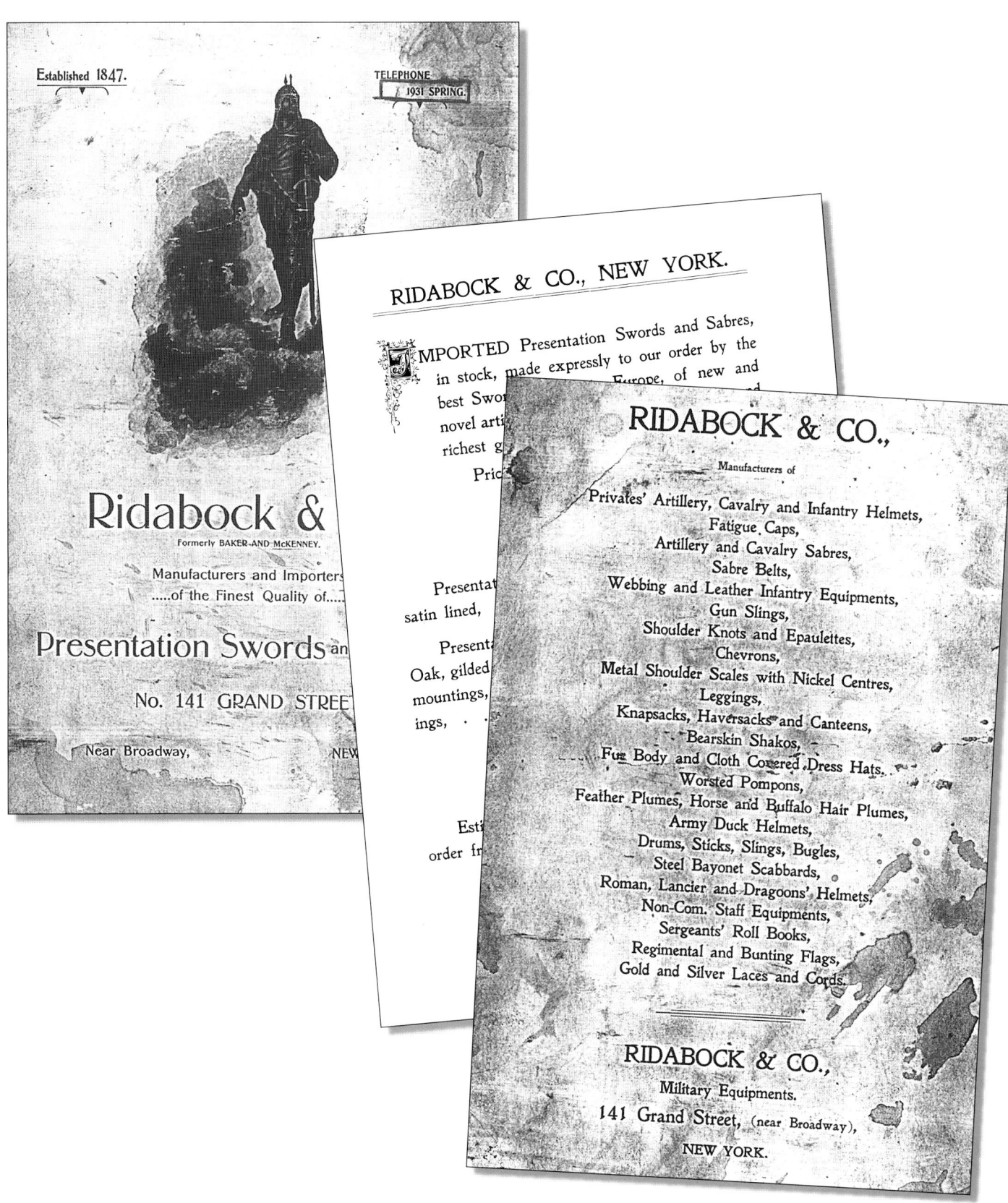

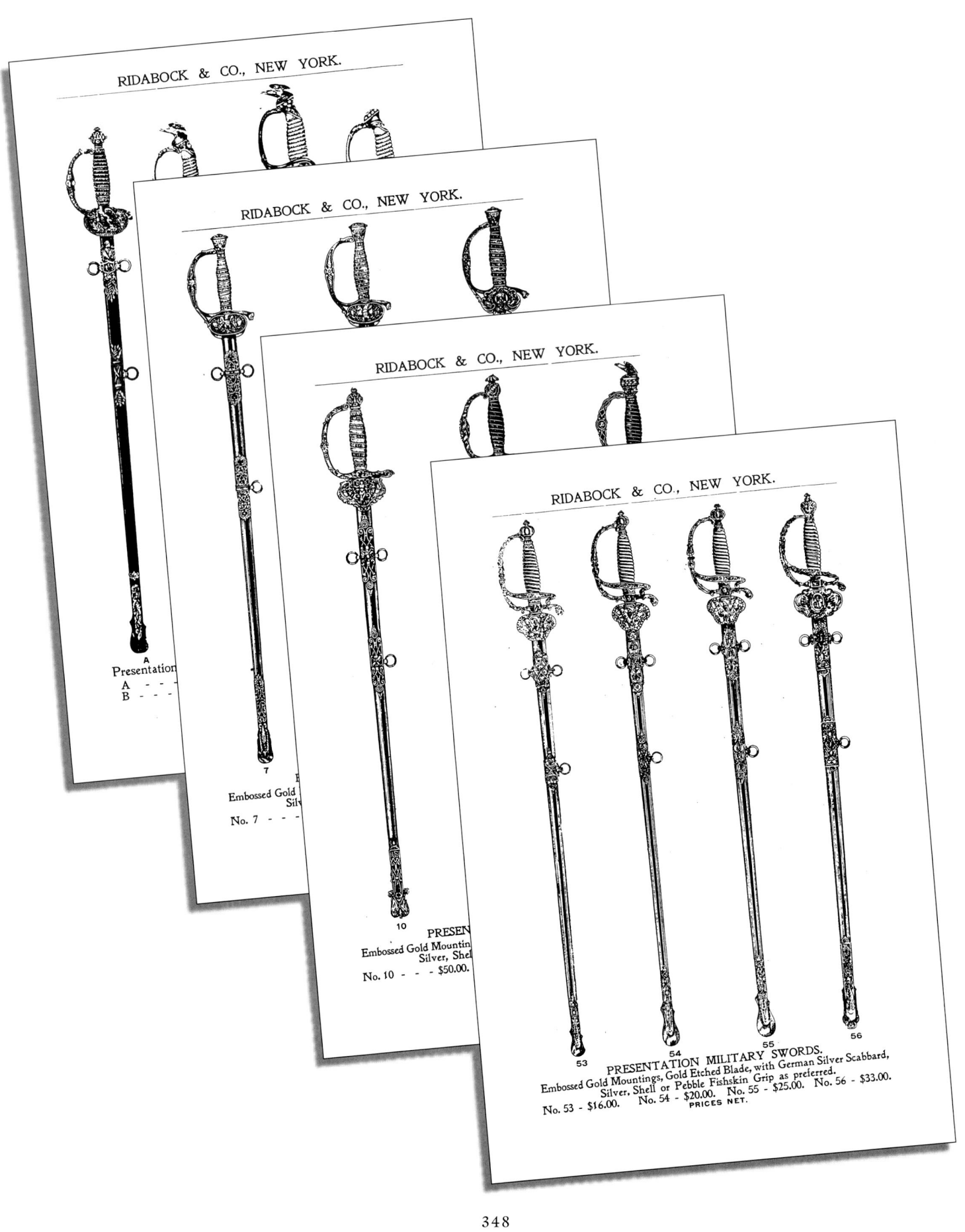

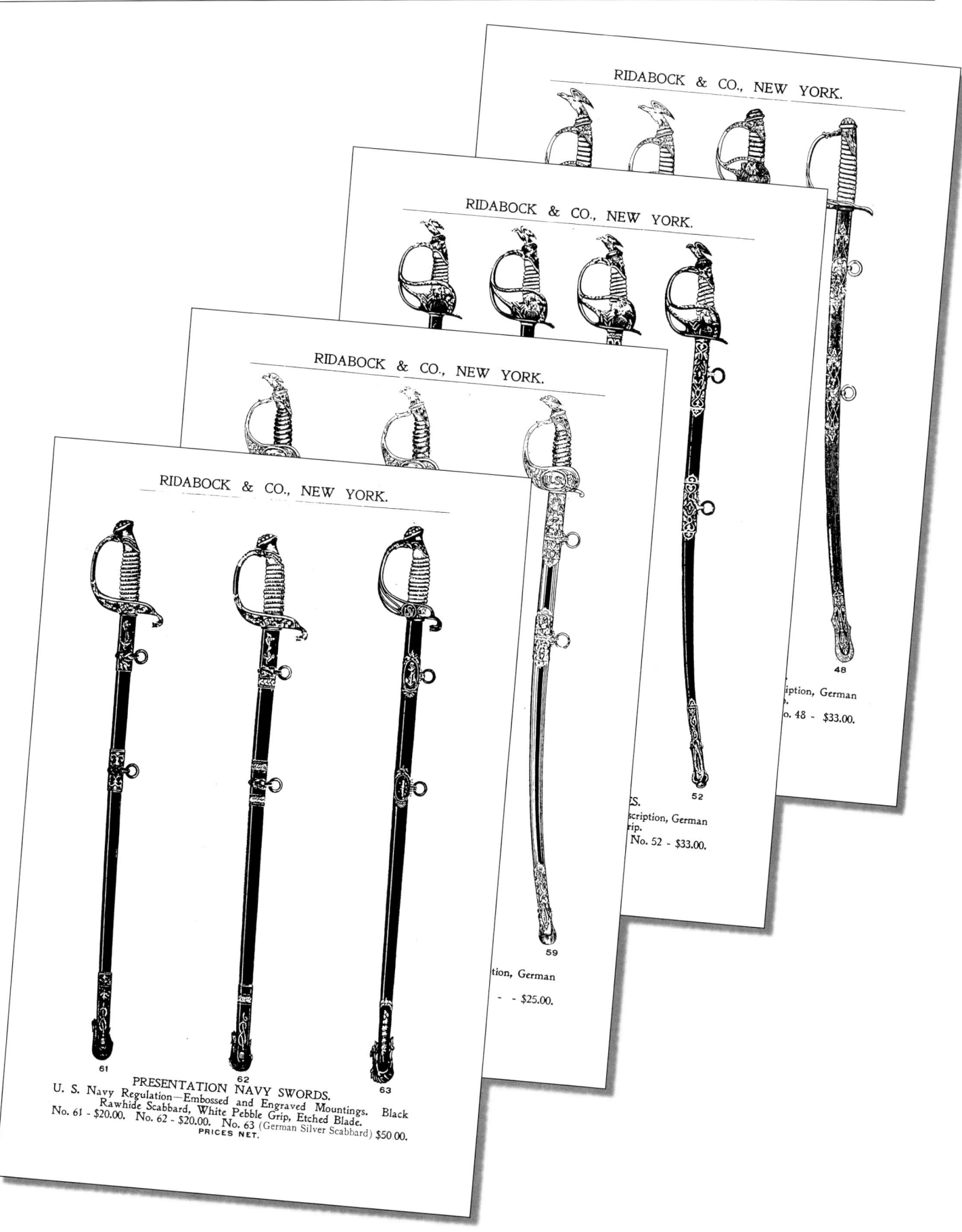

Lilley-Ames Co. 1931 Catalog
(Author's collection)

THE LILLEY-AMES COMPANY - COLUMBUS, OHIO

U. S. REGULATION SABER
The Standard Saber for Officers of the U. S. Army, and College R. O. T. C. Units.

Lilley-Ames Sabers are
100%
AMERICAN MADE

Made complete in our own factories at Columbus, Ohio.

In ordering, advise length of blade desired, and whether or not name panel is desired.

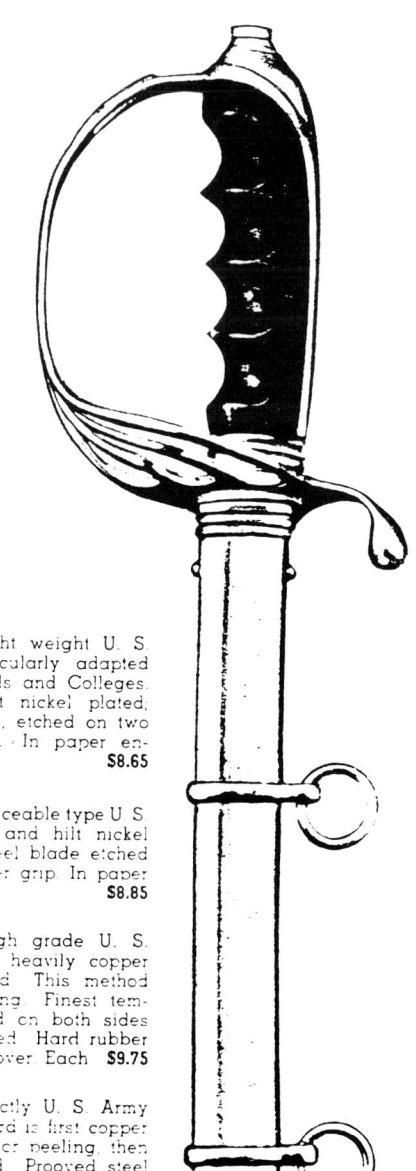

W300 REVERE — A light weight U. S. Army Type Saber, particularly adapted for use in Military Schools and Colleges. Blade scabbard and hilt nickel plated; fine tempered steel blade, etched on two sides. Hard rubber grip. In paper envelope cover. Price, each $8.65

W302 ARMORER — A serviceable type U. S. Saber. Blade scabbard and hilt nickel plated. Fine tempered steel blade etched on two sides. Hard rubber grip. In paper envelope cover. Each $8.85

W304 STANDARD — A high grade U. S. type saber. Scabbard is heavily copper plated, then nickel plated. This method prevents rusting or peeling. Finest tempered steel blade, etched on both sides and extra fine nickel-plated. Hard rubber grip. In paper envelope cover. Each $9.75

W306 REGULATION — Strictly U. S. Army Regulation Saber. Scabbard is first copper plated to prevent rusting or peeling, then extra heavy nickel plated. Prooved steel blade, heavily nickel plated and etched on both sides and back. Extra heavy nickel plating on hilt. Hard rubber grip. In paper envelope cover. Each $11.65

For Chrome Nickel Finish
add $2.00 each.

QUANTITY PRICES ON APPLICATION

ALL PRICES ARE NET

THE LILLEY-AMES COMPANY - COLUMBUS, OHIO

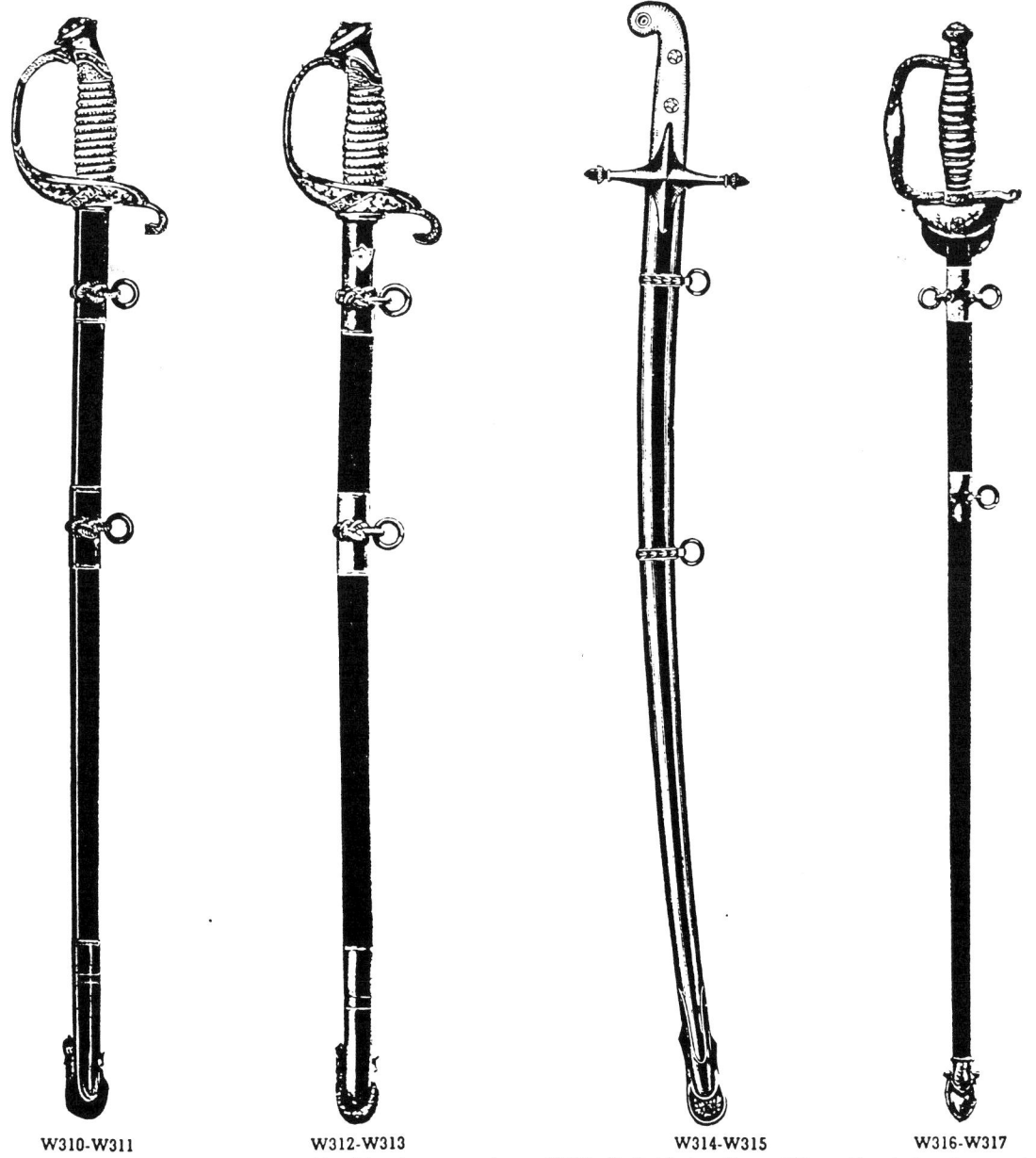

W310-W311 **W312-W313** **W314-W315** **W316-W317**

W310 U. S. Navy Officers Regulation. Metal leather covered scabbard; gold plated mounts and guard; fine tempered steel blade, etched and nickel plated; genuine sharkskin grip. Each **$21.35**

W311 U. S. Navy Officers Regulation. Metal leather covered scabbard; mounts and guard hand chased and extra heavy gold plated and hand burnished; fine tempered steel Prooved blade, nickel plated and etched; genuine sharkskin grip. Each **$28.00**

W312 U. S. Coast Guard Officers Regulation. Metal leather covered scabbard; gold plated mounts and guard; fine tempered steel blade, etched and nickel plated; genuine sharkskin grip. Each **$21.35**

W313 U. S. Coast Guard Officers Regulation. Metal leather covered scabbard; mounts and guard hand chased and extra heavy gold plated and hand burnished; fine tempered steel Prooved blade, nickel plated and etched; genuine sharkskin grip. Each **$28.00**

W314 U. S. Marine Corps Officers Regulation, heavy nickel plated scabbard; gold plated mounts and hilt; fine steel blade nickel plated; genuine ivory grip. Each **$36.00**

W315 U. S. Marine Corps Officers Regulation, heavy nickel plated scabbard; gold plated mounts and hilt; fine steel blade, nickel plated, celluloid grip. Each **$27.35**

W316 U. S. Public Health Service Officers Regulation; metal leather covered scabbard; embossed mounts and guard gold plated; gilt etched diamond blade, genuine sharkskin grip. Each **$21.35**

W317 U. S. Public Health Service Officers Regulation; metal leather covered scabbard; embossed mounts and guard hand chased and heavy gold plated and hand burnished, gilt etched diamond blade, genuine sharkskin grip. Each **$28.00**

QUANTITY PRICES ON APPLICATION

— 3 —

THE LILLEY-AMES COMPANY - COLUMBUS, OHIO

PRESENTATION SABERS

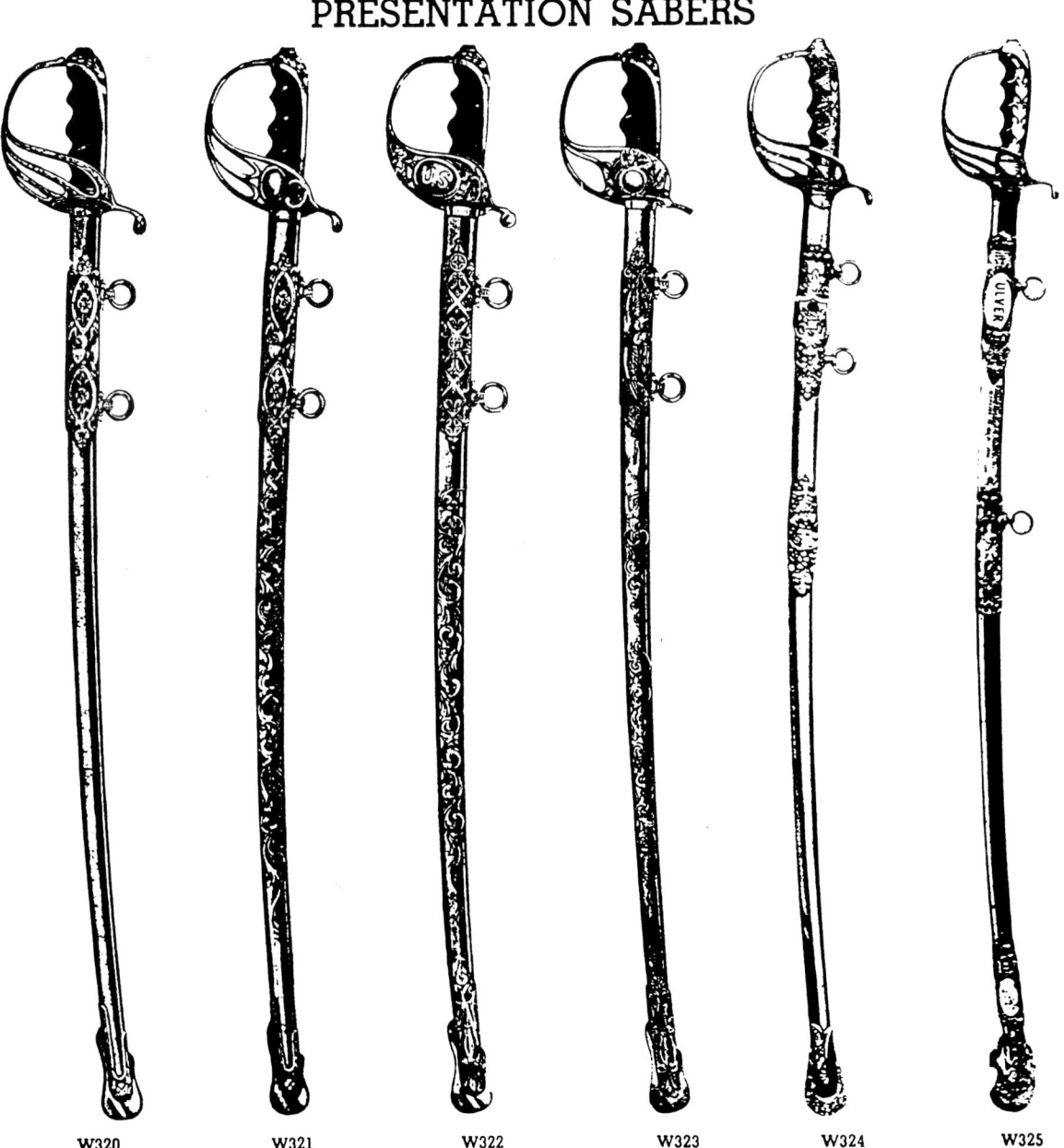

W320   W321   W322   W323   W324   W325

W320 Embossed German Silver Scabbard. Chased Mountings, Black Grip. Blade is plated and etched with appropriate design and includes name etched thereon, each **$30.50**

W321 Embossed and Engraved German Silver Scabbard, Chased Mountings, Black Grip. Blade is plated and etched with appropriate design and includes name etched thereon, each **$24.45**

W322 Embossed and Engraved German Silver Scabbard, Chased Mountings, Black Grip. Blade is plated and etched with appropriate design and includes name etched thereon, each **$40.65**

W323 Embossed and Engraved German Silver Scabbard, Chased Mountings, Black Grip. Blade is plated and etched with appropriate design and includes name etched thereon, each **$45.00**

W324 Extra Heavy Gold Plating, hand chased and engraved, etched nickel plated blade; German Silver Scabbard, Genuine Ivory Grip, ornamented. Each **$110.00**

W325 Extra Heavy Gold Plating, hand chased and engraved, etched nickel plated blade; Steel Scabbard, extra heavy nickel plated, Genuine Ivory Grip etched. Each **$92.00**

QUANTITY PRICES ON APPLICATION

— 4 —

THE LILLEY-AMES COMPANY - COLUMBUS, OHIO

PRESENTATION SWORDS AND SABERS

| ARMY | ARMY | NAVY | NAVY | MARINE CORPS |

W337   W339   W341   W343   W345

W337 Officer's Sword. Extra Heavy Gold Plating; hand chased and engraved; Sterling Silver monogram; U. S. or State Coat of Arms; gold etched and ornamented steel blade; nickel plated steel scabbard, genuine Mother of Pearl grip. Each **$175.00**

W339 Officer's Saber. Extra Heavy Gold Plating; extra fine hand chased and engraved; richly jeweled guard, gold etched and ornamented steel blade; Sterling Silver scabbard, richly hand engraved. Each **$425.00**

W341 Navy Sword. Extra Heavy Gold Plating; hand chased and engraved; gold etched and ornamented steel blade; genuine shark skin grip; fine silk scabbard. Each **$82.65**

W343 Navy Sword. Extra Heavy Gold Plating; extra fine hand chased and engraved; richly jeweled mounts and guard, gold etched and ornamented steel blades; Sterling Silver hand engraved grip; fine bronze scabbard. Each **$300.00**

W345 Marine Corps. Extra Heavy Gold Plating; extra fine hand chased and engraved; gold etched and ornamented steel blade; nickel plated steel scabbard; genuine ivory grip. Each **$155.00**

— 6 —

THE LILLEY-AMES COMPANY — COLUMBUS, OHIO

CADET OFFICERS' SWORDS

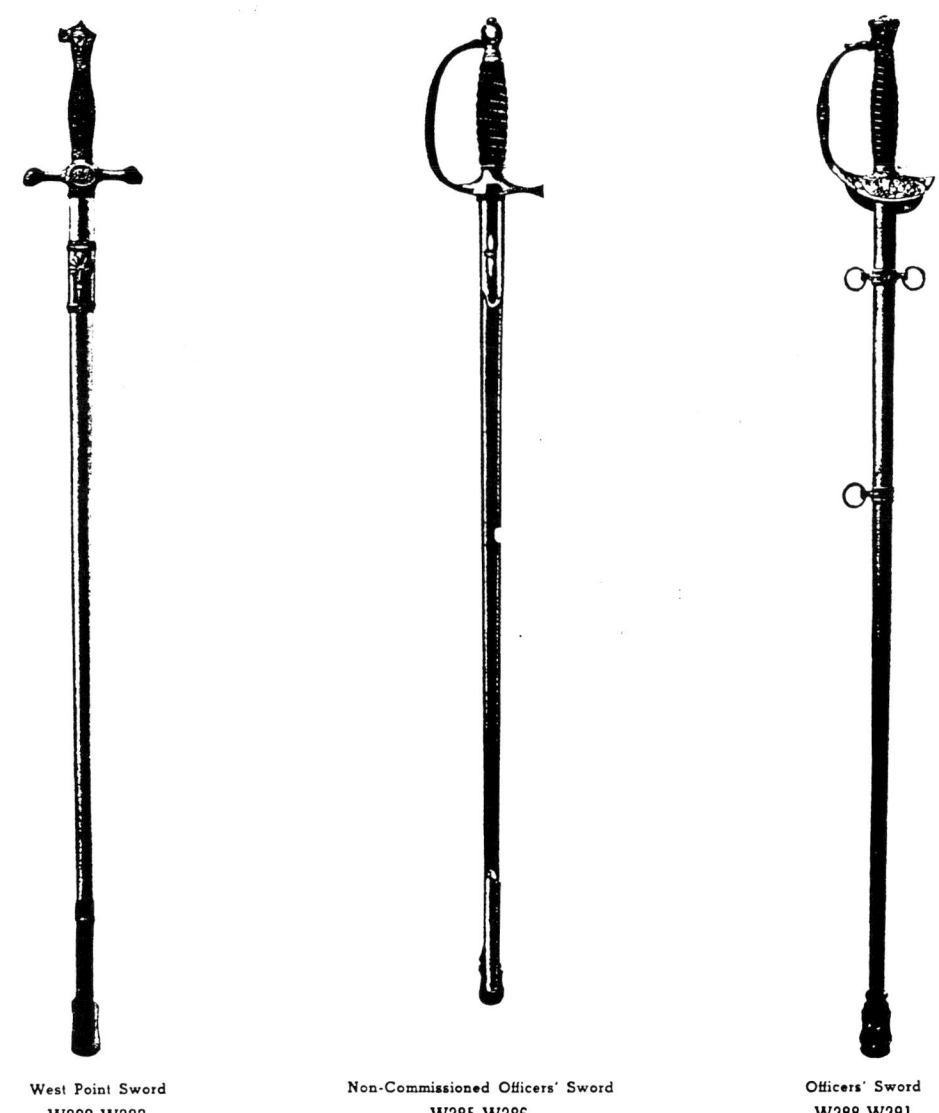

West Point Sword
W380-W383

Non-Commissioned Officers' Sword
W385-W386

Officers' Sword
W388-W391

WEST POINT SWORDS

W380 West Point Regulation Sword, nickel-plated scabbard brass buffed mountings, small oval plain blade, nickel-plated grip, each **$9.00**

W381 West Point Regulation Sword, nickel-plated scabbard, brass buffed mountings, plain diamond blade, nickel-plated grip, each **$9.80**

W382 West Point Regulation Sword, nickel-plated scabbard, gilt mountings, plain diamond blade, nickel-plated grip, each **$11.00**

W383 West Point Regulation Sword; nickel-plated scabbard, gold-plated mountings, etched diamond blade and silver-plated grip, each **$14.00**

QUANTITY PRICES ON APPLICATION

NON-COMMISSIONED OFFICERS' SWORDS

W385 Sword for non-commissioned officers, leather scabbard, brass buffed mountings, steel blade, as illustrated; each **$10.00**

W386 Same sword as W385, with nickel-plated metal scabbard; each **$11.00**

OFFICERS' SWORDS

W388 Officers' Sword, nickel-plated scabbard; polished brass mountings, plain diamond blade, each **$8.90**

W389 Officers' Sword, stationary back guard, good quality nickel-plated scabbard, gilt mountings, etched diamond blade, each **$10.15**

W390 Officers' Sword, stationary back guard; fine quality nickel-plated scabbard, gold-plated mountings, etched diamond blade, each **$14.35**

W391 Officers' Sword, with falling spring back guard, fine quality nickel-plated scabbard, gold-plated mountings, etched diamond blade, each **$14.90**

— 8 —

C.E. Ward Co. 1954 Catalog
(Author's collection)

ANNOUNCEMENT

Since 1920, The C. E. Ward Company has manufactured fine Swords at its New London, Ohio plant.

Facilities for sword production were greatly increased in May of 1951. At that time, Wards purchased the military and fraternal sword and saber assets of The Lilley-Ames Co., Inc. of Columbus, Ohio.

These assets, including all dies, patterns, special machinery, tools, etc., were moved to The Ward Company sword factory in New London, Ohio.

The Lilley-Ames Co., Inc., considered the largest sword manufacturer in the U.S.A., had as its predecessor or merged companies the following: M. C. Lilley Co., established in 1865; The Lilley Co., The Lilley-Ames Co., Columbus, Ohio; The Henderson-Ames Co., Kalamazoo, Mich. and the Ames Sword Co., Chicopee, Mass., founded in 1828.

With the expanded facilities now available, Wards are in position to supply the complete line of military and presentation swords and sabers.

Wards are also equipped to remodel, gold or silver plate and etch military swords and sabers.

THE C. E. WARD COMPANY

MANUFACTURERS

NEW LONDON, OHIO

U. S. Navy Officer's Sword

No. W310

Leather covered steel scabbard; hilt and mounts gold plated; fine tempered highly polished steel blade heavily nickel plated and gold etched on each side with regulation decorative patterns and designs. Regulation grip. Owner's name etched on blade; cloth sword bag included.

Owner's Height Required

THE C. E. WARD COMPANY

MANUFACTURERS

NEW LONDON, OHIO

U. S. Coast Guard Officer's Sword

No. W312

Leather covered steel scabbard; hilt and mounts gold plated; fine tempered highly polished steel blade heavily nickel plated and gold etched on each side with regulation decorative patterns and designs. Regulation grip. Owner's name etched on blade; cloth sword bag included.

Owner's Height Required

THE C. E. WARD COMPANY

MANUFACTURERS

NEW LONDON, OHIO

U. S. Army Officer's Saber

No. W306

Highly polished steel scabbard copper plated, then extra heavily nickel plated; hilt and mounts extra heavily nickel plated; fine tempered highly polished steel blade heavily nickel plated and etched on each side with regulation patterns and designs. Regulation grip. Owner's name etched on blade; cloth sword bag included.

Owner's Height Required

THE C. E. WARD COMPANY
MANUFACTURERS
NEW LONDON, OHIO

5

U. S. Army Officer's Saber For R.O.T.C. Units

No. W306½

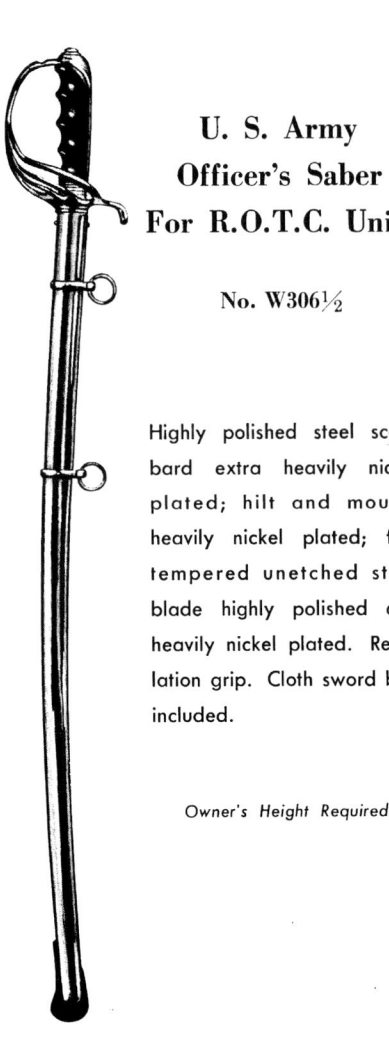

Highly polished steel scabbard extra heavily nickel plated; hilt and mounts heavily nickel plated; fine tempered unetched steel blade highly polished and heavily nickel plated. Regulation grip. Cloth sword bag included.

Owner's Height Required

THE C. E. WARD COMPANY
MANUFACTURERS
NEW LONDON, OHIO

6

U. S. Marine Corps Officer's Saber

No. W314

Steel scabbard, highly polished and heavily nickel plated; guard and mounts gold plated; fine tempered highly polished steel blade heavily nickel plated and etched on each side with regulation patterns and designs. Regulation grip. Owner's name etched on blade; cloth sword bag included.

Owner's Height Required

THE C. E. WARD COMPANY
MANUFACTURERS
NEW LONDON, OHIO

7

Presentation Navy Officer's Sword

No. W343

Brass scabbard highly polished and extra heavily gold plated; hilt and mounts hand chased and extra heavily gold plated; fine tempered highly polished steel blade heavily nickel plated and gold etched on each side with regulation patterns and designs. Coin silver hand engraved grip. Owner's name etched on blade; cloth sword bag included.

Owner's Height Required

THE C. E. WARD COMPANY
MANUFACTURERS
NEW LONDON, OHIO

8

Presentation Navy Officer's Sword

No. W350

Leather covered steel scabbard; hilt and mounts hand chased and heavily gold plated; fine tempered highly polished steel blade heavily nickel plated and gold etched on each side with regulation decorative patterns and designs. Grip as illustrated. Owner's name etched on blade; cloth sword bag included.

Owner's Height Required

THE C. E. WARD COMPANY
MANUFACTURERS
NEW LONDON, OHIO

9

Presentation Navy Officer's Sword

No. W351

Leather covered steel scabbard; hilt and mounts hand chased and heavily gold plated; fine tempered highly polished steel blade heavily nickel plated and gold etched on each side with regulation decorative patterns and designs. Grip as illustrated. Owner's name etched on blade; cloth sword bag included.

Owner's Height Required

THE C. E. WARD COMPANY
MANUFACTURERS
NEW LONDON, OHIO

10

Presentation Navy Officer's Sword

No. W341

Leather covered steel scabbard; hilt and mounts hand chased and heavily gold plated; fine tempered highly polished steel blade heavily nickel plated and gold etched on each side with regulation decorative patterns and designs. Grip as illustrated. Owner's name etched on blade; cloth sword bag included.

Owner's Height Required

THE C. E. WARD COMPANY
MANUFACTURERS
NEW LONDON, OHIO

Presentation Navy Officer's Sword

No. W253

Leather covered steel scabbard; hilt and mounts hand chased and heavily gold plated; fine tempered highly polished steel blade heavily nickel plated and gold etched on each side with regulation decorative patterns and designs. Grip as illustrated. Owner's name etched on blade; cloth sword bag included.

Owner's Height Required

THE C. E. WARD COMPANY
MANUFACTURERS
NEW LONDON, OHIO

Presentation Army Officer's Saber

No. W221

Extra heavily silver plated brass scabbard highly polished and engraved; hilt and mounts hand chased and extra heavily silver plated; fine tempered highly polished steel blade heavily nickel plated and gold etched on each side with regulation patterns and designs. Grip as illustrated. Owner's name etched on blade; cloth sword bag included.

Owner's Height Required

THE C. E. WARD COMPANY
MANUFACTURERS
NEW LONDON, OHIO

Presentation Army Officer's Saber

No. W330

Brass scabbard highly polished, engraved and extra heavily silver plated; hilt and mounts hand chased and silver plated; fine tempered highly polished steel blade heavily nickel plated and gold etched on each side with regulation patterns and designs. Grip as illustrated. Owner's name etched on blade; cloth sword bag included.

Owner's Height Required

THE C. E. WARD COMPANY
MANUFACTURERS
NEW LONDON, OHIO

14

Presentation Army Officer's Saber

No. W332

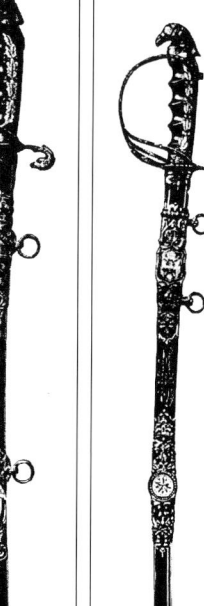

Brass scabbard highly polished, engraved and extra heavily silver plated; hilt and mounts hand chased and gold plated. Coin silver monogram on top mount; fine tempered highly polished steel blade heavily nickel plated and gold etched on each side with regulation patterns and designs. Grip as illustrated. Owner's name etched on blade; cloth sword bag included.

Owner's Height Required

THE C. E. WARD COMPANY
MANUFACTURERS
NEW LONDON, OHIO

15

Presentation Army Officer's Saber

No. W335

Brass scabbard highly polished, engraved and extra heavily silver plated; hilt and mounts hand chased, and heavily gold plated; fine tempered highly polished steel blade heavily nickel plated and gold etched on each side with regulation patterns and designs. Grip as illustrated. Owner's name etched on blade; cloth sword bag included.

Owner's Height Required

THE C. E. WARD COMPANY
MANUFACTURERS
NEW LONDON, OHIO

16

Presentation Marine Corps Officer's Saber

No. W345

Brass scabbard highly polished, engraved and extra heavily silver plated; guard and mounts hand chased, engraved and heavily gold plated; fine tempered highly polished steel blade heavily nickel plated and gold etched on each side with regulation patterns and designs. Grip as illustrated. Owner's name etched on blade; cloth sword bag included.

Owner's Height Required

THE C. E. WARD COMPANY
MANUFACTURERS
NEW LONDON, OHIO

U. S. Marine Corps Non-Commissioned Officer's Saber

No. W635N

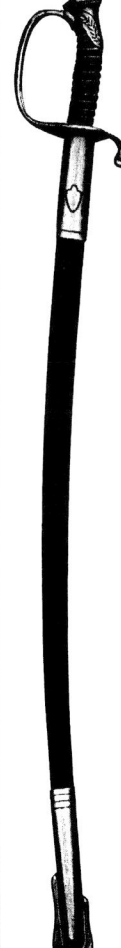

Steel leather covered scabbard; polished and lacquered brass hilt, mounts and hook throg fastener; fine tempered highly polished steel blade heavily nickel plated and gold etched on each side with regulation patterns and designs; grip covered with black leather and wound with gilt wire.

Owner's Height Required

THE C. E. WARD COMPANY
MANUFACTURERS
NEW LONDON, OHIO

Cadet Officer's West Point Style Sword

Nos. W380—W381—W382—W383

No. W380
Steel scabbard polished and nickel plated; tempered unetched oval style steel blade, polished and nickel plated; brass guard and mounts polished and lacquered; nickel plated grip.

No. W381
Steel scabbard polished and nickel plated; tempered unetched diamond style steel blade, polished and nickel plated; brass guard and mounts polished and lacquered; nickel plated grip.

No. W382
Steel scabbard polished and nickel plated; tempered unetched diamond style steel blade, polished and nickel plated; brass guard and mounts polished and gold plated; nickel plated grip.

No. W383
Steel scabbard polished and nickel plated; tempered etched diamond style steel blade, polished and nickel plated; brass guard and mounts polished and gold plated; silver plated grip.

Owner's Height Required

THE C. E. WARD COMPANY
MANUFACTURERS
NEW LONDON, OHIO

Cadet Non-Commissioned Officer's Sword

Nos. W385—W386

No. W385
Black enameled steel scabbard; plain diamond style steel blade, tempered, polished and nickel plated; brass hilt and mounts polished and lacquered; black twist grip wound with gilt wire.

No. W386
Nickel plated polished steel scabbard; plain diamond style steel blade, tempered, polished and nickel plated; brass hilt and mounts polished and lacquered; black twist grip wound with gilt wire.

Owner's Height Required

THE C. E. WARD COMPANY
MANUFACTURERS
NEW LONDON, OHIO

Cadet Officer's Sword

Nos. W388—W389

No. W388
Nickel plated polished steel scabbard; plain diamond style blade, tempered, polished and nickel plated; brass hilt and mounts polished and lacquered; black twist grip wound with gilt wire.

No. W389
Nickel plated polished steel scabbard; diamond style tempered steel blade, polished, etched and nickel plated; hilt and mounts gold plated; black twist grip wound with gilt wire.

Owner's Height Required

THE C. E. WARD COMPANY
MANUFACTURERS
NEW LONDON, OHIO

Military Sword

No. W630

Nickel plated polished steel scabbard; lacquered brass, nickel plated or gold plated hilt and mounts; plain steel blade, tempered, polished and nickel plated; black twist grip.

Owner's Height Required

THE C. E. WARD COMPANY
MANUFACTURERS
NEW LONDON, OHIO

Military Sword

No. W631

Nickel plated polished steel scabbard; lacquered brass, nickel plated or gold plated hilt and mounts; etched steel blade, tempered, polished and nickel plated; black twist grip.

Owner's Height Required

THE C. E. WARD COMPANY
MANUFACTURERS
NEW LONDON, OHIO

23

Presentation Military Sword

No. W632

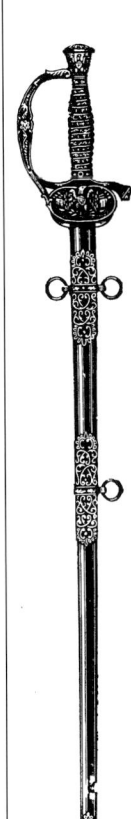

Nickel plated polished steel scabbard; lacquered brass, nickel plated or gold plated hilt and mounts; etched steel blade, tempered, polished and nickel plated; nickel plated grip.

Owner's Height Required

THE C. E. WARD COMPANY
MANUFACTURERS
NEW LONDON, OHIO

24

Artillery Saber

No. W633

Nickel plated polished steel scabbard; lacquered brass, nickel plated or gold plated hilt and mounts; etched steel blade, tempered, polished and nickel plated; black plastic grip.

Owner's Height Required

THE C. E. WARD COMPANY
MANUFACTURERS
NEW LONDON, OHIO

25

Sword Illustrations from the Very Rare F.W. Widmann and William H. Horstmann & Sons Sword Catalogs

Frederick William Widmann was born in Bremen, Germany, in 1795. He immigrated to Philadelphia, PA, in 1816. Widmann was a highly talented military ornamentor, die sinker, and metal worker. He began designing and making distinctive infantry and artillery officer swords around 1821. Many of his swords incorporated the use of eagle-head pommels. His swords and scabbards were very decorative and used patriotic motifs.

Widmann was first located at 115 North Front Street (1816-1828) and then at 98 North Third Street (from 1828 until he died on April 6, 1848). He was located down the street from passementier and military goods dealer William H. Horstmann at 59 North Third Street. Horstmann had also immigrated to Philadelphia in 1816 (born in Cassel, Germany, in 1785). They may even have known each other before arriving in the United States. Widmann bought silver from Horstmann and blades from Solingen, Germany. Widmann sold Horstmann large quantities of military goods and swords.

When Widmann died in 1848, Horstmann bought his stock and equipment. Horstmann also hired Widmann swordsmiths Julius Knecke and Jacob Faser. Widmann had bequeathed his sword design book (catalog) to Faser. Horstmann then expanded his manufactory to include a sword shop in 1849. In 1850 he built a large five-story factory at 5th and Cherry Streets. At first, his sword designs were very similar to Widmann's.

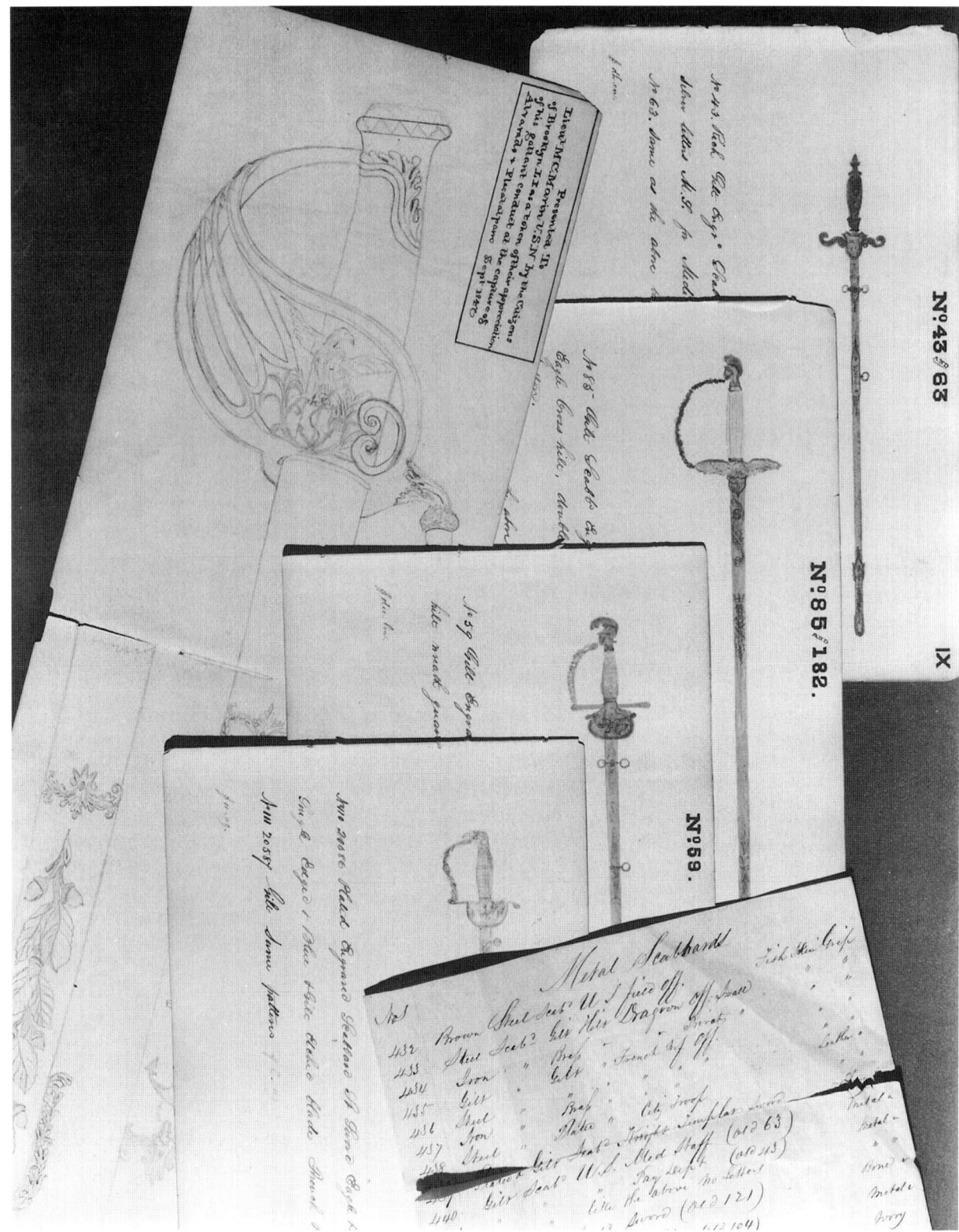

Hand-painted watercolor plates (6" x 9") from the original early 1840s F.W. Widmann factory pattern book (or factory/sales showroom book). Each plate contained details about various finishes (e.g., silver or gilt scabbard and scabbard mountings). The large drawing of a sword hilt contains a neatly lettered rendition of the actual inscription that appeared on the sword when it was presented to U.S. Navy Lt. M.C. Marin for heroism in the Mexican War. The document at the lower right of the photo is a page listing various scabbards that were available with each model. (From the collection of Norm Flayderman)

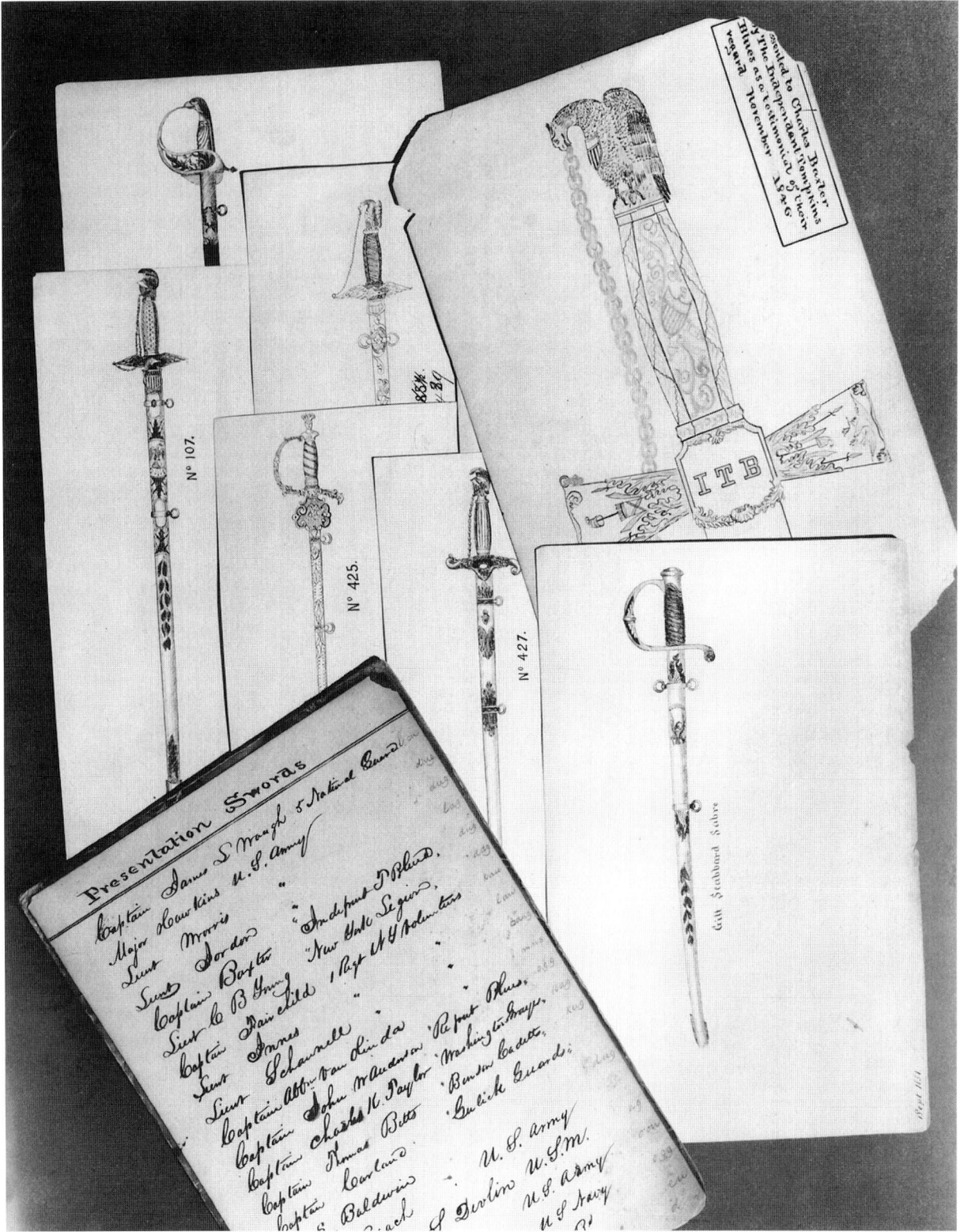

Hand-drawn pen and ink plates (6″ x 9″) from the original September 1851 factory pattern book of Horstmann of Philadelphia, as continued by them after their takeover of the Widmann Company. Drawing in the upper right is the factory artist's rendering of an elaborate presentation sword designed for an elite American militia unit as a gift for one of its officers. The page at lower left lists some of the fancy-grade swords the company made for presentation to various officers for service in the Mexican War. (From the collection of Norm Flayderman)

Mounted Cavalry Saber Exercise Illustrations from an 1843 Philadelphia Sword Manual

(Author's collection)

A

NEW SYSTEM

OF

BROAD AND SMALL SWORD EXERCISE,

COMPRISING

THE BROAD SWORD EXERCISE FOR CAVALRY AND THE SMALL SWORD CUT AND THRUST PRACTICE FOR INFANTRY.

TO WHICH ARE ADDED,

INSTRUCTIONS IN HORSEMANSHIP.

ILLUSTRATED BY

FORTY-FIVE HANDSOME AND EFFECTIVE ENGRAVINGS.

PREPARED AND ARRANGED BY

THOMAS STEPHENS,

PROFESSOR OF BROAD AND SMALL SWORD EXERCISE.

CHAPTER II.

THE BROAD SWORD EXERCISE.

SECTION I.

THE BROAD SWORD EXERCISE—DISMOUNTED.

THE broad sword exercise for Cavalry, to be well performed, should be often practiced when dismounted, by companies or squadrons, formed in line; the tallest men being placed on the right. When the line has been formed for drill, the Instructor gives word—"Eyes right and dress;" "eyes front." The word "Stand at ease" having been given, the pupil is to draw the right foot back six inches, the greater portion of the body resting on the right leg; the hands to be brought together in front of the body, the right hand to grasp the left. This is the position "Stand at ease."

POSITION OF ATTENTION.

The Instructor gives the word, "Attention," and the pupil springs to that position, body erect, arms hanging easily by the sides, palms of the hands turned to the front, heels together, and toes inclined outward.

TO TAKE DISTANCE FOR SWORD EXERCISE.

The right-hand man keeps his post; the remainder left passage, dressing to the right, standing at open interval of about five or six feet apart, will then halt, eyes front. The word is then given, "Prepare for cavalry broad sword exercise." Each pupil or recruit steps from eighteen to twenty inches to the right, standing at open position, imitating that of being mounted.

THE BROAD SWORD EXERCISE—MOUNTED.

The sword exercise of cavalry has three divisions—

3*

arranged in reference to the different combinations of the cuts and thrusts, whether against infantry, cavalry, or both. The motions are all performed by presenting a proper front in the direction whence the attack would be received; and it is always from some quarter of the right or left side of the horse; as it would be impossible to meet an opponent face to face while sitting naturally in the saddle; but can only approach by passing side by side. In this view the motions will be made in directions either on the right or left, where the adversary is supposed to be.

Draw Swords.—Bring the hand smartly across the body to the sword-knot, place it on the wrist, and give the hand a couple of turns inward, in order to make it fast, and at the same time seize the hilt and raise the sword-blade six inches out of the scabbard; by a second motion extend the arm to the right, the point in an elevated position, edge to the right.

One.—Bring the sword hand in front of the cheek; sword erect, edge to the left.

Two.—Bring the sword to the carry, by dropping the arm to the hip; elbow and wrist horizontal, sword erect, with the edge to the front.

SLOPE SWORD.

Loosen the grasp of the handle, let the blade rest against the shoulder, with the edge of the blade-front sloping.

FIRST DIVISION OF PRACTICE.

Carry Sword.—Grasp the handle, and at the same time raise the sword from the shoulder perpendicularly.

No. 1.—GUARD.

Cut One.—Raise the sword arm; the back of the sword in the hollow of the right shoulder; cut from front to rear, on the near side of the horse, at infantry.

Raise the arm full length, sloping the sword over the head, the point bearing over the left shoulder; point lower than the handle, the edge upward.

No. 2.—ASSAULT.

Cut Three.—Carry the sword arm to the right rear, the blade perpendicular; cut from rear to front, on the off side of the horse, at infantry.

Cut Two.—Change the direction of the body, place the back of the sword in the hollow of the left shoulder; cut from front to rear, on the off side of the horse, at infantry.

Cut Five.—Carry the sword arm to the right, bearing the back of the sword against the collar of the coat. Cut from right to left at the bridle arm, or left side, at cavalry.

Cut Four.—Carry the sword hand in the hollow of the left shoulder, opposite the breast; the blade perpendicular, the edge to the rear. Cut from rear to front, on the near side of the horse, at infantry.

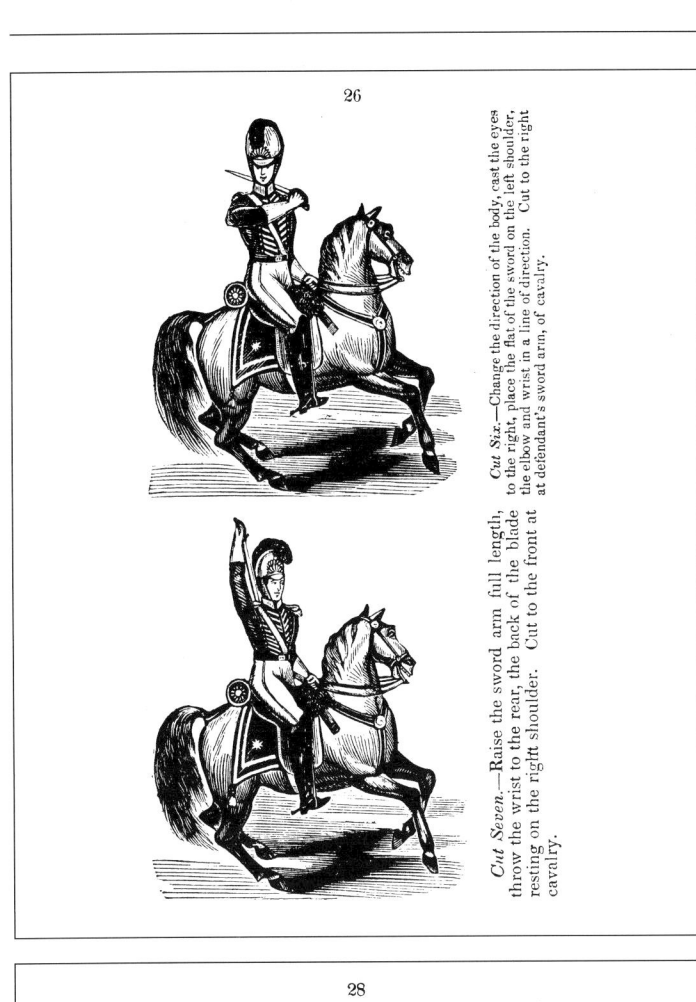

26

Cut Six.—Change the direction of the body, cast the eyes to the right, place the flat of the sword on the left shoulder, the elbow and wrist in a line of direction. Cut to the right at defendant's sword arm, of cavalry.

Cut Seven.—Raise the sword arm full length, throw the wrist to the rear, the back of the blade resting on the right shoulder. Cut to the front at cavalry.

27

First Point.—Raise the sword arm with the hand opposite the right eye; the sword and arm in a line of direction, the edge upward, point to the left front.

POINTS.

Second Point.—Place the elbow inside the right hip-bone, the edge of the sword upward, the point to the right front *point*; raise the wrist and lower the point.

28

Third Point.—Place the heel of the hand on the right hip-bone, the edge to the right front, the point elevated *point*; raise the wrist and lower the point.

FIRST. *To defend the Left Cheek on the left side of the neck.*—*Position*; sword hand carried to the left, the point is to be opposite and above the right eye, the edge to the left front.

GUARDS.—SEVEN ON THE RIGHT.

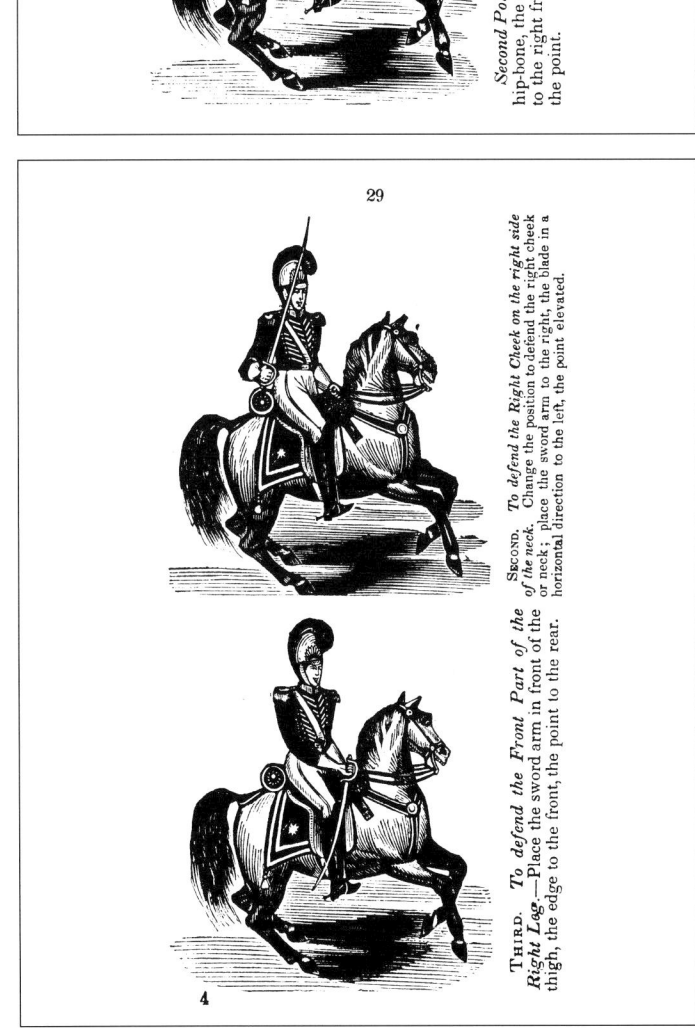

29

SECOND. *To defend the Right Cheek on the right side of the neck.* Change the position to defend the right cheek or neck; place the sword arm to the right, the blade in a horizontal direction to the left, the point elevated.

THIRD. *To defend the Front Part of the Right Leg.*—Place the sword arm in front of the thigh, the edge to the front, the point to the rear.

4

369

MOUNTED CAVALRY SABER EXERCISE ILLUSTRATIONS

FOURTH. *To defend the Hauching Part of the Leg.*—Bring the sword arm in rear of the right leg, the point to the front, edge to the right.

FIFTH. *To defend the Bridle Arm, or Left Side.*—Raise the sword arm directly in front of the brow, the hand over the left shoulder, the edge to the left, the point downward.

SIXTH. *To defend the Sword Arm or Right Side.*—Raise the sword arm to the right, as high as the head; the edge to the front, the point downward.

SEVENTH. *To defend the Head.*—Raise the sword arm full length over the head, the sword directing to the left, the edge upward, the point sloping over the left shoulder.

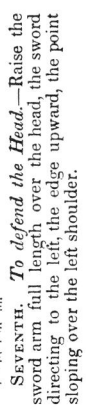

First Parry.—From front to rear, with the back of the sword.
Second Parry.—From rear to front with the back of the sword.

PARRIES ON THE RIGHT.

GUARDS ON THE LEFT.

The same as on the right, only defending the left side. First defending the left cheek; second, defending the right cheek, or neck; third defending the left leg, (rear;) fourth, defending the left leg, (front;) fifth, defending the bridle arm, or horse's hind quarters; sixth, defending the bridle rein, or front part of the body; seventh, defending the head.

PARRIES ON THE LEFT.

First, from rear to front with the back of the sword; second, from front to rear. Carry sword; slope sword.

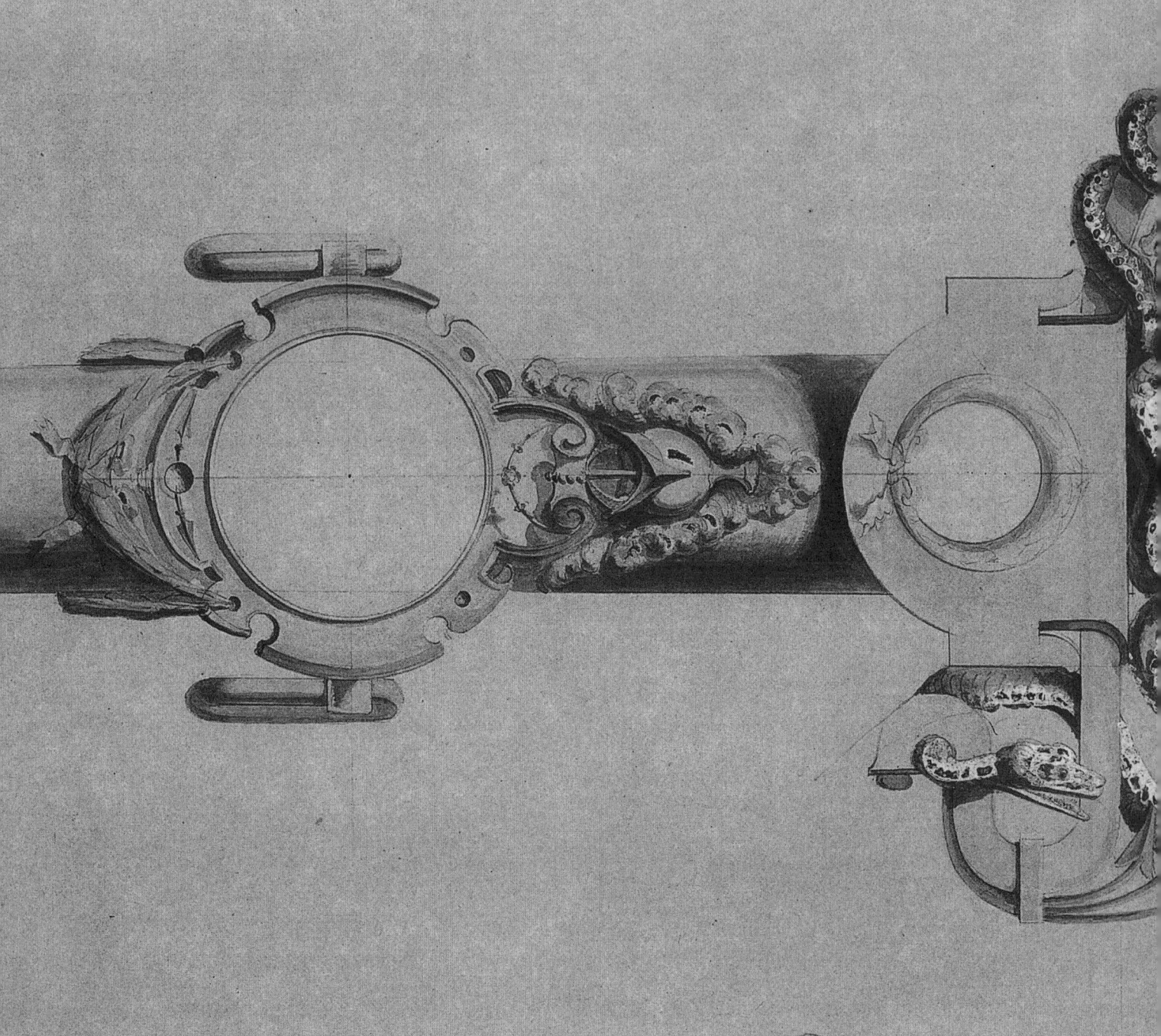